Rev. Jacek Salij, O.P.

OUR FAITH

Rev. Jacek Salij, O.P.

OUR FAITH

Translated by Filip Mazurczak
Foreword by Rev. Jerzy Szymik

Angelicum University Press
Fundacja Świętego Mikołaja
Rome—Warsaw 2023

Angelicum University Press
Fundacja Świętego Mikołaja
Rome—Warsaw 2023

Published by the St. John Paul II Institute of Culture at the Pontifical University of St. Thomas Aquinas in Rome—Angelicum.
Founded at the Angelicum, the St. John Paul II Institute of Culture is run in cooperation with the Saint Nicholas Foundation.
www.angelicum.it/institutes/st-john-paul-ii-institute-of-culture

Angelicum University Press
Largo Angelicum, 1—00184 Rome, Italy
editoria@pust.it—www.angelicumpress.com
Fundacja Świętego Mikołaja
Koszykowa 24/7—00553 Warsaw, Poland
redakcja@teologiapolityczna.pl—www.teologiapolityczna.pl
www.mikolaj.org.pl

ISBN: 978-83-67065-42-9 (print)
ISBN: 978-83-67065-43-6 (ebook)
Managing editors: Marta Broniewska, Mikołaj Marczak, Maciej Wilmanowicz
Translated by: Filip Mazurczak
Copy edited by Agnieszka Gernand, Aeddan Shaw
Designed and typeset by Katarzyna Solecka
Cover: Detail from *The Annunciation*, Jacek Hajnos, O.P. (2023)
Cover design by Design Cooperative TAKŁADNIE, Dariusz Karłowicz

This book has been published with the support of the ©POLAND Translation Program

Table of contents

Our Faith
Rev. Jacek Salij, O.P.

Rev. Jerzy Szymik

FOREWORD

"This cursed dilemma of modern theology is that if it is orthodox, it is craftsmanship, and if it is ambitious, it must be heretical. [...] We need creative and original orthodox theology."

J. Salij, *Dlaczego kocham dogmaty?* ("Why I Love Dogmas")

"In my view, one does not become a great theologian by the fact that he is able to tackle minute and difficult details, but by the fact that he is able to present the ultimate unity and simplicity of the faith."

Benedict XVI, Letter to Cardinal Gerhard Ludwig Müller, July 31, 2017

Faith and Theology

The initial thesis concerning the bond between faith and theology is as follows: if the phenomenon of faith exists, it will always be accompanied by the phenomenon of theology. At the same time, the gravity of Jesus' question hovers over both: "But when the Son of Man comes, will He find faith on earth?" (Luke 18:8). The indissolubility of the bonds between theology and faith makes Jesus' question one about faith, simultaneously a question about theology. Where there is faith, there will be theology...

Father Jacek Salij's theology is in the Augustinian and Thomistic traditions; he rarely refers *expressis verbis* to the Bonaventurian tradition. However, at a deeper level, intellectually and spiritually, the latter is not alien to him, which is and also one in the existential-pastoral inclination of his theological reflection as well as his disputes with neo-Gnostics and the anti-intellectual tendencies of our time. I will recall, then, that St. Bonaventure (1221-1274) claimed that faith becomes theology *propter amorem eius cui assentit*[1]*: out of love for the one it has trusted (literally: with whom it agrees). According to Benedict XVI, this intuition leads us to conclude that "theology would be a great effort that every love must undertake: to better know the one who loves."*[2] In other words, if faith in God and entrusting oneself to God contain the components of hope (trust) and love, which are necessary for its identity and authenticity, it naturally and necessarily strives to know God. For love desires to know the beloved. Meanwhile, for man, a rational being, knowing God cannot take place without the participation of reason (also because the object of faith, or its own attitude, is rational; in fact, it is Reason Itself). This is precisely what theology is: the necessary activity of reason undertaken out of love, without which faith ceases to be itself. This is why theology is necessarily a constant activity of faith and why if there is faith, there will be theology: some form of a theological plant sprouts forth from every mustard seed of faith.

1. Bonaventura, I *Sent proem* q 2 [ad 6 (I 11 b)].

2. J. Ratzinger, *Wiara w Piśmie i Tradycji* (Opera Omnia, Vol. 9/1), ed. K. Góźdź, M. Górecka, trans. J. Merecki (Lublin: KUL, 2018), p. 159 (subsequently: OO 9/ 1). As no official English translation of Joseph Ratzinger's *Opera Omnia* is available, all the quotations are based on the Polish edition, originally used by Fr. Jacek Salij OP.

Bonaventure's conceptualization of the relationship between faith and theology is deeply rooted in the phenomenon of Polish theology and the theological work of Jacek Salij. To repeat, theology is an undertaking of faith in this conceptualization; it is an effort of faith undertaken out of love to understand one's own attitude and substance. If, then, it is undertaken for the sake of understanding, it is done by rational means, or in an ordered form and with the aid of justified principles and logical methods. Here, faith's claims to the truth are fundamental: the essence of faith includes its conviction that it allows man to know what is true (untrue knowledge is not, after all, knowledge; it is not true knowledge) and that this knowledge is to be understood and expressed. It is at this point that theology, which leads to rational reflection on faith, is born. For this, it requires humility and courage (both are equally important) in confrontation with Mystery, whose ultimate fullness cannot be reached by its possibilities or competences. To quote Bonaventure once again: love is the fuel for this undertaking and the source of humble courage.

Thus, theology is sustained by two dynamics: the dynamic of knowing or understanding the truth as well as the dynamic of love, which together direct man towards knowing the One Who loves.[3] Both are proper to faith and are inextricably tied together; they meet and support one another and merge into one epistemic stream that leads to what we call theological knowledge. Love is the eye of theology (to paraphrase Richard of St. Victor's proverb),[4] and what love sees becomes subordinated to the judgment of reason and becomes subjected to the truth whose cognition this entire process serves. Theology as reflection on the faith and "thinking with faith" is irrevocably and essentially bound to the question of truth and its definite

3. *Ibid.*, p. 610. See the constant presence of this thesis in: Congregation for the Doctrine of the Faith, *Instruction on the Ecclesiastical Vocation of the Theologian*, Vatican, May 24, 1990.

4. Grad card (PL 196, 1203). *Op. cit.*: J. Ratzinger, *Jezus z Nazaretu* (Opera Omnia, Vol. 6/2), ed. K. Góźdź, M. Górecka, trans. W. Szymona (Lublin: KUL, 2015), p. 642.

substance. This can be expressed in another way still, from a negative perspective: faith and theology are not interested in the question of how things seem (subjectively) but how they truly (objectively, really) are. It is this concern for the "objectivity" or knowledge (the truth of the object) that strictly binds theology with the entire family of the academic sciences. The academic nature of theology conceived in this way (as a claim to scientific, objective truth) is its unalienable fundament. However, it is not its limit; it does not exhaust its cognitive instruments or epistemological ambitions. And "academic" theology is not the "only necessary" theology. *Scientia fidei* as *scientia sui generis* preserves its own identity and originality not only thanks to its strictly scientific nature and subordination to the methodology of the rational principles of the scientific method but also because of the conviction of the "non-ultimateness" and "partialness" of rational knowledge of the object.

Here, let us add another thought that emerges from almost all of Father Salij's writings: that authentic theological knowledge fulfills its tasks of leading one to the truth when we identify our life with the word of truth which we have encountered. Obedience — for obedience is subordinating one's life to the truth — is life-giving and brings further knowledge, becoming unified with truth and becoming love, thus creating life: "Amen, amen, I say to you, whoever keeps My word will never see death" (see John 8:51). In this way, theology returns with its objective and academic achievements at the level of the subject (subjective level). Herein rests its originality and genius as well as its supreme beauty as science: it is the only synthesis of its kind of what is objective and subjective. Hence the strength of its conviction to persist as a discipline in obedience to what is received (the truth) and not what is invented; and to implement this received truth.

Theology and Faith

Let us concentrate for a moment longer on the relationship between theology and faith, detailing some of its aspects that are essentially present from the perspective of Polish theology.

According to the leading conviction of the Polish school of theology, in a strictly theological sense only faith guarantees objective and full knowledge of things as they truly are. Here, this *solum* is decisive, so let us say this even more firmly: without faith, theology at best becomes religious studies, which is an important discipline but cannot be confused with theology. The last hundred years of theology have provided numerous examples demonstrating that when it is practiced from an agnostic perspective, distancing itself from ecclesial faith, theology's knowledge wanders in the darkness and its language becomes pseudo-scientific gibberish. To put it simply, theology does not "create" faith but rather interprets it and lives off it. Faith comes before theology and is the measure of theology. Meanwhile, theology is the methodological search for the understanding of the word of faith which it did not invent itself but which poses a challenge to human thinking, including theological reason (indeed, faith is never exhausted in it). Theology's auxiliary position with respect to faith leads it, as Joseph Ratzinger writes, "to the appropriate form of modesty, which is a sign of true faith," as in each (true) knowledge worthy of its name "we above all become aware of its limits."[5]

Naturally, maintaining this position (serving faith and based on a substantive deposit given to theology) is for contemporary theology, including contemporary Polish theology, a truly life-giving but exceptionally difficult task. For many decades, there has been a growing tension between the essential claim of the Christian message, which demands faith, and the post-Enlightenment scientific method, which is based on skepticism, autonomy, emancipation, and so forth, up through

5. OO 9/1, p. 249.

extreme rationalism performed using solely the mathematical-scientific methods of research and methodology. At the same time, in the eye of this cyclone, theology fulfills an important task: "It shows in what way faith remains possible and once again becomes necessary when completely respecting the requirements of human reason and its proven cognition. In doing so, it must be critical of the excessively hasty conclusions of reason and considering faith be in critical dialogue with reason and the reverse: it must purify and deepen faith anew in light of reason."[6] At the same time, theology can never become superfluous to either Christianity or people of culture. On the contrary, in the dialogue between cultures, its significance will only grow. However, this can never be done at the cost of a depreciation of the simplicity of faith which places man and his reason before God. For this to not occur, for it to remain the hermeneutic of truth that leads to such areas of cognition to which neither human reason nor any other science can lead, it is necessary for its main root to stem from the theologian's personal prayer and contemplation. Salij frequently recalls this in his writings.

For at least two centuries, it has been evident for the Church that one of the most important tasks of theology is to leave the defensive walls of professional jargon and narrow specializations to respond to the questions of the living person. If this could be reduced to a change of language and a shift in certain methodological emphases, the problem would be minor. Meanwhile, the problem is massive because in the university of today, even in major swathes of all Euro-American civilization, theology is forcefully relegated to the sphere of irrationality unless it decides to "rebrand" itself. To use the language of the times, this means that it ceases to protect its own brand, modifies it, and then expands its target consumer base. To use less fashionable and less ironic language, theology is tempted to sever its ties to faith (which is considered irrational by the dominant

6. *Ibid.*

post-Enlightenment paradigm) and drift towards the future as "rational" faith about the phenomena of religions, spirituality, and culture. Thus, theology should become something akin to "religious archeology for beginners." The cost of opposition is high: theology is perceived as pre-critical naiveté, a bourgeois illusion, or an anachronism accepted with a grain of salt only as a vintage relic. And if it does not become a "modern" discipline, it will be a foreign object in the contemporary progressive *universitas*, which does not allow for exceptions to this "progressiveness."

Contemporary Polish theology deals with this challenge, as does the theological work of Father Jacek Salij. However, we should emphasize that in the most recent spiritual and intellectual condition of Poland, Europe, and the world, new and promising opportunities are opening for theology. It just so happens that over the last two thousand years (the existence of the Church, the Christian faith, the consolidation of theology) of accepting the pressure of history, internal resistance to the "world" (in the Johannine meaning of the term) and pain resulting from everything that in a given time opposes faith or at least ignores it have been essential aspects of the vocation of the theologian;[7] in fact, they are an essential source of theology's development and the strict context of its most important achievements. If the seed does not die, it will not give fruit. Why does this Gospel principle not concern theology, its seed planted in hostile times and circumstances? Naturally — I will once again refer to St. Bonaventure and his *Itinerarium* — this can be accomplished by maintaining the iron principle of good theology, the principle which states that in every era the study of theology needs much more than "reading [...] without fervor, speculation without devotion, investigation without admiration, observation without exultation, industry without piety,

7. J. Ratzinger, *Jezus z Nazaretu* (Opera Omnia, Vol. 13/2), ed. K. Góźdź, M. Górecka, trans. W. Szymona (Lublin: KUL, 2017), p. 447.

[...] understanding without humility."[8] We can read this principle between the lines of Salij's writings and find ample evidence in his very texts.

Our Faith, Our Theology

The question I will cite was posed by Rev. Prof. Czesław Stanisław Bartnik, a theologian half a generation (thirteen years) older than Father Salij who worked alongside Father Jacek in the narrow group of the greatest masters of contemporary Polish theology. Rev. Bartnik called this question "provocative;" here it is: "When speaking of 'Polish theology,' I do not have in mind [...] universal theology written in Polish; theology performed by Poles or in Poland but without its unique traits; the history of the performing of various theological disciplines in our country; the pure reception of theology performed in other countries; or even the contribution of Poles to the development of the great theological systems in the world. I simply ask: Is there such a form of theology that can be described as having a Polish 'pedigree,' a Polish modality of thinking, and a substantive Polish profile? This is a very provocative question."[9]

I believe that this book, together with the entire "Polish Religious Thought" series, is an attempt at answering this question. In any case, there have been at least several such attempts in recent years. I will reference two, each of which expands and deepens the spectrum of perceiving the identity and originality of Polish theology and, at the same time, the Polish *par excellence* of Jacek Salij's theological thought.

8. St. Bonaventure, *The Journey of the Mind to God*, trans. P. Boehmer, OFM (Indianapolis/Cambridge: Hackett Publishing, 1993), p. 2.

9. Cz. S. Bartnik, *Problem "teologii polskiej"*, [in:] *Teologia polska na XXI wiek*, ed. K. Góźdź, K. Klauza (Lublin: KUL, 2005), p. 279.

The first of these only superficially pertains to the sphere of language (the so-called "plan of expression"), but in essence deals with something much deeper, related to theology's "form of expression" but reaching to what—to quote Hans Urs von Balthasar—today we can call theological aesthetics, or the relationship between substance and form, essence with beauty, and *theoria* with *kalos*. Exceptionally interesting and important is the fact that the language in which a large part of Polish theological thought is expressed is that of the belles-lettres. The basic "Polish" means of performing theology in our history was "literary" theology. According to Professor Stefan Sawicki of the Catholic University of Lublin, Polish literature "is a 'theological space' that is especially grateful to interpretation. In it, Polish theological thought can be mainly interpreted: amidst events, attitudes, gnomes, reflections, and letters."[10] This literary science scholar's view was confirmed by the theologian Andrzej Zuberbier: Polish literature is "[...] a *locus theologicus* that is impossible to overlook if one wants to understand Polish theology. And this is not only its history but also our present theological thinking."[11] Hence the methodological proposal in research on the identity of Polish theology: "[...] If one wants to better understand Polish theological thought, one must above all study literature from outside this discipline,"[12] such as the hymn *Bogurodzica*, the lives of the saints, chronicles, Skarga's sermons,[13] and the main works

10. This is a thought "directed towards the incarnation of faith, bearing witness with one's entire self, and thinking of an ethical and social orientation, particularly sensitive to the dignity and worth of the person in the human community." S. Sawicki, *Ethos polskiej literatury, Tygodnik Powszechny* 36(1982) No. 1-21, p. 3.

11. *Sprawozdanie*, [in:] *Chrześcijaństwo a kultura polska. V Kongres Teologów Polskich, Lublin 1416 IX 1983*, ed. M. Jaworski, A. Kubiś (Lublin 1988), p. 142.

12. J. Tyrawa, *W poszukiwaniu tożsamości teologii polskiej*, [in:] *Szkice o teologii polskiej*, ed. S.C. Napiórkowski (Poznań 1988), p. 131.

13. Zuberbier, *Sprawozdanie*, p. 142; W. Łydka, A. Zuberbier, *Teologia w Polsce*, [in:] *Szkice o teologii polskiej*, p. 176. Tyrawa describes the state of Polish theology in the sixteenth century as follows: "[...] The academic community is but one of many, and it is a relatively narrow current of theological thought [...] whereas the extra-disciplinary theological current is very rich in the diversity of its substance and its novel means of posing problems."

of the Romantic bards, "an era of theological theses transcribed to literature."[14] It is no coincidence that Roman Rogowski defended the originality of Polish theology by referring to the writings of Słowacki,[15] while Salij himself said that "the greatest Polish theologian is Cyprian Norwid."[16] Thus, we are faced with the following phenomenon: the theology of a nation which has been Christian for more than a thousand years is to a large extent expressed outside the field of scholarly works, in the form of "literary" theology. In Poland, it is possible to publish books such as *Let Us Pray Using the Words of Polish Poets*,[17], as the distance between the written word and the Word is not great; this goes in both directions.

The second attempt at responding to the "provocative question" above concerns a broader, ideational, and historical panorama of the history of Polish theology during the past hundred years that was written by Rev. Prof. Krzysztof Góźdź, the long-time chairman of the Association of Polish Dogmatic Theologians, although it is the fruit of the research and views of a broader community: the systematic theologians of the John Paul II Catholic University of Lublin.

In the *Lexicon of Polish Dogmatic Theologians of the Twentieth and Twenty-First Centuries*, Góźdź wrote that Polish Catholic theology "was stable until the 1940s, in the spirit of strong Thomistic philosophy, somewhat metaphysical for the most part and recalled the parallel philosophical concept of *philosophia perennis*," and so *theologia perennis*. To put it visually, this theology in a sense resembled the completion of an eternal construction by adding individual bricks, minor elements, the presentation of inviolable traditional construction, and certain adornments. From the 1940s until the Second Vatican

14. E. Bieńkowska, *Powieść i teza*, *Znak*, 30(1978) No. 78, p. 1008. See J. Salij, *Rozpacz pokonana* (Poznań: Wyd. W Drodze, 1983), p. 153-242 (the chapter titled: *Teologia w literaturze*).

15. *"Wszystko przez Ducha i dla Ducha..." Słowacki jako teolog i mistyk*, *Collegium Polonorum*, 11(1987) Vol. IX, p. 119.

16. S. Sawicki, *Ethos polskiej literatury*, *Tygodnik Powszechny* 29(1975) No. 21, p. 4.

17. Ed. A. Koszorz, selected by M. Wiśniewska (Warszawa 1996).

Council, Polish dogmatic theology increasingly metamorphosed into a theology of "earthly realities": a theology of war and peace; historical, national, political, and arbitrary problems; and the defense of the Catholic Church in Poland and around the world. This was related to the tragedy of the Second World War, its cruelties, the inferno of persecutions, and the consequences of two cruel totalitarian systems: German and Bolshevik, respectively. Naturally, we must remember that, apart from a couple years after 1945, Polish theology was not allowed to flourish freely and openly under either the German and Soviet occupations; instead, it limited itself to the verbal and kerygmatic sphere."[18]

Meanwhile, "after the Second Vatican Council Polish theology began to return to its nineteenth century form, which was rather pastoral, humanistic, praxeological, and ecumenical and dealt with the encounter between the supernatural and mundane worlds. It took on a socializing, narrative, and pedagogical nature, attempting to leave the communist ghetto for the broader world, increasingly making use of the legacy of world theology, especially German and, to a lesser extent, French. Finally, in the last years of the twentieth century and in the early twenty-first century, Polish dogmatic theology clearly became divided: into that which was liberal and modernistic and that which sought stable academic foundations in the system of Polish personalism, which increasingly sparred with the post-modern, secularist, liberal, and relativist mentality. One can say that we have a dipolar situation, like it was during the age of the Reformation. At the same time, personalistic theology does not limit itself to polemics but optimistically builds on a grand scale a full, objective, and futuristic vision of the faith and all of reality."[19]

Father Jacek Salij's work forms part of this historical and ideational perspective of Polish theology, actively co-creating the last

18. K. Góźdź, *Słowo wstępne*, *Leksykon polskich dogmatyków XX i XXI wieku* (Lublin: KUL, 2010), pp. 5-6.

19. *Ibid.*, p. 6.

two of the phases described above. Yet this is a work that transcends stereotypes, dependencies, and subordination to the "spirit of the time." This is a work that originally builds a "Salijan" synthesis of Augustinianism and Thomism in the post-conciliar years as well as personalistic theology in the late twentieth and early twenty-first centuries. In both cases, this is on his own terms.

I will discuss this now.

Jacek Salij

One of Father Salij's most important books for Polish theology, *Tajemnica Emmanuela dzisiaj* ("The Mystery of Emmanuel Today"), published in 1989, opens with the following telling confession: "If I were to summarize the very essence of Christianity in one word, I would not hesitate for a moment: Christianity is Emmanuel, God is with us. '[T]he young woman, pregnant and about to bear a Son, shall name Him Emmanuel' (Isaiah 7:14). St. Augustine says that the entire human race was wounded by bandits and gravely ill. Fortunately, the Only Begotten Son of God had mercy on the wretch, took on his nature, and became one of us, after which He dressed his wounds with wine and olives."[20]

This radical Christocentrism — in a three-sentence summary, in a nutshell — that permeates most of Salij's writings essentially comes from the New Testament, St. Augustine, St. Thomas, and so forth; in its form, it refers to the Christological interpretation of the parable of the Good Samaritan. The professor explains that the wine is His blood, while the olive is His Spirit; this is the medicine of Emmanuel.[21]

20. *Tajemnica Emmanuela dzisiaj* (Poznań: Wyd. W Drodze, 1989), p. 7. Unless noted otherwise, the publications in the footnotes are by Jacek Salij, OP.

21. *Ibid.*

This is a unique sign of Father Jacek's theology: theocentric Christocentrism in an Emmanuelian, so to speak with respect to the Bible, format and inclination. We will return to this topic in this preface. "God is with us" is not a neoplasm. Let us recall that it explains that the chasm between God and the world (Isaiah 59:2), filled with darkness and absurdity, lies and murder, violence and disdain, marks our world but has been conquered in the Incarnation.[22] "He is out of His mind," they say of Emmanuel in Mark's Gospel (3:21). "He is out of His mind because of His love for man," Salij .[23] And this mad, loving, permanent presence ("I am with you always, until the end of the age" [Matthew 28:20]) "of Emmanuel among us is called the Church."[24]

"God's selfless and undeserving gift for us is that we are the Church."[25] This is where the miracle of the Church comes from: the wondrousness of Emmanuel. Hence the awe and adoration of God, Christ, and the Church.

If then, it is Emmanuel, then it is the Church ("one cannot be a true Christian outside the Church and outside active participation in the supernatural life of the Church")[26], and as an inextricable element thereof, the Church's sacred faith and knowledge: theology. *Sacra Theo-Logia.*

I.

Father Jacek Salij is above all a theologian of the contemporary Polish Church of the late twentieth and early twenty-first centuries. But first things first.

He was born on August 19, 1942, in Budy, Dubno County, in Volhynia in present-day Ukraine. He was the second child of Józef

22. *Ibid.*, pp. 8-9.
23. *Ibid.*, p. 8.
24. *Ibid.*, p. 11.
25. *Ibid.*
26. *Ibid.*, p. 5.

and Agnieszka née Ostolska. He had an older sister (who died in childhood), three younger brothers, and six sisters. His baptismal name was Eugeniusz, but his religious name is Jacek. After the turmoil of the Second World War, the Salij family settled in Piława Dolna outside Dzierżoniów in Lower Silesia. Eugeniusz entered the Dominican Order in 1960, immediately after his *Matura* exam. He studied at the Dominican School of Philosophy and Theology in Warsaw and Krakow, where he learned dogmatic theology from Romuald Kostecki, OP, as well as Ireneusz Łuczyński, OP, while his master's thesis (*Miejsce mszy świętej w święceniu niedzieli*/ "The Place of Mass in the Celebration of Sunday") was written under the direction of Eugeniusz Gaweł, OP. He took his perpetual vows on November 29, 1964, and was ordained a priest on December 25, 1966. In 1968-1970, Salij continued his studies at the Academy of Catholic Theology in Warsaw under the direction of Henryk Bogacki, SJ (the supervisor of his licentiate and doctoral dissertations) as well as Rev. Ignacy Różycki. Father Salij defended his doctoral dissertation (*Modlitwa za świętych w liturgii rzymskiej*/ "The Prayer for the Saints in the Roman Liturgy") in 1971. Beginning in 1970, he worked as an assistant at the Chair of the History of Dogmas at the Academy of Catholic Theology, and after defending his doctorate he worked as an assistant professor. After defending his habilitation (*Główne kontrowersje teologiczne wokół komunii niemowląt*/ "The Main Theological Controversies Concerning the Communion of Infants"), he became a research associate, and since 1989 he has been an assistant professor of the Chair in Dogmatic Theology of the Academy of Catholic Theology. In 1990, he became an associate professor; in 1996, he was made the director of the Chair of Dogmatic Theology (since 1999, the former Academy of Catholic Theology has been known as the Cardinal Stefan Wyszyński University in Warsaw). In 2000, he received the academic title of a full professor.

For decades, Professor Salij's extracurricular activity has been extensive and fruitful: pastoral, journalistic, cultural, and social. He was a minister to the Cultural Section of the Warsaw Club of Catholic Intelligentsia (1971-1981), a longtime regular contributor to the monthly *W drodze* (since 1973), a co-founder of the *Gaudium Vitae* movement (in 1979), a pastor to teachers engaged in Solidarity (since 1982), and a consultor of the Commission for the Doctrine of the Faith of the Polish Bishops Conference. Since 1971, he has been a member of the Polish Society of Dogmatic Theologians (which for many years functioned as the Dogmatic Section of Polish Theologians) and numerous other societies, committees, and academic societies. He was engaged in the opposition to the communist regime in the 1970s and 1980s. As a signatory to the Letter 59, he expressed his opposition to amendments planned to the Constitution of the Polish People's Republic (in 1975); he also published in underground journals like *Zapis* and *Aneks* and was active in the underground Council of National Education (1982-1989). For this reason, he was harassed; for decades, Salij was denied an associate professorship and even a passport. He became a member of the Council for the Protection of Struggle and Martyrdom Sites of the Polish Nation in 1992 and the PEN Club in 1989. Salij has received numerous prestigious awards. Pursuant to a decision of the President of Poland, Lech Kaczyński, of May 3, 2007, he was awarded the Commander's Cross with Star of the Order of Polonia Restituta, while on November 11, 2017, the President of Poland Andrzej Duda bestowed upon him the Grand Cross of that order. In 2018, he was distinguished with the Medal of the Centennial of the Restoration of Independence. In 1998, he received an award of the Polcul Foundation. In 2004, he became a laureate of the Feniks, an award given by the Association of Catholic Publishers.[27]

27. See Salij Jacek, [in:] *Leksykon Polskich Dogmatyków*, ed. K. Góźdź (Lublin: KUL, 2010), pp. 326-327.

What is most impressive, however, is his output as a writer. Salij is the author of dozens of books, hundreds of academic articles, and if we include his popular and journalist writing, his works are counted in hundreds. For almost half a century (at least since 1973, the beginning of his column *Szukającym drogi* ["For Those Searching for the Way"]), he is one of the most widely read Polish theologians and has had an enormous impact on at least three generations of readers and theological-pastoral students. It is here, in the abundance and quality of his output as a writer, that the notion to publish his collected works, of which this book is a part, was born. This foreword was conceived in a modest way: not as an attempt at describing, analyzing, or interpreting the professor's output (this is a task for researchers) but rather as an introduction to the writings of Father Salij, encouragement to read them, and a kind of flash that opens the entrance to the world of Salij's theology. Here, we are above all interested in a preliminary recognition, simple guidelines concerning methods characteristic of the texts contained in this volume, research preferences, the main substantive emphases, and the author's main areas of research. While reading, we must remember that he is above all a theologian, a professor of dogmatic theology, and a longtime staff member and director of the Chair of the History of Dogmas and Dogmatic Theology. Dogmatic theology is the substantive center of gravity and the golden thread of each of Father Salij's reflections and theses.

2.

In the brief foreword to *The Dilemmas of Our Times*, Father Salij included a lengthy quotation from Denis de Rougemont. He probably chose to do so due to the latter's polemical sharpness and because of the great *laus theologiae* in the other author's text, or because of kinship regarding the view of the fundamental role of *scientiae fidei* for the faith and culture of our civilization with this Swiss historian of ideas and essayist. De Rougemont writes as follows:

I know few occupations more decried in our century, few words which hold less appeal for our contemporaries, and I am not speaking of the uncultivated but of the intellectual elite. You meet great scientists, philosophers, moralists, writers known throughout the world: nine time out of ten, these masters of modern thought confess to you without the least blush, slightly astonished as the question, that they have not read in their lives a single theological treatise. They would be even more astonished if they were told that this is evident in all their work: they would not quite see the connection. I consider that this involves a retrograde attitude, more alarming for the future of culture than the misdeeds of the fascist hordes.

The mind of the Occident and its vocabulary were born of the great theological debates in the centuries of the primitive Church. Our music, our sculpture, our painting were born in the choirs of the churches, while our poetics were composed in the atmosphere of the Manichean sects. Even the great modern philosophies, Descartes and Kant, Hegel, Auguste Comte and Marx, took position on theological issues at their starting point. To be ignorant of theology is to break with the most fruitful tradition of occidental culture. It is therefore to condemn oneself unwittingly to remaking the spiritual discoveries formulated for more that fifteen hundred years by the Fathers of the Church and the great heretics. The theological naiveté of our century is one of the most considerable advantages of the new barbarism.[28]

Salij's great work has been waging a private war against the naiveté and barbarism of "our times" for years (we can hope that this will have public effects). Those two: naiveté and barbarism, have their source in our numerous "dilemmas" contemporary to us. For Salij, the basic weapon in this war is theology (hence the convenience of de Rougemont's quoted thesis).

How does he understand it? How does he do theology?

28. Denis De Rougemont, *The Devil's Share,* chapter IV (Washington, DC: Pantheon Books, 1945), pp. 125-126.

Salij works with dogmatic theology, of course, for he is a specialist and academic professor in this theological sub-discipline. However, what is very important is that he is interested in the interdisciplinary cooperation of dogmatic theology with other fields of theology and, more broadly, with other sciences and, broader still, with art and culture. This is also dogmatic theology that is concerned about its existential implications, about the deep bond between *theoria* and *praxis*, in accordance with Salij's understanding of the uniqueness of Polish theology.

His understanding of theology is very sapiential. In a text that is decisive with respect to this matter, he writes:

> Theology is above all wisdom. Or to be more exact, it is an aspiration towards wisdom, a kind of contemplation of the reality that we see through faith. Thus, theological wisdom can be successfully sought by both professional theologians and persons without an academic background. One must have a living instinct of faith, some sense of touch with respect to the invisible.[29]

In other words, faith and wisdom would be at least as important to the essence of theology as knowledge and expertise, if not even more important. As a side note, here is a relevant gloss that adds a stamp of great authority to this matter. On July 31, 2017, Benedict XVI

29. *Królestwo Boże w was jest*, Poznań 1980, p. 5; this is the continuation and conclusion of this thesis: "If we are to compare the greatest accomplishments, the theology of non-theologians is more vibrant and more directly touches man's soul than the wisdom of professional theologians. It suffices to compare Pascal with Newman, Norwid with Koniński, or Skarga with Woroniecki. I do not intend on postponing professional theology, which is without a doubt unquestionably useful activity. Moreover, without the theology of professionals we would not have neither Pascal, Norwid, nor Koniński; all of them were well-aware of the theological reflection of their times and made ample use of it. It seems, after all, that the theology of brilliant amateurs more directly grows from life, while the wisdom of theologians is based above all on theological knowledge, from which it draws its lifeblood.

I am drawing out these comments to justify my theological writing. For a theologian, this writing is insufficiently professional [...]." *Ibid.*

wrote a brief letter to Cardinal Gerhard Ludwig Müller on the occasion of his seventieth birthday and the fortieth anniversary of his priestly ordination. The letter opens a jubilee book that commemorates that anniversary. The text, full of personal references and reminiscences, warm in tone, and deep in its firm tonation, is essentially a mini treatise on the topic of the essence of theology. To be truly itself, it must lead to wisdom and ultimately be wisdom, a wisdom that transcends merely academic competences, as the pope emeritus writes from the perspective of the tenth decade of his life.

Benedict XVI writes that theology must be something greater than merely the "words of the experts;" it must contain greater wisdom that is capable of "recognizing the limits of a 'simple' scholar's approach." The former Prefect of the Congregation for the Doctrine of the Faith wrote to his successor as head of that congregation (as of 2017): "The prefect [does] not necessarily need to be a theologian, but a sage, who in tackling theological questions would not make specific valuations, but would discern what to do for that [particular] time in the Church." Ultimately, if this is concerned with the greatest good, our salvation, the point is that decisions are undertaken not so much by academic theology as by true wisdom (which encompasses the entirety of the phenomenon of life), which knows "scientific aspects" but furthermore is "able to envisage the entire life of a grand community."[30] Look at this text's second motto: the aim is ultimate unity and simplicity of faith.

And wisdom. It is exactly this shape and dimension that Salij has in mind. In his writing, we are dealing with this process: with wisdom which becomes theology and with theology that becomes wisdom.

Salij has been proposing exactly such a path — towards practical wisdom applicable to everyday life as the theologal aim of faith and theological thinking — for Polish theology and its successors for half

30. All the references in these two paragraphs come from the Catholic Information Agency, January 4, 2018.

a century. Beginning in the 1970s, Salij, inspired by Witold Gombrowicz's views on the topic of freedom and the future of Polish culture, advised that because of our own subordinateness (for we are incapable of instantly overcoming historical and political gaps that separate us from German, French, Italian, or Anglo-Saxon theology) we should add impetus to the development of an original Polish theology.[31] For Polish theological "non-conservative conservatism"[32] (Salij's original expression referring to the ability of creatively expanding views that are faithful to tradition), "popular pressure"[33] protecting Polish theology from innovativeness, and above all the fact that Poles place greater importance on faith and life than even the most brilliant theoretical equilibrations, present a singular opportunity for Polish theology. "Instead of being accountable for someone else's maturity, try to reveal Europe's immaturity [...]. You will find a theory in accordance with your practice," Gombrowicz counseled his compatriots.[34]

This is more or less the advice that Salij has for Polish theology. It is also the kind of theology that Salij performs: in accordance with the principles of existentiality, practicality, and fidelity but full of depth, precision, and courage. If nearly half a century ago Andrzej Zuberbier posed the following task to Polish theology: "Polish theologians will create Polish theology only if they are immersed in global theology,"[35] then Jacek Salij seems to say the opposite in the substance of his various writings: Polish theologians will be immersed in global theology only if they first create Polish theology.

This thesis is original (especially considering advice that contradicts it), powerful, and free of a sense of inferiority. Salij has been going on this path for years: his theology has been socially, politically

31. *Królestwo Boże...*, pp. 141-151 [title of the section: *Zadania teologii dzisiaj*; title of the article: *Sytuacja teologii w Polsce (na marginesie III Kongresu Teologów Polskich)*].

32. *Ibid.*, pp. 146-147.

33. *Ibid.*

34. *Ibid.*, p. 144.

35. *Ibid.*

(in the best meaning of the term "politics," or fighting for what truly makes up our common good) engaged,[36] serving the great cause of Polish reconciliation and the understanding of reality and (post) modernity as well as Christian, Catholic, and Polish identity.[37] For years, he has shared an enormous dose of spiritual and intellectual energy with those "looking for their way" in all the thick jungles of modernity and own life.

However, the essence of his understanding and performance of theology seems to lie in this simple yet imperative sentence: "Theology is above all wisdom."[38] More specifically, to paraphrase his own words: theology is learning wisdom through reflection on the reality that shows us faith. Salij owes his understanding of wisdom itself to Thomas, who in this regard makes generous use of the work of Aristotle and Augustine. We read in the essay *Mądrość i głupota* ("Wisdom and Foolishness") that wisdom "is knowledge considering the deepest causes" (*cognitio per altissimas causas*, to quote Aristotle) and at the same time "knowing what is Divine" (*cognitio divinorum*, to quote Augustine).[39]

Ultimately, then, wisdom consists of knowing God and directing one's life towards Him.[40] This thesis is extremely important to Salij, and one cannot overemphasize how fundamental to his *vitae et theologiae* this synthesis of reason and existence, intellectual theory, and life's practice is. In this way, we must wisely work to improve ourselves and engage our reason in interpreting God's law and subordinating our lives (choices, decisions, actions) to it (God's law, or ultimately

36. See C. Smuniewski, *Chrześcijanie o wojnie. Refleksje inspirowane poszukiwaniem i "odpowiedziami" ojca profesora Jacka Salija OP*, [in:] *Credo Domine. Adiuva incredulitatem meam.* Księga jubileuszowa dedykowana Ojcu Profesorowi Jackowi Salijowi OP, ed. J. Kupczak, C. Smuniewski (Poznań — Kraków: Wyd. W Drodze, 2017), pp. 495-509.

37. See W. Surówka, *Polska Ojca Jacka*, [in:] *Credo Domine...*, pp. 527-541.

38. *Królestwo Boże...*, p. 5.

39. *Eseje tomistyczne*, Poznań 1995, pp. 42, 46.

40. *Ibid.*, pp. 43, 47-48.

God Himself).[41] This is the fullness of everyday and theological wisdom: "God and Christ should be sought not only with one's intellect but also through moral efforts."[42] The opposite of this attitude is foolishness which Salij, inspired by St. Thomas (and, indirectly, by Isidore of Seville) calls the paralysis of the soul (stupor, torpor, immobility), consisting of limiting one's judgments and activities in the narrow framework of only what is mundane. In this way, a pathetic stump of reality cut out of supernatural references is achieved. Only a fool can treat things of this earth as if they were never permeated by the light of the supernatural.[43] Aleksander Fredro, who wrote a two-line poem against fools and foolishness, comes to Salij's rescue; he is quoted by Salij with evident approval:

Great is foolishness' might:
It destroys the earth and reaches hell's heights.[44]

Now, after several decades of his publishing activity, we can see the wisdom-related consequences of his writing exceptionally clearly. We can also see wisdom defined as above according to Thomistic-Augustinian standards. This is thoroughly Gospel wisdom,[45] which at the same time strips one of illusions (sinful ones, or foolishness), brings one back in line, and restores the proper measure of people and objects, one that leads towards God. Many readers "looking for their path" emphasize that with the sleeve of his white habit Father Jacek wiped clean their table of life and words that had been soiled by their own foolishness and that of others, and washed the dirty foam off superficiality, helping them to see further and more deeply.

41. *Ibid.*, p. 60.

42. *Ibid.*, p. 142.

43. *Ibid.*, pp. 49-51.

44. "Głupoty straszna potęga. / Ziemię burzy, piekła sięga." *Ibid.*, p. 50.

45. See, for example: *Świętowanie Pana Boga* [interviewed by A Petrowa-Wasilewicz, J. Borkowicz], Kraków 2001, p. 141 (on his failures and successes), p. 153 (on his own sinfulness and confession), and many others.

His writing is concerned about something much greater than even the most accurate response to any detailed question (with regards to those "looking for their way"). Salij is concerned about the wisdom of his very style of religious and moral thinking. This wisdom and this style are "typically Catholic,"[46] to use his phrase, and free of any eccentricities or sugarcoating. Salij uses no cheap special effects or charlatanism. His writing is Catholic: pure, firm, and nourishing.

3.

The compass of this work invariably and faultlessly points in one direction: towards God. The radical primacy of God is the trademark of these fifty-plus years of Salij's consistently theocentric *scientiae fidei*. We can even call this theology totally theocentric in the sense and meaning that "totality" is synonymous with entirety, with completeness. His underlying idea (and the *leitmotif* of essentially all of Salij's responses to "non-indifferent questions") is the principle taken from the Augustinian spirit and Augustine's writings that in the text *O pochodzeniu władzy od Boga* ("On the Origin of Power from God") is expressed as follows: "Because all of man belongs to God, we must surrender our entire selves to God,"[47] without any restricted enclave. This is precisely explained using the example of "repay to Caesar what belongs to Caesar and to God what belongs to God" (Matthew 22:21). What Caesar wants and demands, Salij explains, "he is entitled to and is our duty only if it is found within our duties towards God."[48] "Caesar" refers to everything apart from God, one's entire life.

And this is only if it fits within our duties towards God.

Not only Augustine but also Aquinas is the patron of such thinking and such an ethos. For Thomas, any anthropological theses are

46. *Pytania nieobojętne* (Poznań: Wyd. W Drodze, 1986), p. 6.
47. *Eseje tomistyczne*, p. 157.
48. *Ibid.*

always and absolutely subordinated to "thorough theocentrism."[49] This is explained particularly emphatically by Salij in the text opening *Eseje tomistyczne* ("Thomistic Essays") titled *Bóg jako dobro powszechne*[50] ("God as a Universal Good;" *bonum universale*). In his view, St. Thomas directs all his spiritual and intellectual efforts towards demonstrating that God is the good common to all (everything and everyone) and in Him lies the ultimate meaning (of everything and everyone).[51] "Every created good is some specific good; only the one God is a universal good," as we read in *Summa Theologiae*.[52]

Salij subordinates the entirety of his theology to this principle; in it he finds the meaning of dogmas. Like Thomas, he understands a dogma as "a conceptualization of God's truth directed towards God Himself."[53] In other words, he distances himself, perhaps as much as is possible, from all "symbolic" theories that try to de-radicalize the "literalness" of the theological word about God and create a neutralizing curtain between the symbol and the thing itself. Meanwhile, the limit of faith, words, and dogma are not sentences and theses but the Reality which they describe.[54] God is the first and the only One in the entire matter of writing about Him and serving Him in such a way.

4.

For the Christian, theocentrism takes on a clearly and unambiguously Christocentric shape. This is a kind of *reductio ad Christum* or, more precisely and perhaps more accurately, *concentratio in Christum*. In other words, the Christocentrism of the Christian faith (not to be confused with Christomonism) is the proper test for the orthodoxy of Theocentrism, which means testing — spiritually, intellectually, and

49. *Ibid.*, p. 26.
50. *Ibid.*, pp. 9-21.
51. *Ibid.*, p. 19.
52. *Ibid.*, p. 20.
53. *Ibid.*, p. 121.
54. *Ibid.*, p. 120.

existentially — if the God in the center (of one's life and thought) is the living, true, trinitarian God, the Father, Son, and Holy Spirit, i.e. the God of Jesus Christ. For years, Salij's theology has been treading exactly this path. Furthermore, Father Jacek has the gift of expressing a complex truth in a uniquely simple way, which is characteristic not only of this dimension of his writings. He writes, for example: "The Christian faith is very simple. To be a Christian, it suffices to encounter Jesus Christ, Who is alive, and become bound to Him."[55] To put it in simpler and more powerful terms: "The Christian faith is Jesus Christ."[56] One hundred percent of his advice for his readers goes in this direction. For example: "We do not believe in Christ because Sacred Scripture tells us so but the Bible is for us Sacred Scripture because of our faith in Christ, the Son of God;"[57] "Just as everything in the Old Testament, it [the passage from Genesis about giants — J.S.] leads us directly to Jesus Christ, the Son of God and our Savior;"[58] "It suffices to separate oneself from Christ in order to [...] become the prey of evil spirits more powerful than we."[59] And so on and so forth. His theology always goes in this direction: the indissoluble convolution of radical theocentrism and equally radical Christocentrism are the trademarks of Jacek Salij's theology.

Naturally, this has its solid fundaments in the history of theology, through which Salij moves with erudition and a weightlessness characteristic of the greats. Of these fundaments, the most important pillars are — to repeat, also in this context — Augustine and Thomas. Their thought is the basic philosophical and theological base for Salij's writings.[60] He reaches for them first, referring to the history and classics of *scientiae fidei*. Some of his statements imply,

55. *Pytania nieobojętne*, pp. 5, 7.
56. *Ibid.*, p. 16.
57. *Ibid.*, p. 55.
58. *Ibid.*, p. 72.
59. *Ibid.*, p. 44.
60. See *Pytania nieobojętne*, p. 33.

in fact, that not only their text or thinking but also their style and faith as well as their very personalities, which were very different, fascinate our author. He is also one of Poland's greatest specialists in Augustinianism and Thomism as well as the author of innovative genre experiments in the area of the popularization of their thought and texts (for example, the famous "interviews" with St. Augustine);[61] the translator and editor of the writings of Augustine and Aquinas (for example, Thomas' *Selected Works*,[62] *Gospel of the Fathers of the Church*,[63] *Lecture on Prayer*,[64] and many others); the author of forewords, contributions, or entire books devoted to the interpretation of these authors; and of attempts to transplant their thought to contemporary questions and problems, interpreting their writing within the context of our *hic et nunc*.

Father Jacek's references to Augustine and Aquinas transcend an ordinary, academic-pastoral, and scholarly-inspirational analysis of their writings. This is a very personal relationship. Salij is inspired not only by the weight and style of their thought but also by the shape of the sanctity of their lives. He is clearly fascinated by a synthesis of these two great Christian figures and their philosophy and theology. According to him, Augustine was "a clever writer, excellent polemicist, and outstanding psychologist who perfectly understood the human soul; he was a master of detail capable of probing the depths of some Biblical statement and shedding unexpected light on some individual word."[65] Meanwhile, Thomas is "a brilliant synthesist," "avoids polemics," and "in general is not concerned about pleasing readers; he writes in an unimaginably formalized way." Salij writes that when he reads him, he "always feels like he is chewing a brick" and "feels respect" for him because any text devoted to his thought

61. For example, *Królestwo Boże...*, pp. 101-106 (*Święty Augustyn o godności płci*).
62. *Dzieła wybrane* (Poznań: Wyd. W Drodze, 1984).
63. *Ewangelia Ojców Kościoła* (Kraków: Znak, 1983).
64. *Wykład Pacierza* (Poznań: Wyd. W Drodze, 1987).
65. *Świętowanie Pana Boga*, p. 100.

"costs me ten times more than any other."[66] In Thomas, he mainly admires his unique combination of the genius of intellect, Gospel radicalism, and down-to-earth common sense. As an example of this synthesis, he repeats several times St. Augustine's simultaneously radical and commonsense advice: "Evil must be avoided under all circumstances, while good must be performed always, but depending on the circumstances;"[67] in other words, neither falling to the supposed determinism of evil nor fanaticism as the supposed service of good are Catholic, Christian, or Divine.

What is particularly valuable in Thomas' philosophical treasury to him is his realism. Salij is an anti-nominalist to the marrow of his bone, which I will discuss shortly. Naturally, Salij — like Thomas himself — is a theologian of the first order, so realism, Thomistic *par excellence* interests him (them) not only as the philosophical background of theology but mainly as an essential dimension of theology itself. "Thomas is a realist," he writes in a text on the natural law, "who is consistently aware of the fact that we are not the creators of reality, but reality comes before our cognition and even before our existence."[68] Elsewhere, in a soteriological text, he writes: "The promise of eternal salvation is something unimaginably greater than an axiological thesis: it is a real offer of salvific power through which God wants to transform us now and in this way bring us closer to ultimate salvation."[69] This is the full (philosophical-theological) dimension of realism borrowed from Aquinas that is continued (developed) in Salij's writings. Supernatural and inconceivable do not mean unreal; on the contrary, the closer one is to the supernatural and inconceivable God, the more realism there is.

66. *Ibid.*
67. *Ibid.*, p. 159.
68. *Eseje tomistyczne*, p. 182.
69. *Ibid.*, p. 87.

And here is an example of realism *a rebours*: understanding sin as an escape into the world of appearances and, furthermore, evil, which demands it not be considered as such,[70] or an escape to infinitely extreme unreality ("through my sin, I can become so uprooted from reality that I live only through appearances").[71]

5.

This is an important thread in Salij's perception of the world and understanding of the entirety of reality, polemically reaching to the above-mentioned nominalism. For him, a born dogmatic theologian spiritually and intellectually brought up on the realistic and orthodox views of Augustine and Thomas, nominalism is the number one enemy and the basic sticking point in the wheels of human cognition and the human way to truth. Salij accuses this philosophical view, born amidst the dispute on the universal in the late thirteenth and early fourteenth centuries (to recall, it comes from Latin: *nomen* = name; its precursors were Abelard and Ockham) and most generally consisting of the reduction of things (the reality of things) to the products of thought or expressions of the tongue, later developed by the Enlightenment empiricists through Kotarbiński and many other postmodernists,[72] of creating in significant spaces in European thought and the life of the West a so-called nominalist mentality[73] ("successfully separating names from things").[74] Its consequences of the processes of secularization in the Euro-Atlantic world are far-reaching.

Salij frequently writes about this, both directly and indirectly. He writes about dealing with Sacred Scripture (when there is no bond

70. *Tajemnica Emmanuela dzisiaj*, p. 8; *Pytania nieobojętne*, pp. 41, 36.

71. *Świętowanie Pana Boga*, p. 15.

72. See P. Janowski, *Nominalizm*, [in:] *Encyklopedia katolicka*, Vol. XIII, ed. E. Gigilewicz et. al. (Lublin: KUL, 2009), Col. 1365-1368.

73. *Eseje tomistyczne*, p. 126.

74. *Słowo wstępne*, [in:] *Tomasz z Akwinu, Ewangelia Ojców Kościoła*, selected and trans. J. Salij (Kraków: Znak, 1983), p. 7.

linking together the word with the matter itself, reading the Bible begins and ends with reading the text, which never attains reality or, above all, does not open itself to the reality of God Himself and not understanding the symbolic structure of speech, it does not allow us to understand the sacramental structure of the Word of God, constantly leading towards unreal literalness and never further);[75] the difficulties of (post)nominalist formation with the appropriate understanding of the reality of God's activity; and the contemporary doubt in the natural law[76] and in salvific intercession.[77] Salij laments that this phenomenon is broad, if not to say, widespread: "in the dispute on the universal, nominalism has emerged victorious in our thinking at the cost of realism."[78]

In the case of Father Jacek himself, this anti-nominalist allergy, however, brings about two positive fruits. First, it effectively protects this professor of dogmatic theology against the disease of theological innovativeness, which to a large extent comes from the insufficiency of realism and the trend towards the relativization with regards to the ambiguity of the element of language (nomens) and at the same time uncertainty with regards to the relationship between things and words. This was quite a bit for a European theologian from the late twentieth and early twenty-first centuries... Second, this naturally leads thinking towards what is real, existential, and poignantly specific, related to the incarnation of the spirit, flesh and blood, and life itself. In other words, it helps to build a bridge between *theoria* and *praxis*. Nominalism (as anti-realism) is in its essence utopian and leads to utopia (hence the mushrooming, in recent centuries, of utopian social models, mostly leftist in nature, directly or indirectly borrowed from nominalist and post-nominalist philosophy). Meanwhile,

75. *Ibid.*, p. 7, 13.
76. *Eseje tomistyczne*, p. 186.
77. *Ibid.*, p. 106.
78. *Świętowanie Pana Boga*, p. 271.

epistemological and ontological realism lead — not necessarily in a straight line, but they do nonetheless — to a theology closer to life.[79]

6.

And precisely this — theology close to life — is the case of Jacek Salij's theology. Naturally, this theoretical dependency between philosophical realism and theological existentiality had to fall on fertile personal (biographical, characterological, pastoral, etc.) soil. It certainly fell on such soil, which was the intention of our author to consistently minister to those "searching for their way." There is a brilliant fragment of his foreword to the *Selected Works* of St. Thomas Aquinas in which Salij writes of Aquinas' "small works," which are "marked by some stigma of immediacy that was formed in response to some question or in relation to some controversy or from the needs of the heart."[80] Next, he quotes his fellow Dominican, Father Marie-Dominique Chenu, who wrote of these same works as follows: "This is why they are so interesting to everyone who wants to recreate the full concreteness of Thomas' intellectual life: we can better know him when we observe what his stance was on a specific controversy; what response he gave to a fellow professor who turned to him with a consultation; how he reacted to a specific writing commission from a friend or the pope; how he defended his fellow brothers against slander; how he justified from a theological or institutional point of view new forms of apostolic work; how his interest in moral problems in relation to economic development was manifested."[81]

79. See A. Nossol, *Teologia bliższa życiu. Wpływ teologii na egzystencję chrześcijańską* (Opole: Wyd. Św. Krzyża, 1984).

80. *Słowo wstępne*, [in:] St. Thomas Aquinas, *Dzieła wybrane*, ed. and trans. J. Salij (Kraków: Znak, 1984), p. 5.

81. M.D. Chenu, *Wstęp do filozofii św. Tomasza z Akwinu* (Warszawa: Akademia Teologii Katolickiej, 1974), p. 359 (*op. cit. Słowo wstępne*, [in:] St. Thomas Aquinas, *Dzieła wybrane*, p. 5).

This passage is brilliant mostly because after many years (Salij quoted Chenu thirty-five years ago, and Chenu wrote this sentence about Thomas more than fifty years ago) this adheres almost completely to "the specificity of Jacek's intellectual life": questions and answers, controversies and consultations, defenses and justifications, arduous investigations, and ethical conclusions. Above all, it is because of the needs of Salij's heart that his seemingly small works are great.

In his "lesser" (and, in essence, major) responses to "those searching for their way" and "asking not insignificant questions," he presents one of the most beautiful faces of professional Polish theology: the wisdom of its service. And Polish theology — sometimes disdainfully and ironically accused of being incapable of inventing a major heresy — is in its essence not interested in getting people to leave the Church; in fact, the opposite is true. In these responses (this is even more evident when they are read in one sitting), Salij is the most original Polish theologian of his generation, situating his theological work at the intersection of dogma and everyday life. In the greatest existential confusion, he finds sunlight, the road to (Gospel) light, and can illuminate the darkness of reason and sometimes the darkness of the heart of the person crushed by the existential burden of blackness, misfortune, and sin, of the person by the cross. One of the secrets to Salij's successful method is that he strips questions of what is superficial (a burst of suffering that blurs the clarity of vision through its pain, a barrier of ignorance, pop culture superficiality, the false suggestions of the world, etc.) and teaches to think Biblically and dogmatically, both internally and from an authentic perspective that does not shirk before the radicalism of faith. Although this is obvious, it must be said that he knows a lot about life's complexities and mysteries. He hunts down the superficiality of our religiosity and constantly struggles to find the form of the depth and shape of truth that would fit it.

I believe he is not always right. In fact, it seems that some of his responses (which are not numerous and are read many years after their initial publication in a dramatically changed context) do not stand the test of time. For example, when he writes about the end of the debate over evolution (which was revived and not only because of extreme "creationism")[82] and civil marriages (so-called concordat marriages changed the circumstances of the problem);[83] when while offering extremely accurate observations on the Index Librorum Prohibitorum he writes that "the law in essence should not interfere into those areas where moral attitudes are shaped"[84] (really?); or on freemasonry (during the last thirty years, we have learned much more about it, and the truth about it is much worse than we had previously thought).[85]

Above all, Salij's theology is wise, prudent, balanced, and rooted in faith and erudition, at the same time trustworthy and trusted by legions of readers. In his advice and suggestions, we find this kind of balance that binds together the traditional with the novel and the painful with what gives hope. This is Father Jacek's permanent contribution to the life of the Church in Poland. To demonstrate his balance and prudence, I will quote several of his statements from an April 2018 interview published in *Gość Niedzielny*: "The volatility of a living organism is part of its beauty, while the faith of the Church is something living. [...] I would not dismiss the fears of traditionalists [...]. Catholics who speak out against the Second Vatican Council are rebellious and sin against the unity of the Church [....]. There are numerous disputes in which both sides are right [...]. We should not worry about the future of the Church; instead, we should worry about

82. *Pytania nieobojętne*, pp. 30-34.
83. *Ibid.*, pp. 172-176.
84. *Ibid.*, p. 269.
85. *Ibid.*, pp. 277-281.

our own salvation."[86] This is Salij in a nutshell. And I will provide one more example. In the 1970s, Father Jacek wrote an article entirely devoted to the topic of praying the rosary. In it, he analytically demonstrated, using several examples, both the virtues and deficiencies (as he called them) of the rosary, concluding the last sentence of his text as follows: "The costs related to the existence of the rosary as an institution seem minor compared to the spiritual worth it adds to the life of the Church."[87] After the long, analytical part of this text, it seemed unclear whether we should pray the rosary or not; there were arguments in favor but also many against, so the matter seemed impossible to resolve until Salij arrived at a simple conclusion.

7.

One of the most interesting threads of Father Jacek's theological work are essays that he himself once called "interdisciplinary attempts"[88] and that to a large extent consist of closely reading the belles-lettres (especially poetry), and their consequences for the research and interpretive interaction between theology and literary studies. This type of text is closely and deeply tied to what has been mentioned above: namely, the concern that theology does not abandon reality and in this way can more effectively serve those who, to quote to the title of one of the professor's most-read books, are searching for their way in the dilemmas of our time. Contrary to popular belief and superficial judgments (such as the notion that poetry is for snobs, etc.), the art of the word is something akin to a sensitive seismograph that records all the tectonic movements (in this case, spiritual, intellectual, and social) of our earth and every one of its eras. Salij the theologian has the temperament of a pastor and a historian, a spiritual therapist and

86. *Wiara jest żywa* (interviewed by M. Jakimowicz), *Gość Niedzielny* 95(2018) No. 16, pp. 28-29.

87. *Królestwo Boże...*, p. 194.

88. *Ibid.*, pp. 217-283.

guide in the labyrinth of the modernity and complications of life, but above all he is — in everything that is mentioned above — a probing and seasoned observer of his age. This is why he needs a seismograph and why his articles and books contain numerous references to poetic texts by St. John of the Cross and Stanisław Barańczak; Antoni Słonimski, Maria Konopnicka, and Anna Kamieńska; Origen and Augustine (treated as poets of the age of the Church Fathers); Cyprian Kamil Norwid, Zygmunt Krasiński, and many others.

In *Teologia Anny Kamieńskiej*[89] ("Anna Kamieńska's Theology"), which many consider to be one of Salij's most important texts, we read: "Poetry's [...] ambition is to achieve something impossible: it seeks truth about the world without the intercession of problems. Thus, the world of poetry lacks the conciseness of the world seen through the spectacles of problems; it contains more antinomy, tension, and unfinished endeavors. But it is a richer and, more importantly, truer world, one that is closer to reality [! — J. S.]. [...] Thus, for example, it is no paradox to me that the greatest Polish theologian is Cyprian Norwid."[90] This is an extremely interesting thesis that for many might prove controversial, but in Salij's work, it is even greater than the mere cooperation of the theological with the artistic. It originates in the uniquely constructed theological aesthetic which is most completely outlined in the essay *Jeśli Bóg jest Artystą...* ("If God Is an Artist...").[91] This text, which was written for an international congress and exhibition in Krakow entitled *Sztuka miejscem odnalezienia się* ("Arts as a Place for Finding Oneself") held in the fall of 1993 is one of the most important voices on the topic of the theology of beauty. In it, Salij proposes the unambiguous and wildly courageous thesis that "ugliness cannot be revealed in a way that strengthens it."[92]

89. *Tygodnik Powszechny* 29(1975) No. 10, p. 4.

90. *Królestwo Boże...*, p. 218. See the fragment of this preface titled: "Our Faith, Our Theology."

91. *Dylematy naszych czasów*, pp. 209-213.

92. *Ibid.*, p. 210.

It is around this thesis that he builds the entirety of his conception of aesthetics, at the same time referring to a powerful phrase from the Book of Revelation directed to Babylon, a Godless city that symbolizes those zones of the world in which God's and man's paths tragically part ways: "No craftsmen in any trade will ever be found in you again" (Revelation 18:22). Such is the tragic finale of Godlessness in the field of beauty: the lack of beauty.

His theological aesthetic is positively founded on the pronouncement that "every shaping of human spaces in a way that would make people feel at home is a form of participation in the work of the Divine Artist."[93] From the negative perspective, the same thesis is as follows: "Every form of filling human spaces with ugliness and false beauty, with despair and attempts at scribbling over (rather than overcoming) despair is a form of opposing the Divine Artist; it is an attempt at building our human world against Him."[94] It was quite courageous to say this in the early 1990s. And this was the voice of a prophet, neither the first nor the last time Salij's work was prophetic.

8.

Two principles — methodologically fundamental but in their internal structure superior to the scientifically methodical characteristic of nature — seem to illuminate all of Salij's theological output: strictly academic, essayistic, homiletic, and advisory.

The first of these is a principle coming from John's prologue *en Arche en ho Logos* (in the beginning, there was Logos). In the alphabet of faith, reason is the beginning and the fundament; it is eternal reason, Divine and of Divine origin. This means that judiciousness and understanding, rationality and a rational (Logos-like) approach constitutively belong to the Christian faith. This rational dynamic of searching for/learning the truth based on Revelation and faith —

93. *Ibid.*, p. 212.
94. *Ibid.*

in addition to the dynamic of love without which nothing that is truly Christian can exist — initiates the phenomenon of Christian theology. This also means for Salij, which was phenomenally expressed by Ratzinger, that "faith does not want to propose to man something like psychotherapy; its psychotherapy is truth."[95] Ratzinger's pronouncement could be the motto of all the responses published in Salij's column *Szukającym drogi* ("For Those Searching for Their Way").

The second principle is the eminently ecclesial nature of all forms of (dogmatic) theology conducted by Father Salij. For him, theology is never merely a private notion; he is too wise for that and knows that "privatizing" it would cause it to lose its weight, gravity, and significance. He knows that for a theologian the Church is not an external organization that is foreign to his thinking. On the contrary, the Church as a subject transcends the narrowness of the individual and is, in fact, an irreducible condition for theology to be theology.[96] Meanwhile, dogma is dogma, not despite ecclesiality or against it (see the first motto of this text) but with it.

Problems related to the sacrament of marriage stand out amidst this rationally, ecclesially, and, at the same time, existentially concentrated dogma. In this area, Father Salij sees a particular need for theological and pastoral assistance. An example of a standard dogmatic text is the brief, dense, and brilliantly written article *Małżeństwo chrześcijan jako udział w paschalnym misterium Chrystusa* ("Christian Marriage as Participation in Christ's Pascal Mystery"), which was first published fifty years ago in *Ateneum Kapłańskie*.[97] Its Biblical-literary counterpoint is *Erotyka Pieśni nad pieśniami w interpretacjach* ("The Eroticism of Song of Songs in Theological Interpretations").[98] Both

95. J. Ratzinger, *Wiara w Piśmie i Tradycji* (Opera Omnia, Vol. 9/1), ed. K. Góźdź, M. Górecka, trans. J. Merecki (Lublin: KUL, 2018), p. 609. See *ibid.*, pp. 609-610.

96. *Ibid.*, p. 610. See *ibid.*, pp. 607-623.

97. 1970 No. 75, pp. 17-28.

98. *Królestwo Boże...*, pp. 222-234.

are a theological fundament and, in fact, standard example of the depth of presentation for individual texts and detailed counseling in marital affairs that are omnipresent in Salij's writings. They contain Salij's most radically and uncompromisingly anti-abortion writings;[99] original observations on the topic of shame;[100] acute comments on the topic of kinds of love that bring one closer to God and those that separate us from God;[101] and the excellent text *Kościół a małżeństwa rozwiedzionych* ("The Church and Divorced Couples"),[102] written in the very middle of the Polish People's Republic, during the early days of Edward Gierek's rule, and which one can excellently read today alongside *Amoris laetitia*, for instance.

This subject matter is strictly related to matters of conscience and freedom, to which he also devotes — explicitly and implicitly — numerous segments of his work. Salij cautions against treating one's conscience as a cape of subjectivism (consolidation in narcissism and the facilitation of doing evil[103]) and advises dealing with it as a valuable and delicate instrument. Above all, one must do so responsibly because the conscience — like any other kind of compass — is prone to destruction. Referencing St. Thomas, Salij repeats that a so-called wandering conscience is no justification for committing evil: "if this happens, we are usually not without fault (S.Th. 1-2 q.19 a.6)"[104] because our responsibility for this situation traces its origins to the processes that destroy the proper functioning of the conscience, which typically does not occur without our freedom and will. Like Thomas, he teaches that conscience "is *preventio praecepti divini ad hominem*, 'the coming of God's commandment to man.' Thus, we are

99. See *Eseje tomistyczne*, p. 148; *Świętowanie Pana Boga*, p. 205.

100. *Pytania nieobojętne*, pp. 182-186.

101. *Ibid.*, pp. 170-171.

102. *Królestwo Boże...*, pp. 107-114. First publication: *W drodze* 1(1973) No. 2, pp. 67-75.

103. *Świętowanie Pana Boga*, p. 313.

104. *Eseje tomistyczne*, p. 56.

obliged to examine our conscience and its consistency with God's law as well as the Christian moral tradition. For sometimes referring to one's conscience is blatant hypocrisy that reeks of pure subjectivism from afar."[105]

Freedom is not an abstract ideological concept but our own, personal, and individual freedom. It consists of staying in God's house, finding a place in His world, and being a child of God, a son or daughter in the Son, and an heir, the exact antithesis of the status and fate of a slave who is in a foreign place and to whom nothing belongs.[106] Hence, obedience to God and His laws is not a danger but a necessary condition for freedom modeled after Christ, Who was the freest of the free "and at the same time emphasized His absolute dependence on the Father."[107] The essence of His freedom rests in this dependency, in His being a Son or Heir. Nothing so accurately illustrated the harsh, conservative, intelligent, and, at the same time, humorous attitude of Father Jacek than his riposte to the comments of a journalist (who suggested that "*in dubio libertas* — in questionable matters choose freedom"), an attitude that in the context of the discussion seemed excessively liberal to Salij: "But are we allowed to be guided by this principle while picking mushrooms? I would strongly discourage that..."[108]

9.

Particularly harsh are Salij's observations regarding freedom and human choices when in his writings (as well as lectures, homilies, interviews, and other public speeches) he touches upon the depraved convenience, bad philosophy, fear, and entanglement in earlier sin that are typical of today's man and lead to a superficial, in his view,

105. *Świętowanie Pana Boga*, p. 313.
106. See *Dylematy naszych czasów*, pp. 212-213.
107. *Świętowanie Pana Boga*, p. 29.
108. *Ibid.*, p. 318.

moral dilemma consisting of the necessity of choosing between committing (moral) evil and experiencing (for example, physical) evil.[109] This is a false dilemma that is incorrectly referred to as a moral one, Salij frequently emphasizes. At least since the time of Antigone and certainly since that of Christ, we know that we do not have to commit evil; there always exists a solution that is one of the forms of martyrdom.[110] Salij harshly opposes Kołakowski's thesis (the philosopher taught that sometimes there is no other possibility than to commit evil, but one cannot be hypocritical), which he considers horrifying and resulting from pagan mythology.[111] He writes: "This world truly is not so rotten that we have no choice. [...] In God's world, there is no situation in which we are forced to commit evil."[112] When there appears an alternative typical of the liberal world in which we must hypocritically choose between committing evil or committing evil without being hypocritical, Salij says: "Faith does not understand such alternatives."[113] Each of us can and should live in accordance with God's will; no one is pressured to choose between one sin and another. Indeed, the cost can be high or even the highest (that of martyrdom), but there does not exist such a thing as "hopeless subjection to evil."[114]

Faith does not understand such alternatives... It is my profound conviction that herein — in the sphere of faith; in its inviolable, mysterious root which is grace but is also subjected to multivarious cooperation with human freedom (in this case, a man, friar, and theologian; this person and not another with his life, fate, circumstances, etc.) — lies the secret of the potency of Salij's theology and all of the writing he has produced as well as his preaching and pedagogical

109. *Dylematy naszych czasów*, pp. 102-103.
110. *Ibid.*
111. *Świętowanie Pana Boga*, pp. 266-266.
112. *Ibid.*, p. 266.
113. *Pytania nieobojętne*, p. 178.
114. See *ibid.*

activity. He treats faith as something deadly (or, better put, life-giving) serious. Salij's understanding of faith is inspired by St. Thomas (who else), as "spiritual agility, whose power initiates within us eternal life and that inclines our minds to acknowledge what does not come naturally to it."[115]

This stunningly beautiful definition, which opens our understanding and practice of faith to the infinite expanse of eternity and God Himself (at a minor cost, the humility of reason, which is a blessed and salvific investment for the human intellect), is particularly dear to Father Jacek, who repeats, analyzes, interprets, and draws conclusions from it on multiple occasions in his writings. He writes that the great question of faith (the greatest of all human affairs) deals with dynamically, holistically directing oneself towards the living God[116] and the personal binding of oneself to God, which Thomas himself compares to the bonds of marriage.[117] Directing faith towards its aim takes place through love; Salij paraphrases and develops in many ways and mutations this Thomistic thesis. Love is greatest of all. Without it, reason and theology, *intellectus fidei*, would be a resounding gong or a clashing cymbal and ultimately nothing (see 1 Corinthians 13:1-2; 13).

In any case, with regards to faith we are dealing with something much, much greater than a worldview or a solely theoretical truth.[118] Faith deals with supernatural spiritual power that transforms man through God (grace) towards the living, eternal, and Triune God. Faith understood as spiritual agility should develop ("progress") but not change; that is to say, it cannot lose its essential identity (it is

115. *Eseje tomistyczne*, pp. 72, 84 (in both cases, Salij wrestles with the translation of the Latin expression in S.Th., of which there are numerous translations; I propose their consolidation, as above).

116. *Ibid.*, p. 73.

117. *Ibid.*, p. 79.

118. *Ibid.*, pp. 87, 141.

constantly "the same but not the same").[119] *Lectio fidei* is without a doubt the central lesson in the professor's school and, at the same time, the source of what is most important in his output.

10.

Now is time for a less theological but more anthropological reflection (although Salij's theology is very much down to earth and relevant to people, as I have pointed out above) on his character, temperament, and inclinations. What can we see from these texts on the topic? In a book-length interview, he summarized his ten-year wait to become a full professor in the Polish People's Republic during the 1970s and, consequently, his ten-year absence from attending faculty councils. "I saved a lot of time in this way. I always admire the wondrousness of Divine Providence above us."[120] On his vows of obedience, he says: "My prior told me to get a driver's license. I protested because I knew I lacked the gift of driving a car well. I got my driver's license, but the last time I drove a car was during my exam."[121] Or: "I love to pray the Imprecatory Psalms."[122] Although he mitigates this commentary somewhat ("I then pray against the sinner who resides within me"),[123] carefully reading Salij's writings (and, therefore, getting to know him a little), the reader comes under the impression that perhaps this prayer is not only for his own conversion...

Father Jacek has the moderate but clear temperament of a polemicist. A careful reader of his writings will easily recall those areas where he struggles against an opinion or thesis contrary to his faith and views and how his writing then becomes harsher... He favorably quotes St. Thomas, who regretted that "his contemporary theologians do not know the contrary doctrines to the degree to which the

119. *Ibid.*, p. 132. See *Wiara jest żywa...*, p. 28.
120. *Świętowanie Pana Boga*, p. 243.
121. *Wiara jest żywa...*, p. 28.
122. *Świętowanie Pana Boga*, p. 23.
123. *Ibid.*

Church Fathers knew the pagan philosophy of their time."[124] He has the same aim as the Angelic Doctor: to defend the faith so that thanks to this knowledge he can "close his opponent's mouth and protect the simple from scandal through a wise response."[125]

Here are some examples of courageous polemics. The first concerns contemporary New Age, an incarnation of ancient gnosis: "abandoning rationale for one's ideological notions, [...] an allergy to prayer and even the mere notion of a personal God, [...] hatred for the Church, [...] a tendency to exaltedly blabber about Christ interspersed with blasphemous blabbering about the true God, Who is the Son of God and Savior."[126] The second concerns Carl Gustav Jung, the father of modern psychiatry who has been virtually canonized in certain circles: "When I read what he had to say about astrology, I thought it to be a ton of rubbish."[127] The third is the beginning of a response to a journalist's question ("What does the term 'parish serfdom' make you think of?"): "Of the arrogance of people who consider the majority of their neighbors to be rabble as well as dividing the world into the center and the peripheries, which I find absurd."[128]

"A good or evil man can be recognized especially by what causes his will to rejoice,"[129] Father Jacek says, quoting St. Thomas. He adds: "A permanent disposition to rejoicing through authentic good is the most infallible sign of a man's rectitude."[130] Fidelity to the Gospel bears the fruits of sweetness and lightness.[131] Such is the fruit of freedom from burdens, worries, and the bitterness of sin: *delectatio*,

124. *Eseje tomistyczne*, p. 140.
125. *Ibid.*
126. *Świętowanie Pana Boga*, p. 298.
127. *Pytania nieobojętne*, p. 136.
128. *Świętowanie Pana Boga*, p. 276.
129. *Eseje tomistyczne*, p. 63.
130. *Ibid.*
131. *Ibid.*, p. 65.

gaudium, the state of satisfaction with life, "rest in the attained good."[132] *Delectatio divina, in Deo.*

***

Decor ordinis, or the beauty of order: in *Contra gentiles*, Thomas Aquinas used this term to call the property of created things to which God grants likeness to Himself.[133] What creates order towards the beauty of Father Jacek's theology is *sensus catholicus* and the *sensus Ecclesiae* of its author. "The life of a Dominican should be unambiguously theocentric," he explained years ago, according to three principles: *Contemplari et contemplata aliis tradere*; *laudare — benedicere — praedicare*; *studium assiduum*.[134] This is translated as: 1. Contemplate and share the fruits of contemplation; 2. Praise God — be kind to people — preach the Word of God; 3. Study constantly.

This book comes from these three principles, and it is about them.

The time of Father Jacek Salij, OP, and his writings are also a great time for the Church in Poland, of which he is an emanation and co-creator.

Katowice, April 4, 2022

132. *Ibid.*, pp. 66, 63.

133. *Ibid.*, p. 100.

134. *Świętowanie Pana Boga*, pp. 133-134.

A THEOLOGIAN IN THE FULL SENSE OF THE WORD

Theology is knowledge of God. There is only one Theologian in the full meaning of this term. He is the One Whom, according to the Gospel, "no one knows [...] except... the Father, and no one knows the Father except the Son and anyone to whom the Son wishes to reveal Him" (Matthew 11:27). Although an ordinary Christian can be a theologian, this can be accomplished only through the participation of His Son, Jesus Christ, in this familiarity with the eternal Father.

If this is the way things are, there is no reason why theology departments should be particularly privileged places of encounter with God. It is difficult to disagree with St. Thomas who writes in his *Commentary on Saint Paul's Epistle to the Ephesians* that a simple woman (*vetula*) can know God better than a learned theologian. As we know all too well, Aquinas had great respect for theologians and did not disparage the academic discipline of theology. He only wanted to warn against a theology that is not immersed in love and does not lead to God.

I would like to recall a certain pamphlet on theologians that is found in the tales of Hasidic Jews. The courtesy with which the criticism is expressed makes it even more biting. According to that tale, the difference between an authentic theologian and someone who limits himself to engaging in theological studies is as follows: "Two people entered a royal palace. One of them studied each room in detail with the eye of an expert, admiring the magnificent tapestries and treasuries of which he could not get enough. The other walked through parlors and rejoiced at one thing: *This is the king's home. Just a couple more steps and I will see my Lord and King*!"

All this image is missing is a greater emphasis on its communal dimension. In this palace, the theologian is someone who tries to show the way to the King and suggest what must be done to encounter and even befriend Him; he wants to help those who are lost and raise the spirits of the discouraged. Above all, a theologian in the true meaning of the word tries to speak of the wonderful King and His kindness and love so that those entering the palace would love Him and dream of encountering Him during their walk there.

Naturally, apart from eternal salvation I desire nothing more than to be a theologian in the full meaning of the word. But am I one? Or am I instead a terrible theologian? This question is the more difficult to answer as there are undoubtedly many terrible theologians, and without a doubt none of them considers himself to be such.

Considering this image, a terrible theologian is someone who falsely presents the way and instead of illuminating it, muddies the waters; he knows little about the fact that the King can be loved and does not instill love for Him in others. A terrible theologian seeks his own glory or the glory of his various "collective I's" and not the glory of the One Who did not seek His own glory (see John 5:44; 7:18; 8:50, 54; 12:43).

To truly be an authentic theologian, it does not suffice to consider oneself as such. St. Paul says in defense of the authenticity of his service in the Church: "For it is not the one who recommends himself who is approved, but the one whom the Lord recommends"

(2 Corinthians 10:18). Am I an authentic theologian in the eyes of the Lord Jesus? How can I recognize this?

I know a few things for certain. First — and psychologists can comment on this however they want; I don't care if they see me as the epigon of a civilization of fear. I simply know that I will not be redeemed at the Final Judgment if the Lord does not have mercy on me. If I add to that the Lord Jesus' measure ("When you have done all you have been commanded, say, 'We are unprofitable servants; we have done what we were obliged to do;'" Luke 17:10), then I am certain that I am not doing everything should.

I am neither a pessimist nor am I trying to tease the reader by ineptly saying what I feel very deeply and what I cannot express in any other way. The question at stake is simple: Do I pray enough? Do I not confuse harmony with comfort, love of neighbor with the desire to be left alone, or the attitude of service with egocentrically looking for myself rather than God? Does not fidelity to the Gospel get mixed up with fear of what is new and unknown or, on the contrary, with the unwise pursuit of the new and unknown? I simply do not know; the Lord Jesus knows this, and herein rests my hope that what is good in me and my work will be accepted by Him and will illuminate with the brilliance of His Divinity, while He fixes everything that is deformed and defective. It is up to me to ensure that my theology is rooted in my own faith and prayer and that I perform it in an attitude of obedience and service.

Second, I know for certain that authentic theology consists of imitating the Lord Jesus in that He did not profess His own teachings: "My teaching is not My own but is from the One Who sent Me" (John 7:16; see 3:11; 8:28). This is why the imitation of the Lord Jesus by exploring the Gospel and illuminating it with the light of the thousands of problems we face today requires intense prayer and more careful listening to not only contemporary problems but above all the faith of the Church. After all, the Son of God did not bring us the Gospel so that it would get lost among a thousand other opinions. In short, I am incapable of imagining authentic theology outside the Church and especially contrary to the Church.

I am certain of a third thing, too: that even the best mothers have a shadow of wicked stepmothers within them. Loving mothers try to remove this shadow, but they only partly succeed. Because we are sinners, Mother Church is also tainted by such a stepmother's shadow. The theologian in particular is called upon to reduce this shadow. Although I want what is best, I certainly sometimes unwittingly cause something contrary.

Thus, I will allow myself to end this reflection with the prayer: God, be merciful on me the sinner! Lord God, have theology under Your protection!

I Believe

WHAT IS FAITH?

Faith Is Something More Than Just a Worldview

Let me begin with two negative theses. Since the Age of Enlightenment, there has been a tendency in our culture to identify faith with a religious worldview. Furthermore, we sometimes encounter the view that faith consists in possessing religious convictions.

If we accept that a worldview is a subjective response to questions about the ultimate meaning of the world and of man, faith usually possesses a dimension of a worldview, but it is something much greater. Let me recall two famous cases when someone who had an indisputably Catholic worldview was nonetheless a non-believer.

The first of these people was St. Augustine, who at a certain point in his search for meaning became convinced that the truth can be found in the Catholic Church, but at the same time he knew that he was still a non-believer. He described his spiritual state at the time in the eighth book of his *Confessions*. The famous *Tolle, lege* scene was the breakthrough. Having heard the voice of a child saying, "Take and read," Augustine opened the Epistle to the Romans and found the words: "[L]et us conduct ourselves properly as in the day, not in orgies and drunkenness, not in promiscuity and licentiousness, not in rivalry and jealousy. But put on the Lord Jesus Christ, and make no provision for the desires of the flesh" (Romans 13:13-14). That was the moment when St. Augustine believed. Previously, he had been afraid of openness to the grace of faith because he knew that he would be too weak to earnestly follow God's commandments. At that moment, he realized that Christ the Lord would support him with His grace. It was then that Augustine became a believer, and his entire life is the best testimony to how deep his faith was and how fully he immersed himself in it.

The second witness to the fact that faith is something more than a worldview is Romano Guardini, one of the greatest Catholic theologians of the twentieth century. When he was a high school student, he was horrified to learn that, despite his enormous religious interests and emotional attachment to the Catholic Church, he was a non-believer because something was not right with his prayer life. That was when his great conversion began. It is no coincidence that Guardini is the author of the argument that, from the spiritual side, people can be divided not so much into believers and non-believers as into those who pray and those who do not. In short, an important symptom (although not its essence) of faith is the search for the living God and finding Him in one way or another.

Faith Cannot Be Reduced to Religious Convictions

Another erroneous belief about faith that the post-Enlightenment mentality would like to impose on believers is the identification of faith with religious convictions. This consists in us, believing Christians, being prohibited (sometimes directly, but usually indirectly) from treating the message of the faith as an objective truth. When, for example, I say that Christ is the Redeemer of all of humanity, I can be admonished with the following words: "Do not say that. At most, you can say that in your opinion or according to the faith of your Church Christ is the Redeemer of all people."

Likewise, if I say that Christ has risen from the dead, I am likely to face the accusation that I am engaged in spiritual imperialism. According to the post-Enlightenment mentality, I can at most say that in my opinion Christ has risen from the dead and that I am greatly convinced this is so.

People who correct us in this way are certainly not aware of the fact that they essentially demand that we renounce our faith. After all, being a Christian means believing that the Son of God has indeed become a man, has indeed died for us on the cross, and has indeed risen from the dead. It suffices to recall the Apostle Paul's firm statement that "if Christ has not been raised, then empty [too] is our preaching; empty, too, your faith," and if Christ had not in fact risen from the dead, then by proclaiming His Resurrection we would be greatly insulting the Lord God for "we testified against God that He raised Christ" (1 Corinthians 15:14-15).

Furthermore, to be a Christian means to seek a personal relationship with Christ and to indeed try to implement such a relationship. Benedict XVI has clearly emphasized this in the preface to his encyclical *Deus caritas est* (which he repeated in the adhortation *Verbum Domini*, 11): "Being Christian is not the result of an ethical choice or a lofty idea, but the encounter with an event, a person, which gives life a new horizon and a decisive direction."[1]

Three Types of Acts of Faith

What, then, is faith? Let us tentatively state that it is an ability to enter real contact with God and with Christ. When we, the Poles, speak of faith, we above all, and perhaps solely, are referring to acts of faith. Language itself inclines us to this. In this case, Latin — which,

1. Unless indicated otherwise, the English translations of all official Church documents (papal documents, papal speeches, conciliar documents, etc.) come from the Vatican's website, Vatican.va.

after all, is the linguistic source of Western Christianity — uses two completely different words: in Latin, "faith" is *fides*, while "to believe" is *credere*. In Polish, both these realities are described using words that have the same root; thus, in practice we seldom distinguish between them.

The tendency to identify faith with its acts (which Pope Benedict XVI had noted in his encyclical *Spe salvi* and on which we will elaborate later) has marked the religious thinking of Western Christians at least since the times of Martin Luther. In order for us to clearly see this difference, I will first define what we are talking about when we mean acts of faith. For that, I will follow St. Thomas Aquinas.

Thomas distinguishes between three types of acts of faith: "I believe that;" "I believe God;" and, finally, "I believe in God." "I believe that" concerns the substance of faith. Namely, we refer to the Living God, Who appeared to us in Jesus Christ with the aid of these acts; they contain not only the truth of God's triune nature and the truth about the incarnation and Redemption, but also all the dogmas of faith related to the Church, the sacraments, and our ultimate destiny. These dogmas concern God's supernatural gifts whose aim is to bring us into eternal unity with God. Thus, in the former aspect faith cannot be replaced with knowledge, as through natural reason we can at most gain knowledge about the existence of God and a general conception of His attributes.

St. Thomas places a great emphasis on the material aspect of faith. If God has indeed given Himself to people in Jesus Christ, He certainly can ensure us infallible access to the truth about this most important work of His love. Thus, Thomas' statement that if the faith of some person were limited to the mind's acceptance of all the truths of the faith taught by the Church, we cannot say of such a person that he is a believer. Such a person merely professes the Catholic worldview; he lacks a supernatural turning towards the Living God, which is essential to faith.

Supernatural faith begins to be implemented at the second level, at that of acts of "I believe God." It begins with the summons of God, Who was first to love us and wants to increasingly surrender Himself to man, to the point of unbelievable closeness in the eternal life. Because this is the summons of God Himself, it makes us capable of responding to it. In other words, this faith is the fruit of God's grace, which incites us to seek God, and which permeates faith. God is simultaneously Someone Absolutely Infinite and Someone Personal; thus, our entering into personal contact with Him is possible only thanks to His initiative, which He undertakes through the gift of grace.

To believe God, grace is necessary for an additional reason. Namely, because of sin, we possess a dark distrust of God that is unfair to Him. Thus, we are inclined to trim the gift of the revealed truth and grace in which God gives us Himself according to our human conceptions and inclinations. It is difficult for us to believe God that His commandments are completely correct and that they are the words of His love which protect our welfare. We are also inclined to suspect God of abandoning us during times of misfortune and affliction. Only the light of grace can illuminate the darkness in which such unfair suspicions are born and incline us towards authentically believing God.

According to St. Thomas, the mere act of faith in God does not bring us closer to eternal life, although it is a work of grace and consists of personally turning towards the Living God. An act of perfect faith, which allows us to know God, and which will culminate in eternally looking at Him face to face, is to believe is such a way that we make God the most important factor in our lives and actions. Only then does faith become a grounded attitude, or a virtue and attempt at surrendering one's whole person to God.

The expression "to believe in God" should be explained well especially to us, Poles, because we typically understand it is the equivalent of *credere in Deum* or, in a sense: I recognize the fact of God's existence. However, *credere in Deum* means something incomparably greater. Namely, it means that I seek to entrust my entire self to God. According to Aquinas, we can be capable of such acts only in a state of sanctifying grace. In other words, to believe in God and to entrust ourselves to God, our faith must be imbued with God's supernatural love. To use Thomas Aquinas' terminology, only *fides caritate formata* can make us capable of such acts of faith.

Personally, I like to illustrate this *credere in Deum* with a reference to marriage; namely, one cannot credibly marry if a man does not believe in his girlfriend or if a girl does not believe in her boyfriend; a marriage will be unhappy if husband and wife do not believe in one another and if they lack the attitude of "I will entrust myself to you for better and for worse." We express something similar in the act of *credo in Deum*: I believe in God, which means that I completely entrust myself to the Lord God.

The Gift Thanks to Which We Are Capable of Acts of Faith

I have presented three types of acts of *credere*. Let us now ask what *fides*, or the faith from which these acts result, is. This can be illustrated most simply with the baptism of an infant. An infant is incapable of making acts of faith, but he already receives the grace of faith in the sacrament of baptism. In the encyclical *Spe salvi* (10) Benedict XVI recalls how the rite of baptism began in the pre-conciliar liturgy: "First of all the priest asked what name the parents had chosen for the child, and then he continued with the question: 'What do you ask of the Church?' Answer: 'Faith.'" In other words, just as an infant is already endowed with reason but does not yet know how to use it, one can likewise receive faith even if one is still incapable of acts of faith. The infant's Christian parents and loved ones will bring him up in an atmosphere of faith in which he will learn to live the faith and become capable of acts of faith.

Let us return to the dialogue opening the ancient baptismal liturgy. When the parents asked for faith for their child, the priest would ask the following question: "'And what does faith give you?' 'Eternal life.'" Benedict XVI comments on this dialogue as follows: "According to this dialogue, the parents were seeking access to the faith for their child, communion with believers, because they saw in faith the key to 'eternal life.' As in the past, this is what being baptized today, becoming Christians, is all about: it is not just an act of socialization within the community, not simply a welcome into the Church. The parents expect more for the one to be baptized: they expect that faith, which includes the corporeal nature of the Church and her sacraments, will give life to their child—eternal life" (*Spe salvi*, 10).

Only considering this distinction between faith and acts of faith can we appreciate the definition proposed by St. Thomas Aquinas that "faith is a habit of the mind by which eternal life begins in us and which makes the intellect assent to things that are not evident." We read that faith is the germ of eternal life in man at the beginning of the eleventh chapter of the Epistle to the Hebrews, which I will briefly discuss in a moment. Now, I will make note of how easily we get by with a false understanding of the idea of the mind's adherence to what is not obvious. Here, Thomas does not state (as both his contemporary admirers and adversaries most frequently maintain) that faith makes our minds capable of accepting statements containing the truths of the faith that do not come naturally to us. Faith above all brings us closer to God Himself and only indirectly towards the statements thanks to which we learn some truth about Him. Thomas said without the slightest hesitation: *Actus credentis non terminatur ad enuntiabile, sed ad rem* ("Now the act of the believer does not terminate in a proposition, but in a thing [reality];" *Summa Theologiae*, 2-2, q. 1, art. 2, ad. 2).

The Real Meaning of Hebrews 11:1

Aquinas was a theologian who carefully avoided showing off his own originality; thus, in the definition of faith that I have just presented we can easily notice that it is a modification of the following formulation from Hebrews 11:1, where faith is presented as *sperandarum substantia rerum, argumentum non apparentium*. Benedict XVI recently asked for the proper understanding of this verse, whose meaning has been completely distorted in Luther's Bible, which reduces faith to deep convictions; namely, in paragraphs 7-9 of the encyclical *Spe salvi*. Benedict XVI's discourse on this topic is not only extremely interesting and skillful; it is furthermore marked by a spirit of authentic ecumenism.

The key term in the original text of this verse is *hypostasis*. "For the [Western] Fathers and for the theologians of the Middle Ages, it was clear that the Greek word hypostasis was to be rendered in Latin with the term *substantia*" (*Spe salvi*, 7); the imperfect Polish translation for both these terms, Greek and Latin, is the term *podstawa* ("basis"). Likewise, *élenchos* (in Polish *dowód*, or "proof"), the second most important term influencing the meaning of this verse, is not subjective but objective in meaning; it indicates a reality that is present within us. Meanwhile, in Luther's Bible both these terms are rendered in a subjective sense. Luther translated *Hypostasis* as *eine gewisse Zuversicht* (a kind of trust or conviction) and *élenchos* as *das Nichtzweifeln* (not doubting). Thus, in Luther's Bible the whole sentence has more or less the same meaning. "Faith is a kind of conviction that hope refers to and not doubting about that which one does not see."

Father Wujek (1599) has translated this statement as follows: *A wiara jest gruntem rzeczy tych, których się spodziewamy, wywodem rzeczy niewidzianych* ("Faith is in essence those things which we expect, the implication of invisible things"). Interestingly, Old Polish translations did not follow Luther's example. Brest Bible (1563): *A wiarać jest grunt rzeczy, których się nadziewamy i okazanie niewidomych* ("To believe is the essence of the things that we hope for and that prove invisible"). Similar, we read in the Gdansk Bible (1632): *A wiara jest gruntem tych rzeczy, których się spodziewamy i dowodem rzeczy niewidzialnych* ("Faith is in essence those things which we expect and evidence for invisible things").

Unfortunately, in the second half of the twentieth century Polish Catholic translations also rendered this verse in the style of Luther. Tyniec Bible: *Wiara zaś jest poręką tych dóbr, których się spodziewamy, świadectwem tych rzeczywistości, których nie widzimy* ("Faith is the guarantee of those goods which we expect and testimony to those realities which we do not see"). Poznan Bible (1974): *Wiara jest mocnym przekonaniem, że istnieje to, czego się spodziewamy, jest świadectwem o wydarzeniach, których nie widzimy* ("Faith is a strong conviction that there exists something we expect; it is testimony to events we do not yet see"). Bishop Kazimierz Romaniuk (1997): *Wierzyć zaś — to znaczy być pewnym, że się otrzyma to, czego się oczekuje; to znaczy być przekonanym o rzeczywistym istnieniu tego, czego się nie widzi* ("To believe, then, means to be certain that one will receive what he expects; this means to be convinced of the genuine existence of that which one does not see").

In his encyclical, Benedict XVI notes that contemporary Protestant exegesis has distanced itself from Luther's understanding of faith. The pope quotes the eminent Protestant Biblical scholar Helmut Köster: "[T]here can be no question but that this classical Protestant understanding is untenable" (*Spe salvi*, 7).

To see faith in its objective dimension and to reject the unilateral reduction of faith only to convictions or to a subjective attitude of trust and confidence makes it possible to recognize faith as the beginning of eternal life. To quote the encyclical *Spe salvi* 7, "Faith is not merely a personal reaching out towards things to come that are still totally absent: it gives us something. It gives us even now something of the reality we are waiting for, and this present reality constitutes for us a 'proof' of the things that are still unseen. Faith draws the future into the present, so that it is no longer simply a 'not yet.' The fact that this future exists changes the present; the present is touched by the future reality, and thus the things of the future spill over into those of the present and those of the present into those of the future."

The truth that eternal life begins in faith was often emphasized by St. Thomas Aquinas. Let us look at Thomas' reflection in the prologue to his *Commentary on the Apostle's Creed*: "The second effect of faith is that eternal life is already begun in us; for eternal life is nothing else than knowing God. This the Lord announced when He said: 'This is eternal life, that they may know you, the only true God, and Jesus Christ whom you sent' (John 17:3). This knowledge of God begins here through faith, but it is perfected the future life when we shall know God as He is. Therefore, St. Paul says: 'Faith is the substance of things to be hoped for' (Hebrews 11:1). No one then can arrive at perfect happiness of heaven, which is the true knowledge of God, unless first he knows God through faith: 'Blessed are they who have not seen and have believed' (John 20:29)."[2]

2. St. Thomas Aquinas, *Expositio in Symbolum Apostolorum — The Apostles' Creed*, trans. Joseph B. Collins, ed. Joseph Kenny, O.P., (New York: Wagner, 1939), https://isidore.co/aquinas/Creed.htm (accessed January 14, 2022).

FAITH AND BELIEFS

Socrates Remains Relevant

When Plato's Socrates was asked if he believed the myth of the kidnapping of Orithyia by Boreas, he responded: "The wise are doubtful, and I should not be singular if, like them, I too doubted" (*Phaedrus*, 4; 229c).[3]

However, as Socrates later explains, both studying myths and distancing oneself from them are a waste of time: "Now I quite acknowledge that these allegories are very nice, but he is not to be envied who has to invent them; much labor and ingenuity will be required of him; and when he has once begun, he must go on and rehabilitate Hippocentaurs and chimeras dire. Gorgons and winged steeds flow in apace, and numberless other inconceivable and portentous natures. And if he is skeptical about them, and would fain reduce them one after another to the rules of probability, this sort of crude philosophy will take up a great deal of time. Now I have no leisure for such enquiries; shall I tell you why? I must first know myself, as the Delphian inscription says; to be curious about that which is not my concern, while I am still in ignorance of my own self, would be ridiculous. For,

3. Plato, *Phaedrus*, trans. Benjamin Jowett, http://classics.mit.edu/Plato/phaedrus.html (accessed January 14, 2022).

as I was saying, I want to know not about this, but about myself: am I a monster more complicated and swollen with passion than the serpent Typho, or a creature of a gentler and simpler sort, to whom Nature has given a diviner and lowlier destiny?"[4]

Therefore, it is not worth distracting oneself with any old beliefs that have nothing to do with posing questions about the meaning of our lives and that in no way help us to shape ourselves. It is even a waste of time to demystify these beliefs because they are outside the categories of truth and untruth as well as certainty and uncertainty, while demystifying them would be an attempt at interpreting them in such alien categories.

This position ultimately led to Socrates' being accused of atheism. It turned out that he was not interested in beliefs outside the realm of truth and untruth because he had truly found God. During his trial, this is how Socrates responded to the accusation that he "does not receive the gods whom the state receives": (Plato, *Apology*). "For I do believe that there are gods, and in a sense higher than that in which any of my accusers believe in them. And to you and to God I commit my cause, to be determined by you as is best for you and me."[5]

I believe that this episode from Socrates' trial could be interpreted considering the Platonic distinction between *doxa* (viewpoint, belief) and *episteme* (cognition). Paradoxically, it was not Socrates but his accusers who were atheists. Gods were the subject of their beliefs (*doxa*). In reality, they were not even concerned about if these gods exist at all or not. They were solely interested if the gods are recognized by the state, while worship of them was a civic obligation. Socrates' accusers were afraid that he had revealed the epistemological emptiness of the state religion. This fear paralyzed them so greatly that they completely

4. *Ibid.*, 229d-230a.

5. Plato, *Apology*, trans. Benjamin Jowett, ProjectGutenberg.org, https://www.gutenberg.org/files/1656/1656-h/1656-h.htm (accessed January 14, 2022).

did not understand Socrates' great discovery: God indeed exists, and as such He is knowable, or accessible to our *episteme*.

The Religions of Antiquity Did Not Know the Concept of Faith

The expression of the world of the gods with the aid of beliefs formulated outside the categories of truth and falsehood were, it seems, something widespread in various religious. Therefore, conquered peoples rejected their religions so easily and instead took up the beliefs and worship of their victors. This is the source of the perennial popularity of various forms of religious syncretism.

The lack of a relationship between beliefs and truth or falsehood is made evident especially when there are attempts at compelling people who truly believe in God to a religion based on beliefs. Neither during the persecution of the Jews during the times of the Maccabees nor during the persecutions of Christians by numerous Roman emperors was any attempt taken to make the persecuted accept the beliefs of the religion imposed on them. There were only attempts to compel them to participate in worship in which they did not want to voluntarily engage. The organizers of such persecutions did not at all notice anything inappropriate in worship imposed on people who did not share their religious convictions.

The astonishment of both the persecutors and the persecuted is a measure of the great discrepancy between two types of religion whose attitude towards the truth is so diametrically different: A judge asked the martyr Polycarp, who was killed around 156: "What harm is there in saying, Lord Cæsar, and in sacrificing, with the other ceremonies observed on such occasions, and so make sure of safety?" (*The Martyrdom of Polycarp*, 8).[6] "But who forbids you to worship him, if he is

6. "The Martyrdom of Polycarp," in: *Ante-Nicene Fathers*, Vol. 1, Alexander Roberts, James Donaldson, and A. Cleveland Coxe, eds. (Buffalo, NY: Christian Literature Publishing

a god, together with those who are gods by nature. For you have been commanded to reverence the gods, and the gods whom all know" (Eusebius, *Church History*, Book VII, Chapter 11, verse 9).[7]

Meanwhile, around 170 Tatian the Assyrian asked in the name of the persecuted Christians: "For what reason, men of Greece, do you wish to bring the civil powers, as in a pugilistic encounter, into collision with us? [...] Only when I am commanded to deny Him, will I not obey, but will rather die than show myself false and ungrateful" (*Tatian's Address to the Greeks*, Chapter 4).[8] In 197, Tertullian wrote: "But with you liberty is given to worship any god but the true God" (*Apology*, 24, 10).[9] Tertullian is greatly surprised that religious worship should require the permission of state authority: "Unless gods give satisfaction to men, there will be no deification for them: the god will have to propitiate the man."[10]

On this matter, both the persecutors and the persecuted were in agreement: worship of the state gods had little in common with the truth.[11]

Co., 1885). https://www.newadvent.org/fathers/0102.htm (accessed January 14, 2022).

7. Eusebius, *Church History*, Book VII, in: *Nicene and Post-Nicene Fathers, Second Series*, Vol. 1, Philip Schaff and Henry Wace, eds. (Buffalo, NY: Christian Literature Publishing Co., 1890), https://www.newadvent.org/fathers/250107.htm (accessed January 14, 2022).

8. Tatian, *Tatian's Address to the Greeks*, in: Ante-Nicene Fathers, Vol. 3., trans. S. Thelwall, Alexander Roberts, James Donaldson, and A. Cleveland Coxe, eds. (Buffalo, NY: Christian Literature Publishing Co., 1885), https://www.newadvent.org/fathers/0202.htm (accessed January 14, 2022).

9. Tertullian, *Apology*, in: Ante-Nicene Fathers, Vol. 3., trans. S. Thelwall, Alexander Roberts, James Donaldson, and A. Cleveland Coxe, eds. (Buffalo, NY: Christian Literature Publishing Co., 1885), https://www.newadvent.org/fathers/0301.htm (accessed January 14, 2022).

10. *Ibid.*, 229d-230a.

11. Prof. Maria Jaczynowska writes that the religion of antiquity "assumes the scrupulous fulfillment of all forms of worship but does not demand faith. Whether or not a man believed in the gods to whom he made sacrifices was his own private matter. However, the mere fact of offering up sacrifices and following the guidelines resulting from auguries were his civic duty" (*Religie świata rzymskiego*, Warsaw, 1990, p. 10). It is also worth noting that the religions of antiquity did not know the concept of faith at all. As R. Bultmann and A. Weiser have noted, Ancient Greek uses the terms "faith" (*pistis*) and "to believe" (*pisteuein*) only in a secular sense (*Theologisches Wörterbuch zum Neuen Testament,* 6,178n). Likewise,

The former tried to save it because behind it was a widely adopted ritual that served the role of a glue that bound society together, while the latter did not participate in it because the mere possibility of venerating false gods filled them with dread, especially since they considered themselves to be the worshipers of the true God and sought to venerate only Him.

Already among the first Christians we can find this tone in the presentation of their faith and in the description of other religions which has been irritating even to Christians since the Enlightenment. The author of the oldest Christian apology said to the emperor Antoninus Pius: "But the Christians, O King, while they went about and made search, have found the truth; and as we learned from their writings, they have come nearer to tru[12]th and genuine knowledge than the rest of the nations. For they know and trust in God, the Creator of heaven and of earth, in whom and from whom are all things, to whom there is no other god as companion, from whom they received commandments which they engraved upon their minds and observe in hope and expectation of the world which is to come. [...] But the rest of the nations err and cause error in wallowing before the elements of the world, since beyond these their mental vision will not pass. And they search about as if in darkness

the Latin term *fides* began to take mean religious faith only in the language of Christianity. Under the direction of Prof. Leokadia Małunowicz, a series of studies on ancient, classic, and new Christian meanings of the term "faith" (*fides*) among the Latin Church Fathers has been written (including S. Szmidt, "Znaczenie wyrazu *fides* u Laktancjusza," *Roczniki teologiczno—kanoniczne* 18/1971, No. 4, pp. 133—142; A. Gołda, "Z badań semantycznych nad łaciną chrześcijańską: *fides* i *fidelis* u św. Opata z Milewy," *Roczniki teologiczno—kanoniczne* 19/1972, No. 4, pp. 172—180).

12. See the testimony of St. Justin (martyred around 165) before a tribunal: "I have endeavoured to learn all doctrines; but I have acquiesced at last in the true doctrines, those namely of the Christians, even though they do not please those who hold false opinions" (*The Martyrdom of Justin*, Chapter 1; in: *Ante-Nicene Fathers*, Vol. 1, Marcus Dods, trans., Alexander Roberts, James Donaldson, and A. Cleveland Coxe, eds. (Buffalo, NY: Christian Literature Publishing Co., 1885).

because they will not recognize the truth; and like drunken men they reel and jostle one another and fall" (Aristides, *The Apology of Aristides*, 15-16).[13]

Faith As Knowledge of the True God

However, the difference between faith and belief is deeper than in the conviction of the religious person about the truth of what he believes. Naturally, such convictions have an important impact on the quality of religious attitudes and actions. For example, the convictions that God Himself gave us the commandments; He assists us through His grace; and that we will someday stand before His tribunal must be positively reflected in the behavior of the person who indeed possesses them. Such a person will appreciate prayer and other forms of becoming bound to God, while his participation in religious rituals will certainly be more than satisfying religious needs or the symbolic confirmation of his membership in a certain culture or society. Conviction of the truthfulness of what I believe could have a tangible impact on my behavior even when I err in my faith.

However, faith is not settled by a conviction of the truth of what it concerns but that it indeed concerns the truth. From this perspective, the mere concept of false faith is just as absurd as that of a rectangular circle, while the possibility of the existence of many faiths is almost as absurd as the possibility of the existence of multiple gods.

Naturally, I am now presenting an approach to faith that seems completely alien to our mentality. From the perspective of epistemology, one can accuse me of appropriating superhuman properties: can an ordinary person have such direct access to the truth that he is

13. Aristides, *Apology*, in: *Ante-Nicene Fathers*, Vol. 9, trans. D. M. Kay, Allan Menzies, ed. (Buffalo, NY: Christian Literature Publishing Co., 1896, https://www.newadvent.org/fathers/1012.htm (accessed January 14, 2022).

capable of not becoming closed off in his convictions which can be verified only to a certain extent?

However, faith is conceived in this way in both the New Testament and the experience of the martyrs: as knowledge of the true God and not only some convictions about knowing Him. Peter did not tell Jesus: "I am convinced that you are the Messiah, the Son of the living God" but: "You are the Messiah, the Son of the living God" (Matthew 16:16). Likewise, the Apostle Paul did not intend to bolster his fellow Christians' conviction that Christ has risen from the dead. Instead, he preached of Christ's resurrection because "if Christ has not been raised, then empty [too] is our preaching; empty, too, your faith" (1 Corinthians 15:14).

Already in the times of the apostles there appeared docetists who denied the incarnation of the Son of God and, consequently, His death and resurrection (see 1 John 4:2n). Thus, it is impossible to imagine one of the apostles saying that there is a difference in convictions regarding Christ between them and the docetists. This matter could appear in such a way to an unbelieving observer. For the Apostle John, it was obvious that we proclaim Christ and persist in Him, while the docetists proclaim falsehoods about Christ and are far from Him (2 John 7-9). Indeed, the non-believer can accuse John's epistemological attitude of usurpation, but this accusation contains the assumption that faith is reduced to merely convictions and that it would be an ordinary delusion to state that faith grants access to the true God and makes it possible to truly know Him.

Can this chasm between the cognitive perception of faith by believers and non-believers be bridged? I see here only one possibility: rejecting the assumption I have presented a moment ago because behind it is the completely arbitrary decision that "God does not exist, and He cannot exist" (it is enough to give it a name to see its limitless naiveté and absurdity). I believe that the only rational view of the non-believer with respect to the cognitive possibilities of faith is agnosticism: "I do not know if God exists or not, but if He does, I cannot rule out the possibility that faith in Him makes it possible to know him."

The second possibility (limiting faith to one's views) does not bridge this chasm between believers and non-believers, although it removes the believers themselves. To be convinced of the truthfulness of Christ's resurrection and to act in accordance with this conviction is not the same as believing in the resurrected Christ. Indeed, such a conviction cannot be considered equal to beliefs that are indifferent to the truthfulness of the message contained within it. It seems, however, that the degradation of faith in the direction of such a belief begins here. Faith reduced to its views is only a small step away from joining the ranks of the practicing non-believers: those who appreciate participation in a religious community and the possibility of fulfilling their religious needs but are little interested in the truth of the faith.

It is very likely that the ranks of today's Christians contain many such (often unintentional) practicing non-believers. We can determine if we are among them through the aid of the following questions: Do I attempt to entrust myself to God? Is He someone close and someone loving to me? Is my faith limited to participation in religious rituals? And the second test: Do I truly believe in eternal life?

Faith Concerns What God Has Indeed Revealed

An example of theological reflection on faith that is contrary to all psychologism (or the reduction of faith to views) is the thought of St. Thomas Aquinas. For our mentality, this reflection is so foreign that even theologians attempt at not noticing what is essential to it. It seems, however, that especially today, when we are increasingly aware of the fact that our thinking about faith has become a slave to psychologism, this reflection especially deserves to be recalled.

According to St. Thomas, human views on God and our ultimate vocation have nothing in common with faith: they are the subject of opinion, not faith. Faith solely concerns that which God has indeed revealed; it is a means of knowing God who reveals Himself to man. Saint Thomas says that it is something internally impossible for faith understood in such a way to come to know something false, for just as the eye knows things by their color and shape and reason accepts conclusions based on their logically resulting from premises, likewise faith knows God through everything that leads to Him because God Himself has made it the subject of His revelation; God cannot error or lead anyone into error. Certainly, faith often lacks psychological obviousness, but it cannot lack certainty, for its basis is the authority of God Himself.

Therefore, if someone only thinks that the theses he proclaims have been revealed by God, such an opinion would be completely free of faith. If one were to hypothetically assume that God did not reveal Himself to people at all, then we would be internally incapable of faith. If our faith contains a tinge of error, it comes from the conjectures of a believer and not from his faith.

Being a means of knowing the God Who reveals Himself, faith ultimately directs itself towards the living God and only instrumentally towards the truths that He has revealed about Himself. Only from this perspective can it be explained why grace, which makes us capable of what we are naturally unable, is necessary for faith. It also becomes logical that faith is prone to evolution and that its essential symptoms are prayer, listening to the Word of God, and giving testimony with one's life (the second part of this statement is expressed by Thomas in the thesis that faith possesses its own dynamism when it is permeated with love). Meanwhile, considering Thomas' teaching about faith all attempts at reducing faith to one's convictions would be completely incomprehensible. Even assuming that these convictions are materially consistent with the revealed truth, they are incapable of bringing us closer to the living God. Faith is, after all — let us finally provide a definition — "spiritual agility, which causes eternal life to be kindled within us" (S. Th. 2-2 q.4 a. L).

As we can see, Thomas even formulates definitions of faith from the position of a believer, while attempts at impartial definitions inevitably fail, so that is the kind of impartiality with which the blind speak of colors. Indeed, we either think that faith is opening to God giving Himself to man, or faith indeed is this, and it indeed leads man to eternal life. In the former case, we would be dealing with a false consciousness of faith rather than with faith, while in the latter case it does not seem that faith is capable of being authentically described in a way other than from the perspective of a man who lives it.

Faith Can Become Degraded to the Level of Beliefs

For three centuries now, cultural mechanisms compelling believers to experience their faith in a way as if it was reduced to some beliefs have been functioning in Europe. The wars and religious persecutions that took place in the early modern era and the exploitation of religious differences for political reasons have inclined the intellectual elites of Europe to renew ancient, pagan models of understanding the religious message. During the Enlightenment, it was nearly universally accepted that the religious sphere is outside the realm of truth and falsehood, while the claims of the Churches to teach the truths revealed by God are an ordinary usurpation. This new but ancient attitude towards religion was expressed in a simple formula that can be easily disseminated that "it is irrelevant how a person believes as long as he acts in a moral upright way."

The preachers of this new dogma, which was supposed to replace all religious dogmas, thought that they had found a magic wand that would bring about widespread harmony. In 1763, Voltaire wrote in his *Treatise on Toleration* (Chapter 21): "The fewer dogmas, the fewer disputes; and the fewer disputes, the fewer calamities."[14] In that age, there was relatively little awareness of the profoundly non-religious (especially political and economic) sources of the wars of religion.

The consistency with which Voltaire denied the Church's teaching any relation to truth and falsehood is demonstrated by the fact that Voltaire proclaims the irrelevance of the central truth of the Christian faith, the truth of the Holy Trinity, on the same page where he wrote the above-cited sentence. Voltaire certainly did not realize that not only the substance of his thesis but also the way in which he had formulated it would cause great anguish to people who took their faith seriously: "Are you [...] possessed of the genealogy of the heavenly family? What is it to you whether the Son was made or begotten, provided that you are faithful to Him; that you preach a sound doctrine, and practice that doctrine if you can?"[15]

For moderate temperaments, the Enlightenment was able to formulate this same thesis in a moderate way. In the famous seventh scene of the third act of Lessing's (d. 1781) play *Nathan the Wise*, posthumously published in 1783, in accordance with the deepest intuitions of religious people he compares faith to a magical ring that "had the hidden virtue him to render/Of God and man beloved, who in this view,/And this persuasion, wore it."[16] From deeply true intuitions, Lessing arrives at a conclusion typical of the Enlightenment: "Let each believe his own the real ring. [...] Let each feel honoured by this free affection. /Unwarped of prejudice."[17]

14. François Marie Arouet (Voltaire), *The Works of Voltaire, Vol. IV of XLIII*, trans. William F. Fleming, https://www.gutenberg.org/files/49726/49726-h/49726-h.htm (accessed January 14, 2022).

15. *Ibid.*

16. Gotthold Ephraim Lessing, *Nathan the Wise*, https://www.gutenberg.org/files/3820/3820-h/3820-h.htm (accessed January 14, 2022).

17. *Ibid.*

Efforts to remove religious truth from the sphere of *episteme* and to transfer them to the sphere of opinion (*doxa*) were continued by the positivists with great engagement. The pickaxe which they used to attempt to strike down faith as the valid means of knowing the spiritual reality (in whose existence most positivists did not believe) was an ideal of clear cognition that could best be written using the language of mathematics as well as the proposal for the empirical verification of that which is known. The apex of this attitude seems to be the thesis of the philosophers from the Vienna Circle who denied religious statements the capacity to express meaning (in other words, they treated it as mumbo jumbo devoid of any substance). In his *Index Verborum Prohibitorum* ("Index of Prohibited Words"), Otto Neurath (d. 1945) included all the key terms of religious language, including the term "God."

The abandonment of any form of religiosity by many Europeans is not the only result of the above-mentioned processes. A significant number of them have remained Christian, but very often their religiosity is reduced to accepting some convictions originating in the Christian faith as well as a vestigial participation in Christian worship.

If the spiritual history of humanity proceeds in a spiral movement, during the past nearly two thousand years we have barely made one circle. In many ways, the present situation resembles the initial situation of the Christian faith. Just as then, the dominant mentality would like to express its attitude towards the most important questions in diverse beliefs that are found beyond the realm of truth and falsehood (the only difference is that there are now more people who are nourished by beliefs inspired by Christianity). Like then, the supporters of diverse beliefs treat each other with far-reaching tolerance. Also like in those days, the dominant mentality is incapable of understanding what faith truly is and has enormous difficulties with tolerating religious believers. The opposition of the believer to limiting faith to the sphere of his views is in diverse ways condemned as an irrational approach and a potential source of religious fanaticism and a danger to mutual tolerance.

In short, just as nearly two thousand years ago, not accepting the reduction of one's faith to the level of views today is likewise often recognized as a threat to building a social order based around mutual tolerance. Perhaps this is the main source of much distrust and many critiques that are leveled against the Church, her teaching, and people who fully identify with the Church in present-day Poland.

If the above description of two fundamentally distinct mentalities somehow reflects our reality, then it seems that a major step forward in building harmonious co-existence in one society would be each side's attempt at understanding the negative image of itself that has been shaped by its opponent. It seems that the representatives of the dominant mentality are more incapable of undertaking such an effort.

Furthermore, it is worth looking for a reasonable *modus vivendi* in which both sides could fully preserve their identity and freedom and more closely study the history of religious intolerance including that which was implemented in the name of religious liberty by those who voiced slogans of tolerance. It is very likely that the unilateral nurturing of memory of acts of intolerance on the part of Christians is a kind of smokescreen intended to cover up the various forms of religious discrimination and compulsion that today's de-Christianized societies apply towards Christians; this includes model democracies.[18]

18. A specific example of the direction in which attempts at limiting religious freedom in a democratic society could go is provided by Prof. Leszek Kołakowski: "When I followed the discussions in the United States on the topic of voluntary prayer in schools, I had the impression that a certain hysterical tone dominated among those who attacked the freedom to say such prayers as if prohibiting a couple students from saying the 'Our Father' during a break between lessons would plunge the country into an abyss of ominous theocracy" ("Bałwochwalsto polityki" ["The Idolatry of Politics"], *Aneks* 44/1986, p. 6).

There Is Also Something Known as Infancy in Faith

In conclusion, I would like to present two observations about the possibility of transforming attitudes of belief into faith. Most likely, every religious person knows how this occurs in the believer based on his or her own experience. Oftentimes, we begin to experience prayer as a real encounter with a loving God only at a certain moment; sometimes, someone's religiosity initially takes on the form of a Christian worldview rather than faith; at other times, some infant in the faith (see 1 Corinthians 3:1; 1 Peter 2:2) does not realize that faith authentically brings us into a new dimension of reality.

Once, a Japanese friend, a zealous Catholic, told me that the significance of conversions undertaken by Asian women should not be overestimated. First, the question of the veracity of faith came to Asia from Europe and, in her view, it is alien to Asian culture; second, for the average Asian woman it is natural that she should share her husband's religion. In her view, the Asian must earnestly live out Christianity for a long time to become a true believer. Perhaps this is why the early Church did not allow the recently baptized to become priests and especially bishops, even if they provided natural evidence of their religious zeal.

Likewise, the phenomenon of the Christianization of entire nations was possible because these nations were incapable of sensing the existence of differences between beliefs and faith and accepted Christianity as a form of new beliefs at a time that was more useful to them. Professor Łowmiański provides a very interesting answer to the question of why "in sources concerning the Christianization of the nations in the early Middle Ages there is no evidence of any attempts at convincing the converted or bolstering the faith of the people about the veracity of the teachings imparted on them." I suspect that my friend from Tokyo would find a series of elements that are very comprehensible to her in Łowmiański's response to this question:

"In accordance with the traditional form of thinking of a pre-literate society that was marked by liberalism and a free collective creativity in the sphere of religion, the ancient Slavs considered every religion professed by any social group to be true, just as they did not doubt the truthfulness of all the divinities that were the subject of worship. The creation of a new divinity is the legal function of a group that makes use of this attribute for which they have justified reasons. The Slavs could not deny that the Christians had this attribute. The God professed in many states could not be untrue. Not encountering any obstacles that were ontological in nature, the missionaries gave a different direction to argumentation, one that aimed to demonstrate the superiority of Christianity over pagan religions."[19]

At least a couple generations are needed for these nations to truly experience the taste of the Christian faith. With regards to individual Christians, already in the apostolic times it happened that some of them never grew out of infancy in the faith (see Hebrews 5:12).

Faith Consists in Truly Growing Close to God

Socrates, who was referenced at the beginning, is most likely an example of a man who found the living God (in this world, this cannot be accomplished in a way other than through faith) without the aid of historical revelation. St. Justin (d. circa 165) would cross out "most likely" from the above sentence, as this is how he wrote about Socrates: "And when Socrates endeavoured, by true reason and examination, to bring these things to light, and deliver men from the demons, then the demons themselves, by means of men who rejoiced in iniquity, compassed his death, as an atheist and a profane person,

19. Henryk Łowmiański, *Religia Słowian i jej upadek* (Warsaw: PWN, 1979), p. 272.

on the charge that he was introducing new divinities; and in our case they display a similar activity. For not only among the Greeks did reason (Logos) prevail" (*The First Apology*, Chapter 5).[20] Naturally, in Justin's statement "demons" refer to the gods that were worshiped in Athens in Socrates' time.

It was only in modern times that we learned to look at the various religions of the world in a Christianomorphic way, treating them in the image and likeness of the Christian religion. After all, Judaism and Islam, which teach their faithful to venerate God the Creator and want people to attain eternal life, are an exception among the different religions (including the historical religions).[21] The aim of such worship was not to bring anyone closer to God (who usually was not identified as the Creator) but to gain his general or temporary favor, while the perspective of perpetual friendship with the Creator did not reach the imaginations of their believers at all. Even the mere idea of faith in which we can grow closer to the living God and grow towards eternal life does not appear in these religions. It is from this perspective that Justin evaluates the Athenian religion from the time of Socrates.[22]

20. St. Justin Martyr, *The First Apology*, in: *Ante-Nicene Fathers*, Vol. 1, trans. Marcus Dods and George Reith, Alexander Roberts, James Donaldson, and A. Cleveland Coxe eds. (Buffalo, NY: Christian Literature Publishing Co., 1885).

21. Both Judaism and Islam are closely tied to God's revelation, which lies at the fundaments of Christianity; after all, the Jews recognize the true God Who revealed Himself through Abraham, Moses, and the prophets. Likewise, Muslims are participants in Abraham's faith and in this faith, as the Second Vatican Council teaches, they "adore the one God, living and subsisting in Himself; merciful and all- powerful, the Creator of heaven and earth" ("The Declaration'on the Relation of the Church to Non-Christian Religions *Nostra aetate*," 3).

22. However, even such religions contain elements that can truly bring one closer to the true God. The conciliar document cited above discusses this as follows: "The Catholic Church rejects nothing that is true and holy in these religions. She regards with sincere reverence those ways of conduct and of life, those precepts and teachings which, though differing in many aspects from the ones she holds and sets forth, nonetheless often reflect a ray of that Truth which enlightens all men. Indeed, she proclaims, and ever must proclaim Christ 'the way, the truth, and the life' (John 14:6), in whom men may find the fullness of religious life, in whom God has reconciled all things to Himself" (*Nostra aetate*, 2).

Justin reasons in accordance with the New Testament principle that "without faith it is impossible to please [God]" (Hebrews 11:6). However, he does not believe in any, not even any Christian, notion of God but in the true God, the Creator of the universe and of all people. Jesus Christ, Who revealed Him to us, only recently became a man for us, but He is the everlasting Logos; "He spoke to us through a son, whom He made heir of all things and through whom He created the universe" (Hebrews 1:2). He is "the true Light, which enlightens everyone [...] coming into the world" (John 1:9). Thus, Justin does not doubt that if Socrates believed in God, then this happened thanks to the One we call the Logos and the Only Son of God.

Whether we recognize the God of some belief or another (even if it is Christian) or if we believe in the true God Who revealed Himself in Jesus Christ and Whom we know only thanks to Christianity makes a major difference. The true God is the Creator of everything: "The heavens declare the glory of God; the firmament proclaims the works of His hands" (Psalm 19:2 and 33:5). Ultimately, God gives Himself to us in Jesus Christ, but He also reveals Himself through His work of creation: "Ever since the creation of the world, His invisible attributes of eternal power and divinity have been able to be understood and perceived in what He has made" (Romans 1:20). As a loving Providence, He is present in the everyday lives of all people: "[T]hough indeed He is not far from any one of us. For 'In Him we live and move and have our being'" (Acts 17:27-28).

If this is so, then all people are called to faith, including those who do not yet know Jesus Christ as a Living Being, both those who will someday meet Him and those who will never do so; both those who do not know Him through no fault of their own and those who consciously reject Him. We are all called to faith, for God loves us all and would like to bring us all to Himself. Faith consists of truly becoming close to God and maturing to eternal life.

FAITH THAT CELEBRATES AND CEREMONIAL FAITH

The Phenomenon of the Weekly Holiday

Only the Biblical religions know religious holidays that are regularly celebrated every seven days (culturally, Islam should be included among the Biblical religions, as it appeared within the realm of clear Jewish and Christian influences). None of the religions of the Far East — neither Hinduism nor Confucianism, Buddhism, or Shintoism — and none of the ancient religions of black Africa or of the Native Americans knows a holiday that would be analogous to the Jewish Shabbos, the Christian Sunday, or the Muslim Friday.

The fact that beginning with our birth we live in a culture stabilized in the rhythm of holidays intertwined with the ordinary days of the week makes it difficult to be astonished at the religious phenomenon of the weekly holiday. Analogously, the average European sees nothing unusual in the message of the first chapter of the Book of Genesis, that God created the sun, the moon, and other celestial bodies. When this statement was first formulated, it was revolutionary in the most literal sense; from it resulted the fact that the celestial bodies were created by God just like everything else and that all who worship them as deities are wrong.

How is the appearance of a holiday like the Old Testament Shabbat revolutionary in the history of the religions of the world? In short, the establishment of a weekly holiday was the practical consequence of the basic promise with which the entire Old Testament is filled: that God wants to enter intimacy with His chosen. Mircea Eliade once wrote that in the religions of ancient Greece man "does not dare to hope that his prayers can establish a certain intimacy with the gods."[23] In this regard, those who worshipped the gods of ancient Greece differed in no way from the adherents of many other religions. The belief about the distance which separates man from divinities can in no way be transcended; it is common to all the non-Biblical religions. Those who profess those religions would never conceive of searching for friendship with God through the aid of prayer and sacrifices. The very idea of friendship with God would probably seem as absurd to them as imagining dry water or hot snow. Their prayers and sacrifices had a more mundane purpose: in this way, they tried to stoke the wrath of the gods and gain their protection. Religiosity constructed in this way would not only lack a need for regular contact with God, but it sometimes experienced fear of excessively bothering God and thus awakening within Him suspicions that we are trying to get too intimate with Him and thus incurring His wrath. In the ancient Greek texts, we can find many testimonies to such fears.

Only the Biblical revelation that man was created in the image and likeness of God Himself, and that God first seeks out a covenant and friendship with people introduced a revolution in the shaping of our contacts with God. The possibility and even the necessity of everyday prayer as well as frequent celebration every couple days as

23. Mircea Eliade, *A History of Religious Ideas, Volume 1: From the Stone Age to the Eleusinian Mysteries*, trans. Willard R. Trask (Chicago: University of Chicago Press, 2014), p. 260.

basic means of our growing close to God and nurturing our friendship with Him have appeared within our imagination.

At this point, it is worth noticing that the contemporary phenomenon of the rejection of religious practices shares many traits with the ordinary regression of the ancient pagan religiosity, when man in principle recognized God, depended on His care, and from time to time sought His help through religious acts but never would have considered becoming a friend of God.

God Wants to Be Our Friend

It seems that the better we comprehend the religious meaning of celebration, the better we will remember that the Christian holidays are a unique manifestation of God's growing close to people and His invitation to intimacy with Him. We must discover anew what the authors of the Book of Deuteronomy were able to notice in such a fresh way: "For what great nation is there that has gods so close to it as the Lord, our God, is to us whenever we call upon Him?" (Deuteronomy 4:7).

Let us try to gain awareness of how often Sacred Scripture speaks of God's desire for man to be His friend, which is unheard of in other religions. We read that Enoch and Noah lived in friendship with God (Genesis 5:22,24; 6:9). Particularly moving are the prayers in which people remind God that 'You, O God, cannot forget that Abraham, our forefather, was Your friend' (see Daniel 3:35; 2 Chronicles 20:7). The greatest mystics are overcome with jealousy when they learn that "[t]he Lord used to speak to Moses face to face, as a person speaks to a friend" (Exodus 33:11). Yet God's offer of friendship is not limited to exceptional people: "The counsel of the Lord belongs to those who fear Him; and His covenant instructs them" (Psalm 25:14). In the name of his entire people, the prophet Isaiah sings of his fascination with God as his Friend: "Now let me sing of my Friend, my Beloved's song about His vineyard" (Isaiah 5:1).

In Sacred Scripture, there are many very insightful images of God's inconceivable closeness to people. "As mountains surround Jerusalem, the Lord surrounds His people both now and forever" (Psalm 125:2). God is compared to a bird that teaches its chicks true freedom and, if necessary, protects them under its wings (Exodus 19:4; Psalm 17:8, 36:8, 57:2, 61:5, 91:4). He is like a shepherd Who "feeds His flock; in His arms He gathers the lambs, carrying them in His bosom, leading the ewes with care" (Isaiah 40:11; see Psalm 23). God is even compared to a nurse, even though Biblical Hebrew did not yet know that term: "The Lord sustains him on his sickbed, You turn down his bedding whenever he is ill" (Psalm 41:4). Especially pregnant is the comparison of God to a loving mother who treats her child with love and concern: "I drew them with human cords, with bands of love; I fostered them like those who raise an infant to their cheeks; I bent down to feed them" (Hosea 11:4; see Isaiah 49:15, 66:13; Psalm 27:10).

The Old Testament constantly speaks of God's growing close to people. In it, there sometimes appear paternal and, from the times of the prophet Hosea, marital symbols related to God. At times, the Old Testament refers to God as our Goel, or our closest relative Who has taken upon Himself the obligation to bring us succor at times of danger. Readers of the Bible do not need to be reminded of how frequent the Old Testament testimonies in which God spends time with His people or with His specific chosen ones are.

Indeed, this entire experience of God as Someone Very Close required a completely new structure of religious worship. It is a religious truism that God deserves a kind of reciprocity on man's part: if God had come so close to us, then we should in turn grow closer to God. Regular prayer, worship, and celebration expresses in a human way our desire that we would like to constantly be close to God and in His sacred presence experience our changing fate. God's coming closer to us is coming closer to people and not objects; it is not something automatic, as God expects evidence from us that we care about being close to Him. The Apostle James writes concisely: "Draw near to God, and He will draw near to you" (James 4:8). "The Lord is near to all who call upon Him, to all who call upon Him in truth" (Psalm 145:18).

Naturally, it is difficult to compare the closeness that God offered to His elect in the Old Testament to the gift of His life-giving presence offered by God in Jesus Christ. This is not only because the True God, the Only Son through Whom the world has been created and Who "sustains all things by His mighty word" (Hebrews 1:3; see John 1:3; Colossians 1:16), has become one of us. In Jesus Christ, we have received completely new access to the Eternal Father that transcends all that is conceivable: "No one comes to the Father except through Me" (John 14:6). Through the power of the Holy Spirit, we become His Body and participants in His Divine filiation. It suffices to recognize that this access to the Father, which was closed off to even the greatest saints of the Old Testament (see Matthew 11:11; 1 Corinthians 3:10n), has been opened to us through faith and baptism (see Mark 16:16) and is implemented especially through the Eucharist, whose celebration and consumption makes us increasingly complete members of the Body of Christ (see 1 Corinthians 10:16). Therefore, celebration of the Eucharist is the very essence of Christian celebration.

Authentic and Inauthentic Celebration

Let us now try to become aware of the basic perversion that endangers religious celebration. Indeed, it turns out that a Catholic can escape from God's closeness not only by ignoring celebration or by becoming negligent in our religious practice, but also through inauthentic celebration.

Thus we are faced with the question of what is the difference between authentic and inauthentic celebration. The response to this question seems simple: celebration is authentic when it indeed sanctifies our everyday life. We celebrate our closeness to God so that it may encompass all of us, including our everyday lives. Celebration cannot be limited to merely celebrating, for then it loses its meaning and becomes a kind of disloyal game with the Lord God: we pretend that we are concerned about His closeness, but we are comfortable with staying far from Him.

In all likelihood, such religious hypocrisy that seemingly seeks out closeness to God yet does not intend to renounce sin could only have appeared in Biblical religions; such hypocrisy attempts to accomplish the impossible and convert to God without abandoning sin. However, Sacred Scripture frequently cautions us against mendacity in giving praise to God. God complains in the Book of Isaiah that this nation "draws near with words only and honors me with their lips alone, though their hearts are far from me/And fear of me has become mere precept of human teaching" (Isaiah 29:13; see Matthew 15:8).

Emotionally engaged prayer cannot help us with this. Only such piety that bears real fruit is authentic: "Even now do you not call me, 'My father, You are the bridegroom of my youth? Will He keep his wrath forever, will He hold His grudge to the end? This is what you say; yet you do all the evil you can" (Jeremiah 3:4-5; Psalm 78:35; Isaiah 58:2-7). "Not everyone who says to me, 'Lord, Lord,' will enter the kingdom of heaven, but only the one who does the will of my Father in heaven" (Matthew 7:21). The Church's teachers have often tied this statement to a verse from the Book of Exodus: "No one shall appear before me empty-handed" (Exodus 34:20; see 23:15).

In a similar way, the prophets exposed the phoniness of our celebration. What good is celebration if we are little concerned about growing genuinely close to God, if we have created an abyss that separates us from God with our sins? (see Isaiah 59:2). What may be the most famous verse on the subject reminds us: "Your new moons and festivals I detest; they weigh me down, I tire of the load. [...] Wash yourselves clean! Put away your misdeeds from before my eyes" (Isaiah 1:14, 16; see Amos 5:21-24, Hosea 5:6).

Apart from the quoted statement ("Not everyone who says to me, 'Lord, Lord'"), two other New Testament texts remind Christians that our prayers and the Eucharist should become harmonized with our everyday life. The earliest Christians associated the first of these texts with celebration of the Eucharist; it comes from the Sermon on the Mount: "Therefore, if you bring your gift to the altar, and there recall that your brother has anything against you, leave your gift there at the altar, go first and be reconciled with your brother, and then come and offer your gift" (Matthew 5:23-24).

In the Didache, a text written at the same time as the Book of Revelation or slightly earlier, this statement by the Lord Jesus was associated with the Sunday Eucharist: "But every Lord's day gather yourselves together, and break bread, and give thanksgiving *(eucharistesate)* after having confessed your transgressions, that your sacrifice may be pure. But let no one that is at variance with his fellow come together with you, until they be reconciled, that your sacrifice may not be profaned" (14:1-2).[24] St. Irenaeus (*Against Heresies*, 4:1, 8:1), Tertullian (*Of Patience*, 12), Origen (*Homilies on Numbers*, 26:2), and St. Cyprian (*The Lapsed, the Unity of the Church*, 13; *On the Our Father*, 23) refer to Jesus' above-quoted statement in a similar spirit.

A close reading of the text of the Didache on the Sunday Eucharist demands that we notice a reference to the Book of Malachi. Namely, this text clearly suggests that Christians who are concerned about the purity of their participation in the Eucharist in this way underscore the truth that is manifested in the Eucharist in Malachi's prophecy about a pure sacrifice given to God everywhere (1:11). By the way, who among us — even priests who celebrate Mass — is today aware of the fact that the first reference, which dates to the time of the apostles,

24. *The Didache*, in: *Ante-Nicene Fathers*, Vol. 7, trans. M. B. Riddle, Alexander Roberts, James Donaldson, and A. Cleveland Coxe eds. (Buffalo, NY: Christian Literature Publishing Co., 1886) https://www.newadvent.org/fathers/0714.htm (accessed January 14, 2022).

to confessing one's sins before receiving the Eucharist was motivated by concern that our "sacrifice may be pure"?

At this point, it is worth recalling that in old Christian texts we frequently encounter the admonition that the hands we raise up to God be clean. The Biblical source of this theme is a statement by the Apostle Paul which has almost become forgotten today: "It is my wish, then, that in every place the men should pray, lifting up holy hands, without anger or argument. Similarly, [too,] women should adorn themselves with proper conduct, with modesty and self-control" (1 Timothy 2:8-9). St. Hippolytus also refers to this text. He cautions that we remain vigilant of the devil because he wants "to oppress and persecute and to maltreat saints, so that they may lift up holy hands while praying to God, seeing that the prayer of the saints furnishes peace to the world but punishment to the wicked" (*Commentary on Daniel*, 24.7).[25] In the first post-apostolic generation, the Epistle of Barnabas instructs: "You shall not go to prayer with an evil conscience" (19:12).

Origen noted that the raising of hands should not be understood in what we would today call a nominalist sense; in essence, we are not only dealing with the external gesture or purely negative sinlessness. Origen explains in his "Homily XI on Exodus": "To lift up the hands is to lift up our works and deeds to God and not to have deeds which are cast down and lying on the ground, but which are pleasing to God and raised to heaven."[26]

Two more of Origen's ideas deserve to be recalled when we ponder the topic of ceremonial faith and everyday life. The starting point of the first of these ideas was the observation that, in the Old Testament, holidays are called "feast[s] of the Lord" (Exodus 10:9, 2 Chronicles 20:20); "festival[s] to the Lord" (Exodus 13:6, 12:14; Deuteronomy

25. Hippolytus of Rome, *Commentary on Daniel*, https://www.pergrazia.com/wp-content/uploads/2019/12/0205_hippolytus_commentary-on-daniel_2010.pdf (accessed January 14, 2022).

26. Origen, *Homilies on Numbers*, trans. Thomas P. Scheck, Christopher A. Hall, ed. (Downers Grove: IVP Academic, 2009), p. 359.

16:10,15); "the Lord's feast[s]" (Leviticus 23:6, 35:30, 41; Exodus 23:14); and "festival[s] before the Lord" (1 Chronicles 8:65; 1 Chronicles 23:31). The prophets never use these names in their speeches denouncing the empty ritualism of celebration. When the prophets speak of celebrations that displease the Lord and which the Lord deplores, they say that they are "your celebrations."

Origen arrives at the following conclusion: Because our celebrations are not always of the Lord, we should always celebrate them so that they may become true celebrations for our Lord. "So, does God have His own feast days? He does. For to Him, human salvation is a great feast. I think that a feast takes place with God through every single believer, through all who are converted to God and make progress in the faith. How do you think it causes Him joy, when the one who had been unchaste becomes chaste, and the one who had been unjust cultivates justice, and the one who had been impious becomes pious?"[27]

In the spirit of this logic, Origen frequently repeats the thesis that every day should be a holy day for the Christian. Likewise, Christians who only participate in the Eucharist on Sundays should act in a way that would make their lives one unending holy day. Origen asks: "Tell me, who come to Church only on festal days, are the other days not festal days? Are they not the Lord's days? [...] God hates, therefore, those who think that the festal day of the Lord is on one day."[28]

On the other hand, it is worth noticing that emphasizing that every day in the life of the Christian should be a holy day led the early Church to celebrate the Eucharist on days other than Sundays and holy days. Origen continues his argument: "Christians eat the flesh of the lamb every day, that is they consume daily the flesh of the word. 'For Christ our pasch is sacrificed.'"[29]

27. *Ibid.*, p. 140.

28. Origen, *Homilies on Genesis and Exodus*, trans. Ronald E. Heine (Washington, DC: Catholic University Press, 1982), pp. 162-163.

29. *Ibid.*, p. 163.

Summarizing this fragment of our reflections, we can say: There is ceremonial faith, which hates God because it consists of feigning closeness to God by people who have grown very distant from Him. There is also the faith that celebrates, for which celebration is becoming filled with God's presence so that it may be as close to God as possible in everyday life.

Naturally, this distinction can be used only to strengthen within oneself and within others the desire to grow closer to God. Those who would refer to this distinction by destroying the slender threads that still bind some Christians to God and the Church are simply spiritual wrongdoers.

Let Us Look at Faith That Celebrates

Let us look a little more closely at the faith that celebrates, or a faith that values the possibility of growing closer to God above everything. Its opposite is ceremonial faith, which we have discussed above. Here, it is worth noting two other perversions of faith. The first of these has become common as the attitude of believers that we call "non-practicing believers." Then, faith is reduced to the fact that someone proclaims the Catholic worldview and maintains a sense of some sort of belonging to the Church. With regards to Thomas' analysis of faith, we can say that such Catholics implement *credere Deum*; however, they do not appreciate the significance of *credere Deo* and *credere in Deum*. In short, their faith lacks a personal turn towards the living God. I think that the following admonition from the Epistle to the Hebrews is addressed to the "non-practicing believers," among others: "Take care, brothers, that none of you may have an evil and unfaithful heart, so as to forsake the living God" (3:12). Let us recall that the Epistle to the Hebrews cautions Christians against "stay[ing] away from our assembly" (10:25). Let us furthermore recall that according to St. Thomas faith that is solely limited to the sphere of convictions (in other words, a faith that is limited to only *credere Deum* and that lacks *credere Deo* as well as *credere in Deum)* does not make one a believer (*Commentary on the Letter of Saint Paul to the Romans*, Ch. 4, Lect. 1, No. 328). The essence of faith in God is not implemented in convictions but in real contact with God, in opening oneself to His love and in the search for salvation within Him.

Another perversion of faith consists of the proud conviction that we can create our own form of contact with God that is independent of the Church. This refers to those Catholics who avoid celebrating closeness to God with the entire Church during Mass, instead claiming that they can much better pray in the confines of the four walls of their home or in nature.

A Catholic who has fallen prey to this error forgets that God "dwells in unapproachable light, and whom no human being has seen or can see" (1 Timothy 6:16) and only "through our Lord Jesus Christ [...] we have gained access [by faith] to this grace in which we stand, and we boast in hope of the glory of God" (Romans 5:1-2). Hence, private prayer which radiates in a Catholic's participation in the Eucharist, which has been established by Christ, is something completely different that private prayer with which a Catholic tries to replace the Eucharist. There is something illogical in someone who considers himself to be a Christian yet practically does not want to affirm the truth that we can gain access to the Eternal Father only in Christ and in the means proscribed by Him.

However, let us set these perversions aside and finally look at faith that celebrates; at faith for which neither convictions nor religious experiences are something autonomous as both are integrally linked to the search for God's real presence and power as well as God's real activity in man. The Lord Jesus spoke of such faith to Saul, who had been thrown down to the ground and sent to preach the Gospel to the pagans, outside Damascus: "that they may turn from darkness to light and from the power of Satan to God, so that they may obtain forgiveness of sins and an inheritance among those who have been consecrated by faith in Me" (Acts 26:18).

Perhaps the most characteristic trait of such faith is the praise of God for His salvific works through both one's speech and a spiritual transformation and spiritual fruits that can be noticed even in the empirical sphere (see Galatians 6:22). We must truly internally experience God's salvific work to possess the attitude about which we read in Psalms: "to be near God is my good, to make the Lord God my refuge. I shall declare all your works in the gates of daughter Zion" (73:28).

Man thus has a spontaneous need to proclaim the blessings he has received from God; he is a bit like a bee that informs the entire swarm of having found a honeycomb. "Come and hear, all you who fear God, while I recount what has been done for me" (Psalm 66:16). "With shouts of joy declare this, announce it; Make it known to the ends of the earth, Say: 'The Lord has redeemed his servant Jacob'" (Isaiah 48:20). "My mouth will speak the praises of the Lord; all flesh will bless His holy name forever and ever" (Psalm 145:21). There are countless such texts in Sacred Scripture (see, for example, 1 Chronicles 16:8-11; Psalm 9:12, 22:23, 35:28, 40:10, etc.).

Sometimes, experiencing God's kindness makes man turn especially towards those who have distanced themselves from God: "I will teach the wicked Your ways, that sinners may return to You" (Psalm 51:15). "In the land of my captivity I give thanks, and declare His power and majesty to a sinful nation. According to your heart do what is right before Him: perhaps there will be pardon for you" (Tobit 13:6).

Most importantly, the normal transmission of the faith to subsequent generations in a way other than in an atmosphere of faith that celebrates, or that which seeks God's presence and power and that experiences God's activity, is inconceivable. Let us closely read the words of Psalm 78 with the eyes of a catechist: "What we have heard and know; things our ancestors have recounted to us. We do not keep them from our children; we recount them to the next generation, The praiseworthy deeds of the Lord and His strength, the wonders that He performed. God made a decree in Jacob, established a law in Israel: Which He commanded our ancestors, they were to teach their children; That the next generation might come to know, children yet to be born. In turn they were to recount them to their children" (Psalm 78:3-6).

Although Sacred Scripture is replete with catechetical pronouncements, we seldom notice them. For the Biblical authors, it is obvious that the truth about the redeeming God should be transmitted from one generation to another in a way that those that transmit it at the same time know it from their own experience: "However, be on your guard and be very careful not to forget the things your own eyes have seen, nor let them slip from your heart as long as you live, but make them known to your children and to your children's children, that day you stood before the Lord, your God, at Horeb, when the Lord said to me: Assemble the people for me, that I may let them hear My words, that they may learn to fear Me as long as they live in the land and may so teach their children" (Deuteronomy 4:9-10; see Exodus 12:24-27; Deuteronomy 6:5-7, 6:20-25, 11:18n; Psalm 22:31, 44:2, 145:4-7, Sirach 6:23-29).

As we can see, the Bible presents the transmission of the faith to children as giving witness to that in which one is already immersed. Experiencing God's closeness, which is realized in the feedback between different kinds of acts of worship and ordinary everyday life, which is treated as service to God, creates an ideal situation in which a witness to God's great works can have all the marks of authenticity. This concerns giving witness to various people, above all to one's own children.

Faith Is Not a Merely Private Matter

The oldest Christian texts present incitements to the shared celebration of the Eucharist as an exceptionally important trait of faith that celebrates. In his *Epistle to the Ephesians* (5:2n), St Ignatius of Antioch argued around 108: "Let no man deceive himself: if any one be not within the altar, he is deprived of the bread of God. For if the prayer of one or two possesses (Matthew 18:19) such power, how much more that of the bishop and the whole Church! He, therefore, that does not assemble with the Church, has even by this manifested his pride, and condemned himself. For it is written, 'God resists the proud.'"[30]

To repeat St. Ignatius' thought in our own words, there can be no doubt that the Church gathered at the Eucharist is something inconceivably greater than the sum of individual Christians. If the individual Christian avoids Eucharistic gatherings and does not value the living Bread, he will inevitably wither. In other words, our boasting of closeness to God would be false if we avoided closeness with our brothers in the faith. The Church is shaped by celebrating the Eucharist. The Apostle Paul formulated the first intuition on this topic: "Because the loaf of bread is one, we, though many, are one body, for we all partake of the one loaf" (1 Corinthians 10:17).

At another point in his *Letter to the Ephesians* (13:1), Ignatius emphasizes this completely new quality of our common growing closer to God in a completely different way. Ignatius is still fascinated by the strength that the Church gains by gathering at the common Eucharist. "Take heed, then, often to come together to give thanks to God, and show forth His praise. For when you assemble frequently in the same place, the powers of Satan are destroyed, and the destruction at which he aims is prevented by the unity of your faith."[31] Naturally, this spiritual strength of the Church is not an illusory glimmer that appears only when the Eucharist is celebrated. Thanks to this

30. *The Epistle of Ignatius to the Ephesians*, in: *Ante-Nicene Fathers*, trans. Alexander Roberts and James Donaldson, Vol. 1, Alexander Roberts, James Donaldson, and A. Cleveland Coxe, eds. (Buffalo, NY: Christian Literature Publishing Co., 1885), https://www.newadvent.org/fathers/0104.htm (accessed January 14, 2022).

31. *Ibid.*

strength, the community of believers as well as its individual believers can successfully face the adversities that life brings to them.

The Didache, which had been written more than a decade earlier, considers the common gathering of Christians to be the best way to protect their faith amidst the growing tide of discord and distraction of the final days: "But often shall you come together, seeking the things which are befitting to your souls: for the whole time of your faith will not profit you, if you be not made perfect in the last time. For in the last days false prophets and corrupters shall be multiplied, and the sheep shall be turned into wolves, and love shall be turned into hate" (16:2n).[32] As we can see, this statement demonstrates a clear similarity with an incitement to "not stay away from our assembly," which is found in Hebrews 10:25.

Indeed, it is not a coincidence that incitements to common celebration are so saturated with summons to persist in the faith as well as be concerned about the faith of one's co-religionists. In this regard, it suffices to have a close look at the fragment of Hebrews 10:23-27 or the last chapter of the Didache. The Sunday Eucharist is simply something much more than a source of faith for each of us and the most exceptional means of renewing closeness to God within oneself. The Sunday Eucharist is and should be the source of faith for the entire participating community and an opportunity for the renewal of our communal closeness to God.

During times of growing secularization, this dimension of the Sunday Eucharist must become the subject of probing attention and pastoral concern. Even sociologists claim that the secularization of contemporary societies consists in the disappearance of social bonds originating in religion and in the fact that faith becomes a solely private matter for individual Christians.

32. *The Didache.*

NON-PRACTICING BELIEVERS

Who Are Non-Practicing Catholics?

The term "non-practicing Catholics" refers to both those who very rarely come to church, as well as those who come to Sunday Mass more or less once a month; it also refers to those who never come to church at all yet would like to receive the holy sacraments before death or at least have a Catholic burial.

There are various reasons why someone might be among the ranks of non-practicing Catholics. Some come from families that seldom or never attended Sunday Mass. Others, meanwhile, learned to forget about Sunday Mass during weekend university courses or due to jobs in which they had to work Sundays. Among our generation, there is also a growing number of Catholics who cease to go to church once they enter non-sacramental unions. It seems, however, that the most common reason for the abandonment of religious practices is entering a milieu in which attending Mass every Sunday is not something natural.

Non-practicing Catholics have diverse attitudes towards the Church. Some have a very strong sense of being Catholics and do not doubt that the Church is their basic spiritual home. Others, meanwhile, are very lukewarm or even harshly critical towards the

Church; not infrequently, their criticism is unjust, but they do not cease to have a real bond with their Church.

A natural consequence of the abandonment of religious practice is neglect of everyday prayer. However, this is not always so. One can avoid attending Sunday Mass but at the same time faithfully observe some sort of regular or even daily prayer ritual. Sometimes, there are people who rarely attend Sunday Mass but like stumbling into a church where they can pray in silence. Anyway, a relatively large number of non-practicing Catholics try to remember prayers.

Why Go to Church?

When asked why one does not attend church if one is a Catholic, a person usually provides one of the following stereotypical responses:

- Why should I go to church? I get nothing out of it.
- Above all, I try to be an honest person, and I'm sure that I'm a better person than many of those who never neglect to go to Mass each Sunday.
- I find Mass boring, and I get the most out of the prayer that I choose myself.

In the fourteenth century, Meister Eckhart gave an accurate albeit off-color response to the excuse that one gets nothing out of going to church: Is God a cow? A cow provides us with milk and calves, and we ultimately eat its meat. Indeed, it is to God that we owe our health; thanks to Him, we have food and clothing. However, God's most important gifts are invisible, and only wise people can recognize and appreciate them. Above all, however, do you really not understand how great an ennoblement of man it is that we can praise God and be His friends?

Let us comment on the second excuse with the following rhetorical question: Do we go to church in order to be better people? Those who believe this are like idealists who claim that girls get married to become more beautiful. Indeed, it sometimes happens that even an ugly woman whom her husband authentically loves is transformed into a beautiful woman. Yet that is not the essential meaning of marriage.

Our relationship with God is similar. We are pleased when it morally ennobles us, but that is not its ultimate aim. Our dedication to God is the beginning and guarantee of eternal life, and the ultimate aim of our relationship with God is to praise Him for eternity (even if this sounds unattractive to the non-believer).

Should I attend Mass every Sunday even if regular prayer or meditation in nature gives me greater spiritual satisfaction? First of all, one factor does not rule out the other: if other forms of prayer enrich you so much, do not abandon them. Meanwhile, I will respond to the above question with the following comparison: The fact that you enjoy the taste of cake is not a reason to abandon your basic meal.

Second, Hans Urs von Balthasar, one of the greatest theologians of the twentieth century, reminds us that the Triune God is accessible to us only when we ourselves become accessible to Him. Thus, it would be greatly tactless toward Him to ignore His invitation to meet with Him and to search for some non-existing access to an unknown God on our own.

In other words, the aim of the sacraments, above all of Sunday Mass, is incomparably greater than the satisfaction of religious needs. The sacraments are real means of meeting Him that have been established by Christ the Lord Himself and ways of becoming filled with His life-giving presence. I recently found Maciej Krzyżak's poem titled *Zaproszenie* ("An Invitation") in the literary journal *Topos*. It explains this aim with endearing simplicity:

every week
God
stubbornly
invites me
to a feast

yet I
am usually
not prepared
I turn my back
to Him
and walk away
without saying farewell
to the comfortable
dangerous
wilderness

This provokes the question: What is the "comfortable, dangerous wilderness" mentioned in this poem? Much can be said on this topic. I was especially moved by the response provided by the Dutch Jesuit Father Eduard Kimman: "For many, losing the habit of attending church means the loss of the habit of listening, understanding, and using religious language. Yet the message of the Bible is transmitted using religious language; the message of Christianity is transmitted using religious language, and we pray and sing using religious language."

A Christian who has himself become so estranged from his own religious community should not be surprised that the Christian faith appears as something from another age to him.

THE APOSTASY FAD

It is only in our times that the term "apostasy" has come to be used in a positive sense. For example, this term does not appear in an appeal to leave the Church that was posted all over Krakow, including on the walls of churches, more than a century ago, in June 1910. It is worth noting that this appeal uses the term "renegades" in the traditional negative sense; however, for reasons that are difficult to comprehend, it is applied to zealous Catholics.

Let us look at the text of this appeal: "Do not be duplicitous; leave the Church! Away with dishonesty in life! Do not be afraid of persecutions. You will be attacked by the clerical international mob with the aid of those renegades who have sacrificed their convictions for the sake of their careers."

It is difficult to identify the aims of that campaign. However, one thing is for certain: its authors wanted to express their hatred for the Church in this way.

In fact, a wave of rejections of the Church took place in Poland during the German occupation in the territories that had been annexed by the Third Reich. In an article by Rev. Jerzy Myszor devoted to the history of ministry in the cathedral parish in Katowice, we can find the following information: "During the occupation, Katowice pastors noted the abandonment of the Church by people who were greatly engaged in the [German Nazi] Party hierarchy, although compared to other cities in Silesia they were not that numerous: there were fifty-one cases in 1941, nine in 1942, and seventeen in 1943."

The truth is that for centuries such terms as apostasy, defection, or betrayal had rather negative connotations in Poland. However, these terms were not applied to mild abandonments that were not influenced by low motives and that were not accompanied by aggression or hatred directed against one's previous religious membership.

The average Pole usually sincerely agrees with the distinction between apostasy and conversion that was proposed by St. John Henry Newman. According to Newman, in spite of appearances, these are not relative terms; that is, it is not the case that those who reject us are apostates while those who come to us are converts. Apostasy and conversion are two spiritually opposed attitudes. Conversion is openness to something new that I had not previously known tied to the desire to maintain as much of what had been dear to me as possible. Meanwhile, apostasy is entering the other camp linked to active hostility to one's previous affiliations.

In our Polish history, we have usually dealt with apostasy in the realm of national belonging. For centuries, it has been the case, and it will probably always be so, that some Poles became Russified or Germanized, while some Russians, Germans, or Frenchmen became Polonized, and no one considered these processes to be national apostasy. We usually used the term "renegades" to refer to people who did not so much drift away from Polishness but instead denied it and became its zealous enemies. It is probably no coincidence that those Germans and Russians who themselves had some Polish ancestry distinguished themselves in their hatred of the Poles. This phenomenon was accurately recognized by Adam Mickiewicz, who described Major Plut as follows in *Pan Tadeusz*:

This Major, by birth a Pole from the little town of Dzierowicze, according to report, had been named Plutowicz in Polish, but had changed his name;

he was a great rascal, as is usually the case with Poles that turn Muscovites in the Tsar's service.[33]

The case with religious apostates is analogous: they had not so much drifted away from the religion in which they had been born but instead broke with it and became its venomous enemies.

Biblical Apostates

The first Biblical reference to apostates is found in the Book of Deuteronomy 13:13-16. There, apostates are called "scoundrels [who] have sprung up in your midst and have led astray the inhabitants of their city, saying, 'Come, let us serve other gods.'" The Biblical authors considered them to be what we would today call a mortal threat to the religious identity of the nation and, consequently, its own existence.

Several centuries later, fear of specific apostates prevented King Zedekiah from abandoning Jerusalem to invaders, which had been suggested to him by the prophet Jeremiah, during the siege of the city: "I am afraid of the Judahites who have deserted to the Chaldeans; I could be handed over to them, and they will mistreat me" (Jeremiah 38:19).

We can frequently read of apostates in the First Book of Maccabees. That was a time of change inaugurated by the conquests of Alexander the Great. Likewise, in the Jewish nation there then appeared tendencies towards the Hellenistic integration that was occurring in the broader world in those days, which would have ultimately led to the entire nation's rejection of its own religion.

The description of what happened then at the beginning of 1 Maccabees is poignant: "In those days there appeared in Israel transgressors of the law who seduced many, saying: 'Let us go and make a covenant with the Gentiles all around us; since we separated from them, many evils have come upon us.' The proposal was agreeable;

33. Adam Mickiewicz, *Pan Tadeusz*, trans. George Rapall Noyes (London: J. M. Dent & Sons Ltd., 1917), p. 226.

some from among the people promptly went to the king, and he authorized them to introduce the ordinances of the Gentiles. Thereupon they built a gymnasium in Jerusalem according to the Gentile custom. They disguised their circumcision and abandoned the holy covenant; they allied themselves with the Gentiles and sold themselves to wrongdoing" (1 Maccabees 1:11-15).

Such people actively opposed their own nation, urging other enemies of the kings from the Seleucid dynasty to intensify their effort to uproot the religion of their fathers. When we read more information about the activity of these apostates (see 1 Maccabees 6:21-21, 7:5-6, 9:23-27, 10:61, 11:21-26), we get the impression that from a human perspective the people of the Covenant nearly dissipated in the melting pot of the nations at the time.

Let us turn to the New Testament. The massive rejection of Jesus by His disciples, who were incapable of believing the truth of the Eucharist, repeated itself throughout the history of the Church on numerous occasions. Fortunately, even in the most dramatic moments there was never a lack of disciples who were faithful to Jesus up to the very end: "As a result of this, many [of] His disciples returned to their former way of life and no longer accompanied Him. Jesus then said to the Twelve, 'Do you also want to leave?' Simon Peter answered Him, 'Master, to whom shall we go? You have the words of eternal life. We have come to believe and are convinced that You are the Holy One of God" (John 6:66-69)

At the end, we find a firm caution against apostasy addressed to Christians threatened with persecution for their faith by the author of the Epistle to the Hebrews: "For it is impossible in the case of those who have once been enlightened and tasted the heavenly gift and shared in the holy Spirit and tasted the good word of God and the powers of the age to come, and then have fallen away, to bring them to repentance again, since they are recrucifying the Son of God for themselves and holding Him up to contempt" (Hebrews 6:4-6).

The Returns of Apostates

To protect her children from apostasy, the Church, being a good mother, cautions that a return to faith may prove impossible. However, she is merciful towards those who have the desire to return. Sometimes, this takes place through the approach of harshness towards apostasy and mercy towards the apostate, as the Synod of Elvira decreed in 305. In canon 22, this synod declared: "If people fall from the Catholic Church into heresy and then return, let them not be denied penance, since they have acknowledged their sin. Let them be given communion after ten years' penance. If children have been led into heresy, it is not their own fault, and they should be received back immediately."[34]

Especially moving are the descriptions of the returns of apostates through martyrdom. Among the martyrs of Lyon (c. 177), whose martyrdom is described in the fifth book of Eusebius of Caesarea's book *Church History*, there was a Christian named Biblias who renounced Christ out of fear of torture. A direct witness to her martyrdom writes: "But the devil, thinking that he had already consumed Biblias, who was one of those who had denied Christ, desiring to increase her condemnation through the utterance of blasphemy, brought her again to the torture, to compel her, as already feeble and weak, to report impious things concerning us. But she recovered herself under the suffering, and as if awaking from a deep sleep, and reminded by the present anguish of the eternal punishment in hell, she contradicted the blasphemers."[35] Biblias bore testimony to the fact that Christians

34. The Council of Elvira, https://web.archive.org/web/20120716202800/http://faculty.cua.edu/pennington/Canon%20Law/ElviraCanons.htm#Discipline%20of%20laity (accessed January 14, 2022).

35. Eusebius, *Church History*, Book V, trans. Arthur Cushman McGiffert, in: *Nicene and Post-Nicene Fathers, Second Series*, Vol. 1, Philip Schaff and Henry Wace, eds. (Buffalo, NY: Christian Literature Publishing Co., 1890), https://www.newadvent.org/fathers/250105.htm (accessed January 14, 2022).

are not guilty of the crimes of which they are accused; she professed that she herself was a Christian and died as one.

The *Menologion*, the official book of the Eastern Church which contains a list of venerated saints, has recorded the return of a high-ranking Persian official who rejected his faith for the sake of his career: "James of Persia was a dear friend of Yazdegerd I, the King of Persia (399-425). He was born a Christian but blinded by his friendship with the king he renounced Christ. When his mother and wife learned of this, they gave him a written notice explaining that they want nothing to do with him for he sacrificed temporal glory over love for Christ. Moved by this, he bitterly lamented his sin. The king fell into a mad rage and sentenced James to a terrible death. He demanded that James be cut into pieces, beginning with his hands and legs down to his shoulders. After such mutilation, he was finally killed with a sword."[36]

Likewise, the Dominican Order can boast of a saint who redeemed his apostasy through martyrdom: Anthony Neyrot, who had been kidnapped by pirates and taken to Tunis, where he was sold into slavery. Anthony decided to trample on his faith, priesthood, and monastic vows and converted to Islam. To drown out his conscience, Anthony began to study the Koran with the intention of promoting Islam among Christians. However, he quickly came to his senses and exactly on the first anniversary of his apostasy, on April 6, 1460, he dressed in a Dominican habit and went to the court of the sultan to publicly profess his return to the Christian faith. A direct witness to those events described them as follows:

> No one is capable of describing the wrath and hatred of which he was the subject or present those slaps in the face and strikes that were administered to him in the cruelest way. Each of the tormentors felt happier with the greater amount of cruelty and savagery he was allotted. It is all the more difficult to describe and believe the consistency and bravery with which

36. Translated from the Polish text by Filip Mazurczak.

Brother Anthony, who constantly proclaimed and praised Christ's name, bore this. He was taken to jail. I immediately wrote him a letter in order to lift his spirits; not because he needed this, but because I wanted to have some contribution to such an important matter. Some of the Genovese merchants who brought him food and clothing did the same. However, he only took a little bit of bread and water, giving the rest to poor Christians and to prisoners who were locked up in this prison.

The following day, he was brought to the leader of the sect who tried to incline him towards error, especially through various promises. Finally, he presented before his eyes the terrible and cruel death that awaited him. However, the good and faithful soldier struck the judge with the same weapon with which the sultan had previously emerged victorious. The judge, who was incapable of rising to his arguments, demanded that he be taken to jail and told that if he would not return to his error within three days and would not publicly proclaim the name of Muhammed, he would die in a terrible way.

He was taken to prison amidst numerous strikes and punches. Three days passed. This was on Maundy Thursday, the day when the Lord Jesus ate the Last Supper with His disciples. On that day, Christ's true disciple was to consume a feast in his heavenly fatherland. He was brought to the judge several times. When admonitions and threats did not work, the judge arrived at the conclusion that nothing can incline him towards this yoke and sentenced him to stoning in an ignoble sentence.

The story of this apostasy and martyrdom reminds us of several seemingly obvious truths, but it would be good to become even more aware of them. First, apostasy can be the case with even very decent Christians and in situations that are objectively not particularly difficult. It suffices for Satan to find some nook in our souls through which he can pass. In the case of Blessed Anthony, that nook was a lack of patience in bearing slavery. Second, noisiness in professing one's new faith is typically calculated to drown out one's internal anxiety rather than a testimony to the deep conviction of one's new views.

Finally, God does not cease to love even those who have betrayed Him, and when He calls someone to martyrdom — even if this is someone naturally weaker than others — He simultaneously strengthens the person with His power.

The Most Common Departures and Returns

However, both rejections of the faith and returns to the faith usually occur without much publicity. Many Catholics do not so much reject their faith as become indifferent to it. They do this for thousands of reasons: because they have ceased to keep the habit of going to Mass every Sunday; because they have become absorbed by debauchery or making money; because they have become addicted to alcohol or drugs; because they are in a non-sacramental union; because they have entered an irreligious milieu; because they have been disappointed by several priests; etc.

Likewise, the circumstances of returns are diverse. Sometimes, God's grace encompasses someone so tangibly that a person simply "must" convert. Great existential experiences, sorrowful and joyful alike, are a common incentive for returns to the Church: the birth or baptism of a child, a child's wedding, unexpectedly surviving a catastrophe, the death of someone close, one's own serious illness, etc. Some returns to the faith and the sacraments take place because of the conversion of a close friend or of one's own child. We cannot enumerate all the circumstances here.

In conclusion, I will recall the poignant caution against apostasy given by John Paul II during his first pilgrimage to Poland, in Krakow's Błonia Park in 1979: "Can one refuse Christ and all that He has brought into human history? Certainly not. It is true that man is free. But the basic question remains: is it licit to do this? In whose name is this licit?"

THE QUESTION OF THE LIGHT OF FAITH

The concept of "the light of faith" has a rich history that is worth studying closely, especially since it is found in the title of Pope Francis' encyclical *Lumen fidei*. A greater understanding of the essence of the light of faith can be facilitated by seeing this concept within the context of structurally related concepts.

Following St. Thomas Aquinas, I would like to distinguish between four radically different concepts of light. I would like to emphasize that I do not plan on presenting the views of anyone other than Aquinas. I am inspired by his conceptualizations, although I do not intend on reconstructing them here.

In Aquinas' works, the basis of the three metaphorical concepts of light is material light, or light in a literal sense. Thomas calls it *lux sensibilis*[37] or *lumen materiale*[38]. It is worth being cautious and not referring the Thomistic term *lumen naturale* to material light, as Thomas almost always refers to the natural light of reason in this way.

In physics class, we were taught that material light is that part of electromagnetic waves that our retinas discern. Considering this,

37. 1 Sent. d.3 q.1 a.2 arg.2.

38. 4 Sent. d. 17 q.1 a.2 q-la 1 sc.

we should distinguish between objective and subjective darkness. Objective darkness is caused by an absence of the above-mentioned waves, while subjective darkness results from the lack of a properly equipped retina. These distinctions are sometimes used in an analysis of the metaphorical concepts of light: it suffices to note how often we use the concept of blindness.[39]

The three metaphors for light are:

1. First, the light of reason. An electronic index of the works of St. Thomas lists 114 uses of the term *lumen intellectus* (and I only checked its use in the nominative), thirty-four uses of the concept of *lumen rationis*, and three uses of the concept of *lumen synderesis* ("the light of conscience;" I will make use of the opportunity to make note of the great depth of the description of the conscience in Sirach 17:8 as "He put fear of Him into their hearts to show them the grandeur of His works").
2. Next, there is the light of faith. Thomas uses the concept of *lumen fidei* thirty-eight times; however, he uses the concept of "the light of grace" (*lumen gratiae*) more often, forty-eight times. For Thomas, the light of grace is the light of faith shaped by love (*fides caritate formata*), or the faith with which we are endowed in a state of sanctifying grace.
3. Finally, we have the light of glory. Aquinas uses the concept of *lumen gloriae* forty-eight times. The light of glory is the capacity to see God in the most literally direct sense, without the aid of any image; in other words, to see God with such directness that is not accessible to us in the present order even while knowing creatures that are inferior to us. No creature inherently has this skill. According to St. Thomas, the light of glory makes the intellect of creation shaped by God: *Lumen gloriae intellectum in quadam deiformitate constituit.*[40]

39. See e.g. S.Th. 2-2 q.15 a.1
40. S. Th., 1 q.12 a.6.

The Light of Reason, or the Capacity to Know Truth and Good

I will begin by sharing my own memories of when I became empirically convinced that even those animals that are most admired by us for their capacity to know the world in which they live are devoid of the light of reason. About a quarter of a century ago, Halley's comet was visible in the sky for several weeks. My friend decided to interest her dog, to which she was so attached that she considered it to be her friend, in this fact. On starry nights, she frequently went on walks with it to turn its attention to this unusual phenomenon. She later said: "I really tried, but I could in no way make my friend notice Haley's comet, which brightened the sky." Its cognitive interests were simply limited to the horizon of its life's needs and possible threats.

We, people, know the truth that transcends this horizon thanks to the light of reason. Likewise, it is only thanks to this that we can distinguish between good and evil. When nuns still lived in my monastery, they kept a female cat with kittens. When one of the cat's offspring grew up, it considered the monastery to be its territory and drove away its mother so effectively that she became completely wild. Nature did not give it memory that this was its mother or understanding that its mother deserves gratitude.

However, let us turn to theology. I will allow myself to recall that the term "the natural light of reason" is even found in one of the dogmatic pronouncements of the Church. In 1870, the First Vatican Council reminded us that thanks to the natural light of reason we can even know God: "God, the beginning and aim of all things, can thanks to the natural right of reason (*naturali humanae rationis lumine*) be known with the certainty of created things" (3004).

The conciliar constitution in which this dogma is found simultaneously turns our attention to the fact that the light of reason can be stirred up and obscured by our moral disorder; it is only thanks to

Divine Revelation that we all can know God at the same time with complete certainty and not a touch of error (see 3005). The Apostle Paul wrote in the first chapter of the Epistle to the Romans that "[t]he wrath of God is indeed being revealed from heaven against every impiety and wickedness of those who suppress the truth by their wickedness" (1:18) and "they exchanged the truth of God for a lie" (1:25).

One could prepare a thick anthology of the observations and instructions of the Church's teachers on the negative impact of sin on the light of reason. Now, I will recall only two wise statements on this topic. Around 180, St. Theophilus of Antioch wrote in his letter *To Autolycus*: "But if you say, 'Show me your God,' I would reply, 'Show me yourself, and I will show you my God.' [...] As a burnished mirror, so ought man to have his soul pure. When there is rust on the mirror, it is not possible that a man's face be seen in the mirror; so also when there is sin in a man, such a man cannot behold God. Do you, therefore, show me yourself, whether you are not an adulterer, or a fornicator, or a thief, or a robber, or a purloiner; whether you do not corrupt boys; whether you are not insolent, or a slanderer, or passionate, or envious, or proud, or supercilious; whether you are not a brawler, or covetous, or disobedient to parents; and whether you do not sell your children; for to those who do these things God is not manifest, unless they have first cleansed themselves from all impurity. All these things, then, involve you in darkness, as when a filmy defluxion on the eyes prevents one from beholding the light of the sun: thus also do iniquities, man, involve you in darkness, so that you cannot see God."[41]

St. Augustine responded to the question of what a sinner who wants to know God must do in a similar way: "Let him become pure,

41. St. Theophilus of Antioch, *To Autolycus, Book I*, Translated by Marcus Dods. From *Ante-Nicene Fathers*, Vol. 2. Edited by Alexander Roberts, James Donaldson, and A. Cleveland Coxe (Buffalo, NY: Christian Literature Publishing Co., 1885.) Revised and edited for New Advent by Kevin Knight https://www.newadvent.org/fathers/02041.htm (accessed January 6, 2022).

that he may be able to see God. Just as if a man could not see because his eyes were dirty and sore with dust, rheum, or smoke, the physician would say to him: 'Cleanse from your eye whatever bad thing is in it, so that you may be able to see the light of your eyes.' Dust, rheum, and smoke are sins and iniquities: remove then all these things, and you will see the wisdom that is present; for God is that wisdom, and it has been said, 'Blessed are the pure in heart; for they shall see God.'"[42]

What is most surprising is that some people have grown accustomed to their darkness and yearning, for the light is alien to them. Jesus said to Nicodemus: "And this is the verdict, that the light came into the world, but people preferred darkness to light, because their works were evil. For everyone who does wicked things hates the light and does not come toward the light, so that his works might not be exposed" (John 3:19-20).

Some are even proud of their own darkness, which they consider to be the most forward-thinking luminosity. The Lord Jesus said the following terrifying words of such people: "And if the light in you is darkness, how great will the darkness be" (Matthew 6:23).

If someone is in love with his own darkness, he can find himself, to use a mathematical metaphor, in darkness squared. This may not only cause him to hide before God, but God may also begin to hide from him. This is poignantly described in the Gospel of John: "Jesus said to them, '[...] Walk while you have the light, so that darkness may not overcome you. Whoever walks in the dark does not know where he is going. While you have the light, believe in the light, so that you may become children of the light'" (12:35-36).

Only God knows why He hides before the sinner who loves his own darkness. Maybe this is because he has reached the zenith of his

42. St. Augustine, "Tractate 1 (John 1:1-5)," in: *Tractates (Lectures) on the Gospel of John*, trans. John Gibb. From *Nicene and Post-Nicene Fathers*, First Series, Vol. 7, Edited by Philip Schaff (Buffalo, NY: Christian Literature Publishing Co., 1888.) Revised and edited for New Advent by Kevin Knight, https://www.newadvent.org/fathers/1701001.htm (accessed January 6, 2022).

depravity? Or perhaps this is to protect them from even greater sin? The truth is that some sinners need aggression against God, which in itself is absurd. Because God is not directly accessible to them, they persecute His presence in people and among people. This aggression reached its peak on Good Friday. As He gave Himself over to His assassins, Jesus said: "[B]ut this is your hour, the time for the power of darkness" (Luke 22:53).

The Light of Faith Is the Light of Neither Convictions Nor a Worldview

The very concept of the "light of faith" contains the necessity for it to be rooted in an authentic understanding of faith. It would be inconceivable to speak and think of faith reasonably if we attempted to reduce faith to possessing religious convictions or to professing a religious world view; in other words, to one of those conceptualizations that the dominant mentality in Europe since the Enlightenment would like to impose.

If faith solely consisted of possessing religious convictions, we would not know how the truth about Christ; we would know neither than He is the Son of God nor that He rose from the dead and redeemed us. Above all, it would be impossible for us to enter a real relationship with Him. Faith reduced to professing the Christian worldview, reduced to a subjective response to a question about the ultimate meaning of the world and of man, would be something even lesser. We cannot see with what transcendence towards us such subjective convictions or views could illuminate us.

In the first chapter of his encyclical, Pope Francis writes that the light of faith "comes from the risen Christ," and thus from unimaginably deeper sources than our views or convictions. Many pages later, Francis writes: "The light of faith is the light of a countenance in which the Father is seen. [...] This means that faith-knowledge does not direct our gaze to a purely inward truth. The truth which faith discloses to us is a truth centered on an encounter with Christ, on the contemplation of His life and on the awareness of His presence" (30).

Number 4 is the heart of this encyclical. There, the pope presents faith whose life comes to us from the resurrected Christ and thus from the future which is transcendent towards us. It can illuminate our entire lives, directing our perspective towards the future, and leading us past the limitations of death. Pope Francis says that this light is so powerful that it cannot come from us.

Let me add Francis' very important comment that the light of faith illuminates not only our entire lives, but also ourselves, and the degree to which we are open to this light essentially depends on the spread of the evangelical message. To quote this encyclical (37): "The light of Christ shines, as in a mirror, upon the face of Christians; as it spreads, it comes down to us, so that we too can share in that vision and reflect that light to others, in the same way that, in the Easter liturgy, the light of the paschal candle lights countless other candles. Faith is passed on, we might say, by contact, from one person to another, just as one candle is lighted from another."

Three Detailed Observations

At the conclusion of this part of the lecture, I will present three important observations by Aquinas, the first of which concerns the relationship between the light of the faith and the light of reason: "[G]ifts of grace are added to those of nature in such a way that they do not destroy the latter, but rather perfect them; wherefore also the light of faith, which is gratuitously infused into our minds, does not destroy the natural light of cognition, which is in us by natuise. For although the natural light of the human mind is insufficient to reveal those truths revealed by faith, yet it is impossible that those things which God has manifested to us by faith should be contrary to those which are evident to us by natural knowledge. In this case one would necessarily be false: and since both kinds of truth are from God, God would be the author of error, a thing which is impossible."[43]

This thesis was repeated by the dogmatic constitution of the First Vatican Council on the Catholic faith (Chapter 4) as well as John Paul II in the encyclical *Fides et ratio*, 34. Thomas did not forget to add that knowledge in the light of faith is much more perfect than knowledge only in the light of natural reason: "Because there is a certain imitation of perfect things in imperfect ones, what is known thanks to natural reason contains certain similarities to what is transmitted thanks to faith. Just as sacred teaching is based on the light of faith, philosophy is similarly based on the light of natural reason. Thus, it is impossible for philosophical pronouncements to be contrary to pronouncements of the faith, but the former come nowhere near the perfection of the latter."[44]

Second, according to St. Thomas, the light of faith is not equally strong in all believers. "We accept the light of God appropriate to our capacity. Faith makes the light of God act within us; however, we must accept this light in a measure appropriate to our capacity."[45]

Third, the light of faith is sometimes obscured by sin within us. The perfection of the act of faith comes from both the mind and the will. Yet faith not shaped by love, when the believer is deprived of sanctifying grace, is incapable of a perfect act.[46]

43. St. Thomas Aquinas, *Super Böethium de Trinitate*, q.2 a. 3; trans. Rose E. Brennan, S.H.N. (q. 1-4) and Armand Mauer (q. 5-6), https://isidore.co/aquinas/english/BoethiusDeTr.htm (accessed January 16, 2023).

44. *Ibid.*

45. "Lumen divinum non recipitur in nobis nisi secundum nostram proportionem; fides autem causatur in nobis ex influentia divini luminis; et ideo oportet quod istud divinum lumen secundum nostram proportionem in nobis recipiatur" (3 Sent. d.21 q.2 a.3).

46. "Quia ergo credere est actus intellectus, secundum quod est motus a voluntate; ad hoc quod iste actus perfectus sit, oportet quod intellectus perfectus sit per lumen fidei, et voluntas sit perfecta per habitum caritatis; et ideo informis fides non habet actum perfectum, et ideo non potest esse virtus" (3 Sent. d.23 q.3 a.1 q-la 2).

The Light of Glory

Naturally, the meaning of the term "light" is purely metaphorical here. "However, since we reach the knowledge of intelligible things from sensible things, we also take over the names proper to sense knowledge for intellectual knowledge, especially the ones which apply to sight, which, compared to the other senses, is more noble and more spiritual, and so more closely related to the intellect. Thus it is that this intellectual knowledge is called *vision*. And since corporeal vision is not accomplished without light, those things whereby intellectual vision is perfected take on the name *light*. [...] Therefore, this disposition whereby the created intellect is raised to the intellectual vision of divine substance is fittingly called the light of glory."[47]

The term "light of glory" originates especially in two Biblical prophesies: "In Your light we see light" (Psalm 36:10) and "Beloved, we are God's children now; what we shall be has not yet been revealed. We do know that when it is revealed we shall be like Him, for we shall see Him as He is" (1 John 3:2); as well as the descriptions of eternal life in the Book of Revelation: "The city had no need of sun or moon to shine on it, for the glory of God gave it light, and its lamp was the Lamb" (Revelation 21:23); and "Night will be no more, nor will they need light from lamp or sun, for the Lord God shall give them light, and they shall reign forever and ever" (Revelation 22:5).

In his *Commentary on Isaiah*, Aquinas wrote that just as the light of reason makes us capable of naturally contemplating invisible realities and the light of faith elevates minds on a pilgrimage to eternal life to supernatural contemplation, similarly the light of glory makes

47. St. Thomas Aquinas, *Contra Gentiles, Book Three: Providence*, Ch. 3, No. 6, trans. Vernon J. Bourke, https://web.archive.org/web/20181014034009/https://dhspriory.org/thomas/ContraGentiles3a.htm#53 (accessed January 6, 2022).

the blessed in heaven capable of seeing God in His essence, and such contemplation is fully and perfectly possible only in the Fatherland.[48]

The light of glory is a gift that absolutely transcends the natural capabilities of even the most perfect creatures; it makes creation God-like with respect to reason.[49] This light cannot be lost because "this light is accepted in an indestructible way, in accordance with nature and the giver and the receiver."[50] "It is somewhat similar to God's intellect;" at the same time, it can make some more similar to God than others.[51]

Of course, "[e]ven though a created intellect is never elevated by the light of glory to such an extent that the distance between it and the divine essence is no longer infinite, yet, as a result of this light, the intellect is united with the divine essence as with an intelligible form; and this union can happen in no other way."[52]

Instead of a Conclusion

Two of the findings above seem particularly important. First, the concept of "the light of faith" is something more than an accidental metaphor; it has a strictly designated place in the series of three hierarchical metaphors that present three different situations of our access to the truth.

Second, the light of faith comes from sources that are incomparably deeper than our views or convictions because, as Pope Francis has aptly written in his encyclical *Lumen fidei*, "it comes from the risen Christ" (1).

48. *Super Isaiam*, cap. 11.1.

49. "Per hoc lumen fit creatura rationalis deiformis" (S.Th. 1 q.12 a.5 ad 3).

50. *Summa contra Gentes*, lib. 3 cap.62 n.5.

51. *Summa contra Gentes*, lib. 3 cap.58 n.3.

52. St. Thomas Aquinas, *Questiones Disputatae de Veritate. TRUTH*, q.8 a.3 ad 14, questions 1-9 trans. Robert W. Mulligan, S.J. (Chicago: Henry Regnery Company, 1952); questions 10-20 trans. James V. McGlynn, S.J. (Chicago: Henry Regnery Company, 1953); questions 21-29 trans. by Robert W. Schmidt, S.J. (Chicago: Henry Regnery Company, 1954); Html edition by Joseph Kenny, O.P., https://isidore.co/aquinas/english/QDdeVer.htm (accessed January 16, 2023).

REASON AND REVELATION

This text is a response to the following letter:

During a conversation on religious topics, someone used the following argument: "I do not recognize any revelation, as I am guided solely by reason," thus clearly implying that his attitude is better because it is more rational. According to this gentleman, those who accept revelation act irrationally, as they accept some source of truth that is independent of their reason. I feel completely terrorized by such a statement because although it is groundless, one does not know what to say in response to it.

I see two major misunderstandings in this gentleman's views. First, he seems to believe that reason is a source of truth. Is it really so? Reason is cognitive dominion that searches for the truth and distinguishes between what is true and what is false, but reason does not establish the truth. Reason merely interprets the truth contained in reality, and it can sometimes err. Naturally, reason is not a dead screen that passively and soullessly reflects reality; it is the cognitive authority of the living human person who becomes actively open to reality. Although this situation gives birth to complicated philosophical problems, it does not change one essential fact: reality, and not reason, is the source of truth.

Thus, we must firmly state that a measure of the rationality of our view of the world is openness to all the possible dimensions of reality.

We should especially become open to those dimensions of reality that seem most essential.

Meanwhile, we often not only close ourselves off from these most essential dimensions of reality, but in fact we claim that such an attitude is rational. Where does this come from? It most likely results from the fact that we confuse rationality with clarity and complete comprehensibility. However, only that which is lesser than our reason, or better still, only that which is a product of our reason, can be fully clear and comprehensible to us. Even dead matter, the sphere of reality that is undoubtedly inferior to man, was fully comprehensible only to nineteenth-century positivists; it ceased to be such when physicists began to study its true nature more closely. If, then, there exist in reality spheres that transcend man and his reason, by their nature they must appear to us as something abysmally mysterious that one can be delighted with and that one would like to love but that cannot be fully understood or named. The demand that limited human reason fully understands that which infinitely transcends it is irrational. Similarly, it is irrational to assume *a priori* that reality is devoid of dimensions that transcend human reason.

I find one more misunderstanding in the views of that gentleman. Namely, he seems to believe that we Christians treat revelation as a source of truth that is independent of reason: that certain truths about ourselves and about the world come from reason, while others result from revelation. What are we to think of the view that certain specific revealed truths which we would be incapable of knowing with our own reason are the subject of reason? It would be difficult to say that this is a false view; it is nevertheless very incomplete. This would be like saying that only mutual declarations of love are the subject of marital love; after all, an essential subject of this love to which everything in this love is reduced is the fact that spouses try to surrender themselves to one another.

What is Divine Revelation? Does this mean that God has revealed Himself to people? That God has revealed Himself to us means that He has opened His interior before us; revealed to us His personal face; spoken to us; professed His love to us. Is it really that irrational to believe that God has revealed Himself to man and that this is how we learned the most essential truth about Him? We cannot even know the interior of a fellow person if someone does not want to open up before us. We can only guess what is taking place inside another person through his acts and works, but only that person himself can provide us access to his interior. How come that our reason must respect the personal structure of another person, but it does not consider the fact that God is Someone Living and Personal?

We can learn much about God through reason: from His presence in various events in our lives and from His works, which like every other great work bear witness to their Artist. However, our reason is incapable of knowing God's interior; learning about God's intentions for us; and entering personal contact with Him. This is possible only under the condition that God Himself would want to open Himself to us.

We Christians believe that God indeed has revealed Himself to us. "In times past, God spoke in partial and various ways to our ancestors through the prophets" (Hebrews 1:1). "For God so loved the world that He gave His only Son, so that everyone who believes in Him might not perish but might have eternal life" (John 3:16). The essence of God's revelation to people was beautifully summarized by the last council in *Dei verbum*, Dogmatic Constitution on Divine Revelation (in this quotation, I omit the numerous Biblical citations): "In His goodness and wisdom God chose to reveal Himself and to make known to us the hidden purpose of His will by which through Christ, the Word made flesh, man might in the Holy Spirit have access to the Father and come to share in the divine nature. Through this revelation, therefore, the invisible God out of the abundance of His love speaks to men as friends" (No. 2).

Please look at the consequences to our faith resulting from the fact that we know God not only from that which we learn about Him thanks to our natural cognitive activity but above all thanks to that which He Himself has revealed to us. What does reason tell us about God? If God exists, He is the very Root of reality, an Omnipresent Being that supports the existence of everything. Thus, reason suggests to us that to even ask the question of whether someone like that exists it does not suffice to ask about His existence in a purely theoretical way; He must be sought out with one's entire self, works, and life's attitude. To see Someone so infinite, we must cleanse our spiritual eyes and renounce all pride. This method of searching for God is suggested only by reason. If we follow these guidelines, through reason we can acknowledge the existence of God; recognize His goodness and love; and yearn for Him to better know Him and somehow grow closer to Him.

However, now when we have recognized God's authentic revelation to people in the Christian good news, our situation with respect to God becomes radically deeper. If God has opened His interior to us, then we are naturally capable of accepting God's revelation to us only to the degree to which we ourselves can open to Him. By opening Himself to us — as a Father Who gave us His only Son, through Whom He calls us to unity with Himself and the Son in the Holy Spirit — God wants to give Himself to us. Can we then accept such an infinite Gift if we ourselves do not want to reciprocate? Naturally, we can surrender ourselves to God only through the power of the love with which He first loved us.

If God had not revealed Himself to us first, we would only be capable of serving Him. Our serving God could at most have some traits of love; however, we would be incapable of truly loving God. After all, what creature can truly love God and become His partner if He does not open before them in His personal secret? "No one knows the Son except the Father, and no one knows the Father except the Son and anyone to whom the Son wishes to reveal Him" (Matthew 11:27).

Thus, there is no other, deeper means of opening oneself to God's revelation than that of personal contact: through prayer, sacramental unity with the Crucified and Resurrected Son of God, fidelity to God's Commandments, and joyful presence in His omnipresence.

At the same time, if our relations with God are not prone to determinism because they are with a Living Person, we must understand that God loves each of us individually, and His love is not stereotypical. Thus, man does not always easily recognize God's love; likewise, it is not always easy for us to comprehend that God's behavior towards us is a sign of His love. Because this is related to our response to true, personal Love, we must be concerned if we are sufficiently faithful to the One who was first to love us, if we give Him our complete, boundless trust. In general, our entire attitude towards God should be openness to Him Who lives, loves, and demands something of us; Who calls us to some things, cautions us against other ones, forgives us, and grants us gifts.

DOGMAS AND FREEDOM OF CONSCIENCE

In general, there are five possible reactions to the truth preached to us. We can: 1) cling to it and consider it to be our internal conviction; 2) become inclined towards it; 3) entertain its possibility; 4) reject it; or 5) be completely indifferent to it. Meanwhile, it turns out that there is a sixth possibility: a given truth can be outwardly recognized without any internal conviction, becoming closed off to the real consequences that would affect me if I had truly opened myself to them.

Little good can be said about the faith of the person who accepts the dogmas of the faith in this way. This sort of person tramples on God's great gift of freedom of conscience; in this way, he degrades both his faith and his personal dignity. He degrades his faith because he is essentially little concerned about its veracity. However, he also degrades his dignity because he acts like a soulless machine that tries to not think about its faith and does not want to implement it in its life; let the "faith specialists" think and believe for me!

However, there is also an authentic approach to the truths and commandments of the faith. This consists in opening my heart to my faith and its convictions, which illuminate my everyday life, feed on my prayer, and increasingly expose before me their depth and internal wondrousness. In this way, the truths and commandments of the faith are for me not only a belief related to my worldview; they become a real sphere where I encounter the living and loving God. Then it is no longer so that my conscience actively and joyfully recognizes and fathoms God's truth, but the Internal Teacher, the Holy Spirit Who gives to the truth recognized by me the power to transform me and bring me closer to God, lives inside of me.

Tadeusz Żukowski prays for such a transformation with brilliant simplicity:

In my conscience
like on a veil
Leave your face
My Beloved.53

Let us note two other anxieties that can affect us in relation to the dogmas of the faith: the fear that obedience to the Church's teaching can endanger our spiritual sovereignty as well as the fear that the Church proclaims dogmas at all. The first of these fears would be much more useful for us if we pointed it in the right direction: if it became within us a fear of becoming prone to social pressures towards both intellectual and moral conformism and if our vigilance and criticism of the various manipulations by the mass media and other means shaping the social climate and its changing fashions were bolstered.

Those who are truly concerned about spiritual sovereignty should notice that today true fidelity to the dogmas of the Church usually requires great courage, while rejecting them is fashionable and lauded. Mere common sense makes us doubt that one can achieve spiritual sovereignty by becoming prone to a sheep-like mentality.

But I digress. It is essential that we notice that spiritual sovereignty is not about becoming isolated from the social experience of the truth. There is a difference between a sheep-like mentality and the search

53. Translated from Polish by Filip Mazurczak.

for truth along with others, benefitting from their experiences and the wisdom that has been accumulated over the centuries. This social dimension of our rootedness in the truth regarding the most important things is emphasized in language: in Greek, "conscience" is *syneidesis*, or "seeing together," while in Latin it is *conscientia*, or "co-knowledge."

In short, those who want to search for the truth about good and evil alone without looking towards those who sought before them or those who search alongside them are probably spiritual brats who are more interested in celebrating their own uniqueness than in finding the truth.

Why does the Church proclaim dogmas at all? We will return to this question. It is very simple: because we truly believe in Christ. We believe that God revealed Himself in Jesus Christ and that Jesus Christ founded the Church in which He is "until the end of the age" (Matthew 28:20). Thus, we no longer need to look for the truth in the darkness, for it comes to us in the light. May we only want to become increasingly open to it and deepen it.

Sometimes, certain people do not like our certainty about the dogmas and the commandments of faith. Fortunately, love for our neighbor does not require that we adjust to his preferences. Besides, if faith is something greater than just a worldview-like game parallel to disbelief there must exist an essential difference between recognizing the ultimate truth by the believer and the non-believer. This difference was aptly noted by Adam Mickiewicz in his "Statements and Comments":

> As long as a spider climbs clinging to a beam
> It is a dogmatic whose system is great, it seems
> Yet when the wind shakes him as the web he descends
> He is no longer a dogmatic but a skeptic in the end[54]

54. Translated from Polish by Filip Mazurczak.

DOES FAITH PERMIT DOUBT?

Let us try to become aware of the difference between uncertainty and doubt, between doubt and skepticism, between dogma and dogmatism. Getting lost amidst these concepts can lead to an attitude of a certain suicide: under the pretenses of concern for the truth, we can kill within ourselves the ability to be open to the truth.

Doubt seems to be something other than mere uncertainty. Uncertainty is an intrinsic characteristic of many of our observations, information, inferences, etc. Oftentimes, it does not negatively affect our mood if we do not feel the need to overcome one uncertainty or another. So what if I start to count crows sitting on a tree branch out of boredom and cannot count them all? What difference does it make if there are ten or eleven crows?

Whereas ordinary uncertainty is a rather static and passive attitude, doubt results from an active attitude towards the observations I have made, the knowledge I possess, and the tradition I have acquired. For doubts to appear within me, the problem must be at least to a degree important in some aspect to me. To doubt that someone is telling the truth, I must be at least a little concerned about what he is saying. The more concerned I am about a matter, the more precisely I would like to investigate how it presents itself in reality. Thus, the Latin saying *dubitando ad veritatem pervenimus* ("doubt is the way to the truth") is correct. The ability to accurately formulate one's doubts about our experiences and convictions as well as the opinions, descriptions, and hypotheses that we take in helps us to distinguish between truth and falsehood and inspires us to pose questions thanks to which we can know the truth more deeply and broadly.

Naturally, there are also unfounded doubts that only obscure the truth that is accessible to us. Sometimes, people have a gift for dispelling such doubts: it had already seemed to us that we were incapable of discerning what was true, while such a person acutely presents the entire problem, distinguishes between important and less important matters, and reliably responds to the posed questions; then the problem is cleared up, and all our doubts are scattered. The opposite also sometimes occurs: someone may have an odd knack for becoming entangled in the most barren doubts that only paralyze his thinking and acting. For example, someone might check his suitcase twenty times before going to the train station to see if he has forgotten to take something; naturally, he has not, but in the process, he has forgotten to buy a ticket.

We can also offend someone with our doubts. Naturally, I understand very well that another person has the right to investigate the credibility of my words and actions, but there are limits that should not be transcended. We sometimes must say to someone dear to us: if you doubt my sincerity, why do you doubt what I say if I have given you no grounds for such doubts?

Whereas doubts concern the sphere of cognition, in their positive form they lead to truth; doubt is something deeper if it is a crisis inside the human person. People overcome with despair, loneliness, and their own sin often confess to priests or psychologists: "I have lost faith in the meaning of life;" "I doubt if anyone needs me any longer;" "I have lost faith that I am capable of changing anything for the better." "I doubt if I can graduate," a student who has flunked an exam yet again may lament. We can doubt someone's friendship or love, our own potential, the meaning of life, or the ideals we profess; we can even doubt ourselves or someone close to us.

Faith that cannot be accepted because of its intellectual dubiousness is only an imperfect form of knowledge. If someone tells me that they have seen a bunch of white crows, I have the right to have my doubts and not believe him. Meanwhile, skepticism opposes the faith that encompasses man to an incomparably greater degree. To tell someone that you have lost your faith in him or that you no longer believe him would be to kill him spiritually. This is especially so if my faith in him bolstered his spirits despite constant failures. To doubt oneself means the same thing as committing spiritual suicide (naturally, I am speaking of doubting oneself as a person not as a chess player or skier). Meanwhile, to doubt some false ideals is like tearing off the chains that hinder my search for the truth and meaning of life.

Let us now pose a question: Do supernatural faith and faith in Christ as well as eternal life allow for doubt or skepticism? If our faith were merely a worldview, it would offend our dignity as rational beings, as we would make it immune to doubt. After all, thanks to doubt we can purify what is correct in our views of that which is wrong; naturally, if we do not allow them to violate the rigors of rationality, doubts facilitate our imbuing of knowledge of the truth. Thus, the non-believer who is only looking for the ultimate truth should carefully study the contents of the faith presented to him and not avoid the doubts that then come to him. The ultimate truth undoubtedly transcends the capacity of human reason, but it cannot contradict it.

Is there a prohibition on doubts to the believer? "Prohibition" is a very inaccurate term. Indeed, faith is real unity with the living God. This unity is as if through a screen, but its reality is confirmed everyday through numerous signs; this unity transcends experience, but it also finds expression in it. Doubts as to whether we will be a good couple are appropriate during a time of courtship, when we are not entirely emotionally engaged with one another. When we already are married, however, doubts are not so much prohibited as they are impossible, for we have become too deeply engaged with each another. Now, only something much deeper can challenge our unity, something proportional to our engagement: namely, doubt. Doubting the point of our relationship is or an existential attitude with which we destroy something of which we had once been convinced would last forever.

Doubting is not something inherently wrong; it is, after all, the only means of leaving false existential engagement. However, it becomes a terribly destructive force if it undermines great and correct engagement within us. Not everyone must be a teacher, but for those who are it would be a terrible thing to doubt the meaning of the witness that a teacher should provide to young people. People can ponder if they want another child, but it would be terrible for a mother or father to doubt the point of being parents of a child that has already been conceived.

It must be clearly said that if a believer doubts the truths of the faith, these are no longer doubts but skepticism, or a state of the spirit in which engagement in the living God has become prone to gradual corrosion. Naturally, I do not call difficulties in faith or even the tempest of darkness in which man tries to not lose contact with the living God skepticism. If Christ indeed is the Redeemer (and not solely according to my private views) and if the Catholic faith indeed offers to people the truth of salvation, then skepticism in faith is something incomparably more serious than intellectual doubts regarding the veracity of the worldview one proclaims.

Someone could level the following accusation to the above reflections: “If doubts related to faith inevitably take on the form of skepticism and if skepticism is something truly so dangerous, then if someone is a believer, perhaps the only solution to these arrangements is to blindly accept dogmas and not think about them at all. However, is such an attitude worthy of a thinking person? Furthermore, if the faith in which someone had already been engaged is false, then with such an attitude he would be sentenced to it forever.”

Hence, our attitude towards the dogmas of the faith should be the opposite of a dogmatic attitude. I understand dogmatism as being isolated in some theory, view, or formula. The dogmatist has no need to study reality, confront his theory with reality, and live out the professed truth in reality; doctrine suffices for him.

If we truly believe the dogmas of the faith, they should be professed in a completely different way. If we truly believe that they contain God's truth (and thus the truth revealing man's ultimate meaning and summoning him to eternal life), then they should be fathomed, while questions related to the current (personal or social) situation should be asked, and the dogmas should be brought into life.

Let us take for example the dogma: "I believe in the resurrection of the body." Here, a mere conviction of reason does not suffice; since Christ proclaims the promise of resurrection, I believe we will be resurrected. This is the bare minimum. I profess this dogma more truly as I open my body and its various dynamisms to the activity of the spirit. Similarly, until I learn to notice the great works of God's power that take place every day, the truth of the faith that God can resurrect our ruined bodies from the ashes will be an abstractly professed formula rather than a dogma for me. I truly explain a dogmatic pronouncement as a dogma only if it becomes an existential truth that I act upon and that affects my life.

People also profess false dogmas. For example, the Nazis professed the dogma that "everything that serves the expansion of the living space for the German nation is good." They certainly acted according to this dogma, which to them was something incomparably greater than a mere ideological conviction. However, dogmas are also prone to verification, although of a different sort than purely theoretical pronouncements (only the theoretical layer of a dogma is prone to logical and ideological verification). If a dogma is false, then professing it and bringing it into life destroys its confessor and spread destruction all around; to use a Biblical expression, "the abomination of desolation."

The opposite is also true: we can recognize the veracity of a dogma if only we do not limit ourselves to it purely theoretical acceptance; it simultaneously humanizes, expands, and deepens us.

Jesus accused His disciples of having "little faith" (see Matthew 6:30, 8:26, 14:31, 16:8). He only incidentally reminded us of the limitations of the intellectual acceptance of His teaching. Weak faith is, above all, faith that is prone to doubt. This is faith in a soul that is afraid of becoming too open to God's truth and power. We should then call to Christ along with the Gospel supplicant: "I do believe, help my unbelief!" (Mark 9:24). I believe, Lord, but only You can break open my soul, which is afraid of completely trusting You!

HOW MANY DOGMAS OF THE FAITH ARE THERE?

And How Many Laws of Nature Are There?

How many dogmas of the faith are there? Is there an official index of dogmas that are professed in the Catholic Church? Let us try to think why no one in the Church has ever made such a list.

A chemistry professor who regularly attends the religious group I lead once asked: And how many laws of nature are there? He proposed the following response: There are as many laws of nature as we need to explain what we have succeeded in knowing in nature. Someone who studies nature is not so much interested in the number of truths that governs it but rather in knowing it, above all knowing it and better understanding what had hitherto been unknown to him.

This analogy seems fitting. There are as many dogmas of the faith as have been recognized by the Church, who tries to preach Christ as faithfully as possible. Just as a scientist is not concerned with establishing the number of laws of nature, although his research helps us to better understand them, but above all focuses his attention on knowing nature better, similarly the Church is above all interested in proclaiming Christ the Lord truthfully and with love; the Church prefers to profess and explain the dogmas of the faith than to merely count them. Indeed, in the Church we believe in dogmas because of Christ, not because of the dogmas themselves.

What is a dogma of the faith? St. Thomas Aquinas says that is a statement that infallibly expressed a truth of the faith and that moves towards that truth (*perceptio divinae veritatis, tendens ad ipsam*). Thus, we do not so much believe in the statement in which a given dogma is expressed but rather in the truth it deserves and that is revealed before us. At the same time, it never suffices to emphasize that the truth of the faith is always greater than the statement in which we express it, for we can absorb it more and more, and it is obvious that we will never fully fathom it.

The Enlightenment mentality that is hostile to faith has imposed on us such an understanding of a dogma of the faith that it is a statement that one must accept without any discussion, even if it seems absurd and one does not understand it. In reality, the situation is completely different with the dogmas of the faith. By indicating the truth of the faith, a dogma invites us to explore it, and only after we have fathomed a truth of the faith can we evaluate its wondrousness and accept it as our own truth.

Let us express this using a simple metaphor. Someone traveling across a desert and chasing one mirage after another will be dying of thirst until he finds real water. A dogma of faith is like pointing towards a well that contains living water; it is like an invitation: "Drink from this; this is the truth thanks to which you will achieve eternal life."

Let us say the same with the aid of another metaphor. A dogma of faith is like a suggestion that the earth is rich in gold, and if you will dig here, then you will certainly find gold, of which there will be more and more. Accepting a dogma and approving the faith contained within it is only the beginning of the spiritual adventure that awaits us thanks to this dogma. A great many Catholics know from their own experience that the dogma in which they had believed for many years only begins to excite them and have a real impact on their life after many years.

What Right Does the Church Have to Make Us Accept Dogmas?

There are two more anxieties formulated in relation to dogmas. What right does the Church have to make us accept dogmas? Maybe this really does violate our intellectual sovereignty? And, besides, can the infallibility that the Church attributes to the dogmas she preaches be a trait of any human statements at all?

Both questions present an opportunity to recall what is absolutely unique and inimitable in the Christian faith. Namely, our Christian faith is not the work of people; its beginning is the gift that humanity has truly (not in some wishful thinking) received from God in the person of His Son. It has become a reality that "God so loved the world that He gave His only Son, so that everyone who believes in Him might not perish but might have eternal life" (John 3:16).

If the Lord Jesus were merely a brilliant sage endowed with exceptional religious charisma, His teaching — much like those of other great figures, including the wisest among them — would not be infallible, and we could correct and complement it. In that case, accepting any dogmas would be evidence of spiritual immaturity or, worse, intellectual enslavement. Thus, it should be unsurprising that non-believers are often completely incapable of understanding how it is possible that their religious friends, whom they sometimes admire for their intellectual independence, nonetheless accept the dogmas of the faith without feeling embarrassed.

The meaning and value of dogmas of the faith can only be discerned in the faith that the Lord Jesus is the Son of God through Whom the world has been created and Who became a man for the sake of our salvation and was resurrected after redeeming us through His anguish and death on the cross. This happened in a specific time and place, but it occurred for the sake of the redemption of all people, of all generations until the end of time.

If the Eternal Father's love is indeed so great that He gave us His only Son, then undoubtedly He gave Him to us in such a way that all people, regardless of the time or place in which they find themselves, could have authentic access to Him and His gifts. Without a doubt, He was capable of being concerned that His Gospel would not be distorted throughout the centuries and millennia.

This is why Jesus Christ summoned His apostles and founded the Church, so that she may be a deposit of truth about Him ("Whoever listens to you listens to Me" [Luke 10:16]) as well as the steward of His forgiveness ("Whose sins you forgive are forgiven them" [John 20:23])" and His real presence in the sacrament of the Eucharist among those who have believed in Him ("Do this in memory of Me" [Luke 22:19]).

Of course, people have various attitudes towards the Church. However, because the Church is truly God's gift (not only according to Catholics) which ensures us a spiritual space where believers have real access to the teaching and grace of our Redeemer and even to the Redeemer Himself, it is good to extend our faith in Him, Jesus Christ, to the Church. Then we will immediately understand that no one imposes upon us the dogmas of the faith but that they are the aid of the Holy Spirit (see John 14:26), impossible to overestimate, so that we may authentically and more deeply understand the Gospel.

Furthermore, we understand that the infallible teaching of the faith is the Church's duty rather than her privilege; it is a duty that is incomparably more important than that of the mushroom picker to distinguish between edible mushrooms and poisonous ones, for the infallibility of mushroom pickers protects life on this earth, while our openness to God's authentic truth or, instead, any forgeries can determine our eternal life.

THE PROCESS OF DECREEING DOGMAS

How does the Church proclaim dogmas of the faith? Is it possible that some of the dogmas we profess could be not proclaimed or be formulated in another way?

Questions Posed in Faith and Outside of Faith

In recent decades, numerous books on alternative history have been written. Such books are more fantasy than history. Their authors, who typically exhibit solid historical knowledge, present such historical scenarios as could have taken place, although real history went in a different direction. In other words, such books are pure speculation. One such author of historical speculation, for example, presented a history of Europe in the late 1930s and early 1940s under the assumption that in 1939 Poland gave in to Hitler's pressures and ceded the Danzig Corridor in Pomerania to Germany. Someone else might present a history of a Poland not threatened by partitions because Sigismund the Old had not agreed to secularize the Teutonic Knights and to the Prussian Homage but instead undertook a strict policy of annexing the Teutonic Order's state to Poland.

The question of "what if?" can be posed to Church history, as well. It can also be asked of those spiritual events in which the Church recognized her faith and proclaimed the dogmas she professes. Indeed, faith does not prohibit us from asking what would have happened if the Council of Nice had not been proclaimed in 325. The question can go further: What would have happened if that council had not decided to accept the symbol of faith? What would have happened if St. Athanasias had died prematurely, and the Church could not have relied on this great defender of the Catholic faith during times of the onslaught of Arianism?

The history of the Church could have gone in different directions, but one thing could not have happened. The Church as the Church could not have distorted the revealed truth and begun to teach something inconsistent with revelation on God and Christ. It could not happen, for example, that an authentic ecumenical council could have rejected the truth of the Holy Trinity or have accepted the heretical teaching that there was only moral unity between the Son of God and the person of Jesus Christ. If something like this would have happened, this would mean that the gates of hell had prevailed against the Church (see Matthew 16:18).

Thus, if works of history present the divinity of Christ the Lord as a belief that had been shaped but could have not been shaped, the truth of the Holy Trinity is presented as a dogma that was shaped accidentally, let us not be deceived, for such thinking is alien to the faith. We believe that God truly loves us, and all the human generations, so greatly that He gave us His Son. If God has given us such a Gift, then He is undoubtedly is concerned that the truth about this would not be distorted or relativized. Likewise, we have no reason to doubt that the Lord Jesus reliably fulfills His promises and gives His Church the Holy Spirit, Who "will teach [Us] everything and remind [Us] of all that [I] told you" (John 14:26).

If things are like this, then the truth of God is the sole property of no one in the Church. Those to whom the Lord Jesus has especially entrusted the faith — the apostles and their successors, the bishops — are neither the owners nor even the stewards of the truth but its guardians. The truth, especially the truths of the faith, is not established; they are sought out, recognized, and accepted.

That was the general attitude of the fathers of the councils during which the dogmas of the faith were proclaimed. Because the summoning of a council was usually caused by a heresy that brought confusion to the Church, bishops gathered at councils looked for arguments in favor of the Church's faith and against heresy above all in Sacred Scripture, but they also carefully studied the ancient writings of teachers recognized by the Church so that they would not abandon the faith professed by previous generations of the Church. No one even entertained the thought that the official teaching of the Church could be established according to one's own whim.

The Dogmas Proclaimed in the Second Christian Millennium

Were similar procedures activated when dogmas were proclaimed in the second millennium of the history of the Church? First, let us recall two important changes that took place in the Church then compared to the first millennium. Much more so than before, the Catholic Church focused on the successor to Peter, the bishop of Rome, and was simultaneously deeply wounded in her Catholicity by the loss of unity with the Eastern tradition.

In particular, three of the newest dogmas are criticized by non-Catholic Christians: the dogma of papal infallibility proclaimed in 1870 by the First Vatican Council; the dogma of the immaculate conception of Mary, which Pope Blessed Pius IX had proclaimed sixteen years earlier; and the dogma of the assumption of Mary, proclaimed in 1950 by Pius XII. The critics of these dogmas ask: On the basis of what premises has the dogma of papal infallibility been proclaimed? Does the fact that two Marian dogmas have been proclaimed by a single person — true, by the pope, but the pope is only one man — not destroy the Church's ancient principle that the revealed truth is a gift granted to the entire Church and that all the bishops must look after it?

I will begin my response to the above questions and anxieties by recalling the especially solemn formula, modeled after dogmatic pronouncements, in which St. John Paul II condemned the crime of abortion: "Therefore, by the authority which Christ conferred upon Peter and His Successors, in communion with the Bishops—who on various occasions have condemned abortion and who in the aforementioned consultation, albeit dispersed throughout the world, have shown unanimous agreement concerning this doctrine — *I declare that direct abortion, that is, abortion willed as an end or as a means, always constitutes a grave moral disorder*, since it is the deliberate killing of an innocent human being" (*Evangelium vitae*, 62).

The above pronouncement cannot be accused of having been proclaimed by a single person, even though it was the pope himself, but by the engagement of the authority of the first teacher of the Church. John Paul II was very careful to underscore that he made this pronouncement in communion with the Catholic bishops after consulting with them and with their unanimous approval.

Analogously, it took many years of consultations with bishops as well as numerous requests to solemnly confirm this truth of the Church directed to the Holy See before the proclamation of both Marian dogmas. Furthermore, it is worth recalling that long before the proclamation of both dogmatic bulls the Church had long celebrated the feast of both Mary's immaculate conception and assumption. It would be difficult to find stronger evidence that both truths had been the subject of the Catholic faith long before being proclaimed as dogmas.

The dogma of the teaching of the infallibility of the successor to the Apostle Peter was proclaimed at an ecumenical council. Then, in 1870, one did not need to have been a prophet to have predicted the downfall of the Papal States. Because the Holy See was losing the political sovereignty that supported its ecclesiastical vocation, this was an attempt to recall the strictly religious meaning of the pope's service in the Church.

On July 18, 1870, 535 council fathers (with only two votes against) voted in favor of accepting the constitution containing the text of the dogma. It is important to know, however, that there were more opponents of the proclamation of this dogma: fifty-five council fathers decided to not take part in the vote at all. Several days before it, they left Rome to not give the impression that they were opposed to the dogma itself, since they were only concerned about not proclaiming it in that very moment. It seemed to them (they would later be proven right) that the anti-Catholic sentiments in the world, which were already great, would be even greater as a result.

The fact is that all Catholic bishops at the time — including those who were opposed to proclaiming this dogma — accepted it. Let us also note that one of the prominent opponents of not the dogma of papal infallibility itself but rather of its proclamation, the Archbishop of Paris, Georges Darboy, died a martyr's death less than a year later.[55]

55. He was shot by the Communards on May 21, 1871. Let us quote a fragment of the archbishop's interrogation before a revolutionary court:

"What is your craft, sir?"

"It is not a craft but a vocation, a moral office exercised by us for the salvation of human souls."

"Stop speaking such nonsense. Instead, tell us what rubbish you say to people."

"We teach faith in our Lord Jesus Christ."

"There are no longer any lords, and we have no lord" (after Grzegorz Kucharczyk, *Francuski Kulturkampf. Walka z Kościołem w III Republice, Miłujcie się,* 2003, No. 2 p. 33).

We will conclude by noting the fact that the dogma of papal infallibility was then formulated with the greatest caution: "The Roman Pontiff, when he speaks ex cathedra, that is, when in discharge of the office of Pastor and Teacher of all Christians, by virtue of his supreme Apostolic authority, he defines a doctrine regarding faith or morals to be held by the Universal Church, by the divine assistance promised to him in blessed Peter, is possessed of that infallibility with which the divine Redeemer willed that His Church should be endowed for defining doctrine regarding faith or morals."[56]

Almost a century later, in 1964, the Second Vatican Council decided it was appropriate to complement the above dogmatic formula with the following explanation: "In matters of faith and morals, the bishops speak in the name of Christ and the faithful are to accept their teaching and adhere to it with a religious assent. This religious submission of mind and will must be shown in a special way to the authentic magisterium of the Roman Pontiff, even when he is not speaking ex cathedra; that is, it must be shown in such a way that his supreme magisterium is acknowledged with reverence, the judgments made by him are sincerely adhered to, according to his manifest mind and will" (*Lumen gentium*, 25).

56. *Pastor Aeternus*, https://www.catholicplanet.org/councils/20-Pastor-Aeternus.htm (accessed January 14, 2022).

I Believe in God

I BELIEVE IN ONE GOD

One can recognize the existence of God without any qualifications yet simultaneously be a non-believer. After all, one can recognize God's existence only because one's reason demands that or because one is terrified by the perspective of the ultimate absurdity of existence. Faith in God is something much more than simply recognizing that God exists. To believe in God means to find the source of light and power in the living God and to encounter Him in various circumstances in life as a Loving Being. I truly believe in God if I know with all the depths of my being that He deserves that all people, including myself, may entrust themselves to Him.

I can believe in God only because He first believed in me. In Sacred Scripture as well as the Church's teaching, God's "faith" in man is called grace or mercy. It should be noted, however, that our conceptions of God's grace are sometimes very far from the truth. This stems from the fact that we seldom compare our conceptions of God with what He has revealed to us in Jesus Christ.

We should above all associate God's grace with a good Shepherd Who looks for His lost sheep; with a loving Father Who suffers because of His prodigal son and Who cannot wait for his return; and with a Doctor and Samaritan Who lovingly cares for the leper or the wounded person and brings him back to health.

My faith in God is possible because God first believed in me even though I am oftentimes very ungrateful towards Him. This meaning is enclosed in the traditional expression that faith in God is a gift of grace. That I can find succor in God and find a loving Father in Him is a grace, as is the fact that I can entrust myself to Him and save my soul, even if I find myself in a situation transcending my human stamina.

It is even more a grace that I can find protection against myself in God, for He has the power to liberate me of my own sinfulness.

This results from the fact that the measure of my faith in God is not the state of my awareness but what has come to be called the state of my soul. Even if calling out "O Lord! O Lord!" filled me with inexpressible sweetness and if my faith threw out evil spirits and performed other miracles, my soul would still be measly if it did not transform me.

On the other hand, even if I were overcome with such darkness that I would no longer sense that God exists, this would not hinder my spiritual maturation; in fact, it could even hasten it if I firmly hold on to the law of love, even when doing so would exceed my capacities and seems contrary to common sense. I would not persevere in such situations in an attitude of true love if I objectively were not close to God and if He had not strengthened me.

What Does "One God" Mean?

The conviction that God is the most perfect of all beings is the source of many erroneous and essential mythological conceptions of God. Indeed, God is Someone infinitely greater than just one of many beings in the universe, perfect or otherwise.

He is the One Who exists in every meaning of the word. Everything else exists because He has called it into existence. Nor is God greater or lesser because He constantly provides all of creation with life. Because He is infinitely perfect, it would be absurd to imagine that He could be greater or lesser.

At this point, it seems fitting to explain what the fact that God is one means. I, this specific person, likewise am only one. As a natural satellite of Earth, the Moon is one in the sense that Earth has no other moons.

God, however, is one in a completely different way. St. Thomas Aquinas says that the mathematical number one can be ascribed to every creature except for God Himself. Indeed, the mathematical number one can be ascribed to an individual being, but God is Someone infinitely greater than an individual being. He engulfs every creature and supports its existence, yet not even the entirety of creation can fathom Him. God is present in His entirety in every being and in every place, simultaneously transcending the entire cosmos of visible and invisible beings. Thus, the mere thought that another god could exist is absurd. Polytheism strips the term "god" of its entire meaning.

How Does This Impact the Truth That God Is One?

It never suffices to emphasize that sin is the main obstacle that separates us from God. Meanwhile, the basic means of coming closer to Him is conversion and making use of the means of displaying our love to Him that are accessible to us. At this point, it is especially worth making note of the fascinating truth that for each of us God is absolutely the Closest Person. He loves me more than any of my loved ones; He is more concerned about my welfare than even I am. "Even if my father and mother forsake me, the Lord will take me in" (Psalm 27:10); this prayer of the Psalmist is repeated in Sacred Scripture in several different ways.

This seems obvious. After all, we owe everything to God, including the fact that we have family members who love us and whom we love. Our very capacity to love comes from Him. He also makes me capable of being concerned about my own welfare. Meanwhile, my sin makes it possible for me to harm even those closest to me, and I seek out my own welfare in an absurd way; namely, by destroying myself and others.

The more I am aware of all this, the more joy the commandment that I should love God with all my soul, heart, energies, and thoughts will bring me. This commandment reveals the most essential truth about both God and ourselves and the reality in which God has placed us. The logic of this commandment can be seen most clearly considering the Great Event that took place two thousand years ago: the only Son of God, Who is one with His Eternal Father, became one of us for our sake and allowed Himself to be crucified for us. Can there be more convincing evidence that the One Who wants us to love Him with all our soul and all our energies selflessly seeks out our welfare?

God Is Omnipotent

In Sacred Scripture, the truth about God's omnipotence is often accompanied by professing that God is the Creator of the universe. The prophet Isaiah calls: "Lift up your eyes on high and see who created these: He leads out their army and numbers [the stars], calling them all by name. By his great might and the strength of His power not one of them is missing" (Isaiah 40:26).

Likewise, the pagans imagined the gods as exceptionally powerful beings. However, because they did not know the truth about the creation of the world, their conceptions of Divine power that had been shaped outside revealed religion differed from the Biblical truth about God's omnipotence with respect to at least two points.

This became apparent in a spectacular way when the chosen people decided to venerate the true God, their Savior from the Egyptian yoke, in the symbol of a mighty bull. God firmly rejected this form of venerating Him since the power of that animal has nothing in common with love and, contrary to God's power, has its limits.

Meanwhile, the truth that God's omnipotence knows no bounds is sometimes expressed in Sacred Scripture through the aid of negating in God the effort we must undertake when we reach the limits of our capabilities: "Do you not know? Have you not heard? The Lord is God from of old, Creator of the ends of the earth. He does not faint or grow weary, and His knowledge is beyond scrutiny" (Isaiah 40:28).

The next two sentences of this pericope tell us that our loving God wants us to participate in His omnipotence: "He gives power to the faint, abundant strength to the weak. Though young men faint and grow weary, and youths stagger and fall" (Isaiah 40:29-30).

Later, the Lord Jesus enlightens us about two specific means of our participation in God's omnipotence: through faith ("Amen, I say to you, if you have faith the size of a mustard seed, you will say to this mountain, 'Move from here to there,' and it will move. Nothing will be impossible for you;" Matthew 17:20) and prayer ("If two of you agree on earth about anything for which they are to pray, it shall be granted to them by my heavenly Father;" Matthew 18:19).

Of What Is the Almighty "Incapable"?

Statements which can also be found in Sacred Scripture that God "must" do some things and "cannot" do others also deserve comment. For example, God "must be true, though every human being is a liar" (Romans 3:4) and "cannot deny Himself" (2 Timothy 2:13). One can come up with a long list of true statements that God "cannot" do something: He cannot err, cause harm to someone, cease existing, lie, and so forth. In summary, God "cannot" not be infinitely good and powerful; He simply "cannot" not be God.

Naturally, it is not the case that God is coerced or compelled into doing anything, nor are there any laws superior to Him that oblige Him (indeed, no such laws exist). After all, the laws of logic as well as moral principles flow from Him and reflect His truth.

What, then, do true statements that God is incapable of something express? Let us notice that in all the statements referenced above, this type of negation has an unambiguously positive meaning, for it precludes the mere possibility of God Himself having flaws or imperfections. We sometimes use such language even with respect to a person: we sometimes that someone is so perfect that he "cannot" botch a task undertaken by him; that he cannot mess something up; etc.

At this point, it is worth recalling the once-popular atheist trap of a question intended to demonstrate that even the notion of God's omnipotence was internally incoherent: Could God create a stone that He could not lift?

Let us pose this question in a more serious way. Indeed, the mere notion of God as Someone Who spends time picking up a stone insults the most elementary intuitions about God and is offensive to Him. One could ask equally stupidly: Could God create a roll that He could not eat?

However, let us take this question seriously and re-formulate it as follows: Could God create a world which He could no longer control? There is only one possible answer to this question: Of course, He cannot because He is truly omnipotent, which means that He is infinitely powerful. Any tendency towards deficiency is contrary to the concept of omnipotence. God's omnipotence consists not in that it can (or even must!) be lacking in something.

"Nothing Is Impossible for God"

Let us now look at several fragments of Sacred Scripture that deal with God's omnipotent love for us people. This means that in His love, God is bound neither by our common sense nor by the limits of the human imagination. When He chose Abraham and decided to grant Him descendants more numerous than the stars in the sky, the fact that His chosen one and his wife had reached an age when people simply cannot conceive children posed no obstacle. This was because nothing is impossible for God.

Later, the angel Gabriel (whose name means "the power of God"!) would reference these words, which foreshadow the coming of the Redeemer. Even though it occurred so quietly that not even Joseph, Mary's virgin husband, had noticed it, the incarnation of the Son of God is a work of God's omnipotence, one even greater than the creation of the world. Thanks to the omnipotent love of the Eternal Father, His Son has taken on our human nature.

Let us return to the Old Testament and recall the order that God gave to Jeremiah during the siege of Jerusalem. It was evident that Jerusalem would fall while the invader would destroy everything before imposing his own order. Meanwhile, God demands of the prophet that he act in an absurd way, as if this were a time of complete peace. God demands that he buys a field with silver and accepts a deed of purchase as testimony that "they shall again purchase houses and fields and vineyards in this land" (Jeremiah 32:15). Jeremiah then understood that God wanted to remind the people that nothing is impossible for the Creator of heaven and earth Who does not abandon His people (see Jeremiah 32:16-44).

Later, Jesus Himself would respond to His disciples' anxiety that only a few would be saved by telling them that what is impossible to people is possible to God.

His Omnipotence and Love Are the Basis of Our Trust

Most importantly, omnipotence in Sacred Scripture is not an abstract trait of a distant God. Naturally, the true God, the Creator of everything that exists, is an omnipotent God, but His omnipotence is expressed in the fact that He benevolently cares for every sparrow and every hair on our heads; however, He cares most for us: "Are not two sparrows sold for a small coin? Yet not one of them falls to the ground without your Father's knowledge. Even all the hairs of your head are counted. So do not be afraid; you are worth more than many sparrows" (Matthew 10:29-31).

Sacred Scripture transmits the truth of this nature of God's omnipotence through testimony rather than through admonitions. It often thanks the Almighty for loving us and caring for us. Such gratitude appears especially frequently in the Psalms: "The joyful shout of deliverance is heard in the tents of the righteous: 'The Lord's right hand works valiantly; the Lord's right hand is raised; the Lord's right hand works valiantly'" (Psalm 118:15-16; see 18:36; 48:11; 63:9).

The Psalmist indicates the fact that God is not indifferent to my fate especially in times of danger: "Though I walk in the midst of dangers, You guard my life when my enemies rage. You stretch out Your hand; Your right hand saves me" (Psalm 138:7). However, entrusting oneself to the powerful God is expressed through both: thanksgiving for having survived as well as a request that God permanently removes the danger (see Psalm 25:15: 31:15-18; 32:6).

It sometimes happens that man does not doubt that God loves us and is omnipotent yet is impatient because he feels as if God has forgotten about us and ignores our sufferings: "For You we are slain all the day long, considered only as sheep to be slaughtered. Awake! Why do you sleep, O Lord? Rise up! Do not reject us forever! Why do You hide Your face; why forget our pain and misery?" (Psalms 44:23-25).

GOD IS THE FATHER, SON, AND HOLY SPIRIT

Let us begin with a question we have indicated above: Why was the truth of the Holy Trinity not revealed in the Old Testament? Why did God not reveal to people that He is the Father, Son, and Holy Spirit during the times of Abraham, Moses, and the prophets? As we recall, a particularly insightful response was provided by St. Gregory of Nazianzus: It is God's custom that He first grants something and only later makes it possible to understand what He has granted.

Let us take a closer look at how the truth about the Son of God was revealed to us. First, there were prophesies, including those that "the young woman, pregnant and about to bear a son, shall name him Emmanuel" (Isaiah 7:14; see 9:5). Next came the moment when the Eternal Father gave us His Son Who became one of us for our sake. However, Jesus only gradually revealed the truth of His Divinity to people. First, He chose His disciples, began to teach like no one else, performed miracles, and gave testimony about His Father. Only after such preparations did He ask His disciples: "But who do you say that I am?" And He seemingly elicited that faith from His disciples. Simon Peter was the first to profess this faith on which the Church must be built and said: "You are the Messiah, the Son of the living God" (Matthew 16:15-18).

The truth about the Holy Spirit was revealed in an analogous way. There was foreshadowing in the Old Testament. During His historical sojourn among humanity, the Lord Jesus frequently prophesied the Holy Spirit: "And I will ask the Father, and He will give you another Advocate to be with you always. [...] He will teach you everything and remind you of all that [I] told you" (John 14:16, 26). Ultimately, the truth about the Holy Spirit was revealed on the Pentecost when that Holy Spirit was granted to the Church.

Only then did the Church — endowed with this Divine Gift — increasingly fathom it. As an example, I will recall a statement by the Apostle Paul that is so characteristic that he probably frequently repeated it, because it appears in an almost identical form in both the Epistle to the Romans and the Epistle to the Galatians: "For you did not receive a spirit of slavery to fall back into fear, but you received a spirit of adoption, through which we cry, 'Abba, Father!' The Spirit itself bears witness with our spirit that we are children of God, and if children, then heirs, heirs of God and joint heirs with Christ" (Romans 8:15-17; see Galatians 4:6).

In short, the mystery of the Triune God boils down to the following question: How is it possible that the one, only, and indivisible God is three truly distinctive Persons? The faith of the Church responds to this question as follows: The Persons of God are close to one another in a proximity that cannot be achieved between created persons so fully that there are no mutual relations between Them (as there are between humans), but each Person is completely the full infinity of His Divinity, in a hypostatic relationship with the two remaining Persons.

The True God — the Father, Son, and Holy Spirit — is a community of Persons so completely and fully open to one another that it would be blasphemous to call Him three gods. Three Persons make up the one and only God in which individual persons completely permeate one another yet do not lose their personal distinctiveness.

On the contrary, their distinctiveness consists of their complete surrender to one another such that for each of them it is inimitable in the sense that only the first Person is the Father, only the second is the Son, and only the third is the Holy Spirit.

Only the First Person Is the Father

"Father" is the name of the first Person. Unlike in the case of the fatherhood experienced by humans, this Fatherhood is not the function fulfilled by Him but is instead the basis for His personal identity. There was never a specific moment when He began to be the Father. He is the Father without a beginning and always in His eternity. The Son is co-eternal together with Him; He is equal to Him in His Divinity and is co-eternal along with the true God.

Herein rests the essence of the Arian error. Initially, the Arians did not reject the truth of the Holy Trinity. However, Arius believed that since the Son is born of the Father there must have been a time when this Son did not exist. The Arians claimed that indeed, the Son is God, but He is inferior to the Father, for He was supposedly created by Him. He is God, they claimed, but He is not really God. It is not difficult to notice that the polytheistic mentality permeated the Christian faith in this way.

At the same time, Arianism was an attempt at describing the mystery of the Holy Trinity through mythological categories. The First Council of Nicaea firmly rejected an explanation of the birth of the Son as an alleged event, as if it had taken place in some primordial past when He supposedly appeared. The teachers of the Catholic faith radically rejected the Arian formulas according to which the Father was older than the Son and that any form of becoming could take place in God.

God is immutable, and He never went through any process of becoming. Each Person is true and equal to the remaining two true

Persons of God, and no intra-Trinitarian origins can be understood as a process of becoming. The birth of the Son as well as the breath of the Holy Spirit never began and do not consist of any changes within the Persons of God. All three Persons are absolutely co-eternal. The mere fact that in His Divine eternity the Son (this comment also pertains, *mutatis mutandis*, to the origin of the Holy Spirit) receives from the Father the entire infinity of His Divinity and had no beginning nor is a change in God in no way reduces or increases the divinity of the Father or of any of the remaining Persons. This is simply how God is, and we must venerate Him on our knees as the One Who is the Father, the Son, and the Holy Spirit.

This truth was wonderfully explained by St. Augustine: only the first Person of the Trinity is the Father, while the second Person is the Son, because He exists not of Himself but of the Father. He explained: "Who is of the Father is not of Himself. If the Son were of Himself, He would not be the Son. He is of the Father. The Father is not of the Son, while the Son is not of the Father. Equal to the Father, He is not of Him, nor is the Father of the Son. [...] Who does not know that God gave birth to God; that the Lord gave birth to the Lord; that the King gave birth to the King; that the Creator gave birth to the Creator; that the Good One gave birth to the Good One; that the Merciful One gave birth to the Merciful One; that the Almighty gave birth to the Almighty? By giving birth to the Son, the Father lost nothing."[57]

As the true God, the Son is not something distinct from the Father; however, He is different than the Father. Through this subtle distinction, St. Augustine demonstrates the real personal distinctiveness of the Son of God and His substantial unity with the Father: "You ask who the Father is. I reply: He is God. You ask who the Son is. I reply: He is God. You ask: who are the Father and the Son? I reply: God. If they ask you about just the Father, respond that He is God.

57. *Collatio cum Maximo Arianorum Episcopo*, 7 (PL 42,726).

If they ask you about only the Son, respond that He is God. If you are asked about Them both, respond that they are not gods but that they are God."[58]

In order to demonstrate the gulf that separates the natural filiation of the second Person of the Trinity from our adopted filiation, Augustine quotes the Lord Jesus' words that "the Father loves the Son and has given everything over to Him" (John 3:35). This means that the Father loves His Son in a completely different way than He loves us: "Does the Father not love John? And yet He has not given all things into His hand. Does the Father not love Paul? And yet He has not given all things into His hand. 'The Father loves the Son: but as father loves, not as master loves a servant; as the Only Son, not as an adopted son.'"[59]

In What Sense Is God Our Father?

Long before Christianity, people within various religious traditions noticed that God treats us as a father would: He looks after us and can be harsh out of concern for our good, but He is patient and forgiving regarding our sins, hoping that we will finally wise up and become rooted in what is good.

To be like a father to you is completely different than to be your father. There is a gulf separating fatherhood in a literal sense and fatherhood in a metaphorical one. We call Jan Kochanowski the father of Polish literature and city councilors the fathers of the city but, naturally, these are metaphorical titles, even if they are supported by outstanding achievements or great significance in a sphere of service to society. In a literal sense, one can be a father only with respect to

58. *Enarratio 1 in Psalmum* 68,5 (PL 36,845).

59. St. Augustine, "Tractate 14 (John 3:29-36)," [in:] *Nicene and Post-Nicene Fathers, First Series*, Vol. 7, trans. John Gibb, ed. Philip Schaff (Buffalo, NY: Christian Literature Publishing Co.), 1888; https://www.newadvent.org/fathers/1701014.htm (accessed February 7, 2022).

one's biological child; strictly speaking, fatherhood consists of transmitting life to someone like us within our own species.

Indeed, for us — and for our very existence — God is Someone incomparably more important than our biological mother and father who have given us life within the same human nature, life to which they had been previously called by their parents. He is the Father Who constantly provides life to all that exists. It is within the sphere of His creative power that we have received life from our parents and we ourselves can transmit it further to our children. Parents provide us with multifarious services of their fatherhood and motherhood, but the Creator provides us with literally everything, including our parents and their ability to be parents.

Nonetheless, it must be clearly said that as the Creator, God is not our father. He is like a father in that He provides us with more than the best human father, but He is not our father. After all, we are creatures, and He is the Creator; we are mortal beings, while He is the infinite God. Fatherhood consists of transmitting life to someone who is like us in nature.

Through Jesus Christ, that which seemed humanly impossible took place: the very Son of God became a participant in our human nature to invite us to participate in God's nature and in God's filiation. The New Testament frequently speaks of our vocation to be children of God. In the Prologue to the Gospel of John, we read of those who believed in the Word incarnate that they have become children of God, after which the evangelist explains how to literally understand that they have been born of God.

This is truly incredible: People born of their parents can be born again, through God Himself! This begins through baptism (see John 3:5; Galatians 3:26-27). Man then becomes truly someone who "may come to share in the Divine nature" (see 2 Peter 1:4) and then "God's seed remains in him" (see 1 John 3:9).

One wants to shout: But this is impossible! Indeed, solely the Only Begotten Son, Who receives from God His entire Divine nature and is the True God equal to Him in everything, is born of God. God Himself cannot do absurd things and cannot make us cease to be creatures. What, then, does the news that man can be born of God and become a participant in His nature mean? What does it mean that man can be a child of God and have access to God as if He were his Father? Why is access to God possible only through Christ?

As we can see, without the Incarnation we would be incapable of truly saying: I believe in God the Father. There can be no doubt that only the Only Begotten Son has real access to His Father, "Who alone has immortality, Who dwells in unapproachable light, and Whom no human being has seen or can see" (1 Timothy 6:16). However, this is why the Son of God has become one of us: so that we who have believed in Him and feed off His own Body would increasingly become one with Him. The more we become with Him, the more truly we become participants in His Divine Filiation, and although we are merely creatures in this way receive access to God not only as the Creator but also as the Father.

Eternal salvation consists of this: "We are God's children now; what we shall be has not yet been revealed. We do know that when it is revealed we shall be like Him, for we shall see Him as He is" (1 John 3:2).

On the eve of His passion, the Redeemer ardently prayed for this unity with us that will take us to the Father for eternal life. The meaning of this prayer of His certainly transcends our popular ecumenical interpretations: "I pray not only for them, but also for those who will believe in Me through their word, so that they may all be one, as you, Father, are in Me and I in You, that they also may be in Us, that the world may believe that You sent Me. And I have given them the glory You gave me, so that they may be one, as We are one,

I in them and You in Me, that they may be brought to perfection as one, that the world may know that You sent Me, and that You loved them even as you loved Me. Father, they are your gift to Me. I wish that where I am they also may be with Me, that they may see My glory that You gave Me, because You loved Me before the foundation of the world. Righteous Father, the world also does not know You, but I know You, and they know that You sent Me. I made known to them Your name and I will make it known, that the love with which You loved Me may be in them and I in them" (John 17:20-26).

THE DIVINITY OF THE HOLY SPIRIT

In the age of the Internet, the typical Catholic must face accusations against his faith more frequently than ever before. Their sheer number, inconsistency, and often striking dishonesty are evidence that their authors and propagators usually are not concerned about convincing others about their beliefs. When we are bombarded with accusations that the Church has covered something up; that she has distorted or incorrectly understood something; or that some new discoveries will strike at the foundations of the Christian faith, it is easy to lose our trust in the Church in general and arrive at the conclusion that it is best to either not care about questions of faith or not be particularly concerned about the Church's teaching in our religious lives.

Yet the Lord Jesus Himself wanted His believers to trust the Church. He said to His apostles: "Whoever listens to you listens to Me. Whoever rejects you rejects Me. And whoever rejects Me rejects the One Who sent Me" (Luke 10:16). If said by anyone else, these words would sound like an audacious usurpation. Thus, those whose religious quest is based on Sacred Scripture yet who in their religious thinking forget about this admonition of Jesus Christ, they at least indirectly reject this truth about Him: the truth that He is the Son of God sent by the eternal Father for the sake of our salvation.

For one cannot truly believe in Jesus and simultaneously accept that the Church He had founded preserved faith in Him by covering up or even distorting certain facts; that His Church completely does not understand His teaching; or that throughout the centuries she distorted His teaching, even if this were not out of ill will. Let us look at this from the perspective of common sense: If God had truly loved us so much that He sent us His own Son, then He certainly saw to it that every subsequent generation of His Church had access to His teaching and to Jesus Himself.

True, Jesus told us that "the gates of the netherworld shall not prevail against [the Church]" (Matthew 16:18) and the Apostle Paul had to caution the faithful: "I am amazed that you are so quickly forsaking the One who called you by [the] grace [of Christ] for a different gospel (not that there is another). But there are some who are disturbing you and wish to pervert the gospel of Christ" (Galatians 1:6-7). Meanwhile, the apostle John did not hesitate to call the wiseacre who distorted the truth about Christ "the deceitful one and the antichrist" (2 John 1:7).

Some of today's builders of the religious tower of Babel like to reference Sacred Scripture. Yet they somehow fail to notice that through the words of the Apostle Paul Sacred Scripture teaches that "the Church of the living God [is] the pillar and foundation of truth" (1 Timothy 3:15). Meanwhile, the Apostle Peter reminds us that "no prophecy ever came through human will" (2 Peter 1:21).

The Holy Spirit, Who ensures that every generation of believers has authentic access to the Word of God, is the source of the Church's teaching authority. The Lord Jesus Himself promised His Church the Holy Spirit: "The Advocate, the Holy Spirit that the Father will send in My name—He will teach you everything and remind you of all that [I] told you" (John 14:26). God always fulfills His promises; thus, He will also fulfill this promise.

Thus, when we hear dozens, or maybe even hundreds of accusations against the faith of the Church, it is worth understanding that their aim is not so much contrasting the Church's teaching with some rival vision, for what competing vision can be formed out of hundreds of mutually contradictory statements and arguments? Their aim is above all deconstruction. They desire the deconstruction of the one and only faith of the Church that has been going on for generations. Through these self-contradictory accusations, they try to force us, Catholics, to concede that our faith is just one of many voices that make up the din of the tower of Babel.

Because we constantly encounter attacks against the Catholic faith, it is good to learn to ignore many of them. Such attacks are numerous and diverse, yet they are so contradictory that it would be a waste of our time and energy to respond to them all. However, in two cases it is worth seeking out responses to arguments against the Catholic faith that we hear: if some accusations were to disturb my own faith and if it is possible that my defense of the Catholic faith would be heard by someone who had begun to doubt it because of that accusation.

Who Is the Holy Spirit?

I wrote the above observations in response to two letters that were addressed to me. The author of one of them strongly denies that the Holy Spirit is someone personal, while the author of the other has major doubts about that and it seems likely to him that God is only some impersonal divine force. Both gentlemen certainly know that not only the Catholic Church but also the Orthodox Church and all the remaining Eastern churches as well as the great majority of the Protestant churches profess that the Holy Spirit is the third Person of the Holy Trinity. However, it seems to them that this faith lacks sufficient Biblical foundation. Thus, both gentlemen requested that I show them Biblical texts that confirm the faith of the Church that the Holy Spirit is Someone personal.

I will begin my response by recalling that even during the times of Jesus' historical presence on our earth "[t]here was, of course, no Spirit yet, because Jesus had not yet been glorified" (John 7:39). The Church received the Divine person of the Holy Spirit only fifty days after Jesus' resurrection (see Acts 2). Thus, we will not look for arguments that the Holy Spirit is Someone personal in the Old Testament.

However, even the Old Testament frequently foreshadows this truth. The truth of the Holy Trinity had not yet been revealed because the Son of God had not yet been given to us, nor had the Holy Spirit been sent to us. However, because the eternal God is the Father and Son and the Holy Spirit, it is not surprising that Old Testament texts emanate the truth of the Trinity in different ways.

Let us once more repeat that in the Old Testament, the truth of the Holy Trinity had not yet been revealed. However, it is difficult to criticize Christians who interpret the verse of Psalm 33:6 in a Trinitarian way: "By the Lord's Word the heavens were made; by the breath of His mouth all their host." For the Christian, this verse spontaneously recalls the Prologue to the Gospel of John, where it is written that everything has been created through the Word that is God.

Analogously, although the Holy Spirit had not yet been clearly revealed, there appears a sense that we should pray to Him in the Old Testament. These are words addressed to the prophet Ezekiel, that he may plead for the resurrection of the dead: "Prophesy to the Breath, prophesy, son of man! Say to the Breath: Thus says the Lord God: From the four winds come, O Breath, and breathe into these slain that they may come to life" (Ezekiel 37:9).

The New Testament contains unambiguous testimony that the Holy Spirit is one of the Persons of God. Let us try to enumerate each one,

1. beginning with the Lord Jesus' promise: "And I will ask the Father, and he will give you another Advocate [Paraclete] to be with you always, the Spirit of truth" (John 14:16-17). Here, the Lord Jesus — our Consoler, Defender, and Advocate, because that is the meaning of the Greek word *Paracletos* — calls the Holy Spirit "another Advocate." Notice that He is the Advocate, not some impersonal force.
2. The Lord Jesus speaks unambiguously of the Holy Spirit as of someone not something in a fragment of John 16:5-15. He is referred to using the masculine pronoun "he" (*ekeinos*) a total of three times, even though in Greek the word "spirit" (*pneuma*) is in the neuter gender.
3. The Apostle Paul writes: "And do not grieve the Holy Spirit of God" (Ephesians 4:30). Can an impersonal force be grieved?
4. The Holy Spirit performs uniquely personal tasks: "He will teach you everything and remind you of all that [I] told you" (John 14:26). With respect to persecutors, "the Holy Spirit will teach you at that moment what you should say" (Luke 12:12).
5. "He will testify to me" (John 15:26); "He will convict the world in regard to sin and righteousness and condemnation" (John 16:8); "He will guide you to all truth. [...] He will glorify Me, because He will take from what is mine and declare it to you" (John 16:13-14). These are typically personal activities.
6. The Holy Spirit "too comes to the aid of our weakness; for we do not know how to pray as we ought" (Romans 8:26).
7. "Do you not know that your body is a temple of the Holy Spirit within you, Whom you have from God?" (1 Corinthians 6:19; see 3:16-17). After all, only one God deserves a legitimate temple.
8. There are various translations of Philippians 3:3. However, because the Greek verb *latreuein* means "to worship," while the noun *Pneumati* has the form of the dative, it seems that the most faithful rendition would be the phrase: "We who worship the Spirit of God."

9. Jesus' words that one can sin against the Holy Spirit and that this is a sin that is incomparably greater than one against the Son of Man, or against the Son of God in His human nature, also suggests that the Holy Spirit is one of the Divine Persons (see Matthew 12:31-32).
10. Let us also make note of those New Testament texts in which all three Divine Persons are mentioned on the principle of equivalence. The Lord Jesus speaks of baptism "in the name of the Father, and of the Son, and of the Holy Spirit" (Matthew 28:19). Furthermore, let us quote the Apostle Paul: "There are different kinds of spiritual gifts but the same Spirit; there are different forms of service but the same Lord; there are different workings but the same God who produces all of them in everyone" (1 Corinthians 12:4-6); "The grace of the Lord Jesus Christ and the love of God and the fellowship of the Holy Spirit be with all of you" (2 Corinthians 13:13).
11. Let us look at this Trinitarian verse of Revelation 22:1: "Then the angel showed me the river of life-giving water, sparkling like crystal, flowing from the throne of God and of the Lamb." Notice that God and the Lamb are different Persons, but the throne is one, for the Father and Son are one God. Meanwhile, the Water flowing from them is, of course, the Holy Spirit. Jesus Himself presented the Holy Spirit in this image when He called: "'Let anyone who thirsts come to me and drink. Whoever believes in Me, as scripture says: 'Rivers of living water will flow from within him.' He said this in reference to the Spirit that those who came to believe in Him were to receive" (John 7:37-39). It is worth knowing that the author of Revelation uses the Greek verb *ekporeuein*, which in Eastern theology has become a technical term referring to the origins of the Holy Spirit.

However, I would like to repeat that we do not have to be capable of responding to all accusations against the faith that we encounter. However, "[a]lways be ready to give an explanation to anyone who asks you for a reason for your hope" (1 Peter 3:15).

THE HOLY SPIRIT AS AN INTERNAL MASTER

The Holy Spirit in the Life and Work of Jesus Christ

Let us begin by recalling that everything that Jesus Christ has done took place in the Holy Spirit. The very term "Christ" is filled with the Holy Spirit, for it means the Anointed or the Messiah. Jesus is the Christ, or the Anointed by the Holy Spirit, as was prophesied (Isaiah 61:1; see Luke 4:18). Let us try to fathom what it means that He is Anointed with the Holy Spirit (see Acts 10:38). This means that He became a man and went through His entire human life filled with the Holy Spirit, or the same infinite Divine Love through which He as the Son of God is united with His Eternal Father.

The New Testament carefully emphasizes the presence of the Holy Spirit in the work of Jesus Christ, in all His most important moments, beginning with the fact that His human conception began in the Holy Spirit. We read in the Gospel according to Matthew: "Joseph, son of David, do not be afraid to take Mary your wife into your home. For it is through the Holy Spirit that this Child has been conceived in her" (Matthew 1:20). The Angel says to Mary in the Gospel according to Luke: "The Holy Spirit will come upon you, and the power of the Most High will overshadow you" (Luke 1:35). In other words, you will become a tabernacle of the Covenant; a tent of the Holy Spirit; a place where the redeeming God is especially present.

Jesus began His public activity in the Holy Spirit. All four Gospels emphasize the presence of the Holy Spirit during Jesus' baptism in the Jordan (for example, Luke 3:22); it is also emphasized in Jesus' later activity (Luke 3:16; 4:1,14,18; 10:21). Furthermore, it was thanks to the Holy Spirit that Jesus endured His Cross and His holy passion: "through the eternal spirit [Christ] offered Himself unblemished to God" (Hebrews 9:14).

Likewise, His resurrection also took place through the power of the Holy Spirit. Here, it is worth remembering that the New Testament makes use of all three formulas: that the Father has resurrected Him (Acts 2:24,32, etc.), that He rose from the dead by His own power (John 10:18), as well as that He was resurrected through the power of the Holy Spirit: "Put to death in the flesh, He was brought to life in the Spirit" (1 Peter 3:18). It is very important to be aware of the fact that Jesus' entire journey on earth — from His conception through His Resurrection — took place in the Holy Spirit; that Jesus fulfilled the work of our salvation in the same infinite and personal Love through which He is united with the Eternal Father as the Son of God; and that the work of our salvation took place within the eternal Love with which God has loved all His creation, especially rational creatures.

The Acting of the Holy Spirit in the Church

Once we become aware of how the Holy Spirit permeates the work of Jesus Christ, we can ask about the acting of the Holy Spirit in the Church. Let us start with Jesus' somewhat mysterious statement that "it is better for you that I go. For if I do not go, the Advocate will not come to you. But if I go, I will send Him to you" (John 16:7). Why was the Lord Jesus' departure a necessary condition for the coming of the Holy Spirit to the apostles and the entire Church?

We will begin our response to this question by noting the closeness to the Lord Jesus with which the apostles were blessed during His historical presence with them. They were fortunate to be able to be His true friends; love and admire Him; listen to His teachings; speak with Him; and ask Him questions and listen to His responses. However, this was ordinary interpersonal closeness only to an extent. To put it more simply, for them, the Lord Jesus was someone from the outside, just like any other person.

Once the Holy Spirit comes, their situation (and ours) becomes incomparably more blessed. Thanks to the Holy Spirit, this inconceivable kind of unity and closeness to Jesus Christ thanks to which we are truly His body became possible. In accordance with what He has prophesied, we can remain in Him and He in us (see John 15:4; 6:56). It is thanks to the Holy Spirit that something so mysterious happens to us that along with the Apostle Paul we can say that "I live, no longer I, but Christ lives in me" (Galatians 2:20). This reality occurs to a much greater extent and much more deeply within us than we realize. This occurs precisely thanks to the Holy Spirit thanks to Whom we are one Body: "For in one Spirit we were all baptized into one body" (1 Corinthians 12:13).

The Spirit of the Father and Son, Who gives life to the Church and Who is Christ's Body, comes to us as the Spirit of filiation. Making us one with the Only Begotten Son, the Spirit teaches us to recognize God's fatherly love for us and to respond to it as we persist in various situations that have been deformed by sin.

In particular in relation to the passion and cross of the Lord Jesus, Christians have sometimes said various unwise things about God the Father: "What kind of Father made His own Son undergo such terrible suffering?" Indeed, the Holy Spirit reveals to us the truth of God's fatherhood: that He loves us in His Son; that without His love we would not exist at all, while His Son experienced His passion on the cross; and that the Eternal Father has not ceased to love us when we became sinners, but He loves us in such a way to make us cease to be sinners.

In short, thanks to the Holy Spirit we can understand both the mystery of our sin as well as the truth of God's fatherly love for us. He "will convict the world in regard to sin and righteousness and condemnation" (John 16:8). When we do not notice God's fatherly love for the world, the Holy Spirit instructs us that this is because we are sinful and live in a world that is to a significant degree influenced by apostasy and infidelity. Furthermore, the Holy Spirit presents this love to us: "As proof that you are children, God sent the spirit of His Son into our hearts, crying out, 'Abba! Father!' So you are no longer a slave but a child, and if a child then also an heir, through God" (Galatians 4:6-7). Naturally, the Holy Spirit causes much more than simply a change of awareness within us; thanks to Him, our relationship with the Father of the Lord Jesus Christ becomes truly child-like.

The Spirit of the Father and Son given to the Church reminds us of everything that Jesus has done for us and what He has taught (John 14:26). Thus, it is in the Holy Spirit that we recognize Jesus' absolute entrustment to His Father; His obedience to and love for His Father. The Holy Spirit incites us to imitate Jesus in the attitude from which flow His words that "My food is to do the will of the One Who sent Me and to finish His work" (John 4:34) and in His attitude expressed in the words that "My teaching is not My own but is from the One Who sent me" (John 7:16). Thus, if the Church persists in the teaching brought to us from the Father through Jesus and despite so much dissent and human sophistry continues to preach and fulfill Jesus' Word truthfully, powerfully, and effectively, that is caused by the Holy Spirit.

The above truths are excellently summarized in the *Catechism of the Catholic Church*: "Because the Holy Spirit is the anointing of

Christ, it is Christ Who, as the head of the Body, pours out the Spirit among His members to nourish, heal, and organize them in their mutual functions, to give them life, send them to bear witness, and associate them to His self-offering to the Father and to His intercession for the whole world. Through the Church's sacraments, Christ communicates His Holy and sanctifying Spirit to the members of His Body" (739).

The Presence and Power of the Holy Spirit in the Liturgy of the Church

Let us also emphasize the presence and power of the Holy Spirit in the liturgy of the Church, especially in the administration of the sacraments to all without exception. Let us begin with baptism and look at this sacrament in light of Jesus' words: "Let anyone who thirsts come to Me and drink. Whoever believes in Me, as Scripture says: 'Rivers of living water will flow from within him.'" The evangelist proceeds to explain: "He said this in reference to the Spirit that those who came to believe in Him were to receive" (John 7:37-39).

This immediately gives rise to the question: From whose interior will those streams of living water flow? From Christ's interior or from that of those who believe in Him? Catholic spirituality loves to respond to these types of questions according to the model of "yes and yes." There is not the slightest doubt that Christ the Lord is the Temple from Whose interior waters flow that are capable of providing hydration to the entire world and restoring the shape of the Garden of Eden to our world as intended by the Creator, which was prophesied by the prophet Ezekiel (Chapter 47). At the same time, those of the Church's teachers who refers Christ's words to me, a baptized individual, are not wrong, for He opened the life-giving source of water in me on the day of my baptism.

This image evidently contains the symbolism of a desert filled with weeds and thorns that we and our earth have become by our distancing ourselves from God, as well as the promise of paradise that Christ wants to make of us by hydrating us with the Holy Spirit. If things are like this and if on the day of my baptism I was granted the source of Living Water called the Holy Spirit, maybe it would be worth asking a somewhat moralizing question: Do I look after this source? Maybe it is neglected and soiled within me?

With regards to confirmation, it is a very important sacrament of the Holy Spirit. The pneumatic particularity of this sacrament is evident especially when we become aware that the relationship between baptism and confirmation is like that between crossing the Red Sea to what would happen on Mount Sinai. Crossing the Red Sea separated God's people from Pharaoh's menace, while they received the Ten Commandments on Mount Sinai and became the People of the Covenant. Both these events prophesied two climactic events of the New Testament: the death and Resurrection of the Lord Jesus as well as the Pentecost.

Baptism includes us in Jesus' transition from death to the Resurrection (Genesis 6:3-14), while thanks to confirmation we become participants in the Gift of the Pentecost (Acts 8:14-17). The Church's Tradition sometimes calls the Holy Spirit the Lawgiver of the New Covenant (see St. Thomas Aquinas, S.Th. 1-2 q.106 a.1), for He writes the Law of Love "not in ink but by the Spirit of the living God, not on tablets of stone but on tablets that are hearts of flesh" (2 Corinthians 3:3). It is the Holy Spirit granted to us in the sacrament of confirmation that allows the faith of our baptism to mature so that we can share it with others. In other words, through the sacrament of confirmation the Holy Spirit especially includes us in the motherhood of the Church, giving birth to increasing numbers of children in Christ.

With regards to the Eucharist, which as the presence of Christ's Sacrifice is the central place in the manifestation and shaping of the

Church, it is also the central place of the activity of the Holy Spirit in the Church. It suffices to be aware that the power of the Holy Spirit sanctifies the gifts of bread and wine so that they "may become the Body and Blood of our Lord, Jesus Christ" (Third Eucharistic Prayer). Meanwhile, consuming the Body and Blood of Christ has the power to allow us to "become filled with his Holy Spirit [and] may become one body, one spirit in Christ" (*ibid.*). Thus, the mystery of the Eucharist, which makes present the Sacrifice of Our Lord, manifests the descent of the Holy Spirit onto His Church, which occurs in time but is also transcendent with respect to time.

With regards to the sacrament of penance, the particular role of the Holy Spirit in this sacrament has been emphasized in the very description of its establishment. As we recall, the resurrected Jesus breathed on His disciples "and said to them, 'Receive the Holy Spirit. Whose sins you forgive are forgiven them, and whose sins you retain are retained'" (John 20:22-23). It becomes immediately apparent that the Lord Jesus' intention here was to repeat the act of creation. According to the description in Genesis, "the Lord God formed the man out of the dust of the ground and blew into his nostrils the breath of life, and the man became a living being" (Genesis 2:7). With the aid of this anthropomorphic description, the Word of God professes the truth that man's spirit is not any manifestation of his carnality, but that man has received it from the Creator Himself; it simultaneously professes that the entirety of man, not only his spiritual element, is a creature of God.

Now, considering the description of the sacrament of penance established by the Resurrected One, it turns out to be something much greater: that not only has the Creator bestowed on man the spiritual element that is transcendent with respect to his carnality, but man is also capable of receiving the Holy Spirit Who incorporates us into Christ and, if necessary, also removes from us all spiritual deformations and makes us into a new creation.

Likewise, it is the Holy Spirit acting in the sacrament of the anointing of the sick Who makes the Christian capable of transforming the sufferings and difficulties of illness into a sacrifice pleasing to God. Meanwhile, in the sacrament of holy orders the Holy Spirit grants the individual Christian the right to participate in the pastoral, priestly, and teaching ministry of Christ the Lord. The Holy Spirit, Whose temple consists of the baptized, also transforms two Christians receiving the sacrament of marriage into a domestic Church, one that should be a place where God is particularly present, a place where sacrifices pleasing to God are given, and a place of particular testimony to Christ both with respect to those who believe in Him and those who do not.

The Holy Spirit Also Directly Acts in Our Interior

The Holy Spirit acts in us not only through the sacraments but also directly in our interior. He is the Cause of our unity in one faith and love; at the same time, each of us is so unique in our faith and in our implementation of our life's vocation: "There are different kinds of spiritual gifts, but the same Spirit; [...] To each individual the manifestation of the Spirit is given for some benefit. To one is given through the Spirit the expression of wisdom; to another the expression of knowledge according to the same Spirit; to another faith by the same Spirit; to another gifts of healing by the one Spirit; to another mighty deeds; to another prophecy; to another discernment of spirits; to another varieties of tongues; to another interpretation of tongues" (1 Corinthians 12:4,7-10).

As we can see, the spiritual richness which the Holy Spirit grants us—each of us in a unique way—is at the same time the richness of the Church. Indeed, this always was a negative criterion thanks to which the Church distinguished between the authentic activity of the Holy Spirit from purely human ideas and activity: Something that is inconsistent with the faith of the Church or that opposes good cannot be a work of the Holy Spirit. The Holy Spirit, Who acts in the interior of each individual Christian, cannot act contrary to Himself; He cannot contradict His own work, which He performs with respect to the entire Church.

At the same time, the Holy Spirit not only leads to the salvation of the Church as a whole but also to that of each of us individually. The Apostle Paul must have frequently spoken about this, because nearly identical expressions appear in two of his epistles: "For those who are led by the Spirit of God are children of God. For you did not receive a spirit of slavery to fall back into fear, but you received a spirit of adoption, through which we cry, 'Abba, Father!' The Spirit itself bears witness with our spirit that we are children of God, and if children, then heirs, heirs of God and joint heirs with Christ" (Romans 8:14-17; see Galatians 4:6).

In brief, we can say that as the internal Master, the Holy Spirit is: 1) The Teacher of the faith; 2) The Teacher of prayer; and 3) The Teacher of our Christian activity. All three truths have already been expressed in the New Testament, from which we receive instructions to listen to the admonitions of the Holy Spirit and not waste His inspiration.

As the internal Teacher of the Faith Who also comes to us from the outside through the teaching of the Church, the Holy Spirit is presented in the greatest detail in the pericope of 1 Corinthians 2:10-16: "[t]his God has revealed to us through the Spirit. For the Spirit scrutinizes everything, even the depths of God. Among human beings, who knows what pertains to a person except the spirit of the person that is within? Similarly, no one knows what pertains to God except the Spirit of God. We have not received the spirit of the world but the Spirit that is from God, so that we may understand the things freely given us by God. And we speak about them not with words taught by human wisdom, but with words taught by the Spirit, describing spiritual realities in spiritual terms. Now the natural person does not accept what pertains to the Spirit of God, for to him it is foolishness, and he cannot understand it, because it is judged spiritually. The spiritual person, however, can judge everything but is not subject to judgment by anyone. For 'who has known the mind of the Lord, to counsel him?' But we have the mind of Christ."

This is why St. Augustine considered himself to be only an external teacher of the faith and deeply believed that his audience would receive the essential teaching from the Holy Spirit, the internal Teacher. "'And you have no need that any man teach you, because His unction teaches you concerning all things' (1 John 2:27) [...] Do not suppose that any man learns ought from man. We can admonish by the sound of our voice; if there be not One within that shall teach, vain is the noise we make. Aye, brethren, have ye a mind to know it? Have ye not all heard this present discourse? And yet how many will go from this place untaught! I, for my part, have spoken to all; but they to whom that Unction within speaks not, they whom the Holy Ghost within teaches not, those go back untaught. The teachings of the master from without are a sort of aids and admonitions. He that teaches the hearts, has His chair in heaven."[60]

Awareness of the fact that the Holy Spirit is the first Teacher of the faith has accompanied the Church throughout her entire existence. This truth was also professed during the most recent council: "To make this act of faith, the grace of God and the interior help of the Holy Spirit must precede and assist, moving the heart and turning it to God, opening the eyes of the mind and giving 'joy and ease to everyone in assenting to the truth and believing it.' To bring about

60. St. Augustine, "Homily 3 on the First Epistle of John," [in:] St. Augustine, *Nicene and Post-Nicene Fathers*, First Series, Vol. 7, trans. H. Browne, ed. Philip Schaff (Buffalo, NY: Christian Literature Publishing Co., 1888), https://www.newadvent.org/fathers/170203.htm (accessed February 8, 2022).

an ever deeper understanding of revelation the same Holy Spirit constantly brings faith to completion by His gifts" (*Dei verbum*, 5).

We have already mentioned that the Holy Spirit is the Teacher of prayers, referencing the texts of Romans 8:15 and Galatians 4:6 that say that we will recognize God as our Father in the Holy Spirit and will be able to call to Him: Abba! In the same chapter of the Epistle to the Romans, the Apostle Paul instructs us that the Holy Spirit present in our hearts says prayers we are still incapable of (Romans 8:26).

Furthermore, the Holy Spirit teaches us how to act in a Christian way. This topic has been presented in greater detail in Galatians 5:16-26. He is "the first installment of our inheritance toward redemption as God's possession, to the praise of His glory" (Ephesians 1:14).

Ultimately, the Holy Spirit, the personal love of the Father and Son, leads us and the entire Church to eternal life: "If the Spirit of the One Who raised Jesus from the dead dwells in you, the One who raised Christ from the dead will give life to your mortal bodies also, through His Spirit that dwells in you" (Romans 8:11). At that time, each of us individually as well as the entire Church will be perfectly one with Christ, for we will be completely filled with the same Spirit that fills Christ and makes Him one with the Eternal Father.

WHERE IS GOD?

In the first episode of Krzysztof Kieślowski's film *The Decalogue*, a boy who had been brought up in a non-religious household asks his believing aunt: "Where Is God?" The aunt takes him in her arms, embraces him, and says: "God is here, and God is wherever people truly love one another."

God Is "More Than Everywhere"

The truth of this scene is deeply moving. At the same time, we must remind ourselves again that the truth about God cannot be closed in any human words or gestures, as it transcends all human means of expression. Sometimes, however, someone deeply fascinated by God can say something so exceptional about Him that it nearly transcends the capabilities of human language.

Probably under the influence of some mystical experience, Beata Obertyńska wrote that "God is more than everywhere" in her volume of poems *Crumbs of Resin*. St. Augustine was thrilled that God is *interior intimo meo*, which can be loosely translated as: "God is closer to me than I am to myself."

Both these beyond-masterful expressions are an echo of Biblical intuitions about God's omnipresence. "Is God indeed to dwell on earth?" King Solomon prayed during the consecration of the Temple. "If the heavens and the highest heavens cannot contain You, how much less this house which I have built!" (1 Kings 8:27).

The Apostle Paul explained to pagan philosophers at the Areopagus: "In Him we live and move and have our being" (Acts 17:28). Meanwhile, in the middle of the second century St. Theophilus of Antioch expressed the truth that God, present in every place, is simultaneously transcendent with respect to all places in the following words: "God [is] by no means to be confined in a place; for if He were, then the place containing Him would be greater than He; for that which contains is greater than that which is contained."

Jesus Himself said that God is closer to me than I am to myself: "But when you give alms, do not let your left hand know what your right is doing, so that your almsgiving may be secret. And your Father who sees in secret will repay you" (Matthew 6:3-4). The Psalmist praised God's love: "Lord, You have probed me, You know me: You know when I sit and stand; You understand my thoughts from afar. You sift through my travels and my rest; with all my ways You are familiar. Even before a word is on my tongue, Lord, you know it all. Behind and before You encircle me and rest Your hand upon me" (Psalm 139:1-5).

Naturally, God's omnipresence must upset the sinner. The first sinner awkwardly tried to justify himself before God: "I heard you in the garden; but I was afraid, because I was naked, so I hid" (Genesis 3:10). We read in the Book of Jeremiah 23:24: "Can anyone hide in secret without my seeing them? —oracle of the Lord. Do I not fill heaven and earth? —oracle of the Lord." St. Augustine asked: "Where is there a place where the One Who is everywhere is absent? Does not Paul remind us of this when he says: *The Lord is near; worry about nothing else*?"

Augustine was thrilled by the fact that God is everywhere because he knew with his entire being that God is Love. When, however, one does not know or does not want to know about this, God's omnipresence can seem frightening, just as it was frightening to the young Sartre. The adulterer from Sirach 23:18-19 also did not want to know of God's omnipresence:

The man who dishonors his marriage bed says to himself, 'Who can see me?

Darkness surrounds me, walls hide me, no one sees me. Who can stop me from sinning?'

He is not mindful of the Most High, fearing only human eyes.

He does not realize that the eyes of the Lord, ten thousand times brighter than the sun,

Observe every step taken and peer into hidden corners.

Yet even the adulterer is encompassed by the Almighty's love, which inclines him to renounce sin and embark on a path leading to life. The sinner Augustine experienced precisely such an encounter with the omnipresent God, which led him to be ashamed of his sin and open to God's love, which ultimately transformed him into a great saint: "And from Thee, O Lord, unto Whose eyes the abyss of man's conscience is naked, what could be hidden in me though I would not confess it? For I should hide Thee from me, not me from Thee. But now, for that my groaning is witness, that I am displeased with myself, Thou shinest out, and art pleasing, and beloved, and longed for; that I may be ashamed of myself, and renounce myself, and choose Thee, and neither please Thee nor myself, but in Thee."[61]

"Who Art in Heaven"

If God is "more everywhere than everywhere" and if He is closer to each of us than we are to ourselves, then what do sacred texts that call Him the heavenly Father (e.g. Matthew 5:48; 6:14, 26, 32) say?

61. St. Augustine, *The Confessions of St. Augustine*, trans. E. B. Pusey (Edward Bouverie), Project Gutenberg, 2013 https://www.gutenberg.org/files/3296/3296-h/3296-h.htm#link2H_4_0010 (accessed February 9, 2022).

If it was already known during the times of the Old Testament that "the heavens and the highest heavens cannot contain [Him]" (1 Kings 8:27), then why does the Lord Jesus so frequently speak of His Father Who is in heaven (e.g. Matthew 5:16, 45; 6:1, 9; 7:11)?

Why does Sacred Scripture so frequently claim that He Who is everywhere is in heaven? Let us recall some of these texts. When the Lord Jesus was baptized in the Jordan, "the heavens were opened [for Him], and He saw the Spirit of God descending like a dove [and] coming upon Him. And a voice came from the heavens, saying, 'This is my beloved Son, with Whom I am well pleased" (Matthew 3:16-17). When He turned to His Father, Jesus characteristically raised His eyes towards heaven. Likewise, the New Testament presents His visible departure from us as entering heaven.

The heaven where God is and where our Lord Jesus Christ sits at the right hand of His Father in His glorious humanity is our eternal destiny. There is our treasure (see Matthew 6:20) and our prize (see Matthew 5:12; Luke 6:23). There, we will find "a building from God, a dwelling not made with hands, eternal in heaven" (2 Corinthians 5:1). The Lord Jesus departed there to "prepare a place for [us]," for "in [the] Father's house there are many dwelling places" (John 14:2).

Where and what is the heaven that these passages describe? King Solomon just explained to us that this is not the same heaven that the astronomers study. In the first half of the third century, Origen clearly taught that "When the Father of saints is said to be in the heavens, we are not to suppose that He is circumscribed by material form and dwells in heaven. Since, in that case, as contained God will be formed to be less than the heavens because they contain Him."[62]

The *Catechism of the Catholic Church* 2794 provides a positive response to the above question: "This Biblical expression does not mean a place ('space'), but a way of being; it does not mean that God is distant,

62. *On Prayer*, XIII, trans. William A. Curtis, https://www.tertullian.org/fathers/origen_on_prayer_02_text.htm (accessed January 16, 2023).

but majestic. Our Father is not 'elsewhere': He transcends everything we can conceive of His holiness." The Apostle Paul tells us the same using an apophatic expression: "the blessed and only Ruler will make manifest at the proper time, the King of kings and Lord of lords, Who alone has immortality, Who dwells in unapproachable light, and Whom no human being has seen or can see" (1 Timothy 6:15-16).

It is impossible to attain "inaccessible luminosity" thanks to one's own efforts. Meanwhile, only Jesus Christ can lead us to the house of His Father. Furthermore, He already brings us to Him in a basic but real way. The Apostle Paul writes about this: "But God, Who is rich in mercy, because of the great love He had for us, even when we were dead in our transgressions, brought us to life with Christ (by grace you have been saved), raised us up with Him, and seated us with Him in the heavens in Christ Jesus" (Ephesians 2:4-6).

What does it mean that heaven is accessible now and that some of Jesus' disciples are already "seated [...] with Him in the heavens"? St. Ambrose, St. Augustine's spiritual father, provides a simple yet convincing response to this question: "Heaven is there where guilt hath ceased, where crimes keep holiday. Heaven is where there is no stroke of death."[63]

"The Farther They Went from Me..."

God's omnipresence is an ontic trait of His relationship with creation. Unfortunately, however, at a spiritual level we can distance ourselves from God, while He can abandon us. In Sacred Scripture, such images are frequently used to describe human sin. For example, God laments in the Book of Jeremiah: "What fault did your ancestors find in Me that they withdrew from Me, went after emptiness, and became empty themselves?" (Jeremiah 2:5). God

63. St. Ambrose, *"On the Mysteries" and the Treatise on the Sacraments*, trans. T. Thompson (New York: The Macmillan Company, 1919), https://oll-resources.s3.us-east-2.amazonaws.com/oll3/store/titles/219/Ambrose_0565.html#lf0565_footnote_nt382 (accessed February 9, 2022).

continues this complaint in the Book of Hosea: "The more I called them, the farther they went from Me" (Hosea 11:2).

It is possible to be far from God yet think one is near to Him: "This people draws near with words only and honors Me with their lips alone" (Isaiah 29:13; Matthew 15:9). One can even be separated from the omnipresent God by a chasm: "Rather, it is your crimes that separate you from your God; It is your sins that make Him hide His face so that He does not hear you" (Isaiah 59:2).

Sacred Scripture also describes man's separation from God from the other perspective. "The Lord is far from the wicked, but hears the prayer of the just" (Proverbs 15:29); "The Lord is on high, but cares for the lowly and knows the proud from afar" (Psalm 138:6). Although one trembles before saying this, growing distant from God can become permanent: "These will pay the penalty of eternal ruin, separated from the presence of the Lord and from the glory of His power" (2 Thessalonians 1:9).

This naturally gives rise to the question: If God is omnipresent in the most literal sense, how can one be so far from Him that He is far from us and that we are even separated from Him by a chasm? Paradoxically, this question can be expressed as follows: How can it be that our earth is not heaven?

The response to this question is as simple as it is painful: the Omnipresent God is Love. If there is no love where it should be present, this means that God is not there. At the same time, it means that a world of appearances far from reality is being constructed there. God complained in the Book of Jeremiah: "[Your ancestors] went after emptiness, and became empty themselves" (Jeremiah 2:5). This is why we are sometimes unhappy and bitter on this earth, and having lost love, we have simultaneously lost God and ourselves and become entangled in the illusory world of appearances.

It would be frightening to think how this would have ended had God not had mercy on us and sent us His Son.

BEING TOUCHED BY THE LOVING GOD

Such Experiences Cannot Be Anticipated

The following letter makes an impact:

"Let me begin with a brief introduction. I am a married woman of approximately forty with a husband and three children and work as an engineer. For a long time, I was a non-believer or, as it is sometimes euphemistically said, a 'non-practicing believer.' I returned to God slowly, taking small steps. The last eight or nine years of my life were a time of intense seeking and regularly attending church, but this was not supported by prayer and receiving the sacraments (out of habit, I received the sacraments twice a year, on Easter and Christmas, which was accompanied by some 'collective' prayer a week before receiving the Eucharist).

Recently, my husband and I traveled to Crete. When we visited some ancient city, I became separated from our group. In the heat, I walked alongside a fence listening to the birds and inhaling the scent of plants and the scorching earth. I thought that this earth had not changed much since the time of the Romans and Bishop Titus, while the Holy Land, where Jesus walked, was probably similar, with the same heat, scent of plants, and singing of birds.

At that moment, I felt God's presence, which was as tangible and certain as the sun in the sky. He was inside me; He was me more than I was myself; He was closer to me than any person, including myself. He was also unimaginable love and mercy. I did not think about my sins at all, for they were simply unimportant amidst this love.

I had already experienced the ecstasy of love between two people, and I had known the joy of motherhood, but this was incomparably greater, more beautiful, and more obvious than all those feelings. I cannot compare God's closeness and presence to anything else. I thought then: 'I see; this is what this is like,' because I thought that this was the finish line, the end, and man's proper place. Although this description is chaotic and inadequate with respect to my experience, at this point words fail.

We slowly grew closer to our group. I thought: 'God, if You are so present inside me, then You must be as present in each of us.' I was choked with a sense of tenderness and love for those people. I approached them and asked: maybe I could take a photo of you? Maybe I could lend you my cap, translate something into English, or lend you my camera? I would have fallen at their feet if they wanted.

What is my problem? It is that, in a sense, I feel chosen. It is clear to me that this is not because of any merits of my own. I think that this entails a certain responsibility, a sense of duty. But how can I recognize God's will? What can I do with this gift so that I do not squander it?

My life has changed so much that I miss God's presence. I eagerly devote my time to prayer and attend Mass two or three times a week because I want to encounter Him again. But is this everything that HE expects of me? I have a certain sense of chaos. I cannot completely devote myself to prayer because I am the mother of three troublesome children.

There must be a reason why I have received this gift. I want to ask once more: how can I recognize the Lord's will? My second question is: how can I return to this moment, the most beautiful moment a person can experience? I miss this so greatly. The thought of death, which I had previously feared so much, no longer frightens me, because I know that I would be greeted with open arms and love after dying."

God, I Want to Love You as Much as I Can!

The author of this letter asks herself a question that is completely understandable considering her circumstances. We, external observers, are interested in one more question: What are the criteria to recognize the authenticity of the spiritual experiences described here? After all, not all spiritual experiences are authentically spiritual; in fact, they can sometimes be caused by our enemy who can pretend to be an angel (see 2 Corinthians 11:14). Personally, I have no doubts that the experiences described above were indeed a wonderful gift from God. I will attempt to explain why I believe this is the case.

According to the author's testimony, her experience was not a love for God that can be explained away as exultation. The fact that this experience was dominated by love and not pleasure, although this woman strongly experienced joy and pleasure, is an important marker of its authenticity. More important, the experience of God's love spontaneously bolstered her love for her neighbors.

A more intense religious life that does not involve avoiding her everyday duties after this experience is the third sign of authenticity. Fourth, she did not have the slightest doubt that she did not deserve this gift from God and that it would be foolish to feel superior to other people for having received it. Fifth, she also knew fully well that these kinds of gifts are an invitation to a deeper engagement in the Church and that they were devoid of temptations to put herself above the Church. The final sign of the authenticity of this kind of experience is the resulting peace or, to be more precise, "love, joy, peace, patience, kindness, generosity, faithfulness, gentleness, self-control" (Galatians 5:22-23).

I would like to make note of one more thing before I pose a question to the author of this testimony. Namely, she does not attempt to repeat that experience of an intense presence of Him Who is Love Itself. Our submission to God is not measured by the intensity of our experiences. When such experiences appear, we thank God for them. But if they do not exist, we are glad that we can truly love Him, even if it does not bring us special satisfaction. Such an experience is a gift from God, but when it disappears, it is also a gift from God because we can more carefully liberate ourselves of self-centeredness in our relationship to God.

The author of the above testimony asks: How can I recognize what God expects of me? Through no merit of her own, she knows what many people who otherwise believe in Christ and pray do not realize: that God's will with respect to us is full of kindness and love and that God is more concerned about my good than I am. This is why the desire to fulfill God's will is something obvious to her. She only fears that she can unwillingly evade God's will.

In the search for a response to her question, I propose to take the Lord Jesus' following words as a basic guideline: "For this is the will of My Father, that everyone who sees the Son and believes in Him may have eternal life" (John 6:40). The Apostle Paul repeats after the Lord Jesus using his own words: "This is the will of God, your holiness" (1 Thessalonians 4:3).

God's will with respect to us is the opposite of any programming. God's will is essentially God's love, which has rested in us, wants to increasingly encompass us, and makes us capable of bearing good fruits and leads us to eternal life.

Naturally, with respect to evil, God's will is categorical: to commit evil is unacceptable. One cannot commit evil even to save one's own life. In this regard, God's will is only categorical because God cares about us and loves us. Furthermore, when fulfilling God's will requires major efforts, God especially supports us.

Meanwhile, with respect to good, God's will is like a mother who brings up her children. It comes to us every day in various events and signs; it incites us to increase our own activity and to make use of our freedom. With respect to good, it is usually not very categorical and permits different variants among which we ourselves choose. It is out of tenderness that God encourages us to not waste away our lives and for us to walk through life doing good deeds. It is only sometimes that man knows with full certainty what exactly God demands of us. However, even then this takes place without compulsion but out of love, with great respect for my freedom.

The most important thing is to make an effort to love God's will, both when it is very clear and when it stimulates us towards doing greater good. Let us make an effort to believe in His love for us with all our hearts. God certainly "deserves" that we completely believe Him.

I was greatly impressed by the observation I once read that the preparation of a single meal by the Blessed Mother was more pleasing in the eyes of the Lord than the martyrdom of St. Lawrence. It is difficult to find a martyr whose death was crueler than that of St. Lawrence, who was certainly filled with great love for God since he emerged victorious from such terrible tortures. One cannot doubt that his death was very precious in God's eyes. The point, however, is that the Blessed Mother was filled with incomparably greater love.

The meaning of this paradoxical comment is to emphasize that, ultimately, what matters in God's eyes is love, and love alone. Naturally, it would be erroneous to ignore the meaning of good deeds. "Faith without works is useless" (James 2:20). However, a good deed is an act of faith only when it is filled with love. The more love it contains, the more pleasing it is to God.

It is telling that after such a distinct experience of feeling God's love, fulfilling God's will above all consists of lovingly performing one's family and professional duties; furthermore, one tries to genuinely notice one's neighbors, whom God places on one's path, every day. Naturally, to fulfill God's will also means to entrust one's failures, disappointments, weaknesses, and dismay to God. To the extent that I am capable, I will do this naturally and simply, without psychological exertion.

Man alone cannot awaken love for God within himself or increase it, for it is a gift from God. Therefore, this gives rise to the question: Am I allowed to want to love God more than other people do? If any of you are faced by this problem, I suggest praying as follows: "Lord God, You know that I love You and that I want to love You as much as I can! However, I would very much like for all other people to love You more than I love You. For me, it suffices that I increasingly love You as much as I can with all my being."

One More Testimony

"One Good Friday, I went to the cathedral after work to confess, but I was dejected by the enormous crowds of people in front of the confessional. Disheartened, I sat in front of an image of the Mother of God. I felt a wave of Benevolence that opened within me some channel like nothing before. Words automatically came to my mind; they arranged themselves without my engagement in a beautiful prayer that I would have never come up with myself.

Unfortunately, after having experienced this state, I am incapable of writing down the words I had said earlier; I simply cannot remember them. How is this possible? I would like to underline that I had never participated in Catholic charismatic renewal before. From today's perspective, I see that through the aid of her charms, sweetness, and kindness the Mother of God brought me to her SON, Who entered Easter like a wind into my heart.

I no longer experience such sweet bliss, although this sometimes still occurs. This is life-giving and healing POWER. Suddenly, I see everything in a different way; I see more and have become aware of various things that I had previously not noticed or understood. I am surprised that I seem so wise to myself. I impress my patients with how I talk to them. One said that I am fantastic; another kissed my hand; yet another cried like a baby. This is insane! Please pray for me that I am capable of surviving the onslaught of this Power. [...]

A recent experience was the strongest, and it struck me with its peculiarity. I had finished seeing patients and filled out all the forms recommended by the reformed health care legislation. I made myself tea and decided to pray a little, because recently I have been praying like crazy, even though in the past I almost never prayed. This was not a chore but something that my heart needed. Therefore, I prayed, and I was suddenly overwhelmed by a tenderness and emotion that caused tears to flow from my face. In my case, tears are very significant because they cause all hang-ups, blockades, and inferiority complexes within me to crumble. I was greatly moved and became defenseless with all my wounds and flaws which had revealed themselves.

Suddenly, I felt so lonely and abandoned that I could do only one thing: fall on my knees and completely submit myself to God. I remembered an instruction from some book that you have to say YES to God. I did this three times. I suddenly felt that I was being lifted by some great force and encompassed by a Love so wonderful and thrilling that I completely submitted to it. This was something fantastic, something that I cannot describe. So much Love only for myself!

I felt that this was the Love of my Father and that I am His daughter. Within my consciousness, there were only the two of us: He, the Creator, and I, His creation. I was so happy! I blossomed and felt beautiful in the fire of this Love. My Father's Love healed my wounds one after another. I melted in this Love. We pervaded one another, and our spirits (my human spirit and His Divine one) mixed. This was the most beautiful communion in the world: God gave Himself through His enormous love, while I took it as if I deserved it.

Let me say more. This great, wonderful God and Creator Who has created me and Who loves me madly asks that I reciprocate His love. Is this not touching? How can one not love such a Father Who is God to boot? I was madly intoxicated with this presence, but "madly" is not the correct word here because I maintained my integrity: I did not melt and I lost nothing, yet I completely became one with God in Love!

All this took place in the spiritual sphere. My body was somewhere far away. I lost my vision and hearing; I moved to a completely different dimension. In my body, I only felt a fire devouring my chest. It was God Who burned away at my interior, which was soiled with sin, but He did not reproach me, nag at me, or complain. This was absolute and unconditional Love. I completely submerged myself in this ocean of Love, much like a child in the arms of its father. God was so personal that I could have tugged at His beard if He had one. However, to be precise, He had neither a beard nor arms.

This experience became increasingly intense. At a certain point, I made a mistake. For a fraction of a second, I became frightened or hesitated. I was afraid that I would not return. This contact became immediately interrupted. I suddenly felt an emotional and physical decline; it was as if I had been pushed into my armchair (in which I had been calmly sitting the whole time). It was over... I regained my vision and hearing, while the fire in my breast flowed to my entire body like a pleasant glow; meanwhile, I sat dumbfounded. However, I did not feel like I had been pushed away. [...] Perhaps God had decided that I could no longer take it and for this reason interrupted our encounter?

After a while, I returned to reality. I quickly returned to life as my face was filled with tears. I suddenly realized that the door to my office was not locked, and if someone had entered and seen me in this state, this would have been quite embarrassing. God sent an armed angel to protect me. What a loving God! He took everything into consideration."

CONTEMPORARY CULTURE'S DETACHMENT FROM GOD

Paganization, or treating one's Christianity as if its meaning only consisted of satisfying our religious needs, is a phenomenon that has accompanied the Church's history from the very beginning. Today, however, this phenomenon has intensified so greatly that there is probably no one who has not noticed it.

This is expressed by the feeling that our bonds with God should be neither very strict nor deep. The god of the pagans is *Deus remotus*, a god who is recognized, with whom one wants to have proper relations, and with whom one searches for deliverance under extreme circumstances but to whom man should not grow too close; in any case, it would be tactless to seek out friendship with him.

There are numerous consequences for this abandoning of God. As a result of the radical limitation of religious practices, man's relationship (and that of Christian societies) to God has radically changed. *Deus remotus* is the opposite of a loving and concerned God; in that case, one ceases to seriously believe in everything that constitutes the essence of the Christian faith. People are no longer so aware that God Himself seeks out man and that His revelation, the gifts of His grace, and His promise of salvation are the subject of the most real truth. Jesus Christ Himself is then no longer experienced as a Living and Loving Being. On the contrary, revealed truths are treated like mythological material that one treats in the way one would treat myths, i.e., in a selective and creative way to infer through their aid what we would never learn.

Likewise, a distant god cannot bring any commandments to people. Although it is remembered that God's commandments were universally recognized (even if they were not universally respected) in the past and even their correctness is recognized, we have learned to see them as merely a symptom of ancient human wisdom. Furthermore, many contemporary Christians likewise approach God's commandments in a selective and creative way. Because a distant god is not a loving god, we lose actual memory of the fact that the commandments are God's loving words addressed to His people.

Furthermore, the awareness that He is the Father of us all is fading, which leads to the revival of a tribal mentality. For us, it is less and less clear that another person is our neighbor, our brother or sister. It suffices to recall the moods of certain contemporary disputes and tensions within political parties, the tone of the radical statements of feminists, or certain conflicts between generations; it is clear from them that many of us do not consider every *homo sapiens* to be human. The painful sense of loneliness and being unneeded that many contemporary people experience is the next consequence of our forgetting that God is love and that without love everything becomes inhuman, cruel, and devoid of meaning.

Unfortunately, contemporary culture — journalism and literature, philosophy and art, law and politics — have led to significant consolidation of this attitude to the world in which God is distant, while ultimate truths are inaccessible to people. Meanwhile, good seems something relative and subject to our arbitrary decisions.

Naturally, if we believe in Christ and His Resurrection, we have no need to panic. The gates of hell will certainly neither defeat the

Church nor subordinate her. Here, I respond only to those tendencies in our culture that participate in the construction of a world that lives as if God did not exist. Yet contemporary culture also participates in the building of God's Kingdom in a very real way.

However, let us return to these paganizing tendencies in contemporary culture that are worth pondering at this moment. It is worth acknowledging and naming the carrot and stick strategy that we can observe with respect to the Church, the main teacher of the truth about the loving God Who seeks closeness with people. On the one hand, the Church is presented as an almost criminal organization whose history is solely one series of terrible crimes and that impedes human freedom and the development of thinking. On the other, the Church is "generously" promised a peaceful existence if she limits herself to her own ecological niche (which, furthermore, is increasingly small) and accepts the fact that today's world must be organized in a way as if God did not exist. These cultural figures and milieus cannot accept a Church that truly believes in Jesus Christ. We must give persistent testimony that the world belongs to God and the Gospel is God's gift to all of humanity.

At the same time, may God save us from our tendencies to isolate ourselves from the world, which wants to honor God only from afar. The early Christians succeeded in avoiding isolationist tendencies as well as the spirit of social sectarianism even during times of persecution. In fact, ancient Christian sources attest to contrary attitudes: the first Christians were fully convinced that they were an integral part of the society that persecutes them and that, being in that society a sign of contradiction and victim of persecution, they rendered a very important service to that society.

This sense of fully belonging to society as well as the desire to vibrantly co-create a common culture should be for us, contemporary Christians, more obvious and easier to attain than for the early Christians.

IF GOD IS NOT TREATED SERIOUSLY

Here, I would like to put forward the thesis that the true God cannot be legitimately accused of anything. When we criticize and accuse Him, we only bolster false conceptions of Him and weaken our own capacity to love Him and unconditionally entrust ourselves to Him.

In our age, it is increasingly fashionable to criticize and accuse God as if we were better and wiser than He, as if we were supra-gods of some sort. Many contemporary people seem to not understand the fact that when we try to correct God's commandments, criticize God's teaching, and accuse God of treating us poorly, we have reached a new acme of pride.

Such an attitude is the opposite of the veneration-filled disputes with God in which the righteous Job or the great leader of God's chosen people, Moses, engaged. Likewise, this has nothing in common with prayer, which sometimes takes the form of a struggle with God that makes man entrust himself to God even more (see Ezekiel 22:30; Colossians 2:1,4:12). For the record, it is worth noticing that the *Catechism of the Catholic Church* emphasizes on at least five occasions that in prayer we sometimes do not hesitate to "ask, beseech, plead, invoke, entreat, cry out, even 'struggle in prayer'" (2629; see 2573, 2584, 2592, 2725).

From where does the audacity to accuse God Himself come? We live in an age when many of us are addicted to accusing others, often unjustly and sometimes without any foundation. Someone who is suffering from such an addiction is not far from being angry with God: Where was God when a tour bus filled with pilgrims fell off a cliff? Does God not see my misfortune? Why does He not listen to my prayers asking for my son to stop drinking? I have been praying for a good wife for so long; does God not hear me? Why does God take a good person who could still live away from this earth, at the same time allowing many wicked people to live healthy and peaceful lives? If God loves us, then why is there so much evil in this world?

Such thinking begins with shaping one's image of God in one's own image and likeness. Before his election as pope, Benedict XVI wrote about this as follows: "We increasingly distort the face of the one God; for example, when we say that all gods are one and the same God. Every culture has its unique form of expression, and it is not a problem if it recognizes God as a person or as an impersonal being or if one calls Him Jupiter, Siva, or something else. It is increasingly evident that God is not treated seriously and that we have abandoned God and only look at the mirror in which we see our own reflection."

In his encyclical on the Holy Spirit (*Dominum et vivificantem*), John Paul II discussed this even more harshly: "Here we find ourselves at the very center of what could be called the 'anti-Word,' the 'anti-truth': For the truth about man becomes falsified: who man is and what are the impassable limits of his being and freedom. This 'anti-truth' is possible because at the same time there is a complete falsification of the truth about who God is. God the Creator is placed in a state of suspicion, indeed of accusation, in the mind of the creature. For the first time in human history there appears the perverse 'genius of suspicion.' He seeks to 'falsify' Good itself; the absolute Good" (37).

What is the practical conclusion of these explanations? If any of us happen to accuse God of something, this would mean that we are immersed in great darkness. None of us is better or wiser than the Lord God. If anything truly good and wise is in us, we have received it from God, Who Himself is Good, Love, and Wisdom. We may not understand Him, but if we begin to accuse Him of something, we immediately see that we are not accusing the true God but a false image of Him that we have created. The true God cannot be accused of anything.

Let us look at the terrible darkness in which man stays who would like to accuse God and who suspects Him of cruelty or indifference with respect to His creatures. Sometimes, our arrogance leads us to accuse God the Father of being cruel with respect to His own Son for having sent Him to die a horrible death on the cross. Instead of looking at the Lord Jesus' Christ and being horrified by what we can do in our sinfulness; instead of loving God for proving at Golgotha that love is stronger than Satan's force directed at Jesus; instead of loving the Eternal Father Who sent His own Son on such an inconceivably difficult mission to save us, in the darkness of our hearts we accuse Him and doubt His love.

In such darkness, man can no longer entrust himself to the Lord God. How can someone who doubts God's love; who suspects He does not love us at all; and who cannot believe with his entire heart that God is Love, entrust himself to God? The Lord Jesus once said: "And if the light in you is darkness, how great will the darkness be" (Matthew 6:23).

This brings to mind the advice of Cyprian Kamil Norwid when faced with the temptation to accuse God: "The god you have made yourselves is an idol in your own chest;" you must "call him to battle and crush him." The return to the Living, True, Loving, and, at the same time, Inconceivable God is possible only under this condition.

I Believe in the Creator of Heaven and Earth

THE BIBLICAL TEACHING ON THE CREATION OF THE WORLD IN LIGHT OF CERTAIN COSMOGONIES

In their cosmogonies, peoples and cultures provide an understanding of reality that is unique to themselves. Myths that present the beginning of the world and of man reveal to us the fundaments on which individual civilizations build their understanding of God, the world, man, and the hierarchy of values.

Here, we will ask how the Biblical truth of the creation of the world by God has influenced and continues to influence European thinking about what is most important to man. A question posed in this way virtually begs for an outline of a comparative background. Thus, we will first look at the three most important extra-Biblical responses to the question of the beginning of the world as well as the worldview hidden in it. In a simplified form, let us call them the Babylonian, Greek, and Hindu responses.

The Myth of Babylon

In the Babylonian cosmogonic myth, the world was created as a result of a struggle between the god Marduk and the female dragon Tiamat. The dragon was particularly angry as her spouse Abzu was first killed insidiously and without a struggle. However, Tiamat loses her confrontation with Marduk and is killed. Marduk cuts her in half "'like a dried fish;' one half became the vault of the sky, the other half the earth."[64] This myth also contains various details on how the slain dragon's various organs were used to create various elements of heaven and the earth.

The spiritual message of this myth seems clear: a world that has been created in this way has its demonic and cursed dimension. Although the creator-god was capable of alleviating and neutralizing this terrifying and destructive nature of the material he used to create the world, absurdity and destruction are integral and indelible dimensions of the reality that Marduk did not create but only submitted to his divine power. However, that senseless reality existed independent of him and was capable of creating increasingly terrifying monsters.

Babylonian theogony and anthropology are in harmony with their cosmogony. A god that engages in a cosmic struggle against the forces of chaos and destruction is, naturally, an integral part of this cosmos; in other words, he is not transcendent with respect to this cosmos. Thus, according to the Babylonian myth, Marduk does not exist from the beginning of time, nor was he always the greatest god. He was born as the last of the gods and demanded the highest

64. Mircea Eliade, *A History of Religious Ideas, Volume 1: From the Stone Age to the Eleusinian Mysteries*, trans. L, 51. Willard R. Trask (Chicago: University of Chicago Press, 2014), p. 71. The struggle between a god and a dragon also appears in many other mythologies. For example, in the Ugarit cosmogony the victory of Baal over the dragon Yam establishes the order and permanence of the seasons of the year (p. 154). In the *Rigveda*, the god Indra kills the dragon Vrtra, liberating the water, heaven, and earth, which had been trapped in this dragon (p. 204).

authority when his grandfather Anu, the god of the heavens, as well as his father, Ea, who cunningly killed Abzu, Tiamat's spouse, were afraid of engaging in battle with the dragon. Most likely, the struggle did not have to end with Marduk's victory. After his victory, Marduk became the founder and lord of the world; however, he is not its absolute ruler. Much like the Greek god Zeus,[65] he is subjected to an impersonal fate greater than himself.

Babylonian mythology's conceptions of humanity are as dreary as its notions of the nature of the world (at least that is how Mircea Eliade evaluates the message of the poem *Enūma Eliš*).[66] The creation of man was closely tied to Marduk's struggle against the dragon: after his victory, Marduk decided to punish those gods who supported her. Kingu proves to be the main culprit. The gods kill Kingu in order to punish him as well as to expiate their own sins. The god Ea — and, therefore, not Marduk, but one of the gods who have lost their leading position — has created man from the blood of the slain (according to one version of the myth, from clay stained by this blood).[67]

Likewise, the message of this myth seems clear: already at the moment of creation man is burdened with guilt for what has been committed in the higher world and is not responsible for his own evil. Thus, humanity's very nature is cursed. In such an anthropology, there is no room for being happy and proud of being a human. The conviction that people have been created like something akin to a garbage bin where the evil committed in heaven is thrown certainly was not conducive to becoming aware of one's human dignity; it

65. See Etienne Gilson, *God and Philosophy* (New Haven: Yale University Press, 2002), pp. 1-37.

66. See Mircea Eliade, *op. cit.*, p. 72.

67. See Norbert Lohfink, *Pieśń chwały* [org. *Das Siegeslied am Schilfmeer*], trans. Jan Doktor (Warszawa: PAX, 1982), p. 57n. The late Greek Orphic myth presents the creation of humanity in a similar way: "'[T]he crime of the Titans,' who dismembered and devoured the young god Dionysos, becomes the origin of man; from their ashes Zeus raised up the present race of men, who thus have a twofold inheritance from god and Titan" (Paul Ricœur, *The Symbolism of Evil*, trans. Emerson Buchanan, Boston: Beacon Press, 1967, pp. 209-210).

influenced an attitude of fatalism and made it difficult to discover the truth that as people we are capable of freedom and love.

The Greek Cosmogony

The Greek cosmogony contains a completely different worldview. It suffices to compare Marduk's struggle against Tiamat with that of Zeus against the Titans and Typhon. Whereas in the Babylonian myth the world was created from the body of a slain dragon, the Greek myth knows no moment of creating the world, which has always existed. Zeus struggles against the Titans and later Typhon because they personify chaos; he struggles against them in order to establish a just order. After victory, Zeus does not kill his opponents but sends them to Tartarus, whose only exit is guarded by hundred-armed giants.[68]

Although suspecting the world of having demonic dimensions is alien to the Greeks, they were nonetheless convinced that matter existing independent of God is eternal. The demiurgic act consisted in the fact that God has shaped shapeless and chaotic matter, introducing order. "From which Anaxagoras derived his theory, when he said that all things had been produced at the same time, and that then intellect had come and arranged them all in order."[69] Diogenes Laërtius, a historian of philosophy who lived in the third century before Christ, wrote: "Plato lays down two primary causes or principles of all things, God and matter, which he also calls mind,

68. See Henryk Podbielski, *Mit kosmogoniczny w "Teogonii" Hezjoda* (Lublin: KUL, 1978), pp. 165-171.

69. Diogenes Laërtius, *The Lives and Opinions of Eminent Philosophers*, XLI, trans. C. D. Yonge (London: G. Bell and Sons, Ltd., 1915), p. 7. See Plato, "Phaedrus," in: Plato, *Symposium*, trans. Benjamin Jowett, http://classics.mit.edu/Plato/symposium.html (accessed February 25, 2022).

and the cause. And he defines matter as something without shape and without limitation, and says that from it all concretions arise."[70]

Plato himself writes in his *Timaeus*: "God desired that all things should be good and nothing bad, so far as this was attainable. Wherefore also finding the whole visible sphere not at rest, but moving in an irregular and disorderly fashion, out of disorder he brought order, considering that this was in every way better than the other."[71] However, the divine creator is limited by the matter existing independently of him. He cannot increase or reduce the amount of matter; furthermore, he must subject himself to its chaos. Plato continues in his *Timaeus*: "[T]he creation is mixed, being made up of necessity and mind. Mind, the ruling power, persuaded necessity to bring the greater part of created things to perfection."

The irreducibility of this myth is expressed in the conviction that all the gods, even Zeus, are subjected to Moirai, or destiny.[72] However, as we can see, not only the mythical gods but even the Greek god de-mythologized by the great philosophers is neither omnipotent nor truly transcendent with respect to the world shaped by him. This even pertains to Aristotle's Unmoved Mover. However, this is logical: if matter exists independently of god, it is logically only partly subordinate to his authority.

What are the consequences of this for the Greek understanding of man? After all, man is not only a spiritual, but also a material being. In fact, the Greeks lack a clear notion of the creation of man. The Greek myths provide several different anthropogonies; however, none includes man's creation by God. The first man is molded from clay by some lower god, Hephaestus, or the Titan Prometheus, or the first people are born of stones that Deucalion and Pyrrha throw at

70. Diogenes Laërtius, *op. cit.*, pp. 137-138.

71. Plato, *Timaeus*, trans. Benjamin Jowett, Project Gutenberg, https://www.gutenberg.org/files/1572/1572-h/1572-h.htm#link2H_4_0010 (accessed February 25, 2022).

72. See Adam Krokiewicz, *Moralność Homera i etyka Hezjoda* (Warsaw: PAX, 1959), pp. 73-96.

one another. We also have at least two descriptions of the origins of people from the teeth of a dragon, while the laborious Myrmonids were simply formed out of ants.

These myths share the conviction that man does not come from God and therefore is not called to intimacy with God. Of course, the gods look after man, but man must accept the fact that his life is ephemeral and filled with anxiety. As perceptively presented by Mircea Eliade, such a pessimistic anthropology led the Greeks to discover a joy of life that was unique to imperfect human existence: "Wisdom begins with consciousness of the finiteness and precariousness of every human life. So the thing to do is to take advantage of everything that can be offered by the present: youth, health, physical pleasures, or occasions for displaying the virtues. [...] Since the gods had forced him not to go beyond his limits, man ended by realizing the perfection and, consequently, the sacrality of the human condition. [...] The joy of life discovered by the Greeks is not a profane type of enjoyment: it reveals the bliss of existing, of sharing — even fugitively — in the spontaneity of life and the majesty of the world."[73]

However, the Greek worldview was open to the notion that the most important aspect of man (namely, the soul, but only the soul) comes from God, and so only the soul is capable of everlasting unity with God.[74] This is why the ancient pagans were so opposed to the Christian truth of the resurrection of the body. Around 176 AD, Celsus fumed: "[F]or such a hope is simply one which might be cherished by worms. For what sort of human soul is that which would still long for a body that had been subject to corruption?"[75] To this, the Christians replied: "But surely it is not without honour for

73. Mircea Eliade, *op. cit.*, pp. 262-263.

74. See Plato, *Phædo.*

75. Origen, *Contra Celsum*, Book V (5:14), trans. Frederick Crombie, in: *Ante-Nicene Fathers*, Vol. 4, eds. Alexander Roberts, James Donaldson, and A. Cleveland Coxe (Buffalo, NY: Christian Literature Publishing Co., 1885); https://www.newadvent.org/fathers/04165.htm (accessed February 25, 2022).

the body to suffer for the sake of godliness, and to choose afflictions on account of virtue: the dishonourable thing would be for it to waste its powers in vicious indulgence."[76] This confrontation between two worldviews becomes even more understandable when we remember that one of the consequences of Greek anthropology was the belief that there are large spheres outside of human activity that are morally neutral.[77]

The Hindu Myth

Let me say a couple words about Hindu cosmogony. A particularly important source to the Hindu worldview is the myth of the creation of the world by the god Prajapati. In the beginning, there was neither existence nor non-existence, space nor sky, day nor night; there was only the god Prajapati. The world was created when Prajapati became aware of his loneliness. According to the great Indian scholar of religion Raymond Panikkar, Prajapati sinned in this reflection on himself. A flaw appeared in the divine unity, so Prajapati wanted for there to be others than himself.[78]

This desire inclined Prajapati to sacrifice himself so that there may be a multiplicity of beings. Thus, the earth and sky as well as celestial bodies and the various creatures of the earth were formed out of Prajapati's body. When all this was over, Prajapati felt terribly exhausted. He suddenly greatly wanted to become united with his creation. According to the myth, this would be manifested in his desire to engage in sexual contact with it. However, since creation had

76. *Ibid.*, (VIII, 50).

77. "And in general, all that which is termed the incontinence of pleasure and is deemed a reproach under the idea that the wicked voluntarily do wrong is not justly a matter for reproach. For no man is voluntarily bad" (Plato, *Timaeus*).

78. See Raymond Panikkar, *La faute originante ou l'immolation creatrice. Le mythe de Prajapati,* [in:] *Le mythe de la peine* (Aubier: Editions Montaigne, 1967), pp. 65-100. With respect to this statement, see p. 73.

begun to exist independently, it was attached to its distinctiveness and feared unity with the creator and even fled from him. This sinful flight from the creator is somehow tied to the fact that the mere existence of creation was the result of sin; namely, it came from that of Prajapati, who began to reflect on his loneliness. If the existence of creation is a sin of both the creator and his creation, then this sin can only be overcome by creation renouncing its own distinctiveness and a return to unity.

The Hindu worldview built around such assumptions does not know a clear distinction between the Creator and creation. In a sense, the entire world is divine, while divinity is a measure of reality. Independent existence is meaningful only to the degree to which a return to the sources of existence takes place in it. Everything that leads to dispersion or that consolidates it is sinful. By becoming dispersed, a being loses its divinity and, therefore, reality. At the same time, all beings, including the gods, are burdened with the sin of dispersion.

It is worth noting that in European culture there likewise appeared intuitions that there was oneness in the beginning. One of the oldest Greek sages known to us by name, Musaeus, said: "There was a time when all the present world/Uprose at once."[79] The emanationism of Plotinus, a philosopher who lived in the third century AD, is particularly well-known. According to him, god's perfection must have spilled outside him and been expressed in the creation of other beings.[80]

79. Diogenes Laërtius, *op. cit.*, p. 6.

80. "The first Principle may indeed be conceived of as a spring (of water) which is its own origin, and which pours its water into many streams without itself becoming exhausted by what it yields, or even without running low, because the streams that it forms, before flowing away each in its own direction, and while knowing which direction it is to follow, yet mingles its waters with the spring." (Plotinus, *Third Ennead*, Book Eight, 10, p. 547; [in:] Plotinus, *Plotinos: Complete Works, v. 2 In Chronological Order, Grouped in Four Periods*, trans. Kenneth Sylvan Guthrie, Project Gutenberg, https://www.gutenberg.org/files/42931/42931-h/42931-h.htm#b_30, accessed March 4, 2022).

The Creation of the World According to the Biblical Description

Let us take a look at the Biblical description of creation. There was something pessimistic in all three cosmogonies described at the beginning of this chapter. According to the Babylonian myth, in the beginning there were hostile and actives forces of destruction symbolized by the dragon Marduk succeeded in defeating. The Greeks, meanwhile, believed that at the beginning there was chaotic and meaningless pre-matter that the demiurge encompassed with his thought and the will of the greatest artist. Finally, according to the Hindu myth at the beginning there was the sin of god himself, who chose what was worse over what was better.

As Mircea Eliade has insightfully noted, "there is a symmetry between the creation of man and the origin of the world."[81] Indeed, all three cosmogonies see something pessimistic in the creation of man. According to the Babylonians, man was created as a sinner burdened by sins committed in the world of the gods. Meanwhile, the Greeks, who had so authentically discovered the joy of life, see man as someone who in his nature is far removed from the gods and therefore devoid of ultimate meaning. Finally, according to the myth of the *Rigveda,* man, like any other creature, was created out of the sin of god himself and therefore possesses an inherent impulse to flee his creator. Furthermore, the god in these three cosmogonies is not truly transcendent with respect to the world. He is a part of it in one sense or another and is subjected to the laws of destiny, while he is forced by some circumstances to create the world.

In all three of these aspects, the Biblical description of creation radically departs from the three cosmogonies presented above. To once again quote Eliade, in the Biblical description there is "no spectacular exploit (combat of the Tiamat-Marduk type), no

81. Mircea Eliade, *op. cit.*, p. 73.

pessimistic element."[82] Most importantly, only the Biblical description speaks of creation in the strict sense of the word. According to the Bible, the Creator completely and fully grants the world creation: He uses no material that exists independent of Him, nor does the act of Creation have anything in common with giving birth, in which the being that gives birth gives something of its own substance to what is being born. In this case, the act of creation is making beings out of nothing; in other words, neither out of oneself nor out of previously existing matter.

It is quite likely that the author of the Biblical description of creation consciously distanced himself from both the Babylonian myth and the Greek beliefs. The first sentence of the Book of Genesis is: "In the beginning, when God created the heavens and the earth—and the earth was without form or shape..." Thus, existence "without form or shape," the equivalent of Greek chaos, was created by God. Eliade also notes that "the primordial ocean is called in Hebrew *tehom*, a word etymologically closely connected with the Babylonian *tiaimat*."[83]

The author's distancing himself from the Babylonian myth is especially evident in the description of the creation of man: God created man out of the clay of the earth, and there can be no talk of man inheriting sin that had been committed in the higher world. Man was created as someone essentially good; we became sinners only later, out of our own fault. Thus, the Biblical description of creation concludes with: "God looked at everything He had made, and found it very good" (Genesis 1:31).

There remains the question of why God decided to undergo the act of creation. The Babylonian Marduk was inclined towards the cosmogonic act because of the prevailing evil that he decided to conquer. The Greek demiurge was compelled to act because of

82. *Ibid.*, p. 164.
83. *Ibid.*, p. 163.

the limitlessness of pre-matter, which needed to become filled with meaning. Finally, Prajapati became aware of his loneliness. What, according to the Bible, inclined God to create the world? There is no other reason than that God is love and wants to give love.

According to research on the chronology of Biblical texts, Israel's faith began with awareness of God's redemptive presence among His people; Israel discovered the truth of creation only from that perspective. In this way, God's act of creation appeared in Israel's consciousness as the first gift of God's love, after which it would receive subsequent gifts.[84] In light of this observation, we can understand the prophets' frequent reference to God's creative power in the texts that proclaim the promise of God's redemptive intervention in favor of His oppressed people.[85] Likewise, the New Testament frequently emphasizes that the Son of God Who wants to fix the world with His love is the same One through Whom the world has been created.[86]

We have already discussed what is most important with respect to the meaning of the Biblical teaching on creation to European culture. Namely, the Biblical cosmogony has determined for us, Europeans, the paradigms of thinking about God, the world, and man. Even when Europeans reject God's existence, the God of the Europeans is a loving God and at the same time omnipotent in every meaning of this world and transcendent with respect to the world. The inability to reconcile this truth about God with everyday reality is sometimes the cause of the rejection of God only in the spiritual milieu that has been shaped by the Bible.

84. See Gerhard von Rad, *Teologia Starego Testamentu,* trans. Bogusław Widła (Warszawa: PAX, 1986), pp. 116-118; P. Gisel, *Creation et eschatologie* [in:] *Initiation a la practique de la theologie,* eds. B. Lauret and F.Refoule, Paris 1983, Vol. 3, pp. 615-624.

85. For example: Isaiah 40:12:29, 44:24-28; Jeremiah 10:11-16; Amos 5:6-9.

86. See John 1:1-3; 1 Corinthians 8:6; Colossians 1:16-20; Hebrews 1:2n. See Hans Urs von Balthasar, *Trójca Święta a stworzenie,* w zbiorze *Kosmos i człowiek* (Poznań: Pallottinum, 1989), pp. 22-30.

Furthermore, contemporary Europe is filled with the strong conviction that the world is initially good while its evil is something that came later. The conviction that once we completely separate it from the entirety of Biblical revelation becomes a source of tendencies to implement pseudo-optimistic utopias that are dangerous to man and his culture. In its essence, the conviction that the world is good and that evil is at least partly removable, and also that the terrible soul-destroying force can be taken away from the evil that overcomes us, seems to be one of the cornerstones of European culture.

Faith in God, Whom absolutely nothing forced into the act of creation and Who undertook this act in complete freedom, seems to be the cultural cause of the fact that our Europe has never lacked (and hopefully, never will lack) people who place the universal over the individual, and for whom the spiritual is more important than the material while freedom is more powerful and significant than necessity.[87] This triple primacy — that of the individual over the universal, spirit over matter, and freedom over necessity — also results from the Biblical conception of man, the Biblical description of creation, and man's fall and redemption.

87. See Joseph Ratzinger, *Introduction to Christianity*, trans. Michael J. Miller (San Francisco: Ignatius Press, 2004).

NATURE AS A GIFT FROM GOD

Nature is a great source of usable goods. Furthermore, close contact with nature is important to our health. Above all, as St. John Paul II has said, "nature is given to man as a subject of admiration and contemplation." Such an approach, however, has to be taught; it is inaccessible to people whose interior is filled with noise, egotism, and other lousy things.

I once saw how a boy who was approximately a year and a half old was incapable of learning to look through a window. He was on a train with his mommy who was trying to interest him in what was happening outside the window. "Look, a cow!" she said and pointed. The boy dully looked at the window and could in no way understand that he had to look through the window, not at it.

Adults sometimes have a similar blockade with respect to nature. Then, it seems to us that forests, for example, exist solely to protect the landscape from desertification, provide wood to make furniture, and maybe to allow us to pick mushrooms and berries as well. Naturally, such blessings of the forest should not be ignored. Yet forests — and the entirety of nature in general — have a greater purpose.

They exist to teach us to enjoy life and to be able to appreciate the fact that our world can be beautiful and colorful and benevolent to us people. A man who knows how to admire and contemplate nature will easily experience the feeling that Jan Kochanowski once expressed:

> Wherever the sun rises and sets every day
> May the world praise its Lord, come what may.

Notice, however, that if the world is like a window through which our spirit can arrive at many wonderful things, then we must take care that this "window" is as clean as possible.

Someone once beautifully noticed that God cares deeply and fully for every creature, even the smallest one. He cares for His child much more than any loving mother; for He provides existence to all His creatures, beginning with the most wonderful angel and including every mosquito and grain of sand. Furthermore, God looks after the world down to the lowest pits of hell, thus even those creatures that reject Him and do not want Him.

We can imitate this wonderful Divine trait. The Lord Jesus even gave us the commandment to love our enemies and persecutors. "Bless those who persecute you! Bless them, and do not curse them!" The Apostle Paul translated this commandment into practical language. It seems very unlikely that anyone could act in such a way without first realizing that such generosity is a trait of God with respect to us who sometimes become His enemies because of our sins.

Meanwhile, with respect to the entire world of nature the imitation of God consists of cultivating within oneself kindness and protectiveness with respect to animals and everything that moves; with respect to trees and plans, rivers and hills, and everything that constitutes our natural environment. Psalm 148 demands: "Praise the Lord from the earth [...] Mountains and all hills, fruit trees and all cedars; Animals wild and tame, creatures that crawl and birds that fly" (7-10).

We, Poles, have numerous wonderfully "ecological" Church hymns. It suffices to recall Christmas carols according to which "the elements sings praise of God" and which claims that "all creation is joyful" with regards to Jesus' birth, summoning the ox and the donkey as well as different kinds of singing birds as its witnesses. Meanwhile, on the days we recall the Lord's Passion "the sun and stars faint/becoming filled with mourning," while in a Marian hymn all of God's most wonderful creation is called to rejoice at the exaltation of Mary: "Praise, flower-filled meadows, green valleys, and hills,/Praise, shadowy woodlets and snaking brooks. [...] May the brooks praise with grateful humming, and the birds with their sweet chirping/And everything that lives and feels — may they all praise Mary along with us."

Those who wrote such hymns and prayed using them must have known that such beautiful and benevolent nature is God's gift to us and that man should imitate God in embracing what is lesser and weaker than we.

It just so happens that arrogance with respect to nature appeared in our European culture along with de-Christianization. People who have grown accustomed to listening to the Bible as the Word of God know that we are to subjugate the earth. Yes, we can make use of it; in fact, we must. Although we are called to subjugate it, we should imitate the Lord Almighty, Whose domination consists of generosity towards His creatures and care for them, as best as we can.

The manner of treating nature as if it were our enemy that must be conquered, subordinated, and tamed in order to use it and force it to serve us appeared only in a de-Christianized Europe. In the classrooms in the 1950s, we watched films about how the brave Soviet man forced the Siberian rivers to flow in the opposite direction. I also remember a certain very arrogant poem that juxtaposed marvelously smoking factory chimneys with barren and useless church steeples. The mentality that created such films and poems was no longer capable of seeing nature as a witness to God's goodness and wondrousness; it looked at it mostly through the prism of utility. Such a mentality was also incapable of making note of its responsibility for the devastation of nature.

It should be noted, however, that just as a terrorist can sometimes become an extreme pacifist, a mentality marked by arrogance towards nature can before our very eyes take on the form of extreme, ostentatious, and even idolatrous respect.

Thus, we should never forget that the Creator Who embraces even His flimsiest creatures with approval and benevolence likewise loves all people, including those who are most deeply lost and even those who hate Him. Therefore, we should not believe defenders of nature whose love for nature is permeated with hatred for any people. They are the heirs to the communists who are seeking out new means of implementing the disgraced ideal of class struggle.

THE "CRUELTY" OF NATURE

Among Polish thinkers, Karol Ludwik Koniński and Czesław Miłosz were perhaps most disturbed by the suffering that characterizes nature. Animals kill and eat one another and die; because they lack free will, they are directed by instinct. Likewise, man often has no choice and must kill pests, or kill to gain nourishment; sometimes, he unwittingly kills small or microscopic beings by his own physical weight. How can this be reconciled with the statement at the beginning of Genesis that everything that God created was good?

What I will say at the beginning is neither an accusation nor a polemic but merely an observation. I would like to notice that people disturbed by this "cruelty" of nature do not deny its beauty, nor are they opposed to saving endangered species of predatory animals. It is only difficult for them to deal with the question of why there is so much struggle for survival and devouring of one another beneath the surface of the often stunning beauty of our forests and rivers, fields and lakes.

The Biblical man did not have this problem, even though he knew all too well that animals eat one another, which is mentioned many times in Sacred Scripture. Furthermore, there are many reasons to think that the Biblical man responded to the beauty of nature differently than we. In such situations, we tend to exclaim: "How beautiful it is here!" Or: "How wonderfully God has created this!" When the Biblical man was impressed with nature's beauty, he sensed that these trees and flowers, animals and birds sing a song of praise to their Creator.

Let us look at Psalm 148 or the Song of the Three Holy Children in the Book of Daniel (Daniel 3:51-90). After reading these passages, St. Irenaeus' statement that God's first revelation before speaking through His Son was the creation of the world no longer seems so mysterious. In a sense, the Biblical man interpreted the beauty of nature as the beauty of the Creator Himself. "Lord, my God, You are great indeed! You are clothed with majesty and splendor, robed in light as with a cloak." These are the opening words of Psalm 104, which is devoted to contemplation of God's creative work.

During this contemplation, the Psalmist is also impressed with the fact that the Creator is capable of feeding this multitude of creatures: "Young lions roar for prey; they seek their food from God." We will devote more attention to this verse in a moment, but first let us continue reading: "[T]he earth is full of Your creatures. There is the sea, great and wide! It teems with countless beings, living things both large and small. [...] All of these look to you to give them food in due time" (Psalm 104:21-27).

Elsewhere, we read that God "gives bread to all flesh, for His mercy endures forever" (Psalm 136:25; see 145:15; 147:9). "Do you hunt the prey for the lion or appease the hunger of young lions?" God rhetorically asks Job: "Who provides nourishment for the raven when its young cry out to God, wandering about without food?" (Job 38:39-41).

In a word, what is sometimes a problem to today's man was a subject of admiration for his Biblical counterpart. He was thrilled by both the deer grazing in the thickets of the desert and the lioness looking at it, thinking about how to satiate itself and feed its young. We do not know if he had any clue as to what our biology teachers tell us: that predators positively influence the health of the animals they hunt because they capture mostly weak and sick specimens, thus engaging in a form of a selection that is beneficial to the species.

We know, however, that when the Biblical man was impressed with the fact that God was capable of feeding all His creatures, he had a strictly designated boundary his admiration could not transcend. Namely, he knew that in no way could the relationship between predators and their prey be applied to interpersonal relations. Predators act in accordance with their nature. Meanwhile, one who is a predator with respect to his neighbor is a scoundrel because we, people, have been created in God's image, and the ultimate law governing our lives should be love.

"Lord my God, in You I trusted; save me; rescue me from all who pursue me," says one of many such Biblical prayers. "Lest someone maul me like a lion, tear my soul apart with no one to deliver" (Psalm 7:2-3). Three pages later, the Psalmist complains that the scoundrels "lurk in ambush like lions in a thicket, hide there to trap the poor, snare them and close the net" (Psalm 10:9). The Apostle Paul deplored the lack of love for neighbor even among Christians: "But if you go on biting and devouring one another, beware that you are not consumed by one another" (Galatians 5:15).

There have been predators among people since the time of Cain. Likewise, for centuries human mendacity has tried to demonstrate that cruelty and injustice towards the weak is neither cruel nor unjust. However, it was only after the appearance of the doctrine that man is one of many animal species and nothing more that there appeared people who openly praised the struggle for survival and saw harshness towards the weak as a factor of social progress. "It is not the wolf's fault that it likes hares," Bismarck said to justify his anti-Polish policies. Friedrich Nietzsche taught that morality, especially the virtue of mercy, was invented by the weak in order to force the strong to be burdened with the former's cowardice and passivity.

The blatant appearance of slogans of the social Darwinism (which had little in common with the noble figure of Charles Darwin himself) in European culture also led to various polemical reactions.

Some, like Max Scheler, argued that disdain for the weak would destroy the fundaments of human culture. Others, like Peter Kropotkin, noted that the struggle for survival was just one of many principles that govern the world of animals and that the principle of solidarity with the weak and helping those members of one's species who are in particular need was equally important in this world.

There also appeared thinkers who — without necessarily being aware of the fact that this was their reaction to social Darwinism — began to be dramatically concerned about the mere fact of the struggle for survival among plants and animals. In Poland, the most outstanding representative of this current was Karol Ludwik Koniński. He was literally terrified by this devouring of one another throughout the biological world. A very spiritually and morally sensitive person, he believed that the honor of being a human is above all the vocation to cease to be the devourer of others and become a defender of everything that is weak, threatened, and endangered.

When we read Koniński's writings on this topic, even if we disagree with them we do not have a need for patronizing comments. I also trust that what I write in a moment — and I shall be radically critical of the anxieties of this great thinker — will not be a patronizing form of patting him on the back, either. I will limit myself to formulating three or four observations.

First, the anxiety that nature is a "great kitchen" where everyone devours everyone results primarily from anthropomorphizing creatures that are not human and whose otherness with respect to us should be noted. If an insect — to use a clichéd example — can have its abdomen eaten by a specimen of a hostile species yet does not cease to copulate with a female, we should in no way speak of suffering.

Yet at least birds and mammals clearly suffer at the hands of their attackers; their entire behavior attests to this. Of course, this is true, and for us this results in the moral necessity to take into account their sensitivity to pain. On the other hand, if calves are capable of walking almost immediately after being born and roosters can run for half a minute after their heads are chopped off, we can infer that the relationship of their brains to the rest of their bodies has a different structure than in people, which likely has a major impact on the quality of the pain they feel.

Someone once tried to convince me that the brain of a mouse caught by a cat secretes some hallucinogenic substance. I am not a biologist, so I do not know if this is true. However, I have no reason to not believe Livingstone, the famous discoverer of the African interior, who wrote in his memoirs that when a lion jumped at him (at the very last moment, it was shot by his travel companion), he felt no fear but instead was overcome with "a sweet readiness to be eaten by that lion."

In any case, the caution against anthropomorphizing the pain of animals seems totally rational.

Second, Koniński and Miłosz were great moralists, and they did not overwhelm us with images of one great cycle of devouring one another in order to promote social Darwinist attitudes. On the contrary, they call us to transcend the biological mechanisms to which we are subjected because of our belonging to one of the species of the animal kingdom; they call us to contrary, even altruistic (and, if necessary, heroic) attitudes. I think that this kind of moralism is capable of reaching even those who reject the ancient wisdom that although man has much in common with the beasts, he is nonetheless a unique creature.

But what if this ancient wisdom — which many today do not appreciate, or even reject — expresses the truth about man? In such a case, an incomparably more correct attitude is to not be surprised at predators or criticize the Creator for allowing predators to exist in His world but instead to praise Him for the fact that He created man — not sheep or wolf but precisely man — for love and that in light of this no man, none of us, can realize his vocation in any way other than through selfless love.

The third comment will be related to the question of whether a Christian can agree — as Czesław Miłosz suggested — that Satan participated in the work of creation and if we are allowed to introduce some Manichean component into our image of God. I would like to mention that according to the Manichean doctrine the kingdom of the spirit has become victim to an invasion of forces of darkness that do not come from the good God and that the work of these forces is the material dimension of reality.

Furthermore, in antiquity there were various gnostic systems that tried to explain the imperfection of our world as having been created not by God but by some bunglers inferior to Him.

Both the Manicheans and the Gnostics had one favorite method of convincing others of the truth of their doctrines. It consisted of convincing their interlocutors that some unpleasant creatures or phenomena — be they flies, lice, vipers, or jackals; extreme cold or scorching heat — are not God's creation. This propaganda technique was frequently exposed by St. Augustine. Here is one of his descriptions:

"Some one or other was suffering annoyance from flies; a Manichæan found him in his trouble, and when he said that he could not bear flies, and hated them exceedingly, immediately the Manichæan said, 'Who made them?' And since he was suffering from annoyance, and hated them, he dared not say, 'God made them,' though he was a Catholic. The other immediately added, 'If God did not make them, who made them?' 'Truly,' replied the Catholic, 'I believe the devil made them.' And the other immediately said, 'If the devil made the fly, as I see you allow, because you understand the matter well, who made the bee, which is a little larger than the fly?' The Catholic dared not say that God made the bee and not the fly, for the case was much the same. From the bee he led him to the locust; from the locust to the lizard; from the lizard to the bird; from the bird to the sheep; from the sheep to the cow; from that to the elephant, and at last to man; and persuaded a man that man was not made by God. Thus the miserable man, being troubled with the flies, became himself a fly, and the property of the devil."[88]

In light of the numerous uncertainties as to whether the entire world was truly created by God, Christians have firmly professed their faith that not only the entire world is God's work but also that everything created by God is good. Meanwhile, Christians responded to the accusation that lice and vipers are not good by claiming that what is bad for man has its good significance in the entirety of creation; furthermore, they can at times be beneficial even to man. I will not go into details, although this problem is truly intriguing; I was once the supervisor of an excellent M.A. thesis on this topic.

In conclusion, I have to explain the famous prophecy that in the times of the Messiah "the wolf shall be a guest of the lamb, and the leopard shall lie down with the young goat; the calf and the young lion shall browse together" (Isaiah 11:6; see 65:25). The Lord Jesus later referred to this prophecy when He told His disciples: "I am sending you like lambs among wolves" (Luke 10:3). Indeed, many of these wolves softened (see, for example Acts 2:37-38); even one particularly brutal wolf, Saul of Tarsus, became particularly mild. One contemporary Biblical scholar is undoubtedly right that these images from the Book of Isaiah "should not be understood in a literal sense, as the inversion of the means of gaining nourishment by the animals under discussion but in the sense of a prophecy of widespread peace."[89]

Indeed, the Church Fathers sometimes conjectured that our sin can negatively influence the beasts. St. Theophilus of Antioch wrote: "For when man transgressed, they also transgressed with him. For as, if the master of the house himself acts rightly, the domestics also of necessity conduct themselves well; but if the master sins, the servants

88. St. Augustine, "Tractate 1," [in:] *Nicene and Post-Nicene Fathers, First Series*, trans. John Gibb, Philip Schaff, ed. Buffalo, NY: Christian Literature Publishing Co., 1888; New Advent, https://www.newadvent.org/fathers/1701001.htm (accessed March 4, 2022).

89. Lech Stachowiak, *Księga Izajasza* (Poznań: Pallottinum, 1996), Vol. 1, p. 263.

also sin with him; so in like manner it came to pass, that in the case of man's sin, he being master, all that was subject to him sinned with him. When, therefore, man again shall have made his way back to his natural condition, and no longer does evil, those also shall be restored to their original gentleness" (*To Autolycus*, Book II, Chapter 17). This is why dogs were terrible beasts in concentration camps, yet they can also do a wonderful job of aiding the blind.

Personally, when I think about the influence of our sin on the predation of animals, I try to adhere to the sober teaching of St. Thomas Aquinas: "In the opinion of some, those animals which now are fierce and kill others, would, in that state, have been tame, not only in regard to man, but also in regard to other animals. But this is quite unreasonable. For the nature of animals was not changed by man's sin, as if those whose nature now it is to devour the flesh of others, would then have lived on herbs, as the lion and falcon. Nor does Bede's gloss on Genesis 1:30, say that trees and herbs were given as food to all animals and birds, but to some. Thus there would have been a natural antipathy between some animals. They would not, however, on this account have been excepted from the mastership of man: as neither at present are they for that reason excepted from the mastership of God, Whose Providence has ordained all this."[90]

90. Thomas Aquinas, *Summa Theologica,* I, q.96, a.1, ad.2, https://www.newadvent.org/summa/1096.htm (accessed January 16, 2023).

INVISIBLE CREATION

The Limitlessness of God's Creation

Regardless of the direction of reality in which we look, its limits are unattainable to us. Looking into the distance, we have every reason to believe that although the most modern telescopes can reach unfathomably far objects, cosmic spaces that are in general inaccessible at this moment of human observation exist outside the scope of such telescopes. Looking into the depths and the smallest amount of matter we are increasingly aware that the moment when we are able to say that we know everything about the structure of matter is infinitely retreating. In this way, even the material world attests to its origins in the infinite God.

Likewise, the fact that man is the only creature on this earth that is capable of recognizing this limitlessness of the cosmos certainly means something. Are we allowed to see this as a sign that we have been created for the infinite God and that, as the Second Vatican Council teaches, man is the only creature on earth that God wanted for Himself?

Recently, we have become so focused on the limitlessness of matter that our interest in the limitlessness of the spiritual world has declined. Indeed, we are aware of our incapacity to completely encompass human history, human thought, or even the human psyche.

Is the world of the spirit limited to man? It is worth realizing that although we know about angels thanks to God's revelation, the most illustrious philosophers of antiquity were convinced of their existence. It was only when translating St. Thomas' *Treatise on Separate Substances* that I appreciated the degree to which the problem of intermediate beings — superior to man yet created by and dependent on God — occupied the minds of Plato, Aristotle, and the other fathers of philosophy.

Christ Is the "Space" of Our Communion with the Angels

Naturally, the essence of the truth about the angels is its religious dimension. I will begin my presentation of this truth with an absolutely central place to the Christian faith; i.e., the participation of the angels in the mystery of the Incarnation and Redemption, which is meticulously emphasized in the Gospels. It is neither a coincidence nor an insignificant detail that it was an angel that announced to us the most wonderful news anyone on this earth had ever heard: that the Son of God would become a man. We hear angels singing of God's glory and peace to His people on Christmas Eve. They appear at the beginning of Christ's public activity and in Gethsemane, the tomb of the Resurrected, and the day of the Ascension.

We will try to look at the meaning of this non-coincidental presence of the angels beside the Son of God, Who has redeemed the human race. Does this not attest to the fact that the Redemption is not a particular matter between God and the inhabitants of the earth but in a mysterious way concerns the entirety of creation? The Old Testament already spoke of the two directions of our unity with the world of the angels, spiritual creatures that are incomparably more perfect than we. The Gospels unambiguously demonstrate that Christ is the center and space of this community with the angels.

Let us look at these two directions of the angels' solidarity with the lost human race. This is most concisely symbolized by the stairway that Jacob saw in his dream: "Then he had a dream: a stairway rested on the ground, with its top reaching to the heavens; and God's angels were going up and down on it" (Genesis 28:12). Angels moving away from us and upwards naturally symbolize the mighty benevolence that pulls us closer to God and that flows from this inconceivable world. Sacred Scripture presents this kindness as angels that carry our prayers and sacrifices to God (Tobit 12:12; Revelation 5:8; 8:3) or as our participation in the perpetual liturgy celebrated by the angels.

The Psalmist calls: "In the presence of the angels to you I sing" (Psalm 138:1). Meanwhile, in Revelation we read: "I looked again and heard the voices of many angels who surrounded the throne and the living creatures and the elders. They were countless in number, and they cried out in a loud voice: 'Worthy is the Lamb that was slain to receive power and riches, wisdom and strength, honor and glory and blessing'" (5:11-12; see 7:11nn). This is why artists often imagined the angels wearing liturgical vestments.

In the image of Jacob's ladder, we likewise see angels that descend from God to us to be our companions, guides, and the defenders in our difficult and dangerous journey. This ministry of the angels has been presented most visually in the Book of Tobit. In the Acts of the Apostles, we read twice about an angel that leads God's friends out of prison. In the story of the conversion of a courtier of the queen of the Ethiopians, we learn that the angel of God can show the way to those who preach the Gospel. The Lord Jesus spoke most generally about the angels accompanying humans: Even the least among us are so dear to God that they have their own angels that "always look into the face of My Father, Who is in heaven." We read in the Epistle to the Hebrews 1:14: "Are they not all ministering spirits sent to serve, for the sake of those who are to inherit salvation?"

How Can We Make the Truth About Angels a Living One?

For many contemporary Christians, the truth about angels smacks of mythology. It is worth noting that this is not a new notion. The Sadducees, who claimed that "there is no resurrection or angels or spirits" (Acts 23:8), thought the same. Personally, I believe that we share something with the Sadducees not only when we directly reject the truth about the existence of the angels but when we virtually do not think about it at all. In the poem *Nie umiem z aniołami* ("I Don't Know How to Deal with Angels") Kazimiera Iłłakowiczówna perfectly expresses the usual problems that this truth poses to contemporary Christians. What should we do? How can we make the truth about angels a living one?

The answer is very simple. It suffices to grow closer to Christ, Who is — let us say this once more — the center and space of our community with the angels. When we grow closer to Christ, we grow closer to His friends and to a greater degree enter "the heavenly Jerusalem, and countless angels in festal gathering, and the assembly of the firstborn enrolled in heaven" (Hebrews 12:22-23). Canto 28 of *Paradiso* in the *Divine Comedy* presents God as a Fire surrounded by nine luminous circles, or nine choirs of angels. Angels are so unimaginably wonderful, deserve our love, and should be our mighty helpers because they are inextricably tied to God and Christ. The Church Fathers compared the angels to rays in God's Sun.

It would be a slight to the angels if we tried to venerate them in a way that would distract our religious focus and make it difficult for our entire selves to turn towards God. "Let no one disqualify you, delighting in self-abasement and worship of angels" (Colossians 2:18). When both Tobits bowed down before an angel, it tried to turn their entire attention to God, Who alone is worthy of praise. Analogously, an angel prohibits the author of Revelation from bowing before it: "Don't! I am a fellow servant of yours and of your brothers the prophets and of those who keep the message of this book. Worship God" (22:9).

The Testimony of the Seers at Fatima on Their Encounter with Angels

True reverence of angels brings us closer to God and is simultaneously a sign of His closeness. In this regard, the testimony of the children of Fatima about their encounter with an angel that preceded the apparition of the Virgin Mary is very moving: "The supernatural atmosphere which enveloped us was so intense, that we were for a long time scarcely aware of our own existence, remaining in the same posture in which he had left us, and continually repeating the same prayer. The presence of God made itself to be felt so intimately and so intensely that we did not even venture to speak to one another. Next day, we were still immersed in this spiritual atmosphere, which only gradually began to disappear."[91]

The results of this encounter were as follows: "From the time that the mysterious light illuminated their souls, they look at the world with different eyes. After seeing angels, the hills and forests, valleys, the sun, people, and sheep look different. The children felt like a traveler returning from afar to whom everything seems different. The angel took them to a land about which they had only had a vague idea. Now, their conception of God has become incomparably greater, as has their repulsion to sin."[92]

Herein rests the meaning of the search for friendly intimacy with the angels: they help us to grow closer to God and bring us farther

91. *Fátima in Lucia's own words: sister Lucia's memoirs*, ed. Fr. L. Kondor (Fatima: Secretariado dos Pastorinhos, 1998), p. 159.

92. In all subsequent cases, where the source of the quotation could not be determined, a decision was made in consultation with the Author not to include a footnote (editor's note).

away from evil. Their absence from our religious life can (although not necessarily must) be a sign of our departure from God. St. Basil once said: "The [guardian] angel will not retreat from us unless we drive him away by our evil deeds. As the smoke drives bees away, and stench the doves, even so, our stinking sin drives away from us the angel who protects our life."[93]

The Benevolence and Power of Angels

Not only poetry but also the most official teaching of the faith speaks of the possibility of becoming similar to angels. Pope St. Gregory the Great said: "You also can deserve to be given this grand title [of an angel]. For each one of you to the extent that you are sufficient, to the extent that you have received the grace of divine aspiration, if you call your neighbor back from wickedness, if he cares to be called upon to do good, if you announce the eternal kingdom or punishment of the errant, not sparing words of holy admonition, you surely are an angel."[94]

Above all, however, we associate angels with a gesture of embracing a weak and helpless or suffering person. This association has become entrenched in language through such phrases as "angelic patience" or saying that a good person is an angel. Let us notice, however, that angelic patience greatly differs from that of people; it is much stronger. Let us take as an example a famous scene from the Book of Daniel: "But the angel of the Lord went down into the furnace with Azariah and his companions, drove the fiery flames out of the furnace, and made the inside of the furnace as though a dew-laden

93. St. Basil the Great, *Homiliae super Psalmos (Homily 16 — On Psalm 33[34])* 33,5 (PG 29,364AC)

94. Sancti Gregorii I Magni Romani Pontificis XL Homiliarum in Evangelia, Libri Duo, Homilia VI.6, http://www.documentacatholicaomnia.eu/01p/0590-0604,_SS_Gregorius_I_Magnus,_XL_Homiliarum_in_Evangelia_Liber_Primus,_LT.pdf (accessed January 16, 2023).

breeze were blowing through it. The fire in no way touched them or caused them pain or harm" (Daniel 3:49-50). It is immediately evident that this angel greatly differs from the Good Samaritan. He is not subjected to the limitations of our human condition.

The might of the angels not only supports God's friends; it is dangerous to evil. The Bible says this so frequently that it is difficult to understand why the truth about the angels as powerful enemies of evil is almost entirely absent from our consciousness. Let us recall the main episodes that make up this tradition. It begins with the cherubim with fiery swords standing at the gates of Eden (see Genesis 3:24). During the time of Exodus, the Angel of Doom killed the first-born sons, while during the time of a threat by an Assyrian king the angel of the Lord sowed destruction among the invading army of Sennacherib (see 2 Chronicles 19:35); the angel also sought revenge against the Godless persecutors of Susanna (see Daniel 13:59). The prayer against villains also speaks of a punitive angel:

> Make them like chaff before the wind,
> with the angel of the Lord driving them on.
> Make their way slippery and dark,
> with the angel of the Lord pursuing them (Psalm 35:5-6).

Above all, in Revelation the angels are frequently presented as the messengers of God's wrath directed against evil. The angels appear in this dual role (as the defenders of good and the avengers of evil) during the final judgment (Matthew 24:31; 13:41).

This tradition was magnificently interpreted by e.g. Antoni Edward Odyniec in his poem "The Angel of Death."[95] May we likewise revive within us this powerful part of the truth about angels. Could we not pray to God that, for instance, He may preempt us of His

95. A.E. Odyniec, *Anioł śmierci* [in:] Odyniec, *Poezye*, Warszawa: Drukarnia Gazety Lekarskiej, 1874, p. 281

judgment? Or that He may send to us His angels that will be unmerciful towards my sin and yours (however painful that might be), but can open up all that is good within us and make us yearn for authentic love?

It seems to me that this should be the substance of, above all, our prayer to our guardian angels. We can also add this element every time we mention the angels in the preface to the Eucharistic Prayer. Let us not be afraid to ask God to send his angelic avengers against us, against everything that is deserving of destruction within us. After all, this would be for our own good.

THE ORIGIN OF MAN IN LIGHT OF FAITH AND SCIENCE

A philosophical hypothesis about the purely natural origin of man had been formulated by Immanuel Kant in 1786, before Charles Darwin was even born. In the treatise *Mutmasslicher Anfang der Menschengeschichte* ("The Purported Beginning of Human History"), Kant supposes that our ancient ancestors became human the moment they became aware of the four following things: 1) an ability to choose their lifestyle, which is unknown to animals; 2) awareness of a certain domination of reason over the instincts; 3) an ability to predict and plan the future with confidence; 4) and their superiority to animals, which, to quote Kant, consists of man's ability to "[say] to the sheep, *Nature gave the skin you wear not for you but for me,* and then took it off the sheep and put it on himself (*Genesis* 3:21)."

However, a richly documented vision of the evolutionary origin of species, including *Homo sapiens,* was first presented by Charles Darwin, especially in his two works: *On the Origin of Species* (1859) and *The Descent of Man* (1871). The theory of evolution struck at the conviction, deeply ingrained in the European consciousness at the time, that man had been directly created by God. Because evolution was initially only a hypothesis that aroused many scientific doubts and because some pundits began to treat it as a tool for promoting atheism, the belief that the doctrine of creation and the doctrine of the evolutionary beginnings of our species were mutually contradictory became quite widespread, among both believers and non-believers. Some Christians who were fascinated with the theory of evolution even lost their faith. In this dispute, many accusations of obscurantism and backwardness were levied against the Church, while religious pundits who spoke out on this topic sometimes gave substance to such accusations. The fact that the popularization of the theory of evolution became the domain of anti-religious activists rather than competent scientists shows how tortuous this debate had become.

An Attempt at Explaining This Strange Controversy

This controversy lasted quite a long time, from the late nineteenth century to the early twentieth. Today, it is difficult for us to believe that it could have taken place at all. What does the dogma of creation say? We believe that the entire world was created by God. That it has been created means that all that exists constantly receives its existence from God. This does not only mean that He created the world in some initial act of creation many millions, or even billions, of years ago. From the perspective of faith, the chronological beginning of the world or when it began to exist is essentially of secondary importance.[96] The essence of the fact that the world has been created is its constant dependence on God in its existence.

96. It is of secondary importance in the sense that for our faith it does not seem terribly important how long the world created by God has existed. We believe that the world has not always existed but that it has had its chronological beginning ("from the beginning of time;" or *ab initio temporis*, as expressed by the Fourth Lateran Council in 1215). Therefore, the fact that the world once had a beginning is important to our faith because we simultaneously believe that it aims for its ultimate fulfillment, towards "a new heaven and a new earth" (see Revelation 21:1).

How does this contradict evolutionary theories or other scientific hypotheses about the structure of the cosmos or its individual parts? The world owes its existence as it is to God, and the qualitative description of it is the domain of science, not faith. If it is in a state of development, in light of faith in the dogma of creation this means that it receives existence from its Creator that makes it capable of development. The formation of galaxies or the appearance of different species of plants and animals by means of evolution is an implementation of the capabilities that matter receives from its Creator. To juxtapose the truth of creation with the theories of evolution is like contrasting the truth that I am God's creation with the truth that I come from my parents.

Why, then, did this controversy appear in the first place? And why did it last for so long? Although the theory of evolution did not oppose the teaching about creation, it was opposed to popular conceptions of evolution at the time. The statement that "the world has been created" was almost universally understood as follows: "at a certain moment, incredibly long ago, God created the world, which means that He made the world exist." In short, the teaching about creation was above all associated with the moment of its existence, while the very essence of this truth became almost completely forgotten: that all creatures are constantly turned towards their Creator so that they can receive their existence from Him. Mythological folk conceptions coincided with deism, which had become widespread among educated people. Consequently, both Christians and non-believers overlooked the essential substance of the teaching on creation. If someone were to say, for instance, that God is the Creator of all animals, in those days almost everyone would have interpreted this as meaning that God once created the first specimens of every species. However, they forgot the basic meaning of this truth: that everything that is alive and everything that exists is at any moment God's creation.

The Gradual Reconciliation Between Theology and the Theory of Evolution

In order to somehow become open to the theory of evolution, at a certain point Catholic scholars came up with a doctrine about divine intervention at the time of the most important changes in evolutionary progress. In particular two moments, they said, absolutely required the Creator's particular intervention: the appearance of life as well as the appearance of the first man, the only visible being that possesses a spiritual element. This doctrine was a major step forward in overcoming the deistic stereotypes about creation, but it was still caught up in them. The mere concept of God's "external intervention" could invite the false conclusion that God is external with respect to the world. Naturally, He is transcendent with respect to the world, and no place can engulf Him, but at the same time He is in His entirety in every place: "In Him we live and move and have our being" (Acts 17:28).

Instead of speaking of "external intervention," would it not be simpler to indicate God's transcendent omnipresence in every place, inside every being, and inside all processes of development? From a religious perspective, we would not have to particularly emphasize the moment of bringing matter to life. With regards to man, not only the first man but in general every man is a person and therefore from the moment we begin to exist God embraces each of us, calling us by name with love and wanting to make each of us worthy of eternal life. Is it possible to emphasize the uniqueness of the relationship between the Creator and man any more? Can we present the distinctiveness of man with respect to all other creatures living on earth any more?

Finding viewpoints that facilitated harmony between the theory of evolution and faith in God the Creator of the universe in ancient Christian writings played an important role in making theologians and priests open to evolution. I have already said that the difficulty of reconciling both truths above all resulted from the false awareness that the truth of creation concerned only the initial moment when the world began to exist. Yet many centuries before the theory of evolution appeared the Church taught that the Creator constantly supports the existence of everything at all times. St. Thomas Aquinas even said that the world had its chronological beginning, but in essence the created world could have always existed, for the essence of its having been created rests not in the fact that it began to exist at a specific moment but in its constant relationship with the Creator, one that could have always existed.

With regards to the topic under discussion, St. Thomas' argument that the majesty and dignity of creatures consists in God granting them not only participation in His existence and goodness but even in His causality — while He does not cease to be the direct cause of the entirety of creation and all individual creatures, He allows creatures to be the causes of others.[97]

The Church Fathers, therefore, created conceptions that would resemble the theory of evolution, which of course would appear much later. For example, in *De Genesi ad litteram*, among others, St. Augustine writes that the Creator deposited in *rationes seminales* objects (the Latin equivalent of the Stoic *logoi spermatikoi*) some internal forces that lead them towards development in some designated direction.[98]

Papal Pronouncements on the Theory of Evolution

One must admit that the Holy See acknowledged that the faith that man has been created by God does not contradict the theory of man's

97. See the chapter titled *Pośrednictwo przyczyn stworzonych w rządach Bożej Opatrzności* ("The Intercession of Created Causes in the Rule of Divine Providence") in Volume 2 of my *Dzieła wybrane* ("Collected Works")

98. St. Augustine, *De Genesi ad litteram,* lib.9 cap.16 (PL 34,406). See J. Łukomski, *Augustyna teoria rozwoju organizmów w świetle współczesnego ewolucjonizmu, Studia Philosophiae Christianae* 7 (1971) No. 2, pp. 151-182.

evolutionary origins relatively late and in a document of low stature: in a speech by Pope Pius XII on November 30, 1941.

Pius XII repeated this in an encyclical, a document of great stature, nine years later. After noting that the theory of evolution belongs to those topics that "although they pertain to the positive sciences, are nevertheless more or less connected with the truths of the Christian faith" (*Humani generis,* 35), we find the following statement: "For these reasons the Teaching Authority of the Church does not forbid that, in conformity with the present state of human sciences and sacred theology, research and discussions, on the part of men experienced in both fields, take place with regard to the doctrine of evolution, in as far as it inquires into the origin of the human body as coming from pre-existent and living matter" (*Humani generis,* 36).

However, it would be a misunderstanding to state that Catholics were not allowed to support the theory of man's evolutionary origins until after the day of the pope's speech on November 30, 1941. Although the general atmosphere in the Church was greatly critical of Darwinism, the Magisterium of the Church never directly opposed this theory, while there were already those who allowed for the possibility that it was the truth among people of the Church in the nineteenth century. This is probably one of the reasons why Darwin's then-controversial *On the Origin of Species* was never on the Vatican's Index of Forbidden Books, despite the fact that many other works found their way to the list all too easily.

It seems, however, that the main reason why the Holy See did not rush to condemn the theory of evolution was the fact that nearly on the eve of the publication of Darwin's *The Descent of Man* the First Vatican Council recalled the old Catholic teaching that *veritas veritati contraria esse non potest,*[99] or "the truth cannot be opposed to the truth." God Himself is the source of both the natural and supernatural truth; thus, there can be no truth contradiction between

99. Thomas Aquinas, *Contra Gentes* 4,8.

science and faith. "Wherefore, the Church is so far from objecting to the culture of the human arts and sciences, that it aids and promotes this cultivation in many ways. For, it is not ignorant of, nor does it despise the advantages flowing therefrom into human life; nay, it confesses that, just as they have come forth from 'God, the Lord of knowledge' [1 Samuel 2:3], so, if rightly handled, they lead to God by the aid of His grace. And it (the Church) does not forbid disciplines of this kind, each in its own sphere, to use its own principles and its own method; but, although recognizing this freedom, it continually warns them not to fall into errors by opposition to divine doctrine, nor, having transgressed their own proper limits, to be busy with and to disturb those matters which belong to faith."[100]

It is worth saying a couple of words about the fact that in the nineteenth century opponents of Darwinian evolution with an education in theology were nowhere as naive as scientistic and anti-clerical propaganda claimed. These people knew perfectly well that the Biblical description of the creation of man presents crucial truths in an anthropomorphic way and that it would be naive to not distinguish the truths of the faith contained in this description from the anthropomorphic forms in which they were presented. This distinction belonged to the most basic textbooks of Catholic theology throughout the centuries of its existence. It was anti-Catholic propaganda that ascribed to the entire Church the conceptions of some Christians that the Creator literally sculpted the first man out of clay. Christian opponents of the theory of evolution had incomparably more important reasons why they opposed this theory. Above all, they were overcome with anxiety that the thesis of the evolutionary origin of our species would become a tool employed to deny man's unique dignity.

100. First Vatican Council, *Dogmatic Constitution "Dei Filius,"* Interdisciplinary Encyclopedia of Religion and Science, https://inters.org/Vatican-Council-I-Dei-Filius (accessed March 8, 2022).

This seemingly naive image of God sculpting man out of clay also contains this theme of man's unique dignity. As far back as around 180, St. Irenaeus found this image to be rich and deep: "God fashioned man with His own hands [that is, the Son and the Holy Spirit] and impressed His own form on the flesh He had fashioned, in such a way that even what was visible might bear the divine form." Therefore, the Only-Begotten Son and the Holy Spirit are the hands of God! The creation of man was the work of the entire Holy Trinity. It is good that this very deep statement can be found in the *Catechism of the Catholic Church* (704).

Meanwhile, this detail of the Biblical description that man has been shaped from the earth reminded the teachers of the Church that man is a part of nature and as such has been particularly called to be a minister to all irrational creatures called to praise God in the name of the entire earth and cosmos. At the same time, the Church Fathers constantly reminded the faithful of the fact that man is something more than merely a part of nature, because God Himself breathed the spirit into the clay of his body.

Both Pius XII and St. John Paul II made note of this moment so that accepting the theory of the appearance of our species by means of evolution we do not treat humans as any other animals. They emphasized man's ontic uniqueness with respect to animals first of all with the aid of the hypothesis that man's immortal soul is not the fruit of biological evolution, but each of us has received it directly from the Creator, and second, by recalling and exploring the Biblical truth that man is the only creature on this earth that was shaped by the image of God Himself and bears likeness to Him.

Of the numerous patristic testimonies that say the same thing on the topic of the human soul as Pius XII in the encyclical *Humani generis*, which indicated the possibility of reconciling the theory of evolution with faith in God the Creator, I will reference two. St. Ambrose (†397) writes in his "Death as a Good": "It is clear that the soul does not die with the body, because it is not of the body. That it is not of the body Scripture teaches in many ways: Adam received the spirit of life from the Lord Our God, and *he was made into a living soul.*"[101]

I quote St. Cyprian (†258) here mainly because his work is a very original attempt at interpreting the prayer: "Thy will be done, on earth as it is in heaven": "For since we possess the body from the earth and the spirit from heaven, we ourselves are earth and heaven; and in both — that is, both in body and spirit — we pray that God's will may be done."[102]

In a message of October 1996 on the topic of the theory of evolution, John Paul II said the same thing as Pius XII in the aforementioned 1950 encyclical. In it, the Holy Father said that certain theories of evolution "are incompatible with Christian anthropology," but only those in which "the human spirit is considered to have been created by the forces of living matter or also as an ordinary epiphenomenon of this matter. They are incompatible with the truth about man; they are also incapable of describing the dignity of the human person."

Meanwhile, those Catholics and other Christians who initially opposed the theory of evolution defended very important truths, above all the truth about the spiritual dimension of our humanity or the truth that the moral law cannot be reduced to the laws of biology; in other words, force is subjected to the moral law and not the reverse.

Purposefulness of the Processes of Evolution or "Chance and Necessity"?

Today, there is a certain tension between the natural sciences and theology because of the question of whether the processes of evolution are directed by some internal purposefulness or, rather, to use Jacques Monod's phrase, "chance and necessity."

101. St. William Theodore Wiesner, *S. Ambrosii De Bono Mortis* (Washington, DC: Catholic University of America Press, 1970), p. 129, 131.

102. St. Cyprian, *Treatises: The Lord's Prayer*, 14-17, https://www.vatican.va/spirit/documents/spirit_20000818_cipriano_en.html (accessed March 8, 2022).

In his pastoral teachings, John Paul II frequently presented evolution from the former perspective. During a Wednesday catechesis on July 10, 1985, he said: "The evolution of living beings that is the subject of scientific research aiming to describe its stages and distinguish the mechanisms acting in it presents a surprising internal purposefulness. This purposefulness which leads all beings in the same direction and over which they have no power and for which they are not responsible makes us think of the Spirit Who is their Inventor and Creator." He spoke similarly in his audiences of January 8 and March 5, 1986.

Tellingly, John Paul II omitted this theme from his message to the members of the Pontifical Academy of Sciences on October 22, 1996, along with the session "The Origins and Evolution of Life," although that he mentioned there both the truth about the creation of man's soul directly by the Creator, and the thesis of the ontological "jump" in the process of evolution that the appearance of *Homo sapiens* was.

The thesis of the purposefulness of evolutionary processes is opposed by scholars dealing with the natural sciences. Rev. Michał Heller recognizes the validity of this opposition: "For the purposes of our discussion it suffices that we recognize such events as random as require probability methods to describe. Not only the birth of life but also many other details related to the construction of our bodies [...] are the result of the cooperation of nature and chance. If a scholar were to say anything else, he would transcend the limits of the scientific method."[103]

According to Father Heller, on the level of faith, or on the basis of truth known thanks to Divine revelation, the thesis of the purposefulness of evolutionary processes can be fully justified: "If, however, a theologian looks at the same process, from his vantage point he has the right to say that in creating the world God had a strategy of embedding chance happenings in the activity of the laws of nature. Naturally, the Creator could have used evolution to realize His aims. The theologian

103. *Bóg, konieczność i przypadek. Z ks. prof. Michałem Hellerem rozmawia Marek Zając, Tygodnik Powszechny*, July 24, 2005.

has the right to say that God acts in the cosmic process of evolution. What the natural sciences see as a blind chance can from the vantage point of theology be God's purposeful activity."[104] I will not try to answer the question of whether this is not perhaps a contemporary version of the theory of two truths. Personally, I believe that it is not.

Questions About Other Human Species and the Problem of Polygenism

Theologians are sometimes asked if the thesis of paleoanthropologists that our species is not the only human species that has lived on this earth poses a challenge to the Christian faith. It seems that the Christian faith is not particularly interested in dealing with the question of the truth of the humanity of the Neanderthals or the peoples of Flores[105] or other extinct human species parallel to *Homo sapiens*. Either they were truly people or they were not, depending on whether the Creator summoned them to eternal friendship with Himself, i.e. if they have been endowed with a spiritual and immortal soul. Neither of these two hypotheses contradicts faith, although each of them can inspire very interesting theological questions.

However, the question of whether our species comes from one or many original strains does pose a problem for theology. In his encyclical *Humani generis*, Pius XII includes a fragment that has become a classic example in discourses on the interpretation of the Church's doctrinal texts: "When, however, there is question of another conjectural opinion, namely polygenism, the children of the Church by no means enjoy such liberty. For the faithful cannot embrace that opinion which maintains that either after Adam there existed on this earth true men who did not take their origin through natural generation

104. See Marcin Ryszkiewicz, *Mali ludzie z Flores — wielkie pytanie antropologii*, *Zeszyty Towarzystwa Popierania i Krzewienia Nauk*, No. 43 (July 2005), pp. 99-127.

105.

from him as from the first parent of all, or that Adam represents a certain number of first parents. Now it is in no way apparent how such an opinion can be reconciled with that which the sources of revealed truth and the documents of the Teaching Authority of the Church propose with regard to original sin, which proceeds from a sin actually committed by an individual Adam and which, through generation, is passed on to all and is in everyone as his own" (37).

The non-theologian is usually surprised by the fact that this pronouncement was then considered to be encouragement to search for the potential reconciliation of the polygenism hypothesis with the Catholic faith. The unambiguous conclusion is that faith only indirectly attaches importance to the thesis of the origin of the family from the first two people. Pope Pius XII teaches that what is most important to the faith in the question of polygenism is the teaching on "original sin, which proceeds from a sin actually committed by an individual Adam." Thus far, we have been incapable of reconciling the polygenism hypothesis with our faith's teaching on original sin.

Immediately after this encyclical's publication, Catholic theology produced many proposals to reconcile the truth of original sin with the polygenism hypothesis. Pope Paul VI was tremendously engaged in the search for an answer to this problem.[106] This discussion became muted with the appearance of the hypothesis that from a biological point of view our species appeared due to chromosomal rather than genetic mutation, and our foremother was "Mitochondrial Eve," likely the daughter of a man in whom such a deep mutation appeared, causing immediate sexual isolation.[107]

106. This problem is presented in detail by Tadeusz Łukaszuk in his book *Związek dogmatu grzechu pierworodnego z monogenizmem w katolickiej teologii ostatniej doby*, (Warszawa: Akademia Teologii Katolickiej, 1976).

107. Józef Życiński cautiously evaluates the significance of this hypothesis to explaining the theological problems under present discussion in: *Hipoteza Ewy mitochondrialnej a monogenizm teologiczny*, [in:] *Słowo pojednania. Księga pamiątkowa z okazji 70. urodzin ks. M. Czajkowskiego*, ed. Julian Warzecha (Warszawa: Biblioteka "Więzi", 2004), pp. 403-412.

The Question of Paradise: Did It Truly Exist?

The traditional teaching of the faith about the state of initial righteousness in which our distant ancestors began their human existence seems difficult to reconcile with the vision of man's evolutionary origins. At least three themes should be considered if we want to respond to the question of whether paradise truly existed in the beginning:

1. The Catholic faith unambiguously teaches that human sin appeared later than man and appeared in our history only because of man's true fault. Denying the above truth would support the difficult-to-accept thesis that God Himself created man as sinful.
2. If paradise did indeed exist, it lasted for an ephemeral moment in human history and pertained to a miniscule number of people (perhaps only two); therefore, the question of paradise seems inaccessible to scientific research.
3. It seems that paleozoological data points towards the existence of diseases and death, predators, and the struggle for survival in the animal kingdom long before man's appearance. This forces us to reject the idyllic conceptions of paradise on earth and instead support St. Thomas Aquinas' thesis, which is dominant in the Christian tradition, describing paradise as a unique situation of our forefathers, a testimony and fruit of their undisturbed friendship with God.
4. The question of paradise, impossible to discuss within empirical sciences, would also be religiously barren if we overlooked its relationship to our current situation with regards to God: Christ is our not only our sole opportunity to regain what is most important, i.e. friendship with God, but we can now regain in Him much of what traditional theology has called the supernatural gifts with which our forefathers were endowed before their lost their sanctity and righteousness.

THE PRIEST OF CREATION

The Prayer of Irrational Creatures

The Psalmist calls: "In the presence of the angels to you I sing" (Psalm 138:1). We try to imitate him during every Mass. At the beginning of the Eucharistic prayer, during the preface, the priest says or sings that we offer this sacrifice "together with the angels and archangels, with all the choirs of heaven."

But God created not only people and angels; He also created an enormous material cosmos. Although on an astronomical scale our earth is a mere speck of cosmic dust, God created countless beings on it, each of which "possesses its own particular goodness and perfection. [...] Creatures exist only in dependence on each other, to complete each other, in the service of each other" (*Catechism of the Catholic Church*, 339-340).

They also somehow pray, although it must be said that the prayer of irrational creatures is one of the Biblical topics we think about very rarely. Here is a fragment of Psalm 98:

> Shout with joy to the Lord, all the earth;break into song; sing praise.
> [...]
> Let the sea and what fills it resound,
> the world and those who dwell there.

> Let the rivers clap their hands,the mountains shout with them for joy,
> Before the Lord Who comes,Who comes to govern the earth
> (Psalm 98:4-9).

In the hymn praising the Creator in the third chapter of the Book of Daniel, all of creation, including the sun, the moon, and the stars as well as creatures that are hostile to humans, is called to prayer:

> Sun and moon, bless the Lord;praise and exalt him above all forever.
> Stars of heaven, bless the Lord;praise and exalt Him above all forever.
> […]
> Fire and heat, bless the Lord; […]
> Cold and chill, bless the Lord; […]
> Frost and chill, bless the Lord; […]
>
> Hoarfrost and snow, bless the Lord;
> Praise and exalt Him above all forever (Daniel 3:62-73).

St. Augustine delighted in this prayer of creation: "[A]ll things cry aloud: the beauty of all things is in a manner their voice, whereby they praise God. The heaven cries out to God, You made me, not I myself. Earth cries out, You created me, not I myself. […] Regard the heavens, it is beautiful: observe the earth, it is beautiful: both together are very beautiful. He made them, He rules them, by His nod they are swayed, He orders their seasons, He renews their movements, by Himself He renews them. All these things then praise Him, whether in stillness or in motion, whether from earth below or from heaven above, whether in their old state or in their renewal."[108]

The ancient Hebrew mentality saw prayer even in the animals' everyday search for food. The Psalmist prays: "The eyes of all look hopefully to You; You give them their food in due season. You open wide Your hand and satisfy the desire of every living thing" (Psalm

108. St. Augustine, "Exposition on Psalm 148," 10, [in:] N*icene and Post-Nicene Fathers, First Series*, Vol. 8, ed. Philip Schaff (Buffalo, NY: Christian Literature Publishing Co., 1888); https://www.newadvent.org/fathers/1801148.htm (accessed March 8, 2022).

145:15-16; see 104:27). God "gives animals their food and young ravens what they cry for" (Psalm 147:9; see 104:21).

The generation of our parents and grandparents were still familiar with such sensory experiences. It was only in recent times that we have forgotten that celestial bodies and the entirety of nature as well as all plants and animals are our fellow creatures. It is difficult to imagine how a Christmas carol about how all of nature rejoices upon the Redeemer's birth could be written today (see "W dzień Bożego Narodzenia" (On the Day of God's Birth): "into the air fly the birds,/ Singing to Jesus praiseful words,/ Then trebles the nightingale,/ And the goldfinch's alto assails"). Most likely, today no author would write a hymn that, like "Chwalcie, łąki umajone" (Praise, O Flowering Meadows), would summon everything that is beautiful in nature to praise Mary. Likewise, it seems unlikely that contemporary religious poetry would try to build on the theme that in light of the Redeemer's Passion "the sun and stars faint/becoming filled with mourning."

"Man Is an Involuntary and Immature Priest"

Regardless of the degree to which we realize this, all of creation — including that which is irrational and inanimate — praises its Creator through its very existence. In a sense, this can be understood as saying that we, who are also creatures although we have been endowed with reason, should supplement this existential prayer of the entirety of creation with conscious prayer, prayer in the unambiguous meaning of the term.

In other words, we humans should in a way lead the prayer of irrational creatures and be like their priests. We should include the unconscious prayer of creatures inferior to us in the prayer of angels and saints as well as our own prayer so that all of creation may praise its Creator.

This human priesthood with respect to the entire material world was expressed by Beata Obertyńska, a poet who unfortunately is little known:

> So what if you someday blow it out in the blink of an eye,
> if when disappearing it will still be itself?
> How I love Your world that passes, how I love it, O Lord!
> I swing it like a living censer before you!

Cyprian Kamil Norwid certainly had in mind our priesthood with respect to irrational being when he wrote that "man is an involuntary and immature priest." Indeed, Norwid was correct in writing that we are not fully aware of this priesthood and we are lousy at carrying it out. Thus, we should be all the more pleased that in recent decades the Church's documents have dealt with this topic more.

The most recent council recalls the Church's teaching on this topic: "Through his bodily composition [man] gathers to himself the elements of the material world; thus they reach their crown through him, and through him raise their voice in free praise of the Creator" (*Gaudium et spes*, 14).

This takes place above all during the Sunday Mass. In *Dies Domini*, his letter on celebrating Sunday, John Paul II writes: "'The Lord's Day' is the day of this relationship par excellence when men and women raise their song to God and become the voice of all creation. [...] Rest therefore acquires a sacred value: the faithful are called to rest not only as God rested, but to rest in the Lord, bringing the entire creation to Him, in praise and thanksgiving, intimate as a child and friendly as a spouse" (15-16).

Our cosmic priesthood, which is realized especially when we celebrate the Eucharist, is painted on the walls of some old churches, especially Gothic ones. Decorated with stars on their vaults and the richness of flora and fauna on the side walls of a church, they visually represent the truth that John Paul II expressed concisely in the second chapter of *Crossing the Threshold of Hope*: "Man is the priest of all creation. Christ conferred upon him this dignity and vocation. Creation completes its *opus gloriae* both by being what it is and by its duty to become what should be. [...] [Man] was created in order to become, in Christ, the priest, prophet, and king of all earthly creatures."[109]

It is worth recalling that in the Old Testament the archpriest praised God in the name of not only the people but also the entire cosmos, which was visually expressed in his liturgical vestments: "For on [Aaron's] full-length robe was the whole world, and ancestral glories were carved on the four rows of stones, and Your grandeur was on the crown upon his head" (Wisdom 18:24). Certainly, the whole world was on Aaron's robe in the sense that it was decorated with likenesses of the sun, moon, and stars, or the entire cosmos. Four rows of twelve precious stones are a symbol of the twelve generations of the sons of Jacob (see Exodus 28:17-21), while during the time of the Church it is a symbol of the progeny of the twelve apostles (see Revelation 21:19n).

"All Creation Is Groaning in Labor Pains Even Until Now"

We read in the Book of Isaiah: "The Designer and Maker of the earth Who established it, as an empty waste did He create it, but designing it to be lived in" (Isaiah 45:18). However, the Creator left the ultimate arrangement of the earth to ourselves so that we could be His collaborators in the work of creation. The way we arrange our lives on earth takes place from the perspective of both entire generations (for example, through the development of agriculture, construction, art, science, and technology) and individual decisions.

109. His Holiness John Paul II, *Crossing the Threshold of Hope*, ed. Vittorio Messori, trans. Jenny McPhee and Martha McPhee (New York: Alfred A. Knopf, 2005), p. 18.

A biting testimony to how powerful our need to improve the world in which we live and to make it more beautiful can be found in Prof. Barbara Skarga's memoirs of a Soviet gulag: "They dress all of us in the exact same navy-blue color. The next day, the cut of the bag-shaped dresses that were distributed was changed; they received embroidered embellishments near the collar and on its sleeves. Those tired, often-hungry women whose entire energy has been depleted have some uncontrollable desire to add more aesthetically pleasing forms of grayness to objects and tools. They want to embellish something, to make it more pleasing."[110]

Unfortunately, we also have a negative tendency to deprive the earth of the meaning and beauty it deserves. When people hate one another, people are sentenced to forced-labor camps, and some children die of starvation while others are not even allowed to see the light; our earth then becomes ugly and terrifying. The earth also becomes ugly because we are constantly turning forests and rivers into garbage dumps, while many things that we produce immediately end up in the dumpster.

We are capable of depriving animals of the true meaning of their existence. It suffices to recall German shepherds in the Nazi concentration camps or some contemporary forms of breeding chickens. Jan Kochanowski once wrote: "From the rising of the sun to its setting let the name of the Lord be praised." Can these words refer to those terrifying dogs or even those poor chickens that spend their entire lives crowded to a space of one square foot? Unfortunately, instead of being priests of creatures inferior to us we are capable of harming them and stripping them of their inherent dignity.

Even inanimate objects have dignity, yet we do not always know how to respect it. Let us express this in a concise, symbolic form: a knife has many good uses (for example, it can serve to slice bread),

110. Barbara Skarga, *Po wyzwoleniu... 1944-1956* (Poznań: Wyd. W Drodze, 1990), p. 113.

and so it is not good to use it as a tool in a battle. Sacred Scripture frequently claims that the earth is besmirched with our sins. This might sound strange and even comical, but it is true that the places where we commit evil acts and the objects we use to commit evil are infected with our sins; it is as if they are defiled by us and are stifled in their existence for God's glory.

The Apostle Paul wrote about this in a famous excerpt from the Epistle to the Romans. "For creation awaits with eager expectation the revelation of the children of God; for creation was made subject to futility, not of its own accord but because of the one who subjected it, in hope that creation itself would be set free from slavery to corruption and share in the glorious freedom of the children of God. We know that all creation is groaning in labor pains even until now" (Romans 8:19-22).

In a word, even for this reason we should convert to God, that He may make our beautiful world even more beautiful. After all, as John Paul II beautifully expressed this in the book *Memory and Identity*, "the beauty of the universe is in a way reflected in God's eyes." In other words, let us try to not obscure the beauty of the world in which the Creator has situated us with our sin.

THE DIGNITY OF MAN FROM THE PERSPECTIVE OF THE TRUTH ABOUT ORIGINAL SIN

The Biblical Description of the Creation of Man in Light of Extra-Biblical Myths

Three radical differences distinguish perhaps all the myths about the creation of man from the Biblical narrative on this topic. Let us begin with a brief overview of the pertinent Mesopotamian, Greek, and Hindu myths.

According to the Sumerian myth, younger gods who had enough hard work on earth forced the god Enki to create man. It turned out that of the first seven people who had from the beginning been destined to a life of hardship and agony, six were botched by the gods, so from the very beginning people had an unenviable fate.[111]

Meanwhile, according to the Babylonian poem *Enūma Eliš* man was burdened with sins that had been committed in the world of the gods at the moment of creation. Let us look at an interpretation

111. Krystyna Łyczkowska and Krystyna Szarzyńska, *Mitologia Mezopotamii* (Warszawa: Wyd. Artystyczne i Filmowe, 1981), pp. 60-67.

of this myth by a renowned contemporary Biblical studies scholar: "There is fault among the gods. Apsu and Mummu are killed, which leads death to enter the realm of existence. Kingu, the leader of the divine rebels, is captured. The congregation of gods sentences him to again serve to remove evil from the sphere of the gods. He is killed for this purpose, and humanity is created from his blood. In this way, the fault of the gods is inscribed in the existence of man, mortal and left to the whims of evil."[112]

We have known the Greek myths about the origins of man for much longer. The first man was made of clay and water by Prometheus, a god of secondary importance (or, in any case, not the highest god). Meanwhile, according to the well-known myth of Deucalion and Pyrrha, humanity was destroyed during a flood and would later be reborn from the stones they throw at one another: "And in a little time, by the interposition of the Gods above, the stones thrown by the hands of the man, took the shape of a man, and the female race was renewed by the throwing of the woman. Thence are we a hardy generation, and able to endure fatigue, and we give proofs from what original we are sprung."[113]

Furthermore, Ovid presents two myths of people who grew out of the teeth of a slain dragon that were sown in the soil.[114] Meanwhile, the hardworking Myrmidons emerged from ants: "Even still do they retain the manners which they formerly had; and they are a thrifty race, patient of toil, tenacious of what they get, and what they get they lay up."[115]

It is worth once more recalling the later Orphic myth of man's creation from the ashes of the divine Dionysos and the ignoble

112. Norbert Lohfink, *Opowiadanie o grzechu pierworodnym*, [in:] idem, *Pieśń chwały* (org. *Das Siegeslied am Schilfmeer*), trans. Jan Doktór (Warszawa: PAX, 1982), p. 58.

113. I am quoting from a relatively late source that comes from the time when Christ walked the earth: Ovid, *The Metamorphoses of Ovid*, trans. Henry T. Riley (London: George Bell & Sons, 1893), pp. 25-26.

114. *Op. cit.*, pp. 86-88.

115. *Op. cit.*, p. 254.

Titans: "'[T]he crime of the Titans,' who dismembered and devoured the young god Dionysos, becomes the origin of man; from their ashes Zeus raised up the present race of men, who thus have a twofold inheritance from god and Titan."[116]

With regards to Hindu myths on the origin of man, its first evident trait is its blatant pantheism. The myth of Prajapati, who was alone at the beginning, explains the creation of the world (and, in this world, the creation of man) through the self-sacrifice of that god. Everything that exists, including the earth and man on earth, came out of Prajapati's decomposing body. In fact, this was more a degradation of existence rather than something positive; the real existence of god became seemingly superficial duration, characteristic of the state of *maya*. Thus, the basic task of everything that came from Prajapati's body or in any case the basic task of man is to try to return to this former divine oneness.[117]

Perhaps the best-known Hindu myth about the origins of man likewise ascribes to man divine origin, but not as the result of degradation. Our forefather was the god Indra's younger and inept god Vivasvat. He was born without any limbs and was unnaturally fat, and his older brothers wanted to remodel him; in this way, Vivasvat became the first man.

The second degradation to which people owe their existence took place thanks to Vivasvat's wife Saranyu. She did not want to be married to this failure of a man, so after giving birth to twins she created a lookalike and presented it to her husband. Vivasvat did not notice this swap, and so Manu, the first man in the full meaning of the word (after all, Vivasvat gained the status of a god), was born.[118]

116. Paul Ricœur, *The Symbolism of Evil*, trans. Emerson Buchanan (Boston: Beacon Press, 1967), pp. 209-210.

117. Raimon Panikkar, *La faute originante ou l'immolation créatrice: le mythe de Prajâpati*, [in:] *Le mythe de la peine*, ed. Enrico Castelli (Paris: Aubier, 1967), pp. 70-88.

118. Władimir Erman and Eduard Tiomkin, *Mity starożytnych Indii*, trans. NN (Bydgoszcz: Pomorze, 1987), p. 21.

Manu married (which was another degradation of what is divine towards what is human) the ten daughters of Virini (also known as Daksha), or Night. This was how the earth became populated.[119]

The Originality of the Biblical Description of the Creation of Man

Let us now compare all these myths with the Biblical account of the creation of man. First of all, the Bible, unlike various mythologies, which all contain numerous inconsistent myths about the origin of man, presents only one account of how man appeared on the earth. Although this account is presented in two forms — a later priestly one (Genesis 1:26-31) and an older Yahwistic one (Genesis 2:4-25) — there is no doubt that both are descriptions of the same event.

The clear awareness that we all come from one root (in fact, from the first couple) has significantly helped us to understand that as humanity we are one family. Karl Jaspers — who, as we know, tended to distance himself from Christianity — saw the origins of this universalizing tendency in a much deeper source: Biblical monotheism. In his view, only professing belief in one personal God Who is transcendent with respect to the universe as its Creator allowed people to see this universe as a whole, as a universe in the eye of its Creator. Faith in God, Who is the Creator and Father of all people, was also possible thanks to the development of the mere concept of humanity as one.[120]

Second, only Divine Revelation says that man has been created by God Himself and that the basic reason for this was God's love. In polytheistic religions, man does not dare to think so highly of himself that he ascribes his existence to the highest god. (I write "the highest god" without capitalizing it because in the myths he also emerged out

119. *Op. cit.*, p. 188.

120. Karl Jaspers, *Nietzsche and Christianity* (Chicago: H. Regnery Company, 1961).

of primordial chaos and therefore is certainly only one of the forces of the world; thus, it would be blasphemous to see him as the True God.)

Polytheists have the courage to explain the beginnings of humanity through God's will under only one condition: if the myth clearly states that this highest god made man into something like a metaphysical garbage bin. In this way, in the Babylonian myth Marduk creates man to place within him the cursed blood of the rebellious god Kingu. Meanwhile, in the Orphic myth Zeus creates man out of Dionysos' divine remains as well as what is left of the ignoble Titans. Likewise, the Australian god Baiame creates man out of his own excrement.[121] As we can see, polytheists did not have a particularly exalted view of themselves.

Naturally, the pantheistic myths do not speak of God's love as the ultimate source of man's appearance. In the pantheistic view of the world, the only reason why things and people appear can be the disintegration of the divine oneness. Thus, these myths present even man's mere existence not as something good but as a result of the degradation of what is divine. Only Biblical faith in the transcendent Creator of heaven and earth makes it possible to know the truth that we exist because we are subjects of God's unique love.

Finally, nowhere outside Divine Revelation will we find the truth that man has been created as someone unambiguously and completely good, or that man has been created in the image and likeness of God Himself (Genesis 1:26), while sin and other evils appeared only later out of our own fault (although not without the influence of sin in the world of spiritual creatures). The mere idea of original sin is alien to origin myths, as are the ideas of creation. The universe and people either emerge out of some god (pantheistic myths) or, more frequently, are created out of primordial chaos, which is sometimes envisioned as a monster that sows destruction and is defeated by a divine demiurge in a cosmic battle (polytheistic myths).

121. *Bogowie — demony — herosi*, ed. Zbigniew Pasek (Kraków: Znak, 1996), p. 65.

Both pantheistic and polytheistic myths present extremely pessimistic images of man: there is much evil in man not because we have brought it upon ourselves but because we have been created in this way. In the pantheistic myths, the mere existence of man (and not only man) attests to divine degradation. Meanwhile, in the polytheistic myths, man is either a "garbage bin" for the evil that had taken place in the world of the gods, the victim of the bungled efforts of the gods,[122] or, finally, carries a particle of that primordial chaos that had been barely subdued by the divine demiurge.[123]

At this point, the mythical consciousness is tellingly consistent regardless of the cultural sphere in which it appears: man is deeply permeated by evil from the very beginning. In light of Divine Revelation, there appears the following explanation of this surprising consistency of the myths in which man is from the beginning immersed

122. An example is the above-mentioned Sumerian myth of the creation of the first seven people. See also the testimony of St. Irenaeus (late second century AD) about the conceptions of the origin of man in Saturninus' gnostic system: "The world, again, and all things therein, were made by a certain company of seven angels. Man, too, was the workmanship of angels, a shining image bursting forth below from the presence of the supreme power; and when they could not, he says, keep hold of this, because it immediately darted upwards again, they exhorted each other, saying, 'Let us make man after our image and likeness.' He was accordingly formed, yet was unable to stand erect, through the inability of the angels to convey to him that power, but wriggled [on the ground] like a worm. Then the power above taking pity upon him, since he was made after his likeness, sent forth a spark of life, which gave man an erect posture, compacted his joints, and made him live. He declares, therefore, that this spark of life, after the death of a man, returns to those things which are of the same nature with itself, and the rest of the body is decomposed into its original elements" (St. Irenaeus, *Against Heresies*, Book I, Chapter 24, trans. Alexander Roberts and William Rambaut, [in:] *Ante-Nicene Fathers*, Vol. 1. eds. Alexander Roberts, James Donaldson, and A. Cleveland Coxe (Buffalo, NY: Christian Literature Publishing Co., 1885); https://www.newadvent.org/fathers/0103124.htm (accessed March 9, 2022).

123. In extreme forms, this is expressed in myths regarding the origin of the first people from the teeth of a slain dragon. See also the myths of the Navajos and Apaches about the goddess Ahsonnutli who sculpted the first people out of wheat and seawater (*Bogowie — demony — herosi*, p. 21); it is worth recalling that, apart from the dragon, the sea is the most common symbol of primordial chaos. Also see the Chinese myth about the creation of the first people out of mud (there is a distinction between the rich and poor; see Mieczysław Künstler, *Mitologia chińska* (Warszawa: Wyd. Artystyczne i Filmowe, 1981), p. 48).

in one form of evil or another. Myths reveal the true defectiveness of our human fate in a surprisingly accurate way, while among the diverse explanations of the source of this defectiveness the myths present a sense of one's own innocence that is typical of sinners and which the psychologically insightful Biblical descriptions of the first sinners point out (Genesis 3:12-13).

In short, even the way in which the ancient mythical consciousness describes our human implication in sin attests to how hopelessly permanent it is. It is easier for us to completely forget about our human, unbelievably great dignity of creatures called to friendship with God Himself than to reject the false conviction of our innocence and recognize our own culpability for the evil in which we are immersed.

The numerous myths about man's origins differ greatly, but they are in agreement with respect to our immersion in evil as well as our refusal to confess to our responsibility for it. This inclines me to propose the thesis that we could know the truth about man's initial dignity and later downfall only thanks to Divine Revelation. Sinners are themselves incapable of love for God; however, they are all too capable of falsely denying their responsibility for the evil for which they are genuinely responsible.

The thesis that without Divine Revelation the truth of original sin would probably never appear within the horizons of our reflections on human nature is clearly stated in the *Catechism of the Catholic Church*: "Only the light of Divine Revelation clarifies the reality of sin and particularly of the sin committed at mankind's origins. Without the knowledge Revelation gives of God we cannot recognize sin clearly and are tempted to explain it as merely a developmental flaw, a psychological weakness, a mistake, or the necessary consequence of an inadequate social structure, etc. Only in the knowledge of God's plan for man can we grasp that sin is an abuse of the freedom that God gives to created persons so that they are capable of loving Him and loving one another" (387).

The *Catechism* goes farther: "We must know Christ as the source of grace in order to know Adam as the source of sin" (388). On the other hand, "we cannot tamper with the revelation of original sin without undermining the mystery of Christ" (389). A demonstration of the truthfulness of these theses would require a separate study.

Why Did Original Sin Encompass All People?

The Catholic faith places enormous emphasis on the fact that the sin of our first parents was a specific event. Thus, it cannot accept the attempt at reducing the account of original sin to the category of a myth, as if this account was solely concerned with emphasizing that we have become too immersed in sin to be able to liberate ourselves of it through our own efforts.[124]

This means that man has left the Creator's hands as a sinless being, internally integrated and spontaneously directed towards his Creator. If this was truly the case, then the first sin in human history was something absolutely inimitable. This was the only sin in our history that was committed by sinless people. Thus, we are incapable of understanding its unique wickedness; after all, all our experience with human evil concerns the evil committed by specific sinners. Naturally, the only sin committed by sinless and holy people at any point in history had to bring about a catastrophe incomparable to the effects of any other sins.

The Biblical description precisely indicates in what this sin consisted. It consisted in the fact that man has rejected an attitude of completely entrusting himself to God and began to suspect God of playing a game that does not necessarily involve our good. Satan told our forefathers: "God knows well that when you eat of it your eyes will be opened and you will be like gods, who know good and evil"

124. Such an interpretation of the truth about original sin is put forward e.g. by Paul Ricœur in the already-quoted book *The Symbolism of Evil*.

(Genesis 3:5). The last fragment of this sentence allows us to infer that man was capable of closing himself off from the truth about good and evil that flow from God; he decided to "determine" what is good and what is evil as if he were a god himself. From that point, every human sin contains these two moments: the lack of entrusting oneself to God and the usurpation of divine authority over the moral law.

Why has original sin encompassed all people? Why do all the descendants of the first sinners enter the world as if they were deprived of communion with God, Who invariably loves us and grants us life? St. Thomas poses a dramatic question: Does our being born into original sin negate the truth of God's word inscribed in the Book of Ezekiel that "the son shall not be charged with the guilt of his father" (Ezekiel 18:20)? However, St. Thomas replies to such a question, one condition must be met for the fault of parents to not spread to their children: they themselves cannot be participants in this fault. Unfortunately, this does not pertain to the sin of our first parents.[125] Why?

In what sense do we all participate in the sin of our first forefathers? When we were children, our catechists explained that when a father loses his estate through gambling, then his children will be poor. This is a shoddy explanation because it indicates that we sometimes bear the consequences of evil performed by others.

A deeper explanation that gives rise to many questions and is most frequently presented by the Church is: Original sin has affected our very human nature, the mere fact of our being human. We no longer have a spontaneous and undisturbed openness to God as Someone Very Close and the Ultimate Source of life and meaning.

St. Thomas says that this universality of original sin results from the fact that as humanity we are much more one body than can be empirically seen: "All people born of Adam can be considered one person."[126] Similarly, we are one spiritual body as the Church, much more

125. *Summa Theologica*, 1-2 q.81 a.1 ad 1.

126. *Ibid.*

so than can be observed. This mysterious yet real unity of humanity to be the ontic grounds on which we can be authentically overwhelmed with the redeeming power flowing from Christ's Cross. In this way, "where sin increased, grace overflowed all the more" (Romans 5:20).

Paul Ricœur is correct and the Pelagians before him were as well that we are capable of inducing sin in one another. The mechanism of the spread of sin through imitation is brilliantly described by Dostoevsky in his novella *The Dream of a Ridiculous Man*. The protagonist of the novella had a dream in which he found himself on a planet that was exactly like our earth except that the people there had fully retained their original righteousness and closeness to God. "It ended with me depraving everyone!" says the protagonist, describing his dream.

Let us cite a fragment of this description: " Like a vile trichina, like a germ of the plague infecting whole kingdoms, so I contaminated all this earth, so happy and sinless before my coming. They learnt to lie, grew fond of lying, and discovered the charm of falsehood. Oh, at first perhaps it began innocently, with a jest, coquetry, with amorous play, perhaps indeed with a germ, but that germ of falsity made its way into their hearts and pleased them. Then sensuality was soon begotten, sensuality begot jealousy, jealousy — cruelty... Oh, I don't know, I don't remember; but soon, very soon the first blood was shed. They marvelled and were horrified, and began to be split up and divided. They formed into unions, but it was against one another. Reproaches, upbraidings followed. They came to know shame, and shame brought them to virtue. The conception of honour sprang up, and every union began waving its flags. They began torturing animals, and the animals withdrew from them into the forests and became hostile to them. They began to struggle for separation, for isolation, for individuality, for mine and thine. They began to talk in different languages. They became acquainted with sorrow and loved sorrow;

they thirsted for suffering, and said that truth could only be attained through suffering. Then science appeared. As they became wicked they began talking of brotherhood and humanitarianism, and understood those ideas. As they became criminal, they invented justice and drew up whole legal codes in order to observe it, and to ensure their being kept, set up a guillotine. They hardly remembered what they had lost, in fact refused to believe that they had ever been happy and innocent. They even laughed at the possibility of this happiness in the past, and called it a dream."[127]

The truth about original sin is much deeper. It does not come to us from the outside, through the imitation of the sins of others or through participation in cultural structures marked by sin. As the descendants of the first sinners, we are spiritually deformed from the very beginning of our existence in the human family. It is not the case that we become sinners only with the passage of time, as we imitate the sins of other people. Thus, Dostoevsky's description barely touches on the mystery of human sinfulness.

However, the perspective of our deep sinfulness which is so appalling especially reveals our unique dignity. This not only means that the Son of God was needed to liberate us from sin and restore our friendship with God. The truth is that human dignity is so great that the Son of God really came to us and liberated us!

The Enlightenment's Denial of Original Sin

We have contrasted the truth of original sin with various myths about man's origins, which contain a very pessimistic anthropology. A couple words should be said about the Enlightenment thesis rejecting

127. Fyodor Dostoevsky, *The Dream of a Ridiculous Man* (1877), trans. Constance Garnett, https://www.online-literature.com/dostoevsky/3368/ (accessed December 16, 2022).

the truth of original sin in the name of the doctrine of the natural benevolence of human nature.

Could such a doctrine appear without the cultural impact of the Biblical truth that "God looked at everything He had made and found it very good" (Genesis 1:31)? Although this is certainly an important question, we will set it aside for a moment. For now, it suffices to notice that not only did the Enlightenment conviction that we are born without original sin (which resulted in numerous eighteenth century tales of kindhearted and sinless "savages") appear in the sphere of Biblical influences but they were also formulated in order to directly oppose the truth of original sin.

Let us recall a famous statement by Jean-Jacques Rousseau expressed in 1762: "The fundamental principle of all morality about which I have reasoned in all my Writings and developed in this last one with all the clarity of which I was capable, is that man is a naturally good being, loving justice and order; that there is no original perversity in the human heart, and that the first movements of nature are always right. I have shown that the only passion born with man, namely love of self, is a passion in itself indifferent to good and evil; that it becomes good or bad only by accident and depending on the circumstances in which it develops. I have shown that all the vices imputed to the human heart are not natural to it; I have stated the manner in which they are born. I have followed their genealogy, so to speak, and I have shown how, through continuous deterioration of their original goodness, men finally become what they are."[128]

Naturally, we cannot abrogate the enormity of the evil that afflicts us with a doctrine that even after Adam's sin we are born as sinless beings. All that can be achieved through such a doctrine is the shaping

128. Jean-Jacques Rousseau, "Letter to Beaumont," [in:] idem., *Letter to Beaumont, Letters Written from the Mountain, and Related Writings*, trans. Christopher Kelly, Judith R. Bush; Eve Grace, ed. (Lebanon: Dartmouth College Press, 2013), p. 28.

of a false consciousness that the sources of this evil are solely external and that they are not in us, either, as we have been born without sin.

It is difficult not to agree with Ewa Bieńkowska, who presents the significance of Rousseau's views to European thinking and its practical consequences as follows: "Nature is not corrupt; man has left the hands of his Creator as a good being. He was depraved by society, which taught him envy, falsehood, and vanity, instilling in him unhealthy appetites. Adam's true downfall is not nature's downfall but the world's culture absorbing phoniness and masks. Rousseau will not profess the return to the primordial state; he knows that this is a chimera and that the process put into motion cannot be reversed. However, the lost brilliance of authenticity can be restored to culture by introducing proper government under which depravity would no longer be possible, as in Sparta or the Calvinist republic of Geneva. In a society organized in this way in which people would regain their innocence as God's creatures, the blemish of sin would be wiped away like an actress's lipstick. Politics is the true name of eschatology."[129]

We already know the fruits of this utopian "eschatology" in whose name the October Revolution took place. Currently, we are in the process of implementing the next revolution. Convinced of our natural benevolence and sinlessness, we are trying to nullify the moral fundaments on which democracy had been hitherto built. The defenders of classic democracy, based on the moral law, are increasingly condemned as the enemies of freedom.

One thing is certain: We will bring upon ourselves many misfortunes if we allow the victory of this new revolution. Reality cannot be deceived. The truth is that we are not sinless and that we also carry the roots of the evil that torments us. Thus, no attempt at building our human world as if we were without sin cannot end well.

129. Ewa Bieńkowska, *Znak* 44 (1992), No. 12, p. 22.

MAN AS GOD'S IMAGE

The Ability to Participate in God's Domination

The truth that man was created in God's likeness appears immediately in the description of man's creation, in the first chapter of the Book of Genesis: "Then God said: Let us make human beings in Our image, after Our likeness. Let them have dominion over the fish of the sea, the birds of the air, the tame animals, all the wild animals, and all the creatures that crawl on the earth. God created mankind in His image; in the image of God He created them" (Genesis 1:26-27).

It seems that this fragment contains the moment of polemics with the idolatrous transfer of authority in God's sphere. If God is the Lord of the earth — as the ancient Babylonians, among others, believed — then only the king is God's image. The Bible is opposed to such a radical division of people into the rulers and the ruled: all people, not only the king, are created in God's image.

The ruler is no god on earth; like all people, he is subordinated to God's law, while his subjects are simultaneously his brothers. This idea was clearly expressed in the Pentateuch, which is the heart of the Old Testament. We read in Deuteronomy that the king "may learn to fear the Lord, his God, and to observe carefully all the words of this law and these statutes, so that he does not exalt himself over his kindred or turn aside from this commandment to the right or to the left, and so that he and his descendants may reign long in Israel" (Deuteronomy 17:19-20).

The first Biblical pronouncement about God's image in man is related to the idea of domination. Naturally, this consists of domination consisting of imitation of the Lord Almighty, Who is a kind, generous, and protective ruler to His creation. If one treats one's domination over nature or people as a destroyer and oppressor, one distorts God's image in oneself; one does not imitate the Almighty Lord, but instead mocks Him.

The Bible returns to these initial intuitions that God's image in man consists of the ability to participate in God's domination on several occasions, such as in the Book of Sirach (17:2-4). It seems that only in light of this initial intuition can one explain St. Paul's allegedly anti-feminist statement: "A man, on the other hand, should not cover his head, because he is the image and glory of God, but woman is the glory of man" (1 Corinthians 11:7). Let us recall that the Bible presents the subordination of women to man, a subjugation that is marked by injury, as the fruit of humanity's downfall (Genesis 3:16), while the fruits of redemption, as the same St. Paul teaches, include the restoration of the essential equality between man and woman: "There is neither Jew nor Greek, there is neither slave nor free person, there is not male and female; for you are all one in Christ Jesus" (Galatians 3:28). What does it mean that a man "is the image and glory of God, but woman is the glory of man"?

I would respond to this question as follows. In the early Church, the religious equalization of men and women paved the way for the social process of emancipation. A tangible sign of this was the refusal of some Christian women to cover their heads. As St. Paul himself notes, the covering of one's head was "a sign of authority" (1 Corinthians 11:10). The apostle certainly wanted to stop this movement for the social emancipation of women, certainly anxious that it could muffle the religious nucleus of the Good News about the liberation of all people, men and women alike. Elsewhere, in the Epistle to Titus, he justifies his demand to respect the family structures recognized in those days in a different way "so that the Word of God may not be discredited" (Titus 2:5). Here, the social subordination of wives to their husbands is religiously justified; it is a reference to the description of the creation of man. Naturally, no essential inferiority results from this, as God does not favor any people over others, and in His eyes even a king is someone not greater than the last of his subjects (see Job 34:18n; Wisdom 6:9; Ephesians 6:10).

Every Man Is Deserving of Great Love

The Book of Genesis deals with one more aspect of the truth of God's image in man. Among the visible creatures, only man has been shaped in God's image, which attests to his unique importance. Therefore, for example, one cannot arbitrarily dispose of human life, which is the property of God Himself: "Anyone who sheds the blood of a human being, by a human being shall that one's blood be shed; for in the image of God have human beings been made" (Genesis 9:6).

In referring to this theme, the Apostle James has noted that in essence every injury against a person is ultimately directed against God in Whose image man is created. Thus, an injury to a neighbor reveals the falsehood of our religiosity: "With [the tongue] we bless the Lord and Father, and with it we curse human beings who are made in the likeness of God. From the same mouth come blessing and cursing. [...] Does a spring gush forth from the same opening both pure and brackish water?" (James 3:9-11).

Let us notice that St. James' thought has an identical structure as the famous sentence in the First Epistle of John: "If anyone says, 'I love God,' but hates his brother, he is a liar; for whoever does not love a brother whom he has seen cannot love God whom he has not seen" (1 John 4:20). The statement of the Apostle James would have been hollow if there was not something Divine in every person. That is why every person is deserving of particular love, for everyone has been created in God's image. This truth is the invisible soul from the Apostle John's statement I have just quoted.

A Summons to Immortality

Finally, there is the third Old Testament perspective on the truth of man's creation in God's image: man is the only one among many creatures that has been called to immortality. The author of the Book of Wisdom evokes this aspect to demonstrate the powerlessness of evildoers plotting against righteous life. Death will not conquer the righteous, even when they are dead: "For God formed us to be imperishable; the image of His own nature He made us. But by the envy of the devil, death entered the world, and they who are allied with him experience it. [...] The souls of the righteous are in the hand of God, and no torment shall touch them. They seemed, in the view of the foolish, to be dead; and their passing away was thought an affliction" (Wisdom 2:23-24; 3:1-2)

Let us note that according to this text man has been created not only in God's image but also as an image of God.

We Have Yet to Achieve Complete Likeness to God

Let us return to the description of the creation of man in the Book of Genesis. Origen, the most outstanding theologian of the Church during her first persecutions, makes note of the difference between God's intention to create man and its implementation. Namely, God decides to create man in His "image and likeness," but ultimately creates man only "in His image." Origen attaches great significance to this detail: In this way, the Creator "conveys no other meaning than this, that man received the dignity of God's image at his first creation; but that the perfection of his likeness has been reserved for the consummation — namely, that he might acquire it for himself by the exercise of his own diligence in the imitation of God."[130]

This great theologian's interpretation is not devoid of a Biblical basis. Indeed, man is a living image of God and should become increasingly similar to his Prototype; however, if he enters the path of wickedness, he can become an increasingly distorted reflection of his Creator. Hence the numerous summons to become similar to God found in Sacred Scripture. "Be holy, for I, the Lord your God, am holy" (Leviticus 19:2; see 11:44; 20:7-8). It is immediately explained that becoming similar to the Holy God consists of venerating one's parents, observing the sabbath, rejecting idolatry, and being concerned for the poor (Leviticus 19:3-10). Jesus Christ Himself made use of this idea in His teaching: "Be merciful, just as [also] your Father is merciful" (Luke 6:36). Meanwhile, in the Gospel of Matthew we read: "So be perfect, just as your heavenly Father is perfect" (Matthew 5:48). This pertains to the perfection of the heavenly Father, thanks to which He presents good not only to the righteous but also the wicked.

The Apostle Peter reveals the unambiguously Christocentric direction in this idea coming from Leviticus. Namely, only thanks to the power of Christ's Blood can we completely reject our sinful behavior and become similar to the Holy God: "Be holy yourselves in every aspect of your conduct, for it is written, 'Be holy because I [am] holy.' [...] [Realize] that you were ransomed from your futile conduct, handed on by your ancestors, not with perishable things like

130. Origen, *De Principiis* (Book III), trans. Frederick Crombie, [in:] *Ante-Nicene Fathers*, Vol. 4, trans. Alexander Roberts, James Donaldson, and A. Cleveland Coxe (Buffalo, NY: Christian Literature Publishing Co., 1885), https://www.newadvent.org/fathers/04123.htm (accessed March 9, 2022).

silver or gold but with the precious blood of Christ as of a spotless unblemished lamb" (1 Peter 1:15n; 18-19).

Meanwhile, the Apostle John takes this idea out of Leviticus to indicate its eschatological direction. We will achieve ultimate likeness to God only in eternity: "We do know that when it is revealed we shall be like Him, for we shall see Him as He is. Everyone who has this hope based on Him makes Himself pure, as He is pure" (1 John 3:2-3).

The Threat of Idolatry

Yet man created in God's image can nonetheless imitate the idols, and then the image of God is gradually distorted in him like those forces that have become the subject of his worship. We read in the Epistle to the Romans: "[T]hey [...] exchanged the glory of the immortal God for the likeness of an image of mortal man or of birds or of four-legged animals or of snakes" (Romans 1:22-23). Here, "the glory of the immortal God" is contrasted with the "likeness and image" of idols. The Creator has deposited that glory in man's interior, as we can read in Psalms: "What is man that you are mindful of him, and a son of man that you care for him? Yet you have made him little less than a god, crowned him with glory and honor" (Psalm 8:5-6). In accordance with the tradition of *kabod Yahweh* (praise to God) in the Old Testament, "the glory of the immortal God" should be understood as God's loving and redeeming presence in man.

A short sentence from the Epistle to the Romans expresses the entire terror of idolatry. This no longer refers to just the external worship of idolatrous images. The essence of idolatry consists of man gradually becoming someone in the image and likeness of his idols. This is an ancient idea, one reaching back to the Old Testament. For example, in Psalm 135:16-18 we read that idols "have mouths but do not speak; they have eyes but do not see; they have ears but do not hear; nor is there breath in their mouths. Their makers will become like them, and anyone who trusts in them." Because idols lack life, those who serve them become filled with death. The Lord Jesus also referred to this idea; He frequently said: "May those who have ears listen." Yet those whose ears are dead like those of the idols will not hear the Word of God.

The ultimate aim of idolatrous worship is always Satan. Indeed, the Church Fathers at times spoke of the image of Satan appearing within us if we do not want to renounce our sins. St. Gregory of Nyssa writes in his *Sixth Homily on the Beatitudes*: "If the divine character is imposed upon us by a virtuous life, it is quite clear that a vicious life takes upon itself the form and features of the adversary (sc. the devil). [...] [L]et us fly from the form of the devil and take upon ourselves the likeness of God. Let us become pure of heart that we may be blessed, as the divine image is formed in us through the purity of our lives, in Christ Jesus our Lord."

May We Not Deform God's Image Within Ourselves

St. Augustine tried to describe this reality of the disappearance of God's image in man in yet another way. His starting point is the Biblical detail that having become aware of their nakedness, our first parents put on animal skins. The saint explains that this was caused by their pride. For them, it was not enough to be similar to God; they wanted to become gods that established the moral law. As a result, they took on the image and likeness of animals. Let us make particular note of St. Augustine's statement that we can choose from one of two situations: we can be similar to God or animals, for we cannot maintain our humanity if we cut ties with our closeness to God:

"For as a snake does not creep on with open steps, but advances by the very minutest efforts of its several scales; so the slippery motion of falling away [from what is good] takes possession of the negligent only gradually, and beginning from a perverse desire for the likeness of God, arrives in the end at the likeness of beasts. Hence it is that being naked of their first garment, they earned by mortality coats of skins. For the true honor of man is the image and likeness of God, which is not preserved except it be in relation to Him by Whom it is impressed. [...] But through the desire of making trial of his own power, man by his own bidding falls down to himself as to a sort of intermediate grade. And so, while he wishes to be as God is, that is, under no one, he is thrust on, even from his own middle grade, by way of punishment, to that which is lowest, that is, to those things in which beasts delight: and thus, while his honor is the likeness of God, but his dishonor is the likeness of the beast, 'Man being in honor abides not: he is compared to the beasts that are foolish, and is made like to them.'"[131]

St. Augustine's reflections above are, therefore, an attempt at fathoming the idea that until we become like Jesus Christ all of us carry the image of the first Adam (see 1 Corinthians 15:49) and that we should throw out the old man "and put on the new self, created in God's way in righteousness and holiness of truth" (Ephesians 4:24).

Let us also recall another insightful observation by St. Augustine. Instead of looking for similarity to the Creator, man, who has been created in God's image, tries to make God similar to himself: "God wants to make you similar to Him, yet you seek to make God similar to you. May God appeal to you as He is and not as you would like to have Him. You are perverted and you want God to be like you, not as He is. If He appealed to you as He is, you would improve and put your heart into trying to imitate Him. Not doing so at the present, you have become prone to perversion" (*Sermon* 9:8).

131. St. Augustine, *On the Trinity* (Book XII), trans. Arthur West, [in:] *From Nicene and Post-Nicene Fathers, First Series*, Vol. 3, ed. Philip Schaff (Buffalo, NY: Christian Literature Publishing Co., 1887); https://www.newadvent.org/fathers/130112.htm (accessed March 9, 2022).

The Son of God Is the Perfect Image of God

All of the above arguments can in a sense be treated as an introduction to the truth for our most important theme: the ideal Image of God does exist in reality. This Image is the Only-Begotten Son, equal to His Eternal Father in His Divinity: "He is the Image of the invisible God, the Firstborn of all creation. For in Him were created all things in heaven and on earth" (Colossians 1:15-16; see 2 Corinthians 4:4). Christ "is the refulgence of His glory, the very imprint of His being, and Who sustains all things by His mighty word. When He had accomplished purification from sins, He took His seat at the right hand of the Majesty on high" (Hebrews 1:3). The second part of the sentence referenced in the Epistle to the Hebrew leaves no doubt as to the fact that the Son of God is the perfect Image of God not only in His Divine nature but also as a man. In fact, He clearly says this Himself: "Whoever has seen Me has seen the Father" (John 14:9).

That brings completely new perspectives (with respect to the Old Testament) for both the teaching about God's image in man and the ability to use images in worship of the True God. It is said in the Book of Exodus: "But you cannot see My Face, for no one can see Me and live" (33:20). This impossibility became fact in Jesus Christ: people could see in Him the perfect Image of God, and not only did they not die because of this, but this event has become the source of life for all of us.

The Only-Begotten Son is the only perfect Image of God and cannot be compared to the sense in which we are images. This difference is wonderfully described by St. Augustine: "As an image, you are an imitator of God, but you are not an image in the same sense as the Son. In the human world, there are also diverse images. The son of a man carries within him an image of his father and is the same as his father, for he is a man just like his father. Meanwhile, your reflection in the mirror is not what you are. Your image is different in your son than it is in the mirror: in your son, your image is substantially equal, while in the mirror it has little corporality yet is some image of you, although not as corporal as your image in your son. Likewise, in the creation the image of God is not what it is in the Son, Who is equal to the Father and is the Word of God, through which everything has happened" (*Sermon* 9:8).

We Must Become Images of the Perfect Image

Only now, in light of revelation about the Son of God as the perfect image of His Father does the truth about the image of God in man take on full meaning. We read in the Epistle to the Romans (8:29): "For those He foreknew He also predestined to be conformed to the image of His Son, so that He might be the Firstborn among many brothers." Thus, the Old Testament ideas that man was called to participate in God's dominion and in God's immortality are barely a foreground to the truth about man as the image of God. The essence of this truth is the news that God calls us and destines us to become similar to His Only-Begotten Son. We are to become images of the Perfect Image; the Eternal Father makes us His sons in His Only-Begotten Son; He makes us participants in His Divine nature. Indeed, the New Testament frequently says that the Father of the Only-Begotten Son also births us to new life (for example John 1:13n; 1 Peter 1:3n, 23-25; James 1:18; 1 John 3:9, 5:18).

Although we are called to reflect God's nature within us, this must happen in our human nature. Just as the Only-Begotten Son is in His Divinity the prototype of this reflection, in His humanity He has likewise become the prototype of the divinized man. In this way, the history of all of humanity is brought together by the two Adams. The first Adam, and along with him all of us, have been created in God's image. Although we have sinned, we have never completely lost God's image in us. The aim of our journey is to resemble the Second

Adam: "The first man was from the earth, earthly; the Second Man, from heaven. As was the earthly one, so also are the earthly, and as is the heavenly one, so also are the heavenly. Just as we have borne the image of the earthly one, we shall also bear the image of the Heavenly One" (1 Corinthians 15:47-49). At the end of time, even our bodies will resemble His glorified body: "He will change our lowly body to conform with His glorified body by the power that enables Him also to bring all things into subjection to Himself" (Philippians 3:21).

For the moment, we should through the power of Jesus Christ throw off ourselves everything that has grown old in the first Adam; i.e., the sinful man: "[Y]ou have taken off the old self with its practices and have put on the new self, which is being renewed, for knowledge, in the image of its Creator" (Colossians 3:9-10; see Romans 6:5n).

When Will We Be Ultimately Similar to Him?

One more aspect of our theme is worth recalling, especially as it is deeply rooted in the consciousness of Western Christianity. Namely, St. Augustine, who saw traces of the Holy Trinity in all of creation, also noted the trinitarian structure of the image of God, which has been impressed in man. Thus, God's image in man consists of memory, reason, and love: memory of our origin in God and our capability to know and love Him. Sometimes, man completely forgets that he comes from God. However, this forgetting is never complete in the full meaning of the word. Man is incapable of completely throwing out of himself the concepts of justice, truth, and good. Even if he had completely distorted them in himself, he always carries these concepts within himselfas a sign that he comes from God. However, although we can distort the image of God within ourselves, we can never renew or fix it by ourselves. This is solely within the authority of the One Who has shaped us in His image. The above ideas have been most completely presented in Book Twelve of St. Augustine's *On the Trinity*.

Man is a living image of God. In order to regain his initial shape and become increasingly like the Prototype, he must want to adhere to Him. "As we said of the nature of the human mind, that both in the case when as a whole it contemplates the truth it is the image of God; and in the case when anything is divided from it, and diverted in order to the cognition of temporal things; nevertheless on that side on which it beholds and consults truth, here also it is the image of God, but on that side whereby it is directed to the cognition of the lower things, it is not the image of God. And since it is so much the more formed after the image of God, the more it has extended itself to that which is eternal."[132] This brings to mind the Augustinian interpretation of the instruction to "repay to Caesar what belongs to Caesar and to God what belongs to God" (Matthew 22:21): The image of Caesar was inscribed on the coin, but God's image is inscribed in you; therefore, give to God what belongs to Him: your entire self (*Exposition of Psalm 103:3*).

However, St. Augustine was not the first to express the thought that we should adhere as closely as possible to the Divine Prototype so that we may completely become God's image. This thought is incomparably more deeply expressed in the Word of God: "All of us, gazing with unveiled face on the glory of the Lord, are being transformed into the same image from glory to glory, as from the Lord Who is the Spirit" (2 Corinthians 3:18). "Beloved, we are God's children now; what we shall be has not yet been revealed. We do know that when it is revealed we shall be like Him, for we shall see Him as He is" (1 John 3:2).

132. St. Augustine, *On the Trinity* (Book XII), trans. Arthur West, [in:] *From Nicene and Post-Nicene Fathers, First Series*, Vol. 3, ed. Philip Schaff (Buffalo, NY: Christian Literature Publishing Co., 1887); https://www.newadvent.org/fathers/130112.htm (accessed March 9, 2022).

I Believe in Jesus Christ

HOW TO TALK ABOUT JESUS CHRIST TODAY?

The first response to this question is suggested in the Epistle to the Hebrews: "Jesus Christ is the same yesterday, today, and forever" (13:8). Today, we should speak of Jesus Christ the same way as always. From the very beginning, there have been attempts to relativize (Matthew 16:14; 1 Corinthians 15:17), mythologize (1 John 4:2-3; 2 John 7), and even slander Him (Luke 7:34; Matthew 27:63).

The Inconsistency of Faith in Jesus with the Rules of Political Correctness

Today's mentality tries to impose on Christians a new form of relativizing Jesus that was probably unheard-of in previous centuries. When some people recognized Jesus as someone akin to John the Baptist, Elijah, or Jeremiah or when they tried to explain the mystery of His Person by situating Him in the same perspective from which they saw Buddha, Socrates, Muhammed, or Gandhi, they explained the phenomenon of Jesus as non-believers. Metaphorically speaking, they believed that the moon was simply one of many streetlamps.

Today, there are growing demands for Christians to renounce their faith that Jesus is the gift of the Eternal Father for all people, that He died for the sins of all people, and that He has the power to lead everyone to eternal life. We are told: "You can believe that Jesus is your Savior; however, it is an act of aggression to say that He is everyone's Savior." Metaphorically speaking once again, we are allowed to believe that the moon is something more than a streetlamp, but we must know that outside the perimeter of your parish He is only a streetlamp.

It is difficult to explain to people who reason in this way that presenting such demands is essentially banning us from believing in Jesus. If He is the Son of God only for us believers or if He has redeemed only us, He is the Son of God and the Redeemer only in our opinion and in reality, is neither.

It turns out that even for people who (usually unwittingly) try to prohibit us from believing in the true Jesus, a simple testimony to this faith makes a great impression. When we respond to their unjustified demands with "I truly believe in the Lord Jesus" or "If He has truly died for our sins, then He also died for the sins of those who do not believe in Him" or "Christ's birth is meaningful only if God has truly given us His Son," then people who had previously tried to confine our faith into the uniform of political correctness devised by intolerant liberalism grow silent or perhaps even become less certain. I would like to note that all three testimonies contain the word "truly."

To Know Jesus, One Must Love Him

Without a doubt, we can find the true Jesus in the Gospels. The Church Fathers above all referenced the Gospels when they had to defend the faithful against the false conceptions of Christ presented by those whose faith was erroneous. Likewise, when we are faced with the relativism with respect to Him today, there is no better way to recall Who Christ the Lord truly is than by immersing oneself in the Gospels and credibly preaching them.

Indeed, the Gospels unambiguously and frequently say who He is, but above all they prevent us from merely dealing with His Person from the vantage point of an observer. We are not allowed to preach the truth about Him — not even the fact that He is the Son of God and Redeemer — without the love that brings us to Him (John 3:16); the love in which He has fulfilled His mission (John 13:1; 15:13); and, finally, the love that He expects of us (Matthew 10:37; John 21:15).

Simply put, our preaching Jesus should be an invitation to love Him and entrust all our concerns to Him. Thus, it would be inappropriate to preach Him to other people without us loving Him first. We should speak about Jesus from the perspective of someone who truly loves Him and wants to love Him more and more.

In this way, we touch upon the main reason why many contemporary Christians are incapable of preaching Christ: they do not know how to speak of Him with faith to even their very own children. Unfortunately, His prophecy is coming true in our times: "[B] ecause of the increase of evildoing, the love of many will grow cold" (Matthew 24:12). Naturally, this does not refer to such love that can be measured by emotions or declarations but love that is a gift from above and grows out of sanctifying grace. Such love directs us to the sources by which we can encounter the loving and living Jesus, i.e. to His words and sacraments. Thanks to this love, we are no longer slaves to sin and can fulfill God's commandments.

Let us recall that Jesus Himself spoke of the crucial meaning for us to love Him more than anyone else: "Whoever loves father or mother more than Me is not worthy of Me, and whoever loves son or daughter more than Me is not worthy of Me" (Matthew 10:37). If someone who was not God demanded such love for himself, that would mean that he is either mad or equal to the devil himself in terms of pride and egocentrism. However, when God demands we love Him "with your whole heart, and with your whole being, and with your whole strength" (Deuteronomy 6:5) and to not even love one's father or mother as much as we would love Him, He in this way demonstrates His selfless love for us. After all, the infinitely perfect God will be neither richer nor happier thanks to our love for Him. Meanwhile, our love for Him verifies, purifies, strengthens, and deepens all our love, including that for our loved ones.

Let us notice that it was only thanks to Biblical revelation that people had the courage to think about the fact that God loves us and wants us to be His friends. Those who professed non-Biblical religions occasionally prayed and made sacrifices to their deities to alleviate their wrath and gain their protection; however, they did not do so too often to avoid suspicions of a desire to become too intimate with them. Biblical revelation was necessary for people to possess a yearning for closeness with God of the sort that we read about in Sacred Scripture: "As for me, to be near God is my good, to make the Lord God my refuge. I shall declare all Your works in the gates of daughter Zion (Psalm 73:28; see 71:5-7; 118:8-9).

Witness to the Father

In general, in the Church we recall the apostles' admonition to not adapt the truth about Jesus to neither our own conceptions nor to anyone's expectations (1 Corinthians 15:12-19; Galatians 1:6-9; 1 John 4:1-3) but to profess the authentic Jesus, the One Who has truly come to us from His Father. Those who preach some other Jesus — not the One Who is the true Son of God and Who has truly become a man — destroy the very meaning of His coming to us.

When we closely read the Gospels, we can find three salvific tasks for whose fulfillment the Son of God became a man. Although all three are ultimately tied to one another, we will recall them here and characterize each one individually, as they reveal three different aspects of the truth about Jesus Christ and all three should certainly be the subject of our faith and our preaching. The Son of God has taken on our humanity to be a Witness to His Father (Matthew 11:27; John 1:18, 6:46, 18:37); dazzle us sinners with the beauty of His (and our) humanity (John 12:46, 8:46, 4:34; Matthew 26:39; Luke 23:34); and, finally, to become our Redeemer and Savior (Matthew 1:21; John 1:29).

He is so reliable a Witness to His Father that "[w]hoever has seen Me has seen the Father" (John 14:9). It was only thanks to Him that we learned Who God truly is, while by looking at Him as He was presented in the Gospels inspired by the Holy Spirit we can verify and correct our various erroneous conceptions of God. Due to our sinfulness, our conceptions of God are at times terribly deformed. We often imagine that God is very distant and is little concerned about us. Or we suspect Him of being unfeeling or cruel; of not being concerned about our straying, the injustices we experience, and our suffering. Sometimes we imagine that, on the contrary, perhaps God wishes us well but is ultimately incapable of helping us. Unfortunately, our understanding of God is in many ways deformed by our sinfulness.

Thus, it is very important to contemplate Jesus and correct our conceptions of God according to this model. It is only thanks to the Lord Jesus that we can properly surmise what it means that God is truly omnipotent, for example. After all, the One Whom the storms and seas obey allowed Himself to be nailed to the Cross. In this way, He not only revealed God's respect for human freedom, even if we dishonorably abuse it, but at the same time He revealed to us that God wants to conquer evil with love, while His omnipotence is most fully revealed in His mercy.

Looking at Jesus, we can see how unfair we are in accusing God of insensitivity to our suffering or straying. It suffices to recall the two situations when Jesus cried (Luke 19:41; John 11:35). Once, He cried over human sin when He cried over Jerusalem's infidelity. Second, He cried over human mortality at Lazarus' tomb. Yet we dare to accuse God, Who is love, of the destruction, harm, and suffering that result from our sins and those of others. Instead of praising God for wanting to encompass us with His simultaneously omnipotent and obedient love while allowing evil because of our freedom, we sometimes prefer to deform our conceptions of God to fit the image of our own sinfulness.

Furthermore, Jesus is the Witness to the fact that the Eternal Father mysteriously suffers due to our sins. His statement that "whoever has seen [Him] has seen the Father" concern all His behaviors, teachings, and miracles, but they especially refer to His holy suffering. Those who look at the Crucified Jesus can understand how greatly our sins wound God Himself. Those who are capable of noticing that the Lord Jesus embraced all sinners — including those who had contributed to His death — with His love even on the Cross will see His loving, merciful, and forgiving face through the suffering face of the Son of God. When preaching about Jesus, we definitely should speak about this more often and more profoundly than we do.

The Perfect Man

Jesus not only reveals to us Who God truly is and does not only correct our conceptions of Him. As the Second Vatican Council has expressed in *Gaudium et spes*, He fully reveals Himself to man as a man. This truth was recalled by John Paul II during the famous words met with thunderous applause in Warsaw's Victory Square on June 2, 1979: "For man cannot be fully understood without Christ. Or rather, man is incapable of understanding himself fully without Christ. He cannot understand who he is, nor what his true dignity is, nor what his vocation is, nor what his final end is. He cannot understand any of this without Christ."

Especially through His coming to us and the Cross, Christ the Lord is proof of the incredible value that man has in God's own eyes.

Thanks to Christ, we have learned that "man […] is the only creature on earth which God willed for itself" (*Gaudium et spes*, 24). How great a treasure man is to the Eternal Father is reflected in the fact that He did not hesitate and "to ransom a slave You gave away Your Son," as we sing in the Holy Saturday liturgy. John Paul II writes in the encyclical *Redemptor hominis* (10): "In reality, the name for that deep amazement at man's worth and dignity is the Gospel, that is to say: the Good News."

However, we will focus our attention on the fact that by becoming a man Christ the Lord went through His earthly life in a perfect way. Thus, we can understand ourselves also in the sense that by contemplating Him, the Perfect Man, we can better understand what it truly means to be man.

Although the Gospels are small books, they contain enough information about Jesus for us to be able to constantly, or at least every Sunday, study His actions and behaviors as well as speeches and instructions to become inspired and imitate Him. After all, He embarked on a path like ours in life in a world greatly deformed by human sin in which the salvation of the truth and beauty of one's humanity can be difficult, sometimes greatly so.

The two fundamental traits that encompass the entirety of our thoughts and attitudes as well as words and actions above all determine that someone is a good person in a beautiful way. Naturally, both these traits characterized Jesus not only to the highest degree but at the same time in a unique way. These traits are: completely entrusting Himself to the Eternal Father and giving Himself to others in a selfless gift of love.

Jesus did not just declare His complete entrustment to His Father; He above all implemented this attitude: "My food is to do the will of the One Who sent Me and to finish His work" (John 4:34). It suffices to recall His prayers during the two most important moments of His life: in Gethsemane (Mark 14:36) as well as the last prayer He offered to His Father immediately before His death (Luke 23:46).

In subsequent generations, thousands and millions of people learned this attitude of unconditional entrustment to God from Jesus, even in situations that seemed helpless from a human perspective. It is worth recalling that not believing God and suspecting Him of a deficit of benevolence towards us constitutes the very essence of our sinfulness; this is the source of the inhuman world which we can create for ourselves and others on God's earth. If not for Jesus, we would not even be able to presume how essential a defense of our humanity is in entrusting ourselves to God.

It is also difficult to imagine that we could so unambiguously and unconditionally formulate the truth that only unconditional love makes up the ultimate meaning of our humanity without faith in Jesus. The famous statement from the conciliar constitution that "man, who is the only creature on earth which God willed for itself, cannot fully find himself except through a sincere gift of himself" (*Gaudium et spes*, 24) certainly has no equivalent outside Christian culture.

There can be no doubt that we have learned this truth about man from Jesus. Thus, when preaching Jesus, it is worth recalling His teaching about selfless love for one's neighbor (Luke 10:29-37), including one's enemy (Matthew 5:43-48), a teaching confirmed by His attitude, even when suffering and when faced with death (John 10:14-15, 13:1, 15:13; Romans 5:7-8; Luke 23:34). Along with the absolute entrustment to the Father, this was Jesus' life's attitude that particularly revealed Him as the Perfect Man. This is why we know ourselves when looking at Him; we learn who we are, how we should be, and our own dignity, vocation, and ultimate purpose.

"We Preach the Crucified Christ"

When we believe in Jesus, we should accept with all our hearts that He is the Redeemer of all people, Who "is expiation for our sins, and nor for our sins only but for those of the whole world" (1 John 2:2). I know from my experience as a preacher that accepting this truth effectively allows us to note that in our own lives even the most perfect, most exalted love is not authentic love if it runs away from the Cross. Unfortunately, we have countless opportunities to see this today. A flight from demanding love is not an uncommon phenomenon today.

We can prepare to accept this truth about the Crucified Christ Who has risen from the dead by seeing in the Gospels how difficult it was for the apostles to accept this truth. The Apostle Peter was incapable of accepting it, although he had just professed his faith in Jesus the Messiah and the Son of God (Matthew 16:16-23). Even seeing Jesus' glory on the Mount of Transfiguration with their own physical eyes was insufficient for the disciples to see the meaning and necessity of the Cross their Master had to experience (Matthew 17:1-18, 22-23).

The Gospels carefully emphasize that Jesus voluntarily suffered; it was a sovereign act of His will to accept the intended outcome of the hatred and ill will directed at Him (Matthew 26:2; John 10:17-18). Previous attempts at murdering Him were unsuccessful because Jesus did not want to then sacrifice Himself this way (Luke 4:29-30; John 7:30, 44; John 8:59; John 10:31, 39). He wanted to enter, in a way, the very center of this inhuman world in which we can change our world through our sins. He voluntarily submitted to the incomprehensible injustice, disdain, and hatred of which we sinners are capable.

He undertook this situation out of love (John 13:1), but what is perhaps also worthy of attention is that amidst all the terrible suffering, mockery, and darkness that He had experienced His love never wavered or grew dimmer. It suffices to recall what He said to the Daughters of Jerusalem (Luke 23:28) and the penitent thief (Luke 23:43) or His prayer of forgiveness for His killers (Luke 23:34). Having found Himself in such darkness, He prayed using the words of the Psalm: "My God, my God, why have you forsaken me?" (Mark 15:34);

persisted in His entrustment to His Father; and died with a prayer of entrustment on His lips (Luke 23:46).

In the center of this cyclone of evil that Satan had unleashed and that He allowed Himself to be thrust into, Jesus turned out to be the same as always: a man completely filled with love for His Father and neighbor. It turned out that there are no places on earth that are so dark that Satan has the last word. It seems that it is much more legitimate to describe the essence of Christ the Lord's sacrifice not from the perspective of the sufferings He endured but rather as love implemented even amidst such terrible sufferings.

It must be clearly stated that the Perfect Man Who was more than human died on the Cross. The greatness of His love was not only founded on the fact that it was not corrupted by evil in the slightest way. He Who died in such an unusual way is the Son of God, equal to the Eternal Father. Since the heroism of ordinary people can cleanse and heal the spiritual atmosphere of entire milieus, it can hardly be doubted that the power of the love that Jesus — the Son of God! — experienced through His passion and Cross is of infinite value. It encompasses the people of all generations (or, to put it in a more cautious way, it can encompass everyone who does not close himself off to it) to liberate them from sin and grant them the grace of participation in God's nature.

Christian faith in Jesus Christ has no analogy in Buddhist convictions about Buddha or Muslim ones about Muhammed. Christ is the deepest fundament and the ultimate culmination of all creation. The New Testament often states this clearly: "For in Him were created all things in heaven and on earth, the visible and the invisible, whether thrones or dominions or principalities or powers; all things were created through Him and for Him" (Colossians 1:16). This is why His taking on our humanity is such an inconceivable gift of God's love for us people and the entirety of creation. This is why the redemption of everything that has been deformed by sin has happened through

His death on the Cross, while the striving of all creation "for the fullness of times, to sum up all things in Christ, in heaven and on earth" (Ephesians 1:10) began through His resurrection.

Christians should first of all be aware of the absolute uniqueness of their faith compared to all other religions. Second, we should not succumb to the pressures of the spirit of this world, which by accusing us of fanaticism, European provincialism, of trying to have a monopoly on the truth, and feeling superior to all who do not share our faith in Christ, would like to force us to adjust our image of Christ to the expectations of the contemporary mentality and consequently renounce our faith in the true Christ. Finally, we should develop within ourselves and cultivate the desire to share our faith in Christ with all who want to listen. In other words, we would be betraying Christ if we were to forget that the Church is missionary in her essence.

"BEGOTTEN, NOT MADE"

Recently, someone asked me: "I have been repeating these words every Sunday for many years, yet I only recently realized how poorly I understand them. Why do we emphasize so strongly during the profession of faith that the Son of God is *begotten, not made*? What does this mean? What do we as the Church profess when we say these words?"

The Only Son of God

Let us begin our search for an answer with another question: Why did the Lord Jesus, Who so frequently spoke of the heavenly Father, refer to Him as "My Father" or "your Father" with such stubborn consistency? He never said that He is our common Father, His and ours. In fact, He once explicitly emphasized that the Eternal Father is His Father and ours in completely different ways: "I am going to My Father and your Father, to My God and your God" (John 20:17).

The answer seems obvious: because He is the only Son of God, the Son of God in the literal sense. Meanwhile, when Sacred Scripture refers to us as the sons or children of God, in older texts this is meant in a metaphorical sense (i.e. that God is like a Father for us, meaning that He loves us, cares for us, forgives us, etc.). It is only in the apostolic texts that this is stated in a much deeper sense: that we are the sons or children of God and therefore are called to participate in the Divine filiation of the Only Begotten Son.

That only Jesus Christ is the Son of God in the full meaning of the word is carefully emphasized in the New Testament. Sometimes, He is called the Only Begotten Son. The Lord Jesus said to Nicodemus: "For God so loved the world that He gave His only Son, so that everyone who believes in Him might not perish but might have eternal life" (John 3:16; see 3:18; 1 John 4:9). Without a doubt, the Only Begotten Son is the true God: "No one has ever seen God. The only Son, God, Who is at the Father's side, has revealed Him" (John 1:18).

The uniqueness of His Divine filiation was confirmed by the Eternal Father Himself in the revelation in the Jordan River: "This is my beloved Son, with Whom I am well pleased" (Matthew 3:17) and on Mount Tabor (see Matthew 17:5). His words can refer to only the one Son of God: "All things have been handed over to Me by My Father. No one knows the Son except the Father, and no one knows the Father except the Son and anyone to whom the Son wishes to reveal Him" (Matthew 11:27; see Luke 10:22).

Arius' Tinkering with the Word of God

When the persecutions of the Church ended in 313 and the number of not necessarily authentic Christians began to significantly increase, the dangerous tendency to subordinate the Christian faith to the pagan mentality appeared. Particularly harmful was the idea of the Alexandrian priest Arius to express the truth of the divinity of the Son of God in the categories of pagan polytheism. Arius did not reject the truth that our Redeemer is God; the testimony of the New Testament expresses this far too clearly for him to have done so. However, the pagans were used to believing in the existence of multiple gods that were not necessarily equal to one another, appeared earlier or later than one another, and were not necessarily compatible with one another. Arius put forward the thesis that although the Son of God is God, He is not an entirely real God, for He has been created by God the Father and is therefore younger and inferior to Him.

The main theme of Arius' writings was an analysis of the concept of the "son." Let us try to reconstruct his arguments: "When you give birth to a son, you had to come first, and only then was your son born. Thus, there was a time when you did not have a son and when you were not yet a father. Furthermore, with respect to your child that has been born, you are greater, wiser, and more powerful."

On the basis of the above analysis, the Arians claimed that the Eternal Father came before His Son and there was a time when He did not have a Son and therefore was not yet a Father; thus, the Son of God is God only in a broad sense, as in reality He is His creation. Naturally, Arius and his supporters referred to Sacred Scripture. However, they did so in a way that "confirmed" their blasphemous theses. They did not seek out the Word of God in Sacred Scripture, but rather support for their views, which were inconsistent with Scripture. In short, they tinkered with the Word of God.

Arius' analysis is correct when we apply it to merely human children. Above all, he does not question the humanity of human children. In fact, this entire analysis assumes that a child born of humans is human. However, when Arius and his supporters suggest applying the same analysis to the concept of the Son of God, they do it based on an opposite assumption. They assumed in advance (which was fundamentally inconsistent with Sacred Scripture) that the Son of God was not truly the Son of God, and even if we call Him God, He is not the true God.

Thus, it is unsurprising that the ecumenical council that convened in Nice in 325 to distance itself from such a radical attempt at distorting the Christian faith very elaborately expressed the profession of faith that the Church believes in Christ's Divinity in the most literal sense: "I believe in one Lord Jesus Christ, the Only Begotten Son of God, born of the Father before all ages. God from God, Light from Light, true God from true God, begotten, not made, consubstantial with the Father; through Him all things were made."

One simply cannot credibly be in the Church yet simultaneously doubt that the Son of God is the true God, co-eternal with and equal to His Father. It is worth emphasizing that the symbol of faith adopted at Nice and complemented by the Council of Constantinople in 381 is the common heritage of the Catholic Church, all the Eastern churches, and the great majority of Protestant communities.

Let us also add that when we reflect on the eternal birth of the Son of God, we stand before the mystery of God, which transcends human reason. This was wonderfully expressed many centuries ago, in 380, by St. Gregory of Nazianzus: "How was He begotten? I repeat the question in indignation. The Begetting of God must be honored by silence. It is a great thing for you to learn that He was begotten. But the manner of His generation we will not admit that even Angels can conceive, much less you. Shall I tell you how it was? It was in a manner known to the Father Who begot, and to the Son Who was begotten. Anything more than this is hidden by a cloud and escapes your dim sight."[133]

Our Participation in Christ's Divine Filiation

Faith would be pointless if we were not concerned about truly believing in Christ but in some distortion of Him. The apostles firmly reminded us of this. The Apostle John writes: "Many deceivers have gone out into the world, those who do not acknowledge Jesus Christ

133. Gregory of Nazianzus, Third Theological Oration (Oration 29, IX), [in:] *Nicene and Post-Nicene Fathers, Second Series*, Vol. 7, trans. Charles Gordon Browne and James Edward Swallow, ed. Philip Schaff and Henry Wace (Buffalo, NY: Christian Literature Publishing Co., 1894), https://www.newadvent.org/fathers/310229.htm (accessed April 6, 2022).

as coming in the flesh; such is the deceitful one and the antichrist" (2 John 1:7). Meanwhile, St. Paul taught: "And if Christ has not been raised, then empty [too] is our preaching; empty, too, your faith" (1 Corinthians 15:14).

In other words, we believe because what we profess is the truth, and if we were to believe something untrue, then we would greatly offend God Himself for not believing in what He revealed to us about Himself. Arius' error led to much confusion in the Church because as Christians we take great care in believing what is true.

If the Son of God were not the true God, then He would not truly be the Son of God, only in some metaphorical sense. If He were a mere creature, even the most perfect creature, He would be neither the Son of God nor God. The very concept of the created God is internally inconsistent. That is why we profess every Sunday: "begotten [because He is the Son] and not made [because He is the true God]."

Considering what has been said above, if the Son of God were not truly God, what would be the point of the promise that we are to "share in the Divine nature" (2 Peter 1:4)? In His inconceivable mercy, the Lord God now makes us increasingly like Christ: "For through faith you are all children of God in Christ Jesus. For all of you who were baptized into Christ have clothed yourselves with Christ" (Galatians 3:26-27). Indeed, we are God's children in only an incipient way, but God's grace within us is "in labor until Christ be formed in you!" (Galatians 4:19). This wonderful teaching would lose its fundament if Christ the Lord were the Son of God only in a metaphorical sense.

The Lord Jesus teaches us that "no one can see the kingdom of God without being born from above" (John 3:3). Without a doubt, He was referring to our being born in God, to our participation in His being born of God: "But to those who did accept Him He gave power to become children of God, to those who believe in His name, who were born not by natural generation nor by human choice nor by a man's decision but of God" (John 1:12-13; see 1 Peter 1:3; James 1:18). Thus, if we have believed in Christ and persist in His grace we possess not only human life, created life, but we contain within ourselves the life of God Himself (a frightening thought!), and our participation in God's nature consists in this. As people, we have been created by God, but by belonging to Christ we experience deification; we become participants in His being born of God.

Naturally, there is an infinite abyss that separates not only the Creator from His creation, but also the birth of the Only Begotten Son and our birth in God. The Only Begotten Son is the True God, while we will never cease to be creatures called into existence out of nothing. He is the Son through His very nature, while we are His adopted children. What a wondrous adoption this is! This consists in God's love making us truly one with Christ. After all, we have received the same Holy Spirit that "scrutinizes everything, even the depths of God" (1 Corinthians 2:10). When we think that the same Holy Spirit also scrutinizes us, thanks to Him we can truly call out to God: "Abba! Father!" (see Romans 8.15; Galatians 4:6).

THE GIFT OF THE INCARNATION AS THE EXALTATION OF OUR HUMANITY

The Second Vatican Council recalls: "The truth is that only in the mystery of the incarnate Word does the mystery of man take on light" (*Gaudium et spes*, 22). Here, the word "mystery" (*mysterium*) is a technical term of the language of faith and indicates that reality described by it is a term that transcends the measure of natural reason, and what is essential in it can be understood only considering Divine Revelation and thanks to grace.

It is worth recalling that John Paul II's famous words pronounced on June 2, 1979, at Warsaw's Victory Square were in essence a commentary on the above-quoted conciliar statement. The pope then said that Christ is "the key to understanding that great and fundamental reality that is man. Indeed, man cannot be fully understood without Christ. For man cannot be fully understood without Christ. Or rather, man is incapable of understanding himself fully without Christ. He cannot understand who he is, nor what his true dignity is, nor what his vocation is, nor what his final end is. He cannot understand any of this without Christ."

Naturally, the council and later the pope were not concerned about the theoretical or practical cognition of who man is but about cognition in faith in Christ and therefore cognition that encompasses the entire person, takes place through listening to the Word of God and implementing it, in seeking out closeness to God and His grace through prayer and the sacraments, through fidelity to the commandments and the imitation of Christ in assuming the Cross every day. In this way, Christ the Lord reveals to us more and more. To borrow a term from the above-mentioned fragment of *Gaudium et spes*, He reveals to us "the mystery of the Father and His love," and in it "fully reveals man to man himself."

Let us say this in slightly more comprehensible language: The revelation of man to man takes place not through some act of transmitting knowledge that is inaccessible to natural reason, but through the activity of saving power within us, which transforms us or frees us from the sins that deform our humanity and leads us to our ultimate destiny.

God's love is the beginning of this revelation of man to man: God not only told us that He loves us, but He loves us in an inconceivable way, for He moved His love to such a degree that "He gave His only Son, so that everyone who believes in Him might not perish but might have eternal life" (John 3:16). In response to such unexpected and measureless love, Pope Leo the Great famously exclaimed in one of his Christmas sermons: "Christian, acknowledge your dignity, and becom[e] a partner in the Divine nature."[134]

The essence of what we receive thanks to the humanity of the Son of God was masterfully summarized by John Paul II: "The redemption of the world [...] is, at its deepest root, the fullness of justice

134. St. Leo the Great, "Sermon 21," [in:] *Nicene and Post-Nicene Fathers, Second Series*, Vol. 12, trans. Charles Lett Feltoe, eds. Philip Schaff and Henry Wace (Buffalo, NY: Christian Literature Publishing Co., 1895); https://www.newadvent.org/fathers/360321.htm (accessed April 6, 2022).

in a human Heart — the Heart of the First-born Son" (*Redemptor hominis*, 9). Such an exaltation of man is, in fact, incredible: God has decided to love us all equally and humanly; He wanted for His Son to become one of us and love us with His human Heart as well!

That is the ultimate truth about man from the perspective of the love of God, Who gave us His own Son. However, love — even the love of God Himself — remains unfulfilled until it is accepted by the beloved and until it makes us capable of loving. We, people, have become capable of recognizing that love is the ultimate horizon of our human life only after having experienced God's inconceivable love, love that culminated in the Incarnation, the Cross, and the Eucharist. More important, we have become capable (or, to put it more cautiously, we are in the process of becoming capable) of accepting and implementing love as the ultimate value and the very fundament of our human dignity.

John Paul II writes about this in the unforgettable fragment of his first encyclical, one that was evidently inspired by the already-quoted text in *Gaudium et spes* (22): "Man cannot live without love. He remains a being that is incomprehensible for himself, his life is senseless, if love is not revealed to him, if he does not encounter love, if he does not experience it and make it his own, if he does not participate intimately in it" (*ibid.*, 10)

The pope continues: "The man who wishes to understand himself thoroughly — and not just in accordance with immediate, partial, often superficial, and even illusory standards and measures of his being — he must with his unrest, uncertainty and even his weakness and sinfulness, with his life and death, draw near to Christ. He must, so to speak, enter him with all his own self, he must 'appropriate' and assimilate the whole of the reality of the Incarnation and Redemption to find himself. If this profound process takes place within him, he then bears fruit not only of adoration of God but also of deep wonder at himself. How precious must man be in the eyes of the Creator, if he 'gained so great a Redeemer.' [...] In reality, the name for that deep amazement at man's worth and dignity is the Gospel, that is to say: the Good News."

I will try to present here this exaltation of man that takes place thanks to the humanity of the Son of God, discussing in turn the four fruits of the gift of the Incarnation mentioned in the *Catechism of the Catholic Church* (457-460): The Word became flesh to 1) save us and reconcile us with God; 2) reveal God's love to us; 3) call us to sanctity, which makes us capable of making a real sacrifice of ourselves when following Christ; and 4) to make us participants in God's nature.

1. The Elevation of Man from the Downfall Through God's Submission

Because of original sin, we as humanity have found ourselves in a state of downfall, i.e., our spiritual situation departs from the Creator's initial intentions for us in diverse ways. This results from our rejecting our friendship and unity with God, Who after all is the source of life and all meaning. Having distanced ourselves from God, we have simultaneously become the victims and creators of various destructive forces that destroy us and our human collectivity and even the world in which our Creator has situated us.

As humanity, we have separated ourselves from one another through walls of hostility, indifference, and false alliances; deception and violence have become the everyday tools of communication with one another. All our values have become prone to disaccord; the truth becomes mixed up with falsehood and is oftentimes separated from love, while our righteousness and mercy become isolated from one another. Our feelings are frequently irrational, while our freedom is too weak for us to control our desires. Furthermore, every person, each of us, is more or less internally fractured: "For the flesh has desires against the Spirit, and the Spirit against the flesh; these are opposed to each other, so that you may not do what you want" (Galatians 5:17). Thus, it is unsurprising that death is the logical end of such a situation (see Romans 6:21).

Naturally, the world has not ceased to be of God due to our sins. However, our evil has greatly distorted it. We have transformed God's world to a significant degree through our disdain for one another and by harming the weak, by sowing hatred, injustice, falsehood, and debauchery; persecuting the righteous; and even shedding innocent blood.

The Son of God did not only accept our humanity. He came to us as one of us and wanted to be with us in such a world that is greatly marked by the curse of sin. He took on every human trait except for sin. "For what the law, weakened by the flesh, was powerless to do, this God has done: by sending His own Son in the likeness of sinful flesh and for the sake of sin, He condemned sin in the flesh" (Romans 8:3).

The Son of God humbled Himself to the degree that, except for sin, He came to participate even in our downfall: "Rather, He emptied Himself, taking the form of a slave, coming in human likeness; and found human in appearance, He humbled himself, becoming obedient to death, even death on a cross" (Philippians 2:7-8). He exposed Himself to all the attacks and madness of evil which we sinners serve, but He did not submit to them to even the smallest degree. True, the forces of evil that dominate our world crushed Him (let us remember, however, that it was His voluntary decision to be exposed to them; see John 10:17-18), but He did not subordinate Himself to them for even a moment. At the Cross — the only cross to which the Son of God allowed Himself to be nailed — love turned out to be more powerful than the entire concentrated power of evil. We have received definite evidence that there is no place on earth where Satan would be capable of overthrowing God's domination.

We contemplate the Cross of Christ the Lord from all possible vantage points. Let us now look at this Cross from the perspective of the exaltation of our humanity. As we have seen, the Son of God's subjecting Himself to death on the Cross led the gift of the Incarnation to extremely radical consequences; not only did He become a man, but He wanted to truly participate in our downfall (however, it must be emphasized that He did not do so with respect to sin).

This Man's victory on the Cross was a victory of our entire degraded humanity. He Himself said: "And when I am lifted up from the earth, I will draw everyone to Myself" (John 12:32). He has the power to lift up all who follow Him from our downfall. All who entrust themselves to Christ and allow themselves to be led by His grace will receive "power to become children of God" (John 1:12). We no longer have to persist in humanity enslaved by sin and Satan. Through Christ, we have been called to "put away the old self of [our] former way of life, corrupted through deceitful desires, and be renewed in the spirit of [our] minds, and put on the new self, created in God's way in righteousness and holiness of truth" (Ephesians 4:22-24).

Naturally, the entirety of man, body and spirit alike, has become degraded due to sin. The entire person experiences exaltation in Christ until we all sit "in the heavens in Christ Jesus" (Ephesians 2:6). Nonetheless, the New Testament likes to speak in a way that makes it seem that the main sphere of the struggle for our humanity and the main location of our victories is our body.

The Apostle Paul implores: "I urge you therefore, brothers, by the mercies of God, to offer your bodies as a living sacrifice, holy and pleasing to God, your spiritual worship" (Romans 12:1). Let us recall a couple more such expressions: "[We are] always carrying about in the body the dying of Jesus, so that the life of Jesus may also be manifested in our body" (2 Corinthians 4:10); "those who belong to Christ [Jesus] have crucified their flesh with its passions and desires" (Galatians 5:24; see John 1:13; 2 Corinthians 10:3; James 3:2; 1 Peter 4:1-2).

The Apostle Paul once wrote that, *pars pro toto*, "we wait for adoption, the redemption of our bodies" (Romans 8:23). Furthermore, now "your body is a temple of the holy Spirit within you. [...] Therefore, glorify God in your body" (1 Corinthians 6:19-20).

In a word, Christ the Lord elevates the entirety of man, including our corporality, out of humiliation. Having lost our friendship with God, not only have our souls become prone to the foolishness that we can replace God with all sorts of invented values; not only axiology has confused us in such a way that we choose evil as if it were good. Likewise, our bodies have found themselves in a pathetic situation, as bitterly described by the Apostle Paul: "For the flesh has desires against the Spirit, and the Spirit against the flesh; these are opposed to each other, so that you may not do what you want. [...] Now the works of the flesh are obvious: immorality, impurity, licentiousness, idolatry, sorcery, hatreds, rivalry, jealousy, outbursts of fury, acts of selfishness, dissensions, factions, occasions of envy, drinking bouts, orgies, and the like. I warn you, as I warned you before, that those who do such things will not inherit the kingdom of God" (Galatians 5:17, 19-21).

The crucified and resurrected Christ has the power to lift our bodies from their humiliation. Thanks to Christ, man becomes united with God, and one of the fruits of this unification is the reconciliation of the spiritual with the corporal in those of us who belong to Christ. Thanks to the grace of Christ, our bodies act as our souls. In Christ, the body no longer struggles against the soul; instead, they cooperate. What is described by the Apostle Paul takes place: "If then you were raised with Christ, seek what is above, where Christ is seated at the right hand of God" (Colossians 3:1).

2. The Culmination of the Revelation of God's Love

The truth of the Incarnation is firmly rejected by both Judaism and Islam. However, many who consider themselves to be Christians and are fascinated by Jesus likewise do not want to accept it. In the times of the apostles, there were the Ebionites, who saw Jesus as someone akin to John the Baptist, Elijah, or Jeremiah (see Matthew 16:14); in other words, they considered Him to be merely a prophet and nothing more. Meanwhile, the docetists acknowledged Jesus' Divinity, but they rejected the truth of His humanity (see 1 John 4:1-3; 2 John 7). In the first centuries of Christianity, the former current was continued by the Arians and Nestorians, while the latter was followed by the adoptionists, the monophysites, or the Monothelites. In modern and contemporary times, the spirit of Ebionitism was expressed in Ernest Renan's *Life of Jesus,* while the spirit of Docetism brings about much confusion through its attempts at separating the historical Jesus from the Christ of faith.

In polemics with intra-Christian attempts at undermining the truth of the Incarnation, it is usually pointed out that without it, Christianity and Jesus' own mission in general become meaningless. One notable attempt at understanding the reasons why many people find it difficult to believe that God truly became man was expressed by John Paul II in his passionate Christmas sermon in 1992. The pope gave these reasons the form of grievances directed at God due to His entry into our world:

"After all, You, God, are beyond everything. You can only be beyond the world; one and only in Your infinite majesty. God, remain alone! Do not bow down to the level of creation! Do not bow down to the level of man! Thus man responds, but he speaks differently, too: Stay beyond the world! Leave the world to man alone! You limit man in this world. We cannot live here together. That is also the response of man who says that such an answer is synonymous with the progress and self-determination of humanity."

The religious studies scholar will see in the above description the idea of *Deus remotus*, the distant God Whose closeness man fears and rejects. According to John Paul II, rejecting the truth of the Incarnation results from a fear of love and a fear of God, Who is Love. At times, it would be more comfortable for us if God were not Love, if He did not love us as He has happened in Jesus Christ.

In the above-mentioned sermon, John Paul II zealously argues: "Brothers and sisters, do not try to ward off God. Do not prohibit God from living amongst us. The One Who was born today is consubstantial with the Father; He is the First-Born of all creation. He comes to what is His. Do not prohibit Him! Let us not think that He should remain alone, clad in unattainable Majesty, but lonesome — beyond the world and outside the world. The world is His, while in the world man is His most of all, as the image and likeness of the Invisible in the visible world. Love is the most appropriate name of God's Majesty, while Love is true when it becomes a gift, when it gives."

In a word, because God "had to" give us His Son, the Son in a way "had to" assume our humanity, and having assumed it, He in a sense "had to" love us until the very end. Naturally, the fact that He "had to" do so was not such a necessity that it would in the slightest degree reduce the voluntary nature of His gift of redemption. He "had to" because of the necessity of love, because love "must" give itself as a gift; this happens in freedom, without which there would be no real gift.

However, true love strives to call the beloved to love and make them capable of loving. Let us recall who we were as the beloved: "But God proves His love for us in that while we were still sinners Christ died for us. [...] Indeed, if, while we were enemies, we were reconciled to God through the death of His Son, how much more, once reconciled, will we be saved by His life" (Romans 5:8, 10). On our earth, where love has so much to say, to consistently love means to take up one's cross and follow Christ. Christ the Lord not only calls us to such love; He has given us a model and makes us capable of it. This is one of the most essential aspects that lift us up from our degrading downfall: thanks to Christ, Who became one of us and persisted in love even amidst the terrible humiliation of the Cross, we can lift ourselves up from our lack of love and learn to love as He loved us.

It is worth noting that in the New Testament, at the level of expressions, the gift of the Incarnation is above all tied to taking on the body. Let us recall several such expressions: "And the Word became flesh and made His dwelling among us" (John 1:14); "For what the law, weakened by the flesh, was powerless to do, this God has done: by sending His own Son in the likeness of sinful flesh and for the sake of sin" (Romans 8:3); "For in Him dwells the whole fullness of the deity bodily" (Colossians 2:9); "For this reason, when He came into the world, He said: 'Sacrifice and offering you did not desire, but a body you prepared for me'" (Hebrews 10:5); "[E]very spirit that acknowledges Jesus Christ come in the flesh belongs to God" (1 John 4:2).

The clear conclusion is that Christ the Lord came to us to restore dignity to that dimension of our humanity which because of our sin has experienced debasement: our bodies. "The body, however, is not for immorality, but for the Lord, and the Lord is for the body; God raised the Lord and will also raise us by His power. Do you not know that your bodies are members of Christ?" (1 Corinthians 6:13-15). It seems that nothing deeper can be said on the topic of the dignity of our human bodies.

3. The Vocation to Holiness, or to Imitate the One Who Became Man

The third of the aims of the Incarnation of the Son of God mentioned in the *Catechism* is the sanctification of our humanity. Sanctity or holiness is a trait that is difficult to define. In the strict meaning of the word, only God is holy. Sanctity is something inconceivably greater than kindness, righteousness, or chastity; the essence of sanctity is in a way obscured by our ignorance. Anne, Samuel's mother, admitted: "There is no Holy One like the Lord" (1 Samuel 2:2).

Although the Old Testament contains a summons to sanctity (see Leviticus 19:2; 20:8), in essence they are promises and prophesies in nature. The first truly holy man was the Son of God, Jesus Christ. The angel that prophesied His birth announced He would be holy (see Luke 1:35). Peter substantiates his remaining by Jesus on the day when nearly all had left Him to the other disciples by arguing that He is the Holy God: "We have come to believe and are convinced that You are the Holy One of God" (John 6:69)

When the Holy One became one of us, it turned out that the sanctity descending from God to our created world consisted of projecting the Trinitarian pro-existence, of giving oneself up in love until the very end: "And I consecrate Myself for them, so that they also may be consecrated in truth" (John 17:19). In the Polish language, the verb *hagiadzein* is translated in two possible ways, also in the above verse: "to sanctify" or "to sacrifice." It is worth knowing that in the New Testament this verb usually simultaneously contains both these meanings: sanctification is based on sacrifice, while sacrifice points towards the sanctity of the one who gives himself to others in love.

Let us now look at both the sanctity of the Triune God and the sanctity of the perfect Man, Jesus Christ. In both cases, sanctity consists of giving oneself entirely until the very end. God's sanctity is realized in the origins of the Divine Persons. By giving birth to a Son, the Eternal Father gives Himself completely to Him; He submits to Him the infinity of His Divinity. By breathing the Holy Spirit, Father and Son completely give themselves to Him; they submit to Him the infinity of their shared Divinity. In this way, Divinity is common to all Three: each Person is the true God, and at the same time all Three are no more God than any other Person at an individual level.

After taking on our humanity, the Son of God on many occasions confirmed His unconditional and complete submission to the Father and to us whom He called brothers in our Father. It is especially worth recalling the Gospel of John in this regard: "My food is to do the will of the One who sent Me and to finish His work" (John 4:34; see 5:19, 30; 6:38; 7:16; 8:28). "And this is the will of the One Who sent Me: that I should not lose anything of what He gave me, but that I should raise it [on] the last day" (John 6:39; see 3:16; 17:12).

In other words, there are no doubts that also as a Man, also through His human will, the Son of God realized an attitude of pro-existence, one of submission until the very end, "even death of a Cross" (Philippians 2:8). However, two observations come to mind here. First, although the Lord Jesus undertook His passion and death by the will of His Father, He did so in complete freedom. He did not have to submit to the explosion of hatred that crushed Him on the Cross. If He wanted, He could have avoided His passion, just as He avoided death during previous attempts on His life (see Luke 4:29-30; John 30:44, 8:59, 10:31, 39). In any case, He had prophesied His passion on many occasions (see Matthew 16:21-23; 17:22-23; 20:17-19). He also said of Himself that He was the Good Shepherd Who "lays down His life for the sheep. [...] No one takes it from Me, but I lay it down on My own. I have power to lay it down, and power to take it up again" (John 10:11, 18).

And one more observation: Although Jesus was the Son of God, in His nature He feared the passion that awaited Him, although He was simultaneously eager to undertake it: "There is a baptism with which I must be baptized, and how great is My anguish until it is accomplished!" (Luke 12:50; see Mark 10:38). After His messianic entry to Jerusalem, He confessed: "I am troubled now. Yet what should I say? 'Father, save Me from this hour'? But it was for this purpose that I came to this hour" (John 12:27). At the beginning of His passion, in Gethsemane, before He voluntarily submitted to the hands of His enemies, He completed an unimaginably difficult spiritual labor to persist in an attitude of perfect pro-existence through His human will. He then begged His Father to withdraw the chalice of suffering yet finished the prayer with: "still, not My will but Yours be done" (Luke 22:42).

Appropriate to this prayer, the human Jesus Christ loved both His own Father (see Luke 23:46) and us to the very end, although we were His enemies (see Romans 5:6-10). He was the first man to go through life on this earth perfectly imitating the holiness of the Triune God, perfectly reflecting intra-Trinitarian pro-existence. It then turned out that the forces of evil are so strong in our sin-tainted world that an attitude of consistent pro-existence would be impossible without "consecrat[ing] Myself for them" (John 17:19).

Jesus was holy in the complete sense of the word. He not only showed us the way to holiness, but He made it possible at all. If the Son of God had not come to us, holiness would be inaccessible. After all, it is not a merely moral attribute. It is the ontic capacity to imitate God in an attitude of consistent pro-existence which we would never be able to attain on our own.

Fortunately, since the Second Vatican Council the Church has frequently spoken of the universal vocation to holiness. John Paul II often emphasized this, especially during his meetings with young people: "Do not be afraid of holiness!" In an apostolic letter, he famously wrote: "To ask catechumens: 'Do you wish to receive Baptism?' means at the same time to ask them: 'Do you wish to become holy?'"[135] Amidst these frequent calls to sanctity, we cannot forget how great an elevation of our human nature it is to be able to strive for sanctity at all.

We "have been sanctified in Christ Jesus, called to be holy" (1 Corinthians 1:2; see 6:11; Hebrews 12:14; 1 Peter 1:14-16). During World Youth Day at the Jasna Góra Shrine in Czestochowa in 1991, John Paul II said that "sanctity is the basic legacy of children of God." If Christ had not made us capable of this, we certainly would be incapable of yearning for such love "as I love you" (John 15:12), nor

135. John Paul II, Apostolic letter *Novo millennio ineunte*, 31.

could we carry one another's burden (see Matthew 11:29) and imitate Him in carrying our cross (see Matthew 10:38; 16:24). As we can read in the *Catechism of the Catholic Church* (456), this is what sanctity consists in.

4. He Became the Son of Man to Make Us Children of God

To be capable of understanding our ultimate human vocation, it is of fundamental importance that we comprehend the words that we repeat during the profession of faith in Christ the Son of God: that He is "begotten, not made." Sacred Scripture calls Him the Father's Only Son (John 1:14, 18; 3:16, 18; 1 John 4:9). This means that there is an infinite abyss between the Son of God and all created persons. Through God's omnipotent and loving will, all creatures have been called into existence out of nothing. However, He is not a creature; He is the Son born of God and not created out of nothingness. He is the infinite God, equal to and co-eternal with the One Who grants Him the infinity of His Divinity in enduring eternity.

The New Testament proclaims a promise we would have to consider mad and absurd if it were not the Word of God: that the Eternal Father wants to give birth to us as His children as well! When faced with this promise, our first instinct is to not want to hear it fully, or even to oppose it. After all, merely being human is so great a gift from God that we are incapable of fathoming its wondrousness! When we think that Christ promises to fully heal our humanity and that through His power, we will be capable of perfect love, we are spontaneously overcome by the feeling that we need nothing more. Since these gifts transcend our imagination, is it even possible for God to give man a greater gift? After all, is not the Son of God the Only Begotten Son? In human terms, it is impossible for anyone else to be born of God! Indeed, we remember that God is our Father, and we are His children. However, we were often inclined to believe that this refers to fatherhood and filiation only in a metaphorical sense.

All our stipulations and opposition are clearly inconsistent with the Word of God. The Lord Jesus clearly says: "[N]o one can see the kingdom of God without being born from above" (John 3:3). There can be no doubt that He is referring to our being born of God. "But to those who did accept Him He gave power to become children of God, to those who believe in His name, who were born not by natural generation nor by human choice nor by a man's decision but of God" (John 1:12-13). God and the Father of our Lord Jesus Christ "gave us a new birth to a living hope" (1 Peter 1:3; see James 1:18). Thus, if we believe in Christ and persist in His grace we possess not only human life, created life, but we have within ourselves the life of God Himself (a awe-filling thought!), and this is what our participation in God's nature consists in. As people, we have been created by God, but by belonging to Christ we experience deification; we become participants in His being born of God. "God's seed" has been planted in us (1 John 3:9). It will grow inside us until the gift of deification achieves the measure intended by our loving Father. "Beloved, we are God's children now; what we shall be has not yet been revealed. We do know that when it is revealed we shall be like Him, for we shall see Him as He is" (1 John 3:2).

Naturally, there is an infinite abyss that not only separates the Creator from His creation, but also the birth of the Only Begotten Son and our birth in God. The Only Begotten Son is the True God, while we will never cease to be creatures called into existence out of nothing. He is the Son through His very nature, while we are His adopted children. What a wondrous adoption this is! It consists in God's love making us truly one with Christ. After all, we have received the same Holy Spirit that "scrutinizes everything, even the depths of God" (1 Corinthians 2:10). When we think that the same Holy Spirit also scrutinizes us, thanks to Him we can truly call out to God: "Abba! Father!" (see Romans 8:15; Galatians 4:6).

The mystery of the Church and the salvation that takes place through her consist in our becoming increasingly one with Christ and growing together to form His Body. How beautifully this was expressed by Christ the Lord Himself: "Remain in me, as I remain in you. [...] I am the vine; you are the branches. [...] I have told you this so that My joy may be in you and your joy may be complete" (John 15:4-11). We can be God's children only through His filiation; after all, He is the Only Son. And if we are "children, then [we are] heirs, heirs of God and joint heirs with Christ" (Romans 8:17). These words dispel all doubts as to our legacy: in Him and with Him we will inherit the Eternal Father Himself Who completely gives Himself to Christ. If created goods will also be our joy, this will be only because the "new heaven and new earth" will be overcome with His Presence in a fullness that is inconceivable to us.

In other words: "What eye has not seen, and ear has not heard, and what has not entered the human heart, what God has prepared for those who love Him" (1 Corinthians 2:9).

In conclusion, I would like to add that such a great elevation is not reserved for only a few. God invites all of us without exception to be one with His Son, Christ, while as St. Hippolytus, one of the oldest Church Fathers, has emphatically explained: "He casts away none of His servants as unworthy of the divine mysteries. He does not esteem the rich man more highly than the poor, nor does He despise the poor man for his poverty. He does not disdain the barbarian, nor does He set the eunuch aside as no man. He does not hate the female on account of the woman's act of disobedience in the beginning, nor does He reject the male on account of the man's transgression. But He seeks all, and desires to save all, wishing to make all the children of God, and calling all the saints unto one perfect man."[136]

136. St. Hippolytus, "On Christ and Antichrist" (3), [in:] *Ante-Nicene Fathers*, Vol. 5, trans. J. H. MacMahon, eds. Alexander Roberts, James Donaldson, and A. Cleveland Coxe

THE LORD OF ALL OF CREATION ON A "SPECK OF COSMIC DUST"

On a Certain Attempt at Debunking Christianity

The enormity of the cosmos studied by astronomers and the mere possibility of the existence of extraterrestrial civilizations is sometimes presented as "evidence" of the absurdity of Christianity. Let me summarize this attempt at debunking Christianity: "The mere notion that in this 'speck of cosmic dust' we have come to call earth there could appear a Lord of all of creation and that this micro, even nano-moment (what is thirty-odd ordinary years against the backdrop of almost fourteen billion years?) of His presence on this 'speck of cosmic dust' and could be of momentous importance to the universe seems like a mockery of common sense! Christianity was born of naive, anthropocentric arrogance!"

I am reminded of two analogous anxieties that Christians felt when faced with the universal dimensions of the message of the Gospel. In the time before the great geographic discoveries, when the Earth seemed immense and impenetrable to people, the possibility

(Buffalo, NY: Christian Literature Publishing Co., 1886), https://www.newadvent.org/fathers/0516.htm (accessed April 13, 2022).

of encounter with rational beings other than humans was entertained. This was written by Pliny the Elder, for instance, in his *Natural History*. St. Augustine carefully recorded various rumors on this topic; however, it does not seem like he lost much sleep over the problem of if such beings exist, if they are people, and if we should preach the Gospel to them if we do meet them. St. Augustine concludes his reflections on this topic with the following: "Wherefore, to conclude this question cautiously and guardedly, either these things which have been told of some races have no existence at all; or if they do exist, they are not human races; or if they are human, they are descended from Adam."[137]

The early Christians were to a much greater degree concerned about the accusations of educated pagans against the teaching on God's omnipotence and omniscience as well as accusations of naive anthropocentrism. Marcus Cornelius Fronto (d. around 166), an educator of the Emperor Marcus Aurelius, fumed: "But the Christians, moreover, what wonders, what monstrosities do they feign! — that he who is their God, whom they can neither show nor behold, inquires diligently into the character of all, the acts of all, and, in fine, into their words and secret thoughts; that he runs about everywhere, and is everywhere present: they make him out to be troublesome, restless, even shamelessly inquisitive, since he is present at everything that is done, wanders in and out in all places, although, being occupied with the whole, he cannot give attention to particulars, nor can he be sufficient for the whole while he is busied with particulars."[138]

137. St. Augustine, *The City of God (Book XVI)*, trans. Marcus Dods, [in:] *Nicene and Post-Nicene Fathers, First Series*, Vol. 2, ed. Philip Schaff (Buffalo, NY: Christian Literature Publishing Co., 1887), https://www.newadvent.org/fathers/120116.htm (accessed April 14, 2022).

138. *The Octavius of Minucius Felix*, https://www.tertullian.org/fathers2/ANF-04/anf04-34.htm (accessed April 14, 2022). Marcus Cornelius Fronto professed the Stoic doctrine according to which providence is merely the gods' control of the law of nature (see Marcus Tullius Cicero, *The Nature of the Gods*, trans. Horace C. P. McGregor (New York: Penguin Classics, 1972). Thus, it is unsurprising that the teaching of Sacred Scripture on God's all-encompassing Providence (see Sirach 16:17-19, 23:18-19, 42:20; Matthew 10:29-30, 12:36) outraged him so.

Meanwhile, Celsus of Alexandria accused Christianity of anthropocentric arrogance. He could not cease to be amazed that Christians can believe in such "nonsense" as the fact that man has been created in God's image and is the subject of God's particular love; that the Son of God Himself has come to save us; and that He will come to the Final Judgment someday. Celsus disdains of such fools, whom he compares "to a flight of bats or to a swarm of ants issuing out of their nest, or to frogs holding council in a marsh, or to worms crawling together in the corner of a dunghill."[139]

Let us imagine, Celsus writes, that worms or frogs have gathered in a puddle and are saying: "And in his fictitious representation, he compares us to 'worms which assert that there is a God, and that immediately after him, we who are made by him are altogether like God, and that all things have been made subject to us — earth, and water, and air, and stars — and that all things exist for our sake, and are ordained to be subject to us.' And, according to his representation, the worms — that is, we ourselves — say that 'now, since certain among us commit sin, God will come or will send His Son to consume the wicked with fire, that the rest of us may have eternal life with Him.' And to all this he subjoins the remark, that 'such wranglings would be more endurable among worms and frogs than between Jews and Christians.'"[140]

The Apex of the Imagination Transcends the Imagination

One need not be greatly perceptive to note that the above-presented "proof" of the absurdity of Christianity is based on one absurd

139. Cf. Origen, *Contra Celsum*, 4,23, *op. cit.*, p. 197.

140. Origen, *Contra Celsum*, Book IV (23), trans. Frederick Crombie, in: *Ante-Nicene Fathers*, Vol. 4, eds. Alexander Roberts, James Donaldson, and A. Cleveland Coxe (Buffalo, NY: Christian Literature Publishing Co., 1885); https://www.newadvent.org/fathers/04164.htm (accessed April 14, 2022).

assumption and one mythological conception. How can one assume *a priori* that truly momentous events (from the perspective of the entirety of existence) either cannot exist or can be legitimized only by an appropriately large material dimension? How can one assume *a priori* that not only the event of Jesus Christ but in general everything that happens in human history is meaningless and that, in any case, lacks ultimate meaning as nothing that occurs in the "speck of cosmic dust" known as Earth simply cannot have absolute meaning? This is ordinary gigantolatry; at a logical level, it is evident *circulus in demonstrando*.

Further: the mere thought of the limitlessness of the cosmos can make anyone's head spin. However, one needs mythological imagination to ascribe to our Earth cosmic marginality. The notion of Earth's marginality could have been meaningful during times when Ptolemaic geocentrism had to be overcome. Empedocles' notion (which was recalled by Pascal) that nothing in the cosmos is marginal because its center is everywhere, for the universe "is an infinite sphere, the center of which is everywhere, the circumference nowhere" seems closer to reality.[141]

Blaise Pascal dramatically understood and was capable of brilliantly describing this "dust-like" place of man, humanity, and even the entire solar system in the infinite cosmos. It is astonishing that "this vast circle [the solar system] is itself but a very fine point in comparison with that described by the stars in their revolution round the firmament. But if our view be arrested there, let our imagination pass beyond; it will sooner exhaust the power of conception than nature that of supplying material for conception. The whole visible world is only an imperceptible atom in the ample bosom of nature. [...] For in fact what is man in nature? A Nothing in comparison with

141. Blaise Pascal, *Pascal's Pensées*, 72 (New York: E. P. Dutton & Co., 1958), Project Gutenberg, https://www.gutenberg.org/files/18269/18269-h/18269-h.htm (accessed April 14, 2022).

the Infinite, an All-in comparison with the Nothing, a mean between nothing and everything."[142]

"The eternal silence of these infinite spaces frightens me."[143] Indeed, contemporary astronomy has shown us something that Pascal did not yet know: that the still-unfathomed cosmos must be measured in millions of light years. It seems that, from a psychological point of view, man fathoms the incomprehensibility of the number ten to the hundredth power same as ten to the millionth power.

Pascal was also capable of showing that this terrifying insignificance of man — and, therefore, of everything that takes place on earth — in the infinite cosmos only increases our "attachment" to a specific, tiny time and space: "I see those frightful spaces of the universe which surround me, and I find myself tied to one corner of this vast expanse, without knowing why I am put in this place rather than in another, nor why the short time which is given me to live is assigned to me at this point rather than at another of the whole eternity which was before me or which shall come after me. I see nothing but infinites on all sides, which surround me as an atom, and as a shadow which endures only for an instant and returns no more."[144]

In other words, Pascal's imagination was painfully perceptive. I know of no other text that presents the insignificance of man and the entire Earth equally suggestively. He was a brilliantly intelligent man who at the same time knew that the apex of the imagination is the ability to transcend the arguments it suggests and to enlighten them with the light of reason. Meanwhile, reason tells us that man has something that is greater than the infinite enormity of the material universe.

Let us quote the most famous observation of this unusual philosopher: "Man is but a reed, the most feeble thing in nature; but he

142. *Ibid.*, 18.
143. *Ibid.*, 206.
144. *Ibid.*, 194.

is a thinking reed. The entire universe need not arm itself to crush him. A vapor, a drop of water suffices to kill him. But, if the universe were to crush him, man would still be more noble than that which killed him, because he knows that he dies and the advantage which the universe has over him; the universe knows nothing of this."[145]

The mere ability to think makes man richer and more important than the entire material universe. Yet man is endowed with something even more wondrous: the ability to love! Thus, Pascal has no doubt that we are absolutely wrong if all we see is that we are smaller than a speck of dust from the perspective of the universe. After all: "All bodies together, and all minds together, and all their products, are not equal to the least feeling of charity. This is of an order infinitely more exalted."[146]

Hence, there can only be one ultimate conclusion about man's place in the material cosmos: "From all bodies together, we cannot obtain one little thought; this is impossible, and of another order. From all bodies and minds, we cannot produce a feeling of true charity; this is impossible, and of another and supernatural order."

Why, though, is the cosmos so unimaginably infinite? It is worth noting that everything that exists, even the measliest creature, is marked by some infinity, which is a sign of its origin in the infinite Creator. Likewise, although Earth objectively is "a speck of cosmic dust," in many ways it is infinite. The fact that we can measure the surface area of oceans and deserts, or the altitude of mountains does not remove the experience of infiniteness whenever we try to directly penetrate it.

Furthermore, we cannot even completely know a lousy mosquito or a measly grain of sand. And we will certainly never get to fully know them. At a time when genetics and molecular physics are dynamically growing, this does not need an explanation.

145. *Ibid.*, 347.
146. *Ibid.*, 792.

Man's interior is also infinite. We will never completely know the person closest to us. In fact, we will never completely know ourselves, except for maybe at the Final Judgment.

According to the testimony of the Bible (although classic philosophy also suspected this),[147] we are also incapable of comprehending the world of spiritual creatures. Even if humanity were completely alone in the material cosmos (which we do not know), then we are but a tiny figment of rational beings, some of which are undoubtedly more perfect than we.

An Event Appropriate to the Entirety of Existence

Pascal's explanations debunk the attempt at questioning Christianity using the "speck of cosmic dust" argument. However, some of us are prone to question Christianity with the supposition that the entirety of existence could be limited to only the infinite material cosmos. Yet Christianity professes faith in God, "Creator of all things visible and invisible." We can cautiously say that the materialist view of the world, which is completely subjected to the research of astronomers and physicists, does not have to express the whole truth about the entirety of existence.

The truth is that even if in Biblical times the material world was conceived in a geocentric way, God and the infinite community of spiritual beings consistently remain the center of the Biblical universe. Accordingly, in its ultimate dimension the Biblical world is not and never was geocentric or anthropocentric.

In other words, Christian sources give no reason to worry if the news of the groundbreaking significance of Christ's work is not tangled up with some naive geocentrism. This anxiety has appeared only because of the materialist reductionism that has affected our common image of the universe in recent centuries.

147. I write about this in the chapter "Invisible Creation."

The New Testament message about Christ's Cross and Resurrection cannot be accused of being only superficially universal; in reality, it is a narrative about a particular event that took place on the "speck of cosmic dust" we have come to call Earth. The New Testament clearly, frequently, and unambiguously expresses that Christ's work encompasses the entirety of existence, above all the world of rational creatures, not only people but angels as well. In short, a response to the "speck of cosmic dust" argument can be found in the New Testament, and it was expressed many centuries before it appeared in the form we know.

Let us look at specific texts. The fact that the angels are present at literally all the important moments of the life and work of Jesus Christ is very symptomatic. An angel announces the Incarnation of the Son of God (Luke 1:26-38) and instructs Joseph about his vocation to virginal fatherhood (Matthew 1:20-21). Angels proclaim Jesus' birth and are the first to rejoice at it (Luke 2:9-14); Jesus' safety is also entrusted to them (Matthew 2:13, 19). We see angels at the very beginning of Jesus' public activity (Matthew 4:11; Mark 1:13). An angel strengthens Jesus during his bloody prayer before His Passion (Luke 22:43). On Easter Sunday, we see angels at the tomb of the Resurrected (Matthew 28:2-7; Mark 16:5-7; Luke 24:4-7; John 10:12); they also appear on the day of His Ascension (Acts 1:10).

It is certainly not coincidental that the angels are so profoundly interested in everything related to Jesus Christ and His work. Does this not attest to the fact that the Redemption is not a particular matter between God and the inhabitants of the earth but in a mysterious way concerns the entirety of creation?

By referring to the image of Jacob's Ladder, the Lord Jesus promised His disciples that He would restore spiritual community with the angels (John 1:51). This community means, on the one hand, powerful benevolence coming from the angels that pulls us towards God and that Sacred Scripture will present in the image of the angels carrying our prayers and sacrifices to God (Tobit 12:12; Revelation 5:8) as well as in that of participation in the eternal liturgy along with the angels (Psalm 138:1; Revelation 5:11-12, 7:11nn).

On the other hand, our community with the angels is also their "descending" towards us to be our companions, guides, and the defenders of our difficult and dangerous path (Matthew 18:10; Acts 5:19-20, 8:26, 12:7-11; Hebrews 1:14).

Christ's Cross and Resurrection also have direct consequences for the world of spiritual creatures itself. To put it visually, we can say that the ultimate healing of wounds caused by the rebellion of Satan and his angels takes place through Christ. He Who descended to our "speck of cosmic dust" two thousand years ago is the Son of God in Whom "were created all things in heaven and on earth, the visible and the invisible, whether thrones or dominions or principalities or powers" (Colossians 1:16).

This is why the Eternal Father sent Him here; this is why He suffered on the Cross to be resurrected to "through Him reconcile all things for Him, making peace by the blood of His Cross [through Him], whether those on earth or those in heaven" (Colossians 1:20).

What will this ultimate healing of wounds after Satan's rebellion consist of? What will the reconciliation of "all things... in heaven," or the entire world of spiritual creatures, with God be like? Biblical texts speak of their destruction (1 Corinthians 15:24); their "despoiling" (Colossians 2:15); and their being "put [...] beneath [Christ's] feet" (Ephesians 1:22). Accordingly, this does not suggest the conversion of the rebels who reject God. Undoubtedly, this is a promise that universal love will dominate and encompass all who desire it thanks to Christ. This will be ultimate and unshakeable love, one that will make it impossible for any hostile forces to disrupt anything. In this sense, they will be ultimately destroyed, despoiled, and put beneath Christ's feet.

This will not so much be the end of times as their fullness. This is understood to mean that it will not concern only a particular episode, which is how human history may appear from the perspective of the cosmos, but it will be the "fulfillment of the world" (*synteleia tou aioniou*). The diversity of Biblical descriptions (Matthew 16:27, 25:31-32; 1 Corinthians 6:2-3; Hebrews 12:18-24; Revelation 21:1nn) leaves no doubt that it will encompass the entirety of existence, which will then achieve its ultimate aim, which at present is inconceivable to us.

THE SON OF GOD'S VIRGIN BIRTH

Jesus' Father Is the Eternal Father

Let us try to above all see how many Divine contents this dogma of the faith contains. The fact that it was included in the credo, or among the most important truths of the faith, demonstrates that this truth is not of secondary significance to Christianity.

What, then, does the truth that the Redeemer has come to earth from a virgin Mother without the participation of a man mean? It is best to read about this directly in the Gospels. Let us open the first chapter of Luke's Gospel and read the description of the Annunciation. This fragment strongly emphasizes the fact that the Lord Jesus did not have a human father. The spiritual significance of this fact is also explained: Mary's Child "will be called Son of the Most High [...]. Therefore, the child to be born will be called holy, the Son of God" (Luke 1:32-35).

Thus, it is clear that the Lord Jesus did not have a human father, for His father is the Eternal Father. He was born of a virgin because He was not an ordinary human. Unlike in our case, His existence did not begin at the moment of conception. He is the eternal Son of God Who became a man for the sake of our salvation.

The description of the Annunciation shows another meaning of our Redeemer's birth from a virgin.. Notice that the evangelist compares the circumstances of the birth of the Lord Jesus to those related to John the Baptist. Indeed, John the Baptist was born of old and infertile parents who had lost hope that they could bear a child. Many great Old Testament servants of God were born in this way. Isaac was born of infertile Sarah; James, the protoplast of Israel, was born of infertile Rebecca; the righteous Joseph was born of infertile Rachel; and Samson, who defeated the Philistines, and the great judge Samuel were also born of infertile mothers.

In the Old Testament, these facts were pregnant with spiritual meaning. Namely, in this way the Lord God reminded His people that the great leaders of the nation, great defenders, or great prophets are His unique gifts for them. Although they were born of people, they were above all gifts of God.

It was pleasing to God for John the Baptist to be born in similar circumstances, for this man was a great gift for God's people, a greater one than even the Old Testament figures mentioned above: "Amen, I say to you, among those born of women there has been none greater than John the Baptist" (Matthew 11:11).

It turns out that John's birth is merely a background for the explanation of the wondrousness of the Lord Jesus' birth. Being born of infertile parents transcends reasonable hope offered by nature, but it is still consistent with nature. Meanwhile, the Son of God was born of a Virgin! God wanted to use this sign to teach us that His Son is His unique Gift for humanity. Another fragment of the Gospels that particularly emphasizes the virginity of the conception of the Lord Jesus offers the following explanation: "For it is through the Holy Spirit that this Child has been conceived in her" (Matthew 1:20).

The Ancients' Mockery of the Lord Jesus' Birth from a Virgin

There is something very intriguing in the fact that the Church places such an emphasis on the truth of the virginity of the Blessed Mother.

I first became aware of this when I realized how much the ancient opponents of Christianity scoffed at this fact. If Mary's virginity were a minor detail for the Gospel message, this truth would have dissolved in the purgatory fire of mockery and jeers that were said about it. Meanwhile, when Christians rebutted these accusations, they realized that faith in Mary's virginity is a test of the authenticity of our faith in Christ.

The accusations went in two different directions. Some saw similarities to pagan narratives of the virgin birth of one mythical figure or another and scoffed: How could Mary, an ordinary and poor girl, have impressed God so greatly that He wanted to have a child with her?[148] Once, St. Justin (d. 166) heard some "good advice" addressed to Christians: "Moreover, in the fables of those who are called Greeks, it is written that Perseus was begotten of Danae, who was a virgin; he who was called among them Zeus having descended on her in the form of a golden shower. And you ought to feel ashamed when you make assertions similar to theirs, and rather [should] say that this Jesus was born man of men. And if you prove from the Scriptures that He is the Christ, and that on account of having led a life conformed to the law, and perfect, He deserved the honor of being elected to be Christ, [it is well]; but do not venture to tell monstrous phenomena, lest you be convicted of talking foolishly like the Greeks."[149]

The second accusation consisted of the slanderous "explanation" that Christian belief in Jesus' virgin birth because they are trying to cover up the act of adultery in which Mary had engaged and whose fruit was Jesus. "[Mary] was turned out of doors by her husband, a

148. That was how Celsus of Alexandria mocked the Christian belief in his book which was published in 177; see Origen, *Contra Celsum*, trans. Frederick Crombie, in: *Ante-Nicene Fathers*, Vol. 4, eds. Alexander Roberts, James Donaldson, and A. Cleveland Coxe (Buffalo, NY: Christian Literature Publishing Co., 1885); https://www.newadvent.org/fathers/04164.htm (accessed April 14, 2022).

149. St. Justin Martyr, *Dialogue with Trypho*, Chapter 67, trans. Marcus Dods and George Reith [in:] *Ante-Nicene Fathers*, Vol. 1, eds. Alexander Roberts, James Donaldson, and A. Cleveland Coxe (Buffalo, NY: Christian Literature Publishing Co., 1885), https://www.newadvent.org/fathers/01285.htm (accessed April 15, 2022).

carpenter by trade, because she was convicted of adultery; that after being driven away by her husband, and wandering about for a time, she disgracefully gave birth to Jesus, an illegitimate child."[150]

In response to the first accusation, Christians noted the radical dissimilarity between pagan myths on the virgin birth and the Gospel truth about our Redeemer's birth. In the Gospel message, there is not a trace of the blasphemous notions regarding the sexual desire of women for some god or of any god's copulation with a virgin. Meanwhile, the virgin birth of the Redeemer expresses a truth that is not even suggested in the pagan myths: that Jesus, a true man, is not an ordinary man but the Son of God Himself, while His coming to us is an act of God's merciful concern for us to save us for eternal life.

Meanwhile, the second accusation was so ridiculous that it sufficed to notice that all the Gospel references to Mary and Joseph without exception emphasize the perfect harmony between them (see Matthew 1:18-25; 2:13-15, 19-23; Luke 2:4-7, 16, 33, 39-51). Meanwhile, the authors of this slander either did not know or forgot out of hatred that "one born of a prostitute" (see Deuteronomy 23:3) could not stand before the Sanhedrin, while Jesus was not only tried before Pilate; He was also tried before this religious court.

Mary Remained a Virgin After Jesus' Birth As Well

The Church not only teaches that Mary and Joseph's marriage was fully virginal but that she did not lose her virginity by giving birth to Jesus. Surprised by how detailed the Church's teaching is in this regard, people sometimes ask with embarrassment if we truly must believe this. After all, how is it possible since she gave birth to Him like any other woman? And why does the Church put so much emphasis on this detail?

150. See Origen, *Contra Celsum*.

Indeed, this is what the Church truly believes. In this way, we affirm our absolute certainty that something without precedent, something that was inconceivable to even the angels, took place: this Son of God, the true God, became a man! This is neither a symbolic message nor a transcendental code. God truly took on human nature and became one of us. And this happened in Mary and through Mary!

It is worth at least occasionally renewing our astonishment that the entry of the Son of God into our human family is something seemingly impossible yet truly happened! This astonishment was poetically expressed by St. Ephrem the Syrian (d. 373): "The Firstborn entered the womb, and the pure Virgin was not harmed. — He stirred and came forth in her travail, and the fair Mother was troubled by Him. — Glorious and unseen in entering, humble and manifest in issuing — for He was God in entering, and He was man in issuing. — A marvel and bewilderment to hear: fire entered the womb; put on a body and came forth!"[151]

Almost twenty years before Ephrem, this was expressed by St. Irenaeus (d. 202), who noted that it was not people but God Who wanted Mary's motherhood to be virginal: "But since an unlooked-for salvation was to be provided for men through the help of God, so also was the unlooked-for birth from a virgin accomplished; God giving this sign, but man not working it out."[152]

St. Thomas Aquinas (d. 1274), who lived more than one thousand years after St. Irenaeus, in a way summarized the teaching of the Church's hundreds and thousands of teachers by writing that Christ

151. St. Ephraim the Syrian, *Hymns on the Nativity*, trans. A. Edward Johnston [in:] *Nicene and Post-Nicene Fathers*, Second Series, Vol. 13, eds. Philip Schaff and Henry Wace (Buffalo, NY: Christian Literature Publishing Co., 1898), https://www.newadvent.org/fathers/3703.htm (accessed April 15, 2022).

152. St. Irenaeus, *Against Heresies* (Book III, Chapter 21), trans. Alexander Roberts and William Rambaut [in:] *Ante-Nicene Fathers*, Vol. 1, eds. Alexander Roberts, James Donaldson, and A. Cleveland Coxe (Buffalo, NY: Christian Literature Publishing Co., 1885), https://www.newadvent.org/fathers/0103321.htm (accessed April 15, 2022). The lengthy twenty-first and twenty-second chapters of this book are completely devoted to the topic of Mary's virginal motherhood.

the Lord wanted to be born in a way that would "reveal both the truth of His body and His Divinity. To reveal the truth of His Body, He was born of a Woman. But to reveal His Divinity, He was born of a Virgin."[153]

Are there any Biblical texts that suggest that Mary remained a virgin after giving birth to Jesus? The Church Fathers referred to the words: "Behold, the virgin shall be with child and bear a Son" (Matthew 1:23). According to the natural order, if she had conceived, that means that she is no longer a virgin; a woman who gave birth is even less a virgin. It was only in Mary's motherhood that the miracle of her conceiving and giving birth as a Virgin took place.

At least three other Biblical texts provided the Fathers with the opportunity to contemplate the truth that by being born of Mary the Son of God did not violate even the corporal marks of virginity. Please do not say: "That doesn't convince me." The statements of the Church Fathers I will now reference are, after all, the fruit of their contemplation of the inconceivable truth that the Son of God wanted to become one of us.

The first of these texts is Isaiah's prophesy:

> Before she is in labor, she gives birth;
> Before her pangs come upon her, she delivers a male child.
> Who ever heard of such a thing, or who ever saw the like?
> (Isaiah 66:7-8)

The spiritual significance of such statements is usually multidimensional. The fact is that St. Irenaeus sees this prophesy as foreshadowing of the unusual birth of Emmanuel.[154] Even the way in which He was born prophesied the beginning of a new world free of sin and its consequences (see Genesis 3:16).

The second text (or, rather, an entire Biblical theme) that gave the Fathers an opportunity to contemplate Mary's virginal motherhood was the perception of Christ as the new Adam, the founder of a new

153. St. Thomas Aquinas, *Summa Theologica*, 3 q. 28 a, 2 ad 2.

154. St. Irenaeus, *The Proof of the Apostolic Preaching*, 54.

humanity (see, for example, Romans 5:12-21; 1 Corinthians 15:21-22, 45-49). St. Gregory of Nyssa (d. 394) said that the birth of this new Adam should significantly differ from the birth of ordinary sinners: "For since she who by sinning brought death down on human nature was condemned to bear children in pain and distress, it was surely necessary and right that the mother of life should originate her childbearing in joy and with joy bring the birth to its completion."[155]

She Gave Birth to the One Who Was to Be Resurrected

Meanwhile, a completely unique meditation has been provided to us by St. Jerome (d. 419) who interprets the prophesy in Ezekiel 44:1-3 about the gate of the sanctuary facing east, which is closed because it is intended for only one Lord, as referring to both Mary and the Tomb from which He rose from the dead without breaking its seal:

"Isaiah even says: 'Who can describe his generation?' (Cf. Isaiah 53:8, LXX) What had Isaiah meant, then, by saying: *'The virgin shall be with child and bear a son'* (Isaiah 7:14)? He is telling us what has happened; but when he says: 'Who can describe his generation,' he is revealing to us the fact that He has been born, but how He has been born, we do not know. Holy Mary, blessed Mary, mother and virgin, virgin before giving birth, virgin after giving birth! I, for my part, marvel how a virgin is born of a virgin, and how, after the birth of a virgin, the mother is a virgin. Would you like to know how He is born of a virgin, and, after His nativity, the mother is still a virgin? 'The doors were closed, and Jesus entered' (cf. John 20:19, 26; cf. Letter 48:21). There is no question about that. He Who entered through the closed doors was not a ghost nor a spirit; He was a real man with a real body. Furthermore, what does He say? 'Feel me and see; for a spirit does not have flesh and bones, as you see I have' (Luke 24:39).

155. St. Gregory of Nyssa, *Homilies on the Song of Songs,* 13, trans. Richard A. Norris Jr. (Atlanta: Society of Biblical Literature, 2012), p. 411.

He had flesh and bones, and the doors were closed. How do flesh and bones enter through closed doors? The doors are closed, and He enters, whom we do not see entering. [...] You do not know how His entrance was accomplished, and you attribute it to the power of God. Attribute to the power of God, then, that He was born of a virgin, and the virgin herself after bringing forth was a virgin still."[156]

I think that considering this meditation it would be quite disrespectful towards the Holy Mother to work on persuading anyone that she persisted in her virginity throughout her life. Cardinal Joseph Ratzinger once wrote: "In the drama of salvation it is not the case that Mary had a part to play before exiting the stage like an actor who has said his lines and departs."[157] That is how Emperor Constantine V (740-775), a well-known destroyer of sacred images, saw the role of Mary, devotion to whom he stridently opposed. He vulgarly compared the Virgin Mother to a purse that is valuable only when it contains gold. According to this blasphemer, her significance ended with the birth of Her Son, after which she became worthless, like a purse without gold. This man clearly understood nothing about God's love for man.

Thus, it is not a coincidence that the Church had to recall the truth about Mary's eternal virginity especially when the truth about Christ was in jeopardy, when the Church was challenged by Nestorianism, Monophysitism, Monothelitism, or Iconoclasm. Pope St. Leo the Great included the following sentence in his 449 Christological letter to Flavian, the patriarch of Constantinople, written within the context of the Monophysite threat: "[Our Lord Jesus Christ] has been conceived of the Holy Spirit in the womb of the Virgin Mother who gave birth to Him without breaching her virginity, just as she had once

156. Jerome, *The Homilies of Saint Jerome (Homilies 60—96)*, ed. Roy Joseph Deferrari, trans. Marie Liguori Ewald, vol. 2, The Fathers of the Church (Washington, DC: The Catholic University of America Press, 1966), pp. 217-218.

157. J. Ratzinger, *Images of Hope: Meditations on Major Feasts* (San Francisco: Ignatius Press, 2006), p. 21

conceived Him in her intact virginity." It is worth mentioning that the Council of Chalcedon considered this letter to be its own document.[158]

By Rejecting Jesus' Divinity, One Cannot Believe in the Virginity of His Mother

The history of the Holy See's assertions of the truth about Mary contains also a Polish thread. In a dogmatic bull dated August 7, 1555, Pope Paul IV cautions the faithful against the teachings of unitarianism, which were spreading in Poland and Bohemia: "[Out of concern for the faithful we admonish] all and each who have hitherto asserted, claimed or believed that [...] that He was not conceived of the Holy Spirit according to the flesh in the womb of the most blessed and ever Virgin Mary, but from the seed of Joseph just as the rest of men; [...] or that the same most blessed Virgin Mary was not the true mother of God, and did not always persist in the integrity of virginity."[159]

Thus, one should not be surprised that because the unitarians rejected veneration of Mary they also doubted Christ's Divinity. It is worth mentioning here that the heated discussion about the Apostles' Creed that took place in German Protestant theology in 1892 and concerned the question of whether one can be a Christian without believing in the virginity of the Blessed Mother was a great boon to so-called liberal theology, which not much later began to sow doubt in Christ Himself in that milieu.

Sometimes, the truth of Mary's virginity gives rise to the following difficulty: Marital relations were conceived by the Creator Himself

158. The list of the Church's official assertions that we believe in the eternal virginity of the Blessed Mother is long: the letter of Pope Hormisdas to Emperor Justin dated March 26, 521; Canon 3 of the Second Council of Constantinople (553); a letter of Pelagius I to King Childebert dated February 3, 557; Canon 3 of the Lateran Synod of 649 under the leadership of Pope Martin I; the symbol of faith of the Sixteenth Council of Toledo (693); and many others.

159. Paul IV, *Cum quorundam*.

as a sign and means in which spouses can express their love for one another, and this pertains to every ordinary marriage.

In response to this argument, we notice that the relationship between Mary and Joseph was not an ordinary marriage. The Eternal Father entrusted His Son to them. He did not "plant Him" but entrusted Him to them, which means that Mary and Joseph knowingly took on the parental duties of the Son of God when He deigned to become the Son of Man for all. It is impossible to entertain the possibility that such an inconceivable vocation was but one of their marital duties. Without a doubt, serving Jesus as parents became the entire purpose of Mary and Joseph's marriage. The lifelong virginity of their relationship was a sign of this.

St. Thomas Aquinas presents four major arguments for why we should reject all notions that Mary engaged in marital sexual relations after giving birth to her Son:

1. "It would be an affront to Christ if He, the Only-Begotten Son of the Father, were not the only Son of Mary and her most perfect Fruit."
2. "This error causes injury to the Holy Spirit Whose tabernacle was the Virgin's womb where Christ's body was formed; it would be inappropriate for this to be later soiled through intercourse with her husband."
3. "This would be an affront to the dignity and sanctity of the Virgin Mother. She would appear as most ungrateful if she were not pleased with such a Son and if she decided to lose the virginity that was miraculously preserved in her through marital intercourse."
4. "It would be great impudence on Joseph's behalf if he desecrated the One who knew from an angel that she had conceived God through the Holy Spirit."[160]

The Church's Virginal Motherhood

If this is such an important truth of the faith, it must make direct reference to our life. First of all, each of us is called to be born in a

160. St. Thomas Aquinas, *Summa Theologica*, 3 q. 28 a, 3 pp.

way similar to Christ; this is the deepest consequence of that truth, one that transcends our imagination. Each of us is called to God's filiation, and one can be born of God only in an immaculate way. "But to those who did accept Him He gave power to become children of God, to those who believe in His name, who were born not by natural generation nor by human choice nor by a man's decision but of God" (John 1:12-13); "Amen, amen, I say to you, no one can see the kingdom of God without being born from above" (John 3:3).

We were first born of our parents; at the natural level, God is our Creator. God summoned us into existence through our parents and constantly supports us in our existence. However, He wants to be more than just a Creator for us; He wants to be our Father. God wants us to be like His Only Begotten Son and to be participants in His Divine nature. Our second birth is birth from God.

A mother is necessary for such a birth and, as in the case of Christ's birth, this is a virgin mother. The Church is the Mother that gives birth to us for God: "Husbands, love your wives, even as Christ loved the church and handed Himself over for her to sanctify her, cleansing her by the bath of water with the word, that He might present to Himself the church in splendor, without spot or wrinkle or any such thing, that she might be holy and without blemish" (Ephesians 5:25—27); "But the Jerusalem above is freeborn, and she is our mother" (Galatians 4:26).

The Church's virginal motherhood is being born of God and for God. Thus, it is unsurprising that from the very beginning the Church has been concerned that signs of her virginal fertility always be abundant. Christians, male and female, who "have renounced marriage for the sake of the kingdom of heaven" (Matthew 19:12), are a sign of this. The Apostle Paul writes: "Now to the unmarried and to widows, I say: it is a good thing for them to remain as they are, as I do" (1 Corinthians 7:8). Meanwhile, the Apostle John writes: "These are they who were not defiled with women; they are virgins, and these are the ones who follow the Lamb wherever he goes. They have been ransomed as the firstfruits of the human race for God and the Lamb" (Revelation 14:4).

True Virginity Is Always Fertile

The virginity of some members of the Church is a sign that the entire Church wants to be completely devoted to God. Thus, true virginity is always fertile. However, such fertility is superior, supernatural, spiritual, and of God. Infertile virginity is no virginity; it is merely spinsterhood. Infertile virginity bears no likeness to the Mother of God's virginity.

In a sense, all Christians are called to virginity: all should submit their entire hearts to God. The Church instructs especially spouses that they should be chaste in accordance with their state. It is thanks to spouses that new people come into the world. Indeed, man is a being worthy of entering the world in a truly human way.

Likewise, when raising a child, human fatherhood and motherhood should be exercised in an atmosphere of chastity. I mean not only chastity in the sense of exercising one's sexuality in a human manner, in accordance with God's law, but also chastity that consists in our efforts to avoid mixing good with evil.

In other words, regardless of whether a Christian is married or unmarried, he is called to imitate the virginal motherhood of the Mother of God. Husbands and wives should work to ensure that their marital community and parenthood be chaste. Meanwhile, those who are not in a marital bond should work so that their chastity is spiritually fertile.

As we can see, the dogma of the faith about the virginal conception of the Lord Jesus is not just some theoretical truth; it bears a very deep relationship to our Christian life.

WHY DO WE VENERATE THE INFANT JESUS?

I decided to deal with this question after receiving the following letter: "I come from a Catholic family, and Christmas was always solemnly celebrated in our home. I will never forget how greatly a crèche with the Infant Jesus at the forefront fascinated me as a child. Last Christmas, I was overcome with the following doubts: Jesus has long ceased to be a child! Is it appropriate that we refer to Him as if He were still a child by singing, for example, 'O, Tiny One' or 'Sleep, little Jesus?' Are we not committing an error by venerating Jesus as a helpless infant in a crèche? After all, He grew up and became someone much more important: our Teacher and Savior. He gave us the Gospel, died for us on the Cross, was resurrected, and is the King of kings and Lord of lords. Please explain to me the point of venerating the Baby Jesus in various novenas and litanies to this Infant or in Christmas carol dialogues with the Infant."

*

Certainly, we all have witnessed, perhaps on many occasions, the enthusiasm and tenderness with which children look at photographs of their parents from their childhood. Usually, they also take great interest in listening to stories from their parents' childhood that have been preserved in their family memory. Parents have long ceased to be children, while their children are greatly fascinated by the fact that they had also once been small and had problems typical of children.

It would be wrong to reduce our religious attitude to the Infant Jesus to a sentimental recalling that the Savior had once also been a child. It seems, however, that this aspect is also worth noticing.

Does veneration of the Infant Jesus contain something more? Let us notice that the Church's liturgy venerates ordinary saints on the anniversary of death because that is when they were born for heaven. Being born into earthly life, however, is the subject of liturgical veneration only with respect to the three holiest people. Apart from the birth of the Lord Jesus, we also celebrate the birth of the Blessed Virgin Mary (September 8th) and John the Baptist (June 24th).

Let us also notice that there is a major difference in our celebrating the birth of the Lord Jesus and that of Mary or John. I don't think anyone would entertain the thought of venerating Mary or John as infants. Neither the liturgy nor the customs of those feast days have any songs or litanies referencing the childhood of those holy persons.

Why? Although both Mary and John were uniquely called to a mission concerning all people to which no one had previously been called, they were merely human. While immaculate from the first moment of her existence because of the Divine motherhood awaiting her, on the day of her birth Mary was not yet the Mother of God; she still had to mature into that mission (see Luke 1:31, 43). Likewise, although John had been freed of original sin in his mother's womb, he would only later become "prophet of the Most High" and "go before the Lord to prepare His ways" (see Luke 1:76; 3:2).

It is completely different with the Lord Jesus, and only with Him. He is the eternal Son of God, "[f]or in Him were created all things in heaven and on earth" (Colossians 1:16). Although His human childhood was immersed in time, much like everyone else's childhood, it is at the same time transcendent with respect to time. This pertains not only to His childhood but also to every subsequent day of His life on earth up through the day of His passion and death on the Cross.

What does it mean that the life of the Lord Jesus, including His childhood, are transcendent with respect to time although they have passed in their historical dimension? The Son of God became one of us for us all, for the people of all nations and generations. He became an infant for us all; He led a hidden life for us all in Nazareth, where He taught and performed miracles; for the sake of us all, He experienced the Cross and Passion, died, and was resurrected.

He is a true man, but He is not merely a man; He is the Son of God Who is equal to the Eternal Father. This is why we, people of all nations and generations, have a real albeit mystical ability to listen to His teaching, experience His miraculous power, become immersed in His passion for us, and become witnesses to His resurrection. Along with Mary and Joseph, as well as the shepherds and the Magi, we can also adore Him as the Infant that was born for us. His childhood is also permanent in the salvific sense.

Indeed, carols such as *Lulajże, Jezuniu* ("Sleep Now, Baby Jesus") can be sung at a merely sentimental level. However, they can and should be sung in faith. We then contemplate the Son of God's love for us which led Him to humble Himself and became a helpless, defenseless child in need of protection. This is why our mystical dialogues with the Infant Jesus contain such warmth and depth.

Let us listen, for example, to the dialogue with the Infant Jesus that makes up the greater part of the carol *W żłobie leży* ("He Lies in a Manger"), which was probably written by Father Piotr Skarga. It is difficult to imagine that such words can be sung in a way other than in the spirit of contemplation:

We: Welcome, Lord! What has happened that you left heaven's pleasures and came down to lowly Earth?

The Infant: My love did it to raise the human up to the heavens.

We: Why are you laid on the hay in the manger, instead of in a crib? Why are you laid with cattle in the stable and not among lords?

The Infant: So that I can save the human, compared to hay, a sinner called a beast.

We: Oh my Lord, all world is your state and serfdom. You are a field flower, why does the world not wish to accept you, although it can?

The Infant: Because the world is used to loving temporal liberties. For me, it makes a bed of cross in animosity.

We: In Rama, Rachel is crying unto the heavens when her sons sink in a bloody bath for no reason.

The Infant: A greater bath awaits Me in an ocean of blood hence they will attain heaven.

We: The three monarch kings leave the Eastern country. They give their hearts with three gifts to You, O Lord.

The Infant: I am happy with their gifts, But I respect their hearts more. May they have heaven for them.

It is sometimes worth referencing testimonies to closeness to the Infant Jesus of some of the great mystics. I shall quote here just the testimony of St. Faustina Kowalska. She writes in her *Diary* (184) that in the Holy Hour she "tried to meditate on Our Lord's Passion. However, my soul was filled with joy, and suddenly I saw the little Infant Jesus. Still, His majesty transfixed me so profoundly that I said, 'Jesus, You're so little, but I know You are my Creator and Lord.' And Jesus replied, 'Yes, I am, and that is why I am with you as a child, to teach you with humility and simplicity.'"[161]

It seems unlikely that Faustina had studied the writings of St. Bernard of Clairvaux, but he wrote the exact same thing that she had directly heard from the Infant Jesus in her prayer: "Behold, 'A Child is set in the midst.' O Little One, desired by little ones! O true Child, but a guileless Child full of wisdom! Let us study to become as this Little One. Let us learn to be meek and humble of heart, lest

161. St. Faustina Kowalska, *Diary*, trans. Teresa Bałuk-Ulewiczowa (Krakow: Misericordia, 2020), p. 154.

the great God should without fruit have become Man and Child; lest He should have died in vain and been crucified in vain."[162]

Faustina and Bernard correctly write the same thing: Only once we become immersed in the gift of the Incarnation and we look at the humility and simplicity of the Infant Jesus do we become capable of truly contemplating the Lord's Passion and are open to its fruits. Let me quote another entry from the *Diary* (332): "When I started Holy Hour, I wanted to immerse myself in the mystery of Jesus' Passion in the Garden of Gethsemane. Then I heard a voice in my soul: 'Meditate on the mysteries of the Incarnation.' And suddenly there was the Child Jesus before me, radiant with beauty. He told me how pleased God was with a soul's simplicity. 'Although My greatness is infinite, yet I abide only with those who are little. I require you to have the spirit of a child.'"[163]

She continues: "One day, when I saw Jesus in the form of a baby, I asked Him, 'Jesus, why do You now come to me in the form of a baby? I still see God, my infinite Lord the Creator lives in You.' Jesus replied that He would keep coming to me in the form of a small child until I learned to be simple and humble" (335).[164]

Such a testimony in fact forces us to yearn for a similar closeness with the Infant. In the year of her death, St. Faustina has the following dialogue with the Infant Jesus: "'Even though You're so small, I know You are God [...] Why do You take the form of a tiny [child] to come to me?' 'Because I want to teach you spiritual childhood. I want you to be very small, because when you're so tiny, I carry you close to My Heart, just as You're holding Me next to your heart now.' Suddenly, I was alone again, but no-one can understand what my soul felt, I was completely immersed in God, like a sponge cast into the sea..." (1481).[165]

162. St. Bernard, *Sermons of St. Bernard on Advent and Christmas: Including the Famous Treatise on the Incarnation Called "Missus est"* (New York: Benziger Bros., 1909), p. 59.

163. St. Faustina Kowalska, *op. cit.*, p. 212.

164. *Ibid.*, p. 213.

165. *Ibid.*, p. 658.

THE BAPTISM OF THE LORD JESUS

The Beginning of the Ultimate Entry Into the Promised Land

The River Jordan has been burned into the memory of God's people. When they were returning from the Egyptian yoke and crossed the Jordan, thus entering the promised land, their forty-year sojourn across the desert ended.

Hence, when John the Baptist began his activity in the desert, people understood perfectly well what was happening. They understood that God would spiritually renew His people in this way. Confessing one's sins with remorse and taking on a baptism of penitence in the waters of the Jordan was a way of confirming their spiritual conversion, a confirmation of their decision that the Lord God would truly come first in their lives.

In any case, John the Baptist constantly emphasized that in this way we are preparing for the coming of the Messiah. All four Evangelists have noted that John emphasized references to Isaiah's summons to prepare the way for the coming Lord and straighten out all paths for His coming.

When Jesus appeared by the Jordan, John recognized Him as the Messiah and meekly recognized that He should retreat because Jesus must grow while he must become smaller. John said that he was not worthy to untie the straps of His sandals; all four Gospels have made note of this. Furthermore, it was John the Baptist who said these words which are repeated during every Mass. Pointing at Jesus, He said: "This is the Lamb of God Who takes away the sins of the world."

Thus, we see how surprised and confused John must have been when Jesus approached him to be baptized. John tries to protest: "You should baptize me rather than the opposite." Jesus, however, does not give in. He says to John: "Stop protesting because righteousness demands this."

Jesus Took the Sins of the Entire World Upon Himself

Naturally, the Lord Jesus did not need a baptism of penitence, for He was immaculate and sinless. He submerged Himself in the waters of the Jordan for an entirely different purpose than penitential sinners. People who were moved by the teachings of John the Baptist received the baptism of penitence to cleanse themselves of their sins, which they had confessed with remorse, and to begin a new life, one in accordance with God's commandments, after leaving the Jordan.

Meanwhile, the Lord Jesus submerged Himself in the waters of the Jordan and was baptized by John to take upon Himself all the evil that penitential sinners symbolically left in those waters. In other words, the Lord Jesus received baptism from John as a sign that He truly wanted to take all our sins, all the sins of the world, upon Himself. The Lord Jesus' baptism in the Jordan confirmed His consent to become the Lamb of God Who takes away our sins and those of the whole world on the Cross, which would redeem us.

The Son of God became a man to be our Messiah and Savior. He received baptism from John and gave testimony that He has taken on the mission of the Messiah and Savior through His human will in a completely conscious and voluntary way. This was a mission that would lead Him to the Cross.

The Son of God's human consent to be the Lamb of God Who would prefer to be killed rather than enter any pact with evil was met with complete approval of the Eternal Father. A voice resounded from heaven: "You are My beloved Son; with You I am pleased." Jesus, the Son of the Virgin Mary, is the same Son of God through Whom the World was created and Who "supports the existence of everything through His mighty Word." In the Jordan, the Eternal Father confirmed the truth of the words that Jesus would later say to Nicodemus, that "God so loved the world that He gave His Son so that everyone who believes in Him may have eternal life." This is why the Church sometimes calls the event of the Lord Jesus' baptism in the Jordan to be His messianic investiture. The Eternal Father Himself confirmed that Jesus is the Messiah and Savior.

Avoid Criticizing God for Being Love!

There sometimes comes a bad moment when we criticize the Lord God Himself for letting His own Son die a terrible death on the Cross. When that happens, we should remember what happened during the Lord Jesus' baptism in the waters of the Jordan. Perhaps we can understand then that we are criticizing God for being Love. It is out of love for us that the Son of God decided to carry our sins to the Cross; He was in no way compelled to do so. It then seemed to Satan that he was the one who had won, although it was on the Cross that Satan was ultimately conquered.

Instead of criticizing God, we should praise Him for being Love. Let us try to analyze what happened in the Jordan then. By receiving baptism from John, the Son of God made the heroic decision to love us until the very end, until His extremely painful death on the Cross.

Meanwhile, the Eternal Father grants Him His full support. A voice from heaven was heard: "You are My beloved Son; with You I am pleased." God's love for people is truly unfathomable. The Apostle Paul later commented on this: "He [...] did not spare His own Son but handed Him over for us all" (Romans 8:32).

By receiving baptism from John, the Lord Jesus took upon Himself the entirety of this spiritual ugliness and moral wickedness that sinners had left in the waters of the Jordan. Thus, He indeed took upon Himself the sins of the entire world, including your sins and mine, to burn them in the fire of love that filled Him on the Cross, even amidst the great suffering when it might have seemed that love was impossible.

Thus, it should be unsurprising that the Lord Jesus also called His death on the Cross baptism. He once admitted to His disciples: "There is a baptism with which I must be baptized, and how great is my anguish until it is accomplished!" (Luke 12:50). When James and John indecently ask the Lord Jesus for an important place in His Kingdom, He responds: "Can you drink the cup that I drink or be baptized with the baptism with which I am baptized?" (Mark 10:38).

How literally Jesus became the Lamb of God Who takes away the sins of the world on Good Friday! How literally was He immersed in terrible suffering and bathed in His own blood! This victorious baptism of our Redeemer — or the victorious crossing of the abyss of evil that befell Him in Calvary's Hill — is the source of His Resurrection and thus of our resurrection as well. The Apostle Paul was right that: "You have been ransomed for a great price!"

Jesus Completed His Redeeming Work in the Holy Spirit

Let us return to the Jordan. The presence of the Third Divine Person, the Holy Spirit, during the Lord Jesus' baptism is symptomatic. All four evangelists have consistently written that He then appeared in the form of a dove. This was a reference to the dove that returned to Noah's ark with an olive branch in its beak. From that point, both the dove and the olive branch are symbols of peace and reconciliation in our culture.

The Holy Spirit descended on the Lord Jesus, Who was being baptized in the waters of the Jordan, in a real, not merely symbolic, way. In this way, the prophetic words that the Holy Spirit would descend on the Messiah and anoint Him were fulfilled (see Isaiah 11:1-2). It is an exceptionally important truth of the faith that the Lord Jesus fulfilled His entire salvific work in the Holy Spirit.

The Holy Spirit, the third Person of the Holy Trinity, is the personal Love of the Father and Son. At the very beginning of the Lord Jesus' salvific activity, during His baptism in the Jordan, the Holy Spirit descended on Him in the visible sign of a dove as testimony that everything that He said and did as a human being took place through the Holy Spirit or the same Love through which He as the Son of God is eternally bound to His Father. Likewise, on the Cross, as the author of the Epistle to the Hebrews (9:14) writes, Christ "through the eternal Spirit offered Himself unblemished to God." Our hearts are anxious to praise God for His mercy: "Oh, the depth of the riches and wisdom and knowledge of God! How inscrutable are His judgments and how unsearchable His ways!" (Romans 11:33).

Jesus' Baptism and Our Baptism

Let us conclude by noting how different the Lord Jesus' baptism is from ours. The Lord Jesus was baptized in the waters of the Jordan; He immersed Himself in the repulsive sins of the world to cleanse the waters of the Jordan and liberate us from our sins. Later, on Good Friday, the Lord Jesus was baptized in His own blood, which fulfilled what the baptism in the Jordan had only portended.

Meanwhile, the baptism during which we were baptized is God's joyous and wonderful gift thanks to which we have become participants in God's nature and the eternal covenant between God and people.

Consequently, you and I and every other baptized person should "live in a manner worthy of the call [we] have received" (Ephesians 4:1). To achieve this, it does not suffice to make an effort; after all, we will not achieve eternal life through our own efforts. We will persist by Christ's side and attain eternal life only if we listen to the Word of God during our entire pilgrimage on this earth and if we make use of the sacrifice and feast of the covenant that is the Eucharist and other means of salvation that Christ has left to His Church. In other words, we should organize our entire lives under the sign of the baptism with which we were gifted at the beginning of our faith.

THE LIGHT OF THE MOUNT OF TRANSFIGURATION

The Truth of Both of Christ's Natures Revealed on Mount Tabor

"His face shone like the sun and His clothes became white as light" (Matthew 17:2). Let us juxtapose this description of the Lord's transfiguration with Moses' request to be able to see His glory (Exodus 33:18-23). Moses does not dare to ask God to show Himself; he merely asks Him: "Please let me see Your glory!" He hears the response: "But you cannot see My Face, for no one can see Me and live." However, God shows kindness to Moses and allows him to see Him "from the back."

The context is indispensable to understanding the meaning of this event. Moses' request does not stem from petty curiosity or a desire to become friendly with God. His people have just committed apostasy by worshiping a golden calf. In this situation, Moses begs God to not abandon His people and continue to accompany them as their Guardian and Defender. In response, God asks His servant to create a stone copy of the shattered tablets of the Ten Commandments and renews His covenant with His people. When, after forty days and forty nights of closeness to God that cannot be described using human language, Moses returns to his people, his face is so illuminated by the testimony of being with God that Aaron and the Israelites "were afraid to come near him" (Exodus 34:30).

Various Church Fathers have interpreted both parts of this event as a foreshadowing of the Messiah. On the one hand, the merciful God Who allows Moses to see Him "from the back" reminded the Fathers of the gift of the Incarnation. It is in Jesus Christ that the true God can be truly seen by us in the present life, albeit not "face to face" but, in a sense, "from the back." Jesus Himself said that when we look at Him, we see the Father (see John 12:45; 14:9), while the Church never doubted that He is the Image of His Father (see 2 Corinthians 4:4; Colossians 1:15; Hebrews 1:3) in a complete and inimitable way but through participation.

On the other hand, Moses' face, which is illuminated with love for God, is only a shadow prophesying Christ the Lord's human face, which radiates with God. Not forgetting to reference the event from the Mount of Transfiguration, Origen writes: "And just as the brightness of the nocturnal light is obscured when the sun has risen, so the glory of Moses is obscured by that which is in Christ," as the light on Moses' face was transient, while Christ the Lord deserved it due to His Divine filiation.[166]

Moses' prophetic encounter with God presaged two aspects of one event that was fulfilled in the Person of the Redeemer on the Mount of the Transfiguration. His face, radiant like the sun, revealed His Divinity, but it also confirmed the ultimate truth and beauty of His humanity, which from the beginning was as our humanity will be at the end of time, "without spot or wrinkle or any such thing, that she might be holy and without blemish" (Ephesians 5:27).

166. See Origen, *Commentary on the Gospel according to John Books 13—32* (341, 335), ed. Thomas P. Halton, trans. Ronald E. Heine, vol. 89, *The Fathers of the Church* (Washington, DC: The Catholic University of America Press, 1993), pp. 406—407.

That is why the spontaneous reaction of the disciples to the Redeemer's Transfiguration, wanting not only to believe in Him but also to love Him, was a need to contemplate His holy face to know and love God and at the same time closely observe Him in the art of being truly human. John Paul II clearly distinguishes between both these aspects of contemplation in his apostolic letter *Novo millennio ineunte*, 23-28.

The Redeemer's Divine Face

Why do we who were not witnesses to Christ's transfiguration speak of the light of Mount Tabor? What is this light? Did it also illuminate us when we did not know how to call it and therefore were not aware of its existence? I would respond by saying that the light of Mount Tabor is the grace of faith and love which allows our loving eyes to look at Christ the Lord as He is presented in the Gospels; His words and actions; and the tiniest details of His actions and holy Passion which He underwent for the sake of our salvation. Thanks to this light, we can truly know more and more Who God truly is and what it means to be a person through love.

"No one has ever seen God. The only Son, God, Who is at the Father's side, has revealed Him" (John 1:18). Naturally, He taught that when He became one of us for our sake and that of our salvation, yet He did not teach only through words but also through Himself, in the various situations He found Himself and that He went through. This is because Jesus of Nazareth the Man is the same Son of God Who is equal to the Eternal Father through Whom the world has been created. By looking at Jesus, we can know the true God.

In this way, we find out many times — incomparably more times than the prophet Elijah, summoned to be a witness to the Transfiguration (see 1 Kings 19:11-13) — that God's omnipotence is full of delicacy and tenderness and is manifested most fully in mercy. When we look at Christ the Lord, we see that God seeks out all of us, even the greatest and most hardened sinners, to save us from eternal death. He is ready to become a suppliant and sometimes acts as if we were showing Him mercy by accepting Him.

At the same time, it is not the case that amidst God's inconceivable love, which is revealed through Jesus Christ, the truth about God's absolute transcendence with respect to all of creation has been suspended. In the Old Testament, the closeness of the infinite and omnipotent but loving God sometimes arouses tremendous fear. Experiencing theophany, the prophet Isaiah calls: "Woe is me; I am doomed! For I am a man of unclean lips, living among a people of unclean lips, and my eyes have seen the King, the Lord of hosts!" (Isaiah 6:5).

On Sinai, God revealed Himself to people amidst storms and fire (see Exodus 19:16-19). In the prophet Ezekiel's vision, not only does God reveal Himself in fire, but the atmosphere of angels subordinate to Him is also filled with fire: "The fire gleamed intensely, and from it lightning flashed. The creatures darting back and forth flashed like lightning" (Ezekiel 1:13-14). The prophet Daniel had a similar vision: "His throne was flames of fire, with wheels of burning fire. A river of fire surged forth, flowing from where He sat; Thousands upon thousands were ministering to Him, and myriads upon myriads stood before Him" (Daniel 7:9-10).

The fire — which, of course, is the fire of God's love, which is so great that it is unbearable to us — is also characteristic of the angels who as the servants of the Resurrected Christ announce to people the news that He is alive. The angel that removed the stone from the Tomb is presented as follows: "His appearance was like lightning and his clothing was white as snow" (Matthew 28:3). "While they were puzzling over this, behold, two men in dazzling garments appeared to them" (Luke 24:4). The Greek term describing the angels' "dazzling" garments comes from the word *astrapé* ("lightning bolt"); thus, these are garments filled with lightning bolts.[167] I would like to emphasize this detail because if we persist in our loving admiration of Christ's Divine Face, we will ultimately become like Him and be filled with love we would certainly be incapable of supporting by ourselves.

Let us notice than on the Mount of the Transfiguration, the disciples, who were close to Jesus and were with Him every day, "fell prostrate and were very much afraid" (Matthew 17:6). We can never overemphasize that the Jesus Who came to us as a helpless Infant needing human assistance and protection, Who was with us "meek and humble of heart" (Matthew 11:29), and Who allowed Himself to be killed and "[w]hen He was insulted, He returned no insult; when He suffered, He did not threaten; instead, He handed himself over to the One Who judges justly" (1 Peter 2:23) revealed Himself to His beloved disciple with the Old Testament attributes of Divinity: "The hair of His head was as white as white wool or as snow, and His eyes were like a fiery flame" (Revelation 1:14). Furthermore, He Himself prophesied that His Divine power and glory would become manifest in His Second Coming: "For just as lightning comes from the east and is seen as far as the west, so will the coming of the Son of Man be" (Matthew 24:27).

We have to note this because it would be a regrettable misunderstanding if, fascinated by the fact that the Son of God Who is equal to the Eternal Father decided to become our brother and even our Servant (see Matthew 12:48-50; John 13:12-16), we decided to identify God's mercy with leniency, God's respect for our freedom with His supposed powerlessness, and God's submission to us with a renunciation of Divinity. The Lord Jesus' transfiguration particularly clearly prophesies that the Lamb Who came to conquer the world's sin is the same transcendent God with respect to all of creation, Who is venerated by creatures "countless in number" and Who is worthy

167. It also seems appropriate to note that the Seraphim from the prophet Isaiah's vision mentioned above (Chapter 6) are literally "burning" (Heb. *sārap* = "to burn," "burning").

"to receive power and riches, wisdom and strength, honor and glory and blessing" (Revelation 5:11-12).

In short, it is not the case that the image of the true and almighty God is reduced to our human measure through contemplation of Christ's Divine Face. Instead, the point is for our humanity to spread more and more and beyond all conceptions so that God can fill up everything. John Paul II spoke of this with conviction: "'Your face, O Lord, I seek' (Psalm 27:8). The ancient longing of the Psalmist could receive no fulfillment greater and more surprising than the contemplation of the face of Christ. God has truly blessed us in Him and has made 'His face to shine upon us' (Psalm 67:1)" (*Novo millennio ineunte*, 23).

Contemplating Christ's Humanity

John Paul II continues: Christ the Lord "reveals to us also the true face of man, 'fully revealing man to man himself'" (*ibid.*). Thus, we will never know ourselves — who we are and why we live — better than by lovingly looking at the One Who became one of us and therefore the most wondrous among us.

Above all, Christ the Lord is living evidence of the incredible value each of us presents to God Himself. Christ "has loved me and given Himself up for me" (Galatians 2:20); these words of the Apostle Paul also apply to me at an individual level, even if I am a great sinner. He died for every prostitute, drug addict, libertine, and egotist on the Cross and would be ready to give His life for but one of them.

St. Augustine was fascinated by God's love for man from which man's exceptional worth flows: "He lifts up the hope of the human race, that it might examine its nature, that it might see what place it has in the works of God."[168]

168. *De agone christiano*, 11:12, https://catholicanalects.blogspot.com/2020/12/taking-up-man.html (accessed January 10, 2023).

Christ is not only evidence of man's astounding value to God but also its source. In the eternal intention of His love, God decided to shape us in the image and likeness of His Son (Romans 5:29; see Genesis 1:26). This is why man has not ceased to be very dear to the loving Father even when God's image imprinted on him is in pathetic state. Despite his sinfulness, man is dear to the Eternal Father to the degree that, as we sing on Holy Saturday, He did not hesitate to ransom a slave and give away His own Son.

In any case, this is not the best way of expressing the fact that through Christ God loves us despite our sinfulness. Instead, it would be more accurate to say that God loves us in Christ against our sinfulness to liberate us from our sins. God's love for man is simultaneously fascinating and frightening. The same Apostle Peter who enthusiastically shouted: "Lord, it is good that we are here" (Matthew 17:4) on the Mount of the Transfiguration also had various other sentiments: "Depart from me, Lord, for I am a sinful man" (Luke 5:8).

Contemplating Christ's humanity also entails learning from Christ what it means to be human. He experienced His historical life as a Perfect Man, which is why John Paul II could say the memorable words: "For man cannot be fully understood without Christ. Or rather, man is incapable of understanding himself fully without Christ. He cannot understand who he is, nor what his true dignity is, nor what his vocation is, nor what his final end is. He cannot understand any of this without Christ."

The truth of the Holy Father's words is simple. We are all human, but the humanity of each of us is obscured by some sinfulness. Unfortunately, some of us are slaves to sin. What does someone who suffers from addiction or who has believed that the laws of economy demand deafness to the suffering of the poor know about what it means to human? What can someone who breaks up his own family or another's know about what it means to be human? Let us set aside the enumeration of our sins, however. I mention them only because they make it easier to be enamored of the Lord Jesus' humility.

The closer I am to God, the more truly human I am. There never was and never will be a man who would be so close to the Eternal Father as the Lord Jesus. Each of us became acquainted with God and His love thanks to our parents or other loving people. The Lord Jesus was the only Man Who from the beginning of His human existence directly knew the Eternal Father as the Absolutely Closest and Most Beloved Person. If closeness to God is a measure of humanity, there never was and never will be a truer human than the Lord Jesus.

We should encourage one another to contemplate Christ's humanity especially since we have an impulse to flee from this attitude. The Lord Jesus Himself noticed this: "[T]he light came into the world, but people preferred darkness to light, because their works were evil. For everyone who does wicked things hates the light and does not come toward the light, so that his works might not be exposed" (John 3:19-20). The Redeemer also positively encouraged us to recognize in Him the Light that illuminates our darkness: "I came into the world as light, so that everyone who believes in Me might not remain in darkness" (John 12:46; see 8:12; 9:5, 12, 35). Naturally, our humanity is more fully healed in this Light.

God Has Only One Hill

Moses and Elijah, who stood next to our transfigured Lord, "spoke of His exodus that He was going to accomplish in Jerusalem" (Luke 9:31). Here, Luke the Evangelist uses the same expression *exodos*, which in the Greek translations of the Old Testament is used to describe the flight from the Egyptian yoke. In other words, Christ the Lord is the new Moses, infinitely more important than Moses because He leads God's people not to the land of Canaan but to the promised land of eternal life.

Not only the destination but also the path of this Exodus is different: Moses led God's people through the desert, while Jesus leads us by dying on the Cross for our sins. Right before the description of the Transfiguration, the Evangelist includes the first prophesy of the Passion and the Lord Jesus' memorable words: "Whoever wishes to come after Me must deny himself, take up his cross, and follow Me" (Matthew 16:24). Thus, His suffering and death on the Cross were not only a sacrifice for our sins; they were also, as the Epistle to the Hebrews 2:10 uniquely expresses, paving the way by the Guide of our salvation.

Let us recall that immediately after descending the Mount of Transfiguration the Lord Jesus healed the epileptic and foretold of His suffering for the second time. The two auguries of His passion are like two buckles that bind together the events on the Mount of Transfiguration. They clearly demonstrate that Jesus' transfiguration can be understood only considering His Passion.

Why does the Lord Jesus, Who intends to ascend the Mount of Transfiguration, call us to take up our Cross and follow Him to Golgotha? The answer is simply: the Mount of Transfiguration and Golgotha are, at a spiritual level, two dimensions of the same hill.

Climbing the hill expresses man's path to God, man's growing closer to his Creator and Redeemer. In its difficult and painful, but, fortunately, short and ephemeral aspect, our growing closer to God is ascending Golgotha. Meanwhile, in its ultimate and eternal aspect, it is the Mount of Transfiguration, a hill filled with the light of God's presence and the joy of friendship with God Himself.

Jesus did not have to ascend the Mount of Transfiguration or Golgotha. The Hill of God's Luminosity is His natural place. Furthermore, He Himself is Light that was not created and the Creator of all luminosity. After all, He is the Only Begotten Son of God, completely unified with the Eternal Father. Sacred Scripture says that He did not make use of the opportunity to be equal with God but humbled Himself and became one of us. It is for our sake that He became human and ascended the Mount of Beatitudes and Golgotha.

It was for our sake that He carried the Cross. Amidst terrible difficulty and suffering as well as insults and abuses He went up Golgotha and suffered the terrible torture of the crucifixion. The fact that the description of His transfiguration is bound together by prophesies of His Passion which are like buckles is an invitation to look at Jesus' Cross as well as our own cross in the light of Mount Tabor.

John Paul II movingly writes about this in chapters 25 and 26 of the already-mentioned apostolic letter *Novo millennio ineunte*: "In contemplating Christ's face, we confront the most paradoxical aspect of His mystery, as it emerges in his last hour, on the Cross. [...] At the very moment when He identifies with our sin, 'abandoned' by the Father, He 'abandons' Himself into the hands of the Father. His eyes remain fixed on the Father. Precisely because of the knowledge and experience of the Father which He alone has, even at this moment of darkness He sees clearly the gravity of sin and suffers because of it. He alone, who sees the Father and rejoices fully in Him, can understand completely what it means to resist the Father's love by sin. More than an experience of physical pain, His Passion is an agonizing suffering of the soul. Theological tradition has not failed to ask how Jesus could possibly experience at one and the same time his profound unity with the Father, by its very nature a source of joy and happiness, and an agony that goes all the way to his final cry of abandonment. The simultaneous presence of these two seemingly irreconcilable aspects is rooted in the fathomless depths of the hypostatic union."

The Sleeping Disciples on the Mount of Transfiguration

On close reading of the description of Jesus' transfiguration, we find an answer to a question that has intrigued perhaps every Christian: Why did the faith of the disciples waver on Good Friday? What did the weakness of their faith consist of that it could not withstand the most difficult trial which was the persecution, insulting, and crucifixion of their Master?

Let us return to the context of what had happened on Mount Tabor. About a week earlier, the Lord Jesus helped His disciples to become aware that they were true believers. He asked them: "But who do you say that I am?" (Matthew 16:15). Previously, the disciples had seen many of His miracles and had frequently witnessed the mysterious authority with which He taught (Matthew 7:29). The Lord Jesus posed this question to His disciples when the opinion that He was an exceptional Person was consistently repeated (Matthew 16:14).

When Peter recognized Him as the Messiah and Son of God in the name of the Twelve (Matthew 16:16), Jesus tried to lead them a step further. He tried to prepare them for the fact that He — the Messiah and Son of God — would suffer and be killed but be resurrected on the third day. However, even Peter, who had just been praised for his faith, turned out to be completely incapable of understanding the prophesy that his beloved Master was awaiting Good Friday but would rise from the dead on the third day (Matthew 16:21-23).

The Transfiguration took place several days later. In this way, the Lord Jesus tried to prepare at least the three disciples closest to Him for the day of His death on the Cross. The fact is that, as we have already said, the repeated prophesy of death and resurrection was the first of two things that Jesus did immediately after descending Mount Tabor.

It turned out, however, that even such a tangible experience of His Divinity as was given to Peter, James, and John on that hill did not help them to recognize the meaning and necessity of the Cross. One of the evangelists writes that they then "were overwhelmed with grief" (Matthew 17:23), while two others "were afraid to question Him" (Mark 9:32; Luke 9:45).

What did the disciples then lack that even seeing God's Divine glory on the Mount of Transfiguration did not stop them from wavering in their faith on Good Friday? This question is very important to each of us because there is no guarantee that any of us will persist in faith until the very end.

To respond to this question, I propose reading Luke's Gospel. We read in this Gospel that the Lord Jesus then took them with Him on the hill "to pray" (Luke 9:28). Certainly, Jesus prayed for a long time because the evangelist writes that the disciples turned out to be lethargic prayer partners and ultimately fell asleep (Luke 9:32). Jesus' transfiguration began while they were asleep, and so the disciples were witnesses to only a small part of what was intended for them on that hill.

They lacked two things on the Mount of Transfiguration. They did not truly accompany Jesus in His prayer; they only half-accompanied Him. Furthermore, they looked into His face too little. If they had not lacked this, then they would not have fallen asleep during His prayer in Gethsemane and they would not have wavered in their faith on Good Friday. Let us notice that although the beloved disciple did not abandon Him at the hour of His crucifixion, even he did not persist until the end, which is clear from the description of his behavior on Resurrection Sunday (John 20:1-10).

How much better would the world be if we were closer to God, if we paid more attention to these two things: if we tried to accompany Jesus in His prayer praising the Father and interceding for sinners more. If only we spent more time looking at Jesus' face and tried to contemplate His holy face more... After all, He Himself said: "Whoever has seen Me has seen the Father" (John 14:9).

Because I have already quoted John Paul II's reflections on this matter from the apostolic letter *Novo millennio ineunte*, I will now quote just two sentences from his encyclical on Divine Mercy (*Dives in misericordia*, 7): "Believing in the crucified Son means 'seeing the Father,' means believing that love is present in the world and that this love is more powerful than any kind of evil in which individuals, humanity, or the world are involved."

Indeed, this is perhaps the most important practical conclusion that flows from the mystery of Jesus' transfiguration: May we gaze at the face of our Lord when He teaches, when He performs miracles, and when He speaks to various people. Let us look at His face in all the situations described in the Gospels. May we also not forget to look at the face of the Crucified One. We must also remember the inimitable opportunity that was given to us: we have access to Him that is so close that He is present with us and for us in the Holy Eucharist.

WHAT DID CHRIST THE LORD'S DEATH GIVE US?

Why did the Lord Jesus agree to die on the Cross? What do such explanations that He died to liberate us from the yoke of sin and save us from hell and damnation mean? In what way has "our salvation been hung on the Cross"?

This question requires us to ponder the essence of Christ's sacrifice. If we say that He made His sacrifice by dying on the Cross, this is, of course, the holy truth, but this expression does not render the spirit of His sacrifice. Christ's giving His life was the substance of His sacrifice, but until we enter its spirit, we will be incapable of grasping what its atoning power consisted of and why we have been redeemed by it.

The Son of God became a man in order to be the first person to completely submit Himself to the Eternal Father. Amidst the enormity of evil that is present throughout our human history and that also takes place in our generation, man's complete submission to God has become impossible. No one needs arguments for this because everyone experiences this through own personal sinfulness. Furthermore, we know how greatly sin can poison social structures, the collective mentality and mores and how great the external pressure of sin is on my attitudes.

The Son of God was a perfectly sinless Man, but He lived in our human environment, which is greatly poisoned by sin. He came to us to give us an example of complete submission to the Father, but this was not easy in our sinful world; we have done everything to pose obstacles to Him in this. The crime that took place on Golgotha consisted not only in the fact that someone completely innocent was killed there; furthermore, everything was done to deprive Him of this innocence or at least tarnish it. We have done everything to stop Him from completely submitting to the Father. Fortunately, we failed, as Jesus Christ was an immaculately righteous man Who completely belonged to the Father until the very end, even during the terrible hours of His Passion.

This is the basic significance of His sacrifice. When we say that He made a sacrifice of Himself to the Father, this simply means that He was completely surrendered to the Father even in the most hostile circumstances. He was completely devoted to the Father even amidst the hurricane of evil that passed through Golgotha. The first Man Who succeeded in going through life on this earth while avoiding even the slightest taint of sin was perfectly obedient to the Father "even [to] death on a cross" (Philippians 2:8). This transcended the capabilities of an ordinary man. Such a complete submission to the Father was possible only because this man was the Son of God.

His heroic submission to the Father brought to all people redemption from sin. What does this mean? Let us become aware that just as evil deeds poison our spiritual environment, every good deed has a certain purifying power. Our good deeds to an extent heal the spiritual atmosphere of our milieus and make it easier for others to do good even though all without exception are irrevocably marked by two imperfections: first, all are to a lesser or greater extent corrupted by human sinfulness; second, the value of all is finite as they are the acts of finite beings.

Indeed, Jesus Christ's righteousness, which He fulfilled on Golgotha, is free of both these imperfections. His fidelity to the Father was not only untainted by even the slightest evil, but its value is infinite: after all, this was a deed of the Son of God, the true God equal to the Eternal Father, performed in His human nature. Thus, the purifying power that flows from Christ's Cross is infinite both with respect to its scope and its intensity. It encompasses (or can encompass if we do not shut ourselves off from it) all people of all generations and is capable of completely liberating us from sin. What had been impossible and would still transcend our abilities if we did so only through our own efforts became possible thanks to the Son of God's coming to earth. The process of restoring our initial beauty to our nature has already begun. Furthermore, the seed of deification is already growing in everyone who opens himself to the radiation of Christ's righteousness.

In this way, His complete submission to the Father was simultaneously a work of the greatest love to people. Indeed, every true submission to God brings good to people. If I, a sinner, submit to God, more evil will dry up within me, while my kindness towards other people will be purified and will revive my ability to do good.

In short, the following two sentences are simultaneously true: that man can be saved only through unity with Christ and that the condition necessary for salvation is our doing good. We will not be saved for our deed because salvation is not merchandise that can be purchased for one thing or another. We will be saved through unity with Christ. To think of salvation that would consist only of happiness but that would not liberate us from evil and make us capable of performing good deeds would be an absurd thought. This is as if a prisoner were to dream of freedom but the notion that freedom would be impossible without throwing off his chains had never come to his mind. Unity with Christ does not mean we do not have to make moral efforts. On the contrary, all who are truly open to Christ's salvific radiation feel even more called to undertake moral efforts.

If I perform good deeds within Christ's grace, they will bear fruit in eternal life; through them, I will genuinely grow in Christ's love and become an increasingly pure person. This will take place not through my good deeds but through the power of Christ in which I perform them. At the same time, grace makes us capable of good deeds. Christ's grace is never barren, though it can be rejected. If I am truly open to Christ's powerful grace, this makes me capable of making sacrifices (i.e. of submitting to God and people even under exceptionally difficult circumstances), self-improvement, and performing good deeds.

I repeat: it is impossible to be open to grace that would not give birth to good deeds. It is true that faith without good deeds can exist. But, as the Word of God says, such faith is empty: "For just as a body without a spirit is dead, so also faith without works is dead" (James 2:26).

Herein rests the mystery why the Church is so concerned that all her children gather around Christ's altar at least once a week, each Sunday. During the Mass, Christ's sacrifice, which can liberate us of our sins and leading us to eternal life, becomes truly manifest. We also understand why the Church encourages her children to listen to the Word of God and participate in the sacraments. For the Word of God and the sacraments bring man into the field of Christ's grace and power, and it is only in the field of grace and thanks to Christ's power that man can imitate Him in His complete submission to the Father.

At the same time, it is important to listen to the Word of God, participate in Christ's only sacrifice, and accept the sacraments in authentic faith, not in a phony way. The difference between faith and phony piety is that faith gives rise to attitudes and actions that are worthy of God's children. Even the loftiest religious experiences are phony piety if nothing results from them.

CHRIST THE LORD'S VICTORY ON THE CROSS

Christ the Lord's victory began on the Cross. He presented His own crucifixion as a victory. "Now is the time of judgment on this world; now the ruler of this world will be driven out. And when I am lifted up from the earth, I will draw everyone to Myself". (John 12:31-32).

The sentence of crucifixion was something much greater than simply a sentence to a cruel, inhuman death. People who sentenced someone to crucifixion were not only concerned about killing someone or even causing him as much suffering as possible before dying. The cross was where the ultimate humiliation of a convict and his actions or ideals took place. The sentence of crucifixion did not end the judgment of the unfortunate convict; it was only the beginning. The true judgment took place on the cross. Shrouded in inhuman suffering and left for the public to view, the unfortunate convict either cursed the day he was born and all his ideals or was filled with powerless hatred and in this way attested to the victory of his enemies.

Yet Christ the Lord died in a completely different way because He was victorious even on the Cross. Despite His terrible suffering,

He was exactly as He had always been, while His behavior was witness to the fact that love is possible even on the Cross. Not only did the way in which He died not compromise His teaching; it greatly authenticated it. Who could blame a convict for forgetting about his own mother amidst the tortures of the crucifixion?

Christ the Lord loved even on the Cross, and He did not only love His Mother. When compassionate women from Jerusalem cried over His suffering, He above all thought about their well-being and said to them: Lament your own lives and the souls of those near to you! He not only forgave the thief his sins but helped him to bear the terrible suffering of being crucified with dignity and with the hope of eternal life. Jesus could look at His killers not only from the perspective of the terrible injury they had done to Him. He could realize that His unfortunate persecutors did not know what they were doing and prayed that the Eternal Father grant them mercy.

In short, Satan wanted to execute judgment upon Christ. He wanted to demonstrate that His teaching about love was an idealistic fantasy that would inevitably collapse when confronted with so-called reality. Yet the exact opposite happened: on Golgotha, judgment was executed on both the world and the ruler of the world, Satan. For Christ the Lord, 'this world' refers to the interpersonal space that Satan had succeeded in arranging and where love and truth must give way to falsehood and violence.

This world was judged on Golgotha; all its powerlessness and barrenness were exposed then. It then became apparent that the power of evil is helpless when confronted with a Man Who holds on to the Heavenly Father with both hands. The power of evil could at most kill His body; it could in no way harm His soul. As long as a person persists in God, Who is the source of all love, the attitude of love cannot be killed within him.

Christ the Lord achieved this victory on the Cross. The Resurrection was a solemn proclamation of this victory. This proclamation was all the more joyous since in our present state as sinners no man is capable of full victory over evil. Jesus Christ, the true Man, is truly one of us. He devastatingly conquered death, as pure love was achieved on this earth amidst conditions that were so extremely hostile to love.

Through His resurrection, He gave us testimony that He, a true Man, is at the same time the true Son of God, and so the victory that He achieved on the hill of His Passion has an infinite dimension: it can be the source of victorious power over evil for each of us. We truly have a reason to rejoice! If Christ has risen from the dead, then not only has the root of evil been irrevocably severed, but our existence has gained meaning for eternal life.

However, we should not be surprised that for many of us the joy of Easter is less apparent than that of Christmas. It is easier to rejoice on the day of one's wedding than when awaiting the birth of a child, although no one can deny that the latter joy is deeper and more mature. Even those who have no intention of undertaking the efforts to accept a promise can rejoice because of it. In short, we are capable of Easter joy only to the degree to which the man that rejects Christ has died inside us and the degree to which the resurrected Christ emerges victorious within ourselves.

Therefore, let us look at the mystery of the rejection of Christ. We will above all see that He was crucified not by bandits or people devoid of any conscience but by ordinary people inclined towards good rather than evil. In fact, the judge who sentenced Him to death truly wanted the trial to end differently. The high priest Caiaphas was not motivated by personal hatred for Christ but by concern that His activity would bring the Roman army to the country, which would have obvious consequences.

It is true that the soldiers made the Sentenced One the subject of their mockery and that the crowd insistently demanded His crucifixion. But is it difficult for us to see a bit of both Caiaphas and the Roman soldiers in ourselves? Have we truly never scoffed at another's confusion, awkwardness, or uniqueness? Is the sense of joy at another's suffering truly alien to us? Does it not sometimes happen that an essentially honest man casts a stone at an innocent man? Oddly enough, stones are usually cast against those we owe something to.

If one of us feels so sinless that he cannot see any of the participants in the murder perpetrated against Christ within himself, he cannot be excused from spiritual kinship to those who helplessly opposed the crucifixion. Pilate's wife who unsuccessfully asked her husband for an acquittal; the merciful Jewish women from Jerusalem who cried over Christ; and Peter who impetuously drew his sword in defense of Christ but lost courage when he better comprehended what was happening: they all are an integral part of the world that crucified Christ. Only the Blessed Mother truly stood at His side; she is the first representative of free people who are wedded to Christ for eternal life.

Considering the above, let us once more compare the joy of Christmas with the joy of the Resurrection. Both are accessible only to those who understand how completely we are immersed in the world and prone to death. Our being restricted to this world cannot even be compared to a serf's bond to his village; it is utterly impossible for us to free ourselves from being destined to death. And Christmas is the message of real hope in this absolutely desperate situation. It turns out that this situation is hopeless only for our human strength. Nothing is impossible for God. How greatly God loves us is shown by the manger in Bethlehem.

The joy of Easter is the joy that this improbable hope is becoming real. We no longer completely belong to the world that has rejected Christ! We have been baptized and therefore carry within us a germ of immortality. The new man, destined for eternal life, is growing within us. Now we can reject this cursed common sense that makes us seek space for the good by making a pact with evil. The resurrected

Christ now liberates our desire for good from our powerlessness, which from a human perspective cannot be remedied.

The fact that Christ has resurrected on Sunday is not incidental. Sunday is both the first and the eighth day of the week. That the light of the Resurrection has illuminated the morning of the first day of the week shows us that by rising from the dead Christ the Lord has initiated a new era in human history, one that will never pass because it is transcendent with regards to history. Through the opening in the tomb of the resurrected Christ, it falls on our earth and will never cease to do so; He is the light of a future age.

This overwhelms us especially when we gather to celebrate the Eucharist. The mystery of the Eucharist is the most royal path, one that increasingly brings us into the light of the Eighth Day which knows no sunset.

"HE SITS AT THE RIGHT HAND OF GOD, THE FATHER ALMIGHTY"

The image of the victorious Jesus Who sits at God's right hand appears a total of twenty times in the New Testament. This very number attests to the fact that an exceptionally important truth about Jesus Christ was expressed with the aid of this image. In the days of the apostles, this image was incomparably more comprehensible than it is to us today, as the image of sitting at someone's right hand was commonly used in informal conversation. It suffices to recall the request of the mother of James and John who asked the Lord Jesus "that these two sons of mine sit, one at Your right and the other at Your left, in Your kingdom" (Matthew 20:21; see Mark 10:37).

Let Us Open the Gospels and Apostolic Writings

The Lord Jesus was the first to use this image in reference to Himself. All three Synoptic Gospels have recorded that after His solemn entry into Jerusalem Jesus explained to the Pharisees that the Messiah is someone greater than a mere descendant of David. He recalled the beginning of Psalm 110 to them: "How, then, does David, inspired by the Spirit, call Him 'Lord,' saying: 'The Lord said to my Lord, Sit at my right hand until I place your enemies under your feet? If David calls Him 'Lord,' how can He be His son?" (Matthew 22:43-45; see: Mark 12:35-37; Luke 20:41-43).

Let us deal with the logic of this argument. If the Messiah is not only a son of David but also His Lord, this means, as the prophet Micah (5:1) wrote, that "[His] origin is from of old, from ancient times."

This image is also found in the solemn Messianic declaration given by the Lord Jesus before the Sanhedrin. In fact, it ultimately inclined the Sanhedrin to sentence Him to death: "Then the high priest said to Him, 'I order you to tell us under oath before the living God whether you are the Messiah, the Son of God.' Jesus said to him in reply, 'You have said so. But I tell you: From now on you will see 'the Son of Man seated at the right hand of the Power' and 'coming on the clouds of heaven'" (Matthew 26:63-64; see: Mark 14:61-62; Luke 22:68-69).

Mark the Evangelist later simply said, without any comment, that after speaking to His disciples Jesus "was taken up into heaven and took His seat at the right hand of God" (Mark 16:19). The Apostle Paul explains to us what specifically this image of sitting at the Father's right hand entails: "which He worked in Christ, raising Him from the dead, and seating Him at His right hand in the heavens, far above every principality, authority, power, and dominion, and every name that is named not only in this age but also in the one to come. And he put all things beneath His feet and gave him as head over all things to the church, which is his body, [a] the fullness of the One who fills all things in every way" (Ephesians 1:20-24; see 1 Peter 3:22).

Jesus said this much more concisely: "All power in heaven and on earth has been given to Me" (Matthew 28:18). This is the power of love that grants us eternal life and is given by the Holy Spirit Himself, as was said in the first sermon said in the history of the Church (by the Apostle Peter). On the Pentecost, Peter said to the crowd gathered at the cenacle: "Exalted at the right hand of God, [Jesus] received the promise of the Holy Spirit from the Father and poured it forth, as you [both] see and hear. For David did not go up into heaven, but he himself said: 'The Lord said to my Lord, 'Sit at My right hand until I make your enemies your footstool'" (Acts 2:33-35).

Various apostles spoke in this vein, that the One sitting at the Father's right hand helps us in diverse ways. Led to a hearing before the Sanhedrin, the Apostle Peter testified that Jesus is the Redeemer of His people, Israel: "God exalted Him at His right hand as leader and savior to grant Israel repentance and forgiveness of sins" (Acts 5:31).

Meanwhile, the Apostle Paul sees Jesus as the One Who sits at the Father's right hand, successfully interceding for us: "Who will condemn? It is Christ [Jesus] Who died, rather, was raised, Who also is at the right hand of God, Who indeed intercedes for us" (Romans 8:34). Thus, if Jesus truly becomes our Hope, then we will ultimately unfailingly attain unity with God: "If then you were raised with Christ, seek what is above, where Christ is seated at the right hand of God" (Colossians 3:1). He promises this Himself in Revelation: "I will give the victor the right to sit with Me on my throne, as I Myself first won the victory and sit with My Father on His throne" (Revelation 3:21; see Matthew 19:28).

We will not discuss every New Testament text in which the image appears; for example, in the Epistle to the Hebrews it appears a total of five times (1:3; 13; 8:1; 10:12; 12:2). However, there is one place in the New Testament that cannot be overlooked. This is an important detail in the account of the death of St. Stephen, the first martyr: "But [Stephen], filled with the Holy Spirit, looked up intently to heaven and saw the glory of God and Jesus standing at the right hand of God, and he said, 'Behold, I see the heavens opened and the Son of Man standing at the right hand of God'" (Acts 7:55-56).

The sermons that concern this verse sometimes note a change in the traditional image: Jesus is not sitting but standing at God's right hand. The Fathers explained that this was because He was holding up Stephen so that he would not grow weak but persist in his martyrdom until the very end. In his sermon on the Ascension, Pope Gregory the Great writes: "It is proper for a judge to sit, while one who struggled or assisted another in his struggle stood. [...] Stephen [...] when engaged in his great struggle, saw a standing Jesus Who supported Him. The grace sent by Jesus fought in his defense so that Stephen could overcome the unbelief of his persecutors on earth." [169]

The Exaltation of Our Humanity

The truth of Christ's exaltation pertains, naturally, to His human nature. Because the Son of God is eternally one with His Father through His nature, and this in no way changed even when "by the power of the Holy Spirit He became man, was born of the Virgin Mary, and became a man."

It was in His human nature that Christ the Lord sat at God's right hand and was exalted above all creation. The author of the Epistle to the Hebrews asks rhetorically: "But to which of the angels has he ever said: 'Sit at my right hand until I make your enemies your footstool'?" (Hebrews 1:13).

On the Feast of the Ascension, Pope Leo the Great wrote in the middle of the fifth century: "[W]e commemorate and duly venerate that day on which the Nature of our humility in Christ was raised above all the host of heaven, over all the ranks of angels, beyond the height of all powers, to sit with God the Father. [...] [Through Faith] the blessed Apostles themselves also [...] had lifted the whole contemplation of their mind to the Godhead of Him that sat at the Father's right hand, and were no longer hindered by the barrier of corporeal sight from directing their minds' gaze to That Which had

169. Sancti Gregorii I Magni Romani Pontificis XL Homiliarum in Evangelia, Libri Duo, Homilia XXIX.7, https://www.documentacatholicaomnia.eu/01p/0590-0604,_SS_Gregorius_I_Magnus,_XL_Homiliarum_in_Evangelia_Liber_Secundus,_LT.pdf (accessed January 16, 2023).

never quitted the Father's side in descending to earth, and had not forsaken the disciples in ascending to heaven. [...] The Son of Man and Son of God, therefore, dearly-beloved, then attained a more excellent and holier fame, when He betook Himself back to the glory of the Father's Majesty, and in an ineffable manner began to be nearer to the Father in respect of His Godhead, after having become farther away in respect of His manhood."[170]

Let us also look at the synthetic presentation of the truth that Christ the Lord sits at the right hand of His Father, offered to us by St. Thomas Aquinas. First, however, let us recall the simple explanation in *An Exposition of the Orthodox Faith*, an excellent summary of dogmatic theology that was written in the first half of the eighth century by St. John of Damascus: "We hold, moreover, that Christ sits in the body at the right hand of God the Father, but we do not hold that the right hand of the Father is actual place. For how could He that is uncircumscribed have a right hand limited by place? Right hands and left hands belong to what is circumscribed."[171]

Meanwhile, St. Thomas Aquinas' lecture in the third part of the *Summa Theologica* (q. 58), which was written in the early 1370s, is worth recalling because it perfectly emphasizes both the exaltation of Jesus Christ's humanity beyond all creation and the promise and beginning of our exaltation in His exaltation:

"Christ is said to sit at the Father's right hand inasmuch as He is on equality with the Father in respect of His Divine Nature, while in respect of His humanity, He excels all creatures in the possession of Divine gifts. But each of these belongs exclusively to Christ. Conse-

170. Leo the Great, Sermon 74 (on the Lord's Ascension, II), I-IV, http://www.clerus.org/bibliaclerusonline/en/ghs.htm (accessed January 16, 2023).

171. St. John of Damascus, *An Exposition of the Orthodox Faith (Book IV)*, trans. E.W. Watson and L. Pullan [in:] *Nicene and Post-Nicene Fathers, Second Series*, Vol. 9, eds. Philip Schaff and Henry Wace (Buffalo, NY: Christian Literature Publishing Co., 1899), https://www.newadvent.org/fathers/33044.htm (accessed April 26, 2022).

quently, it belongs to no one else, angel or man, but to Christ alone, to sit at the right hand of the Father.

Since Christ is our Head, then what was bestowed on Christ is bestowed on us through Him. And on this account, since He is already raised up, the Apostle says that God has, so to speak, "raised us up together with Him," still we ourselves are not raised up yet, but are to be raised up, according to Romans 8:11: "He who raised up Jesus from the dead, shall quicken also your mortal bodies;" and after the same manner of speech the Apostle adds that "He has made us to sit together with Him, in the heavenly places;" namely, for the very reason that Christ our Head sits there."[172]

172. *The Summa Theologiæ of St. Thomas Aquinas* Second and Revised Edition, part 3, q. 58, a. 4, ad 1, 1920, trans. Fathers of the English Dominican Province, https://www.newadvent.org/summa/4058.htm (accessed January 16, 2023).

I Believe in the Holy Universal Church

WHY DO WE NEED THE CHURCH?

Christianity is the only religion whose adherents call themselves the Temple or the Church. A temple is a place where God is uniquely present among people. Let us recall: an omnipresent God! It is due to us that God agrees to be particularly present in a given place.

The essence of a temple was perfectly presented by King Solomon on the day of the consecration of the Jerusalem Temple: "Is God indeed to dwell on earth? If the heavens and the highest heavens cannot contain You, how much less this house which I have built! [...] Listen to the petition of Your servant and of Your people Israel which they offer toward this place" (1 Kings 8:27, 30).

Thus, one should not be surprised that when we speak of the Church, we want to present its "templeness;" we often like to refer to the spiritual substance tied to the only Temple of the true God in the Old Testament, the Jerusalem Temple. The Church implements everything that that Temple had foreshadowed.

Jesus Christ Is the Temple in the Full Meaning of the Word

It is worth realizing that the Lord Jesus is not only the Founder of the Church, the Temple that we constitute. He is the Temple Himself in the full meaning of the word. After all, in His humanity He became the place of God's fullest salvific presence among people. The New Testament often reiterates this. After kicking the moneychangers out of the Temple, the Redeemer said: "Destroy this temple and in three days I will raise it up." The Evangelist notes that "He was speaking about the temple of His body" (John 2:19-21). The Apostle Paul also emphasizes the "templeness" of the Redeemer: "For in Him dwells the whole fullness of the Deity bodily" (Colossians 2:9).

The Evangelists often use temple imagery to present the mystery of the Incarnation. The angel said to Mary: "The Holy Spirit will come upon you, and the power of the Most High will overshadow you" (Luke 1:35). The word "overshadow" must be rendered in a literal sense; it means "to provide shade," and even if we notice an etymological similarity between the words *skia* and *skene*, it means "to cover you with a tent," which is probably a reference to the Tent of Meeting. John the Evangelist also presents the mystery of the Incarnation in the categories of a temple: "And the Word became flesh and made His dwelling among us, and we saw His glory" (John 1:14). In the original Greek, "dwelt" is *eskénosen,* or "pitched a tent."

In What Sense Are We the Church?

If Jesus Christ Himself is the Temple of the New Testament, then we are the Church, or the Temple, as long as we are one with Christ. This is why the Son of God became one of us, to teach us unity with Him; this is why He became a participant in our human nature, in order to allow us to participate in His Divine nature. He descended upon the earth as the most magnificent Temple of God in order to transform all who believe in Him into a Temple or the Church.

Christ's followers are referred to as the Church in the New Testament: "For we are the temple of the living God; as God said: 'I will live with them and move among them, and I will be their God, and they shall be My people'" (2 Corinthians 6:16). A verse later, the Apostle Paul clearly states that the fact that we are the Church is not only a wonderful gift from God but also a challenge: "'Therefore, come forth from them [the idolaters] and be separate,' says the Lord, 'and touch nothing unclean; then I will receive you.'"

The fact that the Church on this earth is only in the process of construction and that God's transforming presence has not yet fully encompassed us is also present in other apostolic pronouncements. The Apostle Paul says to Christians coming from pagan nations: "So then you are no longer strangers and sojourners, but you are fellow citizens with the holy ones and members of the household of God, built upon the foundation of the apostles and prophets, with Christ Jesus Himself as the capstone. Through Him the whole structure is held together and grows into a temple sacred in the Lord" (Ephesians 2:19-21).

To make it clear that the image of the Church being built concerns not only new people who are joining the Church, the apostle adds: "[I]n Him you also are being built together into a dwelling place of God in the Spirit" (Ephesians 2:22). Thus, the Church grows, and she should grow in each of us. God would like to fill each of us more and more with His salvific presence.

Let us notice that Christ, the Temple of God in the full meaning of the word, is called the Cornerstone, or capstone. It is difficult to find a clearer way of emphasizing that the aim of the appearance of this Divine Temple among us was the transformation of each of us into the Temple, or the Church. This brings to mind the stone in Daniel's prophesy that "became a great mountain and filled the whole earth" (Daniel 2:35).

The Apostle Peter directs our attention to another very important dimension of the "templeness" of God's people of the New Covenant. Namely, by addressing us as "living stones" of the Temple built by God, Peter reminds us that in Christ we have become capable of giving ourselves as a sacrifice that is pleasing to God: "Come to Him, a living stone, rejected by human beings but chosen and precious in the sight of God, and, like living stones, let yourselves be built into a spiritual house to be a holy priesthood to offer spiritual sacrifices acceptable to God through Jesus Christ" (1 Peter 2:4-5).

It seems appropriate to recall the gift of the Holy Eucharist. It is the very center of the Temple that we constitute and that is built by including our spiritual sacrifices into the one Sacrifice of our Redeemer.

Christ — Yes, the Church — No?

As we know well, the Lord Jesus Himself gave us the Church. He said in Caesarea Philippi: "[U]pon this Rock I will build My Church, and the gates of the netherworld shall not prevail against it" (Matthew 16:18). The mere fact that He chose twelve apostles so that they may inaugurate His Church — using the model of the twelve sons of Jacob who were the forefathers of the people of the Old Covenant — demonstrates that it was His will to establish the Church, the people of the New Covenant.

Furthermore, the Lord Jesus loves His Church so tangibly that He gave His life for it: "Christ loved the Church and handed Himself over for her to sanctify her, cleansing her by the bath of water with the word, that He might present to Himself the Church in splendor, without spot or wrinkle or any such thing, that she might be holy and without blemish" (Ephesians 5:25-27). Let us notice that the Redeemer loves His Church not because she is beautiful; He loves her so that she may become beautiful.

Furthermore, the Lord Jesus mysteriously identifies with His Church. In the New Testament, we frequently read that the Church is His Body. When He encountered Saul of Tarsus, a notorious persecutor of Christians, outside Damascus, He did not ask: "Saul, Saul, why are you persecuting My followers?" Instead, He asked: "Saul, Saul, why are you persecuting Me?" (Acts 9:4).

Thus, it would be very arrogant to take on an attitude that is popular today: "Christ — yes, the Church — no. I love and admire Christ but nonetheless reject the Church because she is an impediment to my shaping my own religiosity and my own attitude towards Christ." Can one truly love Christ if one rejects His Beloved and Bridegroom for whom He gave His life?

Those who say: "Christ — yes, the Church — no" resemble a Pole who would say: "Polishness — yes, the Polish state — no. My heart is filled with love of my homeland, but don't speak of the Polish state because like any institution it can only ruin everything that is grand."

An anti-institutional scar attests to a great disruption of one's sense of reality. Various imperfections related to the functioning of institutions (which, in general, are inevitable and in certain cases are often open to being repaired and reformed) are used as evidence of the mere existence of an institution's being meaningless or even destructive of the values that a given institution wants to serve.

Another example may serve to illustrate the absurdity of this attitude. Let us imagine a person (or perhaps I am such a person?) who has a very important task to accomplish: raise his children, write a wise book, start a homeless shelter, etc. Let us imagine that this person is seriously ill. It is not the case that his body is an obstacle to his realization of this important task. His illness of which he attempts to cure himself is the obstacle, while the awareness that he has an important task to realize will be conducive to his recovery.

Now, let us apply this example to the topic under discussion. If my reaction to some imperfection of the Church is the attitude of "Christ — yes, the Church — no," then I am similar to a "philosopher" who believes that the best way to get rid of an illness is by killing the patient. Indeed, the patient's death will end his ailment. However, he will not be capable of bringing up his children, writing a wise book, or starting a homeless shelter.

It is very astonishing that a negative attitude to the Church's mere institutional nature appears among Poles as well. Over the past two centuries, our nation's enemies have put great effort into destroying and limiting the institutional dimension of our faith by shutting down monasteries and theological schools; closing churches and religious publications; deporting priests to Siberia and Nazi concentration camps; and destroying roadside religious figures and removing crosses from the walls of schools and hospitals. It would seem that our persecutors' lesson about the institutional importance of grounding our faith in our lives would be never forgotten. It turns out, however, that this is often not the case.

The Church: The Gift of Direct Access to the Lord Jesus

Let us read Jesus' relatively mysterious words: "But I tell you the truth, it is better for you that I go. For if I do not go, the Advocate will not come to you. But if I go, I will send him to you" (John 16:7). This is very intriguing: Why was the Lord Jesus' physical departure a condition necessary for the coming of the Holy Spirit?

The response to this question follows from the truth that the Son of God, equal to the true and eternal Father, is at the same time a true Man. One cannot be a true man in any other way than by becoming immersed in all sorts of human particularity. This is why Jesus was born of a specific mother; lived in a specific time, religion, and culture; and lived and traveled in specific cities.

It is impossible to not realize that during His earthly time spent with us He directly encountered only a tiny fraction of the people of just one generation, even when He was surrounded by crowds. Meanwhile, humanity, to which He gave the words of salvation and for whom He died on the Cross, consists of all people coming from many subsequent generations!

Humanity's greatest geniuses have been incapable of transcending their human particularity. Whether we like it or not, Plato, Buddha, Confucius, Einstein, or John Paul II become someone distant in time, someone who lived a long time ago, to each subsequent generation. With Jesus Christ, however, things are different. Among people, only He is not just a true Man, but He is also the true God Who transcends all particularity.

After His departure to His Father, Jesus gave the Church the Holy Spirit so that — likewise as a Man — He could in a new way be "with [us] always, until the end of the age" (Matthew 28:20). Thanks to the Holy Spirit, God's authentic truth persists in the Church. The Redeemer has told us that the Holy Spirit "will teach [us] everything and remind [us] of all that [He] told [us]" (see John 14:26).

Thanks to the presence of the Holy Spirit in the Church, all believers without exception — regardless of what part of the world and in what time Providence has situated us — have incomparably more direct access to the Lord Jesus than that enjoyed by the apostles during His historical time on earth. When the Lord Jesus was among people, He could have been seen, His teachings could be heard, his miracles could be admired, and He could even be touched and asked about something. However, this was always the case that Jesus was "here," while you, I, he, and she were "there."

After making His sacrifice for our sake, Jesus was resurrected, went to His Father, and sent (and continues to send) the Holy Spirit to His Church. Now, thanks to the Holy Spirit that shapes us into the Church, our unity with Jesus and possible encounter with Him are inconceivably deeper than those of the apostles themselves when they lived with Him every day and when they were capable of directly being with Him. To quote *Sacrosanctum concilium*, the Second Vatican Council's Constitution on the Sacred Liturgy, in the Church, Jesus "[b]y His power [...] is present in the sacraments, so that when a man baptizes it is really Christ Himself who baptizes" (7). He is present in

His Word because He speaks whenever Sacred Scripture is read in the Church. He is present when the Church prays and sings the Psalms, as He Himself promised: "For where two or three are gathered together in My name, there am I in the midst of them" (Matthew 18:20).

In the Church, we have so inconceivably direct access to Jesus that at least on every Sunday we are invited to become truly immersed in the love with which Jesus went through His Passion and death, and we can truly become united with Him through Holy Communion. In the Church, we receive the gift of such direct unity with Jesus that now — at an incipient level, but increasingly so — we are in Him, while He is in us (see 1 John 4:13-16).

And this is the basic response to the question of why we need the Church. This is why Christ the Lord endowed us with the Church, so that all people who have believed in Him — people of all countries, cultures, and generations — may have direct access to Him, His teachings, His grace, His forgiveness, and Himself.

How Can We Talk About Evil in the Church?

In conclusion, I will try to demonstrate a couple of "universal keys" that I use during conversations with people scandalized by evil in the Church. I owe the first key to a teacher who felt very uncomfortable because she constantly heard people speak ill of the Church in her teachers' lounge. At a meeting of the ministry to teachers, she said: "At one point, I realized who was in charge of this smear campaign. He was a colleague who had been living with his third or fourth lover as well as a co-worker who I personally know had undergone two abortions that I know of." Very often, hurling accusations at the Church (sometimes absolutely correct ones) results from an attempt at justifying oneself. This is why evil in the Church — both real evil and that which is slanderously attributed to the Church — brings a sense of satisfaction to sinners who have no intention of converting.

This phenomenon was noted by St. Augustine: "People who are beyond hope pay all the less attention to their own sins, the more interested they are in those of others. They are looking for a chance to tear others to bits, not to put them right. Unable to excuse themselves, they are only too ready to accuse others."[173]

The second key that I like to use in such conversations is a Chinese proverb according to which one tree that falls makes more noise in the forest than the fact that the entire forest is growing. This is true. Evil makes a big ruckus because evil should not exist. Meanwhile, no one is surprised by the existence of good. There is an abundance of good in the Church; however, one should not be surprised that evil, which is a rather unique phenomenon in the Church, is much more visible and usually leads to great scandal. Indeed, the Church should be the last place where evil can be found.

I owe the third key to a certain rabbi who once wrote something like: 'The sins of our Jewish people are more numerous than the sand in the beach, but our people are not hated because of them; they are hated because of their merits.' I think that something analogous can be said of the Church. Indeed, great evil sometimes takes place in the Church. However, this is not why the Church is constantly stigmatized. The Church is disliked and criticized and sometimes even hated above all because she tries to be faithful to the Gospel. This is because she clearly teaches that the commandment "Thou shalt not kill" means "Thou shalt not kill," while the principle "What God has joined together man cannot separate" is as obliging today as it was in the past.

I will conclude by referencing a metaphor proposed by the recently canonized great English convert Cardinal John Henry Newman. Newman became a Catholic in the forty-seventh year of his life. Pre-

173. St. Augustine, Sermon 19.2, trans. Edmund Hill, O.P., [in:] *The Works of St. Augustine. A Translation for the 21st Century*, ed. John E. Rotelle, OSA (Brooklyn, New York: New City Press 1990), p. 378.

viously, he himself was often prone to anti-Catholic stereotypes in his perception of the Church. Once he became a Catholic, Newman liked to repeat that the Church is like a beautiful stained-glass window. Seen from the outside, the stained-glass window, regardless of how beautiful it is, seems to be a meaningless jumble of glass, lead, and dust. In order to admire its beauty, one must come inside. Similarly, in order to see and appreciate the magnificence of God's great gift that is the Church, one must simply come inside.

MARY, THE PERFECT MODEL OF THE CHURCH

Three Reasons Why God Made Mary Immaculate

Even Joseph, Mary's virginal spouse, stood before the mystery of the Incarnation once it had occurred. Mary was the only human witness to the Son of God taking on our human nature. I would like to add that she was an active witness, even a collaborator. In accordance with His tradition of respect for human freedom, God did not intend on imposing Himself upon us, even as our Redeemer.

Why, then, did only Mary's explicit agreement suffice for Him? This detail merits our faith's probing attention, as thanks to it we can learn much about our own situation with regards to Jesus Christ.

This brings to mind the paradoxical comparison of the mystery of the Incarnation to an invasion that God decided to undertake on our earth. This is not a completely arbitrary comparison, since Christ the Lord presents Himself as being more powerful than the "strong man" known as the devil (Luke 11:21-22). In the scene of the Annunciation, the angel presents the Son of God Who was to become the Son of Mary as the King Whose rule would never end.

This strange invasion is marked by complete renunciation of violence, while the only force that God deigned to use in it was humble, authentic love. The beginning of a successful invasion is the conquest of a mighty bridgehead from which it could spread. In the case of this invasion, its dissemination was to be paradoxical. God does not want to impose His Kingdom on anyone; it will be disseminated only wherever people truly want to be open to it.

If we look at the mystery of the Incarnation from this perspective, we can see at least two additional reasons why the Eternal Father, preparing Mary to be the Mother of His Only Begotten Son, made her immaculate, free of all sin, including original sin. The main reason is perfectly evident even outside this perspective: She was to be the Mother of God Himself! She was to be the only person among the billions of people who have ever lived and will live on earth whom the Son of God called "Mommy." After all, the True God Who gave us the commandment "Honor thy father and mother" certainly fulfilled it when He became human, and He did so at a Divine level. It was simply appropriate for the Son of God to make His Mother inconceivably beautiful and immaculate.

But let us look at the two additional reasons. We have said that the beginning of a successful invasion must be the conquest of a strong bridgehead. God decided to implement His Kingdom with great humility and respect for our human dignity, but He would not be God if the design of His powerful love amounted to nothing. His work of the Incarnation and Redemption had to succeed, while the measure of its fruitfulness could have been nothing other than completely voluntary openness to His grace and love. This is why the Eternal Father made Mary, by power of her Son's future accomplishments, immaculate. In this way, He helped her, whom He chose for the mother of the Son of God, accept Him with all her heart.

We sinners do nothing with all our hearts. Even those choices and attitudes that we undertake with the greatest desire and readiness to make sacrifices are always accompanied by some egocentric negligence. Being sinners, we can at most strive to submit our entire selves to God, and thanks to His grace our submission to God can even be greater, but at this point opening our entire selves to God is impossible.

Mary was capable of accepting the Son of God with her entire self. Naturally, she owed this capability not to herself but to God Who had made her immaculate. Nonetheless, it was she who said: "Let it be to me according to Your Word;" she opened her entire self in response to God's intention to give the Only Begotten Son to people as a gift. The most recent council recalled in simple and clear words the universal teaching of the Church Fathers who "see her as used by God not merely in a passive way, but as freely cooperating in the work of human salvation through faith and obedience" (*Lumen gentium*, 56).

Gradually, more and more people began to recognize Him as the Ruler of the Kingdom of God: Joseph, Elizabeth, the shepherds, the Magi, Simeon, and Anna, and, eventually, John the Baptist, the apostles, and growing numbers of believers. Some thirty years later, the world was sufficiently ready for the One Whom He called the Prince of the World to win the decisive battle on Golgotha. Then, Satan's power was radically and definitively curtailed, and the Kingdom of God can now spread to the ends of the earth.

However, there was a moment when only Mary personified the entire Church. The Gospel makes particular note of this. It was noticed long ago that in the Gospel scene of the Annunciation Mary was presented as the Daughter of Zion to whom God's salvific promises were addressed. This is strange because in the Old Testament all the inhabitants of God's city of Jerusalem or the entire people of God and never one individual woman are referred to as the Daughter of Zion. We will try to interpret God's design in this treatment of the individual Mary as the Daughter of Zion through the prophesy of Zephaniah. The substance of this prophesy is astonishingly analogous to that with which the angel came to Mary:

Shout for joy, daughter Zion!
sing joyfully, Israel!
Be glad and exult with all your heart,
Daughter Jerusalem!
The Lord has removed the judgment against you,
He has turned away your enemies;
The King of Israel, the Lord, is in your midst,
you have no further misfortune to fear.
On that day, it shall be said to Jerusalem:
Do not fear, Zion,
do not be discouraged!
The Lord, your God, is in your midst,
a mighty Savior,
Who will rejoice over you with gladness,
and renew you in His love
(Zephaniah 3:14-17).

If we take a closer look at the scene of the Annunciation in Luke, the angel's assurances that "you are full of grace" have no analogies in the above-cited prophesy. It was the fullness of grace that made Mary, an individual woman, capable of personifying the Daughter of Zion, the entire Church. Thus, it is insufficient to say that she accepted the Son of God in the name of us all and that she was then our representative. She perfectly accepted Him with her entire self, in a way no one today would be capable of doing. Thus, it is unsurprising that we so cordially accept the truth of the words inscribed in Luke's Gospel that Mary will enjoy Christ's particular respect until the end of the world: "For He has looked upon His handmaid's lowliness; behold, from now on will all ages call me blessed" (Luke 1:48).

From here follows another, third reason why God made the Mother of His Son absolutely free of all sin. Namely, in the eternal design of His love God has destined the entire Church and each of us in the Church to be especially sinless and immaculate, completely loving Christ in response to His love. When history is fulfilled in eternal life, the entire

Church will stand before Christ "in splendor, without spot or wrinkle or any such thing, that she might be holy and without blemish. [...] [A]s He chose us in Him, before the foundation of the world, to be holy and without blemish before Him" (Ephesians 5:27; 1:4).

Even though we are still sinners, such love, complete and immaculate, from the very beginning comes from the Church towards Christ. Mary has been in the Church much longer than any of us sinners. Meanwhile, God has called us sinners to the Church to transform us into immaculate saints. Accordingly, Mary's figure foreshadows, especially after her assumption, the ultimate vocation of us all. At the same time, she is a living guarantor that there will always be more love for Christ than infidelity and sin in the Church. Indeed, the love that the Church presently directs towards her Redeemer also contains the inconceivable love that binds Mary to her Son.

The Model of Faith

We can learn much about the Church if we closely look at Mary's faith and her virginal motherhood. In both cases, she is an unequaled model for the Church. Mary can be especially aptly described as the model or even leader of faith." The last council presents her in this way several times. "She stands out among the poor and humble of the Lord, who confidently hope for and receive salvation from Him" (Lumen gentium, 55). Below, I will present two more significant conciliar pronouncements on this topic.

The unparalleled intensity of Mary's faith was especially astutely presented by John Paul II in the second and third chapters of the first part of his encyclical *Redemptoris Mater*. There, the heroism of Mary's faith is compared to that of Abraham. Like Abraham, Mary, the Mother of God's people of the New Covenant, "in hope believed against hope." For the reality in which she came to be the Messiah's Mother was plain and filled with danger, as if it contradicted God's promises that "He will be great and will be called Son of the Most High, and the Lord God will give Him the throne of David his father, and He will rule over the house of Jacob forever, and of His kingdom there will be no end" (Luke 1:32-33).

The Gospels very clearly emphasize that Mary was the Mother of the Son of God not only by giving birth to Him and raising Him, but especially because she realized her maternal vocation in deep, heroic faith. Indeed, it is difficult to understand how it is that the Gospel passages that speak of this most clearly were referenced by some Christians to account for their religious indifference to Mary.

Let us look at these two Gospel pericopes. A certain woman wanted to express her great admiration for Jesus' teaching and called: "Blessed is the womb that carried you and the breasts at which you nursed!" And Jesus replied: "Rather, blessed are those who hear the word of God and observe it" (Luke 11:27-28). Jesus responded in a similar way to the news that His Mother and relatives were standing by the house He was in and wanted to see Him: "My mother and My brothers are those who hear the word of God and act on it" (Luke 8:21).

Both these episodes unambiguously demonstrate that one becomes close to Jesus through faith, while He came to our earth so that we all could become close to Him in this way. Even filiation with Jesus and being His mother would mean little if one lacks that spiritual closeness through faith. In both these scenes, this message is clearly present.

One would have to read the Gospels very carelessly to claim that these fragments downplay the meaning of Mary in God's work of salvation. In the same Gospel, we read about Mary: "Blessed are you who believed" (Luke 1:45) and: "Behold, from now on will all ages call me blessed" (Luke 1:48). And also: "And Mary kept all these things, reflecting on them in her heart" (Luke 2:19; see 2:51).

In light of these statements, the Marian significance of both above-mentioned episodes can only be such as explained by the Church's teaching: that Mary was Jesus' mother not only "in flesh," but she realized her motherhood as "the first of 'those who hear the word of God and do it' [...] And therefore does not the blessing uttered by Jesus in response to the woman in the crowd refer primarily to her?" (*Redemptoris Mater,* 20).

There never was and never will be another person in the Church whose faith is purer and deeper than Mary's. For the Church, she is an unequaled model of faith. We become the Church more fully once we become more like Mary in our faith. Especially in situations when reality seems to contradict the Word of God and God's promises, we should wholeheartedly observe Mary, who persisted in her faith even by the Cross.

Besides, it is an understatement that she persisted in her faith by the Cross. The same could be said of the Apostle John or Mary Magdalene. Mary then accomplished something infinitely greater. As the most recent council teaches, she grieved "exceedingly with her only begotten Son, uniting herself with a maternal heart with His sacrifice, and lovingly consenting to the immolation of this Victim which she herself had brought forth" (*Lumen gentium*, 58). This statement is so deep that it is worth referencing it one more time, somewhat more completely: "After this manner the Blessed Virgin advanced in her pilgrimage of faith, and faithfully persevered in her union with her Son unto the Cross, where she stood, in keeping with the divine plan, grieving exceedingly with her only begotten Son, uniting herself with a maternal heart with His sacrifice, and lovingly consenting to the immolation of this Victim which she herself had brought forth."

The Universal Call to Spiritual Motherhood

Let us reference a third pronouncement of the Second Vatican Council that speaks of Mary as the "model of faith": "As St. Ambrose taught, the Mother of God is a type of the Church in the order of faith, charity, and perfect union with Christ. For in the mystery of the Church, which is itself rightly called mother and virgin, the Blessed Virgin stands out in eminent and singular fashion as exemplar both of virgin and mother" (Lumen gentium, 63).

Today, we seem to have forgotten that the Church is our mother and that each of us – not only women but also men – should strive for such maturity in faith in order to be able to give birth to Christ's new children. Let us recall the basic Biblical texts on this topic. The Church as a mother is prophesied above all in the last chapter of the Book of Isaiah. That is also how the Church presents the allegory of Sarah and Hagar in the Epistle to the Galatians: "But the Jerusalem above is freeborn, and she is our mother. [...] Therefore, brothers, we are children not of the slave woman but of the freeborn woman" (Galatians 4:26 and 31).

Especially worthy of attention are those statements of the Apostle Paul in which he attributes to himself various maternal ministrations with regards to the Christians entrusted to him. Indeed, Paul does not hesitate to call himself their father (1 Corinthians 4:15; Philemon 10). At the same time, he is capable of writing: "My children, for whom I am again in labor until Christ be formed in you!" (Galatians 4:19); "Rather, we were gentle among you, as a nursing mother cares for her children" (1 Thessalonians 2:7); "Brothers, I could not talk to you as spiritual people, but as fleshly people, as infants in Christ. I fed you milk, not solid food, because you were unable to take it" (1 Corinthians 3:1-2). Feeding someone with milk and breastfeeding are strictly maternal ministrations, yet the Apostle Paul ascribes them to himself despite being a man.

It is difficult to find more convincing evidence that the image of the Church as the Mother of all believers is not an empty metaphor. This image contains a great exhortation (Cyprian Kamil Norwid would say that this is our collective duty). Namely, the Church will be more a mother the more we believers in Christ will want to share our faith with those who do not yet believe or who are only starting out in their faith. If we do not know how to do this and are incapable of going beyond an elementary school catechesis textbook in our faith, we will contribute to the spiritual infantilization of the Church. The Epistle to the Hebrews contains a surreal but very authentic image of those Christians who are mature in the faith yet must still be fed through a baby bottle: "Although you should be teachers by this time, you need to have someone teach you again the basic elements of the utterances of God. You need milk, [and] not solid food" (Hebrews 5:12).

We will only be capable of genuinely participating in the Church's motherhood if we are capable of imitating Mary's motherhood. The Church has always taken great care to emphasize that her motherhood was virginal. Virginity means unconditional surrender to God and complete openness to God's gifts. The spiritual dimension of Mary's virginity was her faith, which has already been mentioned. Because she was a virgin, she gave birth of the Holy Spirit. Because she was the most faithful of all people, her Divine motherhood was not limited to the corporal birth of Jesus Christ and His upbringing, but it was genuine accompaniment in His salvific work.

Likewise, a necessary condition for our spiritual fertility is to become similar to Mary in her virginity. It should be noted, however, that the number of people whom we have helped in their faith can be testimony to spiritual fertility, but this fertility cannot be measured through simple arithmetic. God's standards are not human standards. St. Therese of Lisieux, who entered a convent almost as a child and spent her entire youth and adult life in a cloister, is the patroness of missions. For it is those who attempt to truly and completely surrender to God who are truly spiritually fertile in their faith. It is above all thanks to them that the Church fulfills her missionary vocation. Thanks to them, the Church preaches the Word of God most effectively and bolsters the needy with her prayer most firmly.

Catholic teaching has always emphasized that particularly important witnesses to and participants in the Church's virginal motherhood are, on the one hand, spouses, and, on the other, men and women who live out vows of celibacy devoted to God. The Church has always reminded spouses that for their parenthood to attain spiritual fertility they need a degree of spiritual fertility that is marked by complete surrender to God. Meanwhile, the Church has constantly cautioned persons who have taken vows of celibacy before God that their living out their vow would be in vain if doing so did not make them fertile for Christ.

Unquestionably, the Church would not notice these great truths if she did not admire the Mother of Christ, who is an unparalleled model for the Church, with love.

"HOW BEAUTIFUL YOU ARE, MARY!"

"Her Spiritual Beauty Encourages Trust and Hope Within Us"

In the Book of Hours, we sing: "How beautiful you are, my friend!" The first Person to Whom Mary is a true friend is her Son Jesus, our Redeemer. All children are younger than their parents, with only one exception: Jesus, the Son of Mary, is the eternal Son of God. In His humanity, Jesus is younger than His Mother. As the Son of God through Whom the universe has been created, He is His Mother's Creator. Because He decided to be born of her as a man, He made her beautiful and immaculate from the first moment of her existence. Thus, there is nothing inappropriate in His calling His Mother His friend.

However, the mere fact that we have learned to sing the Book of Hours in the Church is the best evidence that we who have believed in Jesus Christ and want to be one with Him are also allowed to call Mary our friend.

It is worth knowing that this quote comes from Song of Songs. It is a summary of the particular admiration that the Bride awakens in the Bridegroom. The Bridegroom is enthralled with literally every aspect of his Bride: her eyes, hair, teeth, mouth, temple, and breasts. To put it in simple terms, the Bridegroom calls in Song of Songs: "You are beautiful in every way, my friend, there is no flaw in you!" (4:1-7) In the Book of Hours, this cry of awe concludes with a clear emphasis that she is beautiful for she has been immaculately conceived: "And original sin never corrupted you!"

In his Angelus address on December 8, 1998, Pope John Paul II said: "*Tota pulchra es Maria!* [How Beautiful You Are, Mary!] With these words the Church addresses the Mother of Christ on today's Solemnity of the Immaculate Conception. Mary is the woman preserved from original sin, envisaged and chosen by the Father to become the Mother of the Savior. In giving a human face to the Son of God, who is 'the splendor of the Father's glory' (St. Ambrose), the Blessed Virgin saw shining upon her, as no other creature, the face of the Father rich in grace and mercy. Thus, the Immaculate Conception is an extraordinary gift and an ineffable privilege! As a result, Our Lady, totally preserved from the slavery of evil and the object of God's special favor, anticipates in her life the path to be taken by the redeemed, the people saved by Christ."

One year later, during his Angelus address on December 5, 1999, John Paul II recalled the promise at the beginning of the Epistle to the Ephesians that God wants each of us to become "holy ones who are faithful in Christ Jesus": "Mary, '*full of grace,*' is the realization of all that God wants to accomplish in every person. The Mother of the Redeemer was preserved from sin and filled with divine grace. Her spiritual beauty invites us to have confidence and hope; the Blessed Virgin, all fair and all holy, encourages us to prepare the ways of the Lord and make straight his paths, in order one day to contemplate with her the salvation of God."

Several months later, during his pilgrimage to the Holy Land, John Paul II recalled that the beauty with which Mary shines is a guarantee that the ultimate destiny of the entire Church is one of inconceivably marvelous beauty: "In contemplating the *Theotokos*

[Mother of God], almost at this journey's end, we look upon the true face of the Church, radiant in all her beauty, shining with 'the glory of God which is on the face of Christ' (2 Cor 4:6)."

During his speech in Jerusalem on March 26, 2000, which turned into a prayer, the pope said: "O Advocate, help the Church to be ever more like you, her exalted model. Help her to grow in faith, hope and love, as she searches out and does the will of God in all things (cf. Lumen Gentium, 65). O clement, O loving, O sweet Virgin Mary!"

All of Creation Is Beautiful

Mary is the most beautiful of God's creatures, but beauty is a characteristic of everything that God has created. This was magnificently stated by St. Augustine: "The beauty of all things is in a manner their voice, whereby they praise God. The heavens cry out to God, You made me, not I myself. Earth cries out, You created me, not I myself. [...] Regard the heavens, it is beautiful: observe the earth, it is beautiful: both together are very beautiful. He made them, He rules them, by His nod they are swayed, He orders their seasons, He renews their movements, by Himself He renews them. All these things then praise Him, whether in stillness or in motion, whether from earth below or from heaven above, whether in their old state or in their renewal" (*Exposition on Psalm 148:15*).

Spiritual creatures are even more beautiful. Spiritual creatures are angels and archangels, cherubim and seraphim, and also our spirits as long as we attempt to live in a state of sanctifying grace. Although all these persons are unimaginably beautiful, the beauty of the one whom God chose and prepared to be the Mother of His Son cannot be compared to the beauty of any other creature.

Naturally, God is the Source and Giver of all beauty. Just as we pray: "Only You are holy!" we can likewise call to God in admiration: "Only You are beautiful!" St. Augustine wrote enthusiastically: "Since creation is so beautiful, He Who created it must be that much more beautiful!"

After his conversion, St. Augustine called in gratitude for the gift of faith in his *Confessions*: "Late have I loved you, beauty so old and so new: late have I loved you. And see, you were within and I was in the external world and sought you there, and in my unlovely state I plunged into those lovely created things which you made. You were with me, and I was not with you. The lovely things kept me far from you, though if they did not have their existence in you, they had no existence at all."

If the beauty of creation sometimes pulls us farther away from God, this is an obvious symptom of our sinfulness. Indeed, the Lord God made the world He had created so beautiful that the beauty of creation may awaken within us yearning for the One Who is the same Beauty and Source of all created beauty. Meanwhile, when we think and talk about the beauty of Mary, the most beautiful of all creatures, we cannot imagine that it could pull us farther away from God. After all, the point of her unparalleled beauty is to give us Christ, Who is the Redeemer of us all.

Let us return to the truth that it is God's will that all of His creation may be beautiful. The Lord God expects of us that we will tend to the beauty of our world not only as its guardians but also work to make it even more beautiful. Above all, our souls can and should be beautiful. However, we cannot be indifferent to the material beauty of our world, for the Creator has granted us this world. In the book *Memory and Identity*, Pope John Paul II wrote: "The beauty of the universe is, as it were, reflected in the eyes of God, of Whom it is said: 'God saw everything He had made, and indeed, it was very good' (Genesis 1:31)."[174]

To quote the *Address of Pope Paul VI to Artists*: "This world in which we live needs beauty in order not to sink into despair. It is beauty, like truth, which brings joy to the heart of man and is that precious

174. John Paul II, *Memory and Identity*, p. 83.

fruit which resists the wear and tear of time, which unites generations and makes them share things in admiration. And all of this is through your hands. May these hands be pure and disinterested. Remember that you are the guardians of beauty in the world. May that suffice to free you from tastes which are passing and have no genuine value, to free you from the search after strange or unbecoming expressions."

When the Byzantine emperors began to promote the heresy of iconoclasm in the eighth century and undertook a campaign of stripping churches of all holy images with the aid of the army, Pope Gregory II harshly rebuked Emperor Leo III the Isaurian. The pope explained that it was an elementary obligation of the faith to be concerned that our churches be beautiful. "If anyone should take from you the adornments of royalty, your purple robes, diadem, sceptre, and your ranks of servants, you would be regarded by men as base, hateful, and abject; but to this condition you have reduced the churches, for you have deprived them of their ornaments and made them unsightly. Just as the pope has not the right to interfere in the palace or to infringe upon the royal prerogatives, so the emperor has not the right to interfere in the churches [...]"[175]

St. John Paul II frequently reminded us of the importance to appreciate beauty and strive for it. Many of us remember his exceptionally important speech addressed to people of culture in Warsaw's Church of the Holy Cross on June 13, 1979: "The human spirit lives off love and truth, which gives rise to the need for beauty," he said and recalled two deep statements by Cyprian Kamil Norwid: "What do you know of beauty? [...] 'Tis the shape of Love." Norwid was concerned about the Love that transforms people and the world; thus, he wrote: "Beauty serves to thrill us to work, and work serves for our resurrection."

175. Letter of Gregory II to Leo III, in: Alfred J. Andrea, *Medieval Record: Sources of Medieval History* (Indianapolis/Cambridge: Hackett Publishing 2020), p. 105.

At this point, one is tempted to say: Deep calls to deep (Psalm 42:8), for the canonized pope commented on Norwid's observation on the relationship between beauty, labor, and resurrection with the following words: "Our 'Fourth Bard' was capable of interpreting Christ's Paschal mystery so deeply! He translated it into the language of the Christian life and vocation with such precision. The relationship between beauty, work, and resurrection are the very root of Christian being and activity, *esse et operari*. [...] Your vocation is beauty; you must make objects of beauty. It is your vocation to create beauty in the multifarious matter of human creativity: in the matter of words and sounds, of colors and hues, of the sculptural or architectural blocks, in the matter of gestures with which this most unique material of the visible world, the human body, expresses itself."

"'What do you know of beauty? [...] Tis the shape of Love,'" John Paul II continued in his speech. "Thus, does not beauty remain in some intimate, very real relationship with the One Who loved until the very end, with the One Who revealed the definitive measure of love in the history of man and the world? The ultimate measure — redemptive and salvific. Thus, is the beauty that is your vocation, your labor, and your life's creative pain not found in the hidden yet real bond with the sacrament of Christ's love, the Eucharist?"

The Mother of Beautiful Love

In light of what has been said so far, it can hardly be doubted that beautiful love is the highest form of beauty. This is why the faith of God's people so eagerly refers to Mary, the one who is completely beautiful, as Beautiful Love.

Not every love is beautiful. Indeed, our love can at times be egocentric, possessive, hypocritical, or blind. Even authentic love can be tainted by various deformities in us sinners. The love of the Blessed and Immaculate Mother is crystalline in its authenticity; it is simply perfectly beautiful.

This title, Mother of Beautiful Love, was frequently the subject of Cardinal Stefan Wyszyński's sermons and meditations. To a degree, he was followed by St. John Paul II who in the *Letter to Families* (February 2, 1994) writes:

"The contemporary family, like families in every age, is searching for 'fairest love.' A love which is not 'fairest,' but reduced only to the satisfaction of concupiscence (cf. 1 John 2:16), or to a man's and a woman's mutual 'use' of each other, makes persons slaves to their weaknesses. Do not certain modern 'cultural agendas' lead to this enslavement? There are agendas which 'play' on man's weaknesses, and thus make him increasingly weak and defenseless.

The civilization of love evokes joy: joy, among other things, for the fact that a man has come into the world (cf. John 16:21), and consequently because spouses have become parents. The civilization of love means 'rejoicing in the right' (cf. 1 Corinthians 13:6). But a civilization inspired by a consumerist, anti-birth mentality is not and cannot ever be a civilization of love. If the family is so important for the civilization of love, it is because of the particular closeness and intensity of the bonds which come to be between persons and generations within the family. However, the family remains vulnerable and can easily fall prey to dangers which weaken it or actually destroy its unity and stability. As a result of these dangers families cease to be witnesses of the civilization of love and can even become a negation of it, a kind of countersign."

I would like to conclude by noting that the lengthy twentieth chapter of the *Letter to Families* is entitled "Mother of Fairest Love" and presents the love between Mary and Joseph as a model of authentic love for all spouses.

THE VENERATION OF THE SAINTS AS THE CONFIRMATION OF UNAMBIGUOUS MONOTHEISM

Neither a Continuation nor Modification of Polytheism but Its Opposite

First, let us try to take a position on the fairly widespread view that the veneration of the saints replaced the ancient worship of idols. In fact, the belief that veneration of the saints was in practice merely a continuation of the pagan cult of polytheism is unambiguously debunked by numerous patristic testimonies.

I will begin my overview of them with the description of the martyrdom of St. Polycarp, bishop of Smyrna, which was written in 156 or not long after (*Passio S. Polycarpi,* 17). It appears that, chronologically speaking, it is the first testimony to the fact that even the pagans had noticed that the Christians venerate their saints at a religious level. Polycarp was killed by being burned at the stake. When the Christians tried to retrieve his remains, the governor did not allow them to do so, using the explanation that "lest [...] forsaking Him that was crucified, they begin to worship this one."[176] This brief entry indicates that the pagans (or, in any case, this governor) believed that Christian veneration of the martyrs is a modification of polytheism.

The anonymous author of *The Martyrdom of Polycarp* expresses his astonishment that someone can ascribe such absurd views to Christians. The ancient hagiographer explains: "This he said at the suggestion and urgent persuasion of the Jews, who also watched us, as we sought to take him out of the fire, being ignorant of this, that it is neither possible for us ever to forsake Christ, who suffered for the salvation of such as shall be saved throughout the whole world [...]. For Him indeed, as being the Son of God, we adore; but the martyrs, as disciples and followers of the Lord, we worthily love on account of their extraordinary affection towards their own King and Master, of whom may we also be made companions and fellow disciples!" (*ibid.*). Thus, the distinction between what later theology would call that between *cultus latriae* and *cultus duliae* appeared as early as around 156. The anonymous author continues by explaining that the Christians finally succeeded in retrieving the remains that fire had not completely annihilated. Thanks to this, we possess an exceptional testimony on how the early Church venerated her martyrs: "Accordingly, we afterwards took up his bones, as being more precious than the most exquisite jewels, and more purified than gold, and deposited them in a fitting place, whither, being gathered together, as opportunity is allowed us, with joy and rejoicing, the Lord shall grant us to celebrate the anniversary of his martyrdom, both in memory of those who have already finished their course, and for the exercising and preparation of those yet to walk in their steps" (18).

176. *The Martyrdom of Polycarp,* (17), trans. Alexander Roberts and James Donaldson [in:] *Ante-Nicene Fathers*, Vol. 1, eds. Alexander Roberts, James Donaldson, and A. Cleveland Coxe. (Buffalo, NY: Christian Literature Publishing Co., 1885), https://www.newadvent.org/fathers/0102.htm (accessed May 17, 2022).

I will especially focus on the reflection on this topic by St. Augustine (d. 430). He was very radical in his condemnation of the worship of numerous gods, yet he simultaneously put all his heart in praising the saints that had preceded us in the path to eternal life. St. Augustine's thought is valuable especially because polytheism was then genuinely practiced by thousands of people; thus, Augustine's arguments why the difference between the worship of idols and the veneration of saints is more or less like that between heaven and earth takes on particular significance with regards to the problem in question.

Like earlier Church Fathers, Augustine saw the pagan deities as evil spirits. In Book X of *The City of God*, Augustine explains that the chasm separating polytheism from the veneration of angels and saints consists in that whereas pagan deities or demons are our enemies and want the worst for us, angels and saints are our friends and want what is best for us.

St. Augustine's argumentation is more or less as follows: Only the one God can bring ultimate happiness to His creation. He is the source of the eternal joy of His angels and saints. Thus, because they are good and wish us well, their great desire is to turn our attention towards worship of the only true God. "[I]f [the saints and angels] do love us and desire our happiness, they cannot wish us to be made happy by any other means than they themselves have enjoyed [...]. [T]hey do not wish us to worship them as our gods, but to join them in worshipping their God and ours; nor to sacrifice to them, but, together with them, to become a sacrifice to God. Accordingly, [they] rather love us, and desire us to be as blessed as themselves, look on us with greater pleasure, and give us greater assistance, when we join them in worshipping one God, Father, Son, and Holy Ghost, than if we were to offer to themselves sacrifice and worship."[177]

177. St. Augustine, *The City of God* (Book 10: Chapters 1, 25); trans. Marcus Dods, [in:] *Nicene and Post-Nicene Fathers*, First Series, Vol. 2, eds. Philip Schaff (Buffalo, NY:

St. Augustine asks: "What angels, then, are we to believe in this matter of blessed and eternal life? — those who wish to be worshipped with religious rites and observances, and require that men sacrifice to them; or those who say that all this worship is due to one God, the Creator, and teach us to render it with true piety to Him, by the vision of whom they are themselves already blessed, and in whom they promise that we shall be so?"[178] Thus, the saintly Bishop of Hippo has no doubts that since the pagan deities demand to be worshiped, and only God deserves to be worshiped, then it is clear that these are unclean spirits.

Today, when the Good News that God is love has resounded across the earth for two thousand years, we tend to forget how strongly pagan religiosity was built on fear. People venerated deities simply because they feared them. They feared that if the gods were not appropriately worshiped then they would seek revenge and send upon them some great misfortune. Such atavistic sentiments were also tangible among recently converted Christians who did not yet fully understand that the loving God is truly omnipotent and so sometimes felt tempted to light a candle for the devil. Furthermore, the Christian teaching about good angels sometimes led them to fearfully ask if it was not worth seeking their clemency by worshiping them as gods.

St. Augustine tried to dispel these doubts above all by pointing out their godlessness. He recalled how firmly the apostles Paul and Barnabas (Acts 14:13-18) or the angel from Revelation (Revelation 19:10) opposed being worshiped as gods. "Let no man say, I fear lest the Angel may be angry with me, if I worship him not as my God. He is then angry with you, when you have chosen to worship him: for he is righteous and loves God. As devils are angry if they are not worshipped, so are Angels angry if they are worshipped instead of

Christian Literature Publishing Co., 1887), https://www.newadvent.org/fathers/120110.htm (accessed May 17, 2022).

178. *Op. cit.* (Book X: Chapter 16).

God. But lest the weak and trembling heart perchance say unto itself: If then the demons are incensed because they are not worshipped, I fear to offend them."[179]

This was a quote from the Exposition on Psalm 97. He wrote in a similar vein in *The City of God*: "We ought not, then, to fear that we may offend these immortal and happy subjects of the one God by not sacrificing to them; for this they know to be due only to the one true God, in allegiance to whom they themselves find their blessedness, and therefore they will not have it given to them, either in figure or in the reality, which the mysteries of sacrifice symbolized. Such arrogance belongs to proud and wretched demons, whose disposition is diametrically opposite to the piety of those who are subject to God, and whose blessedness consists in attachment to Him."[180]

The same St. Augustine who said and wrote all this had no qualms about venerating the holy martyrs; he frequently celebrated Masses on the anniversary of their deaths, on which occasion he preached hundreds of sermons, dozens of which have survived until the present. Because many citizens of Hippo worshiped pagan idols in those days, St. Augustine frequently pointed out the chasm between the worship of idols and the veneration we give to our saints.

He writes in Book VIII of *The City of God*: "But, nevertheless, we do not build temples, and ordain priests, rites, and sacrifices for these same martyrs; for they are not our gods, but their God is our God. Certainly, we honor their reliquaries, as the memorials of holy men of God who strove for the truth [...]. [T]he reason why we pay such honors to their memory is, that by so doing we may both give thanks to the true God for their victories, and, by recalling them afresh to

179. St. Augustine, "Exposition on Psalm 97" (10), trans. J. E. Tweed [in:] *Nicene and Post-Nicene Fathers*, First Series, Vol. 8, ed. Philip Schaff (Buffalo, NY: Christian Literature Publishing Co., 1888), https://www.newadvent.org/fathers/1801097.htm (accessed May 17, 2022).

180. St. Augustine, *The City of God* (Book 10: Chapter 26).

remembrance, may stir ourselves up to imitate them by seeking to obtain like crowns and palms."[181]

And here is a fragment of one of St. Augustine's sermons: "And yet, dearly beloved, while those gods are in no way at all to be compared to our martyrs, we don't regard our martyrs as gods, or worship them as gods. We don't provide them with temples, with altars, with sacrifices. Priests don't make offerings to them; perish the thought! These things are provided for God; or rather these things are offered to God, by whom all things are provided for us. Even when we make the offering at the shrines of the holy martyrs, don't we offer it to God? The holy martyrs have their place of honor. Notice, please; in the recitation of names at the altar of Christ, their names are recited in the most honored place; but for all that, they are not worshiped instead of Christ. When did you ever hear it said by me at the shrine of Saint Theogenes, or by any of my brethren and colleagues, or by any priest, 'I am offering to you, Saint Theogenes'? Or, 'I am offering to you, Peter,' or 'I am offering to you, Paul'? You never did; it doesn't happen, it is not permitted. And if you should be asked, 'Do you, then, worship Peter?' answer what Eulogius answered about Fructuosus: 'I do not worship Peter, but I worship God, whom Peter also worships.' Then Peter loves you."[182]

It is very likely that in formulating the above reflection Augustine is indebted to his spiritual father who had also baptized him, St. Ambrose, who in his work *On the Holy Spirit* explained that when we venerate Mary, we do not worship her as a goddess using the following contraposition: *Maria erat templum Dei, non Deus templi. Et ideo ille solus adorandus, qui operabatur in templo*: "Mary was the temple

181. *Op. cit.* (Book VIII: Chapter 16).

182. St. Augustine, "Sermon 273," trans. Edmund Hill, [in:] *The Works of Saint Augustine: A Translation for the 21st Century*, ed. John E. Rotelle (Hyde Park: New City Press, 1994), p. 20.

of God, not the God of the temple. And therefore, He alone is to be worshipped Who was working in His temple."[183]

The Biblical Roots of Specific Manifestations of the Veneration of the Saints

In the second part of this lecture, I will attempt to demonstrate that all manifestations of the veneration of the saints in Church have Biblical precedents. We who believe that Sacred Scripture is the inspired Word of God will find in this confirmation of the truth that veneration of the saints is one of the most important ways of professing our faith in the one God.

Indeed, it seems that five aspects can be identified in the veneration of the saints:

1. By venerating the saints, we want to thank God for so generously endowing His Church in previous generations.
2. Our thanksgiving for the saints is permeated with pleas for God to be as generous to us as He had been to our fathers and mothers in the faith.
3. By venerating the saints, we express our faith that the saints pray for us, and at the same time we ask them to intercede for us.
4. We also express our gratitude and petitions by venerating our saints by, for example, venerating their relics.
5. An important dimension of the veneration of the saints is their imitation. In short, by imitating the saints we learn how we can and should imitate Christ.

We will find all five themes in the Bible, always in perfect harmony with strictly Biblical monotheism. However, let us look at each thread individually.

183. St. Ambrose, *On the Holy Spirit, Book III*, trans. H. de Romestin, E. de Romestin and H.T.F. Duckworth, [in:] *Nicene and Post-Nicene Fathers, Second Series*, Vol. 10, eds. Philip Schaff and Henry Wace. (Buffalo, NY: Christian Literature Publishing Co., 1896), https://www.newadvent.org/fathers/34023.htm (accessed May 17, 2022).

1. The Veneration of Saints as Giving Thanks to God

In a manner of speaking, the entire Bible is filled with thanksgiving for God's great works in the past as well as the fact that in previous generations God inspired people faithful to Him, great leaders of the people and prophets: "Give thanks to the Lord, acclaim His name; Among the nations make known His deeds, proclaim how exalted is His name. Sing praise to the Lord for He has done glorious things; let this be known throughout all the earth" (Isaiah 12:4-5).

In the Book of Sirach, a total of seven chapters are devoted to great elected persons through whom God endowed His people with power and grace (Sirach 44-50). This is how the inspired author introduces his readers to this part of the Biblical book: "I will now praise the godly, our ancestors, in their own time [...]. Yet these also were godly; their virtues have not been forgotten. Their wealth remains in their families, their heritage with their descendants. Through God's covenant their family endures, and their offspring for their sake. And for all time their progeny will endure, their glory will never be blotted out; Their bodies are buried in peace, but their name lives on and on" (Sirach 44:1; 10-15).

We find the same religious respect for our ancestors in the faith in the New Testament: "Remember your leaders who spoke the word of God to you. Consider the outcome of their way of life and imitate their faith" (Hebrews 13:7). In the eleventh chapter of the Epistle to the Hebrews, the great saints of the Old Testament whose lives served as an example of genuine entrustment to God are listed by name. Because an important aim of this epistle is to bolster those persecuted for their faith, the martyrs are especially emphasized (see Hebrews 11:35-38).

To summarize, the saints in the Church are a vibrant summons to thank God for so generously endowing the Church with grace and sanctity, just like in the days of the Old Testament He granted His Chosen People Abraham, Jacob, or Moses. Thus, vibrant veneration of the saints helps us to see the history of the Church as salvation history. Unfortunately, the dominant approach to Church history today is sick and distorted. Beginning with the Reformation and the Age of Enlightenment, the dominant vision has been shaped mostly by those hostile to the Church. If we were to ask most people, including Catholics, of their first associations with the term "Church history," they would probably quickly come up with such terms as "dark chapters," "evil," "crimes," or "the Inquisition."

It is crucial to not only liberate ourselves of these false stereotypes and form a vision of Church history that is more consistent with the historical truth. The history of the Church is at its very core the history of the activity of God's grace, the history of the aspiration of subsequent generations towards eternal life. We have to learn the approach to history that was characteristic of the Biblical man.

The Bible never romanticizes the past; in fact, it speaks very harshly of the sins of our fathers (see 2 Chronicles 30:8; Jeremiah 16:11n). At the same time, the entire Bible is filled with thanksgiving for God's great works in the past as well as the fact that in previous generations God inspired people faithful to Him, great leaders of the people and prophets: "Give thanks to the Lord, acclaim His name; Among the nations make known His deeds, proclaim how exalted is His name. Sing praise to the Lord for He has done glorious things; let this be known throughout all the earth" (Isaiah 12:4-5).

2. "Give new signs and work new wonders" (Sirach 36:6)

Thanksgiving for the great works that God did for our fathers in the faith in a sense demands complementation with a request that God may repeat the work of His power and grace with respect to us as well. The anguished Messiah laments in Psalm 22:5: "In You our fathers trusted; they trusted, and You rescued them." There is a similar prayer in the Book of Sirach: "Thus they will know, as we know, that there is no God but You. Give new signs and work new wonders; show forth the splendor of Your right hand and arm" (Sirach 36:5-7). In the ninth chapter of the Book of Nehemiah, the recollection of God's great works in the past ends with a painful complaint against the present poverty of God's Chosen People. The same prayer in Psalm 44 ends with the dramatic summons: "Awake! Why do you sleep, O Lord? Rise up! Do not reject us forever! [...] Rise up, help us! Redeem us in Your mercy" (Psalm 44:24, 27).

In the past, the great saints were for the Israelites a sign of hope that God can come to the aid of His people even amidst the greatest misery. Moses said to his co-religionists: "The Lord, the God of your ancestors, the God of Abraham, the God of Isaac, and the God of Jacob, has sent me to you" (Exodus 3:15). "Look to Abraham, your father, and to Sarah, who gave you birth [...]. Yes, the Lord shall comfort Zion, shall comfort all her ruins" (Isaiah 51:2-3). With these words, the author of the second part of the Book of Isaiah consoles and offers hope. Meanwhile, during the Babylonian exile Azariah prayed: "Do not take away Your mercy from us, for the sake of Abraham, Your beloved, Isaac Your servant, and Israel Your holy one" (Daniel 3:35).

3. The Saints' Intercession for Us

There is a particularly poignant testimony to faith that the saints intercede for us in the Second Book of Maccabees. In order to give his soldiers courage before a battle whose result would determine if the Hebrews would succeed in defending themselves against the imposition of pagan idolatry, Judas Maccabee told them of the following vision: "Onias, the former high priest, a noble and good man, modest in bearing, gentle in manner, distinguished in speech, and trained from childhood in all that belongs to excellence, was praying with outstretched arms for the whole Jewish community. Then in the same way another man appeared, distinguished by his white hair and dignity, and with an air of wondrous and majestic authority. Onias then said of him, 'This is a man who loves his fellow Jews and fervently prays for the people and the holy city—the prophet of God, Jeremiah'" (2 Maccabees 15:11-14).

The angels also pray for us. In the Book of Zechariah, the angel of the Lord calls: "Lord of hosts, how long will You be without mercy for Jerusalem and the cities of Judah that have felt your anger these seventy years?" (Zechariah 1:12). The inclusion of angels in our prayers in the Book of Tobit as well as Revelation are presented in the image of carrying those prayers to God. The angel Raphael says about his presence in the life of this family: "Now when you, Tobit, and Sarah prayed, it was I who presented the record of your prayer before the Glory of the Lord" (Tobit 12:12).

Let us notice that the angel does not replace them in the prayer but joins this prayer and bolsters it. Similarly, the angel in the Book of Revelation "was given a great quantity of incense to offer, along with the prayers of all the holy ones, on the gold altar that was before the throne. The smoke of the incense along with the prayers of the holy ones went up before God from the hand of the angel" (Revelation 8:3-4; see 5:8). As we can see, the angels and saints pray for us rather than instead of us.

Intercessory prayers carried to God by the saints in heaven as well as our neighbors on earth violate neither the strict monotheism of the Christian faith nor the salvific unity of Christ's intercession. After all, God Himself wants us, His children, to become bound to one another through mutual love. Intercessory prayer is a particularly important form of showing love for one another.

4. The Biblical Source of the Veneration of Relics

Veneration given to the remains of God's great friends has not only its source in Sacred Scripture; its Biblical foundation is also very firm. It suffices to recall the piety with which Joseph carried the body of his father Jacob from Egypt to his family tomb in Canaan (see Genesis 50:1-13). With regards to Joseph himself, Sacred Scripture mentions the transferring of his bones from Egypt to the land of his ancestors five times; thus, this must have been an exceptionally important detail for the ancient Israelites' consciousness (Genesis 50:25; Exodus 13:19; Joshua 24:32; Hebrews 11:22; Acts 7:16).

Meanwhile, according to the Second Book of Kings contact with the bones of the prophet Elisha brought the dead back to life (2 Kings 13:21). This event is undoubtedly an important source of the custom of going on pilgrimages to the tombs of holy Tzaddiks, which is also present in contemporary Judaism.

In Sacred Scripture, we will also find very symbolic accounts of the life-giving force present in the remains of the righteous man. We read in the Book of Sirach of God-fearing judges: "May their bones flourish with new life where they lie, and their names receive fresh luster in their children!" (Sirach 46:12). Three chapters later, we read: "Then, too, the twelve prophets—may their bones flourish with new life where they lie! —They gave new strength to Jacob and saved him with steadfast hope" (Sirach 49:10; see Isaiah 66:13n).

The New Testament has supplemented this intuition by firmly emphasizing that our dignity as children and friends of God extends to our bodies: "Do you not know that your body is a temple of the Holy Spirit within you, which you have from God?" (1 Corinthians 6:19). Furthermore: "If the Spirit of the One Who raised Jesus from the dead dwells in you, the One who raised Christ from the dead will give life to your mortal bodies also, through His Spirit that dwells in you" (Romans 8:11; see Philippians 3:20n).

All these truths were recalled most spontaneously when one of our brothers or sisters in the faith gave his or her life for Christ. Then, it was impossible to doubt that the body of that martyr was a temple of the Holy Spirit in the most unique way. Thus, for believers in Christ it is obvious that this body deserves particular religious respect. We saw this in the description of the martyrdom of Bishop Polycarp of Smyrna.

5. Imitation of the Saints in Sacred Scripture

Naturally, the only One we should absolutely imitate is our Lord Jesus Christ: "Whoever wishes to come after Me must deny himself, take up his cross, and follow Me" (Matthew 16:24). Meanwhile, the New Testament contains frequent appeals to imitate others: Abraham (Romans 4:1-4) and, more broadly, the holy patriarchs: Abel, Enoch, Noah, Abraham, Isaac, Jacob, Joseph, and Moses (Hebrews 11). The Apostle Paul does not hesitate to call himself a model of the imitation of Christ: "Therefore, I urge you, be imitators of me. [...] Be imitators of me, as I am of Christ" (1 Corinthians 4:16; 11:1). In general, Christians should be models for one another: "And you became imitators of us and of the Lord, receiving the word in great affliction, with joy from the Holy Spirit, so that you became a model for all the believers in Macedonia and in Achaia" (1 Thessalonians 1:6-7; see Philippians 3:17).

The idea of imitating the saints comes from the fact that they were the imitators of Christ and thus can in this regard be our teachers.

THE CHURCH AS THE FRUIT OF GOD'S COMPASSION

Let me begin by establishing a couple of definitions. St. Augustine writes (and St. Thomas follows him): "And what is compassion but a fellow-feeling for another's misery, which prompts us to help him if we can?"[184] Meanwhile, to recall John Paul II's moving description, compassion or mercy "signifies a special power of love, which prevails over the sin and infidelity of the chosen people."[185] In other words, God's compassion is God's fidelity to His fatherhood, including when we are unfaithful.

The Church: The Gift of the Redeemer's Real Presence

One cannot doubt that the greatest gift of God's mercy is His giving us His only Son. "For God so loved the world that He gave His only

184. St. Augustine, *The City of God,* Book IX (Chapter 5). See St. Thomas Aquinas, *Summa Theologica*, 2-2 q. 30 a, 1.

185. John Paul II, *Dives in misericordia*, 4.

Son, so that everyone who believes in Him might not perish but might have eternal life" (John 3:16).

The following problem immediately occurs: Historically, the Son of God was with us for only thirty-three years; He spent the rest of His historical life in a country that was culturally peripheral. At most several hundred thousand people, thus relatively few, physically encountered Him. He appeared to only slightly over five hundred people after His resurrection (see 1 Corinthians 15:16). Yet He came to our earth to save people of all generations and every individual person.

Naturally, the gift of the Church is the solution to this problem. Thanks to the gift of the Church, millions and billions of people on earth have access to the incomprehensible mercy shown to us by God through His Son, Jesus Christ.

Because liberal Biblical scholars sometimes professed the theory that the Lord Jesus did not intend to establish His Church (according to this theory, He only professed the ultimate coming of God's Kingdom, which accidentally gave rise to the Church), we must first firmly state all the facts that debunk this theory.

He sometimes directly said that He undoubtedly intended to establish His Church (Matthew 16:18). Meanwhile, His will to establish a Church is also indicated by the fact that He elected twelve apostles to be the fathers of the people of the New Covenant, which is undoubtedly a reference to the twelve sons of Jacob, the sons of the people of the Old Covenant (see especially Acts 1:15-26). Jesus was also concerned that those chosen to be the shepherds of His Church (Luke 5:10; John 21:15-17) would have real authority (Luke 10:16) and real guarantee that they preach His authentic teaching (John 14:26).

Without a doubt, Jesus also wanted to grant graces to His Church. He wanted for His Church to be built by those "born of water and Spirit" (John 3:5; Matthew 28:18; Mark 16:15-16). Jesus gave to His Church the sacrament of penance (John 20:22-23) and above all the sacrament of His own Body and Blood (John 6:27-28; Matthew 26:26-28; 1 Corinthians 23-25). Thanks to these gifts, from then on all people — regardless of the time and place in which they came to live have direct access to Him. To have direct access to Him means to be capable of directly accepting the mercy offered to us by God in giving us His own Son.

It is worth noticing that the access to Jesus granted to us thanks to the gift of the Church is inconceivably more direct than when the Son of God was among people historically. The apostles were fortunate to be able to be His true friends; love and admire Him; listen to His teachings; observe Him perform miracles; speak with Him; and ask Him questions and listen to His answers. However, this was ordinary interpersonal closeness only to an extent. To put it more simply, for them, the Lord Jesus was someone from the outside, just like any other person.

This situation became incomparably more blessed for both the apostles and all believers at the time of the coming of the Holy Spirit. Thanks to the Holy Spirit, this inconceivable kind of unity and closeness to Jesus Christ thanks to which we are truly His body became possible. In accordance with what He has prophesied, we can remain in Him and He in us (see John 15:4; 6:56). It is thanks to the Holy Spirit that something so mysterious happens to us that along with the Apostle Paul we can say that "I live, no longer I, but Christ lives in me" (Galatians 2:20). This reality occurs to a much greater extent and much more deeply within us than we realize. This occurs precisely through the Holy Spirit thanks to Whom we are one Body: "For in one Spirit we were all baptized into one body" (1 Corinthians 12:13).

It is this that Jesus had in mind when He fairly mysteriously said that "it is better for you that I go. For if I do not go, the Advocate will not come to you. But if I go, I will send Him to you" (John 16:7).

Was the Church Established or Made Visible by Christ?

We believe that Christ the Lord is the Redeemer of all people, including those who lived before Him, which is expressed in the truth of His descending into hell (see 1 Peter 3:18-20). Thus, the following question arises: Did Christ the Lord redeem people who lived in the pre-Christian era without the Church or outside the Church?

The thesis that the gift of the Church has accompanied humanity from the very beginning of its history was asked with puzzling frequency by the first Christians. Referencing the New Testament's expression of "the revelation [in Christ] of the mystery kept secret for long ages" (Romans 16:25; Ephesians 3:9-10; Colossians 1:26), they saw the Church parallel to the mystery of Christ: As the Son of God, co-eternal with the Father, became visible to us only at the moment He took on human nature, the Church, which has existed from the beginning of creation, became visible only now, in the last days, thanks to the redemption accomplished by Christ.

In the oldest post-Biblical homily, written in the second century, we read: "So, then, brethren, if we do the will of our Father God, we shall be members of the first Church, the spiritual, — that which was created before sun and moon [...]. [T]he Church is not of the present, but from the beginning. For it was spiritual, as was also our Jesus, and was made manifest at the end of the days in order to save you."[186]

We can find the same notion, that the Church was created before all else, in Hermas' *The Shepherd*, which was written around 150. This especially deserves attention, as the most mysterious fragment of this text, that "[t]he world was created for the sake of the Church," is found in the *Catechism of the Catholic Church* (760). However, let us

186. St. Clement, *The "Second Epistle" of St. Clement,* trans. John Keith [in:] *Ante-Nicene Fathers,* Vol. 9. Edited by Allan Menzies. (Buffalo, NY: Christian Literature Publishing Co., 1896), https://www.newadvent.org/fathers/1011.htm (accessed May 24, 2022).

first recall was Hermas wrote: "'Who do you think that old woman is from whom you received the book?' And I said, 'The Sibyl.' 'You are in a mistake,' says he; 'it is not the Sibyl.' 'Who is it then?' say I. And he said, 'It is the Church.' And I said to him, 'Why then is she an old woman?' 'Because,' said he, 'she was created first of all. [...] And for her sake was the world made.'"[187]

In the middle of the second century, from a purely human perspective there was nothing in the Church that could suggest the theory that *the world was created for the sake of the Church*. Only several centuries later would Christianity become one of the world's great religions. When Hermas wrote these words, the Christians, who were still few in number, were licking their wounds from their recent persecution, while the Church seemed merely a small, fragile boat that could be sunk by any gust of wind.

In short, these words, particularly in that situation, could have been written only by someone who truly believed with all his soul that Christ the Lord is not only some exceptionally wise religious leader but that He is the Redeemer in Whom we can attain eternal life. Without such clear faith in Christ, one cannot even imagine that people have an inconceivably more important duty to fulfill than going through their lives honestly and righteously. To believe that the world was created for the sake of the Church means to believe that the aim of our life is eternal life. Only the Eternal Church can be the purpose of the world's existence.

Hermas' contemporary Justin (d. 167) does not hesitate to speak of Christians living before Christ: "We have been taught that Christ is the first-born of God, and we have declared above that He is the Word of whom every race of men were partakers; and those who lived

187. Hermas, *The Shepherd of Hermas* (Book I), trans. F. Crombie [in:] *Ante-Nicene Fathers*, Vol. 2. Edited by Alexander Roberts, James Donaldson, and A. Cleveland Coxe (Buffalo, NY: Christian Literature Publishing Co., 1885), https://www.newadvent.org/fathers/02011.htm (accessed May 24, 2022).

reasonably are Christians, even though they have been thought atheists; as, among the Greeks, Socrates and Heraclitus, and men like them; and among the barbarians, Abraham, and Ananias, and Azarias, and Misael, and Elias, and many others whose actions and names we now decline to recount, because we know it would be tedious."[188]

Eusebius of Caesarea (c. 260-339) recalls "Christians in deed" who lived before Christ as well as Christianity as the world's oldest religion at the beginning of his *Church History*: "If anyone should assert that all those who have enjoyed the testimony of righteousness, from Abraham himself back to the first man, were Christians in fact if not in name, he would not go beyond the truth. For that which the name indicates that the Christian man, through the knowledge and the teaching of Christ, is distinguished for temperance and righteousness, for patience in life and manly virtue, and for a profession of piety toward the one and only God over all — all that was zealously practiced by them not less than by us. [...] So that it is clearly necessary to consider that religion, which has lately been preached to all nations through the teaching of Christ, the first and most ancient of all religions, and the one discovered by those divinely favored men in the age of Abraham."[189]

It is true that before Christ, God gathered the Church because of His future coming; it can even be found in the "definition" of the Church presented by St. Augustine in his *On the Catechizing of the Uninstructed*, which was written in the late fourth century: The

188. St. Justin Martyr, *The First Apology*, trans. Marcus Dods and George Reith, [in:] *Ante-Nicene Fathers*, Vol. 1, eds. Alexander Roberts, James Donaldson, and A. Cleveland Coxe (Buffalo, NY: Christian Literature Publishing Co., 1885), https://www.newadvent.org/fathers/0126.htm (accessed May 24, 2022).

189. Eusebius of Caesarea, *Church History* (Book I), trans. Arthur Cushman McGiffert, [in:] *Nicene and Post-Nicene Fathers, Second Series*, Vol. 1, eds. Philip Schaff and Henry Wace (Buffalo, NY: Christian Literature Publishing Co., 1890), https://www.newadvent.org/fathers/250101.htm (accessed May 24, 2022).

Church is "the people of God throughout all nations; which Church is His body, wherewith also are united and numbered all the saints who lived in this world, even before His advent, and who believed then in His future coming, just as we believe in His past coming."[190]

For Augustine, this truth was so important that when he wrote his *Retractations* towards the end of his life and compiled an overview of his entire work, he tried to explain the fact that in his youthful work *On the True Religion* he wrote a sentence that gives the impression that Christianity had appeared only recently. Indeed, "what is now called the Christian religion existed even among the ancients and was not lacking from the beginning of the human race until 'Christ came in the flesh.' From that time, true religion, which already existed, began to be called Christian."[191]

This pre-Christian history of the Church even extended into later epochs. For this purpose, Pope Gregory the Great used the parable of the workers in the vineyard: Our Creator "owns a vineyard, the universal Church, which has grown, so to speak, as many branches as it has produced saints, from Abel the righteous to the last one to be born at the end of the world. This father of the family hired laborers to cultivate his vine at daybreak, at the third, sixth, ninth, and eleventh hour, since he had not ceased from the beginning of the world to the end of the world in the end, to gather preachers to instruct the crowd of the faithful. The daybreak for the world was from Adam to Noah; the third hour, from Noah to Abraham; the sixth from Abraham to Moses; the ninth, from Moses to the coming

190. St. Augustine, *On the Catechizing of the Uninstructed*, trans. S.D.F. Salmond, [in:] *Nicene and Post-Nicene Fathers*, First Series, Vol. 3, ed. Philip Schaff (Buffalo, NY: Christian Literature Publishing Co., 1887), https://www.newadvent.org/fathers/1303.htm (accessed May 24, 2022).

191. St. Augustine, The *Retractations*, trans. Sr. Mary Inez Bogan R.S.M. (Washington, DC: The Catholic University of America Press, 1968), p. 52.

of the Lord; and the eleventh hour, from the coming of the Lord to the end of the world."[192]

It is from this fragment that the most recent council has borrowed the expression that the Church is the congregation of God's Chosen People "from Abel, the just one, to the last of the elect" in the Dogmatic Constitution on the Church *Lumen gentium* (2): "The eternal Father, by a free and hidden plan of His own wisdom and goodness, created the whole world. His plan was to raise men to a participation of the divine life. Fallen in Adam, God the Father did not leave men to themselves, but ceaselessly offered helps to salvation, in view of Christ, the Redeemer 'who is the image of the invisible God, the first-born of every creature.' All the elect, before time began, the Father 'foreknew and pre-destined to become conformed to the image of His Son, that He should be the Firstborn among many brethren.' He planned to assemble in the holy Church all those who would believe in Christ. Already from the beginning of the world the foreshadowing of the Church took place. It was prepared in a remarkable way throughout the history of the people of Israel and by means of the Old Covenant. In the present era of time the Church was constituted and, by the outpouring of the Spirit, was made manifest. At the end of time, it will gloriously achieve completion, when, as is read in the Fathers, all the just, from Adam and 'from Abel, the just one, to the last of the elect,' will be gathered together with the Father in the universal Church."

Let us notice that since God initiated the congregation of His Church with Abel the just, this means that mercy was His first response to the downfall of our first parents. The Church Fathers went so far as to say that the punishment that God levied against the first people for their sin was a gift of His mercy. St. John Chrysostom

192. Pope St. Gregory the Great, *Homily 19 of the Gospels*, https://sites.google.com/site/aquinasstudybible/home/matthew-commentary/gregory-the-great-homily-19-of-the-gospels (accessed May 24, 2022).

explained: "[N]o longer did [God] allow Adam in the garden but bade him leave there, showing us that his sole motive in doing this was his love for him. [...] And so the expulsion from the garden was a mark of care rather than necessity. Our Lord, you see, is like this: he reveals his care for us in punishing no less than in blessing, and even his punishment is inflicted for the sake of admonition. Because if in fact he knew that we would not get worse by sinning and escaping, he would not have punished us; but to check our decline into greater evil and to stem the tide of wickedness, he applies punishment out of fidelity to his own loving kindness which is exactly what he did in this case."[193]

Mercy as a Sign of the Church's Authenticity

We, however, should thank God that we know the Redeemer by name, and by visibly belonging to His Church we have privileged access to His teaching and grace, and even to Christ Himself. Thanks to the Gospel preached in the Church, we know the exceptionally

193. St. John Chrysostom, *Homilies on Genesis*, Hom. 18:3 (http://www2.iath.virginia.edu/anderson/commentaries/ChrGen.html). St. Irenaeus wrote of the benevolence that God shows us by making us experience the rotten fruits of our sins: "Long-suffering therefore was God, when man became a defaulter, as foreseeing that victory which should be granted to him through the Word. For, when strength was made perfect in weakness (2 Corinthians 12:9), it showed the kindness and transcendent power of God. For as He patiently suffered Jonah to be swallowed by the whale, not that he should be swallowed up and perish altogether, but that, having been cast out again, he might be the more subject to God, and might glorify Him the more who had conferred upon him such an unhoped-for deliverance, and might bring the Ninevites to a lasting repentance [...] so also, from the beginning, did God permit man to be swallowed up by the great whale, who was the author of transgression, not that he should perish altogether when so engulphed; but, arranging and preparing the plan of salvation, which was accomplished by the Word, through the sign of Jonah, for those who held the same opinion as Jonah regarding the Lord." St. Irenaeus, *Against Heresies* (Book III, Chapter 20), trans. Alexander Roberts and William Rambaut, [in:] *Ante-Nicene Fathers*, Vol. 1, eds. Alexander Roberts, James Donaldson, and A. Cleveland Coxe (Buffalo, NY: Christian Literature Publishing Co., 1885), https://www.newadvent.org/fathers/0103320.htm (accessed May 24, 2022).

important secret of God's mercy: that God, Who has shown pity on us, wants us to be more than just passive recipients of His mercy. Since we have experienced His mercy, it is His will that we show mercy to those who need it (Matthew 18:33). On the other hand, if our hearts are hardened towards the needy, then we ourselves can become incapable of openness to God's mercy (Matthew 25:41-45; Luke 16:19-31).

Thus, in the first generation after the departure of the apostles, St. Ignatius of Antioch wrote that sensitivity to the needs of the poor is an important criterion of the Church's authenticity. The docetists, Ignatius argues, deny the truth of the incarnation of the Son of God, which logically leads to the rejection of the truths of the Eucharist; thus, it is unsurprising that they are not concerned about the poverty of their neighbors.

It is worth knowing this pronouncement in its entirety: "But consider those who are of a different opinion with respect to the grace of Christ which has come unto us, how opposed they are to the will of God. They have no regard for love; no care for the widow, or the orphan, or the oppressed; of the bond, or of the free; of the hungry, or of the thirsty. They abstain from the Eucharist and from prayer, because they confess not the Eucharist to be the flesh of our Savior Jesus Christ, which suffered for our sins, and which the Father, of His goodness, raised up again. Those, therefore, who speak against this gift of God, incur death in the midst of their disputes. But it were better for them to treat it with respect, that they also might rise again."[194]

That the Church's works of charity were not merely symbolic is attested by Emperor Julian the Apostate's testimony, which is filled with hatred towards Christians. In a letter to the pagan High-Priest

194. St. Ignatius of Antioch, *The Epistle of Ignatius to the Smyrnaeans*, trans. Alexander Roberts and James Donaldson, [in:] *Ante-Nicene Fathers*, Vol. 1, eds. Alexander Roberts, James Donaldson, and A. Cleveland Coxe (Buffalo, NY: Christian Literature Publishing Co., 1885), https://www.newadvent.org/fathers/0109.htm (accessed May 25, 2022).

Theodorus, Julian encourages him to organize assistance to the poor that would compete with the Church. Unfortunately, the (probably Christian) copyist grew angry and stopped copying this letter: "For when it came about that the poor were neglected and overlooked by the [pagan] priests, then I think the impious Galilaeans [Christians] observed this fact and devoted themselves to philanthropy. And they have gained ascendancy in the worst of their deeds through the credit they win for such practices. For just as those who entice children with a cake, and by throwing it to them two or three times induce them to follow them, and then, when they are far away from their friends cast them on board a ship and sell them as slaves, and that which for the moment seemed sweet, proves to be bitter for all the rest of their lives — by the same method, I say, the Galilaeans also begin with their so-called love-feast, or hospitality, or service of tables, — for they have many ways of carrying it out and hence call it by many names, — and the result is that they have led very many into atheism… "[195]

I will reference at least one more testimony to demonstrate the considerable importance which the early Church attached to acknowledging the poor. I have in mind the harsh rebuke issued in 596 by Pope Gregory the Great to Bishop Marinianus. Although the epistle to Marinianus has not been preserved, one can infer that it was written in a similar tone as that in which Gregory sent his admonition through Secundus:

"Stir up with such words as you can use our brother the bishop Marinianus: for I suspect that he has fallen asleep. For certain persons have come to me, among whom were some aged mendicants, who were questioned by me as to what they had received and from whom they had received it; and they told me particularly how much had

195. Julian the Apostate, *Fragment of a Letter to a Priest,* trans. Wilmer Cave Wright, [in:] Julian the Apostate, *Works,* vol. 2, LOEB Classical Library 1913, p. 338. Julian issued a similar instruction to the High-Priest Arsacius: *Letter 22,* trans. Wilmer Cave Wright, [in:] Julian the Apostate, *Works,* vol. 3, LOEB Classical Library 1923.

been given them on their journey, and by whom it had been given. But, when I enquired of them what my aforesaid brother had given them, they replied that they had asked him, but had received nothing at all from him; so that they did not get even bread on the way, though it has always been the familiar usage of that Church to give to all. For they said, He answered saying, *I have nothing that I can give you.* And I am surprised, if he who has clothes, money, and storehouses, has nothing to give to the poor. Tell him, then, that with his place he should change his disposition too. Let him not believe reading and prayer alone to be enough for him, so that he should think to sit apart, and nowise fructify with his hand; but let him have a liberal hand; let him succor those who suffer need; let him believe the wants of others to be his own; since, if he has not these things, he bears but a bishop's empty name."[196]

Naturally, the Church is something much greater than a charitable institution. In the Church, sensitivity to material poverty should be a sign of active participation in the service of mercy for eternal life. It is symptomatic that the Church Fathers frequently emphasize this moment when explaining that the Church was born of Christ's pierced side.

Methodius of Olympus, who lived in the first half of the third century, refers Ephesians 5:30, which was presented as a single sentence in his code[197] ("for we are members of His body [*sōma*], of His flesh [*sarks*], and of His bones"), to the mystery of the Incarnation of the Son of God presented in Genesis 2:24, which discusses leaving one's family home in order to become bound to one's spouse. He proceeds to apply the image of the creation of Eve from Adam's rib

196. Pope St. Gregory the Great, "Book VI, Letter 30," [in:] *Registrum Epistolarum*, [in:] *Nicene and Post-Nicene Fathers*, Second Series, Vol. 12, eds. Philip Schaff and Henry Wace (Buffalo, NY: Christian Literature Publishing Co., 1895), https://www.newadvent.org/fathers/360206030.htm (accessed May 25, 2022).

197. As in the editions of the New Testament used by St. Irenaeus, St. Ambrose, Gaius Marius Victorinus, St. John Chrysostom, St. Jerome, Theodore of Mopsuestia, Theodoret of Cyrus, St. John of Damascus, and many other early Christian writers.

to Christ and the Church. According to Methodius, the "rib" of the new Adam, Christ, was given to the Church to make her more like Christ: "[F]or otherwise the Church could not conceive believers, and give them new birth by the laver of regeneration, unless Christ [...] should provide for a certain power being taken from His own side, so that all who are built up in Him should grow up, even those who are born again by the laver, receiving of His bones and of His flesh, that is, of His holiness and of His glory."[198]

The same intuition — that God's power thanks to which the Church exercises the ministry of life and mystery for eternal life flows from the side of the Crucified — can be found in St. Ambrose and other Church Fathers: "From His side, as He slept, God took a rib (cf. Genesis 2:21). For He it is Who slept, took His rest, and rose up; because the Lord protected Him (cf. Psalm 3:6). What is this 'rib'? It is the power of the Lord. For at the very moment that the soldier opened His side, blood and water burst out for the life of the world (cf. John 19:34). This 'life of the world' is Christ's rib; it is the rib of the second Adam. For *'the first Adam was a living soul; the last Adam is a life-giving spirit'* (1 Colossians 15:45). The last Adam is Christ; is Christ's rib; is the life of the Church. Therefore, we are *'members of His body, made of His flesh and of His bone'* (Ephesians 5:30). And perhaps the Lord was speaking of this rib when He said: *'I feel that power has gone out from Me'* (Luke 8:46). The rib has gone out from Christ but without diminishing His body; for this is not a corporeal rib, but a spiritual rib. Now, as you know, the spirit is not divided, but shares—as it wishes—with each one (cf. 1 Colossians 12:11). Regard Eve, mother of all the living (cf. Genesis 3:20).)".[199]

198. Methodius of Olympus, *Banquest of the Ten Virgins*, Discourse 3, trans. William R. Clark, [in:] *Ante-Nicene Fathers*, Vol. 6, eds. Alexander Roberts, James Donaldson, and A. Cleveland Coxe (Buffalo, NY: Christian Literature Publishing Co., 1886), https://www.newadvent.org/fathers/062303.htm (accessed May 25, 2022).

199. St. Ambrose, *Commentary of Saint Ambrose on the Gospel according to Saint Luke*, Book Two, trans. Ide M. Ni Riain (Dublin: Haleyon Press), p. 60. See Gaius Marius Victorinus,

The Church as the Sacrament of the World's Salvation

I will now only briefly mention (I write about this in greater detail elsewhere)[200] another theme that was extremely popular in the ancient Church: that through the Church God shows His mercy to the entire world. Aristides, the oldest Christian apologist who was active in the time of Emperor Hadrian (117-138), wrote: "And to me there is no doubt but that the earth abides through the supplication of the Christians."[201]

He is echoed by St. Justin Martyr (d. 167), his slightly younger co-religionist: "Wherefore God delays causing the confusion and destruction of the whole world, by which the wicked angels and demons and men shall cease to exist, because of the seed of the Christians, who know that they are the cause of preservation in nature."[202] Similarly, Origen writes: "For men of God are assuredly the salt of the earth."[203]

What was behind this seemingly megalomaniac conviction that it is thanks to Christianity that the world has not fallen into complete

Commentary on the Epistle to the Ephesians; St. Augustine, *On Genesis: Two Books on Genesis against the Manichees; and, on the Literal Interpretation of Genesis: An Unfinished Book*, trans. Roland J. Teske, S.J. (Washington, DC: Catholic University Press, 1991); St. Jerome, *Commentary on Ephesians*, trans. and ed. Ronald E. Heine (Oxford: Oxford University Press, 2002).

200. Jacek Salij, *Tajemnica Emmanuela dzisiaj* (Poznań: Wyd. W Drodze, 1989), pp. 75-83.

201. Aristides, *The Apology of Aristides*, trans. D.M. Kay, [in:] *Ante-Nicene Fathers*, Vol. 9, ed. Allan Menzies (Buffalo, NY: Christian Literature Publishing Co., 1896), https://www.newadvent.org/fathers/1012.htm (accessed May 25, 2022).

202. St. Justin Martyr, *The Second Apology of St. Justin Martyr*, trans. Marcus Dods and George Reith, [in:] *Ante-Nicene Fathers*, Vol. 1, eds. Alexander Roberts, James Donaldson, and A. Cleveland Coxe (Buffalo, NY: Christian Literature Publishing Co., 1885), https://www.newadvent.org/fathers/0127.htm (accessed May 25, 2022).

203. Origen, *Contra Celsum*, Book VIII (70), trans. Frederick Crombie, [in:] *Ante-Nicene Fathers*, Vol. 4, eds. Alexander Roberts, James Donaldson, and A. Cleveland Coxe (Buffalo, NY: Christian Literature Publishing Co., 1885), https://www.newadvent.org/fathers/04168.htm (accessed April 14, 2022).

chaos and annihilation? Without a doubt, the inspiration here was Biblical tradition, according to which a handful of righteous can prevail in God's eyes over all the sins of the entire community and stop God's hand which is ready to punish. It suffices to recall Abraham's haggling with God over the salvation of the inhabitants of Sodom (Genesis 18:22-33) as well as other Biblical supplicants (Exodus 32:9-14; 2 Chronicles 30:17-20; Jeremiah 5:1, 14:7-9; Sirach 16:4).

The Book of Ezekiel contains a shocking complaint against the lack of supplicants: "Thus I have searched among them for someone who would build a wall or stand in the breach before Me to keep Me from destroying the land; but I found no one" (Ezekiel 22:30). Only the Son of God turned out to be such a supplicant (Romans 8:34; Hebrews 9:24; 1 John 2:1). The Church should participate in His supplications (Matthew 5:44; 1 Thessalonians 5:17; James 5:16).

At a more universal level, this topic was recalled by the last council, which recalled in *Sacrosanctum concilium*, the Constitution on the Sacred Liturgy (2), that we should show "forth the Church to those who are outside as a sign lifted up among the nations under which the scattered children of God may be gathered together." It is especially worth noting the following comment in *Lumen gentium*, the Dogmatic Constitution on the Church (9): "So it is that that messianic people, although it does not actually include all men, and at times may look like a small flock, is nonetheless a lasting and sure seed of unity, hope and salvation for the whole human race. Established by Christ as a communion of life, charity, and truth, it is also used by Him as an instrument for the redemption of all and is sent forth into the whole world as the light of the world and the salt of the earth."

THE COMMUNITY OF BELIEVERS IN CHRIST

An Institution That Provides Religious Services?

Today, we are confronted with the temptation to treat the Church as an institution that provides religious services. The mere appearance of such a temptation should be unsurprising. After all, today's social life is made up of countless institutions that provide various services. Many of us work for such institutions, while all of us make use of their services. We appreciate service-providing institutions that try to satisfy our needs appropriately, while we criticize services that are performed sloppily and without concern for the client.

In this situation, the temptation to see the Church as an institution that can satisfy our religious needs seems natural. However, this is exactly why this temptation is very dangerous. With respect to a service-providing institution, the client is someone from the outside, even if its services completely satisfy him and he makes constant use of them. Distrust of the institution grows if the services are rendered in an unsatisfactory way or if some competing institution is capable of serving the client better.

We must realize that many Catholics today abandon religious practices or even leave the Church for other religious communities because they have become disappointed with the Church as an institution that renders services: they have been dissatisfied with the priests they have met, they did not see a place for themselves amidst the anonymous crowds that gather at Sunday Mass, or they were frustrated with the poor quality of sermons.

Indeed, it is of great importance that priests properly and lovingly fulfill their pastoral ministry and that the spirit of true brotherhood grows in the parish community. Nonetheless, original sin, which is why the people we have just mentioned leave the Church, leads to treating the Church as an institution that provides services. In a situation in which people are satisfied with the quality of the "ecclesiastical services" rendered, this sin is manifest in a consumer-like attitude to the Church, not feeling responsible for actively participating in the Church's specific problems and treating the Church from the vantage point of an observer, even a benevolent one.

Brothers and Sisters Are More Than Neighbors

In short, it does not suffice to repeat that "we all are the Church;" this expression must be transformed into reality. In pilgrimages in Poland, there is the custom of referring to one another as "brother" and "sister." This custom attests to the fact that we begin to sense that perhaps the greatest challenge the Church faces today is deepening the spirit of mutual brotherhood. Calls to greater responsibility for the Church and to take on the Church's affairs as one's own would be essentially pagan if their fundament were not concern for specific, living persons.

The New Testament contains many testimonies demonstrating that the first Christians wanted to be a community of brothers and sisters. My brother or my sister is a person who is particularly close to me, and I can trust that I am particularly close to him or her as well. Our relationship is marked by spontaneous unselfishness. We cannot even say that we feel obliged to it, as mutual unselfishness is instead something so obvious that we do not even question to what degree it is our duty. Our fraternal closeness is activated especially when one of us is in need. Thus, the basic traits of fraternal bonds are mutual closeness, unselfishness, and solidarity.

The apostles frequently used the terms "mutual affection" or "mutual charity" (see Romans 12:10; 1 Thessalonians 4:9; Hebrews 13:1; 1 Peter 1:22, 3:8). Thus, there is a difference between the love that we owe to all people and the love inside our Catholic community. This does not even refer to the fact that we should love our brothers and sisters in the faith more. Instead, since we are brothers in the faith it should be natural that we are bound together by mutual love and singular concern for the good of the other. Because our brotherhood is realized in faith, we feel a particular need to help one another in our path to God.

This does not necessarily have to be mutual in the sense that if you have helped me, then I will try to repay you. After all, we are bound not by a relationship of mutual interests but by brotherly love. Gratitude for the good I have received from my brother is most often expressed by my trying to give a hand to a brother of mine who currently needs help. Jesus said: "This is how all will know that you are my disciples, if you have love for one another" (John 13:35). Indeed, much love has been placed within us. Thus, if I do not do enough to provide good — including my faith, which is an especially important good — to others, this means that I am to a large degree wasting the love that has been invested in me and am weakening the testimony that our community of faith could give to Christ.

The foundation of building a spirit of community in the Church must be everyone's concern for every individual member of our spiritual community, especially the one that needs help. The apostles recalled this in very specific terms: "My brothers, if anyone among you should stray from the truth and someone bring him back, he should know that whoever brings back a sinner from the error of his way will save his soul from death and will cover a multitude of sins" (James 5:19-20); "We who are strong ought to put up with the failings of the weak and not to please ourselves; let each of us please our neighbor for the good, for building up" (Romans 15:1-2); "Brothers, even if a person is caught in some transgression, you who are spiritual should correct that one in a gentle spirit, looking to yourself, so that you also may not be tempted. Bear one another's burdens, and so you will fulfill the law of Christ" (Galatians 6:1-2).

Loving Individual Brothers but Also Loving Fraternal Love

We thus have what appears to be the most important response to the question of why we all too often feel alien and anonymous in our churches. Unfortunately, the main cause of this rests within ourselves. Namely, if someone comes to the Church mainly to satisfy his religious needs, then it is no surprise that he feels the way people usually feel in institutions that provide services. In order to feel at home in the Church, one must have an authentic relationship of faith with at least several people.

Today, there are numerous initiatives aimed at deepening our sense of community in the faith. Much can be achieved by carefully preparing the liturgy; encouraging the greatest possible participation in the diverse tasks of a parish; and building numerous small communities in the parish. Such initiatives are invaluable, but they can amount to building on shaky ground if we lack what is most important: my concern and yours for the good of the specific man that God has made us encounter. This also pertains to his ultimate good.

Paul the Apostle expressed this truth through the image of the Church as a body: "[S]o that there may be no division in the body, but that the parts may have the same concern for one another. If [one] part suffers, all the parts suffer with it; if one part is honored, all the parts share its joy" (1 Corinthians 12:25-26).

However, the community of believers needs something much more than responsibility for one another. This was expressed in a unique way by St. Thomas Aquinas in his commentary on the Epistles to the Romans 12:10: "[S]o that through charity we not only love the brethren but even love the very charity by which we love them and are loved by them. For if we regard charity as such a great treasure, we will not allow it to be dissolved so easily."[204] In short, for a community to flourish, its members' mutual concern for one another does not suffice; the community must also invest in the community as such. For example, initiatives such as those mentioned above are necessary. On the other hand, in light of St. Thomas' above notion one can clearly see how absurd it is to be concerned for the community but not notice its individual members. Can one truly love with brotherly love and not love one's individual brothers?

Various Ways of Abandoning My Status as a Consumer in the Church

The difference between a community and an anonymous crowd is that the individual members of the former perform designated tasks. The etymology of the Latin term describing community (*communitas*) implies fulfilling tasks together. Let us begin our reflection on

204. St. Thomas Aquinas on Romans, Ch. 12, No. 985, https://sites.google.com/site/aquinasstudybible/home/romans/st-thomas-aquinas-on-romans/chapter-1/chapter-2/chapter-3/chapter-4/chapter-5/chapter-6/chapter-7/chapter-8/chapter-9/chapter-10/chapter-11/chapter-12 (accessed December 16, 2022).

this topic with the widely known pronouncement of St. Paul on the diversity of tasks that God has entrusted to us for the good of this same community of faith: "For as in one body we have many parts, and all the parts do not have the same function, so we, though many, are one body in Christ and individually parts of one another. Since we have gifts that differ according to the grace given to us, let us exercise them: if prophecy, in proportion to the faith; if ministry, in ministering; if one is a teacher, in teaching; if one exhorts, in exhortation; if one contributes, in generosity; if one is over others, with diligence; if one does acts of mercy, with cheerfulness" (Romans 12:4-8; see 1 Corinthians 12:27-30; Ephesians 4:11).

In commentaries on this pronouncement, there are always efforts to emphasize that the summons to active work for the Church pertains not only to her shepherds and not only those Christians whose charism exercised for the good of the community has been in the spotlight. The community of faith is authentically built by spouses who strive for the spirit of God in their families as well as those spouses who remain faithful to their partners who have abandoned them. This community is built by implementing God's principles into one's professional life as well as through patience amidst illnesses and misfortunes. The true builders of the Church also include those who must devote almost their entire spiritual energies to the struggle to regain control over themselves. Who knows if their struggles against addiction, loneliness, or tendencies towards depression is not the widow's mite that God most appreciates?

Many Catholics believe that their possibilities to include a brick in the construction of the spiritual building that is the Church are small or practically non-existent. Those who believe this should rethink the parable of the talents. It is striking that the man who received the least deserves condemnation. Perhaps we most often waste our opportunities to do good when it seems to us that our capacities are small. We should closely read the parable of the talents. Then, we will no longer justify ourselves by claiming that nothing is dependent on us.

Naturally, this does not mean feverishly looking around and wondering what I could contribute to my parish community. Perhaps it would be good to sometimes wonder about the immensity of tasks that need workers in the contemporary Church. So many people abandon the Church or never come to the Church because someone did not give them a helping hand in a time of need. Countless are the people who succumbed to alcoholism because at a moment of misfortune in their lives they lacked support from a friendly and wise soul. How many marriages would not have fallen apart if at least some of their counselors had not given them advice in the spirit of the world but rather in the spirit of the Gospel. One can only imagine the multitudes of parents who would not have to bitterly regret the sin of infanticide if someone had not earnestly explained to them what abortion truly entails. And what can we say of those tasks, perhaps very urgent ones, that have not yet been noticed at the social level?

Indeed, I would be duplicitous to believe that I have no real possibility to transcend my status as a consumer in the Church. The opportunities for active participation in building the community of faith do not even have to be sought; they will find us themselves as long as we are capable of noticing them. In order to undertake the tasks that we are confronted with almost every day, we do not even need to sacrifice time. After all, a word said in the spirit of faith does not take more time than a word in the spirit of this world; at the same time, I can either indifferently stand beside another person or notice his needs. Everything depends on whether my membership in the Church consists of true openness to Emmanuel or rather just the comfort that I can satisfy my religious needs thanks to the Church.

The immensity of spiritual tasks with which the contemporary Church is faced and that are only partly undertaken provokes me to articulate the following three thoughts. First, such a situation demonstrates how deeply we as a community are wounded by the sin of lack of love.

Second, awareness of this situation effectively protects all those whose presence in the Church is not purely passive against pride. Even if I literally burned myself in sacrifice for my fellow brothers, I would take care of merely a drop in an ocean of needs. This inadvertently brings to mind the Lord Jesus' words: "When you have done all you have been commanded, say, 'We are unprofitable servants; we have done what we were obliged to do'" (Luke 17:10).

Finally, the Gospels instruct us to treat seriously everything we do, whether good or wicked: "The person who is trustworthy in very small matters is also trustworthy in great ones; and the person who is dishonest in very small matters is also dishonest in great ones" (Luke 16:10). Thus, from the perspective of my calling to the Kingdom of God it is something quite unimportant if everything is moving along nearly perfectly or, on the contrary, faces numerous obstacles.

It is very important for you and me to actively take part in this construction. The Builder of this Temple is deserving of our trusting His plans and His direction of the construction process. We should not try to relieve Him in this task or to change the process. Likewise, it would be wrong to panic and doubt the meaning of this construction or the possibility to finish this construction due to the enormity of sin and disorder we witness. We will do the best if we trust the Builder of this Temple and if each of us will try to fulfill all His instructions.

THE UNITY OF THE FAITHFUL WITH THEIR BISHOP

The great tumult related to accusations against bishops of having covered up the sexual abuse of minors to which we have been witnesses in recent years forces us to ask (naturally, in the spirit of faith) what a bishop's role is in the Church and how important the unity of the faithful with their bishop is.

Should they be in unity with their bishop even if he is morally ambiguous? What about if their bishop is inept, excessively engaged in politics, does not understand the contemporary world, or gives rise to reservations for some other reason? I will deal with these questions in a moment. However, I will first present the instruction of one of the earliest Christian martyrs who — in words of farewell, for he had been condemned to death — reminded the faithful with great emphasis that one cannot be a true Christian without unity with one's bishop.

The Testament of the Martyr Ignatius

This took place around 108. The old bishop of Antioch, Ignatius, had the possibility to write several farewell letters to neighboring

Christian communities before he was executed. His intention was above all to bolster the faithful in their persisting alongside Christ, protect them from religious disorientation, and encourage them to persist in unity. Today, these letters are an invaluable testimony to the faith with which the Church lived in the first generation after the departure of the apostles.

The believers' maintaining of unity with their bishop was one of Ignatius' greatest concerns; he constantly returned to this topic in his epistles. He wrote to the community in Ephesus: "Wherefore it is fitting that ye should run together in accordance with the will of your bishop, which thing also ye do. For your justly renowned presbytery, worthy of God, is fitted as exactly to the bishop as the strings are to the harp. Therefore, in your concord and harmonious love, Jesus Christ is sung. And do ye, man by man, become a choir, that being harmonious in love, and taking up the song of God in unison, ye may with one voice sing to the Father through Jesus Christ."[205]

Meanwhile, Ignatius wrote to the community in Magnesia: "Since therefore I have, in the persons before mentioned, beheld the whole multitude of you in faith and love, I exhort you to study to do all things with a divine harmony, while your bishop presides in the place of God, and your presbyters in the place of the assembly of the apostles, along with your deacons, who are most dear to me, and are entrusted with the ministry of Jesus Christ, who was with the Father before the beginning of time, and in the end was revealed. Do ye all then, imitating the same divine conduct, pay respect to one another, and let no one look upon his neighbor after the flesh, but do ye continually love each other in Jesus Christ. Let nothing exist among you

205. St. Ignatius of Antioch, "Seven Epistles of St. Ignatius of Antioch," [in:] *The Early Church Fathers and Other Works* (Edinburgh: Wm. B. Eerdmans Pub. Co., 1867), https://www.ewtn.com/catholicism/library/seven-epistles-of-st-ignatius-of-antioch-20957 (accessed May 26, 2022).

that may divide you; but be ye united with your bishop, and those that preside over you, as a type and evidence of your immortality."[206]

To the Trallians Ignatius wrote: "For, since ye are subject to the bishop as to Jesus Christ, ye appear to me to live not after the manner of men, but according to Jesus Christ, Who died for us, in order, by believing in His death, ye may escape from death. It is therefore necessary that, as ye indeed do, so without the bishop ye should do nothing, but should also our hope, in whom, if we live, we shall be found in Him."[207]

Ignatius included several other admonitions written in a similar spirit in his epistles. All of them are a great testimony to how the early Church understood the Lord Jesus' words addressed to the apostles: "Whoever listens to you listens to Me. Whoever rejects you rejects Me" (Luke 10:16). In the Church, the bishops are the successors to the apostles.

Why is the office of the bishop so important to the Church's system? This is because the bishop is the first servant and minister of the Church's greatest treasure: the Eucharist. The gathering of the faithful around their bishop is above all congregating during the Eucharist in one faith and in eating the same bread (see 1 Corinthians 10:17).

Naturally, the Church is not a cluster of communities isolated from one another. As far back as 108, Bishop Ignatius believed that the Church in Rome would preside over our union of love; Ignatius gave testimony to this in the prologue of his epistle to the Church in Rome. This is why in the Catholic Church every Mass is celebrated in unity with the Bishop of Rome, presently Francis, as well as the bishop of the local Church.

Indeed, the Church celebrates only one Eucharist; the bishops are its servants not only in the sense that they themselves celebrate it

206. *Ibid.*
207. *Ibid.*

but also because they ordain priests and ensure that the Eucharist is celebrated with the deserving reverence, in one faith and one Church.

When There Are Reservations About a Bishop

However, we are sinners. Bishops strive for salvation as much as other believers. It has happened, it happens, and it will happen that the sins of a bishop will be greater than those of an ordinary sinner. A bishop can be burdened with transgression that cause great scandal. We must thank God that this happens rarely; however, it does happen. Furthermore, although the majority of bishops teach the authentic faith (see Matthew 18:18), an individual bishop can err in faith and bring about confusion in the faith of the sheep entrusted to him. How should the faithful act in such situations?

There is only one situation when the faithful should abandon their bishop: when he has unambiguously renounced the Catholic faith and severed his unity with the remaining bishops of Rome who in turn are in unity with the successor to St. Peter. In other difficult situations, when the believer has completely fallen out with his own bishop, the spirit of Catholicism demands that he patiently bear this situation (if we are incapable of bringing about change in accordance with the spirit of the Church) rather than rebel against his bishop and deepen divisions within the Church.

There can be diverse situations, but here we will focus on the most difficult ones: when a bishop's behavior gives rise to serious moral reservations. In the early fifth century, such accusations were levied against St. Augustine himself. He was a young bishop when the Donatists publicly reminded the faithful of the sins of his youth in order to curb his constantly growing position.

In his famous *Third Exposition on Psalm 36*, St. Augustine put forth two arguments in his own defense. He articulated both of them in such a way that he did not really defend himself; after all, he had publicly condemned the sins of his youth many years earlier. He directed his first argument to the Donatists who, it is worth knowing, in principle questioned even the importance of the ministry provided by bishops and priests burdened by sin. Augustine reminded them that the Gospel contains an instruction on how to act with respect to teachers who teach well but themselves do wrong: "The scribes and the Pharisees have taken their seat on the chair of Moses. Therefore, do and observe all things whatsoever they tell you, but do not follow their example" (Matthew 23:2-3).

Indeed, he said to the Donatists, various teachers sit on Christ's chair, including those who are in a state of sin. "[A]s long as they teach sound doctrine they are no hindrance to their hearers. Why have you forsaken that chair itself because of the wicked? Return to peace, return to unity which gives you no occasion for scandal. If my words are good, if my deeds are good, imitate me; if, on the other hand, I do not act as I speak, you have our Lord's counsel. Do as I tell you and not as I do; only do not depart from the seat of Catholic unity."[208]

Meanwhile, Augustine counsels Catholics to respond to accusations against him in the following spirit: "Augustine is a bishop of the Catholic Church; he has his own burden to bear, his own account to render to God. I reckon him among the good; whether he is wicked is known to himself, but even if he be good, that is not the ground of my confidence, This above all things have I learnt in the Catholic Church, that my hope must not be placed in a human being."[209]

This rule of the Catholic faith — that we have invested our hope in God, and we try to avoid investing it in any person — seems obvious. It turns out, however, that we sometimes must stringently recall it, especially when we are scandalized by the figure of a priest or

208. *St. Augustine on the Psalms*, ed. Felicitas Corrigan and Scholastica Hebgin (New York: Newman Press, 1961), p. 325.

209. *Ibid.*

bishop who has been morally stained or is burdened by some other flaws that are very difficult to tolerate.

This does not mean that believers should accept the sins of their pastors. Although we are all sinners, we cannot accept sins, neither our own nor those of those we love. Thus, the faithful have the right to expect that their pastors will be distinguished by moral rectitude and deep spirituality. What is more, the faithful have to right to expect of their pastors to "be holy [...] in every aspect of [their] conduct, for it is written, 'Be holy because I [am] holy'" (1 Peter 1:15-16).

The Donatist Syndrome

Unfortunately, opposition to the sins of the shepherds is all too often expressed in the form of authoritative condemnation and from a position of one's supposed perfection. The tendency to react to the sins of our neighbors is perhaps our Polish national flaw. In 1832, Adam Mickiewicz wrote in *The Books and the Pilgrimage of the Polish Nation*:

"Do not incessantly search out the faults and sins of the past. Ye well know that the priest, at confession, warns people against thinking of past sins, and still more against speaking of them to others; because such thoughts and such talk lead again to other sins.

Do not cry, 'Behold! such a stain is upon that man — I must show it to you. Behold! that man has committed such a crime.' Be sure, neither the people will be wanting, whose duty it shall be to detect those stains, nor judges to sit in judgment, nor the executioner to punish them.

In walking through the town, ye do not clean the pavement, although ye see the streets are dirty; nor in meeting a thief, who is caught at his theft, ye do not drag him to the gallows. There are other people, who are appointed to do this.

And such people will never be wanting. When but lately, in one French town, an executioner was wanted, three hundred and sixty-six immediately presented themselves for that office."[210]

The Church is a supernatural institution; thus, the rhetoric of the self-proclaimed guardians of her sanctity can hurt her much more deeply than analogous authoritative condemnations directed towards purely human institutions. Naturally, the faithful are allowed to criticize their bishops or even the pope. After all, sometimes such criticism will do more for the good of the Church than pretending that everything is absolutely perfect. For the Church, it is a dangerous rhetoric that demands the destruction of the ecclesial connection of the faithful to a stigmatized bishop or priest or even to deny his right to administer the sacraments.

Who says "A," will also easily jump to "B." After all, let us listen without emotion to these wildly emotional exclamations that appear in accusations against one priest or bishop or another: "I would never receive communion from the hands of this archbishop!" "How can I be sure that this confessor was not an agent of the secret services under communism?" "I believe in God and always will, but I no longer believe in priests." What perhaps most surprised me amidst all this bitterness was such a high presence of the Donatist mentality among Polish Catholics.

Let us recall what the Donatist schism was. The scandal which started it was caused by the fact that in 312 one of those who consecrated the new bishop of Carthage was Felix of Aptunga, who had been accused of improper behavior during the most recent persecutions. He was accused of having avoided persecution in a sneaky way. Namely, he took advantage of the ignorance of his persecutors, and when they demanded he produce the books of Sacred Scripture, he instead gave them some heretical works.

210. Adam Mickiewicz, *The Books and the Pilgrimage of the Polish Nation* (London: James Ridgway, Piccadilly, 1833), p. 45.

I do not intend on judging this wrongdoing, especially since the opinion at the time was certainly influenced by some *imponderabilia* unknown to us. The fact is that the Donatists professed a thesis that was unacceptable from the perspective of the Catholic faith: that the sacraments administered by sinful priests were invalid, that the Eucharist celebrated by them was invalid, as were baptisms they administered and confessing to them. This suggested that we are saved by the sanctity of the priest who administers the sacrament, not by Christ's grace!

Catholics responded that although the faithful have the right to holy priests, it is not the case that the supernatural efficacy of the sacraments administered by the priest depended on his sanctity. St. Augustine repeated dozens of times in various ways that the Catholic Church teaches us to invest our hope in Christ, not in any person. People were convinced by the ribald metaphor that the grace of God is like the rays of the sun: they do not become soiled or lose their power even when they pass through an outhouse.

The questioning of the validity of sacraments administered by priests in a state of sin led many Donatists to inevitably deny the salvific efficacy of sacraments administered in the Catholic Church. A cold shiver runs down my spine when I recognize a similar logic in some of the reactions I have mentioned above. One will say: "I would never receive communion from the hands of this archbishop!" Then someone else says it more emphatically: "I believe in God and always will, but I no longer believe in priests."

Although Donatism was born of a utopian dream of building a Church consisting of solely pure and holy people, it quickly had to deal with numerous sins in its own ranks. All that it was capable of achieving was a deep disruption of Christianity in Northern Africa for a couple centuries. The devastation caused by Donatism there perfectly paved the way for the victory of Islam in Northern Africa.

Unity with God as the Basis for Ecumenical Efforts

THE PERSPECTIVE OF A CATHOLIC THEOLOGIAN

What Do We Share?

I will begin by enumerating how much the Catholic Church shares not only with the Orthodox Church but also with the overwhelming majority of Protestant communities. We are already in agreement on the fundaments of our Christian faith. All of us believe in one God in the Holy Trinity, in the Father, Son, and Holy Spirit. We all believe in the Son of God, Who for our sake became one of us, granted us the Gospel, and through His passion and death on the Cross redeemed us of our sins, while through His resurrection He opened for us the way to eternal life. Furthermore, we all have been baptized in the name of the Holy Trinity. We also faithfully read Sacred Scripture as the Word of God inspired by the Holy Spirit.[211]

The Catholic Church feels even more closely bound to the Orthodox Church. The shepherds of both our Churches are appointed to

211. St. John Paul II noticed this during an ecumenical meeting in the Lutheran Church of the Holy Trinity in Warsaw on June 5, 1991. "Although we still differ in faith, thanks to the grace of God we are in agreement with respect to the very fundaments of our faith. We all believe in Jesus Christ, the Son of God, Who is our crucified and resurrected Savior; we are all baptized in the name of the same Father, Son, and Holy Spirit."

offices and serve the Church by inclusion in the holy bond of apostolic succession. Thus, in both our Churches the real manifestation of the sacrifice of Christ the Lord takes place during the Eucharist, while the people of God are fed with the true Body and Blood of the Lord. Furthermore, both our Churches greatly venerate the Blessed Virgin Mary. We also both show great respect towards holy images.[212]

Unfortunately, even such closeness in the faith does not preclude mutual or unilateral hostility. Our opponent, the devil, is capable of sowing religious discord among children of the same Church. More than one hundred years ago, Pope Benedict XV cautioned against creating hostile camps within the Catholic Church: "It is, moreover, Our will that Catholics should abstain from certain appellations which have recently been brought into use to distinguish one group of Catholics from another. They are to be avoided not only as 'profane novelties of words,' out of harmony with both truth and justice, but also because they give rise to great trouble and confusion among Catholics. Such is the nature of Catholicism that it does not admit of more or less but must be held as a whole or as a whole rejected. [...] There is no need of adding any qualifying terms to the profession of Catholicism: it is quite enough for each one to proclaim, 'Christian is my name and Catholic my surname,' only let him endeavor to be in reality what he calls himself" (the encyclical *Ad beatissimi*, 24).

We must thank God that at present relations between the Catholic, Orthodox, and Protestant Churches are proper and have been improving. However, it is worth emphasizing and recalling that even when unacceptable things occur in the relations between Churches and communities, both individual Christians and Christian milieus should avoid such hostility. I will recall what St. Augustine advised to members of his diocese on how to act when faced with unjust hostility on the part of the Donatists:

212. The conciliar constitution *Lumen gentium* (15) comprehensively summarizes this.

"Willy-nilly, they are our brethren. Then only do they cease to be our brethren when they cease to say Our Father. The prophet said of certain people: To those who say to you: Ye are not our brethren, say ye: Ye are our brethren (Isa 66:5). [...] Consult the Apostle and you will see that when he speaks of brethren without any qualification, he means to refer only to Christians. [...] They may say: "Go away, we have no connection with you." But we have an undoubted connection with you: we make confession of one and the same Christ, we ought to be in one Body, under one Head."[213]

The Good Fruits of Our Yearning for the Unity of the Church

Let us ask the question: What divides us? Although we profess the most fundamental truths of our Christian truth, we are still a long way's away from communion in the faith. Doctrinal differences seem particularly significant. Furthermore, we are divided by centuries of having lived in isolation from one another, oftentimes amidst mutual hostility. We have frequently hurt one another, and so our historical memory is often very different: each side is more inclined to remember the injury it experienced rather than the injury it caused. Thus, a sense of mutual foreignness, even hostility, was shaped in our Churches and communities.

Naturally, this has changed in the past half-century. Undoubtedly, we have begun to respect one another more. Proselytism, or the use of manipulations and lies in attracting the members of another Church or community, is less frequent. We are also more open to hearing what we have to say to one another. Consequently, we abandon — perhaps not entirely, but tangibly — many unfair stereotypes that we have shaped regarding one another in previous generations.

213. Second Discourse on Psalm 32 (29) [in:] *St. Augustine on the Psalms*, Issue 30, ed. Felicitas Corrigan and Scholastica Hebgin (New York: Newman Press, 1960), p. 142.

At this point, I will reference the appeal to reconciliation that St. Augustine directed to the Donatist bishop Proculeianus: "I ask you, what have we to do with the dissensions of a past generation? Let it suffice that the wounds which the bitterness of proud men inflicted on our members have remained until now."[214]

Notice that St. Augustine does not mention the wounds we have caused to Christians of other Churches or those they have caused us. Augustine speaks of the wounds that we experience in a sense of our own making: the wounds of unjustified prejudices and general hostility to others. We sometimes do not even notice these wounds within us, and so do not think about healing because, as Augustine explains, "we have, through the lapse of time, ceased to feel the pain to remove which the physician's help is usually sought."[215] In short, let us be the heirs of the faith of our fathers and their love for Christ and the Church, but let us not imitate those who err. It seems, however, that we have remembered this principle somewhat over the past fifty years.

Furthermore, thanks to the rather widespread acceptance of ecumenism in recent years, we have learned to view with favor the spiritual and pastoral experiences of other Churches and communities. Sometimes, we even look at them with holy jealousy, which leads us to imitate them. Thus, for example, the piety of our Orthodox brothers reminds us Catholics of the great importance of holy icons in our own devotion. Meanwhile, our Protestant brethren have undoubtedly led to the wonderful renewal of Biblical piety that we can observe among the faithful of the Catholic and, it seems, Orthodox Churches.

On the other hand, after the liturgical renewal that took place in the Catholic Church, many Protestant communities began to renew their forms of worship. As St. John Paul noticed in the encyclical *Ut unum sint* (UUS), 45: "Some, on the basis of a recommendation expressed at

214. Letter 33 — Augustine to Proculeianus, https://www.newadvent.org/fathers/1102033.htm (accessed December 16, 2022).

215. *Ibid.*

the ecumenical level, have abandoned the custom of celebrating their liturgy of the Lord's Supper only infrequently and have opted for a celebration each Sunday." Certainly, the papal saint continues, "due to disagreements in matters of faith, it is not yet possible to celebrate together the same Eucharistic Liturgy. And yet we do have a burning desire to join in celebrating the one Eucharist of the Lord, and this desire itself is already a common prayer of praise, a single supplication."

"There Can Be No Ecumenism Worthy of the Name Without a Change of Heart"

I do not intend to present all the positive changes that took place in the relations between our Churches and communities thanks to the positive ecumenical atmosphere of recent decades. Much good has taken place, and much good is happening. However, it is worth realizing that all these positive changes are in essence only superficial changes if they do not flow from our hearts, which desire constant conversion and seek ever-deeper unity with Jesus Christ. After all, healing that focuses only on removing the symptoms of the disease but not getting to the root of the causes brings little effect.

What can our desires for the unity of Christianity be worth — even if we are ecumenical activists — if we care little about the sin that separates us from Christ and if we lack yearning for ever-deeper unification with Christ the Lord, our Redeemer, and the Redeemer of the entire world (in short, if we lack a desire for sanctity)?

This is clearly taught by the Second Vatican Council. In *Unitatis redintegratio*, the conciliar Decree on Ecumenism, we read: "There can be no ecumenism worthy of the name without a change of heart. For it is from renewal of the inner life of our minds, from self-denial and an unstinted love that desires of unity take their rise and develop in a mature way. We should therefore pray to the Holy Spirit for the grace to be genuinely self-denying, humble, gentle in the service of others, and to have an attitude of brotherly generosity towards them. [...] This change of heart and holiness of life, along with public and private prayer for the unity of Christians, should be regarded as the soul of the whole ecumenical movement, and merits the name, 'spiritual ecumenism.'"

John Paul II deals with the conciliar notion that "there can be no ecumenism worthy of the name without a change of heart" in UUS, 15 and reminds us that this means "personal conversion as well [...] communal conversion." The pope pays particular attention to the sin that permeates our attitude towards our brothers and sisters belonging to other Christian denominations. Frequently, we are incapable of noticing the wonderful works of grace that God performs outside our community or Church; our thinking about others is often marked by pride, lack of an attitude of forgiveness, or unfounded confidence. It is worth noticing that John Paul II speaks of this by thanking the Lord God that we notice some sins and try to convert. He spoke of this thusly:

"Each one therefore ought to be more radically converted to the Gospel and, without ever losing sight of God's plan, change his or her way of looking at things. Thanks to ecumenism, our contemplation of 'the mighty works of God' (*mirabilia Dei*) has been enriched by new horizons, for which the Triune God calls us to give thanks: the knowledge that the Spirit is at work in other Christian Communities, the discovery of examples of holiness, the experience of the immense riches present in the communion of saints and contact with unexpected dimensions of Christian commitment. In a corresponding way, there is an increased sense of the need for repentance: an awareness of certain exclusions which seriously harm fraternal charity, of certain refusals to forgive, of a certain pride, of an unevangelical insistence on condemning the 'other side,' of a disdain born of an unhealthy presumption. Thus, the entire life of Christians is marked by a concern for ecumenism; and they are called to let themselves be shaped, as it were, by that concern" (*ibid.*).

Our reconciliation with God and Christ should be accompanied by our reconciliation with one another. John Paul II dealt with this topic during the ecumenical meeting at the Centennial Hall in Wrocław on May 31, 1997: "Our Churches and Ecclesial Communities need reconciliation. Can we be fully reconciled with Christ without being fully reconciled among ourselves? Can we bear joint and effective witness to Christ if we are not reconciled with one another? Can we be reconciled with one another without forgiving one another? Forgiveness is the condition for reconciliation. But this cannot take place without interior transformation and conversion, which is the work of grace. 'The commitment to ecumenism must be based upon the conversion of hearts and upon prayer' (*Ut unum sint*, 2)."

The Purification of Our Historical Memory

An important sign that we are authentically seeking reconciliation with Christians belonging to other denominations will be the readiness of each Church and community to cleanse itself of its historical memory. Each side should attempt to comprehend its own part of the guilt it bears for the division of Christianity but should also try to look at other Christians with greater objectivity and without unfair partiality. Certainly, this will lead us all to contrition before God and our fellow brothers. Let us trust that we may all be capable of forgiving and asking for forgiveness.

St. John Paul II dealt with this extensively, not only in relation to our responsibility for the division of Christianity in the apostolic letter *Tertio millennio adveniente* (TMA), where he summarized the second millennium of Christianity. Although his words were addressed to Catholics, in essence they pertained to all believers in Christ: "Hence it is appropriate that, as the Second Millennium of Christianity draws to a close, the Church should become more fully conscious of the sinfulness of her children, recalling all those times in history when they departed from the spirit of Christ and his Gospel and, instead of offering to the world the witness of a life inspired by the values of faith, indulged in ways of thinking and acting which were truly forms of counter-witness and scandal" (33).

The pope wrote that we have greatly offended God with those sins "which have been detrimental to the unity willed by God for His People" (TMA, 34). Unfortunately, today we are also not free of these sins. In particular, we should reflect "with a spirit of repentance" on the sin of "intolerance and even the use of violence in the service of truth" (TMA, 35). However, we should also "place [ourselves] humbly before the Lord and examine [ourselves] on the responsibility which they too have for the evils of our day." The pope pays particular attention to the responsibility of Christians for the contemporary atmosphere of secularism and ethical relativism as well as the passivity that sometimes turns into acquiescence to the "violation of fundamental human rights by totalitarian regimes" and the "responsibility shared by so many Christians for grave forms of injustice and exclusion" (TMA, 36).[216]

John Paul II frequently emphasized that although our sins are great, the unity of Christians is genuinely possible. He expressed this in UUS 34: "Even after the many sins which have contributed to our historical divisions, Christian unity is possible, provided that we are humbly conscious of having sinned against unity and are convinced of our need for conversion. Not only personal sins must be forgiven and left behind, but also social sins, which is to say the sinful 'structures' themselves which have contributed and can still contribute to division and to the reinforcing of division."

216. The significance of such ecumenical cooperation was also emphasized by John Paul II in his speech delivered on June 5, 1991, in the Lutheran Church of the Holy Trinity in Warsaw: "As our obedience to the Holy Spirit grows, the external cooperation of our Churches will likewise take on spiritual strength, for example, in our common efforts to protect human life from the moment of conception to natural death or in our common work to achieve such aims as the dignity of every person, labor, justice, peace, freedom, or the protection of the natural environment."

The Vertical Dimension of Our Path to Sanctity

Future historians of ecumenism will certainly be in agreement that in the twentieth century no one emphasized as much as John Paul II that, although believers in Christ are still very divided, they are now bound together by real communion and that, furthermore, mutual communion is growing deeper and should grow deeper still. We could say that this truth is summarized in the fact that we all — Catholics, Orthodox, and Protestants alike — are truly baptized. The recognition of one another's baptism is something more than a mundane fact of ecumenical politeness, for this sacrament initiates our real inclusion in the Body of Christ (see UUS, 42).

Indeed, too much still divides us for us to be able to participate in one Eucharist, but the mere fact that we desire a common Eucharist truly brings us closer to unity. We can already call "Our Father!" to our Lord Jesus Christ in unison. "The common prayer of Christians is an invitation to Christ himself to visit the community of those who call upon him: 'Where two or three are gathered in my name, there am I in the midst of them' (Matthew 18:20)." (UUS, 21)

It is of utmost importance to our ecumenical efforts that they are not limited to meetings, discussions, or even spiritually enriching one another.[217] Authentic ecumenism strives for a common encounter

217. However, this horizontal path to unity is also extremely important. John Paul II spoke about this in detail on January 16, 1998, in a millennial instruction address to Polish bishops on an *ad limina* visit: "Ecumenical activity cannot be limited to prayer for Christian unity in the month of January, but requires a constant effort, dictated by goodwill and the readiness to give a joint Christian witness in today's pluralistic world. We must pray together, speak to one another, and create a sincere atmosphere of human understanding, at both the individual and the institutional levels. We must undertake concrete initiatives so that the ecumenical spirit expressed on various occasions may increasingly permeate the Church's life. In this way, what we can and must do together to show our unity in Christ will become more visible. Christians — in Poland too — must enter the third millennium together, if not completely united, at least more open to each other, more sensitive and more determined on their way to reconciliation."

in Christ (see UUS, 35), and if it is in Christ, it is understood that this should take place through the conversion of the heart and the sanctity of life.

We read in the papal encyclical on ecumenism: "It is necessary to pass from antagonism and conflict to a situation where each party recognizes the other as a partner. When undertaking dialogue, each side must presuppose in the other a desire for reconciliation, for unity in truth. For this to happen, any display of mutual opposition must disappear. Only thus will dialogue help to overcome division and lead us closer to unity" (UUS, 29).

Ecumenical dialogue is only meaningful when it truly leads to unity and takes place before Christ and in Christ. Thus, this should be dialogue in truth, love, and freedom. It would be a terrible misunderstanding if we tried to seek ecumenical agreement through "altering the deposit of faith, changing the meaning of dogmas, eliminating essential words from them, accommodating truth to the preferences of a particular age, or suppressing certain articles of the Creed under the false pretext that they are no longer understood today. The unity willed by God can be attained only by the adherence of all to the content of revealed faith in its entirety. In matters of faith, compromise is in contradiction with God who is Truth" (UUS, 18).

Christ the Lord is the Way, the Truth, and the Life. Thus, John Paul II continues in his teaching on fidelity to God's truth in our path to unity, "who could consider legitimate a reconciliation brought about at the expense of the truth?" We can never strive for a "reconciliation" that would disregard the truth. "A 'being together' which betrayed the truth would thus be opposed both to the nature of God who offers his communion and to the need for truth found in the depths of every human heart" (*ibid.*).

However, love, including ordinary respect for the truth, makes us listen carefully and in good will to the stipulations expressed by brothers from another Church or ecclesial community. Thanks to such an attitude, we ourselves can deepen the truth expressed by us. And we will grow closer to brothers who seem closed off to this truth. It suffices to recall the common declaration of the Catholic Church and the Lutheran Churches proclaimed on October 31, 1999, according to which there are no essential differences in our faith on Christ's justifying grace.

St. John Paul II deeply believed that it was possible to exercise the primacy of the pope in a way that would be in full agreement with Catholic dogma but at the same time could be acceptable to Churches that are critically disposed towards that primacy: "I insistently pray the Holy Spirit to shine his light upon us, enlightening all the Pastors and theologians of our Churches, that we may seek — together, of course — the forms in which this ministry may accomplish a service of love recognized by all concerned." (UUS, 95).

Meanwhile, John Paul II expressed his hope that all believers in Christ could unite in deep veneration of His Mother in his Marian encyclical: "Meanwhile, it is a hopeful sign that these Churches and Ecclesial Communities are finding agreement with the Catholic Church on fundamental points of Christian belief, including matters relating to the Virgin Mary. For they recognize her as the Mother of the Lord and hold that this forms part of our faith in Christ, true God, and true man. They look to her who at the foot of the Cross accepts as her son the beloved disciple, the one who in his turn accepts her as his mother. Therefore, why should we not all together look to her as our common Mother, who prays for the unity of God's family and who 'precedes' us all at the head of the long line of witnesses of faith in the one Lord, the Son of God, who was conceived in her virginal womb by the power of the Holy Spirit?" (*Redemptoris Mater*, 30).

Were the Polish pope's hopes for speeding up the process of the unification of divided Churches naive? One thing is certain: there are no human ways to achieve this aim. Our ecumenical discussions and activities must be filled with not only mutual respect and love but also authentic remorse for the sins of our fathers and ourselves. According to John Paul II, the words of 1 John 1:9-10 undoubtedly refer to ecumenical dialogue: "If we acknowledge our sins, He is faithful and just and will forgive our sins and cleanse us from every wrongdoing. If we say, 'We have not sinned,' we make Him a liar, and His word is not in us." We read in this latter encyclical (34) that a necessary condition for the authenticity of the ecumenical dialogue in which we engage is acknowledgment of our own sinfulness. Only then can we hope that the righteous Jesus Christ will be our Advocate before the Father (see 1 John 2:1).

Apart from an examination of conscience and remorse, we greatly need to pray for unity: "There is a close relationship between prayer and dialogue. Deeper and more conscious prayer makes dialogue more fruitful. If on the one hand, dialogue depends on prayer, so, in another sense, prayer also becomes the ever more mature fruit of dialogue" (UUS, 33).

To summarize, our duty is to seek penitence for everything that separates us from God and ourselves. We must also continue our great prayers for Christian unity. Meanwhile, the Father of all mercy will bring our Churches and us together in a time and in a way that He will consider appropriate.

CATHOLICS AT A PROTESTANT SERVICE

Someone once presented the following problem to me: "I visited my sister who lives abroad. On Sunday, she took me to a Protestant service because the nearest Catholic church was far away even by car. I was most unsettled by the fact that she received communion during this service. When I told her about this, she replied that I shouldn't exaggerate because we are living in a time of ecumenism, and Protestants believe in the same Lord Jesus. I grew silent because I did not know if the Church had an official position on this."

The essence of the Catholic position on the Protestant Lord's Supper was expressed by the last council in its Decree on Ecumenism (*Unitatis redintegratio*). The council's pronouncement is filled with respect for this service, but at the same time it clearly states that the Catholic Church cannot recognize the true Eucharist in it. Therefore, I will begin by referencing the council's pronouncement:

"Though the ecclesial Communities which are separated from us lack the fullness of unity with us flowing from Baptism, and though we believe they have not retained the proper reality of the Eucharistic mystery in its fullness, especially because of the absence of the sacrament of Orders, nevertheless when they commemorate His death and resurrection in the Lord's Supper, they profess that it signifies life in communion with Christ and look forward to His coming in glory. Therefore, the teaching concerning the Lord's Supper, the other sacraments, worship, the ministry of the Church, must be the subject of the dialogue" (22).

It is worth knowing that in this same document the council not only accepts common prayer with our brothers who believe in Christ but are not Catholics; in fact, it encourages it, especially with regards to the prayer for the unity of Christians (8). Why this difference in the approach to the community of prayer and the community of the Eucharist?

There are two reasons. I will deal with the first of these, which has been mentioned in the above statement: "[W]e believe they have not retained the proper reality of the Eucharistic mystery in its fullness, especially because of the absence of the sacrament of Orders."

Along with the Orthodox Churches and other non-Catholic Eastern Churches (that left the Catholic community in the first Christian millennium) and the Old Catholic Churches, we believe that this holiest Mystery is only celebrated validly in Churches led by the successors to the apostles, or the priests ordained by them. Meanwhile, we do not know how to recognize the true Eucharist in the Lord's Supper celebrated in Churches that are unconcerned that their pastors are included in the chain of apostolic succession.

There is also another reason why the Church is hesitant to hasten Eucharistic communion with those Christians who do not share our faith. This reason was most concisely expressed in the conciliar Decree on the Catholic Churches of the Eastern Rite (*Orientalium Ecclesiarum*): "Common participation in worship (*communicatio in sacris*) which harms the unity of the Church or involves formal acceptance of error or the danger of aberration in the faith, of scandal and indifferentism, is forbidden by Divine law" (26).

Thus, the council recalls this in the document because only this cause can be an obstacle to Eucharistic community with the non-Catholic Eastern Churches in which the Eucharist is validly celebrated. The council recalls this in the chapter in which certain possibilities for increasing the sacramental community with our brothers in these Churches are suggested. This was such a far-reaching accommodation of those Eastern Churches with which we are not yet in unity that until today those Churches fear implementing mutuality in his matter.

Let us listen to the council's direct pronouncement: "On the other hand, pastoral experience shows clearly that, as regards our Eastern brethren, there should be taken into consideration the different cases of individuals, where neither the unity of the Church is hurt nor are verified the dangers that must be avoided, but where the needs of the salvation of souls and their spiritual good are impelling motives. For that reason, the Catholic Church has always adopted and now adopts rather a mild policy, offering to all the means of salvation and an example of charity among Christians, through participation in the sacraments and in other sacred functions and things. With this in mind, 'lest because of the harshness of our judgment we be an obstacle to those seeking salvation' and in order more and more to promote union with the Eastern Churches separated from us, the Sacred Council lays down the following policy" (*ibid.*). Then follows an enumeration of the presently possible situations in which sacramental community with Christians belonging to those Church that have maintained apostolic succession is allowed.

In this spirit, canon law establishes the possibilities for sacramental community with non-Catholics. Canon 844, which is quite lengthy, can be summarized in three points:

1. In principle, Catholic priests administer the sacraments only to Catholics, while the believers of the Catholic Church should receive sacramental services only from Catholic priests.

2. Only in very exceptional circumstances are Catholic priests allowed to grant the Eucharist, the sacrament of penance, and the anointing of the sick to non-Catholics who truly believe in the truth of those sacraments, and only in very exceptional circumstances are Catholics allowed to accept those sacraments from non-Catholic clergy (albeit only clergy from those Churches that have maintained apostolic succession).
3. Catholic priests should never administer the sacraments to those Christians who do not recognize the truth of the Body and Blood of the Lord in the Eucharist or the truth of the real absolution of sins in the sacrament of penance and the anointing of the sick. Likewise, Catholics should never receive the sacraments from non-Catholic clergy who are not included in apostolic succession (this above all pertains to Protestant clergy).

When I was writing this text, I looked at both the 1967 and 1993 editions of the *Directory for the Application of Principles and Norms on Ecumenism*. Its instructions are precisely what I have presented. I think, however, that my response will be richer if I reference the documents here.

The 1967 *Directory* presents the problem as follows: "Celebration of the sacraments is an action of the celebrating community, carried out within the community, signifying the oneness in faith, worship, and life of the community. Where this unity of sacramental faith is deficient, the participation of the separated brethren with Catholics, especially in the sacraments of the Eucharist, Penance and Anointing of the Sick, is forbidden. Nevertheless, since the sacraments are both signs of unity and sources of grace the Church can for adequate reasons allow access to those sacraments to a separated brother. This may be permitted in danger of death or in urgent need (during persecution, in prisons) if the separated brother has no access to a minister of his own communion, and spontaneously asks a Catholic priest for the sacraments — so long as he declares a faith in these sacraments in harmony with that of the Church and is rightly disposed. In other cases, the judge of this urgent necessity must be the diocesan bishop or the episcopal conference. A Catholic in similar circumstances may not ask for these sacraments except from a minister who has been validly ordained" (55).

Thus, no Catholic should receive communion in a Protestant church, not only on an ordinary Sunday but even when his life is in danger. The clergy of those Churches have not been validly ordained, i.e., they are not included in the chain of apostolic succession. The same conclusion can be found in the 1993 *Directory* (132).

A truly ecumenical spirit is expressed in respect for the faith and disciplines of other Churches and the expectation of analogous respect for faith and discipline in one's own Church. Thus, all manifestations of unity performed amidst a lack of respect for the faith and discipline of one's own Church or another's are only superficially ecumenical for in essence they are contrary to true ecumenism.

As I have said, in exceptional situations Catholics are allowed to make use of the sacraments of non-Catholic clergy who have been validly ordained. The 1993 *Directory* recalls that Catholics who want to take advantage of this permission should nonetheless respect the faith and discipline of the other Church: "It is recognized, however, that Eastern Churches, on the basis of their own ecclesiological understanding, may have more restrictive disciplines in this matter, which others should respect. [...] Whenever necessity requires or a genuine spiritual advantage suggests, and provided that the danger of error or indifferentism is avoided, it is lawful for any Catholic for whom it is physically or morally impossible to approach a Catholic minister, to receive the sacraments of penance, Eucharist and anointing of the sick from a minister of an Eastern Church. [...] A Catholic who legitimately wishes to communicate with Eastern Christians must respect the Eastern discipline as much as possible and refrain from communicating if that Church restricts sacramental communion to its own members to the exclusion of others" (122-124).

Such is the ecumenical spirit that we try to do nothing according to our own whim. Truly ecumenically inclined Christians are allowed to make use of sacramental ministry in another Church only under two circumstances: if it is in accordance with the faith and discipline of their own Church and if it does not violate the faith and discipline of the Church where they would like to make use of this sacramental unity.

The 1993 *Directory* very beautifully notes that although full sacramental communion has not yet been attained between the divided Churches, there "exists a real, even if imperfect, communion among Christians which can be expressed in many ways, including sharing in prayer and liturgical worship" (104a).

From what I have heard, this still-imperfect communion is very beautifully manifested in some Swedish churches. Namely, Protestants present at a Catholic Mass and Catholics present at a Protestant service enter the line of those receiving communion but when it is their turn, they respectfully bow and depart. And this is the truth: some communion exists between us, but this is not yet full communion.

CHRISTIANS BEYOND DENOMINATIONS?

There are also "ecumenical" initiatives that have led to the creation of new divisions among Christians. One enthusiast of such initiatives says: "We are Christians. We believe in Christ and love Him. We do not want to be Catholics, Protestants, or Orthodox. We are simply Christians, and that's enough for us."

At the end of the twentieth century, when religious education classes were reintroduced in Latvia, a nation of three great Christian denominations, someone suggested that such lessons should transcend denominational borders as doing so would be more ecumenical and, from the vantage point of the state, cheaper. Clear-headed people responded to this with the following argument: Then maybe instead of teaching Lithuanian and Latvian, two languages that are so very similar to one another, separately, let us try to teach both languages simultaneously! And instead of separate Russian, Ukrainian, and Polish classes, how about we teach a synthesis of Slavic languages?

Christ Cannot Be Separated from the Church

Similarly, there can be no synthetic (trans-denominational) faith in Christ the Lord. Indeed, we should thank God that almost all

Christians — the Catholic Church, the Orthodox Churches, and the great majority of Protestant denominations — share the same most important beliefs regarding Christ: that He is the true God, the Son of God equal to the Eternal Father, and that for our sake He became one of us, while through His death on the Cross and resurrection He redeemed us all. However, that is not the whole truth about Him. Believing in Him, we cannot close ourselves off to the truth that He has given us the Church and that He entrusted concern for the Church — who He equipped with multifarious means of salvation — to the apostles appointed by Him and that He constantly grants the Holy Spirit to His Church.

Those who truly believe in Christ the Lord wholly accept His Gospel and do not censor His teachings. If you have heard His words: "Amen, amen, I say to you, before Abraham came to be, I AM" (John 8:58) and have believed in His Divinity, then also believe that He has given the Church the authority to absolve sins: "Whose sins you forgive are forgiven them, and whose sins you retain are retained" (John 20:23). If you believe that He is "the resurrection and the life" (John 11:25), then also listen to His declaration that "upon this rock I will build My Church" (Matthew 16:18) and notice His words in the Gospel: "Whoever listens to you listens to Me. Whoever rejects you rejects Me" (Luke 10:16). If you read the Gospel closely, you will see that Christ the Lord's reaction to the departure of those disciples scandalized by the promise of the Eucharist (see John 6:66-69) does not allow us to reduce this Gift to a merely symbolic interpretation.

In other words, those who say that they believe in Christ but want to believe in Him outside the Church do not believe in the true Christ but in some product of their imaginations, just as those who had mistaken Him for John the Baptist or Elijah, Jeremiah, or another of the prophets did not believe in Him (see Matthew 16:13-14). Nor did the people who acknowledged His divinity but rejected the truth of His humanity (see 1 John 4:2-3). He Himself cautioned us that those who preach Him falsely would appear: "If anyone says to you then, 'Look, here is the Messiah! Look, there he is!' do not believe it. False messiahs and false prophets will arise and will perform signs and wonders to mislead, if that were possible, the elect" (Mark 13:21-22).

In fact, the Apostle Paul wrote that "even if we or an angel from heaven should preach [to you] a gospel other than the one that we preached to you, let that one be accursed!" (Galatians 1:8). Let us pause at this image for a moment. If it indeed happened that an angel from heaven preached to us some different Gospel, without a doubt it would appear beautiful, attractive, and convincing. Certainly, it would imitate the authentic Gospel rather skillfully. However, this would be a false Gospel.

The true Gospel is the good news of Christ Who not only founded the Church (or, more accurately, gave us the Church as a gift), but does much more — He loves His Church: "Christ loved the Church and handed Himself over for her" (Ephesians 5:25). Naturally, Christ the Lord knows well that we, His Church, are sinners. Without a doubt, He does not love us because we are sinners. Instead, He loves us because He wants to free us of sin. From the ultimate perspective, He wants to transform us into "the Church in splendor, without spot or wrinkle or any such thing, that she might be holy and without blemish" (Ephesians 5:27).

A More Universal Religion Than Christianity?

The spiritual sphere resembles material fabric: Once there is one tear, more can quickly follow. Whoever agrees to separate Christ from the Church, even for subjectively noble reasons, becomes prone to going further. Does Christ not distinguish Christians from Muslims and Jews? Must we insist on our faith in Christ? We should appreciate that those who profess all three of these religions share faith in God!

Thus, there is no need to be concerned about Christ; instead, we should rejoice that we all believe in one God!

After adopting the attitude: "God — yes, but Christ — not necessarily," a second temptation follows: But faith in a personal God separates us from the religions of the Far East! Thus, we should perhaps go one step further and take on a more "ecumenical" attitude: "Religion — yes, but a personal God — no."

I am not implying that such an evolution necessarily takes place in the life of all who want to separate their faith in Christ from the Church. However, various people today do indeed proclaim such views: that faith in Christ separates Christians from other believers in God or that in the name of shared religious values faith in the personal God must be rejected as an anthropomorphic superstition. This recalls a telling detail of the parable of the lost sheep: it got lost in the mountains (see Matthew 18:12) looking for what is grand and noble!

Considering such phenomena and such views, it is worth recalling that the Greek verb *diaballein*, which is the root of the word "devil", means "to separate." For this enemy of ours wants to separate everything that God has bound together. He wants to separate husband from wife, truth from love, righteousness from mercy, joy from good, and freedom from truth. He is the cause of death, which of course consists of the separation of the body and soul. He would also like to separate faith in Christ from our membership in the Church, and once he succeeds, he will want even more: to separate faith in God from faith in Christ.

His favorite tactic is to pretend to be the angel of light (see 2 Corinthians 11:14). Humanity needs a religion suitable for modern times, this cunning tempter hisses, and Christianity does not play the role of a truly universal religion; it is too particular! The devil is the master of making false reference to such noble ideals as peace, dialogue, cooperation, and ecumenism. "All religions are equal!" he tells us for he knows well that if we were to adopt this thesis, we would separate religion from truth and deprive faith in God of its essential meaning.

"All religions are equal!" claim the adherents of theosophy and various "progressive" thinkers. "Christianity should discourage preaching that Christ is the Redeemer of all people because this is a form of usurpation with which Christianity attempts to put itself above all other religions." This does not stop theosophy advocates from claiming that they have access to eternal wisdom, which supposedly places them above all religions and gives them the right to judge. I shall try to comment on this attitude. It is worse than pride; it is perversity, plain and simple.

In the 1997 document *Christianity and the World Religions*, the International Theological Commission responds to the above accusation in detail: "[I]t is necessary to affirm that the truth of faith is not at our disposal. In facing a strategy of dialogue which asks for a reduction of Christological dogma to exclude this claim of Christianity's superiority, we opt instead — with the aim of excluding a 'false' claim of superiority — for a radical application of the Christological faith to the form of proclamation proper to it. Every form of evangelization that does not correspond to the message, to the life, to the death and to the resurrection of Jesus Christ compromises this message and, in final analysis, Jesus Christ Himself.

The truth as truth is always 'superior;' but the truth of Jesus Christ, as made clear by our need for him, is always service to man; it is the truth of the one who gives his life for men to make them enter definitively into the love of God. Every form of proclamation which seeks above all and over all to impose itself on its hearers or to dispose them by means of a strategic or instrumental rationality is opposed to Christ, to the Gospel of the Father and to the dignity of the man of whom He has Himself spoken."

HOLINESS AND EVIL IN THE CHURCH

"If the Lord is with us, why has all this happened to us?"

Let us honestly admit that the great topic of "evil in the Church" has become religiously barren to us. Many of us, and above all those who are the most religiously engaged, do not deal with this topic at all. Others criticize the bureaucratization of Church offices, the poor quality of catechesis, the negligence of specific areas of pastoral ministry, the wealth and greed of the clergy, and their excessive or insufficient (depending on the perspective of the one who criticizes) political engagement. We tend to criticize in such a way that it externally reinforces our attitude towards the Church. It rarely happens that our criticism brings good to the Church; however, it leads to the deterioration of our spiritual condition, for it deepens our alienation from the Church.

Yet the topic of "evil in the Church" is truly deserving of our attention. I will try to present its essence from the perspective of the Biblical scene of the call of Gideon (Judges 6:11nn). God's Chosen People were then under the yoke of the Midianites. Gideon was trying to secure wheat from the Midianites' store of plunder when the Angel of the Lord appeared and greeted him with: "The Lord is with you, you mighty warrior!" Such a greeting seems fundamentally false to Gideon. He responds to the angel: "If the Lord is with us, why has all this happened to us? Where are His wondrous deeds about which our ancestors told us when they said, 'Did not the Lord bring us up from Egypt?' For now, the Lord has abandoned us and has delivered us into the power of Midian."

In this consists the essence of evil in the Church. The Church, the people of God, is a place of God's unique presence among people, a powerful and redeeming presence. However, reality seems to contradict this; through their sins, people seem to have forced God to withdraw His presence. The next part of Gideon's story, however, convinces us that God only seemingly had abandoned His people; in fact, He had never ceased to be with them during their slavery, nor did He intend on indifferently gazing at the arrogant domination of the Midianites.

Thus, evil in the Church is the multitude of situations in which we prevent God from showing His powerful love towards us. From an external position, it is easy to criticize the Inquisition or the material status of the clergy. However, our every mortal sin, every addiction, every violation of the sanctity of marriage, every example of indifference towards a needy person, and every case of sowing discord is also a great evil committed against the Church. For in this way we bear false testimony to Christ as if He had not fulfilled His promise of remaining in His Church until the end of the world or as if He were too weak to pour true love into us.

We Can Respond to Every Situation with Good

Let us look at a mundane situation in which petitioners at a parish office are treated cold-heartedly, even rudely, and leave offended that in Church offices people are treated in the same way as in secular ones. Naturally, this does not mean that people in charge of parish offices as well as those that use their services should be so well-mannered that they can hide their indifference towards one another behind a mask of politeness. Although such manners make life easier, they do not transform hearts or make the world better; in fact, they might even consolidate the inhumanity of our relations with one another.

Thus, if I believe that the Church is God's work and not merely another human institution, then I believe that God wants and can transform us so that we can truly love one another. If, then, I work in a parish office, I consider it to be a great gift from God that I have been situated in such a place where I can so often help a fellow man in his path towards God. If it has so happened that as a client, I have been treated cold-heartedly in a Church office, my first reaction will not be condemnation or indignation but pain that such things happen in the Church, which is where there should be the most selfless love. Through such an attitude, I do not add an additional sin, that of a lack of love, through which man so easily reciprocates the harm he has experienced. Love can often suggest a positive activity in favor of healing the scandalous situation that man is not always treated in the spirit of love in the Church.

Cursed and Blessed Thinking About Evil in the Church

Every one of us can experience a moment when we painfully sense a lack of love in the Church. In such situations, it is worth asking Gideon's question: "If the Lord is with us, why has all this happened to us?" Why is there so much sin among us and so little love? If I think about this question not in a rigid, doctrinal manner but as a Christian, I will quickly realize that it is above all addressed to me. As long as my lack of love encountered another's love, I did not even notice that in the Church I am more likely to take than give love. It was only when my lack of love encountered a similar attitude from the other side that I noticed how little love there was among us. And even then I noticed a lack of love not within me but in my neighbor.

The Church is where God's powerful presence among people can be found. However, the Lord Jesus' power is full of humility. He performed the greatest work of His power on the Cross. Although He was killed on it, His love was greater than all the hatred directed towards Him and more powerful than all the world's sin. Likewise, today Christ the Lord is powerful in a humble way. He does not promise us that the Church will be a paradise of mutual love. He promises, however, that He will fill my heart and yours with love and that we will radiate our love onto others if only we are open to His presence. The Kingdom of God begins in the human heart. But if I close myself off from it, I will not notice it even where it authentically exists and acts.

Worse still, a Christian closed off to Christ's transforming power not only becomes a dead member of the Church but begins to be an obstacle for others in their path towards the faith. In turn, Isaiah, Ezekiel, and the Apostle Paul admonish us: "Because of you the name of God is reviled among the Gentiles" (see Isaiah 52:5; Ezekiel 36:20; Romans 2:24). The Lord Jesus sad with anger: "You lock the kingdom of heaven before human beings. You do not enter yourselves, nor do you allow entrance to those trying to enter" (Matthew 23:13).

The lack of love among Christians as an obstacle to the evangelization of the world is an ever-present problem of the Church. The author of the oldest preserved Christian homily deals with it. It is wonderful that in every generation the Holy Spirit finds people who are concerned about this and try to remedy it. But let us first read this text, which is a commentary on the words from Scripture that "[b]ecause of you the name of God is reviled among the Gentiles" (Romans 2:24).

An anonymous author who lived 1,800 years ago asks: "'Wherefore My name is blasphemed; blasphemed in what?' [...] For the nations, hearing from our mouth the oracles of God, marvel at their excellence and worth; thereafter learning that our deeds are not worthy of the words which we speak — receiving this occasion they turn to blasphemy, saying that they are a fable and a delusion. For, whenever they hear from us that God says, 'No thank have ye, if you love them which love you, but you have thank, if you love your enemies and them which hate you' — whenever they hear these words, they marvel at the surpassing measure of their goodness; but when they see, that not only do we not love those who hate, but that we love not even those who love, they laugh us to scorn, and the name is blasphemed."[218]

Without a doubt, this harsh text is truthful. Yet let us recall how many martyrs came from the ranks of these defective Christians in the second century. How great the power of their faith must have been, considering that the Gospel spread to many nations over the course of just a few generations!

The great implication for us is that we can be concerned about the weaknesses of today's Church only in a way that would encourage us to serve God even more zealously. Cursed is the kind of thinking about evil in the Church that leads to panic and sows doubt in God's power, which instead of inspiring greater zeal among us paralyzes and discourages. Such thinking is cursed because it is directly opposed to God's teaching: "'[F]or power is made perfect in weakness.' I will rather boast most gladly of my weaknesses, in order that the power of Christ may dwell with me" (2 Corinthians 12:9).

218. St. Clement, *The "Second Epistle" of St. Clement*, trans. John Keith [in:] *Ante-Nicene Fathers*, Vol. 9, ed. Allan Menzies (Buffalo, NY: Christian Literature Publishing Co., 1896), https://www.newadvent.org/fathers/1011.htm (accessed June 7, 2022).

There Will Always Be Evil in the Church, but We Can Never Accept It

We have now arrived at the moment when, without fear of misunderstanding, we can say the most important thing on the topic of evil in the Church. Namely, we Christians should understand that first of all, the expectation that the Church will cease to be destroyed and paralyzed by the wickedness of her children on this earth is false; second, merely accepting this fact is even more false.

Throughout the history of Christianity, there were numerous utopian aspirations to turn the Church into a community solely consisting of saints. The Catholic Church has always persistently defended the rights of sinners to God and the Church against the Novatians, Montanists, or Donatists. Consequently accused of being lenient towards sin, Catholics responded that we should distinguish between sin and sinners. Sin is the greatest evil that can take place on this earth. It results in important practical consequences that we cannot avoid. The sinner, however, is our neighbor, one who needs the Church's help especially because he is a sinner.

Today, various cults similarly attempt to implement utopian notions of creating a perfect Christianity solely consisting of perfect people. We as Catholics, however, should not be ashamed that the Church consists of sinners. It is important to recall Christ's words that "I did not come to call the righteous but sinners" (Matthew 9:13). The activity of such cults should awaken within us holy fear whether we — under the guise of the good of sinners — do not make light of sin itself. Although the Church will consist of sinners until the end of the world and our sins will harm the Church until the end of the world, sin can never be authorized in the Church. Sin will always be the Church's enemy. It cannot be any different because sin is man's enemy and ruins God's love within us.

The Church Is Holy Because She Sanctifies Sinners

Our reflections on the topic of the mystery of evil in the Church were permeated by the wonderful truth that the Church is holy. Although she consists of sinners, she is holy. She is holy because she is filled with the presence of the One Who "alone [is] holy" (Revelation 15:4). Christ the Lord loves us sinners but hates our sin. This is why He established His Church, to grant her His power and presence to implement this love for us. In other words, He founded His Church to sanctify us sinners, to turn us into saints.

The New Testament speaks of the sanctity of the Church in three dimensions. The Church is holy because our sanctification takes place through her. Naturally, this refers to initial sanctification through the sacrament of baptism. This was wonderfully expressed by St. Paul in his First Epistle to the Corinthians: "[T]o you who have been sanctified in Christ Jesus, called to be holy" (1:2) and thus sanctified yet still called to sanctity. In one of the chapters of this epistle, he wishes to caution the Corinthians that aspiring towards righteousness at a purely human level, without a spirit of love, can easily make one unjust and thus return to his situation from before baptism. Paul writes: "[B]ut now you have had yourselves washed, you were sanctified, you were justified in the name of the Lord Jesus Christ and in the Spirit of our God" (6:11).

But the Church is also holy in the sense that Christ Who is present in her wants to sanctify us even more. "Everyone who has this hope based on Him makes himself pure, as He is pure" (1 John 3:3). "Strive for peace with everyone, and for that holiness without which no one will see the Lord" (Hebrews 12:14). "Like obedient children, do not act in compliance with the desires of your former ignorance but, as He Who called you is holy, be holy yourselves in every aspect of your conduct, for it is written, 'Be holy because I [am] holy'" (1 Peter 1:14-16).

We will continue to be sinners until the end of our time on earth. But if we know why God has called us to the Church, if we search for

Christ's powerful grace, then sin will not dominate within us, and we will sin less and less (Romans 6:12-14). It is in the Church that God realizes His promise from the Book of Micah that He "will again have compassion on us, treading underfoot our iniquities" (7:19).

In short, to be baptized means to be called to sanctity. God wants to make each of us "holy, without blemish, and irreproachable before Him" (Colossians 1:22). The fifth chapter of the last council's Dogmatic Constitution on the Church is devoted to the topic of the universal call to holiness.

To Be Holy Is Also My Duty Towards Others

It is worth realizing that my sanctity is not only God's great gift for myself, as it has initiated my perpetual closeness with God. To be holy is also my obligation towards others. St. Thomas Aquinas writes: "Among the various indications that make the holiness of God known to men, the most convincing sign is the holiness of men, who are sanctified by the divine indwelling."[219]

Meanwhile, the Second Vatican Council recalls the traditional teaching that a particularly convincing testimony to the Church's sanctity is the every instance of surrendering one's life to Christ and, in general, every instance of persisting by Christ's side in a difficult situation: "By martyrdom a disciple is transformed into an image of his Master by freely accepting death for the salvation of the world — as well as his conformity to Christ in the shedding of his blood. Though few are presented such an opportunity, nevertheless all must be prepared to confess Christ before men" (*Lumen gentium*, 42).

There is also a third dimension of the Church's sanctity; namely, that of the Church's sanctity in the ultimate horizon. Although

219. St. Thomas Aquinas, *Compendium Theologiae. Compendium of Theology*, p. II, 8, trans. Cyril Vollert, S.J. (St. Louis & London: B. Herder Book Co., 1947), https://isidore.co/aquinas/english/Compendium.htm (accessed December 16, 2022).

we are still sinners, the Church is already holy. And she is already not only loved by Christ but as a loving Bride reciprocates Christ's love. The Apostle Paul writes: "Christ loved the Church and handed Himself over for her" (Ephesians 5:25). Ultimately, however, Christ the Lord will "present to Himself the Church in splendor, without spot or wrinkle or any such thing, that she might be holy and without blemish" (Ephesians 5:27).

In short, in eternal life we all as the Church will be like His Mother already is to Him: we will completely and without reservation love Him in the full meaning of the word.

The transformation of the Church, which is simultaneously sinful and holy, into a completely holy Church was beautifully described by St. Ambrose (d. 397), St. Augustine's spiritual father: "He, then, whose guilt is remitted is made whiter than snow. So that God said by Isaiah: 'Though your sins be as scarlet, I will make them white as snow' (Isaiah 1:18). The Church, having put on these garments through the laver of regeneration, says in the Song of Songs: 'I am black and comely, O daughters of Jerusalem' (Song of Songs 1:4). Black through the frailty of her human condition, comely through the sacrament of faith. And the daughters of Jerusalem beholding these garments say in amazement: 'Who is this that comes up made white?' (Song of Songs 8:5). She was black, how is she now suddenly made white? [...]

But Christ, beholding His Church, for whom He Himself, as you find in the book of the prophet Zechariah, had put on filthy garments, now clothed in white raiment, seeing, that is, a soul pure and washed in the laver of regeneration, says: 'Behold, you are fair, My love, behold you are fair, your eyes are like a dove's,' (Song of Songs 4:1) in the likeness of which the Holy Spirit descended from heaven."[220]

220. St. Ambrose, *On the Mysteries*, trans. H. de Romestin, E. de Romestin and H.T.F. Duckworth [in:] *Nicene and Post-Nicene Fathers, Second Series*, Vol. 10, eds. Philip Schaff and Henry Wace (Buffalo, NY: Christian Literature Publishing Co., 1896), https://www.newadvent.org/fathers/3405.htm (accessed June 7, 2022).

THE PRIMACY OF PETER IN THE NEW TESTAMENT

The First Witness to Christ Among the Apostles

The New Testament says much about the primacy of Peter. I will begin by recalling that Peter is the first of the apostles that Christ the Lord chose to be witness to His resurrection. When the disciples are on their way to Emmaus from Jerusalem, they find out from the apostles: "The Lord has truly been raised and has appeared to Simon!" (Luke 24:34). Only then does Jesus meet with the remaining apostles (see Luke 24:33-36).

Likewise, when making a list of the Resurrected One's encounters with His friends, the Apostle Paul first mentions Peter, "that He was raised on the third day in accordance with the scriptures; that He appeared to Cephas, then to the Twelve" (1 Corinthians 15:4-5). The moment when Peter is the first among the apostles to witness Christ's resurrection cannot be overestimated. Let us recall what the apostle says about the meaning of this truth amidst the entirety of our faith a couple lines later: "And if Christ has not been raised, then empty [too] is our preaching; empty, too, your faith. [...] If for this life only we have hoped in Christ, we are the most pitiable people of all" (1 Corinthians 15:14, 19).

Furthermore, Peter was the first apostle who believed in Jesus' Divinity and professed this faith in the presence and in the name of the remaining disciples (Matthew 16:15-16). Let me ask rhetorically: From the perspective of God's plan of salvation, could it be of little importance that Peter is the first among the apostles to witness the two most fundamental truths of the Christian faith: that Jesus Christ is the Only Begotten Son of God and that He rose from the dead after dying on the Cross? The Church often emphasizes that the essence of Peter's service is the gathering of scattered disciples around the resurrected Christ and that this is possible only on the foundation of the unified faith that He is the true God, equal to His Eternal Father.

Christ the Lord's Three Words on the Primacy of Peter

Let us recall how Christ the Lord responded to Peter's profession: "And so I say to you, you are Peter, and upon this rock I will build My Church, and the gates of the netherworld shall not prevail against it. I will give you the keys to the kingdom of heaven. Whatever you bind on earth shall be bound in heaven; and whatever you loose on earth shall be loosed in heaven" (Matthew 16:18-19).

It is worth recalling that when the Lord Jesus saw him as the first among the apostles, Peter's faith was still very immature. The Evangelist writes that it became immediately clear that he was still completely incapable of understanding the mystery of the Cross (see Matthew 16:21-23). Furthermore, he betrayed his Master on the day of trial.

Thus, it is even more noteworthy that almost immediately before Peter's betrayal the Lord Jesus repeats His desire for Peter to be the first among the apostles. He said to him during the Last Supper: "Simon, Simon, behold Satan has demanded to sift all of you like wheat, but I have prayed that your own faith may not fail; and once you have turned back, you must strengthen your brothers" (Luke 22:31-32). This statement of the Lord Jesus is the source of the Catholic teaching that one of the basic tasks of Peter and his successors in the Church is to "strengthen your brothers in the faith."

In the Gospel of John, we find one more text demonstrating how important it was to the Lord Jesus to leave the institution of primacy to the Church. This took place after the Resurrection. As if in reference to Peter's three denials of Jesus, He asks Peter three times: "Simon, son of John, do you love me more than these?" Each time, after receiving a positive response from Peter, Jesus repeats: "Tend My sheep" (see John 21:15-17). This event is an important reference point for Catholic reflections on primacy whenever we want to recall that primacy in the Church should above all be fulfilled in love for Christ.

Meanwhile, it is appropriate to mention here that at the moment when the Apostle John was describing this event, Peter had already been deceased for thirty years. It is difficult to find more compelling evidence that John saw the primacy of Peter as a priceless gift from the Redeemer for the entire Church and all her generations.

There Are Countless Testimonies to the Primacy of Peter in the New Testament

The New Testament says even more about the primacy of Peter. Let us look at examples of passages that enumerate the names of all the twelve apostles. The New Testament contains four such catalogues (Matthew 10:2-4; Mark 3:16-19; Luke 6:14-16; Acts 1:13). It is telling that although the apostles are enumerated in various orders in all four lists, Peter is listed first. Matthew the Evangelist even writes: "[F]irst, Simon called Peter" (Matthew 10:2).

There is one more telling moment. When we look at the names of the individual apostles, it becomes clear that some had Semitic names and others Greek ones, but only Peter was given a new name by the Lord Jesus. Furthermore, the Lord Jesus calls him Cephas in Aramaic

(John 1:42), which is the name the Apostle Paul most frequently uses to refer to him (1 Corinthians 1:12, 3:22, 9:5, 15:5; Galatians 1:18, 2:9-14). This is the only example of a name being translated into Greek in the New Testament. In the apostolic Church, Cephas was called Peter, clearly so that Christians who knew Greek would also know that he had received from the Redeemer this name along with his task: "You are Peter, and upon this rock I will build My Church."

Let us notice once more that before Christ's Passion Peter was already considered the leader of the apostles (see Matthew 17:24; Luke 9:32). He is also the only apostle whom the New Testament distinguishes with the label "Peter and the Apostles." The angel says to the women gathered by the tomb of the Resurrected: "But go and tell His disciples and Peter" (Mark 16:7). Meanwhile, the author of the Acts of the Apostles writes: "Then Peter stood up with the Eleven" (Acts 2:14). There are two more, similar entries: "Now when they heard this, they were cut to the heart, and they asked Peter and the other apostles, 'What are we to do, my brothers?'" (Acts 2:37). "But Peter and the apostles said in reply [before the Sanhedrin], 'We must obey God rather than men'" (Acts 5:29).

In conclusion, let us notice how unambiguously Peter fulfills the role of the head of the apostles after the departure of Christ the Lord. He oversees the election of the new apostle who will replace Judas (Acts 1:15nn). He represents the young Church on the day of Pentecost (Acts 2:14nn). Likewise, we later frequently see him as the first in the Jerusalem Church (Acts 3:12nn; 5:3nn; 5:12; 5:29). What is important, Peter makes the decision to baptize the first Gentile (Acts 10), which is of momentous importance to the Church, while the description of this event clearly emphasizes that he did so thanks to the light of the Holy Spirit (Acts 10:9-20). Finally, Peter oversees the Council of Jerusalem.

In a word, the New Testament has very firmly documented Peter's primacy.

THE INFALLIBILITY OF PETER'S SUCCESSORS

The Drive of Fallible People for Infallibility

Let us think about the meaning of the sentence: "People are fallible." This sentence certainly does not express the notion that we are incapable of knowing the truth. It is also not tantamount to saying that it is impossible to achieve certainty in knowing the truth. This sentence only communicates the fact that our knowing of truth can be unreliable, that sometimes achieving certainty does not correspond to the objective situation.

At the same time, man has a kind of drive towards infallibility. Fortunately, this is revealed not only in the arrogant confidence usually evident in ideologies and people who have not the slightest reason to feel infallible. We want, for example, for court rulings to be infallible, hence the scrupulous respect for the principles of law, the attorney and prosecutor at the side of the judge, the appellate system, etc. The ideal of infallibility guides science and is served by carefully crafted methodology, discussions between researchers, and the postulate to verify or falsify the conclusions of research. It is easiest to achieve a state of infallibility in technology: for example, in space flights or, to use the first example that comes to mind, the history of progress in measuring the temperature of blast furnaces.

And yet, despite all the successes that can be attributed to our drive towards infallibility, we do not doubt that the statement: "People are fallible" will always be true. In particular, two circumstances increase the possibility of committing errors in our knowing the truth:

1. If the truth we know is not easily accessible to our cognitive faculties.
2. If it is greater than man, if it belongs to those truths that cannot be possessed but instead themselves come to possess man.

In short, it is easier to be infallible in knowing things than people; infallibility is easier in technical rather than moral activity.

The Infallibility of God

The above comments can help us to consider a second statement: "God is infallible." God is infallible because no truth is to any degree *accessible* to Him; all truths are simply directly and completely *in* Him. The Lord God does not have to confirm truths by reconstructing their elements, drawing conclusions, etc. He simply sees truth in itself. Naturally, He completely and fully sees the whole truth because no truth is greater than He. It is unnecessary to mention that it would be foolish and blasphemous to ascribe the infallibility proper to God to any creature.

Now let us introduce to our reflections to most basic dogma of the Christian faith: that the Son of God, the true God equal to the Eternal Father, became a man for our salvation. Was Jesus Christ infallible in His human nature as well? Of course He was. After all, the human Jesus is the same Person that is infinitely united with the Father and the Holy Spirit. Because He is God, He not only wanted to teach us the truth about God and the way of our lives, but He truly achieved teaching us this. His teaching is completely true and infallible. Although people are fallible, there is not a shadow of fallibility in Jesus Christ the man. At the same time, his infallibility is very humble. He does not use it to show His superiority to others. On the contrary, He has come to serve and seek and save what was lost, while his infallibility is completely subordinated to this purpose.

The Church, the Servant of God's Infallibility

Here is more evidence of the Son of God's infinite humility: He makes ordinary people participants in His infallibility. Although this is difficult to believe, it is clearly stated in the Gospel. He said to His disciples: "Whoever listens to you listens to Me. Whoever rejects you rejects Me. And whoever rejects Me rejects the One Who sent Me" (Luke 10:16). He said this not to exalt them and leave them feeling satisfied but because he wanted the Church to have living plenipotentiaries of His teaching presence. If, then, "the Church of the living God [is] the pillar and foundation of truth" (1 Timothy 3:15), this refers not to the truth that solely expands the mind but rather that which expands the soul, bringing salvation. The infallibility with which Christ endowed His Church in its essence serves the human aspiration towards God and the liberation of man from sin.

Now, it is easier for us to see the absurdity of the accusation that the principle of the Church's infallibility demands that man sacrifice his reason. Yet this principle does not refer to theoretical truth but to the living truth that creates man, and without which man can waste away. I will provide an example. When I speak with someone on the sanctity of human life, I try to get him to acknowledge the principle that human life is absolutely deserving of respect. Until we acknowledge this principle together, we will only be two gentlemen who like to engage in disputes; our discussions will be filled with empty stuff, noise, and darkness. We must accept the principle that human life is something sacred and inviolable for our discussion to turn into a genuine search for truth. It is a strange paradox that until we found the truth, we were only pretending to look for it; we began to seek out the truth in earnest only once we found it. Only then were the previously unexpected depths of the truth about human destiny, human dignity, and the transcendence of the human person with respect to time and space, the laws of biology or sociology, or even consciousness and intelligence opened before us.

In this way, the truths of faith and morality are analogous. Naturally, they must be sought out if one does not know them, if when asking myself the most important questions I am immersed in darkness. The meaning of these truths will be gradually opened before us only once we find them and firmly believe them. The aim of the Church's dogmas is to bring man to places where he can find many truths. This includes the ultimate truth, the truth that liberates man from sin and unifies him with God. The search for truth does not conclude with the recognition of dogmas; in fact, that is only when it begins. Naturally, this is not an ordinary human search. A believer gazes at the truths of the faith in the Holy Spirit and realizes we have received the promise: "He will teach you everything and remind you of all that [I] told you" (John 14:26).

Thus, we should thank the Lord Jesus that He deigned to grant His Church the gift of infallibility. Let us thank Him that the faith of the Church is not immersed in the darkness of ignorance or the noise of conflicting opinions: the basic dogmas of faith and morality are clear. Our thanksgiving will be all the truer once we search for and find God and ourselves thanks to these dogmas.

This is why the Church is so anxious about indifference and heresy; this is why she appreciates the gift of infallibility in teaching the faith that Christ has granted her. If we were to look for an analogy for this attitude of the Church, it contains something of the fear with which we listen to careless pronouncements against the most sacred of moral principles; this fear of ours becomes even greater if those statements are clad in the garments of erudition or concern for the common good.

When Are We All Obliged to Infallibility?

Each and every bishop of Rome is a particular servant of the Church's infallibility. First, however, let me say a few words on this infallibility in the ordinary life to which we are all obliged. Our mentality is scandalized by the mere thought that any human can be infallible. Yet each of us is in a unique way obliged to infallibility. For example, when we go to the forest to pick mushrooms, we are absolutely obliged to correctly distinguish between edible mushrooms and poisonous ones. A nurse must infallibly know that the liquid in her syringe is glucose. If she happened to inject a patient with hydrochloric acid rather than glucose, she could not excuse herself by saying that to err is human.

Indeed, in scientific research erring is an extremely important element of our search for truth. Oftentimes, researchers who propose erroneous hypotheses make crucial contributions to science, for while debunking their incorrect hypotheses many things become clear and we come closer to the truth.

I think that the contemporary mentality does not clearly see the difference between what Gabriel Marcel would call the "having" kind of truth and the "being" kind of truth, between substantive and personal truth. Erring with respect to the substantive truth is a normal and even sometimes blessed thing. Things are different with respect to the personal truth: the truth that determines someone's "to be" or "not to be." In this case, we are absolutely obliged to be infallible.

Today, we are so concerned with the truth that we are all fallible that we barely want to hear that sometimes we ourselves are obliged to infallibility, because there are also errors to which no one has the right. At least the poets still remember this, as Ryszard Krynicki's poem "The Previous Night" shows well:

Last night
I dreamed of a sign in a foreign language

being human

you have the right to err...
but you only have the right to human error,
you only have the right to an error
that you can fix

But you do not have the right to an unfixable error
an error that kills.

If we treat faith in accordance with its nature or, in other words, if we do not play with faith, it pertains to the truth that leads to eternal life. To believe in accordance with what our Lord Jesus Christ has taught us is of supreme importance. In short, in faith we are all obliged to infallibility. If we teach faith to our children, we are not allowed to confuse their little brains and instruct them as things seem to us. In both what we believe and what we teach about the faith we are all obliged to infallibility.

The Charism of the Infallibility of the Bishop of Rome

We can sometimes hear heresies from the pulpit. But it is wrong for a priest to teach something which is inconsistent with the faith. In such situations, we can appreciate how great the charism of the infallibility of the bishop of Rome as the teacher of faith of the entire Church is to all of us believers. The Bishop of Rome and successor to Peter is human like all of us; he is sinful and fallible. When, however, he preaches the faith as the teacher of the universal Church (in other words, when he teaches *ex cathedra*), to recall the dogmatic expression of the First Vatican Council (1870), he "possesses [...] that infallibility which the divine Redeemer willed his Church to enjoy in defining doctrine concerning faith or morals."[221]

221. "Session 4: 18 July 1870—First Dogmatic Constitution on the Church of Christ," [in:] *First Vatican Council*, EWTN, https://www.ewtn.com/catholicism/library/first-vatican-council-1505 (accessed June 20, 2022).

However, we should never forget that papal infallibility is a gift granted to us all; it is like a lighthouse to which we should direct ourselves to avoid getting lost in the faith. Let us notice, however, that one cannot be separated from the other: the first among the bishops, St. Peter, is only a particular servant of the Church's infallible faith. To understand the essence of papal infallibility, we must first greatly value the fact that it is the will of God for the Church to be infallible in the faith at all. When we teach our children about Christ the Savior and His Immaculate Mother, we should not waver in our conviction — if we do this in the faith of the Church — that we are teaching them salvific truths.

This is what the last council says of the infallible faith of the Church: "The entire body of the faithful, anointed as they are by the Holy One, cannot err in matters of belief. They manifest this special property by means of the whole peoples' supernatural discernment in matters of faith when 'from the Bishops down to the last of the lay faithful' they show universal agreement in matters of faith and morals" (*Lumen gentium*, 12).

The infallibility of God's people thus comes from the fact that the Holy Spirit Himself revives the Church community. The Church cannot lose her infallible faith because she will not lose the Holy Spirit: the gates of hell can never prevail against Christ's Church. At the same time, however, the presence of the Holy Spirit in the Church is obscured by our sins. Thus, the unity of the Church, including the unity of our infallible faith, is obscured by our sins. Nevertheless, our sins are incapable of destroying the unity of the Church or depriving her of her characteristic presence. Despite our sins, the unity of the Church is a fact and a fact that is to a large extent visible.

The Bishop of Rome, successor of Peter, is a unique sign and visible knot of the Church's unity. All the bishops along with their flock gather around him, and we all profess the same faith as he. Christ Himself is concerned that Peter's faith is genuine. He prays with Peter "that your own faith may not fail; and once you have turned back, you must strengthen your brothers" (Luke 22:32).

It is by Christ's will that Peter is the first teacher of the infallible faith in the Church. He was given the keys to the Kingdom; Christ Himself implored Him to bolster his brothers in the faith. Thus, Peter was granted the gift of infallibility in teaching the faith because of us all: unity with Peter's faith is a sign of the infallibility of each of us; it is testimony that we do not commit an error in perfectly understanding the Word of God.

Man's infallible faith does not come from himself. This is God's gift, a fruit of the activity of the Holy Spirit in the sinful man. If someone is scandalized by the infallibility granted to Peter (and the infallibility of each of us as long as we profess one Catholic faith in unity with Peter), let him try to notice the root of the dogma of papal infallibility. The root of this dogma is our faith that the Only Begotten Son of God became a Man for our sake and infallibly taught us the paths to salvation, and that it was His will for the infallible paths to salvation to be always known in the Church, despite the contradictory opinions influenced by His Gospel in subsequent generations.

I will conclude this chapter by noticing that in the encyclical *Ut unum sint* (94) instead of the cautious metaphor of the lighthouse we have the dynamic and more Biblical metaphor of a sentinel whose task is particular concern for the unity of the Church in faith: "The mission of the Bishop of Rome within the College of all the Pastors consists precisely in 'keeping watch' (*episkopein*), like a sentinel, so that, through the efforts of the Pastors, the true voice of Christ the Shepherd may be heard in all the particular Churches. In this way, in each of the Churches entrusted to those Pastors, the *una, sancta, catholica et apostolica Ecclesia* is made present."

THE PRIESTLY PEOPLE

The Undeserved Gift of Membership in the Church

The entire following reflection can be reduced to distinguishing between four elements that make up the truth that as the Church we are the Priestly People. God's Word, which clearly speaks of the priesthood of all the baptized, forces us to undertake this topic: "But you are 'a chosen race, a royal priesthood, a holy nation, a people of his own, so that you may announce the praises' of Him Who called you out of darkness into His wonderful light" (1 Peter 2:9; see Revelation 1:5-6; 5:10; 20:6).

We become the priestly people through God's love, which is completely undeserved — and, one is tempted to say, completely unwarranted. In the Old Testament, God frequently confessed to His people that they are His *segullah*: particularly valuable, precious property. "For you are a people holy to the Lord, your God; the Lord, your God, has chosen you from all the peoples on the face of the earth to be a people specially His own" (Deuteronomy 14:2; see Exodus 19:5; Deuteronomy 7:6; 26:28). As we can see, Israel's position among the remaining nations is presented here as akin to the mission that Levi's generation had with respect to the remaining twelve generations (Numbers 3:12; 8:16-19).

We Christians believe that the people of the Old Testament were "priceless property" to God because of Christ Who was born of precisely that people. In any case, the very concept of "priceless property" becomes full comprehensible only considering the Gospel. Namely, it turns out that we are so valuable to God that we "were ransomed from [our] futile conduct, handed on by [our] ancestors, not with perishable things like silver or gold but with the precious blood of Christ as of a spotless unblemished Lamb" (1 Peter 1:18-19). "[W]e await the blessed hope, the appearance of the glory of the great God and of our Savior Jesus Christ, Who gave Himself for us to deliver us from all lawlessness and to cleanse for himself a people as His own, eager to do what is good" (Titus 2:13-14).

Thus, the first priestly trait of God's people is that God has chosen us among all the peoples and nations because we are particularly dear to Him. It is sung to Christ in Revelation: "[F]or You were slain and with Your blood You purchased for God those from every tribe and tongue, people and nation" (5:9).

Let us notice a very crucial understatement: We are particularly dear to God and are chosen among all the nations, but this by no means implies that those who do not belong to the people of God are less dear to Him. Also, it cannot be said with complete certainty that they are just as dear to Him. We simply do not have to know this. It suffices that we try to praise God in the name of all the nations and at the same time invite all to join God's people. We are not allowed to forget that Christ the Lord died for all people.

Although we do not know if those who do not belong to the people of God are equally dear, we do know that our belonging to this people is a unique and undeserved privilege. The people of the Old Testament realized this: "It was not because you are more numerous than all the peoples that the Lord set his heart on you and chose you; for you are really the smallest of all peoples. It was because the Lord loved you" (Deuteronomy 7:7-8). This is emphasized even more by the Apostle Paul with respect to the Church: "Consider your own calling, brothers. Not many of you were wise by human standards, not many were powerful, not many were of noble birth. Rather, God chose the foolish of the world to shame the wise, and God chose the weak of the world to shame the strong, and God chose the lowly and despised of the world, those who count for nothing, to reduce to nothing those who are something, so that no human being might boast before God" (1 Corinthians 1:26-29).

Through Christ, God has proved to us that our value to Him is not only precious but also infinite; in any case, it is priceless. After all, He ransomed us with His own blood: we are "the Church of God that He acquired with His own blood" (Acts 20:28). Christ the Lord introduced another groundbreaking change from the perspective of the Old Testament ideal of *segullah:* not only God's people but also every individual member of this people is of precious value to God. It suffices to recall the parable of the lost sheep or that of the prodigal son.

The Most Unique Access to God

Let us look at the second priestly trait of us all: through baptism, we have received the most unique access to God. In the times before Christ, no one had such intimate access to God as the People of the Old Covenant. The Epistle to the Hebrews presents the difference between the situation of this people with respect to God and our spiritual situation. The author of the epistle notes the almost complete inaccessibility of the Holy of Holies in the Jerusalem Temple: only the archpriest could enter it, and only once a year.

Meanwhile, the Archpriest of the Church, Jesus Christ, entered heaven to constantly intercede for us (9:6-26). At the same time, this Archpriest is Emmanuel, God with us; He is with us every day until the end of the world. Furthermore, He assimilates us in His Body, making us one with Him. Thus, God's intimacy which has become accessible to us in Him is, in fact, unimaginable.

In order to compare the access to God we have received in Christ to that in which the people of the Old Covenant shared, the author of the Epistle to the Hebrews recalls the flight impulse that overwhelmed the people of Israel at the foot of Mount Sinai: "So they took up a position farther away and said to Moses, 'You speak to us, and we will listen; but do not let God speak to us, or we shall die'" (Exodus 20:18-19; see: Hebrews 12:19). Meanwhile, thanks to Christ we can with full confidence and without fear come to "Mount Zion and the city of the living God [...] and God the judge of all" (Hebrews 12:22-24).

At this point, someone might feel tempted by lamentable simplification and attempt to present the greatness of the Christian vocation to closeness with God by downplaying that intimacy with God that was accessible in the Old Testament. Meanwhile, we should proceed in the opposite direction. We should maximally extract the intimacy with God to which the people of the Old Covenant were called and only in considering this show the unimaginable breakthrough caused by Jesus Christ.

The Psalms attest to the great intimacy that God made accessible to people in the Old Testament. No work has yet appeared throughout the history of world literature which would equal the Psalms in terms of the power of heir religious zeal. Let us ponder, for example, the depths of a man who wrote these simple words: "As for me, to be near God is my good, to make the Lord God my refuge" (Psalm 73:28).

It is true that on the pages of the Old Testament God frequently laments the lack of adequate response to His love, but these complaints have not become irrelevant with respect to us who profess Christ: "Since this people draws near with words only and honors me with their lips alone, though their hearts are far from me [...]. I have stretched out my hands all day to a rebellious people, who walk in a way that is not good, following their own designs" (Isaiah 29:13; 65:2).

One likewise cannot doubt that already in the time of the Old Testament God sought such a level of intimacy in His relationship with people that can only be compared to the love that binds together loving spouses or the mutual devotion that exists between parents and a small child. "The Lord calls you back, like a wife forsaken and grieved in spirit, a wife married in youth and then cast off, says your God: For a brief moment I abandoned you, but with great tenderness I will take you back" (Isaiah 54:6-7). "I fostered them like those who raise an infant to their cheeks; I bent down to feed them" (Hosea 11:4).

Only once we realize that humanity's intimacy with God achieved the greatest imaginable zenith in the Old Testament is it possible to somewhat sense the essence of the breakthrough that took place in our relationship with God through Jesus Christ. Namely, thanks to Christ we have been baptized or immersed in the Father, Son, and Holy Spirit. In this way, we are no longer someone from the outside with respect to God. We have begun to be participants in God's nature (2 Peter 14), members of the Body of Christ (Romans 12:4-8; 1 Corinthians 12:31) and have received the Holy Spirit and are transformed into His Temple (1 Corinthians 3:16).

There is no greater honor in this world than to be baptized. To be baptized means to carry within oneself the seed of deification; it means to be called to such intimacy with God as transcends all our feelings and conceptions. Likewise, a priest, bishop, or pope does not receive a greater distinction than the one he received during his baptism. To put it in simple terms, a man cannot receive a greater distinction than the gift of deification. One can wonder if anywhere in the world there is another society where the principle of equalizing upwards is implemented so consistently.

On the other hand, it suffices to probe only a little the mystery of the dignity of a baptized person to see how absurd and decadent it is to be a Christian separated from God. We must treat the state of sanctifying grace like the normal situation of a baptized person.

We are the priestly people because through Christ God calls us to the most unique intimacy with ourselves. Considering this, who are priests and bishops in the Church? What is the sacrament of holy orders? They are servants of God who are called to uniquely serve the Church in her constant growing closer to God. They are the successors to the apostles and their helpers through whose service Christ the Lord truly grants us His salvific power and presence.

St. Caesarius of Arles very accurately explained the meaning of his leadership position in the Church which, after all, does not elevate a bishop above others who have been baptized: "For I am your bishop; I am also a Christian along with you. The former is a name for an accepted office, the latter is the name for a grace received [...] Therefore if it affords me greater pleasure that I was bought along with you than that I have been placed over you, then, as the Lord commanded, I will more abundantly be your servant. Thus I will not be ungrateful for the price [of Christ's blood] whereby I merited to be your fellow servant."[222] (Sermon 232).

At the same time, Caesarius knew that his sacramental ministry and preaching the Word of God would be in vain if Christ Who alone has the power to permeate man's soul and give him life were not present in his pastoral activities: thus, "exteriorly receive the planter and waterer, but interiorly accept the giver of increase. "[223].

The Meaning of Sunday Mass

That is why we must frequently listed to the Word of God and receive the sacraments, for we are people and not angels, and our growing closer to God takes place gradually and is a process. Thus, from the very beginning the Church has placed great importance on prayer

222. Sermon 232, *Saint Caesarius of Arles Sermons,* Vol. III (187-238), trans. Sister Mary Magdeleiene Mueller, OSF [in:] *The Fathers of the Church. A New Translation,* Vol. 66 (Washington, DC: The Catholic University of America Press, 2004), p. 190.

223. *Ibid.*, p. 191.

meetings, especially on gathering at the Eucharist. This was written of the first Christian community that was formed on the day of Pentecost: "They devoted themselves to the teaching of the apostles and to the communal life, to the breaking of the bread and to the prayers." (Acts 2:42). Meanwhile, the Epistle to the Hebrews demands: "We should not stay away from our assembly, as is the custom of some, but encourage one another, and this all the more as you see the day drawing near" (10:25).

It is interesting to look at other arguments that the ancient Christians used to encourage regular attendance of Sunday Mass. These arguments are exceptionally powerful. If someone hears in faith one such argument, he will probably be incapable of willingly abandoning Sunday Mass. Here, for example, is persuasion from the time when the last of the apostles were still alive: "But often shall you come together, seeking the things which are befitting to your souls: for the whole time of your faith will not profit you, if you be not made perfect in the last time."[224] In short, what does it matter that a tree grew beautifully if it has withered before bearing fruit?

Twenty years later, around 108, St. Ignatius of Antioch provided the following arguments: "Let no man deceive himself: if anyone be not within the altar, he is deprived of the bread of God. For if the prayer of one or two possesses (Matthew 18:19) such power, how much more that of the bishop and the whole Church! He, therefore, that does not assemble with the Church, has even by this manifested his pride, and condemned himself. For it is written, 'God resists the proud.'"[225]

224. *Didache*, trans. M.B. Riddle, [in:] *Ante-Nicene Fathers*, Vol. 7, eds. Alexander Roberts, James Donaldson, and A. Cleveland Coxe (Buffalo, NY: Christian Literature Publishing Co., 1886), https://www.newadvent.org/fathers/0714.htm (accessed June 21, 2022).

225. St. Ignatius of Antioch, *The Epistle of Ignatius to the Ephesians*, trans. Alexander Roberts and James Donaldson, [in:] *Ante-Nicene Fathers*, Vol. 1, eds. Alexander Roberts,

Such was the argumentation of St. Ignatius in the fifth chapter of his *Epistle to the Ephesians*. In the thirteenth chapter, he adds another argument: "Take heed, then, often to come together to give thanks to God, and show forth His praise. For when you assemble frequently in the same place, the powers of Satan are destroyed, and the destruction at which he aims is prevented by the unity of your faith."[226]

Thanks to the Eucharist, not only do you and I grow closer to God (or implement more fully the very essence of the priesthood to which we have been called through baptism) but, furthermore, we all as the Church become increasingly united with Christ. This happens to the extent that we already are the only Body of Christ that is nourished by the same Food, "the living Bread that came down from heaven" (John 6:51). It is not the case that you eat one piece of this Bread while I eat another; you, I, and everyone consumes the same Body of our Lord. "Because the loaf of bread is one, we, though many, are one body, for we all partake of the one loaf" (1 Corinthians 10:17).

Thus, it is unsurprising that the ancient Church possessed the following rationale for participation in the Eucharist every Sunday: We are not permitted to skip the Sunday liturgy because this was the equivalent of us wanting to abandon the Church and not caring about being included in the Body of Christ. The *Didascalia*, a document from the third century (PG 1,1021), admonishes a bishop: "Now when thou teachest, command and warn the people to be constant in assembling in the Church, and not to withdraw themselves but always to assemble, lest any man diminish the Church by not assembling, and cause the body of Christ to be short of a member."[227]

James Donaldson, and A. Cleveland Coxe (Buffalo, NY: Christian Literature Publishing Co., 1885), https://www.newadvent.org/fathers/0104.htm (accessed June 21, 2022).

226. *Ibid.*

227. *Didascalia Apostolorum*, Chap. XIII, II.59, ed. and trans. R. Hugh Connolly (Oxford: Clarendon Press, 1929).

Sacrifice Is Fidelity to Love Even When Things Are Difficult

The third priestly trait of God's people is the ability to make sacrifices that are pleasing to God. If someone asked about our first associations with the word "sacrifice," perhaps it would turn out that a sacrifice is above all something unpleasant to us, something we want to avoid. Such associations reveal the same kind of spiritual confusion we encounter when someone associates sexuality primarily with pleasure.

Indeed, the concept of sacrifice contains a moment of overcoming oneself and bearing difficulties. However, the essential message of the very notion of sacrifice is very joyful. It turns out that we can overcome egotism and the power of disorder that act within us and around us because of our sinfulness and that of others. To be able to rejoice in this, one must first realize that man is capable of defying only such an onslaught of evil that does not transcend his power; we can avoid submitting to any onslaught of evil only through the power of Christ.

In short, our ability to make sacrifices pleasing to God is a major opportunity created for us by Christ the Lord: despite numerous obstacles and much darkness, love can emerge victorious in every situation in our lives! Through this perspective, let us consider the burdens, including potential martyrdom, that are related to sacrifice. The difficulties and tribulations that are meaningful and are a sign of hope cannot be compared with those cursed vexations that attest only to the hopelessness and meaninglessness of our lives separated from God. On the other hand, we realize that if evil had not taken root in ourselves and in our world, complete fidelity to the law of love would be something obvious and solely joyful to us; it would not demand that we overcome any obstacles.

Considering the above, we are allowed to say that sacrifice is fidelity to the law of love in our situation as sinners.

Let us now look at the sacrifice of Christ the Lord, for He is the only descendant of Adam who walked the earth with absolute fidelity to the law of love (His Immaculate Mother could so that through the power of His grace and because of His merits). Becoming a man, the Son of God entered our entanglement with sin, although He remained sinless. It turned out that on this earth, inhabited by sinners and flooded by a sea of inhuman structures, even for Him — the Son of God and a fully authentic, sinless Man — it was not easy to persist in complete personal love for the Eternal Father and us people. He suffered the most during those terrible hours of His Passion when the forces of evil furiously attacked Him. But even then, He completely belonged to His Eternal Father and was overflowing with love for all people.

He is the Son of God; thus, His sacrifice can make all of us who want to be His brothers capable of surrendering ourselves to the Eternal Father. Because we are sinful and live among sinners, fidelity to this attitude frequently demands that we transcend ourselves. But we are capable of such an attitude! It is something exceptionally joyful that I, a sinner, am capable of truly loving God and bringing to life the law of love. I am not capable of this on my own; Jesus Christ gives me this capability. He also makes me capable of making sacrifices of myself, sacrifices demanded by fidelity to God in my situation as a sinner living among sinners.

We can frequently read of this in the New Testament. "Whoever wishes to come after Me must deny himself, take up his cross, and follow Me" (Matthew 16:24). Meanwhile, the Apostle Paul writes: "Consequently, you too must think of yourselves as [being] dead to sin and living for God in Christ Jesus. Therefore, sin must not reign over your mortal bodies so that you obey their desires. [...] I urge you therefore, brothers, by the mercies of God, to offer your bodies as a living sacrifice, holy and pleasing to God, your spiritual worship" (Romans 6:11-12; 12:1; see Ephesians 5:2).

The Apostle Paul also indicates that what he preaches to others pertains to himself as well: "No, I drive my body and train it, for fear that, after having preached to others, I myself should be disqualified" (1 Corinthians 9:27).

The entire Church is comprised of priestly people. Thus, Christ has made all of us — also as a community — capable of making sacrifices that fidelity to the law of love demands on this earth. As has been expressed by the Apostle Peter, God builds us into one Church "to be a holy priesthood to offer spiritual sacrifices acceptable to God through Jesus Christ" (1 Peter 2:5).

Unfortunately, I, a baptized person, can treat my ability to make a sacrifice of myself not as a wonderful privilege but as a burden from which I must escape. In this way, I not only personally choose this earth as the place of my ultimate fulfillment and cease to care about eternal life, but I deprive the entire Church of the fragment of priesthood that she deserves of me. Because of such Christians, "the name of God is reviled among the Gentiles" (Romans 2:24).

Our priestly ability to sacrifice ourselves to God grows stronger and deeper thanks to participation in the Mass. After all, this is why Christ the Lord manifests on the altar the Holiest Sacrifice He made on the Cross, that we may join Him and become one with Him in His complete surrender to the Eternal Father. Without a doubt, the Eucharistic sacrifice and feast are at the center of the Church: in it, Christ the Lord gives Himself to us completely, while we try to grow increasingly close to Him. For it is only in eternal life that we will participate in truly complete unification with Him and submit ourselves entirely to the Eternal Father.

Let Us Want to Be Witnesses of Jesus

The Apostle Peter says that we are "a chosen race [...] so that [we] may announce the praises' of Him Who called [us] out of darkness into His wonderful light" (1 Peter 2:9). In other words, the priestly people are a people of witnesses and apostles; we are to "shine like lights in the world" (Philippians 2:15).

Both these apostolic statements (much like the wonderful passage in Ephesians 5:8-13) resound with echoes of Jesus' words from the Sermon on the Mount: "You are the salt of the earth. [...] You are the light of the world" (Matthew 5:13-14). Christians have frequently faced accusations because of these words: indeed, they can easily cause us to elevate ourselves above others or falsely bolster our self-confidence.

If there is some truth in these accusations, then it is our fault. Unfortunately, we are such that we can use even that which comes from God to "spend it on [our] passions" (James 4:3). However, the words about the salt of the earth and the light of the world are pure and truthful. Notice that the Lord Jesus said them immediately after the Beatitudes. Thus, it is not the case that our mere material membership in the Church makes us the salt of the earth and the light of the world. If as Christians we are no different from those whom the Lord Jesus calls "the sons of the world," the latter will mock us because of the Lord's name. We can truly preach God's goodness and be the salt of the earth and light of the world only to the extent that we are immersed in the spirit of the Beatitudes.

In any case, in this very sermon the Lord Jesus gives us an important warning: we are not allowed to do any good only so that people may see and praise us. The Lord Jesus said this admonition in three subsequent topics, which attests to how great importance He placed on it (Matthew 6:1-18). He expects of us that we will be living testimony to His grace and God's benevolence with respect to man both for non-believers and for ourselves. He is the sole Truth; thus, we greatly offend Him if instead of bearing witness to Him we try to deceive others with fantasies that eerily resemble it.

Notice how pointedly the Lord Jesus contrasts witness with false witness. "[Y]our light must shine before others, that they may see your good deeds and glorify your heavenly Father" (Matthew 5:16). These words concern authentic witnesses. Meanwhile, this is what phony testimony is: "[But] take care not to perform righteous deeds in order that people may see them; otherwise, you will have no recompense from your heavenly Father." That is what the hypocrites do "to win the praise of others" (Matthew 6:1-2).

The difference between an egocentric witness and an authentic one is very evident. An authentic witness wants to be transparent. He is above all motivated by the desire for other people to recognize God as the Source and first Cause of all that is good.

The contrast between both witnesses is even greater once we realize that God is praised in a completely different way than man is. Man is praised above all with words; praise of man expresses approval of his conduct or achievements, usually making him feel satisfied and encouraging him to continue his efforts. Meanwhile, words are the last thing in praising God. We praise God above all by being open to His grace and fulfilling His holy will, while words of praise are authentic only when they are the culmination of such an attitude.

The priestly nature of God's people is, therefore, revealed in their spiritual fertility. If we ourselves truly strive for eternal life, we will be for others — in a way that is pleasing to God — living encouragement to want to join us. Karol Ludwik Koniński wrote: "Do not argue against atheism; do not denigrate atheism. Do not exalt yourselves and advertise your own stand. Instead, be nourished by fruits yourselves and give them away for free; if they are sweet and juicy, healthy and refreshing, others will go to your orchard, pick these fruits, and receive nourishment."[228]

There can be no doubts with respect to this. The more spiritual and faithful to God's grace our Church is, the more visible she will be, thus attracting others. On the other hand, we will not be hindered by asking in our examinations of conscience — both individual and social ones — the question of why we forget to share our faith with others or are incapable of doing so.

228. K.L. Koniński, *Wojna. Notatki z dnia na dzień (fragmenty)*, ed. B. Mamoń, *Znak* 1966, No. 9, [95].

FAITH COMES BEFORE THE SACRAMENTS

Can one be a Christian without making a conscious decision? This question is also an argument against baptizing small children. Before I respond to it, let me ask:

Why Do We Baptize Infants?

In short, I would reply with: Because we truly believe in the Lord Jesus! We believe that He truly comes to us in the sacraments and grants us His love, making us capable of following Him as our Shepherd. After all, He came to us and died on the cross for us to, as we sing in a Polish Christmas carol, save the human race.

The Lord Jesus Himself admonishes us to not push our infants away from Him. "Let the children come to Me; do not prevent them, for the kingdom of God belongs to such as these" (Mark 10:14): with these words, Jesus stunned His disciples who had believed that children do not need His blessing. Thus, we baptize infants because we want them to be close to the Lord Jesus beginning with their early childhood and we want them to be brought up in the atmosphere of His grace and love for Him.

Only people can be granted the sacraments. From the very first days of his life, an infant is a person, not merely a candidate to be a person. Therefore, in the Church we do not have any doubts that an infant, just like any other person, is particularly loved by God and the ultimate aim of his life is eternal happiness. True, a very small child does not understand the enormity of the gift he receives during baptism. But such is the nature of the love of God, Who is so concerned about man that He comes accordingly to our present situation.

When I was an infant, God's love overwhelmed me as a person who did not yet know how to use the gift of reason through the sacrament of baptism. With respect to adults, God's love comes to those who can listen to the Word of God "with a generous and good heart, and bear fruit through perseverance" (Luke 8:15). If, then, in His holy Providence God wills that I suffer from dementia in old age, I will not lose the ability to receive the sacraments for I will not lose my humanity just because of my loss of the use of reason. To repeat: God's love seeks out man accordingly to his present situation.

This leads to the following problem: Faith comes before the sacraments, and the sacraments cannot be administered where there is no faith. Thus, we are allowed to baptize small children only when they live among believers and there is hope that they will be brought up in the atmosphere of that faith in which baptism is administered. In the time of the apostles, it was frequently the case that entire families became open to the gift of faith. In those days, a believer in Christ asked to be baptized and received baptism with "all his family" (Acts 16:33; see 11:14; 16:15; 18:8; 1 Corinthians 1:16).

In the first centuries of the Church, baptizing infants was a widespread custom. A decree of the Synod of Carthage from 252 adopted by a gathering of sixty-six bishops has survived. The bishops categorically prohibit postponing the baptism of a child until the eighth day after his birth, for a child should be baptized on the second or third day. Origen, who lived in the first half of the third century, did not doubt that the Church has been instructed by the apostles to baptize small children (*Commentary on the Epistle to the Romans*, 5:9). This could attest to the fact that this was an existing and unquestioned custom. From the very beginning, Christians sensed that they were allowed to — and should — give their children to Christ if they live and grow up in the atmosphere of the Christian faith.

When Baptizing a Child Ceases to Be Something Obvious

What to do when parents who do not believe or who barely believe ask to baptize their child? Can their child be baptized then? Or perhaps such a child should actually be baptized?

As a shepherd, I try to respond to such questions together with the parents who ask for their child to be baptized. If I succeed in starting up a genial conversation, it usually is not difficult for me to explain that administering the sacraments is not a "service for humanity" and that a priest is not permitted to baptize a child if he will be raised by non-believers.

The argument that is then frequently presented ("We will baptize our child now, but he will decide for himself when he grows up") is, from the perspective of a non-believer, logical and understandable, but from the perspective of faith it is unacceptable, as in it faith becomes degraded to the level of a worldview. A worldview can be accepted or rejected. Meanwhile, faith is something more than a worldview; it is entering into a relationship with Christ, Who lives, loves, and saves us.

I know from experience that since supposedly unbelieving parents are asking for their child to be baptized, this means they are not complete non-believers. If I succeed in explaining to them that the baptism of a child requires that he is brought up in an atmosphere of faith rather than merely sending him to religious education classes at the appropriate time, I can usually also convince them to try to ask the great questions and grow closer to Christ once more. At the same time, I try to explain that if I were to baptize their child, but they did not embark on their own path to faith, a dozen or so years later I can expect to hear grievances that I have made someone a Christian without his conscious decision.

The situation of a child who is brought up in an atmosphere of solid faith is completely different. He constantly has the opportunity, relative to his intellectual and emotional development, to confirm, deepen, and love the faith to which he has been called through baptism.

FREQUENTLY BUT WITH DIGNITY

For centuries, the Church has passed on to her faithful two seemingly contradictory summons. On the one hand, we are constantly reminded anew that Christ's words "Take and eat of it; this is My Body" are not only the incantation during consecration but also a challenge addressed to each of us to not avoid Holy Communion. On the other hand, in the Church we try to remember the admonition of the Apostle Paul that "whoever eats the bread or drinks the cup of the Lord unworthily will have to answer for the body and blood of the Lord" (1 Corinthians 11:27).

This admonition should purify our challenge, which in turn should establish the boundaries of the admonition. Unfortunately, today we most frequently hear only the former of these two words; we nearly forget the latter word. Throughout the centuries, we could hear in both the Eastern and Western Churches above all the admonition to not desecrate Holy Communion by receiving it too casually. As a result of fear of not worthily receiving the Blessed Sacrament, frequent reception of Holy Communion was discouraged in practically all of Christianity. Christians seem to have forgotten that genuine religious fear does not paralyze; instead, it encourages positive activity.

The Eucharistic reform undertaken by St. Pius X more than a century ago restored the practice of the frequent reception of Holy

Communion in the Catholic Church. The good fruits of this reform seem indisputable. Unfortunately, however, such is our defective world that some shadow is usually cast on everything that is good. Presently, many among us frequently receive Holy Communion, but unfortunately it happens all too often that as we receive it, we are merely going through the motions, without the proper disposition and perhaps in a state of sin. Our openness to the gift of the Eucharist needs healing, but in such a way that will save the custom of frequent Communion, only purifying it of regrettable abuses.

A Couple of Words on Frequent and Holy Communion

The Church has always spoken of the value of frequent Holy Communion. As an example, I will cite a great teacher of the Greek Church, St. Basil, who wrote in 372: "It is good and beneficial to communicate every day, and to partake of the holy body and blood of Christ. For He distinctly says, 'He that eats My flesh and drinks My blood has eternal life' (John 6:54)."[229]

The great teachers of the Latin Church also encouraged frequent Communion. In the early fifth century, St. Augustine approvingly wrote of the following opinion: "If, however, his sins are not so great as to bring him justly under sentence of excommunication, he ought not to withdraw himself from the daily use of the Lord's body for the healing of his soul."[230]

Despite this, however, the average believer did not rush to receive Holy Communion. Consequently, in 1215 the Fourth Lateran

229. St. Basil, *Letter 93*, trans. Blomfield Jackson, [in:] *Nicene and Post-Nicene Fathers, Second Series*, Vol. 8, eds. Philip Schaff and Henry Wace (Buffalo, NY: Christian Literature Publishing Co., 1895), https://www.newadvent.org/fathers/3202093.htm (accessed June 22, 2022).

230. St. Augustine, *Letter 54*, trans. J.G. Cunningham, [in:] *Nicene and Post-Nicene Fathers*, First Series, Vol. 1, ed. Philip Schaff (Buffalo, NY: Christian Literature Publishing Co., 1887), https://www.newadvent.org/fathers/1102054.htm (accessed June 22, 2022).

Council had to institute the obligation to confess and receive Holy Communion at least once a year. Frequent Communion was not restored by the Council of Trent, even though the conciliar document dated September 17, 1562, unambiguously supports it: "The sacred and holy Synod would fain indeed that, at each mass, the faithful who are present should communicate, not only in spiritual desire, but also by the sacramental participation of the Eucharist, that thereby a more abundant fruit might be derived to them from this most holy sacrifice."[231] How can we account for the fact that St. Pius X's initiative *Sacra Tridentina Synodus*, undertaken in 1902 to restore frequent Holy Communion in the Church, proved to be so effective? In fact, it is so effective that today there is no real need to encourage the faithful to frequently receive Communion. Instead, they should be reminded that if they were to receive it haphazardly or even unworthily, it is better that they do not receive the Sacrament at all.

First, the dominant argument which was used to encourage frequent Communion seems particularly apt. We read in the above-mentioned decree: "[Communion's] primary purpose is not [...] that it may serve as a reward or recompense of virtue bestowed on the recipients. [...] the Holy Council calls the Eucharist 'the antidote whereby we may be freed from daily faults and be preserved from mortal sin.'" People were encouraged to express their veneration for the Eucharist in a new, more appropriate way. The recipient of the words is treated as a deeply religious person, although the argument was addressed to all Catholics. It turned out that persuasion expressed with respect as well as a positive evaluation (even if exaggerated) of those to whom it is directed leads to an almost spontaneous favorable response.

Furthermore, the fact that growing numbers of Catholics have begun to practice the frequent reception of Communion is strongly influenced by the Holy See's official support for the veneration of the

231. *Doctrine on the Sacrifice of the Mass*, Chap. VI, https://www.papalencyclicals.net/councils/trent/twenty-second-session.htm (accessed January 16, 2023).

Most Sacred Heart of Jesus and the related "institution" of the first nine Fridays. Also significant were the great efforts to shape a more intimate attitude to the Eucharist that the Church had to undertake for years in relation to the significant lowering of the age at which children receive their first Holy Communion.

The truth is that throughout the twentieth century — for the first time in 1,500 years — frequent Holy Communion has become second nature to millions of Catholics. We should thank God for this. We must not lose this custom, but at the same time we should not trivialize it by receiving Holy Communion only out of habit while forgetting that Christ the Lord completely gives Himself to us and expects our reciprocity.

When Are We Not Allowed to Receive Holy Communion?

Heartily supporting frequent Holy Communion, the Church has never denied that there are situations when one cannot receive it. The *Catechism of the Catholic Church* (1385) reminds us: "Anyone conscious of a grave sin must receive the sacrament of Reconciliation before coming to Communion." John Paul II elaborates on this topic in the fourth chapter of his encyclical on the Eucharist.

In 2005, the synod of bishops discussed the problem of the unworthy reception of Communion. "Some receive Communion while denying the teachings of the Church or publicly supporting immoral choices in life, such as abortion, without thinking that they are committing an act of grave personal dishonesty and causing scandal. Some Catholics do not understand why it might be a sin to support a political candidate who is openly in favor of abortion or other serious acts against life, justice, and peace" (*Instrumentum laboris*, 73).

In the apostolic adhortation *Sacramentum caritatis* (55), which is something like a summary of that synod, Benedict XVI makes note of another unsettling phenomenon: "Active participation in the Eucharistic liturgy can hardly be expected if one approaches it superficially, without an examination of his or her life." The Holy Father cautions against the attitude of the faithful "that the mere fact of their being present in church during the liturgy gives them a right or even an obligation to approach the table of the Eucharist."

I will refrain from recalling the ancient Church's chilling cautions against unworthy or even sacrilegious Communion. To a certain extent, they led many Christians to abandon regular reception of Holy Communion. However, such notes of warning must be remembered in the hope that we do not abandon regular Communion but receive it worthily so that the Eucharist may deepen our relationship with Jesus.

In the first half of the third century, Origen admonished his audience and his readers: "Let no one go in to this dinner with dirty garments [...] For your garments were washed once when you came to the grace of baptism; you were purified in body; you were cleansed from all filth of flesh and spirit. 'What,' then, 'God has cleansed, you shall not make unclean.'"[232]

"A large punishment awaits those who receive Communion unworthily," St. John Chrysostom cautioned in the late fourth century. "Wherefore it is needful in all respects to be vigilant, for indeed no small punishment is appointed to them that partake unworthily. [...] That which when angels behold, they tremble, and dare not so much as look up at it without awe on account of the brightness that comes thence, with this we are fed, with this we are commingled, and we are made one body and one flesh with Christ."[233]

I will cite one more reference, one that comes from a contemporary of St Augustine, John Cassian. Although written 1,600 years ago,

232. *Homilies on Genesis*, 11:7, [in:] *Homilies on Genesis and Exodus*, trans. Ronald E. Heine (Washington, DC: CUA Press, 2010), p. 365.

233. St. John Chrysostom, *Homily 82 on Matthew*, trans. George Prevost and revised by M.B. Riddle, [in:] *Nicene and Post-Nicene Fathers*, First Series, Vol. 10, ed. Philip Schaff (Buffalo, NY: Christian Literature Publishing Co., 1888), https://www.newadvent.org/fathers/200182.htm (accessed June 24, 2022).

his words continue to resonate with us today: "For many who receive it unlawfully and abusively are weakened in faith and grow sick in mind by catching the diseases of the passions, and they fall asleep in the sleep of sinfulness, never rising from this mortal slumber through a concern for their salvation."[234]

I will also reference an exceptionally harsh admonition from Isidore of Pelusium to a certain Chairemon in the late fourth or early fifth century. We do not know who Chairemon was, nor do we know what specific sins he committed; however, these sins must have been very grave. "It is said," Isidore writes angrily, "that you do everything prohibited and unlawful and yet you are content to stretch forth hands for the Divine mysteries and dare partake of that which is forbidden to you. Such utter shamelessness strikes me with amazement, that taking your fill at the table of demons, you also do not fear to partake of the table of the Lord." (*Book 1, Letter* 170).

When You Are Not Permitted to Receive Sacramental Communion, Receive It Through Desire

The Church sincerely encourages her sons and daughters to supplement their participation in the sacrifice of the Mass with Holy Communion. However, participation in the Mass is meaningful even when we do not receive Communion. This was beautifully described by St. Augustine in the letter we have already cited: "There was no controversy between those two mentioned in the Gospel, Zacchæus and the Centurion; nor did either of them think himself better than the other, though, whereas the former received the Lord joyfully into his house (Luke 19:6), the latter said, I am not worthy that You should come under my roof (Matthew 8:8), — both honoring the Savior, though in ways diverse and, as it were, mutually opposed; both

234. John Cassian, *The Conferences*, 22.V.3, trans. and ed. Boniface Ramsey (New York: The Newman Press, 1997), p. 767.

miserable through sin, and both obtaining the mercy they required. We may further borrow an illustration here, from the fact that the manna given to the ancient people of God tasted in each man's mouth as he desired that it might. It is the same with this world-subduing sacrament in the heart of each Christian."[235]

It suffices to recall that the laws of the Church oblige us to participate in Mass every Sunday, but it does not demand that we receive Holy Communion every Sunday. In his 1947 encyclical *Mediator Dei*, Pope Pius XII explains that receiving the Blessed Sacrament during Mass "is obligatory for the priest who says the Mass, [but] it is only something earnestly recommended to the faithful" (115).

The Church simply does not feel authorized to permit certain Christians to receive Communion, even if they zealously believe in Christ the Lord. This is the rationale Benedict XVI provided in his request that non-Catholic Christians do not receive Communion while attending Mass in a Catholic church. "The Eucharist in fact not only manifests our personal communion with Jesus Christ, but also implies full *communio* with the Church. This is the reason why, sadly albeit not without hope, we ask Christians who are not Catholic to understand and respect our conviction, which is grounded in the Bible and Tradition. We hold that Eucharistic communion and ecclesial communion are so linked as to make it generally impossible for non-Catholic Christians to receive the former without enjoying the latter" (the apostolic adhortation *Sacramentum caritatis*, 56).

Likewise, Catholics who are in the habit of carelessly receiving Communion even in a state of mortal sin must be asked to stand before Jesus' face full of remorse for their sins and in a desire to receive communion, albeit without receiving it. In this way, we do not encourage them to neglect Holy Communion but rather to receive it authentically and with an ardent heart.

235. St. Augustine, *Letter 94*, *ibid.*

THE WEDDING FEAST OF THE CHURCH

We rarely look at the holy Eucharist from the perspective proposed by an anonymous Carthusian monk.[236] The basic thesis of the book is that the Eucharist is a nuptial gift begging for reciprocity and is constantly granted by Jesus to His Beloved, or the entire Church, and each of us, participants in the Eucharist. After all, the Church loves Jesus in such a way that love for Him flows from our hearts. And before the love of the Church for her Beloved comes His love for His Beloved, or the entire people of God, although it is addressed to each of us individually.

That He Himself is the gift in this love and that He expects an analogous gift of our entire selves does not have to be emphasized. Indeed, this goes without saying.

Let us recall that the description of the Last Supper in one of the Gospels begins with the following sentence: "Before the feast of Passover, Jesus knew that His hour had come to pass from this world to the Father. He loved His own in the world, and He loved them to the end" (John 13:1). This love is why Jesus placed himself on the Cross to save us. This love is also why He has granted us the Eucharist forever.

236. Mnich kartuski, *Eucharystia tajemnica ślubna* (Warszawa: Wydawnictwo Fronda, 2005).

One could risk proposing the following definition of the Eucharist: It is the sacrament of the true presence of Jesus, Who loves us completely and invites us to likewise love Him completely. To love completely means to love with one's entire self.

We still are far removed from loving Him fully. Indeed, many of us — even those who deeply feel about His Passion for our sake — do not notice that He went to the Cross to search for those He loved but whom He lost. Sometimes, we are even capable of audaciously accusing the Eternal Father of callousness since it was His will for our redemption to take place through the Cross of His only Son.

Yet on Calvary, the very essence of our sin and our disdain for love as the highest law established by our Creator and Father became apparent. Through our abandonment of God and through our spiritual confusion, we have created a world whose logic consists of injustice, hatred, and cruelty. The height of our collective infidelity as humanity consists in the fact that we were created out of love and to be His Bridegroom, yet we directed all our injustice, hatred, and cruelty against His Son Who came to save us.

Although He was crushed by us, He persisted in His love for us, whom He came to save. At that moment, He loved each of us and loved His Eternal Father in the name of us all. His love for us was truly complete because at that time we were more than his enemies; we were His terribly ungrateful tormentors who paid so terribly for His love. He did not stop loving us even then.

In the name of Jesus Himself, the Apostle Peter consoled the inhabitants of Jerusalem of the generation that physically killed Jesus: "Now I know, brothers, that you acted out of ignorance, just as your leaders did" (Acts 3:17). Without a doubt, these words pertain to each of us as well. This is yet another reason to thank Him for His love which is so merciful. It is impossible to imagine more powerful and equally "absurd" love.

Such an "absurdly" inconceivable love was not merely a passing flash that illuminated the entirety of humanity on Calvary two thousand years ago. It becomes manifest during every Mass; it is granted to us in every Communion. We always grow closer to it whenever we participate in Eucharistic adoration. Indeed, it would be insufficient to say that His love becomes manifest. After all, He Who loves us until the very end is there!

This is why the sacrifice and the sacrament of the Eucharist has the power to transform us sinners into loving friends of our Savior; we rebels surrender to Him entirely, and we who are often unfaithful become Christ's loving and devoted Bridegroom. Without a doubt, the Carthusian monk may help many to discover this exceptionally important dimension of the gift of the Eucharist.

"I Will Speak to Her Heart"

Faith in Jesus Christ is the key without which no one can enter the Divine Paradise that is the Most Blessed Eucharist. Naturally, I mean faith in the true Christ, the Son of God Who is equal to His Eternal Father and Who became one of us for the sake of our salvation.

Let us pause for a moment and ponder this basic truth of our faith: that the Son of God became one of us for the salvation of us all. He is the only Man in human history Who did not begin to exist at the moment of His human conception. He is the eternal Son of God Who took on our humanity out of love for us. After His resurrection, He sends upon all of us who believe in Him His Holy Spirit, thanks to which each of us can enter into such intimacy and unity with Him as was unknown even to the apostles during His earthly life.

Thanks to the Holy Spirit, each of us can, in accordance with His declaration, remain in Him while He remains in us (see John 6:56; 14:4nn); in other words, we complete one another with Him. Because of the Holy Spirit, in Christ we are "one body" (1 Corinthians 12:13), while each of us is individually invited to such closeness with Jesus that the Apostle Paul described with words that can make one suspect that He has grown mad with love: "I live, no longer I, but Christ lives in me" (Galatians 2:20).

Naturally, we receive the gift of the Eucharist in the Holy Spirit and His power. Thanks to this Gift, not only do we lose nothing although we have come to live two thousand years after Jesus fulfilled His salvific mission, but He is accessible to us to an incomparably deeper degree than He was to the apostles when they walked with Him as their teacher.

To comprehend the gift of the Eucharist that is beyond our understanding, in the Church we have come to distinguish the following three dimensions in it: It is the manifestation of the Sacrifice that the Lord Jesus made for each of us on Good Friday. Furthermore, it is the Food thanks to which we can unite with Jesus in an incomparably more intimate way than is possible even between the most beautifully loving spouses. Finally, it is the real Presence of the living, loving, and saving Son of God Who for our sake became our Brother, died for us, and rose from the dead, and now as the Archpriest constantly intercedes for us and wants to be our Guide in eternal life.

Let me try to present this gift, Jesus' inconceivable closeness which we receive in the Eucharist, as we see it from the perspective of each of these three aspects in a few words.

What does it mean that the Sacrifice that the Lord Jesus made on the Cross becomes manifest during the Mass? This sacrifice is the love in which we persist when things are difficult and even when they are very difficult. What Jesus experienced on Good Friday transcends any human conceptions. This was not only unimaginable physical pain. We will never comprehend what it meant to Jesus that He was rejected and mocked by those whom He loved and for whom He made such sacrifices or how He felt about the extreme ungratefulness on the part of those for whom He did so much good, nor will we understand the inconceivable, terrible darkness from whose depth He called: "My God, My God, why have You forsaken Me?"

Yet even then His love for His Father and for us, whom He chose as His brothers and sisters, remained unambiguously pure and was not obscured to the slightest degree. It suffices to recall that He constantly thought in the categories of the good of others (see Luke 23:27-28; John 19:26-27), including the criminal (see Luke 23:43) and His own killers (see Luke 23:34). Completely devoted to His Father even amidst terrible suffering and darkness, He died saying: "Father, into Your hands I commend My spirit" (Luke 23:46).

During the Mass, Jesus not only becomes truly present among us, the baptized who have gathered around His altar as one Church, in the form of bread and wine, but He stands in the powerful, inconceivable love that overcame Him on the Cross and led to our resurrection. At least once a week, on Sunday, each of us can become immersed in His sacrificial love, include in it our small and defective sacrifices, and be bolstered so that we can measure up to the summons to love, including difficult love. This is what our participation in the one and only Sacrifice of Christ the Lord consists in.

Let us look at the Eucharist in its second aspect: that it is Nourishment. We have been given the formula: "Take and eat... Take and drink..." From the very beginning, they were a source of scandal. Once Jesus proclaimed the establishment of the Eucharist, His audience were offended: "How can this man give us [His] flesh to eat?" (John 6:52). People continue to be scandalized by the fact that Jesus gives us Himself to eat until the present day: who has not heard the accusation that the Eucharist is a civilized form of cannibalism?

One sentence by the Apostle Paul illustrates the uniqueness of this Food: "The Bread that we break, is it not a participation in the Body of Christ? Because the loaf of bread is one, we, though many, are one body, for we all partake of the one loaf" (1 Corinthians 10:16-17). Let us notice that when we receive Communion, it is not the case that each of us receives only a small part of the Body of the Lord. Even if millions and billions of people receive Communion and even if this were to continue for a thousand subsequent generations, each of us receives the whole Body of Christ. This means that thanks to this consumption we all are, or increasingly become one Body.

Thus, likewise from this perspective the Eucharist is the gift of inconceivable love. The Body we eat is Christ Himself. This is not the dismembered body of what once had been Christ. When we receive Communion, each of us consumes Christ, the entirety of Christ. Thanks to this Nourishment, each of us can more truly refer to ourselves the words of the Apostle Paul that I no longer live but Christ lives within me. Thanks to this Nourishment, each of us, though many, makes up one Body.

Unlike other foods, this wondrous Nourishment is not prone to assimilation. On the contrary, it transforms us into itself. St. Augustine saw this even before his conversion. "I am the food of grown men," he heard the mysterious voice of Christ the Lord say in his interior. "Grow, and you shall feed upon Me; nor shall you convert me, like the food of your flesh into you, but you shall be converted into Me."

In other words, as we have said, by receiving Holy Communion we enter a mystery of incomparably greater intimacy than that which takes place through the most beautiful marital love. After all, a husband and a wife will never attain such unity that they permeate one another. Meanwhile, we become the Body of Christ in the sense that He is in Me (and in every person who belongs to Him) and I in Him; at the same time, He is in us, and we are in Him.

The mystery of unity with Christ the Lord and the process of us who believe in Him becoming His Body should be explained above all by Trinitarian *perichoresis*, the circumintercession of the three Divine Persons. Just as each Divine Person is infinitely found in the other two Persons — and in this way the Three are the only God —

similarly, the more each of us belongs to Christ, the more unity there is with Him. At the same time, the more each of us belongs to Christ, the more fully we are distinct from everyone else and at the same time co-create the Body of Christ more fully.

Likewise in the third aspect — as the true, real, and personal presence of the Redeemer among us — the Eucharist is above all a gift of God's love for us people. It suffices to become aware of how many people come to the tabernacle each day to gain strength, be filled with peace, find consolation, and restore their hope. Here, I would like to recall an anonymous person immersed in adoration of the Blessed Sacrament so deeply that she unknowingly made a great impression on Edith Stein, who was not yet a believer, and had a major impact on her conversion.

Is there a place in the Church (both in the lowercase and uppercase meaning of the word) that can be associated more with God's promise than that in the Book of Hosea? "Therefore, I will allure her now; I will lead her into the wilderness and speak persuasively to her" (2:16): God says these words about the unfaithful Bridegroom; that is, about both the entire pilgrim Church and each of us.

The Eucharistic presence of the Redeemer fulfills most completely the promise from the Book of Jeremiah (31:33-34) that after the New Covenant

> I will place my law within them,
> and write it upon their hearts;
> I will be their God,
> and they shall be my people.
> They will no longer teach
> their friends and relatives,
> "Know the Lord!"
> Everyone, from least to greatest, shall know me

God did not promise doctrinal anarchy. Instead, He promised the most intimate access to Him. Naturally, He is sufficiently omnipotent to follow up on this promise in diverse ways, also without the aid of the Eucharist. One thing is certain. When faced with the Blessed Sacrament, we no longer have the desire to pompously pontificate about the faith. Man is then overcome with a desire to most fully participate in the faith of the Church, be pleasing to his God and Redeemer, and to want to express his love for Him.

Various Retreats from the Eucharist

Now let us pose an intriguing question: How is it possible for someone to simultaneously believe in Christ yet avoid the Eucharist? Three forms of retreating from the Eucharist seem particularly evident, so we will begin contemplating this question with them.

There are Catholics who have grown accustomed to rarely attending Sunday Mass. Some say that they simply get nothing out of Mass because they always "experience the same thing in church and grow bored," while others complain of the poor quality of the sermons. It is worth noting that the phenomenon of abandoning religious practices in many ways resembles the return to old pagan religiosity, when man in principle recognized God, counted on His protection, and occasionally resorted to Him through religious practices, but would never consider becoming God's friend. In that case, going to church every week — because such a mentality understands only so much of the Sunday Mass — seems too much and feels like unnecessary imposition on God.

Another form of retreating from the Eucharist is the practice of avoiding Holy Communion by Catholics who regularly attend Sunday Mass. I am not referring to those who are not allowed to receive Holy Communion but whom the Church encourages to receive it at least by desiring it. This lack of Eucharistic hunger among believing Catholics, which I should not like to attempt to explain, is astonishing. Some receive Communion only once a year and are motivated by the obligation of Church law.

There are also seemingly less clear forms of retreating from the Eucharist. Some claim to not like Sunday Mass but frequently stumble into a church when there are no people because they say they pray better then. Yet no prayer can replace participation in Christ's sacrifice. In fact, when we take a closer look at this perspective, it often turns out that those who avoid the Mass but frequently visit churches for a moment of prayer are looking for prayerful silence rather than an encounter with the One Who waits for us in the tabernacle.

The phenomenon of retreat from the Eucharist was recorded in the apostolic Church. The author of the Epistle to the Hebrews saw this on the one hand as related to a crisis of love for one's neighbor and, on the other, as weakened expectation of the Lord's glorious coming: "We must consider how to rouse one another to love and good works. We should not stay away from our assembly, as is the custom of some, but encourage one another, and this all the more as you see the day drawing near" (10:25). In other words, here we have a rather typical drama of retreating from zealous faith: Those who love little are also little concerned about loving more.

A radical admonition addressed to those Christians who have grown accustomed to regularly abandoning Eucharistic assemblies was written around 108 by St. Ignatius of Antioch, who was sentenced to a martyr's death. Those who avoid attending the Eucharist first of all close themselves off to God's great gift of the Church and, second, build their hope in themselves rather than God or Christ. "May no one stray!" Bishop Ignatius writes. "Let no man deceive himself: [...] For if the prayer of one or two possesses such power, how much more that of the bishop and the whole Church! He, therefore, that does not assemble with the Church, has even by this manifested his pride, and condemned himself. For it is written, 'God resists the proud.'"

In this book, I have on several occasions emphasized that faith in the truth of the Eucharist demands confirmation in our concern for the poor and needy. In other words, even if we partake of the Eucharist every day, we can retreat from it through an egotistical attitude of life that is far removed from the love of one's neighbor.

The Eucharist Means Thanksgiving

Let us look once more at the great gift of the Eucharist from the perspective of the fundamental ingratitude that characterizes us sinners. Let us begin by recalling the truth that we live completely immersed in God's gifts, a truth that is obvious to every Christian. Everything we are, everything that surrounds us, and everything we use is a gift from God. Likewise, our very existence as well as all our physical, mental, intellectual, and spiritual gifts and strengths come from God. The people both close to us and far from us who make up our human environment are God's gift. Every day, we receive abundant gifts from God that are necessary to live. Our immersion in God's gifts is perhaps best illustrated by our need for air, without which we would be incapable of living for even a few minutes. The existence of a creature that would not owe everything to God's gifts is metaphysically impossible.

Meanwhile, after original sin we do not meet even the two most basic requirements of gratitude. Gratitude does not consist of empty words of thanks or currying favor with one's benefactor. It is above all an appropriate reception of gifts in accordance with the intention of those who offer them as well as remembering thanks to whom we have come to participate in them. Meanwhile, the minimum requirement of gratitude is to at least refrain from active ingratitude, which consists of using gifts contrary to the intentions of those who give them, or even against them. And we do not even meet these two requirements of gratitude to the Greatest Giver. We constantly abuse His gifts, use them in ways that are inconsistent with His will, and even use them against God Himself.

The first Man Who went through life with a perfectly Eucharistic attitude was the Son of God, Jesus Christ. Everything that was human in His nature — which, of course, He took on for the sake of our salvation — and the entire environment in which He lived as well as everything He used He received, like other people, from the Eternal Father. However, unlike us, He accepted all these gifts with perfect gratitude, in a way that is consistent with the will of the Giver.

It then turned out that all of God's gifts are given to man so that man may ultimately accept God Himself as a gift and then completely surrender himself to God. Jesus Christ the man accepted the Eternal God literally with His entire human nature and similarly completely surrendered to Him.

Furthermore, it became apparent how difficult it is for sinners living on this earth to persist in a Eucharistic attitude. For Jesus Christ, an attitude of complete surrender to the Father at one point began to mean the bloody prayer in Gethsemane, the Stations of the Cross, and the Passion on the Cross.

At the same time, it became apparent that the who surrenders to the Eternal Father becomes a gift for other people. On the Cross, the Lord Jesus completed His total surrender to the Father and to us, His brothers and sisters.

Jesus of Nazareth the man is the only Son of God. Thus, the attitude of perfect thanksgiving He manifested in His life, and especially on the Cross, became a watershed in the history of man's relationship with God. His act of thanksgiving is an act of a Person of God, and thus it is of infinite value and has the power to effectively influence every man, regardless of the time and place of his situation.

Now everyone who grows closer to Jesus can receive from Him this attitude of thanksgiving in which He persisted even on the Cross. He Himself provided us with a model form of growing close to Him and becoming transformed into people who give thanks: He "took Bread, and, after He had given thanks [*eucharistesas*], broke it and said, 'This is My body that is for you. Do this in remembrance of Me'" (1 Corinthians 11:24).

At the same time, it cannot be emphasized enough that even if we were to participate in the Eucharist every day, we still carry within us the old man. If we try to live in fidelity to grace, he is increasingly weak within us and is no longer the lord of our lives. At the same time, as long as we pilgrims head towards eternal life, the old man in each of us has not completely died. An attitude filled with the love of our entire selves giving thanks does not yet overwhelm us. Thanks to the Eucharist, we are gradually reinforced in such an attitude.

THE FINAL TRIAL OF THE CHURCH

A fragment with this title can be found in the *Catechism of the Catholic Church*; it begins with the following statement: "Before Christ's second coming the Church must pass through a final trial that will shake the faith of many believers. The persecution that accompanies her pilgrimage on earth will unveil the 'mystery of iniquity' in the form of a religious deception offering men an apparent solution to their problems at the price of apostasy from the truth. The supreme religious deception is that of the Antichrist, a pseudo-messianism by which man glorifies himself in place of God and of his Messiah come in the flesh" (675).

Is the Conqueror of Death, Hell, and Satan Weak?

The footnotes in this concise fragment contain eight statements from Sacred Scripture, including the Lord Jesus' unsettling question: "But when the Son of Man comes, will He find faith on earth?" (Luke 18:8). In fact, this is not a complete list of the Biblical references to the last trial of the Church. For example, it does not contain the Lord Jesus' prophesy from His eschatological speech, although it seems to be

Christ's most important prophesy on this topic: "Then they will hand you over to persecution, and they will kill you. You will be hated by all nations because of My name. And then many will be led into sin; they will betray and hate one another. Many false prophets will arise and deceive many; and because of the increase of evildoing, the love of many will grow cold" (Matthew 24:9-12).

Under the influence of such statements, we are overwhelmed with more and more unsettling questions. Since even Christ's followers will be subjected to persecution — and, worse yet, we cannot be certain that our faith and love will not grow cold, so perhaps even we will break down and depart — then what do Christ's words that "I have conquered the world" (John 16:33) mean? Did He truly conquer it since this world is still capable of causing such grave harm to both the Church and her individual believers?

If He has conquered the world that is His enemy and ours, why does He still allow it to be victorious? If those who believe in Him lose their faith, what do the words mean that He said about His sheep that "[n]o one can take them out of My hand" (John 10:28)? If departure from the faith will take on the form of an avalanche before His final coming, what does His victory consist of?

And there is one more question: If at the end of our human history evil will particularly prevail, does this mean that the world has been programmed for this purpose? Did the One to Whom all power on heaven and earth has been given (Matthew 28:18) not want to make use of that power? Why? What does this mean?

Not Supporters but Co-Victors

Sometimes, the best way of searching for a response to a difficult question is by asking another question. Let us try this method and ask why so many testimonies to the persecutions of the Church and Christ's adherents do not lead to any doctrinal anxieties on the pages of the New Testament. After all, the inspired authors have no doubts that Christ the Lord is the ultimate and irrevocable Victor over death, hell, and Satan! Why, then, do the pages of the New Testament not even contain any traces of the question of how it can be that the ultimate Victor permits the persecutions of His disciples and supporters?

On the contrary, the New Testament calmly states that "all who want to live religiously in Christ Jesus will be persecuted" (2 Timothy 3:12). There, we frequently find the admonition that "[w]hoever wishes to come after me must deny himself, take up his cross, and follow Me" (Matthew 16:24) as well as the reminder that "[i]f they persecuted Me, they will also persecute you" (John 15:20).

Around 108, the old bishop of Antioch, Ignatius, who had been sentenced to a martyr's death, shed priceless light on this problem. Namely, having hope that thanks to Christ's grace he would emerge victorious from a martyr's death, Ignatius wrote to the then-young bishop Polycarp: "It is the part of a noble athlete to be wounded, and yet to conquer."[237] The following question automatically comes to mind: What about Christians who broke down when faced with persecution, when they were beaten, and lost? Unfortunately, the response here is rather clear: Such a person was only a superficial Christian, which became apparent amidst persecution. Naturally, we must meekly add: "Therefore, whoever thinks he is standing secure should take care not to fall" (1 Corinthians 10:12).

In other words, Christ the Lord, the ultimate Victor, permits persecutions and defections because He does not need supporters; He wants us to be His co-victors. He is concerned that we may participate in His victory over death, hell, and Satan in unity with Him, in unity with His Cross and the mockery He faced, bolstered by His grace.

Moving witness to this truth was presented by St. Thomas More (d. 1534), the English martyr from the time of Henry VIII. When

237. The Epistle of Ignatius to Polycarp, https://www.newadvent.org/fathers/0110.htm (accessed December 16, 2022).

he was harassed with the demand to express his approval for the subjugation of the Church to the king of England, he underwent anxiety-filled days. One time, after an interrogation before a commission of lords, Thomas returned to his home joyful and relaxed. His son-in-law, who accompanied him, in fact thought that the danger to St. Thomas More's life and limb had passed. Great was his astonishment when his father-in-law explained to him why his joy was so great: "In good faith I rejoice, son, that I had given the devil so foul fall, and that with those Lords I had gone so far, as without great shame, I could never go back again."[238]

Only God knows how many of those who carried their cross and imitated Christ "shall also be united with Him in the resurrection" (Romans 6:5) as well as how many contenders belonging to Christ were beaten or even killed yet won! Without a doubt, this is "a great multitude, which no one could count, from every nation, race, people, and tongue" (Revelation 7:9).

An Ancient Story About the Apostle Bartholomew

We have not yet dealt with the question of why "before Christ's second coming the Church must pass through a final trial that will shake the faith of many believers." Two truths cannot be breached while looking for a response to this question. First, nothing "will be able to separate [...] from the love of God in Christ Jesus, our Lord," such adherents of His who truly and completely belong to Him (see Romans 8:39). Second, just as the conversion of Nineveh ended the danger to the city resulting from a verdict of God Himself (see Jonah 3:4-10), the same can happen to the final trial that awaits us. However, this can happen only if we convert — on the scale of all humanity.

238. *The Life of Thomas More: A Biography by William Roper*, https://www.famous-trials.com/thomasmore/999-roperbiography (accessed December 16, 2022).

The response of Sacred Scripture to the question of why this trial will occur is as simple as it is mysterious: "But woe to you, earth and sea, for the Devil has come down to you in great fury, for he knows he has but a short time" (Revelation 12:12).

We must immediately reject the interpretation according to which in the final days Christ's authority over the Church or world would decrease. "Jesus Christ is the same yesterday, today, and forever" (Hebrews 13:8). Not Christ's power, but our devotion to Him will then decrease. This rightly causes us to be fearful. Thus, we should cling to Him even more strongly. We should implore Him in accordance with the words of the Eucharistic hymn: "Permit me not to be separated from You." Let us try to implement (not through declarations but through our entire lives) the summons with which St. John Paul II inaugurated his pontificate: "Open the doors to Christ!"

Considering this, will Satan's authority over our earth increase? Satan's terrible power and simultaneous powerlessness with regards to those who belong to Christ is excellently presented by the old Christian tale about the Apostle Bartholomew.[239] Namely, when the resurrected Christ appeared to the apostles, Bartholomew asked Him: "Lord, show us this adversary of the people. [W]hat power he has that he spared not even you, but caused you to be hanged upon the tree." To this, the Lord Jesus responded: "You are asking for that which you are unable to look at." Next, the remaining apostles began to ask Him: "Lord, let us behold him." "Since this is what you want," Jesus then said and commanded that the devil be brought to them. Five hundred sixty angels brought forth a powerful, fire-breathing beast tied down with fiery ropes. The apostles were terrified. Next, Jesus demanded of Bartholomew: "Come near, Bartholomew, and trample with your feet on his neck." Bartholomew feared and apologized, "I did not know what I was asking of you!" To this, the Lord Jesus

239. Cf. The Gospel of Bartholomew, [in:] *The Apocryphal New Testament*, trans. M. R. James (Oxford: Clarendon Press, 1924).

responded: "Go and tread upon his neck." When Bartholomew grew closer to the beast, the devil turned into jelly trembling with fear.

I tried to find another text that would equally wisely present to us the very essence of the truth about our enemy: that he is very powerful, and we are incapable of defending ourselves against him on our own. At the same time, we are completely safe, and it is the devil who fears us when we are near the Lord Jesus.

It seems to me that I have found precisely such a text, which was written by the great poet Adam Mickiewicz, a two-line poem entitled "Night Bird":

> Satan hunts in the dark, for he is a nocturnal beast;
> Hide from him in the light, for there he won't notice you in the least.

I Believe in Eternal Life

ETERNAL LIFE: A GIFT FROM GOD AND THE AIM OF OUR JOURNEY

It was only in the New Testament that the promise of eternal life was clearly proclaimed. It was clearly and frequently preached by Jesus Christ because He was the One Who would redeem us and open for us the path to eternal life and happiness. Therefore, I will begin the following discourse by recalling that in the Old Testament the promise of eternal happiness was almost unknown; I would like to emphasize, however, that it would be an exaggeration to purport that it was completely unknown.

The Haziness of Eschatological Conceptions in the Old Testament

In the Old Testament, especially in its most important books, the question of man's fate after death is barely outlined, while the answer to this question is highly imprecise. This is understandable. After all, it was not the time to preach to people about the joy of eternal life when achieving it was completely impossible. Christ would only come later.

We read in the Old Testament that the dead are in some Sheol, or an abyss, a sad place far from God that is not true life but some sort of half-existence. "Do you work wonders for the dead?" the Psalmist asks dolefully. "Do the shades arise and praise you? Is Your mercy proclaimed in the grave, Your faithfulness among those who have perished?" (Psalm 88:11-12)

This passage as well as related ones (see Psalm 6:6; Isaiah 38:18; Baruch 2:17) reveal to us two important truths. First, even if the man of the Old Testament knew little about life after death, he nonetheless knew that death was not the annihilation of man. Second, these passages present to us something very important about the mystery of death. Death, as the Biblical account of man's fall tells us, is a fruit of sin. However, it is not our corporal death that is the worst part of death. Death was related to becoming separated from God, practically forever. This is why before Christ's coming Sheol was above all a sad place, as the above passages mention.

However, in the Old Testament man did have hope for eternal life, which illuminated his conception of Sheol. Here is a fragment of Psalm 73:23-28, for example:

> Yet I am always with You;
> You take hold of my right hand.
> With Your counsel You guide me,
> and at the end receive me with honor.
> Whom else have I in the heavens?
> None beside You delights me on earth.
> Though my flesh and my heart fail,
> God is the rock of my heart, my portion forever.
> But those who are far from You perish;
> you destroy those unfaithful to you.
> As for me, to be near God is my good,
> to make the Lord God my refuge.
> I shall declare all your works

Later texts of the Old Testament contain clear prophesies of life after death; however, their aspectivity is noticeable. Let us look, for instance, at this well-known passage from the Book of Wisdom: "The souls of the righteous are in the hand of God, and no torment shall touch them. They seemed, in the view of the foolish, to be dead; and their passing away was thought an affliction and their going forth from us, utter destruction. But they are in peace" (Wisdom 3:1-3). The aspectivity of the above quote — which had clearly been formulated using categories of Greek mentality — consists in the fact that the author does not mention the promise of the resurrection of bodies at all.

Meanwhile, whereas the Old Testament authors speak of the resurrection, it seems that they do not notice that the essence of this situation will be our immersion in God and the deification of our entire humanity. To confirm this observation, I will quote what is perhaps the most powerful Old Testament passage about resurrection, which comes from the Book of Daniel: "Many of those who sleep in the dust of the earth shall awake; Some to everlasting life, others to reproach and everlasting disgrace" (Daniel 12:2).

Regardless, the promise of eternal life is almost absent from the Old Testament. Those references that are found in the Old Testament are unclear and generic. Naturally, we Christians know why this is so: Christ had not yet come; humanity had not yet been redeemed; and eternal life was not yet truly accessible. In short, it was not yet time to preach the promise of eternal life.

It must also be emphasized that the eschatological conceptions of the Old Testament never evoke associations with consumptive happiness. In particular, the Psalms contain numerous declarations that completely submitting oneself to God Himself and remaining in His presence is the greatest source of joy in our lives. "Taste and see that the Lord is good; blessed is the stalwart one who takes refuge in Him" (Psalm 34:9). In another Psalm, we read: "As the deer longs for streams of water, so my soul longs for You, O God. My soul thirsts for God, the living God. When can I enter and see the face of God?" (42:2-3).

Someone could argue that these passages do not directly mention eternal life. However, they undoubtedly open us to eternal life; they somehow demonstrate what man's ultimate vocation constitutes. For how else can we understand the Psalmist's words: "When can I enter and see the face of God?" Perhaps the direct object of these yearnings could have been visiting the Jerusalem Temple once more, such as in the enthusiastic shouts of Psalm 71:22-23: "That I may praise You with the lyre for Your faithfulness, My God, And sing to You with the harp, O Holy One of Israel! My lips will shout for joy as I sing Your praise; My soul, too, which You have redeemed," or in the contemplative prayer in Psalm 73:28: "As for me, to be near God is my good, to make the Lord God my refuge. I shall declare all your works."

However, it is difficult to deny that yearning for a visit to the Temple is not the ultimate horizon of all these above-quoted exclamations. Such yearnings flow from deeper ones, from yearning for eternal friendship with God.

Christianity Cannot Exist Without Faith in Eternal Life

In the New Testament, the truth about eternal life is frequently and very clearly proclaimed. Jesus seriously responds to the question: "Teacher, what must I do to inherit eternal life?" (Luke 10:25; see Matthew 19:16). He cautions that "How narrow the gate and constricted the road that leads to life. And those who find it are few" (Matthew 7:14; see Luke 13:23-24). He promises that "everyone who has given up houses or brothers or sisters or father or mother or children or lands for the sake of My name will receive a hundred times more and will inherit eternal life" (Matthew 19:29).

The promise of eternal life as well as the admonition to not lose it through one's own fault is the subject of many of the Lord Jesus' parables: about the workers in the vineyard (Matthew 20:1-6), the guests to the wedding feast (Matthew 22:2-14), the faithful and unfaithful servants (Matthew 24:45-51), the foolish and wise virgins (Matthew 25:1-13), and the talents (Matthew 25:14-30). During the Final Judgment, the elect will hear the joyful verdict: "Come, you who are blessed by My Father. Inherit the kingdom prepared for you from the foundation of the world" (Matthew 25:34), while the Judge will reject the villains: "Depart from me, you accursed, into the eternal fire prepared for the devil and his angels" (Matthew 25:41).

Likewise, in the epistles of the apostles the promise of eternal life is almost constantly invoked. The Apostle Paul promises: "I consider that the sufferings of this present time are as nothing compared with the glory to be revealed for us" (Romans 8:18). Meanwhile, in the Epistle to the Philippians we read: "But our citizenship is in heaven, and from it we also await a Savior, the Lord Jesus Christ. He will change our lowly body to conform with His glorified body" (3:20-21). Paul did not forget about his — and everyone's — vocation to eternal life when faced with encroaching martyrdom: "From now on the crown of righteousness awaits me, which the Lord, the just judge, will award to me on that day, and not only to me, but to all who have longed for His appearance" (2 Timothy 4:8).

The image of the victorious crown must have been quite popular in the apostolic Church since we also find it in the epistles of the apostles Peter and James as well as in Revelation (see 1 Peter 5:4; James 1:12; Revelation 2:10). Meanwhile, the Apostle Barnabas (who is probably the author of the Epistle to the Hebrews) expresses the hope of eternal life by cautioning that we might not achieve it: "Therefore, let us be on our guard while the promise of entering into His rest remains, that none of you seem to have failed" (Hebrews 4:1). Meanwhile, for the Apostle John the essence of eternal life consists of looking at God, Who will make us like Him (see 1 John 3:2; 1 Corinthians 13:12).

Faith in eternal life is so frequently and unambiguously expressed on the pages of the New Testament that the attitude of those Christians who declare affiliation in Christ and the Church but at the same time confess to a lack of interest in the very question of eternal life or in what awaits us after death is truly astonishing. "For me," they say, "the Christian faith is already such a great treasure to which I owe so much that I am essentially little concerned if eternal life exists or if, instead, nothingness awaits us after we die."

Such an attitude cannot be reconciled with authentic Christianity. It should be pointed out to such post-Christians that the Apostle Paul clearly distanced himself from such an approach to faith in Christ: "If for this life only we have hoped in Christ, we are the most pitiable people of all" (1 Corinthians 15:19). The apostle explains that even the event of Christ's Resurrection would be meaningless if it were not the beginning of the resurrection of us all: "But if Christ is preached as raised from the dead, how can some among you say there is no resurrection of the dead? If there is no resurrection of the dead, then neither has Christ been raised" (1 Corinthians 15:12-13).

In short, without seriously believing in eternal life one cannot be a Christian. In its essence, the Christian life is the path to eternal life, the path to ultimate resurrection. Pope Gregory the Great accurately observed: "he is a foolish traveller who sees pleasant meadows on his journey and forgets where he is going."[240]

Only Christ Can Grant Us Eternal Life

Why was the first generation of believers in Christ so confident that God wants to grant eternal life to all people? It is easy to respond

240. Gregory I, *Forty Gospel Homilies*, Homily 14, trans. David Hurst OSB (Kalamazoo, MI: Cistercian Publications, 1990), p. 112.

to this question: Because they truly believed that Jesus Christ is the Son of God and Redeemer. If faith in eternal life were not based on this fundament, it would be an empty faith, an ordinary human conviction and one of many beliefs thanks to which people from different cultures try to make guesses about what is inaccessible to our cognitive faculties.

Only because Jesus is the eternal Son of God Who, having become one of us, redeemed us on the Cross can we truly say that "[t]here is no salvation through anyone else, nor is there any other name under heaven given to the human race by which we are to be saved" (Acts 4:12). The Apostle Paul said the same thing albeit using different words when he said: "For there is one God. There is also one mediator between God and the human race, Christ Jesus, Himself human, Who gave Himself as ransom for all" (1 Timothy 2:5-6). Meanwhile, Jesus' frequently referenced words: "I am the resurrection and the life; whoever believes in Me, even if he dies, will live, and everyone who lives and believes in Me will never die" (John 11:25-26) could have been said only by the Son of God and Redeemer, or a liar and a fraud. "We have come to believe and are convinced that You are the Holy One of God" (John 6:69).

Achieving eternal life would be completely inaccessible to us if God did not want to grant it to us, for it absolutely transcends the limits of human nature. It was only the post-Christian mentality that introduced to our thinking the arrogant opinion that anyone who lives an honest life deserves eternal life. This misunderstanding became possible once Christians, having abandoned the notion of eternal life within the categories of friendship with God and eternal unification with Him, began to see it as a consumptive achievement.

Indeed, moral rectitude is a necessary condition to receive this gift. However, even if we were completely sinless, we would not be deserving of eternal life. After all, we are only creatures! We could never attain with only our natural strength this unimaginably strict unification with God that is filled with love and that Sacred Scripture presents as seeing God "face to face" (1 Corinthians 13:12), sharing in God's Divine nature (see 2 Peter 1:4), standing before God's face (see Ephesians 1:4), and being "heirs of God and joint heirs with Christ" (Romans 8:17).

And we are not without sin. Without God's forgiveness, none of us can achieve the moral rectitude in which we can stand before God's Tribunal without fear. "If we say, 'We are without sin,' we deceive ourselves, and the truth is not in us" (1 John 1:8). Instead, Jesus Christ "is expiation for our sins, and not for our sins only but for those of the whole world" (1 John 2:2). The admonition resulting from the parable of the Pharisee and the tax collector, which demonstrates that our conceptions of moral rectitude can be very far removed from how God sees them, will always remain relevant. It is worth noting that the criminal crucified alongside Christ who converted on the day of his death heard Jesus say: "Amen, I say to you, today you will be with me in Paradise" (Luke 23:43).

God Wants to Redeem the Entirety of Man

God is the Creator of all of man, of our bodies and our souls. Because he created the entirety of man, He also wants to redeem his entirety. It suffices to recall how firmly the Lord Jesus defended the truth about resurrection in His discussions with the Sadducees. Influenced by the dominant pagan mentality in those days, the Sadducees rejected the truth about the resurrection of bodies. Faith in the resurrection seemed irrational, outdated, and backwards to them. They were so certain they were right that they did not even bother to provide rationale for their views. Instead, they replaced arguments with mockery. Rather than persuasion, they preferred to scoff at those who believed in the future resurrection.

They came up with the story of a woman who was married to seven brothers, one after another, and buried the seventh husband. They asked the Lord Jesus: "Whose wife will she be at the resurrection?" It seemed that thanks to this little story they had thoroughly ridiculed both the promise of resurrection and Jesus Himself, Who proclaimed such "foolishness."

Then, the Lord Jesus calmly and respectfully explained wherein their error rested. The Sadducees believed in God and, furthermore, recognized the basic books of the Old Testament. Thus, the Lord Jesus kindly demonstrated to them that by rejecting God's promise of the future resurrection they essentially destroyed their faith, even if that was not their intention.

It is worth recalling this short sentence in which the Lord Jesus provides to the Sadducees two great explanations of where their error lay: "[Y]ou do not know the Scriptures or the power of God" (Matthew 22:29). In other words: "Dear Sadducees, by mocking the promise of resurrection you are mocking the Word of God. You believe that Sacred Scripture is the Word of God. Try to notice that Sacred Scripture, or God Himself, teaches us about the future resurrection. And God is truthful and omnipotent. If He promised something, then He did not lie, and He certainly did not want to lead us into error. Furthermore, do not forget, dear Sadducees, that God is omnipotent; nothing is impossible in Him, and fulfilling this mystery will not be beyond His power."

Through the words "You do not know the Scriptures or the power of God," the Lord Jesus summons the Sadducees to test their own faith. He tells them more or less this: "You claim to believe in God and respect Sacred Scripture. And that is probably true. However, such faith seems limited to declarations. Truly believe in God, the truthful and omnipotent God; believe in His omnipotent love. And then you will also love His truth, including the truth that the pagans do not like."

The Lord Jesus pointed out to the Sadducees one more error in their conception of God. God allowed Himself to be known, the Lord Jesus says, as the God of Abraham, Isaac, and Jacob. It is not the case that God was God only when they lived on this earth. Likewise, it is not so that God is only the God of only Abraham's soul, Isaac's soul, and Jacob's soul. The true God is not the God of the dead but of the living. If He has chosen us as His friends, He will never allow us to cease existing. If He granted to us, His friends, bodies, this was not so that we could live in our bodies for merely several decades of our temporal lives. God is the God of the living, not of the dead. Thus, He has the power to resurrect our bodies, degraded by sin and death, like Christ's resurrected Body.

The Lord Jesus frequently said that our bodies are likewise destined for eternal life. "For just as the Father raises the dead and gives life, so also does the Son give life to whomever He wishes" (John 5:21). This is why when doing good deeds, we should not have in mind human gratitude: "blessed indeed will you be because of their inability to repay you" (Luke 14:14).

The Lord Jesus proclaimed to us the promise of His future resurrection very emphatically in His Eucharistic speech: "For this is the will of My Father, that everyone who sees the Son and believes in Him may have eternal life, and I shall raise him on the last day" (John 6:40; see verses 44, 51, 53-54, 58). Perhaps only His words before bringing Lazarus back from the dead resounded more emphatically (see John 11:25-26).

Thus, it is unsurprising that the Apostle Paul would later write that if we were to reject the resurrection of the dead, we would be "false witnesses to God, because we testified against God that He raised Christ, Whom He did not raise if in fact the dead are not raised" (1 Corinthians 15:15).

The Path to Eternal Life Leads Through the Cross

It is worth noting one more important aspect of the truth about eternal life: that the path to eternal life leads through the cross. We can frequently read of this in the New Testament. "Whoever wishes to come after Me must deny himself, take up his cross, and follow Me." All the apostles unanimously recalled this. The Apostle James writes: "Consider it all joy, my brothers, when you encounter various trials" (James 1:2). The Apostle Peter's teaching was similar: "In this you rejoice, although now for a little while you may have to suffer through various trials" (1 Peter 1:6). Again, the Apostle Paul writes: "For this momentary light affliction is producing for us an eternal weight of glory beyond all comparison" (2 Corinthians 4:17).

We may ask a few simple questions: What is the cross? Is the cross tantamount to suffering? Why does the New Testament ascribe such great significance to the cross? Although the cross is often related to suffering, its essence is not so much suffering as it is love.

Let us look at the model, Christ the Lord's Cross. On the Cross, our Redeemer experienced terrible suffering, but the most important part of His sacrificial offering was not so much His suffering but the fact that He persisted in love amidst such horrible suffering: He was completely devoted to His Father and filled with crystal pure love for all people, including His murderers. In Christ, Satan did not find even a single particle for himself. Also on the Cross, Jesus was completely filled with love.

To carry one's cross means to persist in love even in the most difficult circumstances. We live in a world in which evil still has a lot to say. There remain within us many dark dynamics that push us to make bad choices, and also the external world is filled with forces that try to oppose love being the ultimate horizon of human attitudes and actions. Thus, to carry one's cross means to not submit to these dark forces. To carry the cross is to imitate Christ the Lord in His absolute "yes" to our Father in heaven; it is the unconditional faith that love is the greatest value, greater than even our earthly lives. To carry one's cross means to know with one's entire self that we do not need to fear "those who kill the body but cannot kill the soul" (Matthew 10:28).

Even if we did not know Christ, such an attitude would pave the way for a blessed openness transcending temporal values. Meanwhile, by believing in Christ the Lord, the Son of God and our Redeemer, we can see increasingly clearly that, just like He turned out to be the ultimate victor on the Cross, our consistent fidelity to love leads to the glory of resurrection.

A Superficial Conflict

During this discourse, it is possible to notice a superficial conflict in the New Testament's teaching on eternal life. On the one hand, its accomplishment utterly transcends the capability of our human nature, but on the other the Lord Jesus Himself and, following Him, the apostles unambiguously teach that we will receive eternal life as a reward for fidelity to God's commandments.

In only the Sermon on the Mount, the Lord Jesus several times mentions the reward for our good deeds that awaits us (or that we have lost). The Lord Jesus concludes His enticement to patiently accept afflictions due to Him with: "Rejoice and be glad, for your reward will be great in heaven" (Matthew 5:12). Meanwhile, those who are incapable of selfless love (Matthew 5:46) as well as those who do good only because of human opinions "have received their reward" (Matthew 6:2).

The apostolic epistles contain instructions that God "will repay everyone according to his works" (Romans 2:6) and that "each will receive wages in proportion to his labor" (1 Corinthians 3:8). Meanwhile, the Apostle John cautions: "Look to yourselves that you do not lose what we worked for but may receive a full recompense" (2 John 1:8).

In the Book of Revelation, the One Who calls Himself "the Alpha and the Omega, the first and the last, the beginning and the end" prophesies: "Behold, I am coming soon. I bring with me the recompense I will give to each according to his deeds" (22:12).

How can we explain these two seemingly contradictory truths: on the one hand, salvation is without a doubt absolutely and completely a gift from God but, on the other, we undoubtedly deserve salvation because of our good deeds for which salvation will be a reward?

This conflict is only superficial. Of course, God is the complete giver of eternal life and happiness. However, He gives His gifts to creatures as He created them. He created us in His image and likeness; He made us persons, or beings that He loves in particular and that He wants to love Him. When God created us as persons, He granted us reason, made us capable of responsibility, and summoned us to freedom. In the extraordinary design of His love, God decided to elevate us above our status as creatures and make us something akin to gods, true participants in God's nature. Thus, it is clear that the implementation of such a great metaphysical intention transcends the possibilities of human nature and is possible only thanks to God's supernatural gift.

That is why the truth consists of both statements: Because eternal salvation absolutely transcends the capacities of human nature, it is completely God's gift. Because God truly loves us, He grants us this gift, carefully respecting our personal dignity: thus, He grants it in such a way that His grace makes us capable of receiving this gift as free people.

It is never enough to emphasize that our accomplishments are in no way partners of God's grace; they are its fruit. Outside God's grace, we would be thoroughly incapable of deserving eternal life.

THE MAGNIFICENCE OF GOD'S JUDGMENT

The Yearning for God's Judgment

Let us look at those passages in Sacred Scripture in which God's Tribunal is presented as a joyful and yearned-after event. Here is a passage from Psalm 96:11-13:

> Let the heavens be glad and the earth rejoice;
> let the sea and what fills it resound;
> let the plains be joyful and all that is in them.
> Then let all the trees of the forest rejoice
> before the Lord Who comes,
> Who comes to govern the earth,
> To govern the world with justice
> and the peoples with faithfulness.

In a world that has separated itself from God and become dominated by various idolatrous powers, nothing is as it could and should be. The Second Vatican Council accurately described this as follows: "For without the Creator the creature would disappear" (*Gaudium et spes*, 36). Whenever we cease to take God into account, not only do we know little about who we are and why we live but also everything that makes up our world becomes somewhat distorted and deprived of authenticity.

This is why the prophesy of God's coming to His property arouses such joy not only among God's friends but in all of creation. Translated into the language of theological discourse, the thrilling vision of Psalm 96 can be presented using the following definition: God's Tribunal is God's powerful and loving entry into our human affairs to restore good to all that belongs to Him and to prevent evil from further prevailing.

Thus, it is unsurprising that faith in fact makes us yearn for God's Judgment. The New Testament contains testimony that among the first Christians this expectancy was often so great that they were "hastening the coming of the day of God" (2 Peter 3:12), which to us today is even more puzzling since the Apostle Peter immediately noted that on that day the illuminated heavens would "be dissolved in flames and the elements melted by fire." Peter continued to explain that we would like to hasten the coming of that day because "according to His promise we await new heavens and a new earth in which righteousness dwells" (verse 13).

It cannot be denied that although we truly believe in Christ, we sometimes fear His coming to the Judgment instead of wishing to hasten the arrival of that day. Such an approach was insightfully analyzed by St. Augustine in his commentary on the above-quoted Psalm: "We love Him, and yet we fear lest He come. Are we sure that we love Him? Or do we love our sins more? Therefore, let us hate our sins for their own sake, and love Him who will come to punish our sins. He will come, whether we like or not: for because He comes not just now, it is no reason that He will not come at all. He will come, and when you know not; and if He shall find you ready, your ignorance is no hurt to you."[241]

241. St. Augustine, "Exposition on Psalm 96," trans. J.E. Tweed, [in:] *Nicene and Post-Nicene Fathers*, First Series, Vol. 8, ed. Philip Schaff (Buffalo, NY: Christian Literature Publishing Co., 1888, https://www.newadvent.org/fathers/1801096.htm (accessed July 21, 2022).

In a general audience catechesis given on September 18, 2002, St. John Paul II recalled that in its first dimension the prophesy of the coming of the Lord for the Judgment was fulfilled through the event of Christ's Birth and His salvific death on the Cross. He then came to us in His truly Divine power and redeemed the entire world. He came to grant Divine support to everything that is open to His love. At the same time, on Good Friday Christ the Lord exposed the ultimate powerlessness of evil: although in that hour of darkness the forces of evil did everything to defeat Him, they utterly failed. Thus, for centuries the Church has rejoiced because of her Lord and Judge Who, to repeat John Paul II's expression, "reigns from the height of the Cross — a throne of love and not of dominion."

Regardless, these two comings of the Lord and Judge — first in human weakness and finally in Divine majesty — are tied to one another. The very logic of our faith demands that we, who already "saw His glory, the glory as of the Father's only Son, full of grace and truth" (John 1:14), yearn and want to yearn even more and more authentically for the day when "everything is subjected to Him, then the Son Himself will [also] be subjected to the One Who subjected everything to Him, so that God may be all in all" (1 Corinthians 15:28).

The Perfect Implementation of the Eternal Design

In the Gospels, God's Judgment is compared to a harvest (see Matthew 13:30). In one of His parables, the Lord Jesus explains: "He who sows good seed is the Son of Man, the field is the world, the good seed the children of the kingdom. The weeds are the children of the evil one, and the enemy who sows them is the devil. The harvest is the end of the age, and the harvesters are angels" (Matthew 13:37-39).

The harvest is essentially a positive one-time event that is the culmination of the waiting for crops. The metaphor of the harvest contains the message that neither the world nor its history is accidental.

Our world has some positive meaning to be implemented and some aim to be achieved. This is not only the final aim but also the ultimate one, the ultimate completion.

If it is final, then it is eternal. In a word, the Day of Judgment will be the Day when the magnificence of God's creative work will be finally revealed. For all of creation (hence the presence of the angels in the descriptions of the Final Judgment) it will become obvious that God has brought the designs of His love with respect to the entire creation to a perfect end and no dark forces could pose an obstacle to Him.

Here, it is also worth noting that in the original Greek the Gospel term "end of the world" that appears in the Lord Jesus' parables had a depth that its English equivalent lacks. *Synteleia* can be better rendered as "culmination" or "fulfillment" than "end." Therefore, the Day of Judgment will not so much be the "end of the world" as its fulfillment.

A farmer awaiting his harvest had to first sow the seed in his field. Similarly, the world is moving towards its ultimate maturity because its Creator has given it such a direction of development. We can say that the history of all of creation is a giga-event that cannot be fully comprehended by the human mind. Its beginning was God's design of love thanks to which everything was called into existence. Its culmination will be in leading this design to a perfectly implemented end, to the appearance of "new heavens and a new earth in which righteousness dwells" (2 Peter 3:13).

The author of Revelation clearly lacked words to sufficiently express his awe for the ultimate shape of the work of the Divine Artist that we will see on the Day of Judgment:

Then I heard every creature in heaven and on earth and under the earth and in the sea, everything in the universe, cry out:

> 'To the one who sits on the throne and to the Lamb
>
> be blessing and honor, glory and might,
> forever and ever.'

> The four living creatures answered, 'Amen,' and the elders fell down and worshiped (Revelation 5:13-14).

God's plan for each of us has an analogous structure. Each of us is not only a member of our families and the various other communities to which we belong. We are not only a particle of our generation and all of humanity, a particle of the entirety of creation. God has loved me and each of us individually for the sake of each of us. He loved me before I came into being, and because He loved me, I exist. The Apostle Paul mentions this at the beginning of the Epistle to the Ephesians: "Blessed be the God and Father of our Lord Jesus Christ, Who has blessed us in Christ with every spiritual blessing in the heavens, as He chose us in Him, before the foundation of the world, to be holy and without blemish before Him" (Ephesians 1:3-4).

And this is God's love intended for my ultimate purpose: I am to be holy and immaculate before God for all of eternity. At the Final Judgment, I, who still am sinful and imperfect, will appear as God's masterpiece. God has billions and billions of us, yet each of the saved will then appear as an unimaginably original and inimitable masterpiece of God's love. We will be a personal masterpiece, incomparable to the works of human artists. Meanwhile, a person can achieve bedazzling beauty if he learns from God Himself to find himself through selfless giving of oneself. It is with this beauty that the saved will shine during the Final Judgment.

Yet We Fear This Judgment

And yet we are fearful of God's Judgment. The Lord Jesus Himself cautioned us that during this judgment some would be rejected and would hear: "Amen, I say to you, I do not know you" (Matthew 25:12); "Depart from Me, you accursed, into the eternal fire prepared for the devil and his angels" (verse 41). We can also find frightening expressions concerning this judgment in the apostolic epistles: "By your stubbornness and impenitent heart, you are storing up wrath for yourself for the day of wrath and revelation of the just judgment of God" (Romans 2:5; see 2 Peter 3:7).

Furthermore, other questions make us anxious: Indeed, we count on God's mercy, but will God also absolve us of those sins of which we are not aware? And even if the Lord Jesus pardoned my sins in the sacrament of penitence, will my conscience be examined of them during the Final Judgment, especially if they have led to injuries that could not be remedied? And there is one more question: Can the saved expect that their sins which God has pardoned will be forgotten and no one will know about them?

Let us begin with the latter question. Before becoming true friends of God, some saints committed great sins and even crimes. Not only did David seduce another man's wife, he insidiously killed her husband. Peter denied his master, while Mary Magdalene led a life so sinful that Luke the Evangelist did not even attempt to describe it; he only used the harsh expression that thanks to the Lord Jesus "seven demons had gone out" from her (Luke 8:2). All three became great saints, while in heaven they undoubtedly rejoice that their sins are told from thousands of pulpits each year, for these are also the accounts of their conversion and their experience of God's mercy.

Indeed, salvation consists in the fact that we will be completely filled with God's love: I will be completely worthy of love and will love everyone and everything that is deserving of love. There will then disappear the reasons why we highly value the possibility of hiding our various private affairs. I will not even feel shame for the evils I had once committed for they will have been overcome. Evil that is atoned, forgiven, and replaced with even greater good is no longer the subject of shame because its memory is filled with joy and the praise of the mercy of God Who did not allow for my perdition.

However, the fact is that some Biblical pronouncements on God's Judgment terrify us. I would like to recall the general tone with which the Good News was preached. The Gospel is one great promise of salvation and a summons to become open to it. The Lord Jesus said of His mission: "For the Son of Man has come to seek and to save what was lost" (Luke 19:10). The parables of the Prodigal Son and of the shepherd looking for his lost sheep as well as the spiritual promise contained within Christ's healings and His saving of the adulteress, the numerous tax collectors, and the thief crucified alongside Him, and above all His death and resurrection all attest to His infinite mercy.

Thus, all of the Lord Jesus' difficult pronouncements that can arouse fear or even terror we can authentically understand only once we recognize the word of love within them. When He said that I can be condemned at God's Judgment, He did so in order that I will never experience this and to save me from this terrible possibility.

Once, a sermon on God's Judgment by my fellow Dominican, the late Father Rajmund Koperski, made a great impression on me. He said that during His Judgment God will ask each of us one question: *Do you love me?* It will be impossible to lie and pretend during this judgment; there, man will speak the whole truth. Those who respond to the question of *Do you love me?* with "Yes, Lord, you know that I love You" (John 21:16) will immediately be among the saved. God will ask the others: *Will you at least let Me love you?* Those who respond to that question in the affirmative will go to purgatory, where God's love will encompass them even more until they completely love their God and Redeemer, becoming capable of being face to face with God. The notion that someone could respond to this question with an arrogant "no" is indeed terrifying.

It seems to me that this scene is, in fact, a brilliant summary of the Biblical teaching on God's Judgment.

I BELIEVE IN THE RESURRECTION OF THE BODY!

The Promise Rooted in the Truth About Creation

The truth about the resurrection of the bodies is found only in those religions that profess the truth that God is the Creator of all that exists. Let us look at an example of a radical difference between the Christian faith in eternal life and the resurrection of the bodies on the one hand and the ancient Greek eschatology on the other. The concept of the creation of the world by God was unknown to the Greeks. The Ancient Greeks believed that in the beginning there was chaos, some self-generated pre-matter that a divine demiurge had to first embrace with thought and order or transform it into the cosmos. This demiurge, however, was not a creator; he was only someone who gave meaning to initial meaninglessness; he imposed some order on the primeval chaos. It was only thanks to Biblical revelation that we learned that literally everything in existence comes from God.

At the starting point, distinctiveness leads to excessively far-reaching consequences. If what is Divine is good and if God has created everything, then everything is good; such logic seems to be present in all the religions. The author of the description of creation carefully emphasized this, on several occasions noting the goodness of everything that God called into existence: “God looked at everything He had made and found it very good” (Genesis 1:31). Evil, the Bible teaches, appeared only because some creatures endowed with intelligence knowingly opposed God. In its nature, evil is secondary with respect to good; if there were no good, there would also be no evil. Evil is like a cancer that eats away at good, for it needs good to exist.

The Greek vision was entirely different. According to the Greeks, eternal and un-created chaos, or matter, which also includes the body, is neither good nor evil for it neither comes from God nor opposes Him. There were many areas of life that the Ancient Greek treated kindly (they were even capable of vigorously enjoying them), but he did not measure them in terms of good and evil. The Ancient Greeks believed that only spiritual things come from God. In other words, if a Christian sees human reality as good mixed with evil and this mixture pertains to both man’s spiritual and corporal sphere, then the Ancient Greek tended to see it as spirit mixed with matter.

How does this affect eschatology? For the Ancient Greek, salvation consisted of liberating the spirit from the bonds of the body, while for the Christian, salvation is the liberation of good from the bonds of evil. According to the Greek conception, salvation therefore pertains only to the spirit, while we Christians believe that the entire man will be saved. The Christian hope for salvation consists in that the spirit is united with God, and thus being healed, strengthened, and elevated, it will raise the body with it.

What has come from God should return to God: we have come from God irrespective of our will, so let us freely return to Him. Because all of man came from God, all of man should return to Him. The promise of resurrection, then, rests in the mere fact of man’s creation and will be fulfilled despite our sinfulness; this is thanks to the salvific coming of the Son of God and His death and resurrection.

Indeed, the Ancient Greeks lacked a clear notion of the creation of man. The Greek myths provide several different anthropogenies; however, none includes man's creation by God. The first man is molded from clay by some lower god, Hephaestus, or the Titan Prometheus, or the first people are born of stones that Deucalion and Pyrrha throw at one another. We also have at least two descriptions of the origins of people from the teeth of a dragon, while the laborious Myrmonids were simply formed out of ants.

These myths share the conviction that man does not come from God and therefore is not called to intimacy with God. Of course, the gods look after man, but man must accept the fact that his life is ephemeral and filled with anxiety. As perceptively presented by Mircea Eliade, such a pessimistic anthropology led the Greeks to discover a joy of life that was unique to imperfect human existence: "Wisdom begins with consciousness of the finiteness and precariousness of every human life. So the thing to do is to take advantage of everything that can be offered by the present: youth, health, physical pleasures, or occasions for displaying the virtues. [...] Since the gods had forced him not to go beyond his limits, man ended by realizing the perfection and, consequently, the sacrality of the human condition. [...] The joy of life discovered by the Greeks is not a profane type of enjoyment: it reveals the bliss of existing, of sharing — even fugitively — in the spontaneity of life and the majesty of the world."[242]

However, the Greek worldview was open to the notion that the most important aspect of man, namely the soul, but only the soul, comes from God so that it may be capable of everlasting unity with God. This is why the ancient pagans were so opposed to the Christian truth of the resurrection of the body. We should not be surprised by this: since they did not know the truth about creation, they were

242. Mircea Eliade, *A History of Religious Ideas Volume 1: From the Stone Age to the Eleusinian Mysteries*, trans. Willard R. Trask (Chicago: University of Chicago Press, 2014), pp. 262-263.

incapable of seeing their bodies as a gift from the Creator Himself, a gift given to us forever, even if we temporarily lose it when we die. Indeed, thanks to Divine revelation only the Biblical man began to thus look at his body.

Sacred Scripture on the Resurrection of Bodies

Already in the Old Testament faith in the resurrection of bodies was very clearly formed. In the Book of Daniel, we read: "Many of those who sleep in the dust of the earth shall awake; some to everlasting life, others to reproach and everlasting disgrace" (Daniel 12:2). It is worth recalling that the Hebrew language did not yet have a term for "all;" when this term had to be expressed, the word "many" was used.

The Psalmist is also a witness to faith in the future resurrection: "For You will not abandon my soul to Sheol, nor let your devout one see the pit. You will show me the path to life, abounding joy in Your presence, the delights at Your right hand forever" (Psalm 16:10-11). It is worth recalling that this Psalm was referenced by the Apostle Peter in the first general sermon that was preached in the history of the Church (see Acts 2:25-28).

Exceptional testimony to this faith was the description of the martyrdom of the seven brothers from the times of the Maccabees. Faith in resurrection gave those people the strength to surrender their lives in defense of God's law: One of these martyrs said to his persecutor: "[T]he King of the universe will raise us up to live again forever, because we are dying for His laws" (2 Maccabees 7:9). Similarly, the other martyr said when dying: "It is my choice to die at the hands of mortals with the hope that God will restore me to life" (2 Maccabees 7:14).

Meanwhile, the mother of these heroes of the faith knew well that that fundament of faith in the future resurrection is faith in God, the Creator of everything: "I do not know how you came to be in my womb; it was not I who gave you breath and life, nor was it I who arranged the elements you are made of. Therefore, since it is the Creator of the universe who shaped the beginning of humankind and brought about the origin of everything, He, in His mercy, will give you back both breath and life, because you now disregard yourselves for the sake of His law" (2 Maccabees 7:22-23).

The fact is that in Jesus' time faith in the resurrection was already deeply ingrained in the consciousness of God's people. It was doubted only by the Sadducees, who were the representatives of the fraction of the Jewish community that was most open to the Greek mentality. In the Gospel, we read that the Sadducees said "that there is no resurrection" (Matthew 22:23). One day, they came to the Lord Jesus with a story they had made up in order to mock the faith, that of a woman who was married to seven subsequent brothers and finally buried the seventh. Whose wife will she be after the resurrection?, they asked Him mockingly, thinking that they had successfully discredited that truth.

The Lord Jesus briefly provided them with two arguments: "You are misled because you do not know the Scriptures or the power of God" (Matthew 22:29). First of all, "you do not know the Scriptures" because you, the Sadducees, recognize Sacred Scripture, and there you will find the promise of resurrection, which means that God Himself promises this to people. Second, "you do not know [...] the power of God": after all, God is omnipotent, and since He Himself promised that we would rise from the dead, He has the power to fulfill this promise.

The truth about resurrection was an essential part of the Lord Jesus' message of salvation: "Amen, amen, I say to you, the hour is coming and is now here when the dead will hear the voice of the Son of God, and those who hear will live" (John 5:25). Jesus not only promised them resurrection; He is the source of resurrection. He said to Martha four days after the death of her brother: "I am the resurrection and the life; whoever believes in Me, even if he dies, will live" (John 11:25). This is because He is life and resurrection, while the Eucharist is the nourishment for eternal life: "Whoever eats My Flesh and drinks My Blood has eternal life, and I will raise him on the last day" (John 6:54).

Resurrection was the subject of preaching the Gospel to the extent that audiences felt as if the apostles above all preached to them the resurrection: "While they were still speaking to the people, the priests, the captain of the temple guard, and the Sadducees confronted them, disturbed that they were teaching the people and proclaiming in Jesus the resurrection of the dead" (Acts 4:1-2). Even on the Areopagus in Athens, when the Apostle Paul reached the intellectual elites of this city, he did not neglect to provide them with testimony about the future resurrection, although he could have predicted that in this way, he risked rejection and mockery (see Acts 17:32).

Because in the first generation of the Church many pagans believed in Christ, naturally some of them tried to run from this truth and adapt it to the pagan mentality. The Apostle Paul always reacted firmly to such attempts: "But if Christ is preached as raised from the dead, how can some among you say there is no resurrection of the dead? If there is no resurrection of the dead, then neither has Christ been raised. And if Christ has not been raised, then empty [too] is our preaching; empty, too, your faith. Then we are also false witnesses to God, because we testified against God that He raised Christ, Whom He did not raise if in fact the dead are not raised. For if the dead are not raised, neither has Christ been raised, and if Christ has not been raised, your faith is vain; you are still in your sins. Then those who have fallen asleep in Christ have perished. If for this life only we have hoped in Christ, we are the most pitiable people of all" (1 Corinthians 15:12-19).

When Hymenaeus and Philetus later tried to mask their doubts about resurrection and adorn them with beautiful and pious words, the Apostle Paul firmly stated that they "have deviated from the truth by saying that [the] resurrection has already taken place and are upsetting the faith of some" (2 Timothy 2:18). Notice that this was written by the same apostle who frequently taught that our resurrection has already been set into motion: "If then you were raised with Christ, seek what is above, where Christ is seated at the right hand of God. Think of what is above, not of what is on earth" (Colossians 3:1-2; see Romans 6:4; Ephesians 2:4-6, 5:14).

The Dignity of the Human Body

Why were the pagans so offended at the mere mention of the resurrection of bodies? Why was it difficult for some Greeks to believe in this truth even after believing in Christ? Erroneous views almost always contain a grain of truth. Therefore, let us pose the following question: What truth would the intuitions of the ancient pagans reflect if the corporal and Divine spheres were essentially separated from one another and if there were no point of contact between them?

What truly separates man from God and from what is Divine is sin. The ancient pagans were little aware of their sinfulness. Thus, they recognized the truth about our degradation resulting from our sins in a deformed way. It seemed to them that this degradation is a consequence of our corporeality. The stoics went so far as to propose that the wise man should extinguish within himself all feelings because they come from our corporeality; Plotinus, the creator of Neo-Platonism, was openly ashamed to have a body.

These philosophers accurately sensed the debasement in which man found himself. They were incorrect in seeing this as connected to our corporeality. Meanwhile, it is not our bodies but our sinfulness that degrades us. The body is a great gift from God. Sin degrades us as well as our bodies. This happens when man desecrates his body through debauchery or drunkenness or by losing control over his fears and feelings. The Apostle James even said that our bodies experience debasement because of the sins of the tongue: "The tongue is also a fire. It exists among our members as a world of malice, defiling the whole body" (James 3:6).

Meanwhile, faith in the resurrection of bodies is not only a matter of doctrine that we Christians recognize and preach. For this faith to not be empty and barren, we must ensure that our bodies will also truly be temples of the Holy Spirit (1 Corinthians 6:19). We must now work on restoring our bodies' dignity. Naturally, our efforts can be effective only in Christ and thanks to His grace.

In what do these efforts consist? The Apostle Paul gives us a general directive: "For just as you presented the parts of your bodies as slaves to impurity and to lawlessness for lawlessness, so now present them as slaves to righteousness for sanctification" (Romans 6:19). In practice, this means that we use our arms, legs, and tongue to do good and not evil; we subject our sexuality to the moral law and surrender it to the service of true love; our fears, feelings, and desires should be entrusted to God and filled with love for our neighbor; and we should transform all our illnesses, sufferings, and other tribulations into a cross that brings us closer to God.

I will respond to all who fear that this program of restoring dignity to our bodies and expressing our faith in the future resurrection transcend human capabilities in three points. First, nothing is impossible for God; thus, we should greatly count on God's grace in our efforts. Next, this program seems excessively difficult or even impossible only from the position of an external observer. If we accept it as a program for our lives, living according to it will become something sweet and light even if on various occasions we become aware of our weakness. Finally, to embark on our efforts to improve ourselves and persist in them we should help one another; herein lies the mystery of the communion of saints.

If it is difficult for someone to believe in the future resurrection of bodies, he should try to become sensitive to God's power, which transforms man, including our corporeality, today. Already today man can transcend evil, which tries to subordinate us. Children can already have pure parents, while our bodies do not need to be governed by wrath or passion but by reason and God's peace. Man can already become less prone to manipulation and objectification, increasingly regaining his personal subjectivity. Already today Christ the Redeemer wants to miraculously transform the wounds of our sins into signs that beg for sacrificial love. Our bodies can already enjoy their initial purposefulness intended by the Creator: they are themselves temples of the Holy Spirit and are to express and reveal souls filled with God.

Those who experience this (even just a little, by sensing and desiring) will recognize the validity of the teaching about the ultimate resurrection in the internal logic of the Christian faith. They will also understand somewhat more deeply why Christ's path to resurrection led through the Cross. It is impossible to attain that anticipation of resurrection that the Apostle Paul mentioned in the above-quoted passage of Colossians 3:1 without entering on the Stations of the Cross along with Christ. After all, we are immersed in death. Entering this dimension of resurrection demands transcending the limits of death, which have been designated by the forces of evil and disorder. Naturally, transcending these limits hurts; it is a cross. This is why it is so important that we attempt to transform all our tribulations into a cross and help our neighbors go through theirs.

Therefore, when the thought that the resurrection of bodies is extremely improbable comes to our minds, we should not only ask if we truly believe in Christ, the Son of God. We should also fear that we are insufficiently transformed by the power of the Resurrected Redeemer compared to what could be possible thanks to God's grace. Perhaps I fear the hardship of effective attacks against the boundaries of death that separate me from God? We should intensify our spiritual efforts. At the same time, this should make us trust even more in the mercy of the One Who died on the Cross for us and as the First-born among the dead wants to bring us into a reality which transcends evil and death.

We Will Become Similar to the Resurrected Christ

Let us ask one final question: Do we know anything about what our existence in our resurrected bodies will be like? We can find a response to this question in the Epistle to the Philippians: "But our citizenship is in heaven, and from it we also await a Savior, the Lord Jesus Christ. He will change our lowly body to conform with His glorified body by the power that enables Him also to bring all things into subjection to Himself" (Philippians 3:20-21).

Thus, if we want to know more about the state of our bodies after resurrection, we should look at the resurrected Christ. The faith of the Church recognizes the following four traits in the glorious body of Christ the Lord: His body was completely filled with God's presence (*claritas*) and transfigured (*subtilitas*); thanks to the latter trait, He could come to His disciples in His real body despite closed doors. His body was marked by transcendence with respect to space (*agilitas*); this is why the Resurrected One did not have to travel in order to appear in Jerusalem and later the Sea of Galilee. Finally, His resurrected body was free of suffering and inaccessible to any forces hostile to Him (*impatibilitas*).

We can start attaining all four of these traits even now (naturally, for the time being, only in an incipient and invisible way). Meanwhile, during the Final Judgment our corporeality will attain its ultimate purposefulness, ultimate meaning, and beauty, and we will be visibly similar to our resurrected Lord.

Thus, it is worth longing for our bodies to likewise be in heaven. It is worth constantly delighting in the fact that our bodies will then be inconceivably close to God, inconceivably filled with love for God. Sometimes, I ask myself: In what will our happiness in heaven consist? Everything that Sacred Scripture says on this topic transcends our imagination. From my own experience I know how wonderful it is to live in a state of sanctifying grace, even if we fall seven times a day. However, we can in no way imagine how much more wonderful it would be to be completely free of sin once we will be "holy and without blemish before Him" (Ephesians 1:4).

On earth, "to be near God is my good, to make the Lord God my refuge" (Psalm 73:28) and we know something about what it means to be filled with love for God. However, we are incapable of imagining our closeness with God when we will be with Him "face to face" (1 Corinthians 13:12). On earth, we experience in many ways a foretaste of the fact that "God is Light" (1 John 1:5) because faith illuminates everything that is important to us. In heaven, God will be our Light in an inconceivably tangible sense. Now, we simply flourish when we can imitate God and His various attributes, when we can imitate Him in His mercy. There, "we shall be like Him, for we shall see him as He is" (1 John 3:2). In short, we can hardly make an effort to understand the magnificence of heaven because "[w]hat eye has not seen, and ear has not heard, and what has not entered the human heart, what God has prepared for those who love Him" (1 Corinthians 2:9).

Thus, it is difficult to imagine that we can truly treat the promise of eternal life differently than by growing in our prayer lives and yearning to pray as authentically as possible. It is difficult to imagine faith in the future resurrection in a different way than by giving our bodies for the service of good, opening our bodies to obedience to God's commandments, and attending to the sick and suffering bodies of our neighbors in service of mercy.

WILL WE FIND OUR LOVED ONES IN ETERNAL LIFE?

We often ask this question when someone dear to us dies. On the one hand, it is clear to us that the afterlife will be completely different than life here on earth. On the other, we are incapable of imagining happiness in heaven without dear and beloved people close to us.

What Does the Faith of the Church Say About This?

A very ordinary response to this question can be found in the prayers of the Mass for the dead. For example, during the Mass for his deceased parents the priest asks God: "unite me with them in the joy of the saints." Meanwhile, in another prayer he says: "reward their difficulties and allow me to see them in the joy of the eternal light."

During a Mass for a deceased child, the Church prays that "we may someday participate with them in the joy of eternal life." During such a Mass, the following request is said of that child's parents: "let them see [their child] in Your Kingdom with joy once again."

The prayer for deceased spouses seems particularly deep: "unite them in eternal life in the fullness of Your love." The hope that people close to one another will find each other in eternal life also appears in many of the Church's prayers for the deceased: "lead him/her along with the saints to the eternal feast of Your Kingdom;" "to that he/she may live with Your saints in the glory of the resurrection;" "so that he/she may happily participate in eternal happiness along with his/her brothers." These and similar expressions are often repeated in these prayers.

In this way, awareness of the Lord Jesus' teaching on eternal life is reflected in the Church's consciousness. Here is the image of the feast to which He (Who appears in this passage in the third person, as the household owner) will invite all He will find prepared on the day of His coming: "Amen, I say to you, He will gird Himself, have them recline at table, and proceed to wait on them" (Luke 12:37). It is difficult to imagine a feast without its participants being close to one another.

On another occasion, the Lord Jesus speaks of eternal life as remaining in the house of the Father: "In My Father's house there are many dwelling places" (John 14:2). Unfortunately, there are houses in which people who are alien to one another live. However, such a situation is inconceivable in the house of the One Who is Love itself. We should closely read what God Himself says of His house, to which He invites us: "I will live with them and move among them, and I will be their God, and they shall be My people" (2 Corinthians 6:16; see Ezekiel 37:27).

In the shortest terms: it would be absurd to think that the love of our dear and dearest should end at the moment of death. God's love, which will fill us in eternal life to an extent that transcends our present conceptions, is a love that gives, not one that stifles. We already know that the more we love God the truer our love for God is and the more authentically we will love those dear to us. In eternal life, when our love for God is full and perfect, our love for one another will attain its ultimate shape and the fullness of its truth.

This was magnificently described by St. Cyprian, Bishop of Carthage, a martyr who lived in the third century, in his short piece *Mortality*: "[Heaven is our] native land [...] A great number of our dear ones there await us, parents, brothers, children; a dense and copious throng longs for us, already secure in their safety but still anxious for our salvation. How great a joy it is both for them and for us in common to come into their sight and embrace! What pleasure there in the heavenly kingdom without fear of death, and with an eternity of life the highest possible and everlasting happiness; there the glorious choir of apostles, there the throng of exultant prophets, there the innumerable multitude of martyrs wearing crowns on account of the glory and victory of their struggle and passion, triumphant virgins who have subdued the concupiscence of the flesh and body by the strength of their continency, the merciful enjoying their reward who have performed works of justice by giving food and alms to the poor, who in observing the precepts of the Lord have transferred their earthly patrimony to the treasuries of heaven! To these, beloved brethren, let us hasten with eager longing! let us pray that it may befall us speedily to be with them, speedily to come to Christ."[243]

What About Defective or Even Wasted Love?

It is good to be aware that even if we share the deepest bonds with someone, our love is sometimes marked by various deficiencies. The very sacrificial love of a mother or father can possess traits of egocentrism, misunderstanding one's child, or unwise lenience. The love of spouses, even that which evokes human admiration, can be wounded by laziness, incorrect submissiveness, or some other darkness.

If God grants us eternal life, we will not only find our loved ones, but we will in fact find them in such fullness that is inaccessible to us in our present lives. We read in the Catechism of the Catholic Church that our closeness to one another will not be "wounded any longer by sin, stains, self-love, that destroy or wound the earthly community" (1045).

243. St. Cyprian, *Mortality*, NTSLibrary, http://www.ntslibrary.com/PDF%20Books/MORTALITY%20by%20St%20Cyprian.pdf (accessed July 22, 2022).

Thus, there is an important practical conclusion resulting from our faith that our relationships can and should survive, be purified, and perfected in eternal life: We should now notice and remove from our love for our dearest ones everything that is imperfect, egocentric, and not pleasing to God. It would be terrible if during God's Judgment it turned out that my love even for my spouse or biological child lacked anything worthy of surviving.

In conclusion, we may ask ourselves a particularly difficult question. It sometimes happens that a biological son or daughter distances him or herself so much from his or her parents, becoming completely alienated from them and being indifferent to their parents suffering. Even more frequently, marriages fall apart in what seems to be a unilateral way: until the end of his or her days, only one of the spouses feels an attachment to the one who abandoned him or her. Can people hope to find their loved one in eternal life? Will estranged brothers, wounded friends, and the victims of complicated conflicts in which sometimes no one did anything wrong ever find one another?

The one who is truly tormented by such questions must know that the answer greatly depends on his own attitude. The response can be a verbal "yes," but, unfortunately, one's attitude can simultaneously say "no." Everything depends on whether I become insulated in my sense of injury, in holding a grudge and recalling my grievances or if I instead do everything to open my heart to my neighbor whom I have lost. Many attempts at reconciliation between people are unsuccessful because those who yearn for reconciliation most often unknowingly do much to preclude it.

It is also worth remembering that eternal life is the ultimate horizon of our reconciliation. If, facing God, I wish for reconciliation and if I purify my prayer for reconciliation so that it is truly selfless, I am allowed to hope that God will ultimately reconcile us, even if it were to happen after death.

HOW TO SHOW LOVE FOR THE DECEASED?

In the encyclical *Spe salvi*, Pope Benedict XVI writes: "The belief that love can reach into the afterlife, that reciprocal giving and receiving is possible, in which our affection for one another continues beyond the limits of death — this has been a fundamental conviction of Christianity throughout the ages, and it remains a source of comfort today" (48).

It is worth being aware that we can show love for our deceased loved ones not only by praying for them. Naturally, praying for the deceased is exceptionally important; indeed, it deepens our communion with them before God. The Church particularly encourages us to remember them during the Eucharistic sacrifice. However, there are many other ways we can — and sometimes even should — show love for our deceased loved ones.

We Can Be the "Proxies" of Our Deceased Loved Ones

I will begin with a testimony. I once read in a text by the Polish ethnographer Oskar Kolberg that, according to the customs of the rural population of Mazovia, a funeral procession stopped by a chapel or a roadside cross. Then, one of the loved ones of the deceased asked the funeral's participants to forgive him all the wrong he may have done to them. This custom required that the participants outshouted one another with proclamations such as: "May he forgive us if we harmed him!" "We have nothing against him!" "May the Lord Jesus show him mercy!" "May he rest in peace!" And so forth.

I recalled this custom during the funeral of a certain artist. I concluded this portion of the funeral sermon by encouraging its participants to spiritually reconcile themselves with the deceased while making the sign of peace but also that we all, the participants of this funeral, may reconcile with one another and forgive all the injuries that could have accumulated within us. I said: "Let us treat this as something akin to our gift for the deceased who in God's eyes may be worth even more than our prayers."

I did not know that many people who had been estranged from one another were participants in the funeral. If I had known that, perhaps I would not have made such a blunt summons to reconciliation. The truth is that I later heard many say that the rain of God's grace literally poured onto the funeral's participants. People gave testimony to many authentic reconciliations that had taken place during that funeral. Even today, it sometimes happens that someone recalls that summons to giving to one another the sign of peace as an unforgettable experience and great miracle of God's grace.

However, an ordinary way of making good decisions in the name of someone dear to the deceased, in a way in his name, is paying his debts and fulfilling all his other obligation as well as fixing the reparable injuries he had caused someone if he had not forgotten to close accounts with his neighbors before departing from our world. Love suggests to us that during God's Judgment it will be easier if we do not neglect this.

Furthermore, it often happens that someone's intuition suggests that I should "facilitate" doing good even after someone's death.

Sometimes, this was resolved institutionally; thus, for example, during the funeral of a wealthy person his family was expected to give alms to the poor. In some monasteries, the deceased monk "received" his meal for forty days after his death; it was later given to someone truly hungry. Today, the family of the deceased sometimes asks his friends and acquaintances to support some noble institution, usually a charity, instead of bringing flowers. Sometimes, the loved ones of the deceased fund a scholarship for a poor student, for example. Yet only God knows how many good deeds are done when people are inspired by their deceased loved ones without boasting to anyone. Then, we usually have the sense that good fulfilled in this way "counts" as an accomplishment of the deceased.

Do the Deceased Pray for Us?

Do the deceased know what is happening to us with whom they were bound on earth? And: We pray for them, but do they pray for us? We sometimes ask each other these questions. The answer must sometimes be sought from the perspective of the truth of the communion of saints.

There are two things we know for certain. Without a doubt, we should pray for our deceased loved ones, remembering that the efficacy of our prayer depends on if when interceding for them to God we are in a state of sanctifying grace. If sin reigns within us, it frustrates the efficacy of our prayers. Usually, we spontaneously suspect this, and people often have a great need to entrust their deceased loved ones to God. Without any external encouragement, they receive the sacrament of penance and receive Holy Communion, believing that their prayers for the deceased will in this way become more effective. Such conversions are undoubtedly the most beautiful victory from the tomb that certainly "counts" as an accomplishment of the deceased.

There is one more thing we know for certain: that the deceased who are allowed to see God's face are actively interested in everyone they loved during their earthly lives. Without a doubt, they pray for them. They are complete in God and truly participate in God's truth and love. However, the Church's teachers add one qualification here: The efficiency of not only our prayers for the dead but also their prayers for us are significantly reduced (or even thwarted) by our sins. Even if I had very holy parents who are ultimately united with God, their prayer for me can be of limited help if I live in sin and have no intention of converting. In short, if the prayer offered in my intention by my deceased who are completely holy is to be effective, I must love God and try to grow in holiness.

If, however, my loved ones are still in purgatory, do they know what is happening to me? Do they pray for me? That we do not know. The greatest theologians say that they probably do not. However, the Church has ultimately never spoken out on this topic; thus, it is better we do not answer these questions than risk a false answer. The most important thing is to not forget to pray for our deceased loved ones.

THE GIFT OF PURGATORY

Clinging Is Not Always Faithful

Someone once asked me to present Biblical passages that he could point out with his own finger when debating Jehovah's Witnesses on the topic of purgatory. I will show such passages shortly, but I would first like to say a few words about reading Sacred Scripture as the Sadducees did. We know from the Gospels that the Sadducees rejected the truth of the future resurrection, which they accounted for by the fact that Moses' Pentateuch (the Sadducees only recognized the Pentateuch as Sacred Scripture) is silent about this truth. Every Biblical scholar would confess that the Sadducees are right. Indeed, the entire Pentateuch does not contain a single sentence that directly mentions the resurrection.

The Lord Jesus criticized this kind of clinging to the letter of the sacred text and quoted to the Sadducees a sentence from the Pentateuch in which if they know how to read God's Word in faith notice the truth about the resurrection: "And concerning the resurrection of the dead, have you not read what was said to you by God, 'I am the God of Abraham, the God of Isaac, and the God of Jacob'? He is not the God of the dead but of the living" (Matthew 22:31-32).

Such a Sadducee-like tendency to reject everything in the Word of God that is not said directly and is clearly manifested in the sacred text became apparent in the first generation of the Church that lived without the physical presence of the apostles. Testimony to this is found in the words of St. Ignatius of Antioch, who in 108 wrote: "When I heard some saying, If I do not find it in the ancient Scriptures, I will not believe the Gospel; on my saying to them, It is written, they answered me, That remains to be proved."[244]

One time, I spoke to a certain girl who had many grievances towards the Church for condemning the use of drugs. After all, she said indignantly, Sacred Scripture says nothing on this topic, whereas in the Far East (at least according to her; I earnestly doubt this is the case) some Buddhists use drugs for religious purposes. Meanwhile, another girl told me about a "pious" boy who tried to convince her to go to bed with him, arguing that nowhere in Sacred Scripture is there a prohibition against premarital intercourse. Meanwhile, I frequently encountered the statement (which I think was influenced by the doctrines of Jehovah's Witnesses) that love for one's fatherland is a pagan invention, for the New Testament never mentions it.

I presented particularly drastic examples of the "Sadducee" approach to Sacred Scripture. However, generally speaking, the temptation to read the Bible in this way greatly increased, including among Catholics, beginning in the fifteenth century. In that century, the dominant philosophy in the European mentality was nominalism, or such a philosophical formation that is more interested in the phenomena of reality than in the root of these phenomena and in what imbues them with deeper meaning. In relation to the text, this rigorous formation is limited to contents directly contained in words

244. St. Ignatius, "The Epistle of Ignatius to the Philadelphians," trans. Alexander Roberts and James Donaldson, [in:] *Ante-Nicene Fathers*, Vol. 1, eds. Alexander Roberts, James Donaldson, and A. Cleveland Coxe (Buffalo, NY: Christian Literature Publishing Co., 1885), https://www.newadvent.org/fathers/0108.htm (accessed July 22, 2022).

and sentences and in general is not at all interested in the deeper meaning that the text indicates. In short, this is a "horizontal" rather than "deep" formation. Indeed, nominalism is the common root of both the Protestant principle of *sola Scriptura* (the principle that the text of Sacred Scripture is solely the source of the truth of faith) and Catholic apologetics that responded to a Biblical quotation used to oppose some Catholic truth with two other Biblical quotations to support that truth.

Purgatory: A Gift of God's Mercy

I promise to present the Biblical quotations on the existence of purgatory in a moment. However, I recommend first closely reading the Epistle to the Romans 6:3-14. By a "close read," I mean such an interpretation of Sacred Scripture as that by the Lord Jesus in the above-mentioned discussion with the Sadducees. Namely, reading Sacred Scripture is close when the inspired sentences do not rigorously close us off in their literal sense but instead lead towards a more complete truth about God.

The above-mentioned passage from the Epistle to the Romans speaks of baptism as the immersion of the old man, the sinful man, in death. This old man must die within us so that the new man, who is of God, may live within us. In accordance with this description, a truly Christian life consists of gradually killing the old man so that God's man may more fully possess me. It would be ideal if that old sinner ultimately died within me on the day of my departure from this world. Then, I would be wholly and completely a man of God and would immediately experience the joy of seeing my God face to face. What will happen if at the moment of death, I am a man of God, but part of the old sinner remains within me? This is not an abstract question. Indeed, it would be abstract if I were fully and completely faithful to God's grace. Unfortunately, however, that is not the case.

Sometimes, we can see with the naked eye that people very evidently filled with God's grace have not freed themselves of their weaknesses and sins until the end of their days.

In the Catholic Church, we believe that in His mercy God allows all His friends who had not completed the dying of their sin to be able to do so in the other world. We refer to purgatory as the process of the complete purification of sins that God completes in all who have left this world in a state of sanctifying grace and still need such purification. We are deeply convinced that our faith directly stems from the apostolic teaching on Christian life as the growing dying of our sin.

Specific Biblical Rationale

We also find confirmation of this faith in the Gospel. Christ the Lord Himself cautioned us against incurring debts that we will have to repay in the afterlife: "Settle with your opponent quickly while on the way to court with him. Otherwise, your opponent will hand you over to the judge, and the judge will hand you over to the guard, and you will be thrown into prison. Amen, I say to you, you will not be released until you have paid the last penny" (Matthew 5:25-26). Christ said something similar in His parable of the merciless debtor: "Then in anger his master handed him over to the torturers until he should pay back the whole debt. So will my heavenly Father do to you, unless each of you forgives his brother from his heart" (Matthew 18:34-35).

Thus, the accusations of Protestant fundamentalists that we made up our teaching on purgatory are even more painful. If they do not find this truth in Sacred Scripture, it is a matter of their own faith and conscience, but why are they so aggressive towards the faith of others? Can they not instead focus on everything that is positive in their own faith? Protest and polemics still seem to be the main means of their religious engagement.

However, let us return to these sacred texts in which we, Catholics, find testimony to purification after our deaths. When discussing sins against the Holy Spirit, thus a completely different topic, the Lord Jesus differentiates between the pardoning of sins in this world (in this age) as well as in the future world (Matthew 12:32). Biblical scholars say that He used the rabbinical differentiation that was the basis of the prayer for the deceased. Among the Jews in those days, prayer for the dead was already widespread. It is worth noting that the Gospels have no traces of information that the Lord Jesus, Who so clearly opposed the Sadducees' attempts at debunking the promise of resurrection, was opposed to these prayers.

Indeed, the Gospel contains no indications that the Lord Jesus prayed for the deceased or encouraged such prayer. However, the reason for this is obvious. We should notice that without exception all of Christ the Lord's encounters with the deceased that are described in the Gospels end with raising them from the dead! The Gospels simply present Christ the Lord Who reveals Himself as the Son of God and Victor over death. The Gospels do not at all discuss the question of how He has conquered death in light of the fact that faith in Jesus does not protect us from corporal death. And the truth of purification after death appears only in response to this question.

Going further, the first Christian communities rejected circumcision. Slightly later, they ceased to celebrate Shabbat and to distinguish between pure and impure foods, but nothing indicates that they attempted to reject the prayer for the deceased, which had been present in the Jewish tradition for at least two centuries (see 2 Micah 12:43-46). On the contrary, the Apostle Paul himself prayed for the deceased Onesiphorus who had helped him greatly during his imprisonment in Rome as well as during his stay in Ephesus. He prays as follows: "May the Lord grant him to find mercy from the Lord on that day" (2 Timothy 1:18). Meanwhile, hundreds of early Christian tombstones with the names of the deceased inscribed on them have survived to the present. We can find detailed information about this in every textbook dealing with early Christian archeology as well as in professional encyclopedias.

For a Catholic, prayer for the deceased is an obvious postulate that results from the truth about the communion of saints. Not only do we believe this; it is the subject of our everyday experience that the greater God's love is within us, the closer we grow to one another and the more capable we are of showing one another love. For us, it is unfathomable that death could contain such dark power that it can sever the unity of God's children; after all, Christ the Lord is the Victor over death! If God is pleased that we who live on this earth pray for one another, how could He not be pleased that we pray that the deceased can be in full unity with Him as soon as possible?

THE FIRE OF PURGATORY

Someone once presented his problem as follows: "It isn't the case that I reject the Church's teaching on the fire of purgatory. I want to believe in the Church as the teacher of faith without qualification. However, I cannot deny that this truth seems improbable to me. If someone accused the teaching about the fire of purgatory of being an example of mythological thinking, I would be incapable of responding."

It would be pathetic if someone understood the sentence: "I believe in the Church's teaching without qualification" as: "I believe in the Church's teaching without reflection." The above letter is to me pleasant evidence that such a mixture is practically impossible. After all, those who identify with the Church's teaching without qualification should in their understanding deepen their faith; confront their faith with their knowledge about reality, which is prone to change; and they should also pose questions about the faith, both those that automatically come to mind and those that come from the outside. I believe that only someone who does not treat his faith seriously can believe the Church's teaching without reflection.

God Who Reveals Himself in Fire

With regards to the fire of purgatory, we should naturally free ourselves of all the symptoms of mythological thinking. Referring to Sacred Scripture is the best protection against sliding into mythological conceptions. It is worth recalling how often fire appears in Biblical descriptions of God coming to man.

God appeared to Moses in a flaming bush that did not cease to burn (Exodus 3). During the journey of the Israelites to the Promised Land, "[t]he Lord preceded them, in the daytime by means of a column of cloud to show them the way, and at night by means of a column of fire to give them light. Thus, they could travel both day and night" (Exodus 13:12; see Numbers 14:14). Fire also accompanied those memorable events in which God's Chosen People received the Ten Commandments: "Now Mount Sinai was completely enveloped in smoke, because the Lord had come down upon it in fire" (Exodus 19:18). God's Shekinah sometimes took on the form of fire, thanks to which God signaled His benevolent and salvific presence among people: "On the day when the tabernacle was erected, the cloud covered the tabernacle, the tent of the covenant; but from evening until morning, it took on the appearance of fire over the tabernacle" (Numbers 9:15). In Isaiah's famous vision, the lips of the prophet are purified by a burning coal taken from the altar (Isaiah 6:6-7).

Let us notice that even if God's fire is sometimes the cause of fear (as was the case especially during the revelation on Sinai), it is always a sign of God's gifts and transcends human expectations.

Likewise, in the New Testament we encounter this mysterious fire, which is a sign of God's presence. On Pentecost, the Holy Spirit appeared to the apostles as "tongues as of fire" (Acts 2:3). Revelation twice mentions the victorious Christ using: "His eyes were like a fiery flame" (1:14; 19:12). Meanwhile, the Epistle to the Hebrews simply states: "For our God is a consuming fire" (12:29).

The Image of St. John of the Cross

I think it suffices to recall these sacred passages so that using the intuition of the faith we can begin to guess what the fire of purgatory is: man's encounter with God after death will be akin to immersion in fire. When man is truly devoted to God but not yet completely devoted to Him, then he will experience the unimaginably intimate encounter with God after death as something simultaneously wonderful and painful. It is wonderful because it is a true encounter with the One Who is Love itself, an encounter undoubtedly deeper and fuller than that which the greatest mystics achieved on earth.

At the same time, this must be a very painful encounter, for man will then see how little room he has for God compared to the potential with which he was created. Man will also see the part of himself that has unfolded in a false direction: he will most earnestly want that which is unworthy of eternal life within him to be burned by this Divine fire. Unimaginable fascination with God Who is Love will arouse within man the great desire to enter that fire so that, regardless of the enormous pain, he will be cleansed of what is unworthy of God and will expand as much as possible to become completely filled with God.

In any case, the experiences of the mystics allow us to imagine the fire of purgatory in this way. St. John of the Cross (d. 1591) compared the love of God that fills man during contemplation to being thrown into a fire. At first, it is very painful, until it destroys what should be burnt within man. However, as man becomes increasingly like God, being in this fire fills man with joy that is incomparable to anything else. St. John of the Cross writes about this at length in *Dark Night of the Soul*, especially in Chapters 4-10 of the second book.

Here, I will summarize the lengthy metaphor on which the holy mystic elaborates in Chapter 10. When man finds himself in God's love, it encompasses him like a fire encompasses wood. Just as a piece of wood that then becomes like fire, man becomes like God and is completely overwhelmed with His holy presence.

John of the Cross writes: "Fire acting upon wood begins to dry it out by driving out the moisture and causing it to lose the water it contains within itself. Then the fire begins to make the wood black and unsightly. At the same time, it causes the wood to give off a bad odor. Then as it dries little by little, it brings out and drives away all the dark and unsightly accidents which are contrary to the nature of fire. Finally, it begins to kindle it externally and give it heat, and at last transforms it into itself and makes it as beautiful as the fire. In this respect, the wood has neither passivity nor activity of its own, save for its weight, which is greater; and its substance, which is denser than that of fire, for it now has within itself the properties and activities of fire. Thus, it is dry, and it dries. It is hot and it heats. It is bright and it gives off brightness. And it is much less heavy than before. All these properties and effects are caused in it by the fire."[245]

Naturally, this is only a comparison. However, the next part of his deduction attests to how dear this comparison was to St. John. "In this same way we have to philosophize with respect to the divine fire of contemplative love which, before it unites and transforms the soul into itself, purges it of all its contrary accidents. It drives out its unsightliness and makes it black and dark so that it seems more unsightly and abominable than it had been before. The divine purgation is removing all the evil and vicious temperaments which the soul has never perceived because they were so deeply rooted and grounded in it. But now that they are to be driven forth and annihilated, these things reveal themselves and become visible to the soul, because it is so brightly illuminated by this dark night of contemplation. (It is no worse than before, however, either in itself or in its relationship with God.) As it sees within itself that which it did not see before, it becomes clear to it that not only is it unfit to be seen by God, but deserves His abhorrence, and that He does indeed abhor it. By this

245. St. John of the Cross, *Dark Night of the Soul: and Other Great Works* (Alachua: Bridge-Logos Publishers, 2007), p. 182.

comparison we can now understand many things concerning the purpose for the purgation of the soul.

[...] [These afflictions] are felt as though they come from the weakness and imperfections which belong to the soul. Without such purgation, the soul cannot receive its divine light, sweetness, and delight; even as the log of wood, when being acted upon by the fire, cannot immediately be transformed until it is made ready. This is why the soul is greatly afflicted."[246]

That such an extrapolation of St. John's own spiritual experiences to the situation of the soul after death is not arbitrary is attested by the Apostle Paul himself, who also speaks of a mysterious immersion in the fire that will occur on "the Lord's day," in its eschatological dimension: "[F]or no one can lay a foundation other than the one that is there, namely, Jesus Christ. If anyone builds on this foundation with gold, silver, precious stones, wood, hay, or straw, the work of each will come to light, for the Day will disclose it. It will be revealed with fire, and the fire [itself] will test the quality of each one's work. If the work stands that someone built upon the foundation, that person will receive a wage. But if someone's work is burned up, that one will suffer loss; the person will be saved, but only as through fire" (1 Corinthians 3:11-15).

The Fire of God's Presence

All reflections on our situation after death would be sterile and audacious attempts at cleverness if they do not help us in understanding our situation with respect to God more deeply. It is also worth contemplating the nature of the fire of purgatory, above all so that we may immerse ourselves as much as possible in the fire of God's presence in our present lives. Currently, we can barely tolerate a tiny bit of that fire, but we can already experience both its types of activity. On the one hand, it is a fire of delight that kindles within us ever-greater love

246. *Ibid.*, 182-183.

for God; on the other, it is a fire of blessed pain, a fire that eats away at God's enemy who continues to reside in each of us.

When commenting on the words of a Psalm, St. Augustine (d. 430) mentioned the first activity of this fire: "From the gleam before Him, His clouds passed, hail and coals of fire" (Psalm 18:13). Augustine's words are simple, but they tell us practically everything: "They, who were already dead, abandoned by the fire of good desire and the light of righteousness, and who remained in coldness and darkness, re-enkindled and enlightened, have come to life again."[247] Here, each of us can only ask ourselves if God's fire is already burning within us. For perhaps, as we sometimes sing, "our hearts are [still] cold as ice?"

If, however, God's fire is burning within me, it will undoubtedly purify me as well, at least initially. When commenting on a sentence already quoted in this letter (Hebrews 12:29), Origen notes: "But let us reflect that God does indeed consume and utterly destroy; that He consumes evil thoughts, wicked actions, and sinful desires, when they find their way into the minds of believers; and that, inhabiting along with His Son those souls which are rendered capable of receiving His word and wisdom."[248] In another of his works, Origen writes: "But when He is said to be a consuming fire, we inquire what are the things which are appropriate to be consumed by God. And we assert that they are wickedness, and the works which result from it, and which, being figuratively called wood, hay, stubble, God consumes as a fire."[249]

247. St. Augustine, "Exposition on Psalm 18," translated by an anonymous scholar, [in:] *Nicene and Post-Nicene Fathers, First Series,* Vol. 8. Edited by Philip Schaff (Buffalo, NY: Christian Literature Publishing Co., 1888), https://www.newadvent.org/fathers/1801018.htm (accessed July 26, 2022).

248. Origen, *De Principiis*, trans. Frederick Crombie, [in:] *Ante-Nicene Fathers*, Vol. 4, eds. Alexander Roberts, James Donaldson, and A. Cleveland Coxe.(Buffalo, NY: Christian Literature Publishing Co., 1885), https://www.newadvent.org/fathers/04121.htm (accessed July 26, 2022).

249. Origen, *Contra Celsum*, Book IV, trans. Frederick Crombie, [in:] *Ante-Nicene Fathers*, Vol. 4. eds. Alexander Roberts, James Donaldson, and A. Cleveland Coxe (Buffalo, NY: Christian Literature Publishing Co., 1885), https://www.newadvent.org/fathers/04164.htm (accessed July 26, 2022).

Unfortunately, herein lies the cause for many of our departures from God. We have become so accustomed to our sinfulness that we sometimes protect it as if it were our greatest treasure and the source of our personal identity. We are afraid of growing too close to God because we subconsciously grasp the truth of the words that "as wax is melted by fire, so may the wicked perish before God" (Psalm 68:3). On the one hand, we want the old sinner within us to die, but on the other we are afraid that this will hurt. In this way, we are neither completely devoted to God (unfortunately), nor do we (fortunately) completely abandon Him.

We simply are incapable of acknowledging how great an opportunity it is that God wants to fill us with His presence, which destroys everything deserving of destruction and kindles the love that truly loves with one's whole heart, strength, energies, and thoughts.

I will conclude by quoting the deep intuition on the topic of the fire of purgatory expressed by the Swiss mystic and convert from Protestantism Adrienne von Speyr (d. 1967): "The first step in the fire, and it is perhaps the most painful one, is the realization of one's own sin. One is spared nothing there; one's knowledge has to be complete. Only then is it replaced by prayer, before finally being erased by the fulfilment of that prayer. The knowledge remains, but it is no longer painful [...] There is, though, one thing that remains or perhaps arises for the first time in the fire: prayer. And from now on it is the kind of prayer that rises up only against sin, against all sin, period — no longer only against one's own — because sin stands for Christ's suffering — the prayer is heard, accepted, and becomes liberation — not only from sin, but from all its bonds, and at the same time this means that the fire is at an end. The way can be long, but there is only this one exit. The prayer that just now was still supplication becomes a song of praise; it accompanies the soul — the soul now purified through the fire — from the fire into heaven. No soul comes to Christ otherwise than praying."[250]

250. Adrienne von Speyr, *Lumina and New Lumina,* trans. Adrian Walker (San Francisco: Ignatius Press, 2008), pp. 63-64.

HOW TO SPEAK OF ETERNAL DAMNATION?

Above all, as long as Sacred Scripture remains the basis of the teaching of the Christian faith, or until the end of the world, the issue of damnation cannot be avoided. It appears too frequently and too clearly in sacred texts for it to be omitted from the Church's teaching.

The Lord Jesus Himself Spoke the Most About Hell

What is more, above all the Lord Jesus Himself spoke about eternal damnation. Hans Urs von Balthasar — though one can ask how he succeeded in harmonizing Jesus' teaching with his own inquiries in the book *Dare We Hope That All Men Be Saved?* — noted that it was necessary for Christ the Lord to clearly profess the promise of eternal life for us to be able to speak of the danger of its irretrievable loss:

"Jesus proclaims His message of love in relation to this first Jerusalem, irremediably condemned to the unquenchable fire of God's wrath (Jer 7:20), and He does not do so without opening even more horrible abysses than were ever foreseeable by the Old Testament. There, being blessed or happy, like being cursed or lost, could have a meaning only in temporal terms; as long as heaven (Heb 11:40) was not open, there could not be a hell (but only a predecessor to both: Hades, Sheol). It is only when that heaven has been opened that eternal hell opens for the first time."[251]

Hans Urs von Balthasar spoke even more firmly: if not for Christ the Lord's redemptive sacrifice, hell would be the destiny of us all, and it was revealed on Golgotha how terrible it truly is: "Indeed, it is in the God-forsakenness of the Crucified One that we come to see what we have been redeemed and saved from: the definitive loss of God, a loss we could never have spared ourselves through any of our own efforts outside of grace. [...]

Instead, it is the reality that the God-forsaken One experienced in an eminent way because no one can even approximately experience the abandonment by God as horribly as the Son, Who shares the same essence with the Father for all eternity. Thus, both of our eternal lots lie together in His hand: precisely because He is our grace, He is also our judgment; He is our judge and at the same time our Redeemer. As Christians, we know that the sins committed in the face of acknowledged love weigh imponderably more heavily than those committed in ignorance."[252]

After explaining why only Jesus' teaching clearly contained the truth of eternal damnation, we should recall that He most frequently expressed it using three metaphors. The first is the metaphor of being thrown outside, into the darkness, and thrown into jail (Matthew 8:12, 22:13, 25:30, Revelation 22:10); next, the metaphor of anguish and fire (Matthew 18:8, 25:41; Mark 9:47n; Hebrews 10:27); and, finally, the metaphor of loss, death, and ruin (Matthew 7:13; Luke 13:3-5; Galatians 6:8; 2 Thessalonians 1:9).

The Lord Jesus also spoke of eternal damnation without the use of metaphors. False disciples who proclaim Him with their lips

251. Hans Urs von Balthasar, *Love Alone Is Credible*, trans. D. C. Schindler (San Francisco: Ignatius Press, 2004), p. 76.

252. *Ibid.*, p. 52.

but not their hearts will hear the following terrible words from His mouth: "I never knew you. Depart from Me, you evildoers" (Matthew 7:23). Meanwhile, in His pronouncements on sins against the Holy Spirit, a synonym of eternal damnation are the strong words that such sin "will not be forgiven, either in this age or in the age to come" (Matthew 12:32). An analogous tone resounds in the words of the Apostle Paul: "Do not be deceived; neither fornicators nor idolaters nor adulterers nor boy prostitutes nor sodomites nor thieves nor the greedy nor drunkards nor slanderers nor robbers will inherit the kingdom of God" (1 Corinthians 6:9-10; see Galatians 5:19-21).

What Is the Essence of Hell?

It seems that the main reason why some Gospel warnings against eternal damnation have grown muffled in the teaching of today's Church[253] results from attempts to debunk the currently popular accusation that Christianity has created a civilization of fear.

In this context, it is worth recalling the view of Karl Jaspers, himself a non-believer, who pointed out the essentially positive dimension of the traditional fear of hell and claimed that a non-believer should also — under the threat of falling into existential mediocrity — nurture a fear analogous to the Christian fear of hell: a fear of wasting one's existence. According to Jaspers, both getting rid of this fear and its prevalence in our interior are terrible alternatives. This fear should be within us, but it should be overcome by an attitude of constantly turning towards what is most deeply positive.

This voice of a philosopher who essentially did not believe in hell but defended the fear of hell is quite interesting: "If fear of hell is for countless souls the basis for the choice of good over evil, it rarely tends

253. However, let us make note of the clear presentation of the teachings of the faith on this topic in the *Catechism of the Catholic Church*, 1033-1037. See John Paul II's speech during his general audience on July 28, 1999, titled: "Hell as the Ultimate Rejection of God."

to be solely fear of a supposed reality. Rather, this fear, encoded in the image of hell, can make us aware of the deeply existential motivations for the choices of our own existence. Existential anguish is the basic trait of the awakened man. The calm that results from a denial of hell does not suffice; this calm must result from positive trust, a basic constitution of the soul following from good will which always overcomes fear. Where anguish disappears, man is only superficial."[254]

Hell as the irreversible wasting away of oneself (for example, the final and irreparable inability to love) is undoubtedly the deepest perspective on this topic that is possible in the horizon of a non-believer. The perspective of faith — fully supporting the above expression — goes unimaginably further: Hell is irreparably finding oneself outside of God's presence, "separated from the presence of the Lord and from the glory of His power" (2 Thessalonians 1:9).

Thus, the dreadfulness of this situation is recognizable only to the degree to which we understand who God, Whose presence is entirely absent from hell, is for man. However, we can never comprehend Who God is for us; how, then, can we fully understand what separation from Him is? In short, hell is certainly a more terrible state than we can think and understand; this is probably why the Lord Jesus Himself depicted it using the terrible images found in the Gospels.

The lack of these images in the description of the state of eternal separation from God and merely emphasizing this separation does not make this description less terrifying, unless someone has no idea that God is Love and the source of all meaning.

Let us look at two descriptions presented with true feminine subtlety. Here is Simone Weil's apophatic description: "At death, some disappear into the absence of God and others disappear into the presence of God. We cannot conceive this difference. That is why

254. Karl Jaspers, *Was ist Philosophie? Ein Lesebuch* (München: Dt. Taschenbuch-Verlag. 1980), p. 203.

the representations of heaven and hell have been elaborated, so as to have an approximation which the imagination can grasp."[255]

This was understood in a very analogous way by Beata Obertyńska:

> I understand neither heaven nor hell... This is all
> Too big for my mind, which is narrow and lame
> I will either be close to Your name
> Or very far.

Some have even tried to paradoxically describe this frightening and irrevocable absence of God as a state filled with joy and satiation for people, who neither need God nor yearn for Him. "The only place outside heaven," C. S. Lewis speculated (I do not know if he had already accepted the teachings of Christianity), "where you can be perfectly safe from all the dangers and perturbations of love is hell."

If we carefully look at the great diversity of expressions with which the state of ultimate meaningless is expressed, we can clearly see that they concern the same unfortunate situation. Thus, hell is a state of ultimate license and disobedience (C. S. Lewis), "a real pantheon of all those who consider themselves to be gods" (J. Guitton), and the state of "extreme egoism" and "utter loneliness" (J. Ratzinger).

St. Thomas Aquinas described hell in a negative way, as the opposite of eternal joy. "[M]an's ultimate happiness, as regards his intellect, consists in the unobstructed vision of God. And as regards man's affective life, happiness consists in the immovable repose of his will in the first Good. Therefore man's extreme unhappiness will consist of the fact that his intellect is completely shut off from the divine light, and that his affections are stubbornly turned against God's

255. Simone Weil, *First and Last Notebooks: Supernatural Knowledge*, trans. Richard Rees (Eugene, OR: Wipf and Stock Publishers, 2015), p. 142.

goodness. And this is the chief suffering of the damned. It is known as the punishment of loss."[256]

However, perhaps the deepest intuition on the essence of hell was formulated in the patristic era. Thus, the fire of hell would be the same infinite Divine love that is the joy of the saved (it is unsurprising that few in the Church deal with this thought). Pope Leo the Great said: *Quod erit iucunditas mentibus nitidis, hoc erit poena maculosis*; this pronouncement is found in the breviary (Monday of the twenty-third week of Ordinary Time). "What will be joy for clean souls will be a punishment for tainted ones."

In short, man can achieve such a denial of God that with all his being he does not want God to exist. But God simply is. And He cannot cease to be God. He cannot cease to be omnipresent Love. Indeed, here on earth man can proclaim His non-existence or his own will that he does not want anything to do with God. Yet after death God will truly directly stand before each of us. One cannot be there without the omnipresence of God's Love. To the condemned, God's absence would consist of an all-encompassing protest against the fact that God is Love and that we are immersed in this Love.

Hell Begins Here and Now

Senatores boni viri, senatus — mala bestia. "Individual senators are good people, but the senate is a wicked beast." I think that we can use the intuition contained in this proverb to describe the spiritual state of our age. Even if many of our contemporaries are people close to God, that does not change the fact that, unfortunately, we live in an age of an enormous abandonment of the living and true God.

256. St. Thomas Aquinas, *Compendium Theologiae. Compendium of Theology*, p. I, 174, trans. Cyril Vollert, S.J. (St. Louis & London: B. Herder Book Co., 1947), https://isidore.co/aquinas/english/Compendium.htm (accessed December 16, 2022).

Many people have the desire for God to not exist, and perhaps even more people conceive God in a pagan way: as a wise, powerful, and good being that exists somewhere far away and to whom we can call out in exceptional situations (one's wedding, the birth of one's child, one's funeral, the holidays) or in whom they can look for succor during difficult times.

If one lives as if God did not exist or as if He were very distant, such a situation is evidently going in the direction of what we described above as hell. After all, the essence of hell is being far from God and becoming closed off to His presence. In such a situation, silencing Gospel admonitions against eternal damnation — or, in fact, deceiving heathens (yes, there are authentic heathens among Catholics) with the promise of universal salvation — can only serve as a consolidation of the hell we begin to build here on this earth.

Thus, it should be unsurprising that separation from God leads us to existential confusion, just as we should not be surprised that if a man is not satiated, he is hungry. There are many symptoms of this confusion in our life today. Growing support for abortion and euthanasia; the falling apart of even the most basic family ties and the crisis of all forms of social authority; the growing sense of the meaninglessness of life and the plague of drug addiction; the immersion of millions of people in destructive loneliness and the declining understanding of social service: these are the most blatant examples of evidence that the civilization of death is standing at our gates.

Reality is simply Divine; it is completely immersed in the presence of the loving God. We lack the power to decide that we do not want God to be so close and that we instead prefer He be far away. When we begin to create a world that is far-removed from God, this simply means that we are running away from reality; then, we are running not only from God but also from ourselves and even from meaningfully rejoicing at temporal values. Sooner or later, it turns out that we have situated our lives in some dimension of deception where nothingness and death dominate.

God responds to our rebellion in a truly Divine way: "What fault did your ancestors find in Me that they withdrew from Me?" (Jeremiah 2:5). He gave us His Only Begotten Son to save us. Likewise, God does not want to condemn any of us; He wants to lead each one of us to salvation (see John 3:17; 1 Timothy 2:4, 4:10). However, just as a hungry man will not be satiated by merely talking about food but instead must begin to eat, similarly by listening about universal salvation we will not leave the gates of hell into which entire societies have been clearly entering. We must simply convert to God and place all our hopes in Him.

Let us summarize the last part of our reflections: To ensure our talk of eternal damnation is not ideological but instead a true discussion of faith, we must find in it a place to become aware of how bad and incompatible with the deepest needs of human nature it is for man to be separated from God. Furthermore, we must more clearly see how many unnecessary and cursed bills we pay for wandering far from God.

Indeed, there is something blessed in the fact that there is no true happiness outside God. The Church Fathers sensed that what Sacred Scripture calls God's wrath is in essence a sign of God's love for sinners and a sign of His care for rebels. St. John Chrysostom explains: "[N]o longer did [God] allow Adam in the garden but bade him leave there, showing us that his sole motive in doing this was his love for him. [...] And so the expulsion from the garden was a mark of care rather than necessity. Our Lord, you see, is like this: he reveals his care for us in punishing no less than in blessing, and even his punishment is inflicted for the sake of admonition. Because if in fact he knew that we would not get worse by sinning and escaping, he would not have punished us; but to check our decline into greater evil and to stem the tide of wickedness, he applies punishment out of fidelity to his own loving kindness which is exactly what he did in this case."[257]

Similarly, the fact that, having separated ourselves from God, we have introduced so much absurdity, falsehood, and death into our lives is a sign of God's concern for us rather than God's abandonment of us. Having recognized the beginnings of hell on this earth, we can in a sense have empirical evidence that our true hope lies only in God, and in this way, we can avoid eternal hell.

The Teaching on Damnation as the Word of Love

However, admonitions against eternal damnation will be a dead and harmful truth for us if we do not see that they are the word of God's love for us. Every sentence in the Gospels is the word of love. Likewise, when the Lord Jesus tells us of eternal damnation, it is the word of His love for us.

What does this mean and what are the implications for the preaching of the truth? This means that we are to preach the news of salvation rather than informing people that if they do not attain salvation they will end up in hell; thus, we should not lie to people that the Gospel teaching about eternal damnation is simply the Lord Jesus' way of frightening His children with the bogeyman.

The basic truth of our preaching must be the news that Jesus wants to and can save us. "For the Son of Man has come to seek and to save what was lost" (Luke 19:10). The parables of the Prodigal Son and of the shepherd looking for his lost sheep as well as the spiritual promise contained within Christ's healings and His saving of the adulteress, the numerous tax collectors, and the thief crucified alongside Him, and, finally, His death and resurrection: in short, the entire Gospel is one big promise of salvation and a summons to become open to it.

257. St. John Chrysostom, *Homilies on Genesis*, Hom. 18:3 (http://www2.iath.virginia.edu/anderson/commentaries/ChrGen.html, accessed December 16, 2022).

The summons to salvation is also permeated with Christ's admonitions against eternal damnation, just as road signs informing of traffic problems and dangers are permeated with the promise of driving safely. Similarly, the admonitions of the mass media against poisonous mushrooms are filled with the hope that mushroom pickers will bring home baskets full of solely edible mushrooms.

If the aspect of love contained in Christ's teaching on eternal damnation were lost on us, we would not preach the truth but some imitation, forgery, or sham. Indeed, true love uses harsh and unpleasant means if there is no other way to bring those we love to reason. The human heart can become overgrown with fat or turn to stone. It can become de-sensitized to the degree that it does not understand the most basic moral and spiritual principles. Then, the only solution is to take out a hammer to shatter this stone and reach a living heart.

The Lord Jesus could reach even such hardened hearts; to do so, He used various means. He could directly tell the Pharisees that they were a tribe of vipers and whitened tombs; He cautioned us all against the eternal fire. These are the ultimate means through which He tried to reach hardened hearts immune to other arguments. He used them because He loved us; He was indifferent to the fate of neither the Pharisees nor anyone else. After all, it was love that made Him frequently speak of eternal damnation. No one wants hell to be empty more than Jesus.

St. John Chrysostom commented on the notions of an empty hell, on notions that the teaching on eternal damnation is only a pedagogical technique on God's part very accurately: "But if He does punish, and still you say it is a matter of threat, and on that account become more slothful, if it were really but a threat, would you not become more supine? If the Ninevites had known it was a matter of threat, they would not have repented. But because they repented, they cause the threat to stop at words only. Do you wish it to be a threat only? You have the disposal of that matter. Become a better man, and it stops only at the threat. But if, which be far from you! Thou despises the threat, you will come to the experience of it. The men before the flood, if they had feared the threat, would not have experienced the execution of it. And we, if we fear the threat, shall not expose ourselves to experience the reality."[258]

Sometimes (however, very rarely!) we can, I think, say to someone: "You are going straight to hell; eternal damnation awaits you." This can be said to a man who angrily says to his infirm mother: "When will you finally croak?" Or to someone who cynically and shamelessly takes advantage of another's helplessness. And to a sexual pervert who demoralizes children. However, the aim of such harsh words is not to give a verdict but to lead someone to come to his senses. The aim of telling someone that he will go to hell is to save them from hell. Thus, this very powerful word is not just a defense of those who experience harm but at the same time a work of love towards wrongdoers.

Saving People Facing Eternal Damnation

The above reflections clearly demonstrate that a theologian or priest who simply preaches that some people will be saved while others will be damned would render a bad service to Catholic orthodoxy. The truth about eternal damnation cannot be preached from the perspective of an accepting observer. Eternal damnation must be conceived of as something that should happen to neither myself nor anyone else. Love even suggests that if anyone were to encounter damnation, it would be best that it were I before anyone else.

This is how the great mystics understood this truth. St. Catherine of Siena prayed: "Better were it for me that all should be saved, and I alone (saving ever Thy charity) should sustain the pains of Hell, than that I should be in Paradise and all they perish damned; for greater

258. St. John Chrysostom, *Homily 3 on Philemon*, https://www.newadvent.org/fathers/23093.htm (accessed January 16, 2023).

honour and glory of Thy name would it be. [...] If Thy truth and Thy justice permitted it, I would that Hell were utterly destroyed, or at least that no soul ever more should descend thither, and if (so I were still united to Thy charity) I were put over the mouth of Hell to close it, in such wise that none should ever more enter it, much would I rejoice, so that all my neighbours might thus be saved." [259]

Some prayer testimonies to the struggle for the souls of hardened sinners recall Jacob's struggle against God (Genesis 32:25-33) or the famous verse of Ezekiel 22:30: "Thus I have searched among them for someone who would build a wall or stand in the breach before Me to keep Me from destroying the land; but I found no one."

St. Margaret Maria Alacoque wrote: "[The Lord] often placed me in this painful condition, and He once showed me the chastisement He was about to inflict on some souls; but I cast myself at His Sacred Feet saying: 'O my Savior, I beseech Thee rather to wreak Thy vengeance upon me and blot me out of the Book of Life than to permit these souls which have cost Thee so dear to perish!' And He answered: But they love thee not and cease not to afflict thee. 'It matters not, my God, provided they love Thee, I will not cease entreating Thee to pardon them.' Let Me do as I will, I can bear with them no longer. Embracing Him still more closely, I replied: 'No my Lord, I will not leave Thee till Thou hast pardoned them.'"[260]

St. Sister Faustina had the premonition that through her prayer she liberated many endangered souls from the mouth of hell. Once, after one of her prayers for the unrepentant sinners, she had the following vision: "When I had finished Adoration, halfway to my cell, I was suddenly surrounded by a pack of big black dogs jumping and howling, wanting to tear me to pieces. I noticed that they weren't dogs

259. Edmund Gardner, *Saint Catherine of Siena* (London: JM Dent and Co., 1907), pp. 14-15.

260. St. Margaret Mary Alacoque, *The Autobiography of St. Margaret Mary,* 100 (Charlotte, North California: Tan Books, 2012).

but devils. One said angrily, 'We are going to tear you to pieces for having taken away so many souls from us tonight.' I replied that if it were the will of the most merciful God, they could tear me as much as they wanted, for I rightly deserved it, since I was the most wretched of sinners, but God was ever holy, just, and infinitely merciful. At these words all the devils said together, 'Let's run, for she is not alone, the Almighty is with her.'"[261]

The victorious struggle in which St. Thérèse of Lisieux engaged as a child for the soul of a certain criminal initiated within her the desire to constantly fight for the salvation of souls endangered by eternal damnation, a desire that would last all her life: "After this unique grace, my desire to save souls grows each day, and I seemed to hear Jesus say to me what he said to the Samaritan woman: 'Give Me to drink!' It was a true interchange of love: to souls I was giving the *blood of Jesus*, to Jesus I was offering these same souls refreshed by the *divine dew*. I slaked His thirst and the more I gave Him *to drink*, the more the thirst of my poor little soul increased, and it was this ardent thirst He was giving me as the most delightful drink of His love."[262]

In his encyclical *Mystici Corporis Christi*, Pope Pius XII, perhaps influenced by the apparitions in Fatima, wrote the following, which is something like a summary of this great mystical tradition: "This is a deep mystery, and an inexhaustible subject of meditation, that the salvation of many depends on the prayers and voluntary penances which the members of the Mystical Body of Jesus Christ offer" (44).

In the contemporary Church, we can instead observe a crisis of the spiritual attitude that forced many of God's friends to offer prayers of petition for those who seem most threatened by the loss of salvation. We can ask if this crisis attests to the fact that within ourselves

261. St. Faustina Kowalska, *Diary*, trans. Teresa Bałuk-Ulewiczowa (Krakow: Misericordia, 2019), p. 206.

262. St. Thérèse of Lisieux, *Story of a Soul: Study Edition* (Washington, DC: ICS Publications, 2005), pp. 155-156.

the germ of individualism deforms even our hope for salvation or if it instead is the effect of the spread of an easy hope for universal salvation and, consequently, neglecting the danger of losing salvation.

We should notice that a recognition of the truth about eternal condemnation that is accompanied by easily accepting the existence of hell is false. However, being "consoled" by notions that hell is probably empty, especially if this attitude is accompanied by a lack of personal engagement so that salvation which God grants us in Jesus Christ reaches all, including those who are completely closed off to it, may be even farther removed from the truth.

Both attitudes — accepting the existence of hell and rejecting its existence — lead to false conceptions of God and, subsequently, distort our religious attitude towards Him. Wherever the existence of hell does not lead to religious opposition, the image of God as a harsh Ruler easily flourishes, while fear can become one of the most important dimensions of religiosity. Meanwhile, if people are convinced that hell does not exist, the mercy of God, Who wants to heal and fill even the greatest sinner with His loving presence, can easily be misunderstood as God's leniency towards the evil we commit. Thus, this is ultimately an attitude of hopelessness with respect to the possibility of our liberation from sin; man can then only rely on God's leniency to lead him to a happy finale.

If we reject both extremes of this dilemma, what should our attitude be? Personally, I would greatly like for hell to be empty. I know that the Lord Jesus Himself wants this. I know one thing with complete certainty: even if it indeed is empty, I can end up there. Thus, I should surrender myself with all my heart and all my actions to the Lord Jesus so that I will not end up there, and I should do everything so that no one would end up there!

THE ULTIMATE HORIZON OF OUR COMMUNITY OF BELIEVERS

May We Never Reject Unpopular Truths

By, for example, opposing divorces and denying the sacraments to people who formed relationships with someone else while their spouses are alive, does the Church not act against her own interest? After all, the Church alienates many people in this way!

Everyone has heard similar arguments. They seem particularly convincing in societies that have grown accustomed to the fact that various political parties seek out social support and popularity by responding to various collective expectations. Has the Church's instinct of self-preservation been weakened? Why does she not want to reject those elements of her teaching that are contrary to the expectations of a great many people?

Naturally, it sometimes happens that some priest or bishop may begin to value social expectations towards the Church over the teaching and spirit of the Gospel. In the conviction that in this way he is protecting the Church and keeping many people in her, such an "enhancer" of the Lord Jesus degrades the Church to the level of such groups whose survival and significance depend on gaining an appropriate number of supporters and keeping them in its ranks.

Meanwhile, if it was Christ Who founded the Church, and if the Church is a Kingdom not of this earth (see John 18:36), there must be some resulting consequences. It is not our task to worry if the Church will successfully survive the tempests of history or another revolution of consciousness; let us leave such concerns to Jesus. Instead, we should tend to what belongs to us. It suffices to find light for every day of our lives in the Gospel; to try to make use of the eternal goods that God placed in His Church; and to try to be that light and share these goods with others as much as possible.

If people leave the Church, that is certainly oftentimes our fault as well: perhaps we lack fraternal love; perhaps her faith is taught too cold-heartedly; perhaps we cannot ultimately listen to those expectations with respect to the Church that are in accordance with the spirit of the Gospel. All this should be the subject of our examinations of conscience and our efforts to improve.

However, woe unto us if we try to keep those who want to leave the Church through flattery and "updating" God's teaching to make it fit contemporary tastes. It suffices to recall how the Lord Jesus Himself acted when His teaching did not match the tastes and expectations of His audiences and so "many [of] His disciples returned to their former way of life and no longer accompanied Him" (John 6:66). He made no attempts at keeping them through flattery or by adjusting His teaching. He only turned to the Twelve: "'Do you also want to leave?' Simon Peter answered Him, 'Master, to whom shall we go? You have the words of eternal life.'"

Christianity Cannot Exist Without Faith in Eternal Life

These words are absolutely crucial to understanding the service of Christ the Lord and His Church: "You have the words of eternal life!" To imagine the Church and Christian life without faith in eternal life is like imagining marriage without the spouses' sense of closeness to one another. If it sometimes happens that even children are incapable of bringing spouses closer to one another and that they continue to feel alien to one another, we interpret this as something perverted and unnatural, as something that should not happen. Equally perverted and unnatural is membership in the Church without deep faith in eternal life.

Let me try to explain this by referring to what is perhaps the Lord Jesus' least-known parable. Let us recall it in its entirety: "Which of you wishing to construct a tower does not first sit down and calculate the cost to see if there is enough for its completion? Otherwise, after laying the foundation and finding himself unable to finish the work the onlookers should laugh at him and say, 'This one began to build but did not have the resources to finish'" (Luke 14:28-30).

If I tried to be a Christian without belief in eternal life, I would act like a person with the resources to only build a shack but who begins to build a palace: such a person invests all his money and plenty of time into something meaningless. Given the man's possibilities, he may not even succeed in building the foundations!

The Apostle Paul was absolutely right when he wrote: "Let us eat and drink, for tomorrow we die" (1 Corinthians 15:32). If there is no eternal life, why should a husband and wife who find it difficult to live together work on combating difficulties and consider that they were united by God Himself? After all, it would be much easier if both went their ways and tried to build happy family lives anew. If everything ends on this earth, then our efforts to subordinate our bodies to our souls are truly meaningless: does it not suffice to live honestly and not harm anyone? It is worth realizing how much logic there is in contemporary departures from the ethics of the Gospel. Such departures appear as a consequence of doubting eternal life.

It is only in the horizon of eternal life that Gospel ethics take on mighty truthfulness. Here are several of the most frequently repeated imperatives of this ethics: "For if you live according to the flesh, you will die, but if by the spirit you put to death the deeds of the body, you will live" (Romans 8:13); "Do not store up for yourselves treasures on earth, where moth and decay destroy, and thieves break in and steal. But store up treasures in heaven, where neither moth nor decay destroys, nor thieves break in and steal" (Matthew 6:19-20); "And do not be afraid of those who kill the body but cannot kill the soul; rather, be afraid of the one who can destroy both soul and body in Gehenna" (Matthew 10:28).

If our hope for eternal life is in vain, such teachings are abysmally stupid; worse, they are extremely harmful. For if someone is amused by tilting at windmills, one can avoid interfering; in fact, one can favorably look at such eccentric behavior. However, if someone begins to preach to others that tilting at windmills is the best way of life and, furthermore, if such a madman finds followers, he becomes dangerous. After all, the wings of a windmill are not made of rubber; they can shatter many a fool who took the summons to tilt at windmills seriously. The Apostle Paul spoke of this clearly: "If for this life only we have hoped in Christ, we are the most pitiable people of all" (1 Corinthians 15:19).

Let us not be afraid to notice the following weakness of Christianity compared to all other religions. If Christ is not the Son of God; if He did not rise from the dead; and if He cannot grant us eternal life, then all the good that the Church has contributed and continues to contribute to human history does not counterbalance the harm she does to humanity by preaching the deceptive ideals of the Gospel. If that were the case, then the ancient pagans who considered Christians to be "enemies of the human race" were right. If that were the case, we should satisfy our religious needs in some other religion (perhaps Buddhism would be best, for it seems most pleasing among the non-Christian religions). For "if Christ has not been raised, then empty [too] is our preaching; empty, too, your faith" (1 Corinthians 15:14).

Christ, however, has risen from the dead! He was truly resurrected! And His sheep "follow [Christ]. [He will] give them eternal life, and they shall never perish. No one can take them out of [God's] hand" (John 10:27-28). If, then, Christ has risen from the dead, then His Church is the community of "those who were being saved" (Acts 2:47). If Christ has risen from the dead, then the ethics of the Gospel can be preserved, while every time it is implemented it truly changes the face of our earth. If Christ has risen from the dead, there is perhaps no greater contradiction of the principles of common sense than belonging to the Church without believing in eternal life.

What should a Christian whose faith in eternal life is undergoing a crisis then do? I think that the source of such a crisis is always acting according to some other ethics than that of the Gospel. Even if such an ethics were 95 percent consistent with Christian ethics, it is the ethics of the children of this world (even if they are very noble and otherwise deserving of admiration). A Christian who wants to renew his faith in eternal life must become a "madman" who treats the Gospel, the entire Gospel, literally. The Divine power he will then experience as well as the practical efficiency of Gospel ethics will fill him with the joyous certainty of eternal life.

Origen beautifully expressed this around 233 in his work *On Prayer*: "If, accordingly we would be ruled over by God, by no means let sin rule in our mortal body nor let us obey its commands when it calls our soul forth to the works of the flesh that are alien to God, but let us mortify our members that are on earth and bear the fruits of the Spirit that the Lord may walk in us as in a spiritual garden, ruling alone over us with His Christ."[263]

263. Origen, *On Prayer*, trans. William A. Curtis, https://www.tertullian.org/fathers/origen_on_prayer_02_text.htm (accessed July 27, 2022).

We Are the Next Particle of the Eternal Church

The horizon of eternal life is understood as meaning that the Church is a much greater community than all we who believe in Christ. This is said most clearly in the Epistle to the Hebrews: "No, you have approached Mount Zion and the city of the living God, the heavenly Jerusalem, and countless angels in festal gathering, and the assembly of the firstborn enrolled in heaven, and God the judge of all, and the spirits of the just made perfect, and Jesus, the mediator of a new covenant" (12:22-24).

Thus, we, who constitute the Church on earth, are merely novices in this ultimate Church that God builds for all eternity. This is why our particle of the Church is called the pilgrim Church: we are only on our way, only in the process of maturing to eternal life. "[B]ut when the perfect comes, the partial will pass away [...]. At present we see indistinctly, as in a mirror, but then face to face" (1 Corinthians 13:10, 12).

It is not the case that we on earth constitute one Church, while another one, the ultimate Church, is in heaven. We, who are on a pilgrimage to eternal life, constitute one Church along with all those who already can look at God face to face. It would be unthinkable that our pilgrimage may not interest our elder brothers and sisters who already are completely united with Christ. This intercession of the saints for us is even more valuable since their unification with Christ is complete.

When I pray for you, my prayer is effective only to the degree to which I am united with Christ. It is true that here on earth the degree of man's union with Christ can be great. The Apostle Paul could have called without hypocrisy: "I live, no longer I, but Christ lives in me" (Galatians 2:20). Christ the Lord prayed that we would here on earth unite with Him and one another more in Gethsemane: "And I have given them the glory you gave Me, so that they may be one, as We are one, I in them and You in Me" (John 17:22-23). However, complete and total union with Christ is only a gift of the future age.

How powerful, then, must the prayer of all the saved be since Christ completely embraces them? In a sense, it would be insufficient to say that Christ and all the saints pray for us. More: only Christ prays for us! The saints do not pray for us alone; Christ prays through them. The Church in Heaven is already completely and totally the Body of Christ. This is not in the sense that the saints have lost their personal identity in Christ; in fact, the opposite is true. Christ Himself prays for us in the sense that they are one with Christ in a manner that is inconceivable to us and that the same Holy Spirit Who prays in Christ the Son of God prays in them.

For the above to not become beautiful but empty words, we must once again pose the following question: If Christ Himself intercedes for us and if the entire Church of the saved prays for us in Christ, then why are we still so sinful? Herein lies the humility of the omnipotent God: He has created us without us, but He has too much respect for us to save us without us. It is I who must invite Him to me. No saint nor even Christ Himself can replace me in that. Christ the Lord says in Revelation: "Behold, I stand at the door and knock. If anyone hears my voice and opens the door, [then] I will enter his house and dine with him, and he with Me" (3:20).

PERSONAL INDEX

J